Lynn Buchanan
80168086

# DECISION MAKING UNDER UNCERTAINTY:

## Models and Choices

**Charles A. Holloway**
Stanford University

**PRENTICE-HALL, INC., Englewood Cliffs, New Jersey 07632**

*Library of Congress Cataloging in Publication Data*

HOLLOWAY, CHARLES A
Decision making under uncertainty.

Bibliography: p.
Includes index.
1.—Decision-making—Mathematical models. I.–Title.
HD30.23.H64 658.4′033 78-31920
ISBN 0-13-197749-0



Printed in the United States of America

10 9 8 7

PRENTICE-HALL INTERNATIONAL, INC., *London*
PRENTICE-HALL OF AUSTRALIA PTY. LIMITED, *Sydney*
PRENTICE-HALL OF CANADA, LTD., *Toronto*
PRENTICE-HALL OF INDIA PRIVATE LIMITED, *New Delhi*
PRENTICE-HALL OF JAPAN, INC., *Tokyo*
PRENTICE-HALL OF SOUTHEAST ASIA PTE. LTD., *Singapore*
WHITEHALL BOOKS LIMITED, *Wellington, New Zealand*

**To Christy, Debbie, Susan, and Stuart**

# Contents

## APPENDICES

# Preface

The goal of *Decision Making Under Uncertainty: Models and Choices* is to present the methods, concepts, and ideas of decision analysis at a level that can be understood by students, managers, and analysts who do not have extensive backgrounds in mathematics. The treatment is intended to be fundamental in two senses. On the one hand, it is introductory and covers the basics of modeling, probability, and choice. On the other hand, it includes discussions of the foundations or assumptions behind the procedures. The latter are particularly important for those who intend to use the methods as a basis for decisions, because the usefulness of the procedures and the information conveyed by the models depends on these assumptions.

The material has grown out of teaching an introductory course in quantitative methods to students in a Masters of Business Administration program over a number of years. The decision to turn the material into a book was influenced by several factors. One is a firm conviction, based on experience teaching the material, that the concepts and topics covered are important for anyone who faces complex problems. Another factor is that modern treatments of economics, finance, accounting, marketing, and operations management are coming to rely on these concepts. Therefore, this material can be an important addition to a curriculum. A third factor is that a course built around these topics can be fun to teach, since many of the problems are intrinsically interesting to a wide spectrum of students.

The basic approach is to lay out the options available for dealing with decisions under uncertainty. These options have been divided into those associated with developing models of decision problems and those associated with the choice process. The material on models presents a standard introduction to probability, but in the context of decisions. The material on choices covers the fundamentals of preference or decision theory.

The book can be used in several ways. One method of use is in a basic course on decisions under uncertainty that covers an introduction to probability, model building, assessment of probabilities, revision of probabilities, value of information, options for choosing, preference theory, and organizational arrangements for dealing with risk such as risk sharing, diversification, and incentive systems. Special topics such as decision making with multiattributes can also be included. If the book is used in this way, it can provide all the background in probability required for an ensuing course in statistics that concentrates on estimation, hypothesis testing, regression analysis, and other statistical procedures.

It can also be used for a course on decision theory following a course that provides an introduction to probability. Depending on the extent of the prior coverage, the probability chapters can be left out completely or used selectively. For instance, if probability has been taught in conjunction with a course in statistics, the material on model building, classical and subjective concepts of probability and assessment procedures may be retained. This type of course would extend the basic ideas of probability learned in statistics and introduce new concepts such as revision of probabilities and value of information. The course could then concentrate on the options for choice, preference theory, and organizational issues.

Another possibility is to use the book for a course that is limited to an introduction to probability. The decision focus allows the fundamentals to be covered in an interesting setting. Moreover, it raises questions about the nature of probabilities and their assessment that focus student interest on the axioms. The instructor's manual contains detailed outlines and assignments for each of these suggestions.

A number of features have been included to help students learn the material and to give instructors flexibility. Part 1 is both an introduction and a brief first pass through the subjects. This serves several purposes. It gives students an overview so that realistic and interesting problems can be used when the details of probability and model building are studied. From a pedagogical perspective, the second pass through the material, provided by Parts 2 and 3, reinforces and extends the coverage in the first pass. By including this overview, instructors who want to emphasize either probability models or choice, but not both, can assign Part 1 to establish quickly a common base of knowledge. The text attempts to minimize the problems of integrating the various parts by including block diagrams at the beginning of each chapter that indicate how the material fits into the overall framework of the book, and a summary at the end of each chapter.

The only formal mathematical prerequisite is a knowledge of basic algebra (calculus is not used). However, some general facility with quantitative reasoning will make the material easier to understand. Special sections with single bullets ● have been provided for those who want more examples and explanation. No new topics are introduced in these sections. Sections with two bullets ● ● are for students who want to learn about additional or more advanced topics. Since practice is important for learning this material, a large number of new problems and cases have been included. Most of them represent realistic problems for decision makers. The problems in the text are supplemented by additional problems in the instructor's manual.

Many people have contributed to the ideas and material found in this text. As anyone who has taught part of a multiple section course knows, the development of a course is really a joint effort. It is certainly true in this case. Michael Harrison and David Kreps have been involved longer and more intensively than others. The material covered and ideas for presentation reflect their inputs over several years. Perhaps more importantly, they have pushed me to learn more about the subject than I ever would have learned on my own. I am especially indebted to them. They and others who have taught the course have also made direct inputs to the problems and cases (many of which first appeared as examination questions) included at the end of the chapters and in the instructor's manual. Charles Bonini, Joseph Blackburn, Joel Demski (even though he never taught the course), James Freeland, Jack Moore, Evan Porteus, and Oscar Serbein have each contributed to these problems and to the development of the course. I am grateful to them and to Stanford University, the copyright holder on some of the problems, for allowing me to include this material. I am also grateful to Professor Paul Vatter of Harvard for allowing me to include the Morris Manufacturing Company case, which is an adaptation of the Western Manufacturing Company case that he wrote.

The contents and presentation have benefited from detailed reviews by the following professors: Charles Bonini (Stanford), James S. Dyer (UCLA), J. Michael Harrison (Stanford), Charles H. Kriebel (Carnegie-Mellon), Michael R. Middleton (University of San Francisco), J. S. Milutinovich (Temple), Paul J. Schoemaker (Wharton), and Don Wehrung (British Columbia). Their contribution is happily acknowledged. There are, of course, a great number of individuals who have contributed to developing the theory of decision making under uncertainty. Many have been identified in the text. The pioneering work, in making the theory available to decision makers, done by Professors Ronald Howard, Howard Raiffa, and Robert Schlaifer has been particularly influential and is reflected in the material included.

I am indebted to the many students who struggled through early versions of these chapters and provided valuable suggestions. In particular I would like to thank Michael Bloom and Andy Corty for their extensive comments. A special note of gratitude goes to Ursula Kaiser, who cheerfully and skillfully typed the first draft in syllabus form, and to Laurie Yadon and Marilynn Rose, who did the same for later versions. I also thank Marian Hartstein, Ron Ledwith, Mike Melody, Curt Novak, Elinor Paige and Judy Rothman, the people at Prentice-Hall who helped with this project, and my father, Dr. Heber Holloway, who read the galleys for the entire manuscript. Finally, I want to express my appreciation to Stanford University and the Graduate School of Business for providing the setting that allowed me to undertake this task.

Charles A. Holloway
*Palo Alto, California*

# PART 1

# Introduction and Basic Concepts

# 1

# Introduction to the Analysis of Decisions

Decisions imply choices among alternatives. They form an important part of our experiences. In some cases we make decisions automatically or in a programmed manner. For example, we rarely make conscious comparisons of alternative routes when traveling to and from familiar destinations. Instead, we rely on programmed decisions to select the route. Managers decide on production quantities using *rules of thumb*. Bond traders buy and sell millions of dollars worth of securities using procedures that are largely automatic. These programmed procedures or rules of thumb are efficient in terms of the effort or cost of making the decision. And often they produce good decisions, especially when similar decisions are made repeatedly. In these cases experience allows us to develop good decision-making procedures.

In other cases we make decisions using instinct or intuition. Instinct is used when severe time pressure precludes any other mode. For instance, if, while driving along a street, you are suddenly confronted by a bicyclist, you must decide to stop or turn left or right to avoid a collision. A manager in a negotiating session may have to decide quickly how far the other side can be pushed without placing himself/herself in a poor position. Intuition or instinct also is used when the differences among the various alternatives are minor. In these cases the cost of a more formal analysis is not warranted. Even when alternatives have important differences, some decision makers prefer to make most of their decisions using intuition. To some extent it is part of their managerial style.

## USING ANALYSIS

The use of analysis is an alternative to making decisions in a programmed manner or completely instinctively. In one way or another the pros and cons of each alternative are investigated. Expert advice and available data are factored into the choice. Analysis is used when decisions are complex and alternatives differ substantially from each other. These are often *one-of-a-kind* decisions.

They can take a variety of forms. One example is establishing a policy for a recurring set of decisions. For instance, purchasing decisions can be analyzed in detail to establish a rule for reordering. Some decisions arise either once or so infrequently that no policy or procedure is developed for them. Although these decisions may not arise often, they can be crucial to the success of an organization. Analysis involves a conscious, purposeful effort directed at determining the proper choice for these decisions. As we will see, this *does not* rule out using intuition but allows intuition to be used along with the other inputs to an analysis.

## THE NEED FOR SOME PHILOSOPHY

This book is concerned with decisions that are approached using some form of analysis rather than those made in a programmed or instinctive manner. The methods and concepts presented here are intended to clarify and simplify decisions. The aim is to help decision makers to make better decisions. The book addresses both the *philosophy* and the detailed *methods* of the analytical process. At first glance it may seem contradictory to include philosophy in a book about decision making. After all, decision making is a very down-to-earth task. Managers and others faced with tough decisions usually have a practical outlook. The problem with leaving out the philosophy is that it is needed to ensure that the *analytical methods* are *used properly*. The approach taken here is fundamental, starting from primitive notions of information and individual preferences. The purpose is to provide decision makers with a clear understanding of both the *limitations* and potential *benefits* of formal analysis. The concepts are illustrated by concrete problems throughout the book. Since concepts such as risk, uncertainty, and information form the basis for the modern theories of economics, finance, accounting, marketing, and operations management, this fundamental approach will also provide a background for these subjects.

Methods and techniques for modeling decisions and choosing among alternatives are described in detail. There is no single best method for every situation, so the available options are presented. Under conditions that can be precisely defined, individuals who follow the procedures will make choices consistent with their own preferences.

## SOURCES OF COMPLEXITY

There are four things that can make a problem complex enough to make some form of analysis attractive: (1) a large number of factors, (2) more than one decision maker, (3) multiple attributes, and (4) uncertainty (see Figure 1.1). When one or more of these characteristics is present, it is often impossible to keep in mind and think about all the important aspects of a problem.

### A Large Number of Factors

Problems that have a large number of factors are common in both business and government. Examples of this class of problems in finance (e.g., calculation of the rate of return for an investment with alternative means of borrowing and paying back money), accounting (e.g., determining production costs), and operations (e.g., selecting the best mix of products for a plant) are

**FIGURE 1.1**

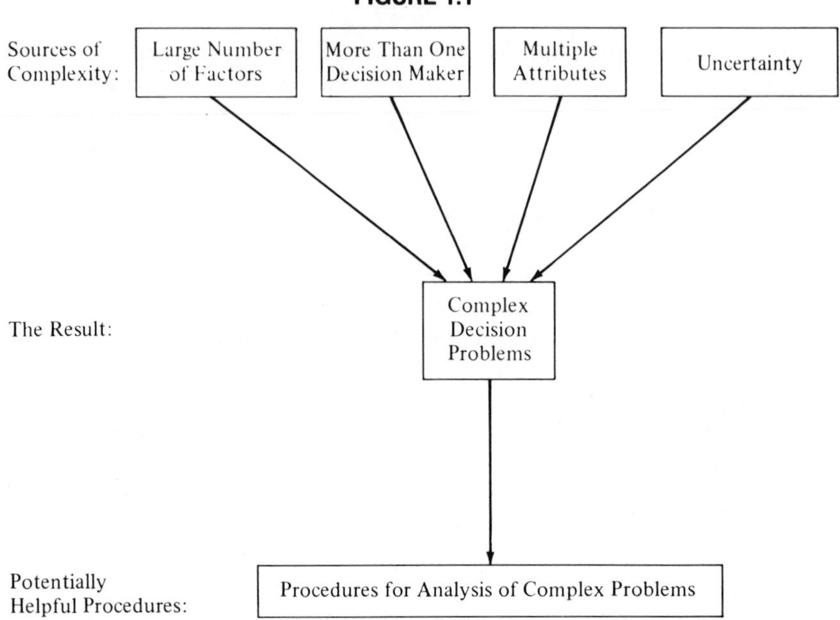


illustrated in discussions on uncertainty. But no attempt is made to present the specialized techniques found in texts on finance, accounting, or operations management. Optimization techniques for deterministic problems (e.g., linear programming) are also left to texts on *operations research* and *management science*.[1]

### More Than One Decision Maker

When more than one decision maker is involved, the problem of *choosing* an alternative can be very difficult. Social choice theory and the theory of games offer some help on these problems. Neither will be covered here. The selected references at the end of this chapter provide a guide for those who are interested in reading about these topics.

### Multiple Attributes

Multiple attributes are common in decision problems, particularly in government. Chapter 20 includes a discussion of this class of problems.

Uncertainty is the main topic of this book. Some of the complications presented by uncertainty are introduced below.

[1]See, for example, H. M. Wagner, *Principles of Operations Research* (Englewood Cliffs, N.J.: Prentice-Hall, 1969).

## THE PROBLEMS IN CHOOSING UNDER UNCERTAINTY

Why are decisions under uncertainty worth studying? Why are they any different from other decisions? We just get as much information as possible, determine the consequences of each alternative, and then choose the best. It all seems very straightforward. But when problems are complicated by uncertainty, each of the phases described above (gathering information, assessing consequences, and making a choice) is also complicated. How much and what kind of information do we want? What do we mean by information anyway? Which consequences are important? How can they be assessed when uncertainty is present? Do we even know what *best* means when things are uncertain? The concepts and procedures discussed here will help answer these questions.

### Evaluating Decisions Under Uncertainty

The basic dilemma is illustrated by thinking about how to evaluate the quality of a decision when uncertainty is present. The obvious choice is to look at the results from a decision. After all, we are really interested in what we get as a result of a decision, not the analysis or decision itself. The owners of a company that has lost a lucrative contract are not likely to find much solace in being told that they did a good analysis and their bid price was a good choice. A political candidate who lost votes by deciding to speak in favor of disarmament just before a war broke out may not be interested in hearing that the decision was a good one in light of the facts available when it was made. The problem with this approach to evaluating decisions is that, as long as uncertainty is present, it is possible to have outcomes with unfavorable consequences even when "good" decisions have been made. If the outcomes are controllable, there is no uncertainty. Uncertainty, by definition, rules out guaranteeing that the best outcome is obtained. Therefore, results or outcomes by themselves are not enough to evaluate a decision when uncertainty is present. To illustrate these ideas, consider the following simple example:

**Example 1.1**

During a business trip to Nevada, your associate, Mr. Green, who is extremely wealthy, becomes wildly enthusiastic over gambling. During the trip his enthusiasm is matched by his luck and he wins $100,000. On the plane coming back he is still excited about gambling and asks if you will play blackjack with him. Considering yourself a poor card player and remembering that you are somewhat short of cash, you decline. After several other suggestions which you refuse, Mr. Green, in a last effort to get you to play, proposes the following gamble. "See the priest sitting across the aisle? Well, let me propose the following. We will ask him to flip a coin from his pocket. You call it in the air. If you win, I'll pay you $20,000. If you lose, you pay me $1,000." Because Mr. Green is wealthy to start with and because he has already won

$100,000 during the week, you know you will not "feel bad" if you should win, even with the difference in payoffs. In fact, you decide that an extra $20,000 to him is probably close to the same as the $1,000 is to you and your spouse. Finally, you accept the proposition. The coin is flipped and you lose.

On returning, you announce to your spouse that you invested some money in a one-time gamble with Mr. Green and lost $1,000. Your spouse is understandably upset and disappointed at the loss and lets you know in no uncertain terms.

From your standpoint, there was clearly a bad outcome in this case (i.e., the consequences associated with the outcome were unfavorable). Your spouse is reacting to the news of the bad outcome. The question is, does the bad outcome reflect the quality of the decision you made to participate in the gamble? Would you be satisfied to have your spouse judge you using the outcome alone as evidence? Or would you want to explain the circumstance of the gamble in an effort to demonstrate that the decision you made was sound, even though the outcome was bad?

The distinction between *good decisions* and *good outcomes* is important when dealing with decisions under uncertainty. It places the focus back on the process of decision making. If it is difficult to judge the quality of a decision *after the fact*, how can we cope with the process of making a choice before the outcomes are known? To understand this problem a little better, we consider *choices* in general.

### Making Decisions Under Uncertainty

When alternatives have *known* outcomes and consequences are described by a *single measure*, then making a choice is an easy task.[2] For example, assume that one alternative will result in a contribution to profit of $10,000 to be paid in 1 week, and another a contribution to profit of $5,000 to be paid in 1 week. If the only consequence of interest is contribution to profit measured in dollars and the outcomes are guaranteed, say by the federal government, there is no difficulty in deciding on the first alternative. This would be true even if the second alternative had a contribution of $9,999. But when uncertainty is present, the choice becomes more difficult. An example will clarify these difficulties.

[2]The terms *outcome*, *consequence*, and *measure* can sometimes be used interchangeably. However, at other times it may clarify things to think about them separately. Uncertain events have a set of possible outcomes. For instance, if a coin is flipped, one outcome is *heads*. When there is no uncertainty, there is only one possible outcome. Decision makers are interested in the *consequences* associated with various *outcomes*. If you received a prize for every head in a coin flip, the consequence of a head would be the prize. If the prize involves a sum of money, the natural way to *measure* the *consequences* is in terms of dollars. Another name for the measure used to describe the consequences of an outcome is *evaluation unit*. When more than one aspect of a consequence is important, we can discuss the various *attributes* of a consequence. Chapter 2 discusses these issues in more depth.

**Example 1.2**

Assume that two investment alternatives are available. The first involves purchasing a share of an oil drilling syndicate. The second consists of investing in a new shopping center. The investment in each case is $10,000. Also, in each case the properties will be sold once they have been developed. Therefore, both will "pay off" in approximately 1 year. In both cases the money received is uncertain. A thorough investigation has convinced you that the possibilities are as follows:

| *Oil Drilling* | | *Shopping Center* | |
|---|---|---|---|
| *Chance* | *$ Received* | *Chance* | *$ Received* |
| $\frac{1}{4}$ | 0 | $\frac{1}{4}$ | 4,000 |
| $\frac{1}{2}$ | 10,000 | $\frac{1}{2}$ | 14,000 |
| $\frac{1}{4}$ | 100,000 | $\frac{1}{4}$ | 24,000 |

Which would you choose? The choice is not obvious as it was when there was no uncertainty. The simple preference statement, "I prefer more money to less," no longer provides a basis for choosing between the alternatives. The amount received depends on both the alternative chosen and the outcome of the uncertain event. Two people who both agree they prefer more money to less might reasonably disagree on the choice in this example. A new element, called *risk*, enters the decision with uncertainty. The ideas involved in choosing under *certainty* are so simple and familiar that we rarely think about them. These ideas and underlying assumptions become more important when we try to make decisions under *uncertainty*. In fact, they are important enough that one of the major thrusts of the remainder of the book is to lay out options available for helping people make decisions when uncertainty is present.

## PREVIEW

Complications from uncertainty extend to all phases of the decision-making process. It would be nice if we could just ignore the uncertainty. And sometimes we can. But even casual conversations with businessmen and government officials indicate that their lives are filled with uncertainty. Such statements as "I am paid to take risks" and "If I knew for sure what was going to happen, my job would be a cinch" are common. Insurance and investment banking are examples of industries that have been created to deal with uncertainty and risk. Syndicates and partnerships are organized to share risks among individual investors. As the world becomes "smaller," changes in one country's governmental policies can affect business in other countries. Thus, political uncertainty is becoming important for many businesses. The pervasiveness of uncertainty has led to developing the methods presented here.

A comprehensive treatment of decision making under uncertainty is provided. The analytical process is separated into two parts: *models* and *choices*. Figure 1.2 shows the basic organization. Models provide descriptions of decision problems. When uncertainty is present, these models use the theory of probability. Once the decision problem has been modeled, a choice must be made. The options available to a decision maker for making choices are presented.

**FIGURE 1.2**

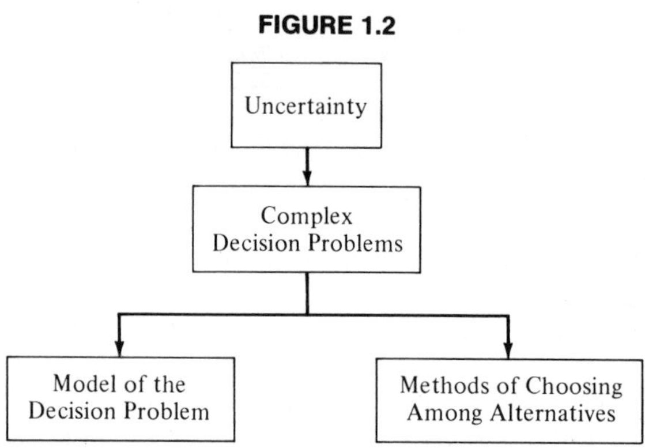


The book is organized into three parts. Part I, consisting of the first six chapters, covers the basic ideas. The purpose is to present quickly the options, concepts, and techniques. It is intended to provide an overview of the process of decision making under uncertainty. Part II and Part III build on this overview.

Part II, consisting of Chapters 7 through 15, covers models under uncertainty in depth. The topics fall into two broad classifications. One is a thorough treatment of the concepts, rules, and techniques for manipulating probabilities. Here the use of probabilities in the model-building process is emphasized. The other is a discussion of how the probabilities required for inputs to the models can be obtained. Procedures based on theoretical, empirical, and subjective assessments are covered. Bayesian revision techniques that allow empirical evidence to be combined with other prior information are also presented.

Part III, Chapters 16 to 20, discusses the choice process under uncertainty in detail. Procedures for assessing preferences in the face of uncertainty, attitudes toward risk, basic behavioral assumptions, risk sharing and incentives, and multiple attribute problems are covered.

Although the presentation of the overview in Part I requires some repetition, the two-pass approach has significant advantages. For one thing, Part I provides the motivation for studying probability. It allows the details of Parts II and III to be placed in context when they are studied. For people who are familiar with some of the material on probabilities, it also allows selective reading.

The fundamental concepts are presented in some depth to provide the background and understanding required to judge the relevance of analytical techniques in specific problems. In some cases the application will be straightforward and noncontroversial. In others, there may be legitimate disagreement on the proper method of analysis. The purpose of presenting a range of techniques is to emphasize the options available in analyzing a decision. Fortunately, in many problems the initial modeling phase leads to a clear choice. The use of the techniques should be guided by the answer to the question: What is the alternative to the analysis? If a simpler procedure, including no analysis at all, is adequate, you should use it.

## SUMMARY

This book is about models and methods of analysis for decisions complicated by uncertainty. Concepts such as probabilities, risk, and information, applicable in economics, finance, marketing, accounting, and operations management, will be developed. Methods and techniques for modeling and analyzing specific decision problems will be discussed in detail.

A major difficulty in making decisions under uncertainty is that "good" decisions can have "poor" outcomes, and vice versa. Uncertainty adds the dimension of risk, complicating the choice process. The objective of this book is to lay out the options available to a decision maker or analyst faced with a complicated problem. To accomplish this, we will consider the fundamentals of both modeling and decision making under uncertainty.

## ASSIGNMENT MATERIAL

**1.1.** Discuss three different approaches to decision making and give examples of when you might use each.

**1.2.** Give an example of a decision problem in which you would not want to be judged solely on the outcome.

**1.3.** Describe how a "good" decision can result in a "poor" outcome.

**1.4.** Describe why knowing which outcome you prefer is not adequate for making a choice under uncertainty.

## SELECTED REFERENCES ON MULTIPERSON DECISIONS


ARROW, K. J. *Social Choice and Individual Values*. New York: Wiley, 1951.

BUCHANAN, J. M., AND G. TULLOCK. *The Calculus of Consent, Logical Foundations of Constitutional Democracy*. Ann Arbor, Mich.: University of Michigan Press, 1962, Chaps. 10, 11, 12.

LUCE, R. D., AND H. RAIFFA. *Games and Decisions: Introduction and Critical Survey*. New York: Wiley, 1967, Chap. 14, pp. 327–345.

QUIRK, J., AND R. SAPOSNIK. *Introduction to General Equilibrium Theory and Welfare Economics*. New York: McGraw-Hill, 1968, Chap. 4.

RAIFFA, H. *Decision Analysis: Introductory Lectures on Choices Under Uncertainty*. Reading, Mass.: Addison-Wesley, 1968, Chap. 8, pp. 220–228.

SEN, A. K. *Collective Choice and Social Welfare*. San Francisco: Holden-Day, 1970.

WILSON, R. "An Axiomatic Model of Logrolling." *American Economic Review*, Vol. 59, No. 3, June 1969.

# 2

# The Analytical Approach

Psychologists, sociologists, economists, and mathematicians have all studied the process of making decisions. It will come as no surprise that they have different ideas about the process. The approach presented here—the *analytical approach*—relies primarily on concepts and procedures developed by economists and mathematicians. Perhaps more accurately, the approach has been developed by a subset of economists and mathematicians who are often called decision theorists or management scientists. The approach is characterized by formal, logical statements and procedures. Its use is motivated by problems that are hard to think about because of their complexity.

The fact that *other* approaches have been left out does not mean they have nothing of value to bring to decision making but simply that this book is about quantitative, analytical methods. We will study the techniques in detail. However, before getting started, there is an overall or big-picture issue to discuss: we must have clearly in mind what *can* be expected from analytical methods and quantitative analyses and, just as important, what *cannot* be expected from them.

## THE QUANTITATIVE/ANALYTICAL APPROACH

### The Modeling Phase

The quantitative/analytical approach looks for relationships between inputs (or decision variables) over which managers have some control and outputs (or consequences) in which managers have an interest. It tries to establish reasonably precise quantitative expressions for these relationships. The result of these two steps is a *model* that can be used to determine the consequences of different decisions. Schematically such a model can be represented as shown in Figure 2.1.

Examples of decision variables are price, production quantity, and capital expenditures. Consequences are often measured in terms of profit, sales, or costs. Exogenous inputs might include general economic conditions or government tax policy. The model *links* alternatives to their consequences.

**FIGURE 2.1**

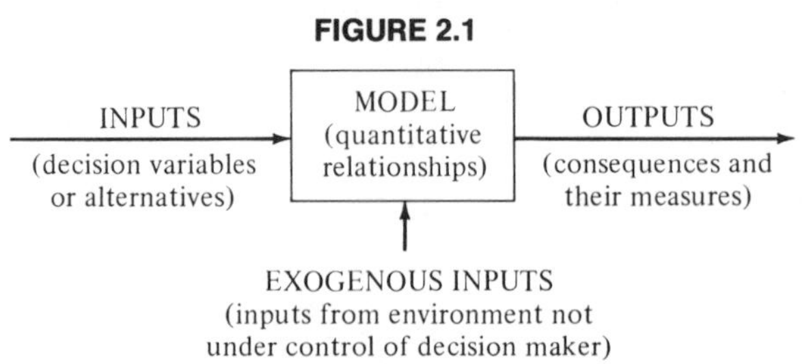

### The Choice Phase

Next, the information from the model is used to make a *choice*. During the choice phase analytical procedures can be used to help relate the consequences to the decision maker's *preferences* or *values*. This phase is simple when there is certainty and consequences are described by a single measure, but it can be very difficult when uncertainty is present or the consequences involve more than one important attribute.

## DECOMPOSITION

The overall approach, then, tries to connect what we have control over with our preferences. But, how does it work? Quantitative methods imply numbers. Choices clearly depend on individual values. Even in the modeling phase, judgments may be required. How can these values and judgments be included in a quantitative procedure? The detailed answer to this question will take most of the book to present. However, the overall *strategy* can be explained. It is simple: *divide and conquer*. The term used to describe this strategy is *decomposition*. Rather than eliminate judgment, the entire thrust is to make judgment easier to apply. Complex problems are broken down into smaller problems. Decisions are made for the smaller—hopefully easier—problems. The decisions for these smaller problems are combined (using mathematical manipulations) to provide a decision to the original complex problem. The benefit of decomposing the original problem is that *judgment* often can be applied more easily using the decomposed problem. For example, a simple estimate of profitability can use estimates of revenue from the marketing department and costs from the accounting department. These estimates can be combined using simple algebra to determine profit. It is no secret that marketing staffs must use judgment in developing a revenue projection (the projection may, in fact, be the result of further decomposition). Similarly, accountants and auditors know that judgment plays an essential role in developing cost estimates.

A simple example may help to make the decomposition/recomposition ideas clear.

**Example 2.1**

Assume that you are faced with the choice between two alternative means of providing the data-processing capacity for your organization. Both alternatives would be supplied from the same company and require the same input and output capabilities. The methods of entering data, formats, and equipment are identical, as are the printing devices required for output. Also, the operating systems and software packages (computer programs) are the same. The difference involves the method of acquiring the actual computer processing and storage capabilities. In both cases all processing, with the exception of input and output operations, will be done outside your organization.

Alternative 1 consists of a contract for unlimited access to processing time up to a maximum of 100 hours per month. The contracting company has enough experience with the data-processing requirements and characteristics of jobs in organizations similar to yours that they are willing to contract directly on total hours used independent of the mix between input–output activity and central processing unit use. The cost for this fixed block of service is $8,000 per month. Under alternative 1, storage for data files and programs is also provided on a fixed-charge basis of $2,000 per month for 50 million bytes (a unit of information for computers) of storage.

Alternative 2 consists of supplying both processing time and storage on a demand basis. The rate for processing time (again independent of the mix between input–output and central processing unit time) is $2/minute and the storage cost $\$6\times 10^{-4}$/byte-month.

The choice between the two alternatives obviously depends on the amount of storage and processing time required by your organization. A reasonable way for you to proceed in the analysis would be to contact the users to determine their needs for the upcoming year. For purposes of illustration, assume that there are two users in the organization, payroll/accounting and operations. After discussion with the payroll/accounting department you determine that the computer will be used to keep track of all payroll information for both salaried and hourly employees and to calculate weekly payrolls, including deductions for withholding, insurance, savings plans, and so on. The department head states that past usage indicates weekly processing time for this task to be 8 hours. He says storage requirements depend on the number of employees. Each employee requires a record that takes 1,000 bytes. There are 3,000 employees. Other data storage and software take an additional 2 million bytes for the payroll/accounting department.

Operating department usage varies considerably over the year. During periods of heavy demand in the first 3 months of the year, the department head indicates they must perform an analysis 5 days/week, which requires 2 hours/day. During the next 6 months the analysis only needs to be run twice a week (2 hours for each run) and for the last 3 months, as demand picks up, it is run three times per week. He claims that storage requirements are constant at 5 million bytes.

An analysis follows.

COMPARISON BETWEEN DATA-PROCESSING ALTERNATIVES

| *Alternative 1:* Fixed Processing Time and Storage | | | *Annual Cost* |
|---|---|---|---|
| A. *Processing Time:* | 100 hours/month | | |
| | (\$8,000/month)×(12 months) | | $ 96,000 |
| B. *Storage:* | 50 million bytes | | |
| | (\$2,000/month)×(12 months) | | 24,000 |
| | | *Total* | $120,000 |

*Alternative 2:* Processing Time and Storage on Demand

A. *Processing Time:*

1. *Payroll/Accounting:*

*Demand:* (8 hours/week)×(52 weeks/year) = 416 hours/year

*Cost:* (416 hours/year)×(60 minutes/hour)× ($2/minute) $ 49,920

2. *Operations:*

*Demand:* January–March
(2 hours/day)×(64 days) = 128 hours
April–September
(4 hours/week)×(26 weeks) = 104 hours
October–December
(6 hours/week)×(13 weeks) = 78 hours
310 hours

*Cost:* (310 hours)×(60 minutes/hour)×($2/minute) 37,200

*Total Processing Time Cost* $ 87,120

B. *Storage:*

1. *Payroll/Accounting:*

*Demand:*

Variable: (1,000 bytes/employee)×(3,000 employees) = $3\times10^6$ bytes/month

Fixed: $2\times10^6$ bytes/month

Total Demand: $5\times10^6$ bytes

*Cost:* ($5\times10^6$ bytes/month)×($\$6\times10^{-4}$/byte-month)×(12 months) $ 36,000

2. *Operations:*

*Demand:* $5\times10^6$ bytes/month

*Cost:* ($5\times10^6$ bytes/month)×($\$6\times10^{-4}$/byte-month)×(12 months) 36,000

*Total Storage Cost* $ 72,000

*Total* $159,120

This analysis is straightforward and presents a case for choosing alternative 1 as long as the capacity meets or exceeds the demand. This can be checked easily. The maximum demand for processing time occurs during the first 3 months of the year: payroll/accounting = (8 hours/week)×(5 weeks) = 40 hours; operations = (2 hours/day)×(23 days) = 46 hours. This sum is less than the 100 hours maximum per month, and hence the fixed capacity is adequate to service the demand. Similarly, the 50 million bytes of storage is more than adequate to cover the 10 million bytes of demand.

### The Use of Decomposition

The decomposition used in this analysis is obvious. But since our purpose is to consider in detail the use of analytical methods, three points are worth emphasizing. *First*, note how the decomposition is used. In evaluating alternative 1 the annual costs were calculated by multiplying the monthly cost by the number of months. While this is a completely trivial calculation, it is an instance of decomposition. The calculation breaks up the quantity of interest (annual cost for alternative 1) in the following way:

$$\text{Total annual cost} = \text{Annual processing cost} + \text{Annual storage cost}$$
$$\text{Annual processing cost} = (\text{Monthly cost}) \times (\text{Number of months})$$
$$\text{Annual storage cost} = (\text{Monthly cost}) \times (\text{Number of months})$$

The calculations for alternative 2 are also simple. Costs are decomposed into demand and cost per unit. The method of recombination is obvious. Processing costs and storage costs are calculated by multiplying demand times the cost per unit for each month. The totals are obtained by adding the costs. The procedure is trivial in this deterministic example. However, as we will see, when uncertainty is present, the decomposition and recombination are not so obvious.

### Different Ways to Decompose

The *second* point is that there are a number of different ways to decompose this problem. For instance, in determining demand for payroll/accounting, the number of hours per week was multiplied by 52 to obtain hours/year. Another option is to find the number of hours per run and multiply by the number of runs per year. The estimate for demand could have been decomposed further by considering weekly demand to be the sum of daily demands. The *proper* level of decomposition depends on the problem. At one extreme the alternative could be evaluated without any decomposition. The annual costs could be guessed at without any calculations. Once the data are obtained, it is not likely that a decision would be made without calculating the annual costs for each alternative as shown here. However, before gathering the data, we might reasonably consider making the choice without an analysis to save the cost of gathering the information and doing the analysis. For this problem most people would agree to undertake the analysis suggested above. But as the costs of information and analysis increase, the option of choosing without doing the analysis becomes more attractive.

### The Use of Judgment

The *third* point to emphasize is the use of judgment. Earlier the claim was made that quantitative methods do not eliminate judgment. Rather, they allow it to be applied more easily. If a choice were made without analysis, it is clear that the decision maker would be using judgment. The question is, does the analysis eliminate the judgment? The answer is clearly no. The judgment is shifted from the overall choice to the inputs of the quantitative analysis. For example, the inputs—*hours per week for payroll/accounting*, *number of analyses per week*, and *time per analysis for the operations depart-*

*ment*—were obtained from department heads, using their judgment. Using these figures to calculate costs involves a judgment on the part of the decision maker.

## THE ROLE OF MANAGERS

The need for judgmental inputs means that managers as well as specialists must be involved in the analytical process. In addition, a decision to initiate a quantitative study can only be made by a manager with authority to allocate funds. Leaving these decisions in the hands of specialists who have a vested interest in analysis is certainly not an attractive prospect.

Experience also indicates that close liaison between managers and specialists is important even after initiation of an analysis. Otherwise, as the analysis proceeds, the problem perceived by the manager may not be the same as the problem being addressed by the analyst. Using the results of an analysis effectively also depends on involvement of both managers and specialists. Too often managers are presented with thick reports using methods and assumptions they do not understand, leaving them in the unenviable position of either disregarding the efforts of the staff or accepting them on blind faith.

## THE USE OF ANALYTICAL PROCEDURES

During the last two decades, the use of analytical procedures has increased dramatically. One of the main reasons is the increasing complexity of the problems in both the private and public sectors. This complexity pushes the unaided human mind to its limits.[1] The availability of large high-speed digital computers has allowed those interested in analytical procedures to develop a formidable set of tools. The result is a cult of analysis based on decomposition, logic, and rationality.

This cult has been criticized on a variety of grounds. The basic effectiveness of analytical reasoning has been questioned and alternatives to the analytical styles of thought proposed.[2] But even if progress is made on alternative styles of thought, analytical processes are not likely to be completely abandoned. Another criticism is that analytical procedures fail to account for all aspects of a problem. This is a different type of criticism. It is

[1]See A. Newell and H. M. Simon, *Human Problem Solving* (Englewood Cliffs, N.J.: Prentice-Hall, 1972); and J. March and H. A. Simon, *Organizations* (New York: Wiley, 1958).

[2]See H. J. Leavitt, "Beyond the Analytic Manager," *California Management Review*, Spring–Summer 1975; and J. March, "The Technology of Foolishness," in H. J. Leavitt et al. (eds.), *Organization–Environment Relations in the Future* (New York: Praeger, 1974).

based on an *assumption* about the role of quantitative methods, which is, at the very least, open to serious question. Specialists in management science and nonspecialists alike have a tendency to treat an output from an analysis as an objective solution to a decision problem. This interpretation is not only misleading, but almost always incorrect. One of the main reasons for the back-to-basic-principles approach taken here is to lay bare the assumptions underlying the analytical processes. An understanding of the basic principles will not only make it easier to use the procedures but, more important, ensure that there is no misunderstanding about their role in problem solving.

### Analytical Procedures as Information Generators

Since analytical procedures are based on decomposing decisions so that judgments can be made more easily, it is clear that individuals, not the procedures, make the decisions. If the output of an analysis is not a decision, what should we call it? It is simply *information*. In principle, using a very sophisticated model or analysis is no different from summarizing data by computing an average. Both supply information. In one case the information may be in the following form: Based on available data, the average number of arrests per day in San Francisco during April is 50. In a more sophisticated model, the information may be in this form: Based on available costs and capacities, the minimum cost, assuming that all manufacturing is done internally, results from a production mix of 500 type A units and 300 type B units. Thinking about the output as information helps to place quantitative/analytical methods in the proper perspective. In particular, it makes clear that use of these techniques must compete on the basis of cost and effectiveness with other information alternatives, including gathering no additional information or making no formal analysis.

### Implementation of Decisions Based on Analysis

Implementation involves acting on the decisions that were made on the basis of an analysis. In some cases the decisions may require changes in an organization. There is substantial interest in this topic among proponents of analytical methods.[3] A variety of directions are being pursued, including behavioral and organizational research and the design of interactive computer systems with graphical displays.

A basic problem is that because of the complexity, many decisions are not immediately recognized as the best course of action by those who are affected. For example, if a thorough analysis of the costs and benefits indicates that a new purchasing policy should be instituted, it is unlikely that those involved will react by saying: "Of course. Why didn't I think of that?"

[3] See the list of selected references at the end of this section for a description of some of the work.

The complexities of the problem and the fact that different groups are affected in different ways will prevent this from happening. As a result, the decisions may never be implemented unless some specific effort is made to explain the policy and gain the acceptance of those affected. As simple and self-evident as it may be, the most important step in implementation is recognizing the importance of existing organizational constraints on the decision process.

One difficulty in dealing with implementation is that it is not always clear what constitutes an implementation failure. One type of failure might involve the rejection of a specific recommendation by someone higher in the organization. We could argue about this being regarded as a failure. An analyst or manager who recommends one action which is rejected, may have done an excellent job if he has correctly assessed the consequences. After all, preferences for consequences are individual in nature and agreement will not always be reached. In other cases the analysis may include only one aspect of the problem. The individual making the decision may use the analysis as one of many inputs in the overall decision process. Success or failure in these situations should not be tied to implementation of a specific recommendation but rather to use of the analysis as part of the decision process.

## ●● STEPS IN THE OVERALL PROCESS[4]

The overall process of problem solving can be described in three steps: developing alternatives, creating a model to evaluate alternatives, and making a choice.

### ●● Developing Alternatives

This is a crucial part of problem solving, since choices obviously are limited to the set of alternatives considered. For many problems—particularly complex, one-of-a-kind decisions—there may be only a few alternatives considered. For instance, in locating a new facility, it is likely that only two or three alternative sites will be considered in depth.

An important impact of quantitative methods on alternative generation is to reduce the time and cost needed to evaluate an alternative. In many cases computer models can rapidly evaluate alternatives. This can help an individual develop insights leading to new alternatives or leading to changes in the problem formulations. The thrust of much of the work on interactive computer programs is to foster these insights by rapid feedback and easy communication between the individual and the computer. Alternative generation is a creative process that must involve the individual. There is a large

[4]Sections labeled ●● include more advanced or detailed treatment.

amount of evidence that the process is not always, or even most often, analytical.[5] On the other hand, the use of analytical models to evaluate alternatives can aid the process.

## ●● Creating the Model: Describing the Consequences

The output from a model used to evaluate alternatives must describe the consequences in terms that are meaningful to decision makers. This can be done in several ways. One possibility is a verbal description, presenting in rich detail various aspects of the consequences. The position papers of government agencies use this type of description. These verbal descriptions can use a broad spectrum of words, conveying different shades of meanings. In some cases supplementing the verbal descriptions with pictures is particularly effective.

When alternatives have significant differences on some aspects of the consequences, comparison using verbal descriptions is difficult. Developing specific *attributes* and *measures* that can be directly compared may make comparison easier. The fewer attributes required to describe adequately the alternatives, the easier the comparison becomes. Consequences are sometimes easier to describe in the private sector because a single profit figure is often adequate.

**Determining the Essential Features.** When several aspects of the consequences are important, developing attributes and measures can be a difficult task. The idea is to capture the *essence* of the consequences in a few, measurable attributes. There are three steps in the process. The first is to decide what constitutes the essence. Such terms as *goals* and *objectives* are often used to describe things that are important in a problem and hence are a guide to what is essential. The idea is that if something does not relate to an objective, it cannot be essential and therefore can be left out of the description.

When more than one person is involved, individual differences can result in disagreement on the goals and objectives. However, in determining the essential features of an alternative, it is (at least theoretically) possible to consider objectives held by any participant. In fact, even diametrically opposed objectives can be included if we refrain from specifying which *direction* is preferred. For instance, if the decision involves development of open land for an industrial park, the amount of *industrial development* could

[5]In addition to the Leavitt, Newell and Simon, and March references previously cited, the interested reader may wish to pursue: (a) J. S. Bruner, J. J. Goodnow, and G. A. Austin, *A Study of Thinking* (New York: Wiley, 1956); (b) P. Keen and J. McKenney, "How Managers' Minds Work," *Harvard Business Review*, May 1974; (c) P. C. Wason and P. N. Johnson-Laird, *Psychology of Reasoning, Structure and Content* (Cambridge, Mass.: Harvard University Press, 1972); (d) P. C. Wason and P. N. Johnson-Laird, *Thinking and Reasoning* (New York: Penguin, 1968).

be included as an important aspect. Some people will place a positive value on more industrial development and others a negative value.

Goals and objectives are psychological concepts involving an individual's preferences. They are often hierarchical in nature, with overall features subdivided into more specific ones.[6] To prevent misunderstandings that might occur from the use of such terms as goals and objectives—which carry with them connotations of directions and preferences—we can substitute *essential features* for the terms *goals* and *objectives*.

**Determining the Attributes.** The second step in describing alternatives is to provide a link between the psychological concepts of objectives, goals, and essential features and the objective world of alternatives. This link is provided by *attributes*. Attributes are characteristics or properties that are related to goals and objectives. For example, if the feature under consideration were *industrial development*, one attribute associated with the concept might be *economic activity*. Another might be *depletion of open space*. There may be others, depending on what the psychological concept "industrial development" means to an individual.

**Developing Measures.** A measure is a quantitative scale used to describe the relative levels of an attribute. Another term used is *evaluation units*. To be useful, a measure must have a high correlation with the attribute it is describing. For example, a measure for the attribute *economic activity* might be *number of new jobs*, and a measure for *depletion of open space* might be *acres*. Another requirement is that the scale value of the measure must be available for each alternative under consideration. To be useful in describing an alternative, a measure must be both highly correlated with the attribute and available for each alternative.

If a set of attributes and measures can be obtained, it contributes toward the choice process in two ways. First, it serves as a convenient summary of the *important* characteristics of the decision problem at hand. Second, it makes comparisons and *trade-offs* among attributes easier to make. Notice that the statement is not that the comparisons are *easy* but *easier*. These comparisons can still be extremely difficult.

### ●● Creating the Model: Relating Alternatives to Consequences

The traditional role of analysts, and consequently of analyses, has been gathering data about the consequences of various alternative actions. This means establishing the relationships that link alternatives to consequences—described in terms of attributes and measures of interest. In a quantitative analysis these relationships form the model. Methods for creating these

[6]See J. R. Miller III, *Professional Decision Making* (New York: Praeger, 1970), for an extensive discussion of the process of developing goals, attributes, and measures.

models when uncertainty is present will be discussed in detail throughout the book.

A short hypothetical example will serve to illustrate the model-building process when multiple attributes are important.

**Example 2.2: Creating a Model**

The manager of the Tetons Area Rapid Transit (TART) was charged with the responsibility of bringing high-quality transportation to the Tetons National Park and surrounding area. His initial step was several months of protracted discussions with potential bidders on a transportation system. Two months later he received bids and descriptions from two contractors.

Contractor *A* recommends an overhead monorail system. The system is all electric; the towers are gracefully designed and vary in height from 10 feet to 20 feet off the ground. The cars are entered from a series of platforms which have parking lots on the first two levels, and the lobby and ticket booths on the third level, which is the entry level for the monorail cars. Each car is designed like a lounge with seats facing forward, backward, and toward the middle. Each seat is an individual unit designed to provide a comfortable ride. The system is fast, taking approximately 30 minutes to complete a one-way trip. The estimate of capital costs for construction of the towers is $70 million, with the purchase of the cars another $30 million. Operating costs are projected to be $10 million per year. The engineers have spent considerable effort to ensure a trouble-free design.

Contractor *B* has come up with a plan which he feels will harmonize with the rustic, rugged western landscape. It is a surface rail system using the conventional two-track configuration. Power is supplied by coal, which is readily available in this part of the country. The train cars are fashioned after the parlor cars of the 1890s but are designed using modern materials for safety and durability. The system is designed to take 40 minutes to complete a trip. However, before starting back, a 10-minute wait is necessary for refueling. Engineers estimate that the rail system and stations will cost $40 million. The equipment is projected to cost an additional $40 million, with operating costs at $7 million per year.

The manager is faced with a choice between these two systems. He has been told to recommend one of the two systems to his superiors.

These descriptions serve as an example of verbal descriptions of two alternatives—obviously they could be greatly expanded. A description of the consequences using a set of attributes and measures is illustrated in Figure 2.2 (no claim is made for completeness, as the purpose is to illustrate attributes and measures). The measures used include judgmental scales (like comfort) and objective measures (like dollars and minutes). We will not pursue the question of how various scales can be constructed; however, careful design of the attributes and measures can make the choice easier.[7] With the attributes and measures suggested in Figure 2.2, the next step is to provide the link to the alternatives. We will not attempt to describe this phase here. Some of the

[7]See Miller, *Professional Decision Making*, or R. Keeney and H. Raiffa, *Decisions with Multiple Objectives* (New York: Wiley, 1976).

**FIGURE 2.2**

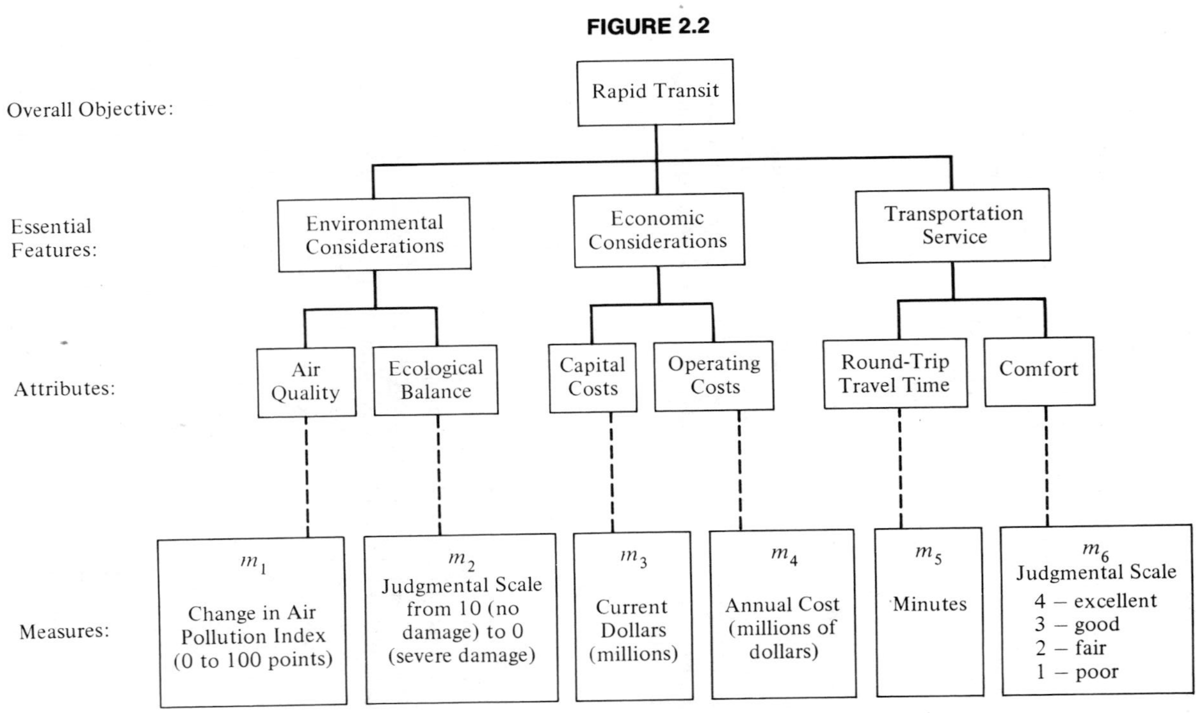
Overall Objective:
Rapid Transit
Essential Features:
Environmental Considerations
Economic Considerations
Transportation Service
Attributes:
Air Quality
Ecological Balance
Capital Costs
Operating Costs
Round-Trip Travel Time
Comfort
Measures:
$m_1$ Change in Air Pollution Index (0 to 100 points)
$m_2$ Judgmental Scale from 10 (no damage) to 0 (severe damage)
$m_3$ Current Dollars (millions)
$m_4$ Annual Cost (millions of dollars)
$m_5$ Minutes
$m_6$ Judgmental Scale
4 – excellent
3 – good
2 – fair
1 – poor

information such as costs and travel time is directly available. The other must be obtained through additional analysis. If the process were completed, we might obtain the results shown in Table 2.1.

**TABLE 2.1**
**Estimated Level of Measures for Salient Attributes**

| | $m_1$ | $m_2$ | $m_3$ | $m_4$ | $m_5$ | $m_6$ |
|---|---|---|---|---|---|---|
| *Alternative A* | 0 | 7 | 100 | 10 | 60 | 4 |
| *Alternative B* | 10 | 8 | 80 | 7 | 90 | 3 |

### ●● Making the Decision

This is the final step in the process. Difficulties encountered when uncertainty is present have been described in Chapter 1. When more than one attribute is required to describe the consequences of the alternative, the problem of deciding can also be difficult. Procedures for dealing with these problems are discussed in Chapter 20.

## SUMMARY

The basic strategy behind the analytical approach to decision making is *decomposition*. The first level of decomposition is separating the decision problem into two phases: the *modeling* phase and the *choice* phase. The model links alternatives to consequences. The choice process links the consequences to individual preferences. The purpose of decomposition is to make it easier to apply the judgments required in a decision—not, as sometimes supposed, to eliminate judgment. There are always different ways to decompose a problem. In many familiar cases the decomposition is trivial (e.g., breaking up profit into revenue minus costs). In other cases—particularly when uncertainty is present—the creation of a model can be challenging.

The proper use of these analytical procedures requires participation of both managers and specialists. To participate effectively, the limitations as well as the benefits of these procedures must be understood. This accounts for the *basic* approach taken in the book.

The overall process of problem solving can be described by three steps: developing alternatives, creating a model to evaluate alternatives, and making a choice. Creating the model consists of describing the consequences—possibly in terms of multiple attributes—and relating each alternative to the consequences. The process of creating a model and making a choice becomes complicated when there is uncertainty or multiple attributes. The techniques for dealing with these complications when uncertainty is present provide the main focus for the remainder of the book.

## ASSIGNMENT MATERIAL

**2.1.** Explain how decomposition can facilitate making a decision.

**2.2.** Explain the difference between a *goal* and an *essential feature*.

**2.3.** What is the relationship between an *objective* and an *attribute*?

**2.4.** What two conditions must be satisfied for a *measure* to be useful?

**2.5.** Consider the following statement: "The use of subjective judgments is inconsistent with using analytical techniques." Explain why you either agree or disagree with the statement.

**2.6. Antenna Systems**

Antenna Systems was founded in 1967 to take advantage of the growing market for television antenna facilities to service cities where reception was poor or the population was too small to support a full range of television stations. Thomas Brent founded the firm after studying civil and electrical engineering in college and gaining 3 years of experience working in the Facilities Planning Division of a major television network. Because of his background, Brent decided to focus initially on the construction of facilities and not their operation. His long-range thinking included the operations aspects of the business, but for the present he felt he needed more experience and capital to make both construction and operation profitable.

For these reasons, Brent adopted the firm policy of selling community-antenna facilities as soon as they were constructed. In developing a new location, the company obtained a franchise from the city government, and then, before committing any resources to actual construction, tried to interest local businesspeople and investors in forming a company to purchase and operate the facility as soon as it was completed and checked out. If Brent failed to organize a local group that would contract for purchase of the facility on satisfactory terms, he preferred to forfeit the franchise rather than tie up his limited working capital for an indefinite period of time.

On June 1, 1971, Antenna Systems held only one franchise for system installation. Work on this project was drawing to a close and would be completed within a week. Early that morning a small electronics distributor approached Brent and asked if he would supply him with 50 VHF antennas. Although Antenna Systems did not normally manufacture antennas for external distributors, it did maintain the necessary manufacturing capability since it regularly produced such antennas for its own use. The electronics distributor thought he could sell the 50 antennas during the next year. Based on his own estimated selling price the distributor offered to pay $100 per antenna.

Brent took the proposition to his production foreman and asked him how much he thought it would cost to make 50 units. The foreman replied that he did not know offhand but at least 1 week of the company's production time would be required. Raw materials for the last similar antennas had cost $42 per unit and the housing for the transducer had been purchased for $45 per unit. Referring to the latest monthly operating report (Exhibit I), the foreman said it looked like a losing proposition to him, since the margin would not likely be enough to carry the overhead.

*Exhibit I*

*Operating Report*
*May 1971*

| | |
|---|---:|
| Salaries | $2,000 |
| Payroll | 2,500 |
| Rent | 200 |
| Utilities | 50 |
| Supplies and equipment | 1,500 |
| Miscellaneous | 250 |
| Total | $6,500 |

After looking at the operating report Brent asked the foreman to determine how many hours he thought it would take to produce one antenna, using a member of their normal work crew (paid at $5 per hour), and to give him the report that afternoon. After some analysis of standard operating costs, the foreman reported: "I am confident that after we get the process set up, one unit could be made in 1 hour by one man. But the setup would take about another 60 hours." With this new information Brent returned to his office to decide whether to take the job.

*Questions*

1. What would you do if you were Brent?
2. In your analysis, where did you use decomposition?
3. If you were Brent, would you be satisfied with the level of decomposition you were able to use in the analysis? If not, what additional information would you like?

## 2.7. Leslie Electronics, Inc. (A)

Leslie Electronics, Inc., is a small electronic components manufacturer located in Mountain View, California. It was founded in 1963 by Donald Leslie (B.S., M.S.E.E., Rice Institute of Technology). Before coming to California, Leslie had worked for 3 years as a design engineer with Texas Instruments. Leslie Electronics produces very specialized electronic subassemblies that are sold to larger electronic companies for inclusion in their final products.

Late in August 1972, Leslie was contacted by Sidney Roth, president of Audio Concepts, Inc., of Santa Rosa, California. Audio Concepts was a firm engaged in the construction of music recording studios both for independent and major recording companies. Roth is about to sign a contract to construct a recording studio complex in San Francisco, and has asked Leslie if he can supply approximately 100 electronic portasols at $1,000 each.

Leslie is inclined to take the job, since his plant will be operating at a fairly low capacity until the first of November, when work on an RCA contract is begun. Leslie Electronics has never produced portasols before, but it has produced a closely related product and Leslie feels that there is no technical problem standing in the way. He called Hans Sturdevant, his plant engineer, into his office, and told him of Roth's offer.

"I think we should accept the offer, especially considering how slow things are in the plant," Sturdevant said. "I figure that one worker could assemble one in about 10 hours. At our wage rates we could figure that's about $50. The raw materials would be about $450 per portasol. As for the housings, there are two possible ways we can go. We could buy them at $300 each—they are quite similar to the ones we bought for that small General Electric contract—or we could buy a mold and make them ourselves for about $50 each. The mold would cost us around $17,500, but of course we'd have it if we ever need to make additional portasol housings."

*Questions*

1. What should Leslie do?
2. How would Leslie's decision change if Roth had asked for 50 instead of 100 units?
3. At what number of units would Leslie be indifferent as to which method he used?
4. If Leslie decides to purchase the mold and make the housings, how many units must he sell to start making a contribution? How many units must Leslie sell to make a profit if he decides to buy the housings?
5. How was decomposition used in your analysis?

## SELECTED REFERENCES ON IMPLEMENTATION


CHURCHMAN, C. WEST. "Theories of Implementation," in Randall L. Schultz and Dennis P. Slevin, eds., *Implementing Operations Research/Management Science*. New York: American Elsevier Publishing Company, Inc., 1975, pp. 23–30.

DOKTOR, ROBERT, RANDALL L. SCHULTZ, AND DENNIS P. SLEVIN, eds. *The Implementation of Management Science*. Amsterdam: North Holland Publishing Co., 1979.

HAMMOND, J. S. "The Roles of the Manager and Analyst in Effective Implementation." *Sloan Management Review*, Vol. 15, No. 2, 1974.

HUYSMANS, J. H. *The Implementation of Operations Research*, New York: Wiley, 1970.

MCKENNEY, J. L., AND P. G. W. KEEN. "How Managers' Minds Work." *Harvard Business Review*, May–June 1974.

RADNOR, M., A. H. RUBENSTEIN, AND D. A. TONSIK. "Implementation in Operations Research and R&D in Government and Business Organizations." *Operations Research*, Vol. 18, No. 6, November–December 1970.

RADNOR, M. AND R. NEAL. "The Progress of Management Science Activities in Large U.S. Industrial Organizations." *Operations Research*, Vol. 21, March–April 1973.

# 3

# Modeling Under Uncertainty – Diagrams and Tables

When complexity due to uncertainty leads to formal analysis, decomposition and analytic methods may offer some help in two areas. The first is in the representation or modeling process, and the second is in the choice process. This chapter discusses two procedures for modeling: decision diagrams and payoff tables. These procedures are helpful in structuring the decision problem in order to define the possible *outcomes*. We also illustrate how *evaluation units* are assigned to each *outcome*—that is, how *measures* are used to describe the *consequences* of each outcome. Figure 3.1 shows where the topics fit into the overall discussion.

## BASIC CONCEPTS AND TECHNIQUES

Decision diagrams, or *decision trees* as they are often called, and payoff tables are nothing more than graphical or tabular representations of the possible outcomes. These possible outcomes are determined by the uncertain events and available alternatives. The power of the procedures lies in simplicity and intuitive appeal. Although we will discuss several rules and conventions, a

**FIGURE 3.1**

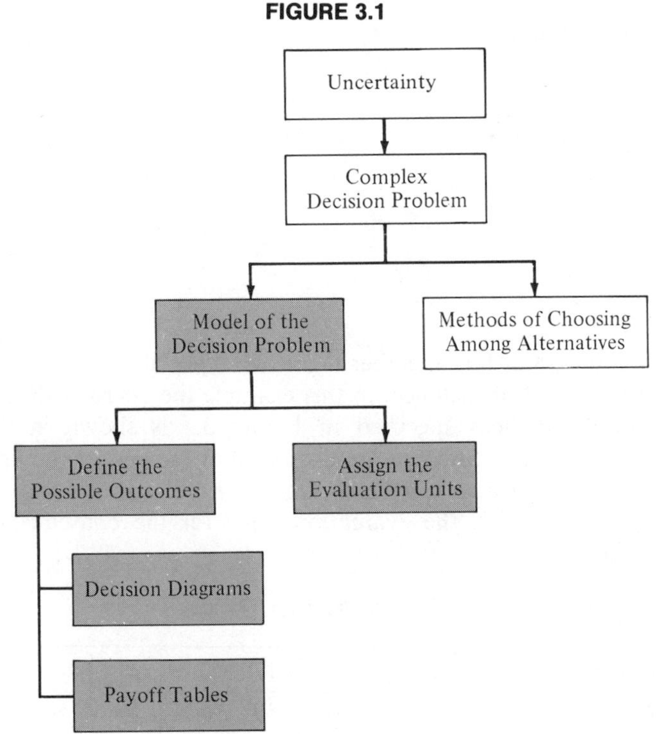

decision diagram is just a chronological picture of what can happen for each decision alternative. It is a tool to help structure problems when uncertainty is present. More than anything it is a practical aid to straight thinking.

There are usually several different models that can be used to represent a decision problem. Besides providing a *correct representation* of the decisions and uncertain events, a model should make it easy for the decision maker to *input judgments*. In this chapter we will concentrate on the more technical aspects of correctly portraying the decision problem. In later chapters, where options are presented for obtaining probabilities, we will discuss diagramming to make it easy to apply judgment.

## DECISION DIAGRAMS

### Diagramming Conventions

Decision problems under uncertainty are made up of *decisions* and *uncertain events*. By convention the diagrams use a □ to represent a decision and a ○ to represent an uncertain event. Figure 3.2 shows a hypothetical *decision node*. Each branch represents a single alternative. Figure 3.3 shows the *event nodes* for a coin flip and the roll of a six-sided die.

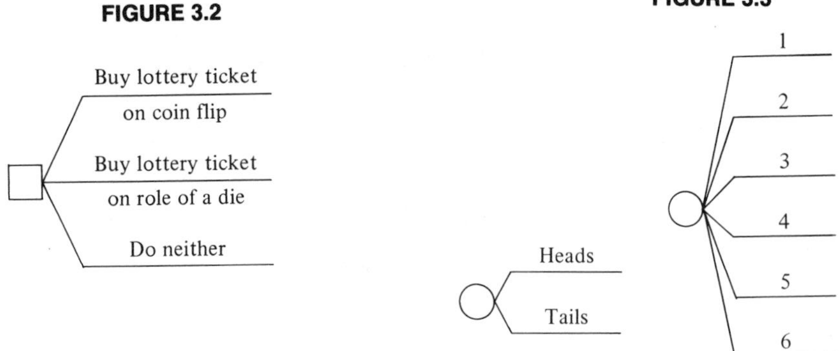


Decision diagrams link together these two types of nodes to represent the possible outcomes. For instance, in this example the decision diagram corresponding to the choices specified in Figure 3.2 is shown in Figure 3.4. Consequences for each outcome are displayed at the end of the branches. If either lottery ticket in the example costs $1 and the payoffs for the outcomes are shown in Table 3.1, the evaluation units for the consequences are as shown on Figure 3.4.

**TABLE 3.1**

| *Outcome* | Head | Tail | 1 | 2 | 3 | 4 | 5 | 6 |
|---|---|---|---|---|---|---|---|---|
| *Payoff* | $2 | $0 | $1 | $0 | $2 | $0 | $0 | $3 |

**FIGURE 3.4**

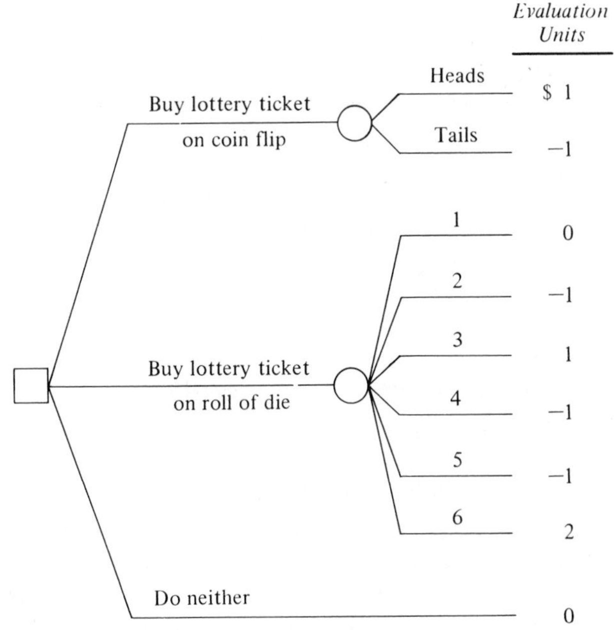


### Guidelines and Rules for Diagramming

Diagrams such as Figure 3.4 are very easy to construct. In some cases, however, the structuring problem is more difficult. In these cases guidelines and rules are helpful in keeping things straight. The guidelines and rules stated below will be illustrated by an example and explained further later in the chapter. Read them through quickly and then go on to the example.

Guidelines and Rules for Diagramming

1. Identify the *immediate decision* and *alternatives* to be considered.
2. Determine an *evaluation date* for the consequences of the immediate decision.
3. Identify all uncertain events that can *directly affect* the *consequences* of the alternatives that make up the *immediate decision*.
4. Identify all *future decisions* that can directly affect the consequences of the alternatives that make up the immediate decision.
5. Identify all uncertain events that may *provide information* that can affect any future decision.
6. Outcomes and alternatives at any node must be *mutually*

*exclusive* (i.e., no more than one can possibly occur or be chosen).
7. Outcomes and alternatives at any node should be *collectively exhaustive* (i.e., at least one must occur).
8. Diagram events and decisions *chronologically*, using the date at which the decision maker learns of the outcome or must make the decision.
9. Two or more event nodes not separated by a decision node, or two or more decision nodes not separated by an event node, can be interchanged.

The Recreational Properties Incorporated example given below will be used to illustrate the rules and guidelines for decision diagramming. Read it through to understand the problem before proceeding to the discussion. (You might like to try diagramming it before reading the discussion.)

**Example 3.1: Recreational Properties Incorporated**

In the spring of 1975, Peter Larson, the President of Recreational Properties Incorporated, was faced with an important decision. He was concerned because the course of action chosen could have a significant impact on the company's operations and opportunities over the next 2 years. The shareholders had invested a total of $15 million 5 years ago with the objective of participating in recreational land development. Their strategy had been to acquire land parcels or options to purchase properties with recreational potential. They often consolidated several parcels and obtained leases from the U.S. Forest Service or Bureau of Land Management to create a desirable recreational property. Once the land had been obtained, they either sold it to another developer or made initial improvements themselves and then sold. They had a policy against operating any resorts and would only undertake 1 to 2 years of initial development, including roads, sewers, and the core facilities (a few condominiums, tennis courts, golf course, ski hill, etc.). Initial development was aimed at demonstrating the potential rather than completely exploiting it.

The problem facing Larson involved a set of land parcels in the White Mountains, located approximately 100 miles from a large metropolitan area and near two well-developed ski areas. The elevation varied from 7,000 feet to 10,000 feet, and snowfall from December to March was usually between 20 and 35 feet. Summer recreation was also possible since the property was split by a river and had good access (15 minutes) to a lake big enough for water skiing and sailing. Recreational Properties had put together three different parcels to create the White Mountain Ski area. These parcels controlled the access to the east side of White Mountain, which was owned by the Forest Service. The three parcels were controlled through options that expired on June 1, 1975. Total purchase price was $10 million. The Forest Service had not yet agreed to a long-term lease arrangement. In fact, the government had not even agreed to lease the mountain for development as a ski area.

When Larson had purchased the options, almost a year ago, he thought that a Forest Service lease would be obtained within 3 months. The Forest Service at that point had agreed in principle with the use of White Mountain for skiing. Shortly after the options were purchased and before any public hearings on the lease issue, a group of conservationists had filed suit to stop construction of a ski resort 50 miles north of White Mountain. Their injunction was obtained by showing that the environmental impact report, used as a basis for the construction permit, was inadequate. Since the Forest Service had been involved in the preparation of the report, and the agency was also leasing part of the land to be used in the development, the injunction was directed at the Forest Service as well as the developers. Because of the suit, the Chief Forester refused to consider any new lease permits until the outcome of the suit was known. He felt that there might be precedents which would serve as guidelines for future leases.

On the other hand, the White Mountain area was substantially different and a decision to halt the northern development permanently would not necessarily block the White Mountain development. For one thing, White Mountain was close to existing ski resorts and the area was already heavily affected by visitors, while the development to the north was closer to wilderness areas. Access also argued for White Mountain, as good roads already existed and the travel time was approximately $1\frac{1}{2}$ hours less to the major population center.

Larson believed that the situation was out of his control. He had already pursued all the political lines available to him and the answer was consistent: "You'll just have to wait until the suit is settled. There is nothing we can do." The suit was not scheduled to be heard until mid-August, which meant the options would expire before Larson would know about the Forest Service lease. Larson had discussed extensions with each of the three property owners. After more than 2 months of negotiation, he had obtained a firm commitment from each of the landholders which would extend the option for 6 months, until December 1, 1975. The price of this option was $150,000 and the purchase price was raised to $11 million. The basis for the increase in purchase price was a bona fide offer to the three of them for $11 million by another investor. If Larson does not pick up the new option within 5 days (April 10, 1975), the owners will sell it to the other investor, contingent on Larson not exercising his original option. The other investor has agreed to sign a note for $11 million, plus $300,000 interest due in March 1977.

This extension was not all that Larson had hoped. He was sure the court decision would be made within the next 4 months, but he knew that no matter which way the court decided, a series of public hearings would have to be held before the Forest Service would decide on the lease. This process would take a minimum of 6 months. If he did not obtain a lease, the value of the land would be substantially less. In fact, he estimated that the value would be $8 million and he would have no alternative but to sell.

To further complicate the problem, Larson's preliminary analysis of the best way to handle the property if a lease were obtained from the Forest Service was not conclusive. He was considering two alternatives: (1) sell the property without any development, and (2) install access roads, sewers, three ski lifts, and build the first wing of the lodge designed for the area. The first alternative would undoubtedly take over a year and Larson estimated that the land would sell for $15 million. One reason the second alternative was attractive was that construction could be completed during that same year. Larson knew of several individuals who could do a good job of organizing and managing the skiing activities. By selling the project after 1 year of operation, there was a good chance that considerably greater profit could be realized than with just the raw land, and without any significant change in the timing of the sale. The added cost for this development would be approximately $5 million.

The critical factor was the popularity of the facility. Larson and his consultants felt confident that the hill would prove attractive to the intermediate and advanced recreational skier. However, popularity would depend somewhat on the snow conditions. Relatively warm weather and wet snow would severely affect the quality of the skiing in several bowls. Thus, if the winter had more than the normal amount of wet snow and warm weather, the resort would compare relatively poorly with other ski areas. Larson had worked up two sets of figures, one assuming a good reputation and the other assuming a poor reputation (see Table 3.2).

**TABLE 3.2**

| *Reputation* | *Net Income for First Year* | *Selling Price* |
|---|---|---|
| Good | $ 100,000 | $22 million |
| Poor | −200,000 | 18 million |

If he did not follow through on the White Mountain property, Larson was skeptical about finding another large investment during the next year or so. He knew how long it had taken to develop this one and believed he would keep his assets in liquid securities while he tried to develop another property. Based on past experience he would expect to earn $1.5 million during the comparable time period.

What he needed was some way to combine all the important factors so that he could decide whether to pick up the option.

### Immediate Decision Alternatives—Guideline 1

The first guideline states that the immediate decision alternatives should be identified. In Larson's case, his immediate choice involves the option renewal. The alternatives described in the problem are:

1. Purchase the new option.
2. Exercise the old option before June 1, 1975.
3. Do neither (in which case the land will be sold to the other investor).

The alternatives should not be restricted to those associated with White Mountain. Obviously, if we have left out an available alternative associated with some other investment, we could make a serious mistake, say by buying the option when we would have been better off investing in a shopping center. In this case Larson has stated that he plans to invest his available assets in liquid securities if he does not accept one of the White Mountain options. The first node of the diagram can be drawn as shown in Figure 3.5.

**FIGURE 3.5**

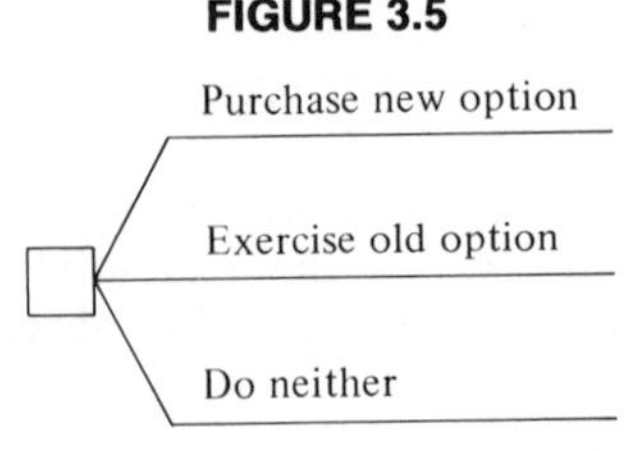

### Determine the Evaluation Date—Guideline 2

The evaluation date should be the same for all alternatives under consideration. In Larson's case he will know about the suit in mid-August 1975 and will require at least 6 months more to obtain the Forest Service lease, which takes us to February or March 1976. With either of the two options discussed, Larson has one more year before he can sell the property, putting the evaluation date near March 1977. Therefore, the uncertain events and future decisions between April 10, 1975, and March 1977 will be included on the diagram.

### Uncertain Events That Affect the Consequences of the Initial Alternatives—Guideline 3

These events are discussed below for each initial alternative.

**Uncertain events associated with purchase new option.** The *Forest Service Decision* on the lease will affect the price Larson can demand for the property. If the lease is obtained and the initial development completed, the *reputation gained* will affect the profitability of the venture. These two uncertain events directly affect the consequences of the *purchase new option* alternative.

**Uncertain events associated with exercise old option.** The events that affect this alternative are the same as those for the *purchase new option* alternative.

**Uncertain events associated with do neither.** According to Larson, there is no uncertainty associated with this alternative. In actual practice there would, of course, be uncertainty involved with his investment of $10 million. What is important is the magnitude of the uncertainty. If there is substantial uncertainty, it should be explicitly included.

### Future Decisions—Guideline 4

The decisions facing Larson after the initial decision, shown in Figure 3.5, and before the evaluation date are discussed below.

**Future decisions associated with purchase new option.** Once the court ruling is made, Larson will have to decide between purchasing the three parcels and letting them go. If he decides to purchase the land and obtains a lease, he must decide whether to take on the initial stages of development or sell without additional investment.

**Future decisions associated with exercise old option.** In this case there is a future decision involving the initial development if a lease is obtained. Another decision that could be included here is the possibility of selling to the other investor, who offered to pay $11 million plus $300,000 interest in March 1977. On the other hand, this alternative *can be seen* to be inferior to the *do neither* alternative and hence can be omitted from the diagram (it results in a net contribution of $\$11.3-\$10=\$1.3$ million, versus $1.5 million for the *do neither* alternative). This point comes up often in creating a decision diagram. When can a branch safely be *left off*? The answer is, whenever you can see clearly that it is inferior to another alternative. Individuals differ in their ability to "see clearly" enough to eliminate branches. The best advice is to include alternatives if there is any doubt. The process of analysis will quickly eliminate inferior branches.

**Future decisions associated with do neither.** No future decisions.

### Uncertain Events That Provide Information for Future Decisions—Guideline 5

Only one uncertain event falls into the information category. It is the court decision and it can only affect a future decision if the new option is purchased. In this case the outcome can affect the decision to purchase the land. If the new option is not taken, the court decision cannot affect any decision, since the land is either purchased or not and the development decision only depends upon whether the Forest Service ultimately grants a lease.

### Mutually Exclusive and Collectively Exhaustive Requirements—Guidelines 6 and 7

Guidelines 6 and 7 are technical requirements to maintain the logic of the diagram. We can check the nodes as they are developed. In Figure 3.5 each alternative is mutually exclusive. Larson would never *purchase new option* and *exercise old option*. Neither could he *purchase new option* and *do neither* or *exercise old option* and *do neither*. In the first case logic dictates that both would not be chosen. In the other cases it is physically impossible to choose *do neither* and one of the purchase options. Since these three alternatives are the only ones Larson believes are available to him, they are collectively exhaustive and satisfy guideline 7.

### Diagram Events and Decisions Chronologically—Guideline 8

Although it is not always necessary to diagram events according to a strict chronological order, it is almost always good practice. The important thing to remember is that the event timing corresponds to when the *decision maker* learns of the outcome. The results of the analysis of Larson's problem so far are shown by the decision diagram in Figure 3.6.

**FIGURE 3.6**

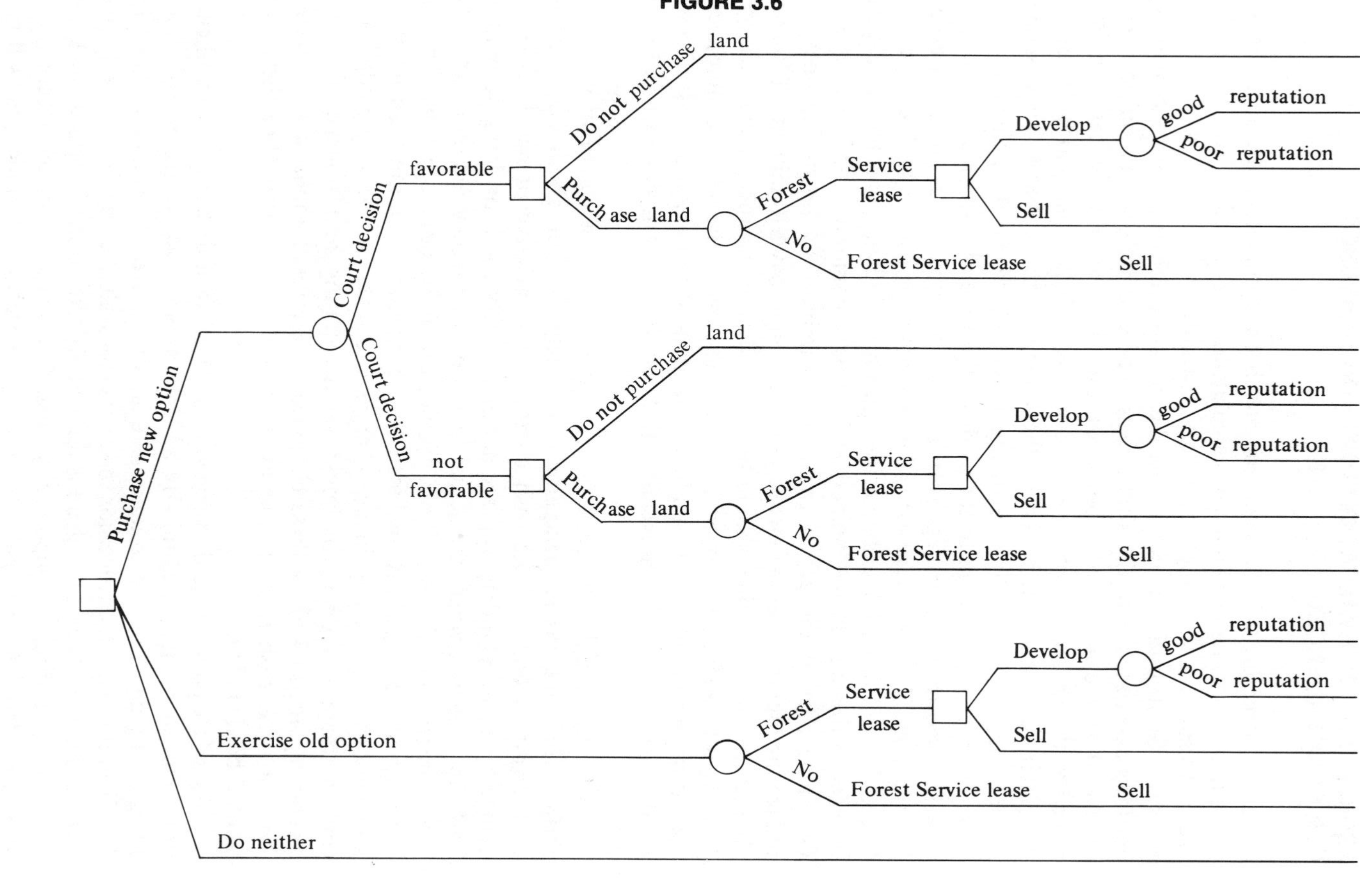
Purchase new option
Court decision
favorable
Do not purchase land
Purchase land
Forest Service lease
Develop
good reputation
poor reputation
Sell
No Forest Service lease
Sell
Court decision
not favorable
Do not purchase land
Purchase land
Forest Service lease
Develop
good reputation
poor reputation
Sell
No Forest Service lease
Sell
Exercise old option
Forest Service lease
Develop
good reputation
poor reputation
Sell
No Forest Service lease
Sell
Do neither

## ASSIGNMENT OF EVALUATION UNITS OR MEASURES FOR CONSEQUENCES

Once the structure of the problem has been completed, the measure or evaluation unit to be used must be calculated and assigned to each end point. We will usually use a single monetary attribute, *contribution*, with a dollar measure. Contribution is defined as the net cash inflows minus the net cash outflows associated with the alternatives. The cash inflows and outflows can be placed at the appropriate points on the diagram and the net cash flow placed at the end points of the diagram. The cash flows should be placed at the point on the diagram where the commitment is made. They should include all costs, including financing costs and taxes, if applicable. They represent the actual commitment made at the time of a decision or the cash flow received (positive or negative) from the outcome of an uncertain event. For instance, if the *exercise old option* alternative is chosen by Larson in the Recreational Properties example, he must pay $10 million. This is a cash transfer to the current landholders and a cash commitment on Larson's part. Obtaining part of the actual cash, say $5 million, by borrowing does not reduce the fact that Larson incurs an obligation to pay $10 million. If finance charges are incurred, they should be included. For instance, if these charges amounted to $0.9 million over the life of the project, the actual commitment should be increased to $10.9 million. Assuming that Larson uses all his own capital, we can place the monetary values on the diagram as shown in Figure 3.7.

Keeping straight the cash flows used to calculate *contribution* can be difficult in some cases. Generally, it will help to think about the decisions and events in terms of the cash commitments (positive or negative) represented by each. The diagrams are not particularly good for doing accounting *cash flow analyses*, where the actual timing of the inflows and outflows to the day is important. These analyses should usually be done separately and the net financing costs, if any, included on the diagram. The same is true of tax calculations. Calculating finance charges and taxes can be very complicated and is treated in depth in books on accounting and finance. To avoid becoming sidetracked by these complications, we will almost always neglect both of these cash flows in our examples. Of course in practice these *costs* should be included.

As a last point, note that *opportunity costs* are not cash flows and hence not included on the diagram. By an opportunity cost we mean cash flows foregone by deciding not to undertake an alternative. According to the rules for diagramming, each decision node includes all the *opportunities* (alternatives) available. Therefore, there is no need to take "other" opportunities into account by adding an opportunity cost. For example, in the Recreational Properties problem, if Larson decides to exercise the old option, he will give up the opportunity of making $1.5 million. This is *not* included as a cost of exercising the option, because it is not a true cash flow associated with that

**FIGURE 3.7**

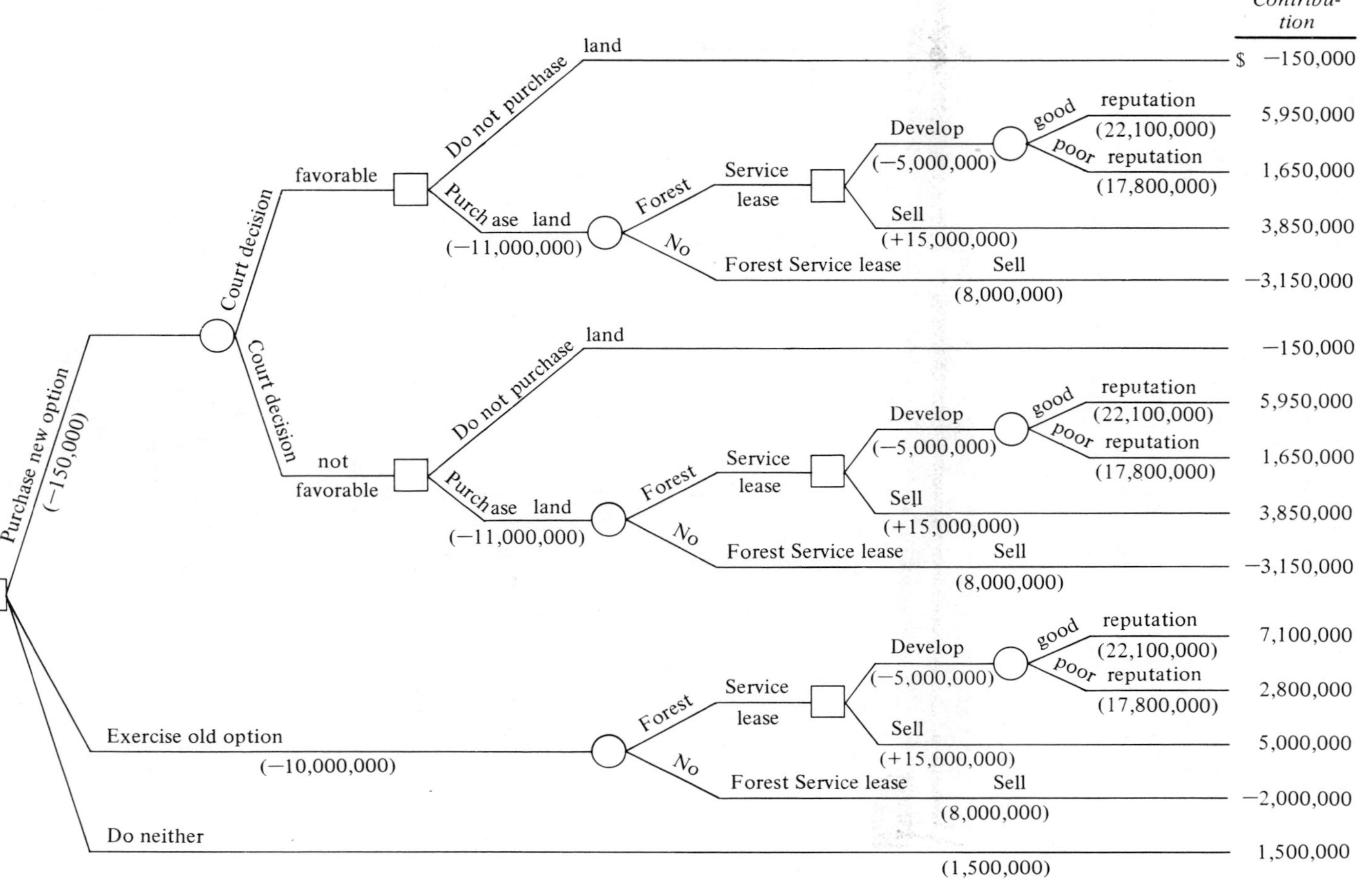

Contribution
Purchase new option
(−150,000)
Court decision
favorable
Do not purchase land
$ −150,000
Purchase land
(−11,000,000)
Forest Service lease
Develop
(−5,000,000)
good reputation
(22,100,000)
5,950,000
poor reputation
(17,800,000)
1,650,000
Sell
(+15,000,000)
3,850,000
No Forest Service lease
Sell
(8,000,000)
−3,150,000
Court decision
not favorable
Do not purchase land
−150,000
Purchase land
(−11,000,000)
Forest Service lease
Develop
(−5,000,000)
good reputation
(22,100,000)
5,950,000
poor reputation
(17,800,000)
1,650,000
Sell
(+15,000,000)
3,850,000
No Forest Service lease
Sell
(8,000,000)
−3,150,000
Exercise old option
(−10,000,000)
Forest Service lease
Develop
(−5,000,000)
good reputation
(22,100,000)
7,100,000
poor reputation
(17,800,000)
2,800,000
Sell
(+15,000,000)
5,000,000
No Forest Service lease
Sell
(8,000,000)
−2,000,000
Do neither
(1,500,000)
1,500,000

choice. This *opportunity* is taken care of by the separate branch labeled *do neither*, which would result in the cash flow of $1.5 million.

We can now see one of the most important sources of simplification provided by decision diagrams: each end point represents a completely certain state (at least as far as the approximation represented by the model is concerned). For instance, the top branch in Figure 3.7 represents a state of the world defined as: *Larson purchases option*; *court decision is favorable*; *land not purchased*. With these conditions specified we can use a deterministic model to evaluate the consequences—in this case $-150,000.

## PAYOFF TABLES

Payoff tables are sometimes easy to use for decision problems that have only one stage: that is, a single decision node followed by a single uncertain event node. Guidelines for using payoff tables are given below. Read them quickly and then go through the example.

### Guidelines for Using Payoff Tables

1. Check that only a single decision node exists, followed by an uncertain event (i.e., there is not a sequence: decision followed by uncertain event followed by decision, etc.).
2. Check that the uncertain event has the same set of outcomes for each possible alternative (i.e., the different alternatives result in different consequences for the outcomes, not in different outcomes).
3. Label a column for each alternative and a row for each outcome of the uncertain event.
4. Place the "payoff" or evaluation units for the consequence associated with each alternative/outcome pair in the indicated cell of the table.

**Example 3.2: Payoff Tables**

The buyer for a large wholesale clothing store must decide on orders for the fall season. Although there are many items, a new line of dresses will constitute a major part of the line. The distribution of sizes has been determined based on historical patterns; however, the total number of dresses to order is a problem. Only a single order can be placed, and it must be placed 4 months in advance. The dresses will be sold to retailers in lots of 200 dresses. Based on available evidence for this year and past data, the buyer expects demand to be between 1,000 and 2,000 dresses. Dresses will also be purchased in increments of 200 dresses and the cost per dress is $80. The wholesale price during the fall season has been set at $180 per dress. Units not sold during the fall season will be disposed of at a price of $20 per dress.

**TABLE 3.3**
**Payoff Table for Contribution**

| | *Order Quantity* | | | | | |
|---|---|---|---|---|---|---|
| *Demand* | 1,000 | 1,200 | 1,400 | 1,600 | 1,800 | 2,000 |
| 1,000 | 100,000 | 88,000 | 76,000 | 64,000 | 52,000 | 40,000 |
| 1,200 | 100,000 | 120,000 | 108,000 | 96,000 | 84,000 | 72,000 |
| 1,400 | 100,000 | 120,000 | 140,000 | 128,000 | 116,000 | 104,000 |
| 1,600 | 100,000 | 120,000 | 140,000 | 160,000 | 148,000 | 136,000 |
| 1,800 | 100,000 | 120,000 | 140,000 | 160,000 | 180,000 | 168,000 |
| 2,000 | 100,000 | 120,000 | 140,000 | 160,000 | 180,000 | 200,000 |

### The Table Construction

The payoff table is shown in Table 3.3. The alternatives for the single ordering decision are shown across the top of the table. The possible outcomes of the uncertain event on sales are shown down the left-hand margin. Guidelines 1 and 2 are satisfied, so the payoff table adequately represents the decision problem.

### Calculation of Contribution

If we assume that the evaluation unit is *contribution*, we can determine the contribution for each combination of order quantity and demand as follows:

Demand less than order quantity:

$$\text{Contribution} = (\text{Demand}) \times (180) + (\text{Order Quantity} - \text{Demand}) \times (20) - (\text{Order Quantity}) \times (80)$$

Demand greater than or equal to order quantity:

$$\text{Contribution} = (\text{Order Quantity}) \times (180 - 80)$$

### Decision Diagram Representation

Any problem that can be modeled using a payoff table can also be represented by a decision diagram. Figure 3.8 is the decision diagram corresponding to this problem. For single-stage problems, payoff tables have the advantage of a more compact representation.

## ● MORE ON DECISION DIAGRAMMING[1]

Decision diagramming is intended to be an aid to laying out alternatives and their consequences for a decision maker. The rules and guidelines may look imposing at first. If so, a little practice will make them clear. In fact, the *process* of creating a decision diagram is really quite straightforward. The

[1]Sections labeled ● include additional examples and discussion of material covered earlier.

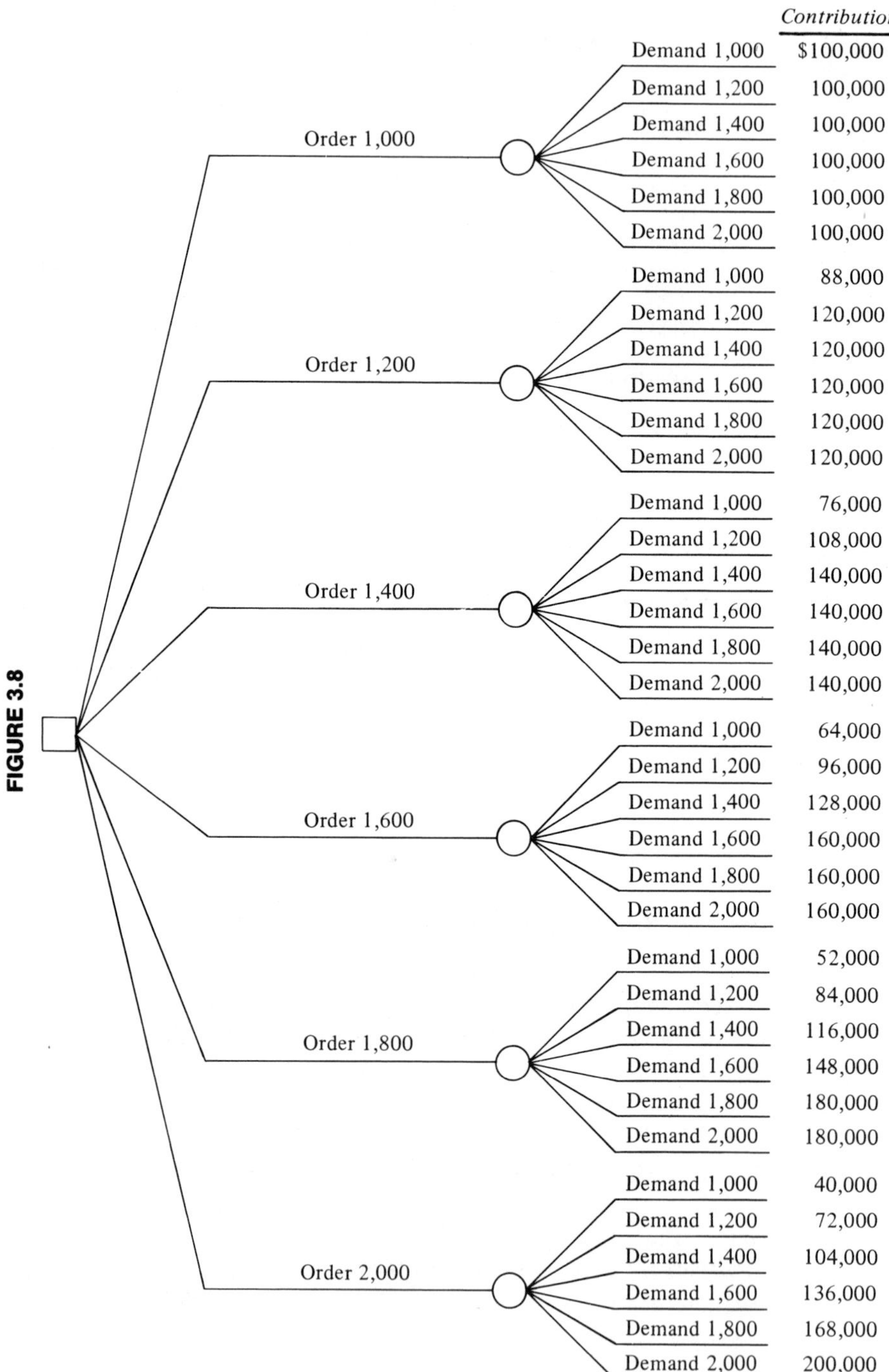

Contribution
Order 1,000
Demand 1,000 $100,000
Demand 1,200 100,000
Demand 1,400 100,000
Demand 1,600 100,000
Demand 1,800 100,000
Demand 2,000 100,000
Order 1,200
Demand 1,000 88,000
Demand 1,200 120,000
Demand 1,400 120,000
Demand 1,600 120,000
Demand 1,800 120,000
Demand 2,000 120,000
Order 1,400
Demand 1,000 76,000
Demand 1,200 108,000
Demand 1,400 140,000
Demand 1,600 140,000
Demand 1,800 140,000
Demand 2,000 140,000
Order 1,600
Demand 1,000 64,000
Demand 1,200 96,000
Demand 1,400 128,000
Demand 1,600 160,000
Demand 1,800 160,000
Demand 2,000 160,000
Order 1,800
Demand 1,000 52,000
Demand 1,200 84,000
Demand 1,400 116,000
Demand 1,600 148,000
Demand 1,800 180,000
Demand 2,000 180,000
Order 2,000
Demand 1,000 40,000
Demand 1,200 72,000
Demand 1,400 104,000
Demand 1,600 136,000
Demand 1,800 168,000
Demand 2,000 200,000


**FIGURE 3.8**

rules are necessary to make sure the model is complete. But once you have the idea, you will follow the rules automatically. Remember, we are just trying to create a model that is a *good approximation* of the decision faced. As you proceed with the model, you will have to use judgment as to what to include and to leave out. Model building is an *art*, not a science. The rules are there to prevent you from making logical mistakes.

### • The Process of Decision Diagramming

We have divided the work of decision diagramming into two stages so far. First, specify the possible outcomes by linking together the decisions and uncertain events. Second, assign evaluation units to each end point—or outcome. The first stage can be done in three steps.

**List initial set of alternatives.** The alternatives to choose among are listed. At this stage it usually pays to think about all possibilities, although alternatives that are obviously inferior should be left out.

**Pick an evaluation date.** All alternatives should have the same evaluation date. It is the point in time when the major effects of the initial decision have been completed.

**Develop sequence of uncertain events and decisions for each alternative.** Starting with each of the initial alternatives, merely "walk through" the future events and decisions for the alternative. We are just trying to put down all the possibilities that flow from the alternative. To illustrate the type of questions you should ask during this process, consider the Recreation Properties example. Assume that you are an analyst trying to help Larson structure his problem. The conversation might go like this:

You: Mr. Larson, you apparently have three alternatives: purchase the new option, exercise the old option, do neither. If you can't think of any more, let's see what the possible consequences are for each one.

Larson: At this point, these are my three options. So let's proceed.

You: Let's assume you decide to purchase the new option. What happens next?

Larson: Well, lots of things happen. I have to come up with the $150,000, call my lawyer to draft the agreement, and then contact each member of the syndicate.

You: These are all things that *must* be done if you are to purchase the new option. What I had in mind is, what is the next thing that will occur after you complete the purchase?

Larson: Then I wait around for the court to decide on the injunction. There is really nothing I need to do until after that decision. There is no chance that the Forest Service will rule on the lease until after the court decision, and I certainly will not make a decision on buying the land until after the court ruling. [The first uncertain event node is identified.]

You: O.K. The first thing that will happen is the court ruling. If the ruling is favorable to you, then what?

Larson: Then I have to decide whether to buy the land. Unfortunately, I know the hearing process will not be completed before my option runs out. [A subsequent decision node is identified.]

You: I assume that if you decide not to buy the land, that is the end.

Larson: Yes. [One branch of the decision node is explored.]

You: What if you decide to buy the land?

Larson: Then I wait for the Forest Service ruling on the lease.

You: What are the possibilities?

Larson: They have been through this thing so many times that I am sure their decision will be final. They won't delay it or restudy it. The ruling will either give me a lease or deny it. [Another uncertain event node is identified.]

You: If you don't get a lease, then you have no choice but to sell?

Larson: That's right. [The consequences of one outcome are determined.]

You: But what if you get the lease?

Larson: I'm faced with another decision on the best way to sell the property. I can either do some initial development or just sell. [Another decision node.]

You: What are the advantages of developing?

Larson: Well, if I sell it at that point without development, I think I can get close to $15 million. That would provide me with a nice profit. But if I put in the initial development, and things go well, I could get quite a bit more for it.

You: What if things don't "go well"?

Larson: Then I would be better off selling without developing. Of course, I won't know how well the development will be accepted until after it is developed.

You: As far as you can see now, it will either have a good or a poor reputation?

Larson: That's right. [Another uncertain event node, associated with the develop alternative.]

You: And in either case you will sell it after 1 year?

Larson: Yes, my investors have made it clear we are not in the business of operating resorts.

This set of questions has explored all the possibilities for the *purchase new option* branch when the court decision is favorable. A similar "walk-through" will identify the possibilities for an unfavorable decision and the other two initial alternatives. These questions can obviously be asked of oneself, so there is no need for a decision maker and a separate analyst. The important thing in this process is a very practical, *what-will-I-run-into-next* point of view. If you take this point of view and are sure to explore all the separate outcomes and alternatives at each node, the model will satisfy all the rules and usually be a good approximation of the decision. The next few sections discuss particular aspects of the rules and conventions that are sometimes troublesome.

### • What Qualifies as a Decision Node?

To qualify as a decision, the alternatives must include an *irreversible commitment* or *allocation* of resources. If not, the choice of one alternative over another could be changed at no cost. This would mean that no real decision is required. For example, suppose you have been offered the use of a vacation cabin by a friend at a reasonable rate. Your friend states that the cabin will be available for a weekend 2 weeks hence and if you do not use it, no one else will (your friend is not interested in offering it to anyone else). After checking your calendar you decide to accept the offer. In the middle of the next week suppose your schedule changes, causing you to call your friend and cancel the cabin. Although described as a decision, your acceptance of the offer would not qualify as a decision in our framework. Without an irrevocable commitment (you could change your mind without incurring any cost), no decision, as defined here, was made. This restriction on what qualifies as a decision prevents cluttering diagrams with tentative choices that are reversible at no cost and hence are equivalent to the option of waiting until some commitment is required.

### • Alternatives That Are Unknown at the Decision Point

Obviously, only those alternatives known to be available at the time the decision is made (the time at which the irrevocable action is taken) can be considered as part of the initial set. By "available" we mean an alternative that can be chosen by the decision maker. If you *think* another option may be available later but it is not available at the time the decision is made, it cannot be included in the set of initial alternatives. One of the initial alternatives is usually *choose none of the above*. In other words, wait. By waiting past a decision point some opportunity will be foregone (if not, no real decision is made), but you may have other options or opportunities later. If these possibilities are well defined they can be included in the diagram with the appropriate delay conditions.

These future options may be particularly important when the evaluation date is distant and available alternatives represent long-term resource commitments. Where specific uncertain events will affect the availability of future opportunities, they may be displayed explicitly along this *wait* branch. If no specific uncertain events and future opportunities are known, the evaluation of the *wait* alternative can take into account a *normal* set of consequences that one would expect over the time horizon. For instance, if *normal* returns of 10% are available, they can be used to evaluate the *wait* alternative.

### • Inferior Alternatives

Not all available alternatives need be included. Those which can be eliminated as inferior without resorting to the full analysis suggested here should not be added. On the other hand, if some doubt exists, it is better to include the alternative and let the analysis aid in its evaluation. After all, the entire purpose of the analysis is to eliminate inferior alternatives. In the end all but the most preferred will be eliminated.

## • Evaluation Date

The evaluation date should be the same for all alternatives under consideration. Although in some cases the effects of a future decision will go on indefinitely, it is obviously impossible to include sets of uncertain events and decisions indefinitely. The decision problem must be delimited by choosing an evaluation date so that the *major* uncertainties and future decisions which affect the consequences of the immediate decisions are included. Remember, the analysis will always deal with a simplified approximation of the real world. The important thing is to provide a good approximation.

### •• Alternatives with Extended Evaluation Dates

If alternatives extend over a considerable length of time, the modeling and choice problems become more difficult. Some of these problems are discussed in later chapters. A technique often used when consequences are realized at different times is discounting back to present value.[2]

The present value of a cash payment, $C$, received $t$ periods in the future, is usually less than the payment itself. If the payment were available now, it could be invested in a government-insured savings account and earn interest at the rate of $i$ per period. Therefore, we calculate the present value as the amount that would have to be invested now to accumulate to a value of $C$ in $t$ periods.

$$\text{Present Value} = \frac{C}{(1+i)^t}$$

There are some difficulties associated with this approach. When payoffs and costs are incurred at different times, we actually have a multiple attribute problem. The use of discount rates is not always appropriate for taking the differences into account. Preferences for income, for instance, may not be captured by the constant, linear trade-off implied by using present-value techniques. Differences in the time when uncertainty is resolved can also complicate the problem. These problems are discussed in Chapter 18.

## • Mutually Exclusive Alternatives

A common error that violates mutually exclusive alternatives can be illustrated by slightly extending the Recreational Properties problem. Assume that Larson has another investment alternative, in a beach resort on Maui. Further assume that he cannot extend his option at White Mountain. Therefore, he can buy land at White Mountain or not and he can buy land in Maui or not. At first glance it might seem reasonable to diagram this as shown in Figure 3.9. However, these alternatives are not mutually exclusive, since he

[2]See J. C. Van Horne, *Financial Management and Policy*, 4th ed. (Englewood Cliffs, N.J.: Prentice-Hall, 1977), Chap. 2, for a discussion of present values.

FIGURE 3.9

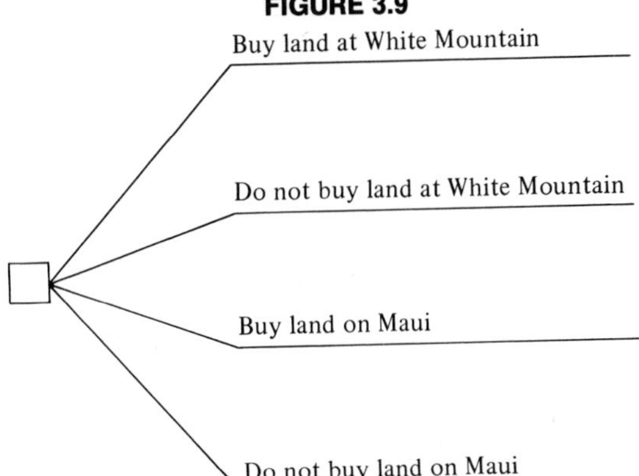


FIGURE 3.10

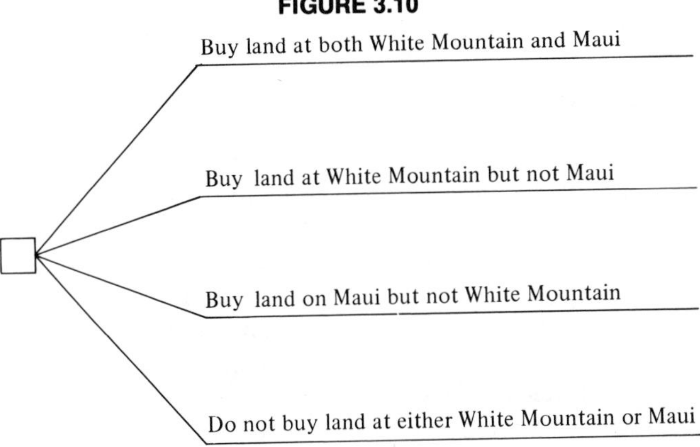


can obviously both *not buy land at White Mountain* and *not buy land on Maui*. If we assume that Larson has the capability of investing in both projects simultaneously, the proper set of alternatives is shown in Figure 3.10.

### • Mutually Exclusive Outcomes

In defining uncertain events, the same type of thing can happen. For instance, assume that in talking with his lawyer, Larson was told that outcomes could be *favorable* or *unfavorable* from the district court. However, if the decision is favorable to Larson, the conservationists might decide to appeal. Diagramming the court outcome as shown in Figure 3.11 would be incorrect, because the events *favorable* and *appealed by conservationists* are not mutually exclusive. This set of outcomes can be correctly diagrammed as shown in Figure 3.12 if we assume that an appeal from the conservationists will only be a possibility with a district court decision favorable to Larson.

FIGURE 3.11

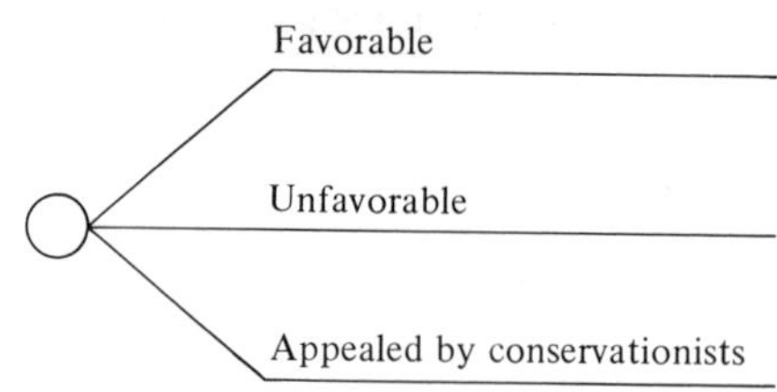


FIGURE 3.12

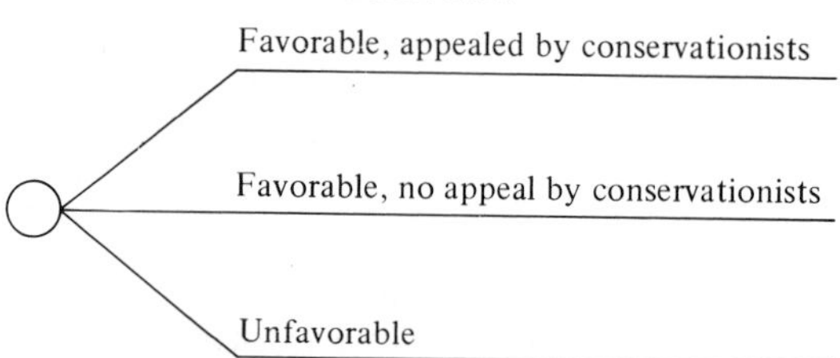


## ● Ordering of Events and Decisions

Ordering events and decisions chronologically not only aids intuition but is usually necessary for a logically correct diagram. The important consideration is the position of uncertain events that provide information for future decision nodes. The diagram must correctly portray the timing of the resolution of the uncertainty. The uncertain events should be positioned to reflect the time the outcome is revealed to the decision maker. For instance, assume that as vice president of marketing for a manufacturer, you are trying to decide on a new pricing policy. For purposes of discussion, call the two alternatives under consideration *raise prices* and *no change*. Your major competitor is also trying to decide on its new pricing policy. Figure 3.13 depicts the problem.

Sometime later you learn that your competitor has decided on a new policy but will not announce the decision until *after you have made a choice.*

FIGURE 3.13

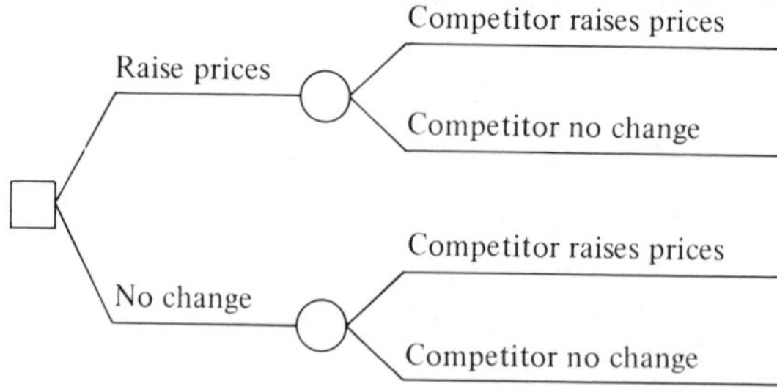


Has your problem changed? The answer is *no*. You still do not know the outcome of your competitor's policy decision. Therefore, Figure 3.13 describes your problem. The problem specified in Figure 3.14 indicates you will know the competitor's decision prior to making yours. Therefore, it is *not* the problem you face. In this simple example it is unlikely that anyone would be confused. However, in more complex problems it is easy to go astray unless you think clearly about the *time* at which uncertainty is resolved for the *decision maker*.

**FIGURE 3.14**

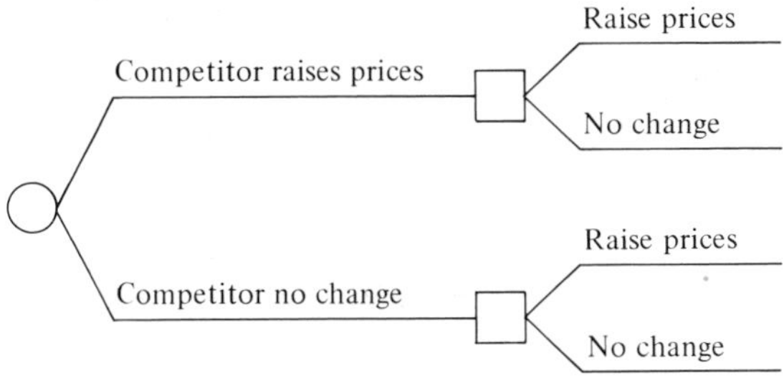


### ● Exceptions to Chronological Order

When two or more events occur without being separated by a decision node, their order can be changed without affecting the validity of the diagram. As we will see when we begin to provide information on probabilities of events, this flexibility can be useful. When two or more decisions are not separated by an event node, they can also be interchanged or made into a single node. The possibilities can be illustrated by reconsidering Figure 3.10. Figures 3.15 and 3.16 are both equivalent to Figure 3.10.

## OVERALL PROCESS

Creating a decision diagram requires knowledge of the process of diagramming and knowledge of the problem. In some cases an analyst knows about the process and a manager about the problem. Developing a diagram is virtually always an iterative procedure, with the analyst asking a series of questions, making preliminary diagrams, and returning to discuss the diagram with the manager. The process will very likely sharpen the manager's perception of the *real* problem. Like any abstraction of a real-world setting, the diagram is only an approximation of the actual problem. The ultimate authority on the acceptability of the approximation is the individual who must make the decision. If it is close enough to the real decision problem to portray the essential features accurately, and yet simplified enough to improve individual judgments, it can be a valuable aid to the decision maker. In many settings this initial part of the modeling process may clarify the problem to the point that the desired choice is obvious. When we are fortunate enough to have this happen, no additional analysis is necessary. In the following chapters we will discuss how the model can be completed by adding information on probabilities and then how it can be used to make a choice.

**FIGURE 3.15**

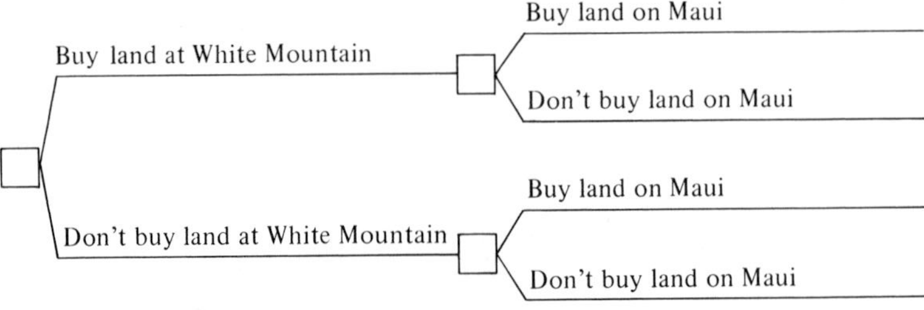


**FIGURE 3.16**

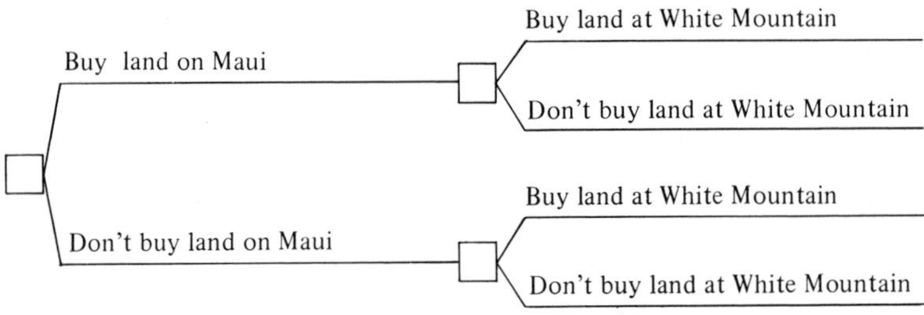


## SUMMARY

Models representing decision problems can help clarify the problem and lead to a decision. This chapter covers two stages in the model-building process: *defining the possible outcomes* and *assigning evaluation units*. The first involves displaying the structure of the decisions and events that determine the outcomes. *Decision diagrams* and *payoff tables* provide a means for displaying the structure. There are conventions, rules, and guidelines for creating these decision models. The rules are intended to make the models logical and complete; the guidelines and conventions to make them easier to use. The process can be thought of in three steps: *list initial set of alternatives*, *pick an evaluation date*, and *develop a sequence of uncertain events and decisions for each alternative*. The result of using these steps is a model showing the possible outcomes from each alternative.

*Assigning evaluation units* involves describing the consequences of each possible outcome by a quantitative measure. Usually, we will use *contribution* as the evaluation unit. *Contribution* is calculated by summing the positive and negative *cash flows* for each alternative.

The last stage of the model-building process is the assessment of probabilities for the uncertain events. This topic will be introduced in Chapter 4. Once the model is completed, it can be used to help make a *choice* among the initial set of alternatives. Chapter 5 introduces the choice problem.

## ASSIGNMENT MATERIAL

### 3.1. Pine Mountain Resort

In the spring of 1971, Monte Upshaw, the head of a syndicate of investors interested in developing recreation property, was trying to decide about the development of the Pine Mountain Ski area. The site, located in the northwestern corner of the state, was an ideal location for a ski area.

The question now seemed to be how to best develop the area. Two major alternatives were under consideration:

1. Go ahead now with a full-scale development. This would involve building access roads, and substantial investment in skiing facilities.
2. Begin with a small-scale development. This would involve access roads into only a part of the area, and a smaller-scale ski development. This could be expanded after 1 year if demand seemed to warrant it.

Because the syndicate members believed in moving from one project to another, they had agreed to sell at the end of the second year of operation. Therefore, the operating time horizon was limited to 2 years.

Upshaw recognized that the degree of success would depend upon the trends in skiing. There was also some question about the population growth in the northern part of the state. Would this growth continue at the past rate or drop off (or perhaps accelerate)?

As can be seen from the discussion above, there was considerable uncertainty about the extent of the use of the facility if it were built.

The major economic considerations involved the costs of constructing the roads and facilities, and the revenue that would accrue from the facilities (less operating costs).

Although estimates of usage of the facility had been made, the actual usage rate was quite uncertain. Rather than try to come up with one number estimate, Upshaw decided upon three general levels of usage—*high*, *medium*, and *low*. Costs, revenues, and sales prices were calculated for each level. The results are shown in Table 3.4. Trends in population, skiing popularity, and competing facilities were taken into account in making the estimates in Table 3.4.

The usage level achieved in year 2 would not necessarily be the same as in year 1. Upshaw felt that if usage in year 1 is *high*, then year 2 usage could be either *medium* or *high*. If year 1 usage is *medium*, the second year could be either the same or *high* or *low*. If the first year has *low* utilization, year 2 could be *low* or *medium*.

Upshaw recognized that the expenditures involved a substantial financial commitment for his syndicate and was concerned about the risk involved. At the minimum he wanted a good way to display all the decisions and possible outcomes.

**TABLE 3.4**

**Costs, Revenues, and Sales Prices**

A. *Construction Costs* (Roads and Facilities)
   1. Full development now: $5 million
   2. Small development now: $3 million
   3. Expansion after one year: $4 million

B. *Net Revenues and Sales Prices*
   1. Full-Size Facility (originally full size or expanded. Expansion can be completed in the off season so that full-size facility revenue will be realized beginning in year 2 if expansion is undertaken at the end of year 1).

| *Usage* | *Revenue Less Operating Cost Each Year* | *Sales Price Based on Usage in Year 2* |
|---|---|---|
| High | $1.0 million | $5.0 million |
| Medium | 0.5 million | 2.5 million |
| Low | 0.1 million | 0.5 million |

   2. Small-Scale Facility

| *Usage* | *Revenue Less Operating Cost Each Year* | *Sales Price Based on Usage in Year 2* |
|---|---|---|
| High | $0.5 million | $2.5 million |
| Medium | 0.4 million | 2.0 million |
| Low | 0.1 million | 0.5 million |

Draw a decision diagram representing Upshaw's decision problem. Place the monetary consequences on each end point of the diagram. Do *not* try to solve the problem.

## 3.2 Computex Corporation

Computex is a new company in the computer peripheral equipment field. It has one product which has been marketed and is in the process of developing a new graphical display terminal. The chief engineer, Mr. Renap, has developed two approaches to the design. One is rather conventional and would fill out the line with little development expense ($50,000) but would not be much different from other products on the market. The other possiblity involves a radical departure from terminals now available. It is January 1977 and if the company is to proceed with development of the graphics terminal as part of the normal R&D effort, it must make some decisions now. The radical approach depends upon the development of a special display screen, which in turn depends critically on the quality of a new coating material. Renap's investigation of this new coating material leads him to believe that there is about a 30% chance that it will be high quality, 50% medium, and 20% low quality. He will not know for sure until July, 6 months from now. If the company pursues the radical approach, it will have to make a commitment now to develop the prototype. This effort is expected to cost $30,000 over the next 6 months. If the company makes a commitment to develop the prototype, two options will be open to the company after learning about the material quality. They can continue with the development at an additional cost of $100,000 or revert to a conventional approach which can take advantage of some of the prototype work already completed and be finished for an additional $40,000. If the company does not pursue either approach now, it could begin a crash program in July and finish the conventional approach with a total cost of $100,000.

The sales manager investigated the market for the new product and found that it would be sensitive not only to the overall approach, radical versus conventional, but also to the characteristics that result from the qualtity of the coating material. He has also determined that because of the rapid obsolescence factor in this field, the life cycle of either product will be 2 years. His sales forecasts, given below, reflect this factor and are estimates of net contribution (excluding development cost) over the 2-year sales period.

| | |
|---|---|
| Radical—high quality: | $300,000 |
| Radical—medium quality: | $200,000 |
| Radical—low quality: | $100,000 |
| Conventional: | $150,000 |

Diagram the problem faced by Computex, showing cash flows and the net contributions for each end point. Do *not* try to determine the best action for Computex.

## 3.3 Haggard Productions, Inc.

Ferlin Haggard, a patron of the arts and fast-buck promoter is considering backing a Broadway play for the upcoming season. The list of prospective plays has been narrowed to the following two: *Cabernet*, a musical adaptation of *The Grapes of Wrath*, and *How to Succeed in Business Without Dying*, a melodrama based on *The Godfather*.

From back issues of *Variety*, Haggard has determined that musicals of the Cabernet type are *hits* (or successful) 20% of the time and *flops* (or failures) 80% of the time. He similarly learned that melodramas are hits 30% of the time.

Haggard's current financial resources are quite limited; his net liquid assets amount to only $750,000. As a result, he can afford to produce only one play for the coming season. However, Haggard does have the option of previewing *one* of the plays in New Haven before deciding which, if either, play he would like to produce for the Broadway (New York) stage. Since the time before the season begins is too short to allow Haggard to preview both plays in New Haven, he does have the option of previewing one play and producing the other for Broadway.

The costs and revenues associated with the two plays are given below. No revenues will result from a New Haven preview.

| | *Cost of New Haven Preview* | *Additional Cost of New York Opening (with New Haven Preview)* | *Cost of Opening in New York (bypassing New Haven)* | *Revenue if Hit* | *Revenue if Flop* |
|---|---|---|---|---|---|
| *Cabernet* | $200,000 | $500,000 | $600,000 | $4,000,000 | $300,000 |
| *How to Succeed* | 75,000 | $275,000 | $325,000 | $1,000,000 | 100,000 |

Haggard has observed that of the *hit* musicals on Broadway that were previewed in New Haven, 80% were hits in New Haven; of the musicals that flopped in New York and were previewed in New Haven, 40% were hits in New Haven. Of the hit melodramas in New York that were previewed, 90% were hits in New Haven; 60% of the previewed melodramas that flopped in New York were hits in New Haven. While Haggard may find preview results useful, he feels that the accuracy of this kind of test is not high enough to compel him in all cases to act in accordance with the preview result.

Diagram the decision problem facing Haggard. Place net contribution values on each end point. Do *not* try to determine the probabilities associated with the uncertain outcomes or determine which choice is best.

## 3.4 Department of Housing and Urban Development

As the head of the Western Region of the U.S. Department of Housing and Urban Development, Jean Bidwell faces a dilemma. Her redevelopment responsibility allows her the flexibility to purchase land for new projects and she has just been approached by a major landholder in downtown San Jose who offered a one-block parcel for a low price, $1,000,000. The conditions were that the purchase must be completed by December 1, 1976. This parcel was one Bidwell plans to include in a redevelopment package. The dilemma arises because all the approvals for the redevelopment have not been obtained. Two are required. First, the local city council must approve the plan, and second, a federal panel must approve the plan prior to erecting any new building. However, Bidwell has complete authority to purchase land and tear down existing buildings prior to final approval for constructing the new buildings. Therefore, she has the authority to purchase the land and, if she purchases the land, the authority to tear down the existing buildings. Of course, if the ultimate outcome of the review process is no redevelopment, the property will have to be sold.

Her discussions with the city manager and city council members indicate that a final vote either supporting the plan or rejecting it will come in March 1977. The federal panel's decision, which will also be either "yes" or "no," would come 3 months later. At this point the city council is split on the plan, with three "yes," three "no," and one undecided. Bidwell thinks the undecided member will ultimately vote "yes," but she is not sure. After discussion with her aide, Jim Hudson, she decides that there is a 0.75 chance that the undecided council member will vote "yes." She does not think any of the other members will change their votes. As far as the federal panel is concerned, she thinks there is a 0.8 chance they will confirm the city council's recommendation if it is to go ahead. Of course, if the city council votes "no," the project is dead and the federal panel is not involved.

Bidwell is tempted to act now because her planning estimates indicate that if she waits until after the council's vote, the land will cost her $1,200,000, and if she has to purchase it as late as June 1977, it will cost $1,500,000. Moreover, there is a potential advantage to tearing down the existing buildings during the month of April because of a seasonal lull in construction during that month. Her estimates are that the cost during April (which is the earliest the buildings would be torn down even if the land is purchased now) would be $200,000, and after June the cost would be $300,000.

If the project is not approved, Bidwell expects a drop in land values, so that selling the land after cancellation would net $800,000 if the buildings are not down and $900,000 if the buildings are down. (Clearly, if either the city or panel says no, she will sell the land in the state it is in. That is, if the buildings are still up, she will not tear them down before selling.) After much discussion with Jim Hudson, Bidwell also concludes that her actions will not affect the vote of either the city council or the federal panel. That is, their decisions will be the same regardless of whether she purchases the land now or later or begins the process of tearing down the buildings now or later.

Diagram the problem faced by Bidwell, laying out her alternatives and the uncertain events she faces. Value each end point using *dollar costs*. *Warning*: Because of the nature of this problem and the fact that the benefits of the redevelopment project are not included, the higher costs will be associated with the outcomes where both the city and panel vote "yes." *Do not* try to place all the probabilities on the diagram or solve the problem for a best strategy.

## 3.5 Morris Manufacturing Company

On January 15, 1972, the monthly meeting of the Morris Manufacturing Company's Board of Directors was held at the company's offices in Oakland, California. All four directors were present. From the chair, Charles Blake, the president of Morris Manufacturing, began the meeting by informing the directors of the background of negotiations with the Dayton Electric Products Corporation. Dayton was a manufacturer of heavy-duty industrial equipment, and the home office and principal manufacturing facility was located in Los Angeles, California.

"In 1965 Dayton asked us to determine whether a heavy-duty overhead crane with a 50-ton capacity could be built. The crane was needed to move one of a series of new generators from the construction area to the testing shop, a distance of about 600 feet. Our design engineer, John Stiles, did some figuring for us and wrote them that such a crane could be built for about $200,000. Dayton then decided not to make the capital investment at that time but to continue to use its old, but serviceable, crane. During the next 5 years we checked with them from time to time, and found varying degrees of interest in a new crane.

"Then last year Dayton indicated definite interest in resuming serious talks. We drew up some tentative plans based on the gauge, capacity, height, and other specifications of their overhead track, and sent the plans to Carl Mosley, Dayton's chief engineer. Mosley approved the plans and, as usual, we took this as an assurance that the track was a normal, level, industrial installation, permitting the proposed simple six-wheel design for the crane. In spite of a general increase in costs in the interim, John Stiles was able to submit again the original bid of $200,000. The order was placed, and our production costs finally turned out to be $150,000. The crane was shipped on September 25, 1971, on schedule.

"Unfortunately, Dayton's track foundation was not adequate for a six-wheeled crane of this capacity, and began to bend and crack. Dayton would not accept the crane and returned it at a cost of $5,000 to us. John then undertook an engineering study and concluded that the cost of rebuilding the crane with a 12-wheel design would be about $160,000. A further review of the costs developed no useful shortcuts. On October 15, a revised total price of $350,000 was offered to Dayton.

"No firm reply was received by the end of October, so I arranged for a meeting with Dayton's general manager, Bob Hendricks, and Carl Mosley. John Stiles went down to Los Angeles with me, and the first thing we did was look at the damaged rails. They had already repaired the track and were again operating their old crane. Right away, we could see that the rail structure was completely inappropriate for the six-wheel design, and that it could not stand the pounds-per-square-inch loads generated by six wheels. Apparently that had not occurred to Carl Mosley, since their existing crane was of an "antique" 10-wheel design, and he figured that we would know how many wheels a crane should need. Well, we really should have inspected the tracks, since this rail design is as old as Dayton's crane.

"Hendricks said that he thought that $350,000 was a greater investment than Dayton could consider. He felt that a suitable crane should cost about $280,000, and thought that he could get a competitive bid for about that much. We left the meeting with the understanding that we would review the design to see if costs could be reduced enough to get below the quotation of October 15. Both Hendricks and Mosley indicated that there was "no big rush" for us, and I suspect that they may be willing to keep plugging along with that old dinosaur they're using now."

There was a knock at the door, and John Stiles entered. "I've asked John to give us some further information on this matter," Blake said, "and I would like to give the floor to him at this time."

"Thank you, Mr. Blake. We quoted Dayton a figure of $350,000 based on our present estimate of the costs of modification and the production cost of the original crane. Now, though, with an indication that a suitable crane at $280,000 would probably be acceptable to them, we could reconsider. But I would like to remind you that it would have been impossible to have built a 12-wheeled crane originally for $280,000. I would say that there is an even chance that we'd get the order at $280,000, since nobody else could build a 12-wheel for any less. At a lower figure of $220,000, say, I'd bet on a 90% chance of getting the order. At the higher price of $350,000 I'd say we'd have only a 25% chance of getting the order."

"What about trying to sell the crane to someone else, instead of trying to sell it to Dayton?" asked one of the directors.

"There's some chance of that," Stiles replied. "I know of another company, Stern Industries, that might take the crane off our hands. I'd guess there is a 30% chance they would purchase it—but the price we could get is a different matter. I'd say that three prices are possible: $100,000, $150,000, and $180,000. Presuming that Stern does, in fact, purchase the crane, I think the most likely sales price is $150,000; we have about a 7 out of 10 chance of getting that amount. On the other hand, there is the possibility that their purchasing agent, Judith Hirtenstein, might force us to take $100,000 for the crane—about a 2 out of 10 chance, I'd say. Finally, we stand about a 1 in 10 chance of making off with the $180,000 figure. In addition to a lower selling price, another drawback is that just to get a salesman out there and to prepare the sale would cost us about $10,000, and *then* we're at the point I mentioned above of either getting the sale or losing it. Also, if we try initially to sell to Stern, we will eliminate any chance of selling the crane to Dayton.

"If we do decide to go all out in trying to sell the crane to Dayton, we're going to have to develop a good, revised design. I figure that this will cost us about $20,000. No matter what bid price we try, if they reject it, we can always try to sell the crane to Stern. With the time delay I'd guess that we'd have only a 15% chance of selling the crane to Stern. If we can sell it, I think that the price and chances that I mentioned earlier would be the same."

"How about scrapping the beast, John," asked Blake.

"I've been thinking about that, too. I think we should consider scrapping the crane at any point that things start looking too expensive and risky. We could salvage at least $50,000 from it, and we would certainly avoid a lot of uncertainty."

At this point Charles Blake thanked John Stiles, excused him from the meeting, and turned to the other directors. "As you might suspect, there is the possibility of pressing Dayton on the legal point that they studied and approved our plans for the initial crane, and that they, therefore, must accept the crane as designed. However, I think that this is a very poor idea, since the last thing we want to do is become involved in a lawsuit over this thing. There is the possibility that a growing company like Dayton will be a source of future business for us, but not if we sue them."

Draw a decision diagram representing the problem faced by Morris Manufacturing Co. Use net contribution to value each end point. Do *not* try to determine all probabilities or solve the problem.

## SUPPLEMENTARY REFERENCES


BROWN, R. V., A. S. KAHR, AND C. PETERSON. *Decision Analysis for the Manager*. New York: Holt, Rinehart and Winston, 1974, Chaps. 16 and 17.

SCHLAIFER, R. *Analysis of Decisions Under Uncertainty*. New York: McGraw-Hill, 1969, Chaps. 2 and 3.

# 4

# Introduction to Probability

Probabilities distinguish decision models under uncertainty from other models. Decision diagrams, with end points labeled by the chosen evaluation unit, provide the structure linking alternatives to outcomes and their consequences. Probabilities are required to complete the description of the uncertain events. This chapter introduces the basic definitions and concepts of probability. The emphasis is on the *information* provided by probabilities. The details of how probabilities are obtained and used in calculations are the subject of Part II of the book. Figure 4.1 shows how the material fits into the overall discussion.

**FIGURE 4.1**

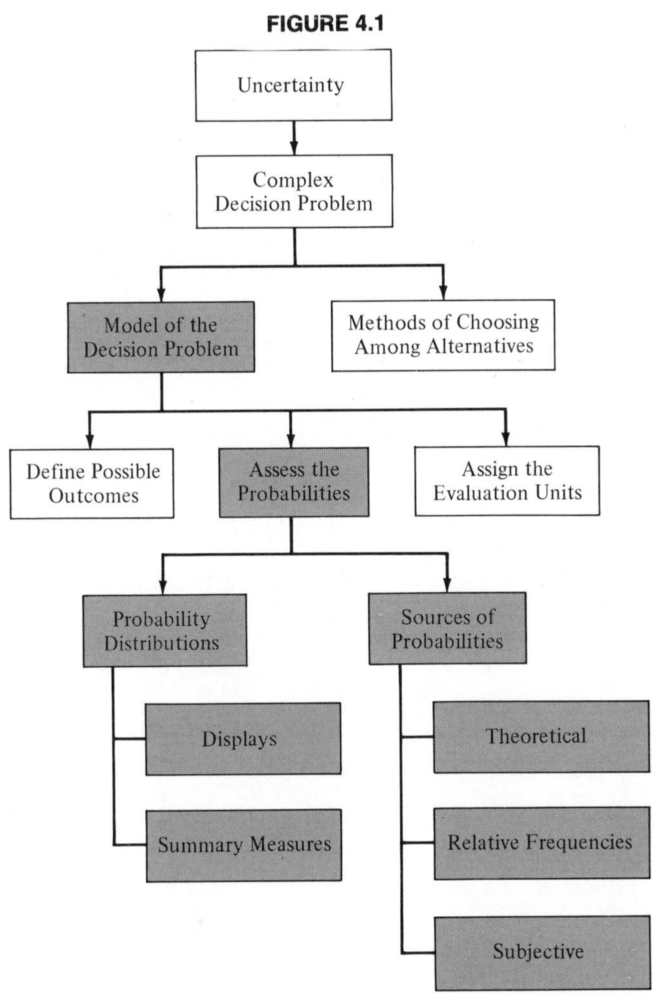

## BASIC CONCEPTS AND DEFINITIONS

When uncertainty is present, the chance of any outcome occurring is described by a probability. In most cases probabilities are easy to understand. With a little help, our intuition about probabilities can be extended to cover rather complex decision problems. To start with, consider a simple example.

**Example 4.1**

Assume that you have a batch of five *widgets* just off your production line. The quality control supervisor has checked them and found two defective units. Before the defective units could be removed from the batch, they were mixed together with the good units. A customer calls and asks to have a widget shipped immediately. The only widgets you have on hand are the batch of five with two defectives. Retesting would take too long. You know that if you ship a defective unit, you will have to pay \$10 to replace it. However, for an extra cost of \$5, you can buy a good widget from a retail store and send it to the customer. You have two alternatives if you want to comply with the customer's request for immediate shipment: select a unit at random from the batch of five and ship it, or buy one at a retail store.

A decision diagram of the problem, using incremental costs as the evaluation unit, is shown in Figure 4.2. To complete the model we need the probabilities for the uncertain event on the unit shipped, if one is chosen from the batch of five. From the information in the problem, we would say the probability that any particular unit is shipped is $\frac{1}{5}$. The following definitions will allow us to discuss the use of probabilities in more detail.

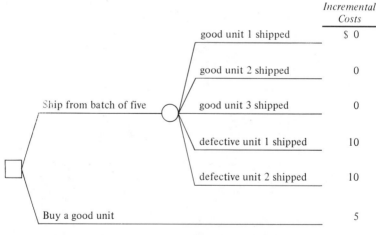

**FIGURE 4.2**

| Decision | Outcome | *Incremental Costs* |
|---|---|---|
| Ship from batch of five | good unit 1 shipped | \$ 0 |
| | good unit 2 shipped | 0 |
| | good unit 3 shipped | 0 |
| | defective unit 1 shipped | 10 |
| | defective unit 2 shipped | 10 |
| Buy a good unit | | 5 |

### Set

> **Set**
>
> ***Definition:*** *A **set** is a collection of objects called **elements**.*

In our example the five widgets that are candidates for shipping form a set. The elements of the set are *good unit 1, good unit 2, good unit 3, defective unit 1,* and *defective unit 2.* The letters from A to D in the alphabet are another example of a set. Each letter is an element and the collection is a set. Sets can be written in two ways. For the alphabet example we have:

1. List each element: $S = \{A, B, C, D\}$
2. Describe a rule: $S = \{\text{first four letters in the alphabet}\}$

Elements need not be simple objects like letters or widgets. If we are contemplating developing a new product and need to examine the products of competitors, the set of interest consists of the collection of competitors' products (e.g., when considering color television, $S$ = {RCA, Sony, Zenith, etc.} or $S$ = {all competing color television sets}).

### Subset

**Subset**

***Definition:*** *A* ***subset*** *is any collection of elements from a set.*

For instance, in our example, *good unit 1* and *good unit 2* constitute a subset of the widgets.

### Uncertain Event

**Uncertain Event**

***Definition:*** *We have discussed* ***uncertain events*** *throughout the book. They represent the* ***processes*** *or* ***objects*** *that are uncertain. In some settings (especially in statistics) they can be described as* ***experiments****.*

For instance, in our example, the random choice of one unit from the five can be thought of as an experiment. The flip of a coin is an uncertain event that can also be described as an experiment. Uncertain events that are not naturally described as experiments will be illustrated later.

### Outcome Space (or Sample Space)

**Outcome Space (or Sample Space)**

***Definition:*** *The* ***set*** *of all possible outcomes of an* ***uncertain event*** *is called the* ***outcome space****.*[1]

[1]This could just as easily be called the *set of outcomes* rather than outcome space. Use of the term "outcome" or "sample space" corresponds to terminology used in many discussions of probability and statistics and is more descriptive when events have outcomes measured by continuous scales.

For example, if two coins are tossed, we have the outcome space $\{HH, TH, HT, TT\}$. We will usually use the greek letter Ω, capital omega, to denote an outcome space. In a decision diagram the outcome space for any uncertain event is represented by the branches leaving the uncertain event node.

For our example, the outcome space is the set Ω = {good unit 1 shipped, good unit 2 shipped, good unit 3 shipped, defective unit 1 shipped, defective unit 2 shipped}. Each element can be thought of as a point, as shown in Figure 4.3.

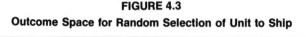

**FIGURE 4.3**
**Outcome Space for Random Selection of Unit to Ship**

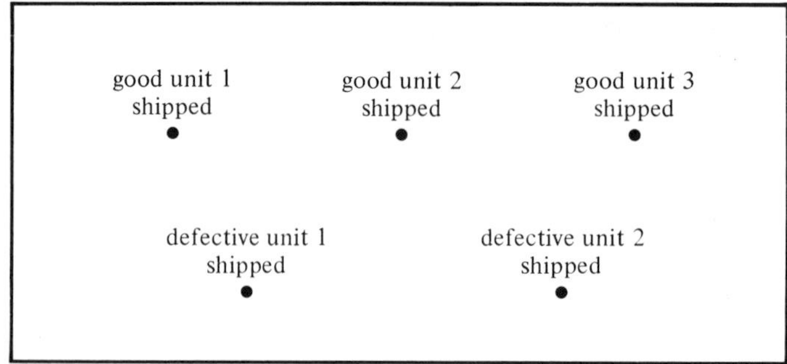


### Event

**Event**

***Definition:*** *A* ***subset*** *of outcomes in outcome space is called an* ***event****. Note that this is not the same as an uncertain event. The term* ***uncertain event*** *refers to the process, object, or experiment that is uncertain. The term* ***event*** *refers to a subset of the possible outcomes from an uncertain event.*

For instance, the outcome *good unit 2 shipped* from the selection process in the example is an event. The subset of outcomes $S$ = {good unit 2 shipped, good unit 3 shipped, defective unit 1 shipped} is also an event. In some cases the term *simple event* is used for subsets consisting of a single element.

Figure 4.4 shows the event {defective unit 1 shipped, defective unit 2 shipped}. In this case we can describe the event naturally as *defective unit shipped.*

### Occurrence of an Event

**Occurrence of an Event**

***Definition:*** *We say that an event* ***occurs*** *if any of the outcomes in its collection of outcomes occurs.*

**FIGURE 4.4**

**Illustration of Event: Defective Unit Shipped**

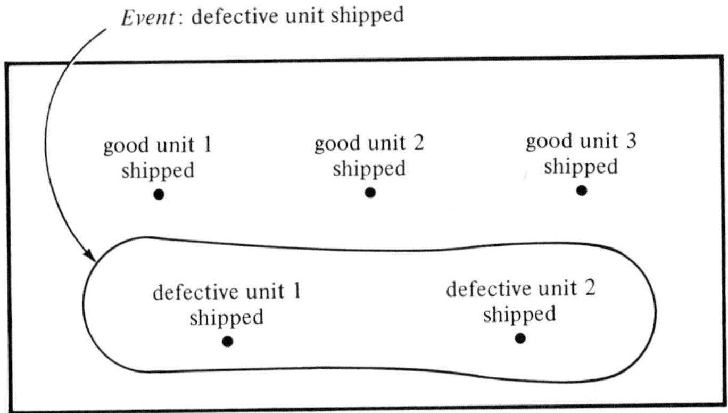


For instance, if we have the event *defective unit shipped* as defined in Figure 4.4, we say it occurs if either defective unit 1 is shipped or defective unit 2 is shipped.

### Complement

> **Complement**
>
> ***Definition:*** *The* ***complement*** *of an event consists of the subset of elements in the outcome space that are not included in the event.*

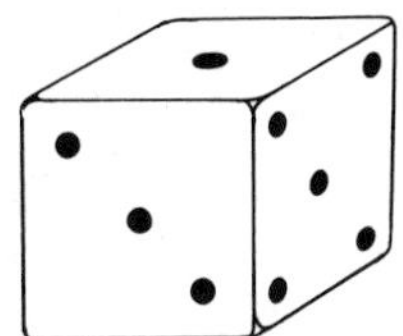

For example, if we defined the event $D = \{0 \text{ defectives}\}$ in a production lot of size 3, the complement of event $D$, written $\sim D$ and read "not $D$" is given by $\{1, 2, \text{ or } 3 \text{ defectives}\}$. The idea of a complement can be illustrated using a *Venn* diagram. Think of rolling a single six-sided die. Figure 4.5 shows a Venn diagram for the uncertain event, *one roll of the die*. Each dot represents an element in outcome space (a possible outcome of the roll). We define event $A = \{3,4,6\}$. The complement of $A$ is $\sim A = \{1,2,5\}$. Taken together, $A$ and $\sim A$ constitute the entire outcome space for the roll of the die.

**FIGURE 4.5**

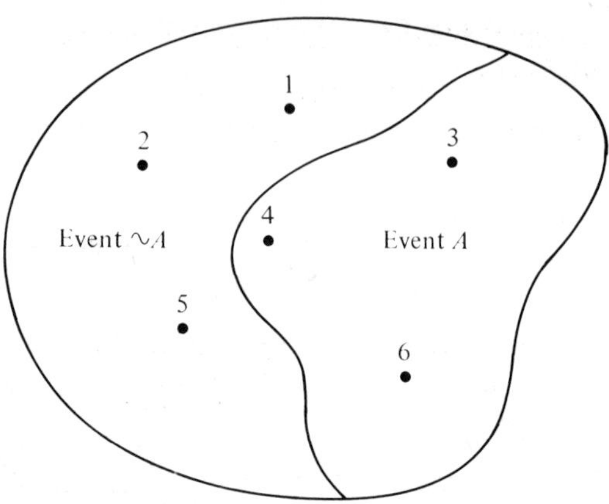


## Union

> **Union**
>
> ***Definition:*** *The **union** of two events, say A and B, consists of those elements of the outcome space that are elements of A or B or possibly both. The union is written $A \cup B$.*

When more than two events are involved, say $A_1, A_2, A_3, A_4$, the union consists of those elements that are elements of at least one of the events $A_1$, $A_2$, $A_3$, and $A_4$. For example, if $A = \{3,4,6\}$ in the roll of a die and $B = \{1,2,3\}$, $A \cup B = \{1,2,3,4,6\}$. This union is displayed in Figure 4.6.

**FIGURE 4.6**

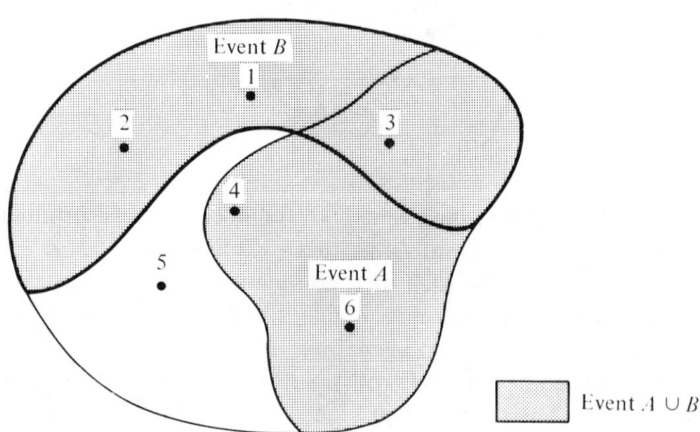

### Intersection

> **Intersection**
>
> ***Definition:*** *The* ***intersection*** *of two events, say A and B, consists of those elements that are common to both A and B. The intersection is written as $A \cap B$, or, when the meaning is clear in discussing probabilities, (A, B).*

When more than two events are involved, say $A_1, A_2, A_3, A_4$, the intersection consists of those elements that are elements of each of the events $A_1$, $A_2$, $A_3$, and $A_4$. In the die-rolling example, $A = \{3,4,6\}$ and $B = \{1,2,3\}$; $A \cap B = \{3\}$. This intersection is shown in Figure 4.7.

**FIGURE 4.7**

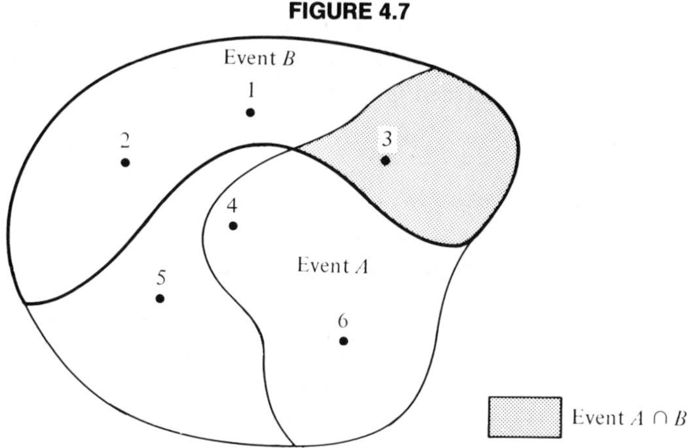


### Null (Empty) Set

> **Null (Empty) Set**
>
> ***Definition:*** *The* ***null set****, represented by the Greek letter, $\phi$, phi, is the set without any elements. When an event is the null set, it is impossible.*

### Mutually Exclusive

> **Mutually Exclusive**
>
> ***Definition:*** *Two events are said to be* ***mutually exclusive*** *if their intersection is the null (empty) set. That is, they have no element in common.*

**FIGURE 4.8**

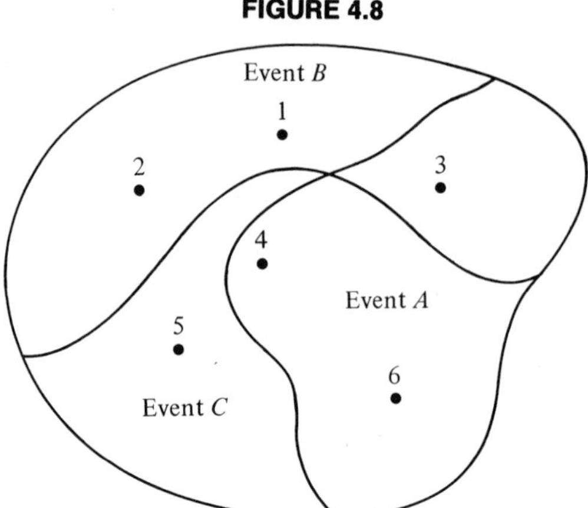


In the die-toss example, if we define event $C = \{5\}$, then events $A$ and $C$ are mutually exclusive. When events are not mutually exclusive, such as events $A$ and $B$, they can both occur (see Figure 4.8).

### Collectively Exhaustive

> **Collectively Exhaustive**
>
> ***Definition:*** *Events are **collectively exhaustive** if taken together they make up the entire outcome space. This means that at least one of the events must occur.*

The sets $A$, $B$, and $C$ in Figure 4.8 are collectively exhaustive events.

## TECHNICAL REQUIREMENTS FOR PROBABILITIES

### Notation for Probabilities

> *The **probability** of event $A$ is written $P(A)$.*

### Conditions on Probabilities

Let $A$ and $B$ be *any* two events defined on outcome space $\Omega$. A probability measure assigns real numbers such that:

1. $P(A) \geqslant 0$, $P(B) \geqslant 0$.
2. If $A$ and $B$ are mutually exclusive, $P(A \cup B) = P(A) + P(B)$.
3. $P(\Omega) = 1$.

These conditions merely require that the probability of any event defined on $\Omega$ is greater than or equal to zero; if two events are mutually exclusive (i.e., have no elements in common), the probability of either one or the other (their union) is the sum of the probabilities assigned to each event separately; and the probability of the event that is the entire outcome space (i.e., all possible outcomes) is 1.

In the die-tossing example, the conditions mean that the probability of any outcome must be greater than or equal to zero. If we let $D_1=\{1\}, D_2=\{2\},\ldots,D_6=\{6\}$, then $P(D_i)\geqslant 0$ for $i=1,2,\ldots,6$. The *subscript* $i$ defines which of the outcomes from 1 to 6 the event represents. If we agree that the probability of any outcome is $\frac{1}{6}$ (because each has an equal chance and there are six possibilities), $P(D_i)=\frac{1}{6}$. With $A=\{3,4,6\}$, the second condition requires that $P(A)=P(D_3)+P(D_4)+P(D_6)=\frac{3}{6}$. (Note that outcomes are mutually exclusive and event $A=D_3\cup D_4\cup D_6$.) If event $E$ is defined as $\{1,2\}$, the second condition requires that

$$P(A\cup E)=P(A)+P(E)=\tfrac{3}{6}+\tfrac{2}{6}=\tfrac{5}{6}$$

The last condition specifies that

$$P(\Omega)=P(D_1)+P(D_2)+P(D_3)+P(D_4)+P(D_5)+P(D_6)=1$$

### Notation for Summations

Rather than writing out each term in a summation, a shorthand notation is used.

$$\sum_{i=1}^{6} P(D_i)=P(D_1)+P(D_2)+P(D_3)+P(D_4)+P(D_5)+P(D_6)$$

### Limitation of the Technical Requirements

These conditions are technical requirements that have to be satisfied for the rules of probability to be used. They say nothing about the *meaning* of probability in general or about particular statements such as "the probability that it will rain tomorrow is 0.7" or "the probability of a head in a coin toss is 0.5." Later in this chapter we discuss three views of probability that are based on three different ideas about the meaning of probabilities. For now we will rely on our intuitive notion while discussing how probabilities can be displayed.

## PROBABILITY DISTRIBUTIONS

Probability information is displayed by *probability distributions*. There are several ways the information can be presented. In this section we discuss probability distributions for discrete outcome spaces.

### Probability Density Function

When the outcome space of an uncertain event consists of a finite number of discrete points, the probability associated with *each* point can be listed. This form for a probability distribution is called a *probability density function.*[2] For example, if we consider a single roll of a fair, six-sided die, the probability density function can be written

$$P(X=1)=\tfrac{1}{6}$$
$$P(X=2)=\tfrac{1}{6}$$
$$P(X=3)=\tfrac{1}{6}$$
$$P(X=4)=\tfrac{1}{6}$$
$$P(X=5)=\tfrac{1}{6}$$
$$P(X=6)=\tfrac{1}{6}$$

where we have introduced $X$ to stand for the number of spots showing. Therefore, $P(X=1)$ should be read: "The probability that the number of spots showing is 1." The same information can be displayed by a graphical plot of the probability density function, as shown in Figure 4.9.

**FIGURE 4.9**

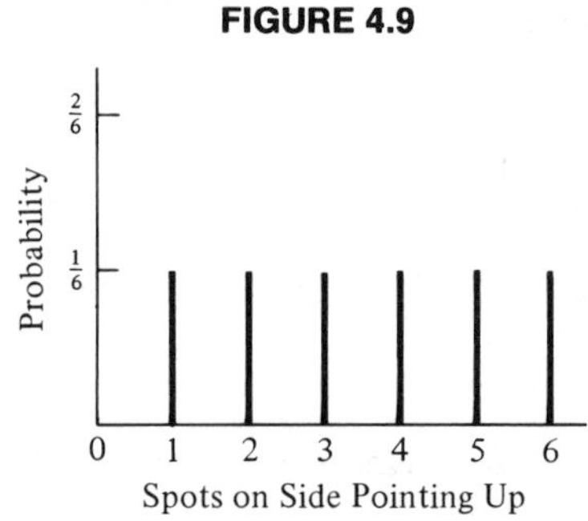


As another example, consider two tosses of a fair coin. Suppose that we are interested in the number of heads in the two tosses. The diagram of the uncertain event is shown in Figure 4.10. Each of the four outcomes shown (which can be written $HH$, $TH$, $HT$, and $TT$) has an equal chance. Therefore, each has a probability of $\frac{1}{4}$. To be completely formal we can define $Y$ to be the number of heads in two tosses.

$$\text{Event } \{Y=0\}=\{TT\}$$
$$\text{Event } \{Y=1\}=\{TH, HT\}$$
$$\text{Event } \{Y=2\}=\{HH\}$$

[2]For discrete events this is sometimes called a *probability mass function.*

**FIGURE 4.10**

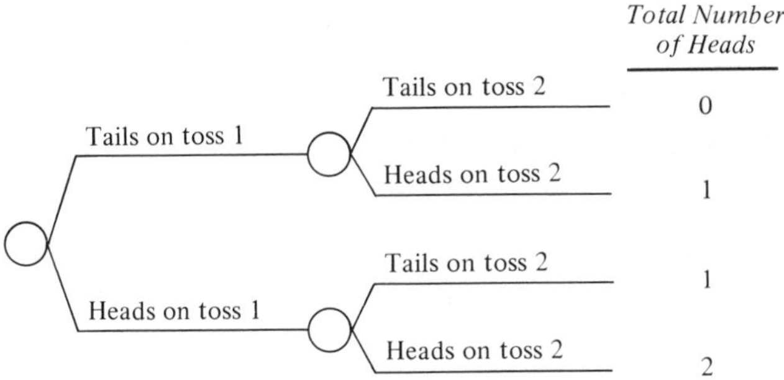


The probability density function for $Y$ is

$$P(Y=0)=P(TT)=\tfrac{1}{4}$$
$$P(Y=1)=P(TH)+P(HT)=\tfrac{1}{2}$$
$$P(Y=2)=P(HH)=\tfrac{1}{4}$$

It can be plotted as shown in Figure 4.11.

**FIGURE 4.11**

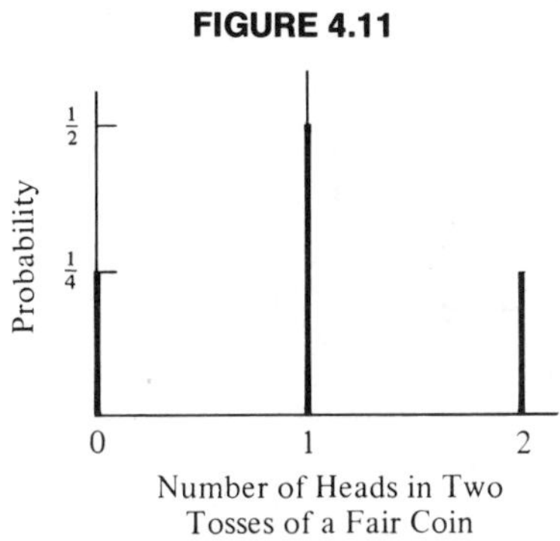


### Cumulative Probability Distribution

A probability distribution can also be displayed using a *cumulative distribution* (sometimes called a *cumulative distribution function*). It can be defined to cumulate in either of two ways. If we let $X$ stand for the numerical value associated with the outcomes of some uncertain event (say the number of spots showing on the single toss of the die described above) and $x$ stand for some specific value (in the die example, $x$ can take on six values: $x_1=1$, $x_2=2, x_3=3, x_4=4, x_5=5, x_6=6$), then the cumulative distribution is the probability that a given value or less is obtained. This is written $P(X \leqslant x)$. For the single toss of a die, the cumulative distribution is as follows:

$$P(X \leqslant 1) = P(X=1) = \tfrac{1}{6}$$
$$P(X \leqslant 2) = P(X=1) + P(X=2) = \tfrac{2}{6}$$
$$P(X \leqslant 3) = P(X=1) + P(X=2) + P(X=3) = \tfrac{3}{6}$$
$$P(X \leqslant 4) = P(X=1) + P(X=2) + P(X=3) + P(X=4) = \tfrac{4}{6}$$
$$P(X \leqslant 5) = P(X=1) + P(X=2) + P(X=3) + P(X=4) + P(X=5) = \tfrac{5}{6}$$
$$P(X \leqslant 6) = P(X=1) + P(X=2) + P(X=3) + P(X=4) + P(X=5) + P(X=6) = 1$$

Cumulative distributions can also be plotted. Figure 4.12 is a plot of the cumulative distribution for the die example.

**FIGURE 4.12**

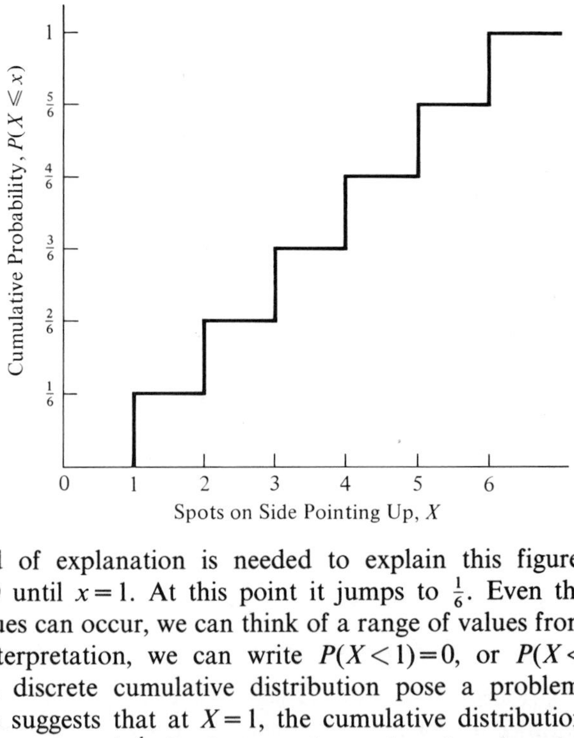

A word of explanation is needed to explain this figure. Notice that $P(X \leqslant x) = 0$ until $x = 1$. At this point it jumps to $\frac{1}{6}$. Even though only six discrete values can occur, we can think of a range of values from 0 to 6. With such an interpretation, we can write $P(X < 1) = 0$, or $P(X < 1.5) = \frac{1}{6}$. The jumps in a discrete cumulative distribution pose a problem because the vertical line suggests that at $X = 1$, the cumulative distribution takes on all values between 0 and $\frac{1}{6}$. In fact, we know it only takes the value $\frac{1}{6}$. To emphasize this, cumulative plots for discrete random variables are sometimes displayed as shown in Figure 4.13. Since there is some benefit to using the original plot with the vertical lines, we will continue to use it; however, the meaning of the jumps must be kept in mind.

The cumulative distribution provides the same information as the density function, and one can be derived from the other. Starting with the density function, the cumulative distribution is calculated for each discrete outcome

FIGURE 4.13

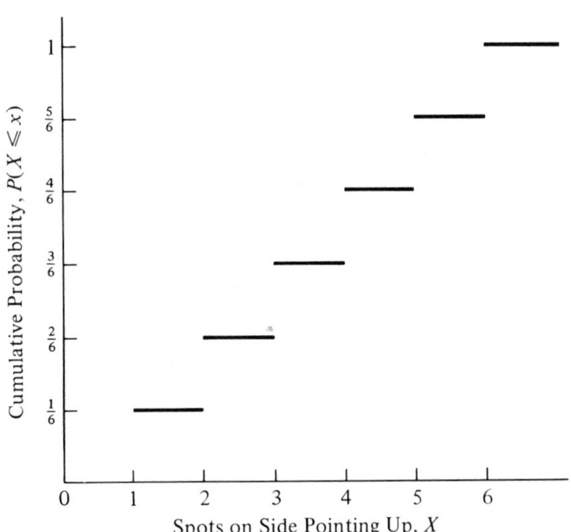


using the relationship

$$P(X \leqslant x_n) = \sum_{i=1}^{n} P(X = x_i)$$

The notation $\Sigma_{i=1}^{n}$ indicates the sum over elements beginning with the element indexed 1 and ending with the element indexed $n$. That is,

$$\sum_{i=1}^{n} P(X = x_i) = P(X = x_1) + P(X = x_2) + \cdots + P(X = x_n)$$

Starting with the cumulative distribution, the probability density function is calculated using

$$P(X = x_n) = P(X \leqslant x_n) - P(X \leqslant x_{n-1})$$

For the die-tossing example we can calculate

$$P(X = 4) = P(X \leqslant 4) - P(X \leqslant 3) = \tfrac{4}{6} - \tfrac{3}{6} = \tfrac{1}{6}$$

The cumulative distribution is particularly useful for considering such questions as: "What is the probability that profit is less than or equal to zero?". These questions are couched directly in terms of cumulative probabilities. For instance, the probability that there are less than or equal to four spots on a roll of a die can be read directly off the cumulative plot as $\frac{4}{6}$.

The second way to define a cumulative distribution just reverses the cumulating procedure—that is, the probability that a given outcome or *more* is given. This is written $P(X \geqslant x)$. For the die example, we have

$$P(X \geqslant 1) = P(X=1) + P(X=2) + P(X=3) + P(X=4) + P(X=5) + P(X=6) = 1$$

$$P(X \geqslant 2) = P(X=2) + P(X=3) + P(X=4) + P(X=5) + P(X=6) = \tfrac{5}{6}$$

$$P(X \geqslant 3) = P(X=3) + P(X=4) + P(X=5) + P(X=6) = \tfrac{4}{6}$$

$$P(X \geqslant 4) = P(X=4) + P(X=5) + P(X=6) = \tfrac{3}{6}$$

$$P(X \geqslant 5) = P(X=5) + P(X=6) = \tfrac{2}{6}$$

$$P(X \geqslant 6) = P(X=6) = \tfrac{1}{6}$$

This cumulative distribution is plotted in Figure 4.14.

**FIGURE 4.14**

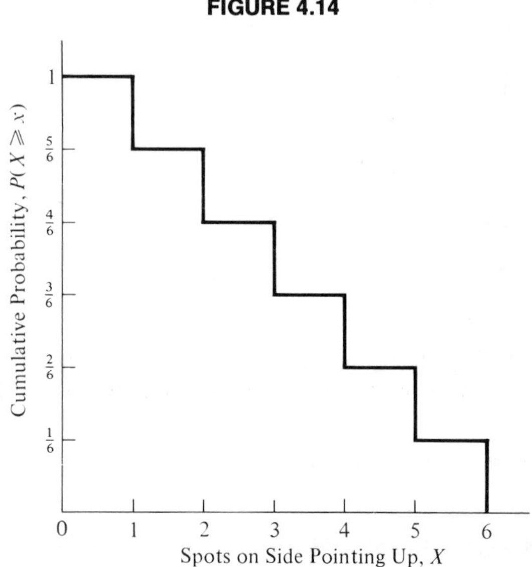


## SUMMARY MEASURES FOR PROBABILITY DISTRIBUTIONS

Probability distributions can be summarized without giving a complete density function or cumulative distribution. The two most useful parameters are the mean and standard deviation.

### The Mean of a Probability Distribution

The *mean* of a probability distribution is closely connected with the *average* value. Averages are calculated for attributes of some population. Suppose that we are interested in the ages of people in a group made up of the tenants in a new apartment building. The results of a survey are given in Table 4.1.

**TABLE 4.1**

| *Age* | *Number of Tenants* |
|---|---|
| 21 | 8 |
| 22 | 15 |
| 23 | 22 |
| 24 | 28 |
| 25 | 27 |
| Total | 100 |

The average age of the group is

$$\begin{aligned}\text{Average Age} &= \frac{21(8)+22(15)+23(22)+24(28)+25(27)}{100} \\ &= 21\left(\tfrac{8}{100}\right)+22\left(\tfrac{15}{100}\right)+23\left(\tfrac{22}{100}\right)+24\left(\tfrac{28}{100}\right)+25\left(\tfrac{27}{100}\right) \\ &= 23.51\end{aligned}$$

Now assume we want to select one tenant at random from the group and determine his/her age. This is an uncertain event with five possible outcomes. If we define $X$ to be the age of the person selected, the probability distribution is

$$\begin{aligned}P(X=21)&=\tfrac{8}{100}\\ P(X=22)&=\tfrac{15}{100}\\ P(X=23)&=\tfrac{22}{100}\\ P(X=24)&=\tfrac{28}{100}\\ P(X=25)&=\tfrac{27}{100}\end{aligned}$$

The *mean* of this distribution is defined as the sum of the outcomes "weighted" by the probabilities:

$$\begin{aligned}\text{Mean} &= 21\left(\tfrac{8}{100}\right)+22\left(\tfrac{15}{100}\right)+23\left(\tfrac{22}{100}\right)+24\left(\tfrac{28}{100}\right)+25\left(\tfrac{27}{100}\right) \\ &= 23.51\end{aligned}$$

This expression for the mean age of the distribution is just exactly the same as the average age. The difference is that a *mean* is a parameter of a probability distribution and an *average* is a parameter of some population.

As another example consider two tosses of a fair coin. The probability density function for the number of heads is given in Figure 4.11. The mean is

$$\begin{aligned}\text{Mean} &= 0\left(\tfrac{1}{4}\right)+1\left(\tfrac{1}{2}\right)+2\left(\tfrac{1}{4}\right) \\ &= 1\end{aligned}$$

In this example we do not naturally think of a *population* and its *average*. However, the *mean* is defined as shown. We might think about the *mean* as the *average* number of heads per trial *if* the two tosses were repeated a large number of times.

## Expected Values

The *mean* is also called the *expected value* of the probability distribution. If we define $X$ to be the quantity describing outcomes of an uncertain event with $n$ discrete outcomes, then the expected value is written

$$E[X] = \sum_{i=1}^{n} x_i P(X = x_i)$$

where the $x_i$'s are the values associated with the $n$ points in outcome space. For instance, if $X$ is defined to be *contribution*, the $x_i$'s are the specific values of contribution that can be obtained, and $E[X]$ is described as the expected contribution.

## Mean or Expected Value

**Mean or Expected Value**

***Definition:*** *The* ***mean*** *or* ***expected value*** *of a probability distribution on X with outcomes* $x_1, x_2, \ldots, x_n$ *is defined to be*

$$\text{Mean} = E[X] = \sum_{i=1}^{n} x_i P(X = x_i)$$

The mean is a measure of central tendency in a probability distribution. It is designed to locate the center, or middle, of the possible outcomes.

## Standard Deviation and Variance

The *standard deviation* and the *variance* convey the same information. The standard deviation is used most often. It has the advantage that its *units* are the same as the mean. That is, if the units describing the outcomes are "quantity sold," the standard deviation is given in terms of "quantity sold" also. Units for the variance are the "square of quantity sold." The standard deviation is a relative measure of dispersion around the mean. A distribution with twice the standard deviation of another is, in a sense, twice as *spread out*.

## Variance

**Variance**

***Definition:*** *If we let X be the outcome of an uncertain event with n discrete outcomes, the* ***variance*** *is defined to be*

$$\text{Variance} = \sum_{i=1}^{n} (x_i - E[X])^2 P(X = x_i)$$

Since $E[X]$ is just the mean, the variance is a measure of dispersion about the mean. Distributions with outcomes far from the mean will have higher variances than those with outcomes near the mean, all other things being equal. Similarly, distributions with high probabilities for extreme outcomes will have higher variances than those with low probabilities for extreme outcomes, all other things being equal.

Consider the die-tossing and coin-tossing examples (see Figures 4.9 and 4.11). We would expect the variance of the distribution associated with the toss of the die to be the greater since it is more spread out. The variances calculated below bear this out.

**Die-toss example**

$$E[X] = \tfrac{1}{6}(1) + \tfrac{1}{6}(2) + \tfrac{1}{6}(3) + \tfrac{1}{6}(4) + \tfrac{1}{6}(5) + \tfrac{1}{6}(6) = 3.5$$

$$\begin{aligned} \text{Variance} &= \tfrac{1}{6}(1-3.5)^2 + \tfrac{1}{6}(2-3.5)^2 + \tfrac{1}{6}(3-3.5)^2 + \tfrac{1}{6}(4-3.5)^2 \\ &\quad + \tfrac{1}{6}(5-3.5)^2 + \tfrac{1}{6}(6-3.5)^2 \\ &= \underline{2.92} \end{aligned}$$

**Coin-toss example**

$$E[X] = \tfrac{1}{4}(0) + \tfrac{1}{2}(1) + \tfrac{1}{4}(2) = 1$$

$$\begin{aligned} \text{Variance} &= \tfrac{1}{4}(0-1)^2 + \tfrac{1}{2}(1-1)^2 + \tfrac{1}{4}(2-1)^2 \\ &= \underline{0.5} \end{aligned}$$

### Standard Deviation

> **Standard Deviation**
>
> ***Definition:*** *The* ***standard deviation*** *is the square root of the variance.*
>
> $$\text{Standard Deviation} = \sqrt{\sum_{i=1}^{n} (x_i - E[X])^2 P(X = x_i)}$$

**Die-toss example**

$$\text{Standard Deviation} = \sqrt{2.92} = 1.71$$

**Coin-toss example**

$$\text{Standard Deviation} = \sqrt{0.5} = 0.707$$

By specifying the mean and standard deviation, much of the important information can be given for an uncertain event.

## THE MEANING OF PROBABILITIES

The technical requirements and methods of displaying probability distributions for an uncertain event have been introduced. We have relied on our intuition to provide basic probabilities for simple uncertain events such as tossing a die or coin. But, *exactly* what is the meaning of a probability? How can we assess probabilities? Is there a basic definition that we can always use? Unfortunately, there are no simple answers to these questions. There are different views on the basic concept of a probability. These views are sometimes labeled *classical* (theoretical, symmetrical), *relative frequency* (limiting frequency), and *subjective* (personal).[3] The first two views—classical and relative frequency—are associated with an *objective* concept of probability.

## CLASSICAL VIEW OF PROBABILITY

The classical or theoretical view of probability relies on conditions of symmetry and the principle of insufficient reason. The idea is that symmetry allows one to argue that, in the absence of any information to the contrary, all events are regarded as being equally probable. The obvious example is the throw of a six-sided die. Symmetry exists because all six sides are the same. Using the principle of insufficient reason, the probability of any side pointing up is $\frac{1}{6}$. The classical view is formalized by the following definition.

**Classical Probability**

***Definition:*** *If an uncertain event has n* ***mutually exclusive***, ***equally likely***, *and* ***collectively exhaustive*** *outcomes, and if event A contains* $n_A$ *of these outcomes, then the probability of event A is* $n_A/n$ [*i.e.*, $P(A)=n_A/n$].

Examples of the use of this definition are easy to find and often involve games of chance. The die and coin toss previously discussed fit this category. The examples below illustrate how the definition formalizes our intuitive results and discuss some potential pitfalls.

Consider the toss of a standard six-sided die. The outcome space is $\Omega=\{1,2,3,4,5,6\}$. Define event $A=\{1,6\}$. Therefore, $n=6$, $n_A=2$, and $P(A)=\frac{2}{6}=\frac{1}{3}$.

Suppose that we are interested in the probability of obtaining at least one head in the two tosses of a fair coin. An eighteenth-century mathematician, d'Alembert, argued that the probability was $\frac{2}{3}$, on the following grounds. The

[3]For extensive discussions comparing these views, see, for example, B. deFinetti, "Probability Interpretations," *International Encyclopedia of the Social Sciences* (New York: Macmillan, 1968); L. J. Savage, *The Foundations of Statistics*, 2nd rev. ed. (New York: Dover Publications, 1972); and B. deFinetti, *Theory of Probability*, Vol. I (New York: Wiley, 1974).

outcome space is $\Omega = \{0 \text{ heads}, 1 \text{ head}, 2 \text{ heads}\}$ and the event of interest, $A = \{1 \text{ or more heads}\} = \{1 \text{ head}, 2 \text{ heads}\}$. Therefore, $n = 3$, $n_A = 2$, and $P(A) = \frac{2}{3}$. It is clear that he misinterpreted the symmetry in the problem. As we showed in Figure 4.11, the three elements in the outcome space are not equally likely. The outcome space that consists of symmetrical elements is $\Omega = \{HH, HT, TH, TT\}$, where $HT$ stands for the outcome heads on the first toss and tails on the second toss. We can now redefine event $A = \{HH, HT, TH\}$. Therefore, $n = 4$, $n_A = 3$, and $P(A) = \frac{3}{4}$.

Consider the probability of drawing an ace or a spade from a shuffled deck of cards. The outcome space is $\Omega = \{52 \text{ cards}\}$ and event $A = \{\text{ace or spade}\}$. Therefore, $n = 52$, $n_A = 4$ (number of aces) + 13 (number of spades) − 1. A common mistake involves improperly counting the number of elements in $n_A$ by failing to recognize the overlap (i.e., one ace is also a spade). The probability of $A$, $P(A) = \frac{16}{52} = \frac{4}{13}$.

### Criticism of the Classical View

Those adhering to the relative frequency view and the subjective view criticize this method of obtaining probabilities. The relative frequentists just reject outright the idea of using the principle of insufficient reason. Subjectivists generally have two complaints. The first also involves the principle of insufficient reason. They argue that it is extremely unlikely that situations will arise in which individuals will not have had some experience which will influence their feeling about the chances of events. Their second complaint is that it is not always obvious when the appropriate symmetry conditions exist.

From the point of view of decision making, these criticisms have two important implications. The first is that the number of problems where the classical view will yield probabilities is limited. There are many more situations in which we would all agree that symmetry does not hold than those in which we would agree that it does hold. The second is that determining the existence of the appropriate symmetry and the applicability of the principle of insufficient reason requires judgment. For instance, the assumption that heads and tails of a coin satisfy the theoretical definition requires that the events $H$ and $T$ are collectively exhaustive. What about landing on an edge? This, of course, could be taken into consideration by expanding the outcome spaces to include {Head, Tail, Edge}. But this violates the equally likely assumption. Even if we were sure that the coin could not land on its edge, we might still be concerned about asserting equal chances, since the coin could be bent, or could be heavier on one side, or the tosser might affect the outcome.

Coin flipping may seem rather remote from the type of managerial decision problems we claim to be addressing—and it is. The point is that even in something as simple as coin tossing, judgment must be brought to bear when the classical method is used to determine probabilities. The important question is, how much judgment? Or perhaps even more to the point, is an individual more comfortable making these judgments than some others? One of the great advantages of discovering a situation in which the classical definition applies is that individuals may feel more comfortable about their judgments (surer, if you will) than in other settings.

### Limitation of the Classical View

Regardless of your belief in the appropriateness of this as the fundamental view of probability, its applicability is limited. In terms of our simple gambling problem, what is the probability of heads with a bent coin? If you are a retailer deciding on the number of units to order, what are the probabilities of selling various quantities? In a manufacturing setting, what is the probability of obtaining a defective unit from each process? If you are director of an Internal Revenue office, what are the probabilities of finding errors in various classes of returns? None of these probabilities can be determined using the classical approach, since the "equally likely" assumption does not hold. We need another view of probability to answer these questions.

## RELATIVE FREQUENCY

The relative frequency view of probability relies on counting the number of occurrences of an event. We can think of collecting data by counting how many times an event occurs in a fixed number of trials. Since the relative frequency of a particular event taken from a small number of trials can be different from that obtained with a large number of trials, the *probability* of an event occurring is taken to be the relative frequency as the number of trials becomes very large. The concept is formally defined below.

### Relative Frequency Probability

**Relative Frequency Probability**

***Definition:*** *If an uncertain event occurs a large number of times, m, the outcome at each trial is independent of previous outcomes, and event A occurs* $m_A$ *times, then the* ***probability*** *of A is taken as equal to its* ***relative frequency,*** $m_A/m$ [*i.e.,* $P(A) = m_A/m$].

The concept corresponds generally with our intuitive feeling about probabilities. For example, if a lopsided coin is flipped 100 times and turns up heads 70 times, we are tempted to say that the probability of heads is $\frac{70}{100}$, or 0.7. Similarly, if records of the demand for a product on a daily basis over a month are as shown in Table 4.2, the relative frequencies are often used as the probability for each level of demand.

**TABLE 4.2**

| *Demand (Units)* | *Number of Times Demanded* | *Relative Frequency or Probability of Demand* |
|---|---|---|
| 0 | 2 | 0.10 |
| 1 | 4 | 0.20 |
| 2 | 4 | 0.20 |
| 3 | 6 | 0.30 |
| 4 | 2 | 0.10 |
| 5 | 2 | 0.10 |
| | 20 (days) | 1.00 |

### The Conditions and Required Judgment

The relative frequency of an event may vary significantly with the number of trials, $m$. For example, if we have a series of 10 flips of a coin which result in $(H, H, T, H, T, T, H, H, H, H)$, the probability of heads based on relative frequency after each trial is shown in Figure 4.15.

Just as in the classical case, the relative frequency concept requires judgments. One important judgment, illustrated by Figure 4.15, is the number of trials needed to determine accurately a probability. This question is partially addressed by classical statistics and will not be covered here in detail. The requirement of independent trials is also important. In some processes the outcome of the $m$th trial is heavily influenced by the outcome at trial number $(m-1)$. Perhaps the most important issue, requiring judgment when relative frequencies are used, is that of comparability. Data collection in one setting may or may not be a good guide in another setting. For instance, if the demand data shown in Table 4.2 have been gathered during the month of December, are they a good predictor of demand during January?

**FIGURE 4.15**

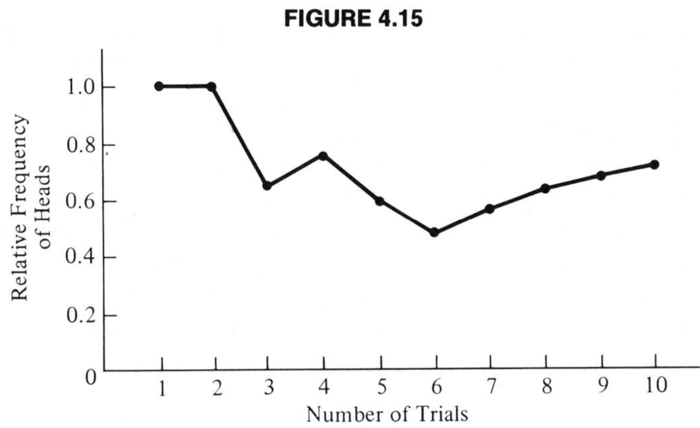

### Limitation of the Relative Frequency View

The relative frequency concept requires situations in which a large number of repeated, independent trials are available. The classical concept requires a set of collectively exhaustive, mutually exclusive, and equally likely events. Decision makers are often faced with questions that cannot be modeled using either of these views of probability (e.g., situations that have never been encountered before and may never occur again). Should a new product be introduced? What price should be paid for a company in an acquisition? Will a new manufacturing process be successful? What is the probability of obtaining a contract with a given bid? Will a weapons system meet its specifications? If problems such as these are to be analyzed, another concept of probability is often required.

## SUBJECTIVE PROBABILITIES

Subjectivists claim that the basic notion of probability is intuitive and that any attempt to confine it to either the classical or relative frequency view is unnecessary. In discussing the outcome of a case, a lawyer might say, "I think it is more probable that the judge will rule the evidence to be admissible than not." A doctor might assert, "The probability of a full recovery is better than 80%." An expert in labor negotiation might say, "I think it is more likely that the first offer will be accepted than the second." A subjectivist would claim that the meaning of these statements is evident and the use of probabilities is a natural and intuitive way to communicate when outcomes are not known with certainty. Others argue that the statements are meaningless since the terms "more probable" and "probability of 80%" are not well defined. Subjectivists assert that all we need to do is stick with the intuitive concept and provide means for sharpening it.

### Difference Between Objective and Subjective Views

The fundamental disagreement involves the precise meanings of these probability statements. Objectivists retreat to settings where they can rely on idealized conditions of symmetry or a large number of trials to explain meanings. Even if these idealized settings exist in a decision problem, they cannot be verified without resorting to personal or subjective judgments. The subjectivists, therefore, assert that acceptance of these probabilities really reflects the knowledge of the person using them. This highlights the major difference in interpretation between objectivists and subjectivists: objectivists interpret probabilities as characteristics of identifiable physical processes; subjectivists interpret them as the *state of knowledge of a given individual.*

To illustrate the difference between these two views, consider the following simple example. Assume that we are involved in betting on the outcome of a coin flip with a group of people. Some people are objectivists and others subjectivists but all want to examine the coin to determine if it is "fair." After this examination, everyone is convinced that the probability of a head on any particular flip is 0.5. Now assume that the coin is flipped and allowed to fall on the floor. Before going over to look at the outcome, suppose that we ask those involved what they think the probability of a head is now (after the flip but before observation). An objectivist who considers probabilities to be a characteristic of a physical process might reply: "It is either zero or 1; we just don't know." A subjectivist would disagree, saying: "It is still 0.5. Nothing has changed. Since I do not know the outcome, my state of knowledge is the same and hence my probability assessment is the same." A subjectivist could further argue that differentiating between before and after the coin toss is logically meaningless. In an atemporal sense, heads on the coin flip is either true or false. Whether the actual state is hidden from us by the fact that it will occur in the future or because we have not yet walked over to look is immaterial. The example also points out how the usefulness of probability is extended in decision-making settings by adopting the subjectivist view. If you hold a lottery ticket that pays $1.00 if heads comes up, and after the flip but before observing the outcome, you are offered $0.51, how would you respond? A subjectivist would be able to use the 0.5 probability assessment in making a decision. The objectivist would have to invent some other way to consider the offer.

Adoption of the subjectivist view does not preclude considering objective evidence. What it does is recognize explicitly that even probabilities obtained using theoretical or relative frequency views involve judgments. The judgments reflect the knowledge of the individual using them. Hence, the probabilities themselves are subjective and based on an individual's state of mind. Moreover, adopting the subjective view extends the concept of a probability to many important problems that cannot be conveniently modeled in terms of "equally likely events" or "repeated trials." A subjective probability is a quantification of personal uncertainty. It is characterized by a number between zero and 1, representing an individual's degree of belief in an outcome of an uncertain event. The assessment zero indicates a belief that the event is impossible and 1 indicates a belief that it is certain.

### Assessment of Subjective Probabilities

Even if we accept the view that probabilities are subjective as a *concept*, there is still the practical problem of measurement. How are they obtained? This problem is highlighted when subjective probabilities are used to communicate among individuals. What exactly do we understand when a legal expert says: "I think the chance of a favorable verdict is 75%?" What does a 75% chance mean to the lawyer? How are intuitive notions translated into a quantitative probability?

Methods for assessing probabilities can be placed in two camps. One suggests asking for a probability directly. For instance, a marketing manager might be asked directly for the probability that sales exceed a certain level. The other recommends that probabilities be obtained indirectly from a series of choices. By making choices between two uncertain events, a probability can be deduced. The assessment problem occurs because individuals have feelings about probabilities that are not usually directly expressed in terms of numbers. That is, we may have definite feelings about the probabilities associated with an uncertain event but not have these feelings "coded" in terms of probabilities. Procedures for subjective assessment are discussed in detail in Chapter 12.

Verifying that a theoretical or relative frequency concept is appropriate is a particularly good method of assessment. This is not abandoning the subjective view of probability, because verification of an objective model requires several subjective judgments. Often these judgments are easy to make. Objective evidence is effective in convincing others and, appropriately, the goal of most studies. When objective evidence is not available, the next best alternative is usually to turn to an expert for help (of course, the "expert" may be yourself). For example, in dealing with a court case, the president may turn to the financial vice president for information on the financial consequences of various outcomes and to the legal staff for subjective assessment of the probabilities of various outcomes. In settings such as these, the lack of *objective* probabilities may be regrettable, but decisions must be made. As discussed in Chapter 12, these subjective probabilities can be rigorously defined. Assessment procedures are aimed at helping to develop a consistent set of probabilities when more objective models are not available.

### The Use of Subjective Probabilities

Whether subjective probabilities should be used in a particular case depends on the problem and the availability of other alternatives. From a practical point of view, a decision maker always has a number of options, including asking someone else to make the decision. Choosing to gather more information opens up options on the type of information to obtain. The type of information used most often is deterministic (i.e., it neglects the uncertainty). When uncertainty is present, using a deterministic model can lead to poor choices. An alternative short of actual probability assessments is the specification of a most likely value and a range (best and worst cases). In some cases this may be adequate. The obvious next step is to ask about the likelihood or probability of the worst or best case. Once this question is asked, uncertainty is being considered explicitly. The question now becomes: "Where can the probabilities be obtained?" Regardless of which of the three concepts is used, judgment is required. Objective evidence should be used when available, but in its absence subjectively assessed probabilities may provide the best option for the analysis.

## SUMMARY

Probabilities are used to describe the chances of outcomes in uncertain events. The following terms are used in discussing probabilities:

*Set:* collection of objects called elements
*Subset:* collection of elements from a set
*Uncertain Event:* the process or object that is uncertain
*Outcome Space:* the set of all possible outcomes of an uncertain event
*Event:* a subset of outcomes in outcome space
*Occurrence of an Event:* when any outcome in the subset defining the event occurs
*Complement of A:* the subset of outcome space not included in the event $A$
*Union of A and B:* the set of elements that are contained in $A$ or $B$ or both
*Intersection of A and B:* the set of elements that are contained in both $A$ and $B$
*Null Set:* the set without any elements
*Mutually Exclusive:* the intersection is empty
*Collectively Exhaustive:* the union is the entire outcome space

To qualify as a probability, the following technical requirements must be satisfied. For *any* events $A$ and $B$:

1. $P(A) \geqslant 0$, $P(B) \geqslant 0$.
2. If $A$ and $B$ are mutually exclusive, then $P(A \cup B) = P(A) + P(B)$.
3. $P(\Omega) = 1$.

Probability information is displayed by *probability distributions*. There are two different forms of probability distributions: *probability density functions*, which specify the probability for each discrete outcome, $P(X = x_i)$; and *cumulative probability distributions*, which specify the probability for a given value or less, $P(X \leqslant x_i)$ [or, if cumulated the other way, a given value or more, $P(X \geqslant x_i)$]. Either of these can be presented in tabular or graphical form.

A probability distribution can be summarized by its parameters:

$$\text{Mean or Expected Value} = E[X] = \sum_{i=1}^{n} x_i P(X = x_i)$$

$$\text{Variance} = \sum_{i=1}^{n} (x_i - E[X])^2 P(X = x_i)$$

$$\text{Standard Deviation} = \sqrt{\sum_{i=1}^{n} (x_i - E[X])^2 P(X = x_i)}$$

There are three different views of probability:

*Classical Probability:* If an uncertain event has $n$ mutually exclusive, equally likely, and collectively exhaustive outcomes, and if event $A$ contains $n_A$ of these outcomes, then $P(A)=n_A/n$.

*Relative Frequency Probability:* If an uncertain event occurs a large number of times, $m$, the outcome at each trial is independent of the previous outcomes and event $A$ occurs $m_A$ times, $P(A)=m_A/m$.

*Subjective Probability:* A subjective probability is a number between zero and 1, representing an individual's degree of belief in the outcome of an uncertain event.

A major distinction between the subjective and objective views of probability is that subjectivists interpret probabilities as the state of knowledge of an individual, while objectivists attribute them to characteristics of physical processes. As shown by Figure 4.1, the assessment of probabilities is the last step in the modeling process that includes specifying the outcomes and assigning evaluation units.

## ASSIGNMENT MATERIAL

**4.1.** Describe two collections of objects with which you are familiar in terms of set notation.

**4.2.** Specify the outcome space for an uncertain event consisting of flipping a coin 3 times in succession.

**4.3.** For the outcome space in problem 4.2, what elements would you assign to the event "two heads"?

**4.4.** Specify the outcome space for an uncertain event consisting of rolling a pair of six-sided dice. Define the event "7 spots showing" on this outcome space.

**4.5.** Consider rolling two six-sided dice. Which of the following pairs of events are mutually exclusive?

(a) The sum of the two is less than or equal to 6; the sum of the two is equal to or greater than 6.
(b) The sum of the two is 7; one 3 and one 4.
(c) One die is 4; one die is 6.
(d) The sum of the two is greater than 7; the sum of the two is less than or equal to 7.

**4.6.** Consider drawing a card from a standard deck of playing cards. Which of the sets of events described below are mutually exclusive?

(a) Hearts; spades
(b) Ace; king
(c) Jack; spade
(d) Diamond; club; neither

**4.7.** Which of the following sets of events are collectively exhaustive?

(a) In a soccer game: win; lose.
(b) Considering the weather: sunny; rainy.
(c) Considering tossing two dice: the sum of the two is 12; the sum of the two is less than 12.

(d) Considering flipping a coin three times: more than 1 head; less than or equal to 2 heads.

**4.8.** Which of the density functions in Figures 4.16 through 4.18 qualify as probability distributions? Why or why not?

(a)

**FIGURE 4.16**

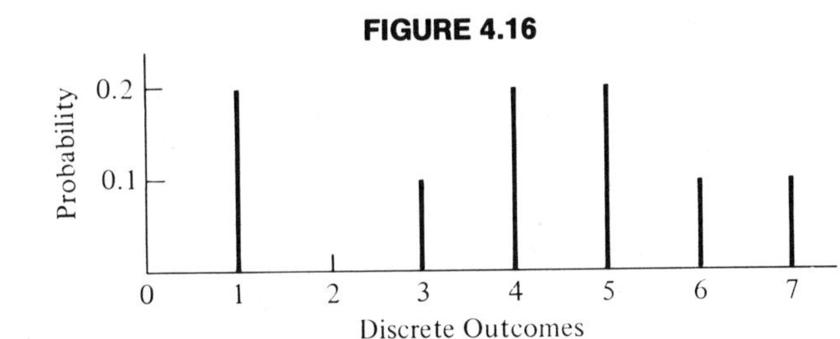


(b)

**FIGURE 4.17**

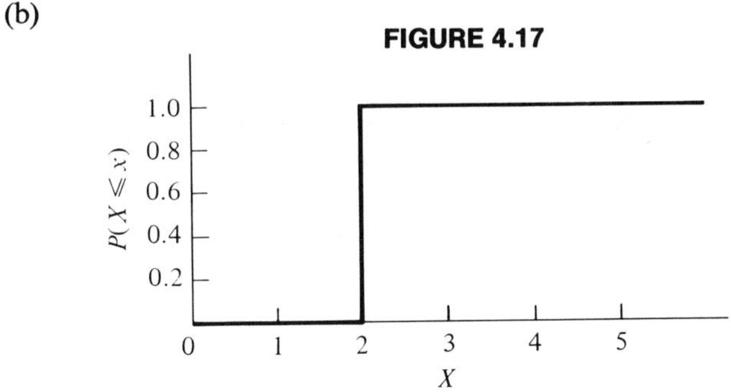


(c)

**FIGURE 4.18**

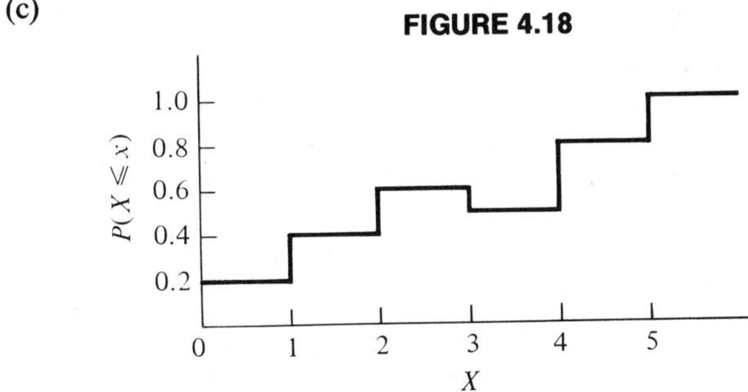


**4.9.** Assume that you have been selected to play in a game using a dodecahedron (a solid figure having 12 sides). The game will involve betting on which side or combinations of sides from four tosses comes up when the dodecahedron is rolled. The day before the game one of the four dodecahedrons used to play the game is given to you.

(a) Explain in detail what someone would do to determine probabilities using the classical concept.

(b) Explain in detail what someone would do to determine probabilities using the relative frequency concept.

**4.10.** What is the basis for saying that the theoretical and relative frequency concepts require subjective inputs?

**4.11.** In a meeting on state resources, the size of the state of Alaska became important. It was not possible to determine the area during the meeting. One person, a geographer, was asked, "In your opinion, what is the probability that the area of Alaska is greater than 600,000 square miles?"

(a) How would someone who believed the classical view of probability was the only valid concept react to such a question?
(b) How would someone who believed the relative frequency view of probability was the only valid concept react to such a question?
(c) How would someone who believed in the subjective view of probability react to such a question?

**4.12.** A retailer has kept track of weekly demand for washing machines under normal conditions (i.e., excluding holidays, sales, etc.). The results are given in the following table:

| *Demand* | *Number of Weeks Observed* |
|---|---|
| 0 | 12 |
| 1 | 18 |
| 2 | 25 |
| 3 | 22 |
| 4 | 13 |
| 5 | 7 |
| 6 | 3 |

Use the relative frequency concept of probability to do the following.

(a) Display the probability density function for demand during a week.
(b) Plot the cumulative distribution function for demand during a week.
(c) What is the probability that demand is 3 units?
(d) What is the probability that demand is less than or equal to 3 units?
(e) What is the probability that demand is greater than 1 unit?

**4.13.** Consider a deck of playing cards with the ace and face cards (king, queen, jack) removed. Do the following using the classical concept of probability.

(a) Plot the probability density function for the number on a single card randomly drawn from the modified deck.
(b) Plot the cumulative distribution for the number on a single card randomly drawn from the modified deck.
(c) What is the probability that the card drawn is either a 5 or 6?
(d) What is the probability that the card drawn has a number between 3 and 7?
(e) What is the probability that the card drawn has a number less than 4?
(f) What is the probability that the card drawn has a number greater than or equal to 6?

**4.14.** Given the cumulative distribution in Figure 4.19:

(a) Plot the probability density function.
(b) Plot the cumulative distribution for $P(X \geqslant x)$.

FIGURE 4.19

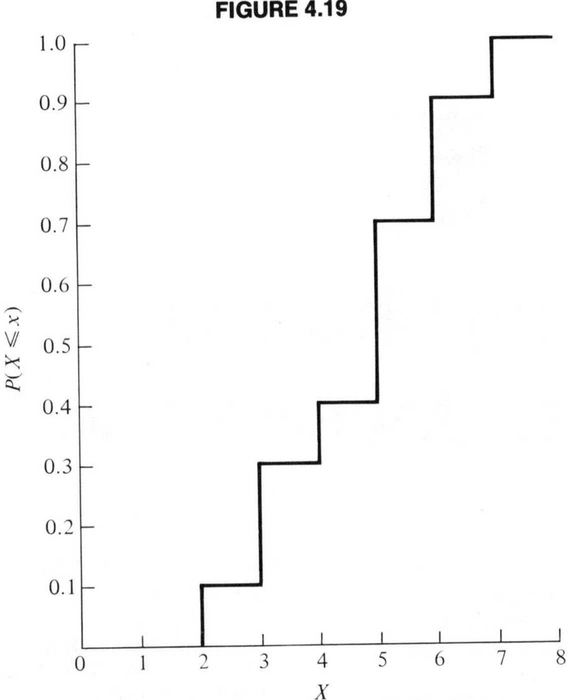


**4.15.** Calculate the expected value of the following probability distribution.

$$\begin{array}{ll} P(X=5)=0.2 & P(X=9)=0.3 \\ P(X=6)=0 & P(X=10)=0 \\ P(X=7)=0.3 & P(X=11)=0.2 \\ P(X=8)=0 & P(X=12)=0 \end{array}$$

**4.16.** Calculate the expected value of the following probability distribution.

$$\begin{array}{ll} P(X=1)=0.10 & P(X=5)=0.15 \\ P(X=2)=0.15 & P(X=6)=0.10 \\ P(X=3)=0.25 & P(X=7)=0.05 \\ P(X=4)=0.20 & \end{array}$$

**4.17.** What are the *means* for the probability distributions in problems 4.15 and 4.16?

**4.18.** Calculate the standard deviations for the probability distributions in problems 4.15 and 4.16.

**4.19.** Calculate the mean and standard deviation for the probability distribution in problem 4.12.

**4.20.** Calculate the mean and standard deviation for the probability distribution in problem 4.13.

**4.21.** Calculate the mean and standard deviation for the probability distribution in problem 4.14.

# 5

# Making Choices Under Uncertainty

Even if a complete model is developed for a decision problem under uncertainty, the choice can be difficult. As discussed in Chapter 2, a simple expression of preference on the units used to evaluate the consequences is usually not enough. The uncertainty means that you cannot be sure which outcome will result from a chosen alternative. This *risk* adds a complication. Individual attitudes toward risk differ. We can think about two aspects of the problem: How can we understand the risk involved? Once we understand the risk, how can we evaluate it to make a choice? This chapter discusses the options available to decision makers, starting from the simplest and moving to the more complicated. The easy answers to ways of choosing among

**FIGURE 5.1**

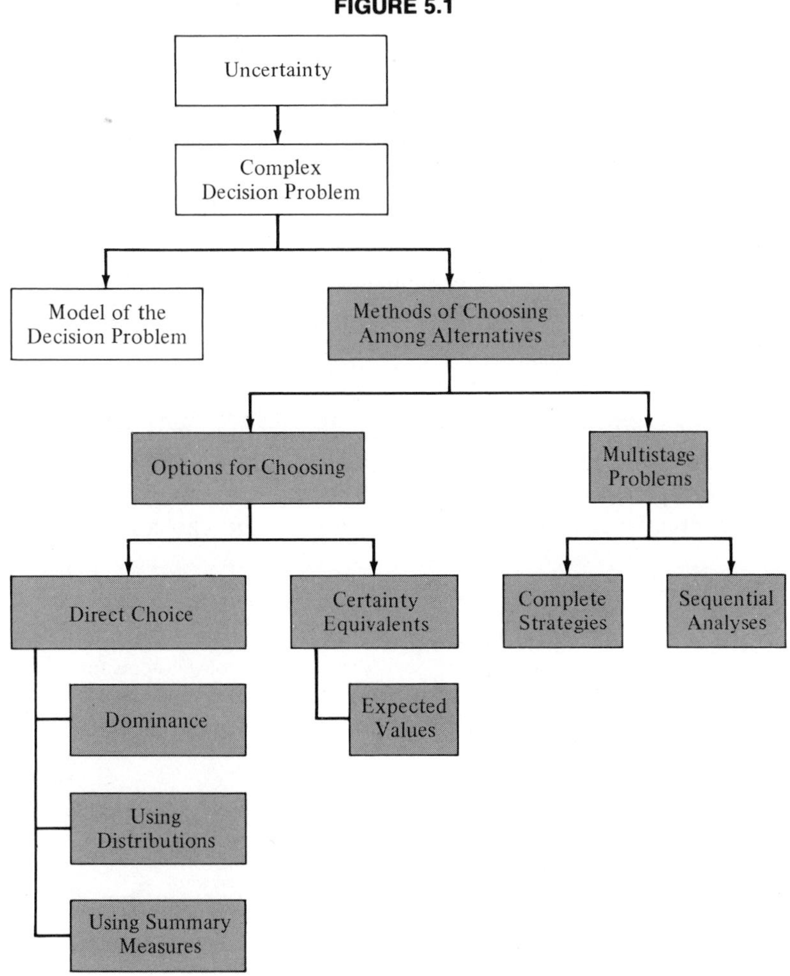

uncertain alternatives do not hold up in many situations. To provide a solid foundation we will emphasize the concepts as well as the techniques. The purpose is to explain the difficulties so that you will be able to judge which of the options you should use in any situation. Figure 5.1 shows how the material fits into the overall organization of the book.

## DIRECT CHOICE

The most basic method of choosing between two alternatives is to compare them directly and, using some intuitive process, select one over the other. In some cases decision makers may find this method adequate. However, as the complexity of the problem increases, we often find it hard to keep all the important factors in mind. This drives us to decompose the choice problem. To illustrate direct choice and its problems, consider the following example.

**Example 5.1**

As a manufacturer of special instruments you are considering two new products. The first is a temperature recording and transmitting device (TRT). The technology required for a successful design is not yet available but you believe it is within the capability of the engineering staff. After careful assessment you decide the probability of success is 0.5. The second product is a pressure sensor (PS). The sensor would fill out your product line. No new technology is required, but you feel there is still a 0.2 chance the design will fail. Resource limitations do not permit both products to be designed. A simplified model of the decision problem is shown in Figure 5.2. Consequences are evaluated in terms of present value of contribution over the product lifetime.

The difficulties with making a choice directly are apparent even in this simple problem. As the decision maker you are called on to process simultaneously information about the chances of success and the importance of the possible consequences. When dominance exists, the choices can be made easily.

**FIGURE 5.2**

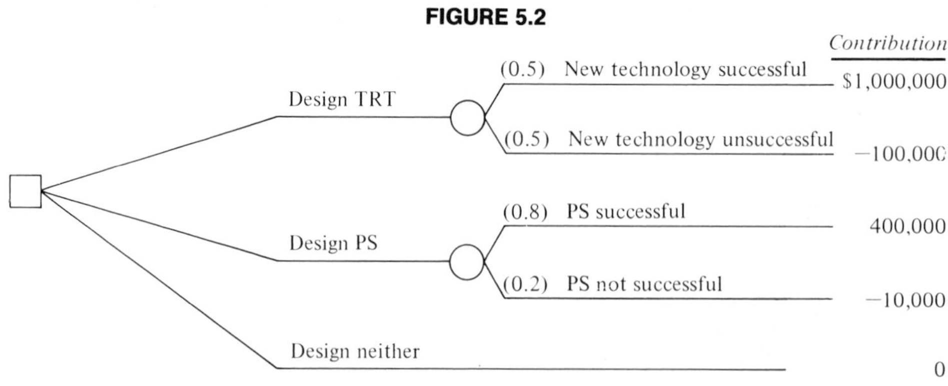

### Outcome Dominance

There are two ways outcome dominance can arise. The first is when the worst outcome for alternative *A* is at least as good as the best outcome for alternative *B*. In this case *A* dominates *B*.

As an example, change the instrument manufacturer's problem described above so that a failure in the new technology results in a modified TRT design. With this design, assume that the contribution would be $400,000 rather than $−100,000. This revised alternative is shown in Figure 5.3. In this case *design TRT* dominates *design PS* and *design neither* because $400,000 is at least as good as the best outcome for the other two alternatives and, if it is successful, the $1,000,000 is better than either of the others.

Outcome dominance can occur in a slightly different form when two alternatives are followed by the same uncertain event. That is, the alternatives differ only in the consequences associated with the outcomes. In this case if, in an outcome-by-outcome comparison, alternative *A* always is at least as good as alternative *B* and is strictly preferred for at least one outcome, then *A* dominates *B*. The rationale is obvious: by choosing *A* you can never do worse than by choosing *B*, and you may do better. This is illustrated in Figure 5.4.

The worst payoff for the *plant corn* alternative, $2,500, is not at least as good as the $5,000 payoff for the *plant wheat* alternative. However, for each weather outcome, the *plant corn* alternative is at least as good as the *plant*

**FIGURE 5.3**

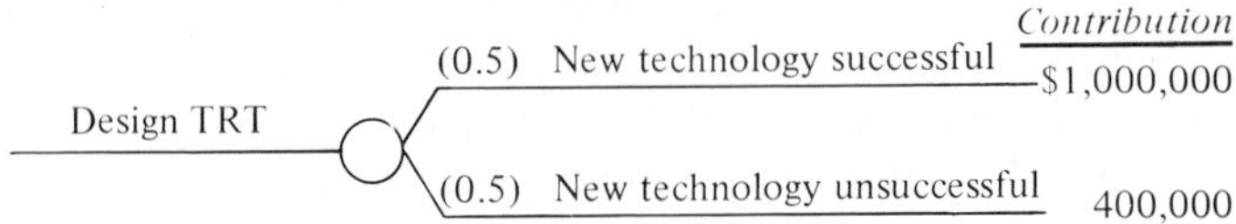


**FIGURE 5.4**

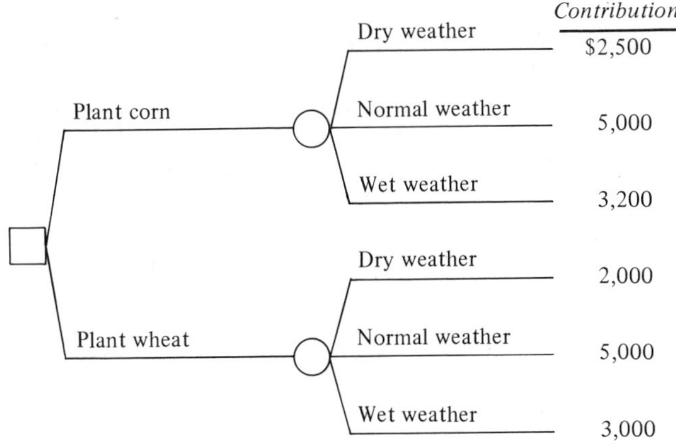

*wheat* alternative and in two cases the payoffs are strictly better for the *plant corn* alternative. Therefore, *plant corn* dominates *plant wheat*.

> **Outcome Dominance**
>
> ***Definition:*** *If alternative A is at least as preferred as alternative B for each* ***outcome****, and if A is strictly preferred to B for one outcome, then A dominates B.*

## Probabilistic Dominance

A slightly weaker form of dominance is also useful for making choices directly.

> **Probabilistic Dominance**
>
> ***Definition:*** *If for any values of the evaluation units (in which more is better) the probability of alternative A achieving that value or more is greater than or equal to the probability of alternative B achieving that value or more, then A* ***dominates probabilistically****. The case in which the probabilities are equal for A and B for all values of the evaluation units is an exception. In this case, based on the probability distributions, A and B are equivalent.*

A probabilistically dominated alternative can have an *actual* outcome that is better (more preferred) than the *actual* outcome from the alternative that dominated it. Nevertheless, probabilistic dominance is a compelling reason for choosing one alternative over another. The following example illustrates this concept and shows how probabilistic dominance can be recognized using cumulative probability distributions.

### Example 5.2

As the product manager for a large company, you are in the position of choosing one of three new products to be marketed. Development and prototype production have been completed as well as pricing studies (see Table 5.1). Only one product can be introduced. Market research studies have determined that the discrete probability distributions for sales of each product shown in Figures 5.5, 5.6, and 5.7 are good approximations.

**TABLE 5.1**

| *Product* | *Unit Price* | *Unit Cost* | *Contribution per Unit* |
|---|---|---|---|
| *A* | $2.50 | $1.50 | $1.00 |
| *B* | 6.00 | 4.00 | 2.00 |
| *C* | 3.75 | 2.25 | 1.50 |

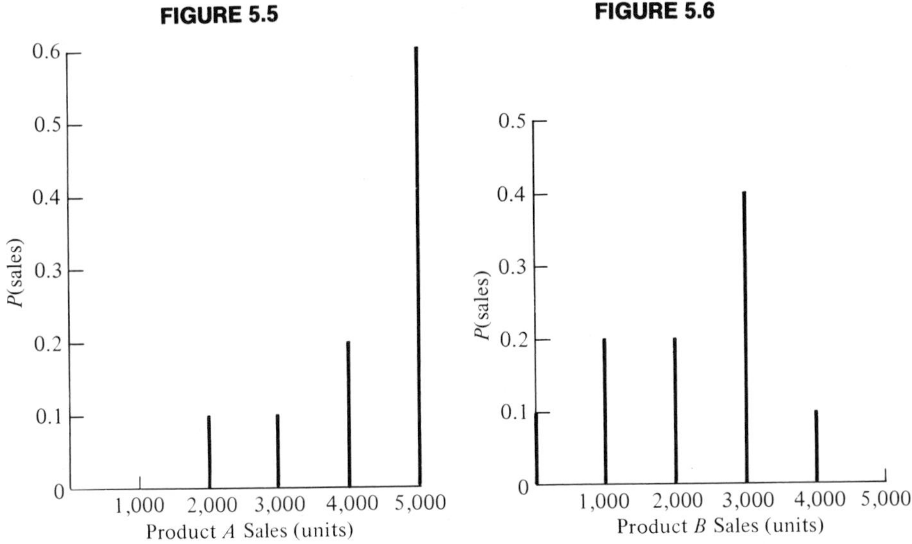


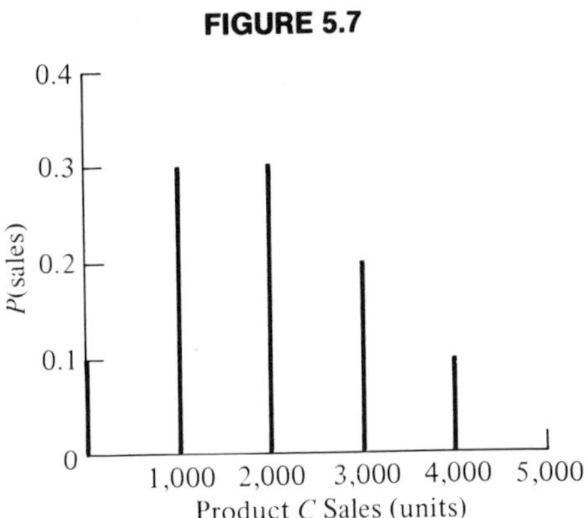


The problem can be diagrammed as shown in Figure 5.8. The probability density functions for the *contribution* of each alternative are shown in Figure 5.9. Figure 5.10 shows the cumulative probability distributions for contribution (probability of a given contribution or *more*) for the alternatives *product B* and *product C*. From Figure 5.10 we can see that the alternative *product B* is above and to the right of the alternative *product C* except over the range $0 to $1,500, where they are equal. Therefore, *product B* has a greater probability of obtaining a given value of contribution or more than *product C*, except over the range $0 to $1,500, where they are equal. This means that *product C* is probabilistically dominated by *product B*.

Now assume that, for some reason, you actually produce both *B* and *C*. It may turn out that the contribution from *C* is $6,000 and the contribution

**FIGURE 5.8**

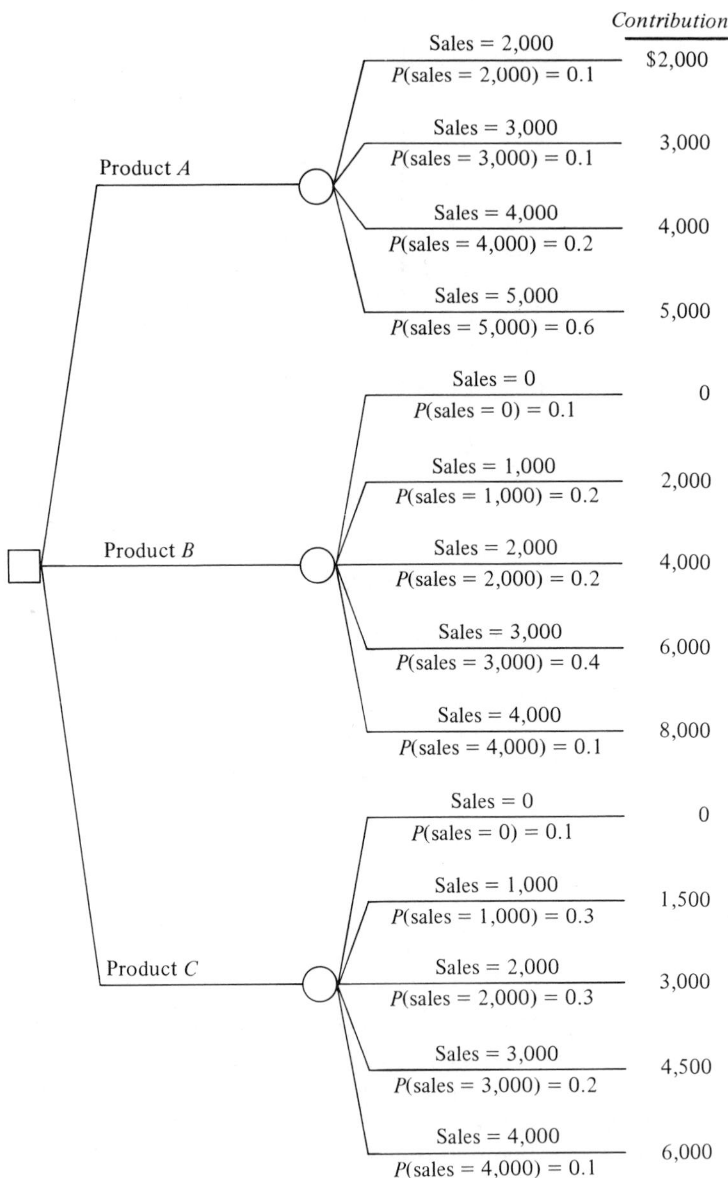
Contribution
Product A
Sales = 2,000
P(sales = 2,000) = 0.1
$2,000
Sales = 3,000
P(sales = 3,000) = 0.1
3,000
Sales = 4,000
P(sales = 4,000) = 0.2
4,000
Sales = 5,000
P(sales = 5,000) = 0.6
5,000
Product B
Sales = 0
P(sales = 0) = 0.1
0
Sales = 1,000
P(sales = 1,000) = 0.2
2,000
Sales = 2,000
P(sales = 2,000) = 0.2
4,000
Sales = 3,000
P(sales = 3,000) = 0.4
6,000
Sales = 4,000
P(sales = 4,000) = 0.1
8,000
Product C
Sales = 0
P(sales = 0) = 0.1
0
Sales = 1,000
P(sales = 1,000) = 0.3
1,500
Sales = 2,000
P(sales = 2,000) = 0.3
3,000
Sales = 3,000
P(sales = 3,000) = 0.2
4,500
Sales = 4,000
P(sales = 4,000) = 0.1
6,000

**FIGURE 5.9**

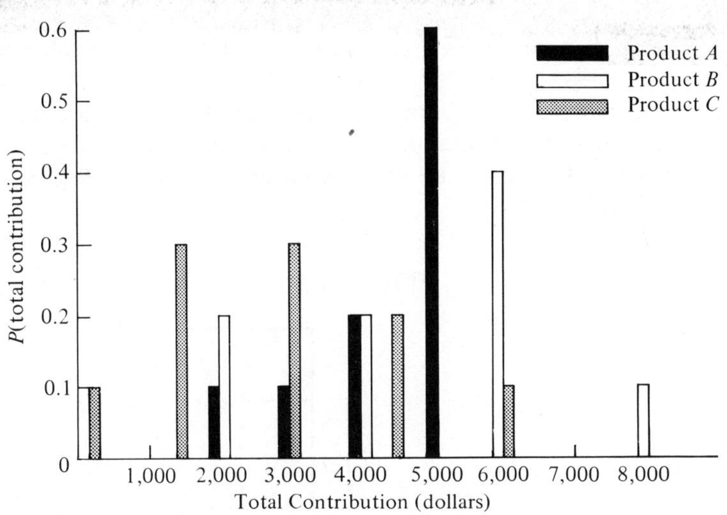


**FIGURE 5.10**

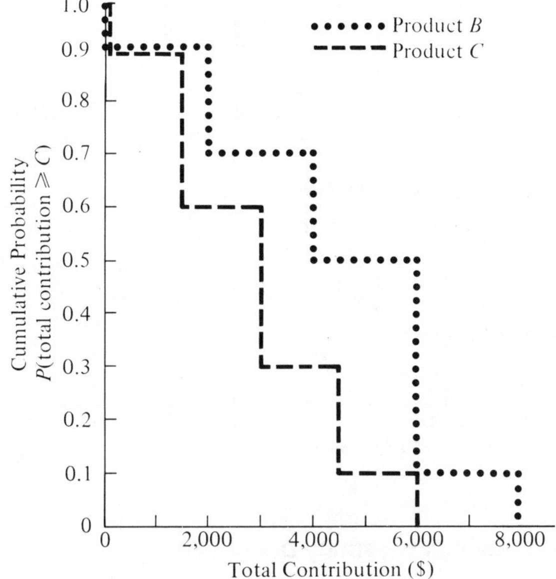

from *B* is only $2,000. This situation illustrates that a *probabilistically dominated* alternative can have a better actual outcome than the alternative that dominates it. With *outcome dominance* this type of reversal could not occur.

Figure 5.11 is a plot of the cumulative probability distribution for a given contribution or less for all three alternatives. Dominance of *product B* over *product C* is seen using this figure by recognizing that *product B* is below and to the right of *product C*.

**FIGURE 5.11**

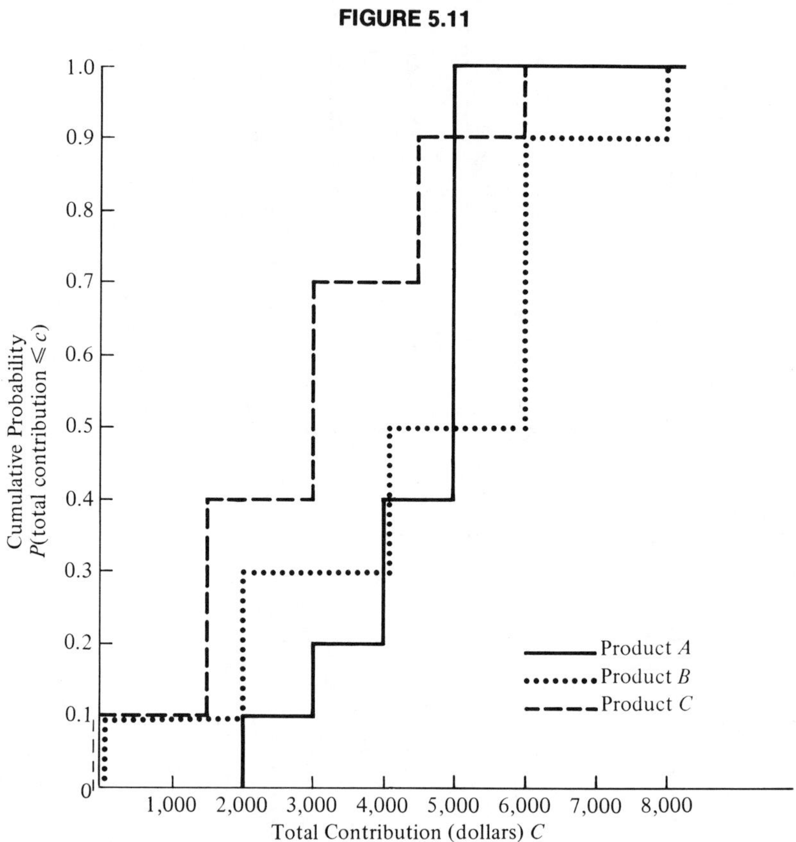


### Direct Choice Using Probability Distributions

Without dominance the decision maker has to try to understand the uncertainty and risk of each alternative. A probability distribution for each alternative, in terms of evaluation units, contains *all* the information; however, it usually is hard to look at probability distributions and internalize the *risk* and *opportunities* of various alternatives.

In Example 5.2 we would look at Figures 5.9 and 5.11. Product *C* can be eliminated by dominance. Using Figure 5.9 to compare products *A* and *B*, we could note that product *B* has higher probabilities for low outcome than *A* does. But it also has high probabilities for outcomes above the best possible outcome with *A*. The decision maker must weigh the risks of low outcomes against the chance of high outcomes and choose one of the products.

The same information can be obtained from the cumulative distributions for contribution, shown in Figure 5.11. The plots are easier to use for such questions as: "What is the probability of reaching a certain level of contribution?" For instance, consider a contribution of $3,000. The probability that product *A*'s contribution is less than or equal to $3,000 can be read directly as 0.2. For product *B* the probability is 0.3. Therefore, *B* has a greater chance than *A* of being lower than or equal to $3,000. The decision maker can use this type of question to understand the uncertainty in the alternatives. On the basis of this understanding, a choice is made. Which would you choose in this case?

### Direct Choice Using Summary Measures

Rather than try to assimilate the entire probability distribution for contribution, comparisons can be made on the basis of summary measures. The obvious measures to include are the *mean*, the *standard deviation*, the *maximum*, and the *minimum*. The cumulative probabilities for "important" levels of contribution may also be included. In the product development example, the comparison might be made using Table 5.2. We see that *B* has a slightly higher mean. But it also has a higher standard deviation, indicating more uncertainty (the distribution for *B* is more spread out than for *A*). The minimum shows that with *B* there is a chance of making nothing. With *A* the minimum is $2,000. On the other hand, *B* might yield as much as $8,000, while the maximum for *A* is $5,000. The last two rows confirm that there is more *downside* risk and *upside* potential in *B*. With direct choice this information is processed by the decision maker and a choice made.

**TABLE 5.2**

| *Measure* | *Product A* | *Product B* | *Product C* |
|---|---|---|---|
| Mean contribution | $4,300 | $4,400 | $2,850 |
| Standard deviation | $1,005 | $2,332 | $1,704 |
| Minimum contribution | $2,000 | 0 | 0 |
| Maximum contribution | $5,000 | $8,000 | $6,000 |
| Probability of contribution less than $3,000 | 0.1 | 0.3 | 0.4 |
| Probability of contribution more than $5,000 | 0 | 0.5 | 0.1 |

### Direct Choice Using Aspiration Level

Another suggestion for making direct choices is to base the comparison on some "level that is *important* to obtain"—an aspiration level.

> **Aspiration-Level Criterion**
>
> ***Definition:*** *Maximize the probability of achieving some aspiration level.*

The idea is that there may be some aspiration level that is very important to a decision maker. Amounts over the aspiration level are of little or no importance. To illustrate, assume that in the example discussed above, the decision maker feels that it is extremely important to make at least $3,000. Table 5.3 shows the probability of achieving this level or greater for each alternative (see Figure 5.11). Using the aspiration-level criterion, product *A* would be chosen.

**TABLE 5.3**

| *Product* | *Probability of* $3,000 *or More* |
|---|---|
| *A* | 0.9 |
| *B* | 0.7 |
| *C* | 0.6 |

If the direct comparison of probability distributions is too difficult, two other methods for choosing are available. *Certainty equivalents* are easier to use in some cases. More important, they offer the possibility of further decomposition. Summarizing the probability distributions by *means* or *expected values* is the easiest method. However, it may neglect important aspects of the problem. These options are discussed next.

## CERTAINTY EQUIVALENTS

Certainty equivalents have three advantages over direct choice: (1) the comparisons may be easier because they are made between a probability distribution and a certain quantity; (2) once the equivalences have been made, the choice is easy, because higher values (for desirable consequences) are preferred to lower values; and (3) the process of determining certainty equivalents can be further decomposed. The disadvantages of the procedure are that it may be time consuming and difficult to understand.

**Certainty Equivalent**

***Definition:*** *The* ***certainty equivalent*** *for an uncertain event is that certain value, in terms of the evaluation units, which a decision maker is* ***just*** *willing to accept in lieu of the gamble represented by the uncertain event.*

To illustrate the concept of a certainty equivalent, we will consider a simplified example.

**Example 5.3**

You operate a helicopter service in Seattle, Washington. The majority of your business is involved with short runs from a downtown location to the airport and charters for people who need to visit different spots in the local area. You are approached by a ski lodge in the Canadian Rockies to fly skiers to untracked, powder snow in inaccessible areas. The contract is lucrative but your mechanic warns that the engine is not rated for extremes in temperature and moisture which might be encountered in very bad weather. After some discussion you are able to ascertain that engine failure would not endanger the pilot or passengers because the craft would always make it back to a base camp before completely losing power. On the other hand, the damage to the helicopter would require an expensive repair job. Figure 5.12 is a diagram of the problem you face.

**FIGURE 5.12**

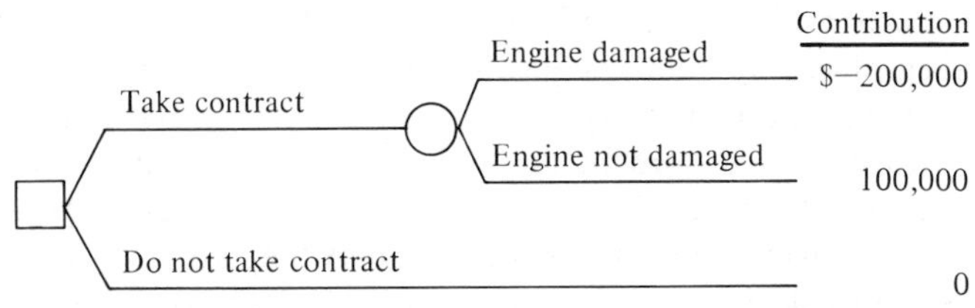


The idea behind using certainty equivalents is straightforward. A certainty equivalent for the uncertain event on engine damage in Figure 5.12 is a profit value that is *equivalent* to the uncertain event. The *equivalency* is in the mind of the decision maker. It means that the decision maker is indifferent between facing the uncertain event and taking the profit value specified by the certainty equivalent. Since the decision maker is indifferent between the two, we can substitute the certain value for the uncertain event. Then the contract decision is easy. We choose the alternative with the highest profit figure. In this case, if the certainty equivalent is greater than $0, we choose *take contract*. If it is less, we choose *do not take contract*. If it is exactly $0, we are indifferent between them.

A certainty equivalent is a *decision*, not an *estimate*. If you are the decision maker, it is the value you *decide* to *just* accept in lieu of facing the uncertain event. It is *not* in any sense an *estimate* of what you think you will receive.

### The Insurance Analogy

Are managers capable of making certainty equivalent decisions? To answer this, place yourself in the position of the helicopter operator, and assume that you are considering the contract. You are faced with an uncertain event. The outcome will either cost you $200,000 or give you a $100,000 profit. As you are considering this set of circumstances, assume that an insurance agent walks into your office and offers you the following contract:

1. If you take the contract to fly skiers and end up with less than $10,000, I will make up the difference. That is, if the engine is damaged, I will pay you $210,000.
2. If you take the contract to fly skiers and end up with more than $10,000, I will take the excess. That is, if the engine is not damaged, you will pay me $90,000.

This means that no matter what the outcome is, you end up with $10,000. In essence, the insurance agent is offering to buy your uncertain event for $10,000, since this is the amount you receive regardless of the condition of the engine.

Without considering whether you would take the contract, is this a reasonable decision for an individual to make? It is just a matter of purchasing insurance. The premium is conditional on the outcome. The probability of engine damage is obviously one of the important factors in making such a decision. Clearly, if you thought the engine were very likely to be damaged, you would be more interested in the insurance proposal than if you thought it unlikely. Many business managers indicate that they are used to making this type of insurance decision. Those who are not often see it as a reasonable decision to have to make.

For the sake of discussion, assume that you agree you could make this decision. If you can make the decision for the $10,000 figure, then presumably you can also make it for other values the insurance agent might suggest. The reply to at least two possible offers should be the same for everyone. If the insurance agent offered $100,000, you would surely accept, since this is what you would receive under the best outcome. On the other hand, if he offered you $-200,000, you would reject it since you can never do worse than $-200,000 and there is some chance of receiving $100,000. Therefore, conceptually, we could start at $-200,000 and ask for your decision (at which point you would reject), then ask for your decision at $-180,000, $-160,000, and so on. Since we know that when we reach $100,000 you will accept, there must be some value between \$ −200,000 and \$100,000 at which you stop rejecting and start accepting. For purposes of discussion, assume that you decide you would just accept the insurance offer at \$20,000. That is, if the offer were less than \$20,000, you would refuse it. In this case the *take contract* branch can be replaced by a certain \$20,000. The comparison between the two alternatives is now easy, since you prefer \$20,000 to \$0.

### Properties of Certainty Equivalents

This example illustrates three properties of certainty equivalents that deserve emphasis. First, the decision to reject the offer at all prices below \$20,000 and accept for \$20,000 (and of course any price above) means that you are *indifferent* between a guaranteed \$20,000 payment and the uncertain event represented by the *take contract* branch. This is precisely the *definition* of a certainty equivalent. Second, it illustrates that certainty equivalents are *decisions*, not estimates of what will be received from an uncertain event. The uncertain event in the example will either yield \$100,000 or \$ −200,000. Third, at least for some simple problems couched in terms of insurance decisions, the decision is a reasonable one to ask managers to make.

### Assessing Certainty Equivalents

Certainty equivalent decisions may be *possible* to make, but that does not mean that they are easy. They require a decision maker to process information of two different types simultaneously: (1) information on the probability that a set of outcomes will occur, and (2) information on the consequences of the outcomes as measured by the evaluation units (e.g., contribution in dollars). The only simplification over direct choice is that uncertain events are compared with a single certain outcome. The decision maker must determine how the uncertainty and consequences interact and relate them to a certain outcome.

### Procedures for Assessing Certainty Equivalents

One way to assess certainty equivalents is to consider the uncertain event and decide directly. For example, assume that you are the lucky owner of a lottery ticket that pays \$10,000 if a fair coin lands with heads up and nothing if it lands with tails up. You might just think about the lottery and decide that you would accept an offer of \$4,000 to buy the ticket, but no less.

Certainty equivalents can also be assessed by a series of direct choices. The procedure is described below using a general uncertain event in Figure 5.13. The uncertain event is represented by a "fan." Think of the evaluation units as a contribution in dollars. $C_{max}$ is the best outcome and $C_{min}$ the

FIGURE 5.13

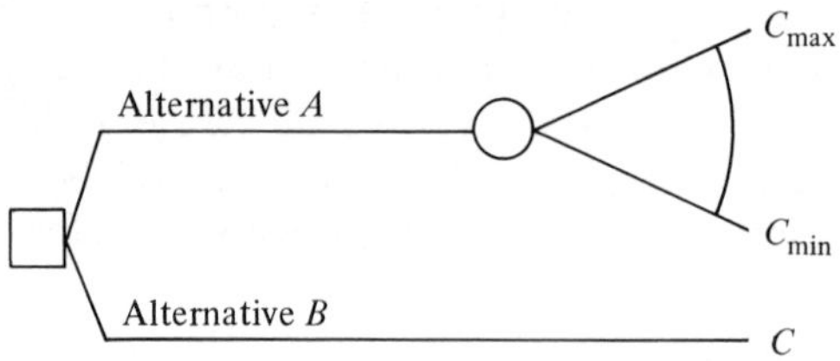


worst. Because neither the specific outcome nor the probabilities are provided, we cannot actually assess a certainty equivalent. However, the general procedure is given below.

> Procedure for Assessing Certainty Equivalent
>
> 1. Choose a value of $C$ between $C_{max}$ and $C_{min}$.
> 2. Consider the decision between alternatives $A$ and $B$ in Figure 5.13 and make a direct choice.
> 3. If you choose $A$, increase $C$ by some amount and repeat the process. If you choose $B$, decrease $C$ by some amount and repeat the process.
> 4. Vary $C$ until you are just indifferent between alternatives $A$ and $B$ (i.e., you would just as soon have $A$ as $B$). This value of $C$ is your certainty equivalent for the uncertain event.

**Example 5.4**

A friend, Phil, owns the lottery ticket shown in Figure 5.14. If heads comes up on the toss of a fair coin, he wins $10,000. If tails comes up he gets nothing. He has several offers to buy the ticket and asks your help in determining his certainty equivalent for the lottery.

First you show Phil the diagram in Figure 5.14 and explain that you are going to offer him the choice between alternatives $A$ and $B$ for a series of $C$ values. He is to respond by choosing either $A$ or $B$.

FIGURE 5.14

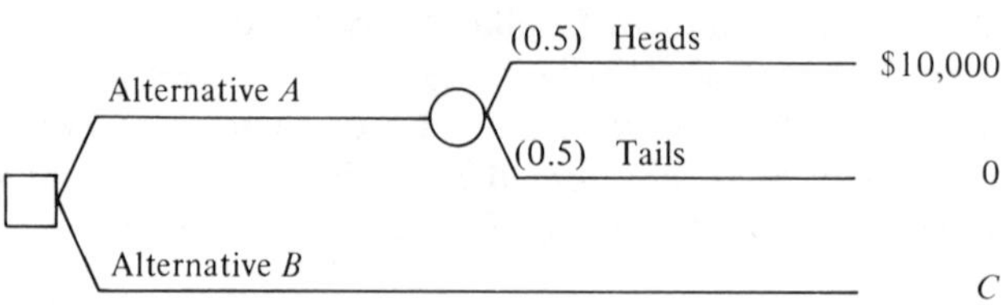

You: Which alternative do you choose if $C = \$2{,}000$?

Phil: That's easy. I choose *A*.

You: OK, what if $C = \$6{,}000$?

Phil: That's easy, too. I choose *B*.

You: How about $C = \$4{,}000$?

Phil: Well, that's a little harder, but I'd take *A*.

You: What if $C = \$5{,}000$?

Phil: This is getting tougher. If $C = \$5{,}000$, I would take *B*.

You: I'm going to make it even harder. What is your choice for $C = \$4{,}500$?

Phil: $C = \$4{,}500$. That's tough. I don't know which to choose. I guess it wouldn't make any difference to me.

You: If you mean that, your certainty equivalent is \$4,500.

Phil: Yes, I mean it. The more I think about it, the more I am convinced. I am indifferent between *A* and *B* for $C = \$4{,}500$.

### Certainty Equivalents for Complex Uncertain Events

Certainty equivalent decisions are not too difficult for simple uncertain events like the lottery discussed above. However, if the uncertain events are more complex, they become very difficult. For instance, if we just consider the roll of a die rather than flipping a coin, we might have a lottery like the one shown in Figure 5.15.

In this case it is almost impossible to process the information and think about a certainty equivalent decision. Fortunately, we can decompose the certainty equivalent decision. The decomposition will allow us to calculate certainty equivalents for more complex uncertain events based on certainty equivalent decisions for simple uncertain events. Chapter 6 describes this procedure.

**FIGURE 5.15**

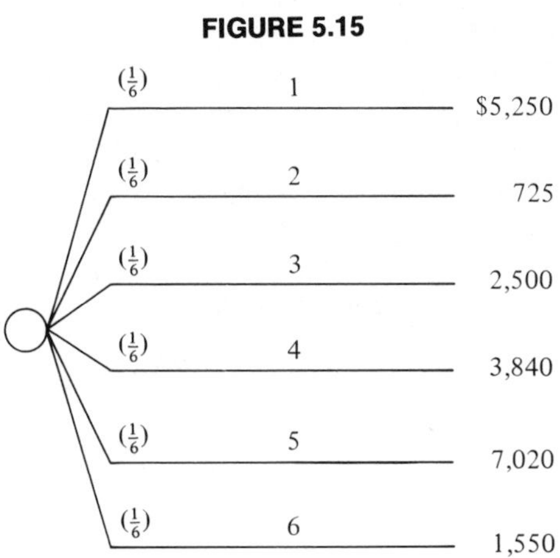

## USING MEANS OR EXPECTED VALUES

If probability distributions are summarized by their means or expected values, direct comparison is easy. For desirable consequences the alternative with the highest expected value is chosen. Referring back to Example 5.2, we have:

**Product *A***

$$\text{Expected total contribution} = (0.1) \times (\$2{,}000) + (0.1) \times (\$3{,}000) + (0.2) \times (\$4{,}000) + (0.6) \times (\$5{,}000) = \boxed{\$4{,}300}$$

**Product *B***

$$\text{Expected total contribution} = (0.1) \times (0) + (0.2) \times (\$2{,}000) + (0.2) \times (\$4{,}000) + (0.4) \times (\$6{,}000) + (0.1) \times (\$8{,}000) = \boxed{\$4{,}400}$$

**Product *C***

$$\text{Expected total contribution} = (0.1) \times (0) + (0.3) \times (\$1{,}500) + (0.3) \times (\$3{,}000) + (0.2) \times (\$4{,}500) + (0.1) \times (\$6{,}000) = \boxed{\$2{,}850}$$

Based on the means, product *B* is chosen. This certainly simplifies the decision process. The question is whether it leads to the choice of the most preferred alternative. For instance, the high probabilities of low outcomes with *B* may cause a decision maker to prefer *A*.

### Expected Values and Certainty Equivalents

Using expected values to summarize the probability distribution amounts to using them as certainty equivalents. For the decision shown in Figure 5.16, involving a coin flip, the expected value of alternative *A* is \$50,000 [(0.5) × (\$100,000) + (0.5) × (0) = \$50,000], and the expected value of alternative *B* is \$45,000 [(1) × (\$45,000) = \$45,000]. Therefore, if expected values are used as a basis for choosing, *A* is chosen. For *B* to be equivalent to *A* using this procedure, *B* would have to result in a certain \$50,000.

The problem with this approach is that most individuals would choose alternative *B* when offered the choice in Figure 5.16. This implies their

**FIGURE 5.16**

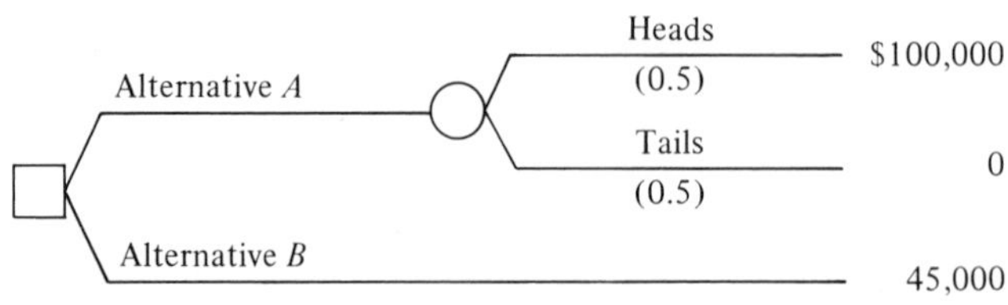

certainty equivalent for *A* is less than \$45,000. Therefore, using expected values in this problem would not result in the choice preferred by most people.

### Attitudes Toward Risk

We can describe an individual's propensity to take risk on the basis of his/her certainty equivalent for alternative *A* in Figure 5.16. For certainty equivalents less than \$50,000, the behavior is called *risk averse*. For a certainty equivalent of \$50,000, we say that the behavior is *risk neutral*. If the certainty equivalent is greater than \$50,000, we call the behavior *risk seeking*. Each individual's certainty equivalent reflects a particular attitude toward the risk. There is no reason to expect everyone to decide on \$50,000 or any other value for the certainty equivalent. If some people are willing to sell for \$30,000, we can not accuse them of being irrational as we might if they told us they preferred a certain \$30,000 to a certain \$50,000.

Means or expected values *are* certainty equivalents for the special case of risk neutrality. Therefore, when a decision maker is risk neutral, choices can be made by comparing expected values. There are situations in which a decision maker is likely to be risk neutral—or at least *approximately* risk neutral. Decisions involving small amounts of money and repeated trials are two cases where the assumption of risk neutrality is often made. Part III of the book discusses these issues in more detail.

## ● Pitfalls in Calculating Expected Values

When expected values are appropriate for making choices because of risk neutrality, we must be careful to calculate them correctly. A natural suggestion is to economize on the modeling effort by just using "best estimates" instead of probability distributions for uncertain events. The idea is that "best estimates" will be *means* and, therefore, adequate for the analysis when expected values are used to make choices. Since probability distributions are usually required to calculate means, it is not clear that any real economy results from using means as inputs. Moreover, in some cases, using means as inputs to a model will not provide the correct expected value. To illustrate, consider the following example.

**Example 5.5**

You are interested in determining the rate of return for a new project. Your analysis indicates there is some uncertainty about both the required investment and the contribution. The investment required will be \$100,000 with probability 0.3 or \$50,000 with probability 0.7, and the contribution will be either \$150,000 or \$75,000 with 0.6 and 0.4 probabilities, respectively. Therefore, expected investment $= 0.3 \times \$100{,}000 + 0.7 \times \$50{,}000 = \$65{,}000$, and expected contribution $= 0.6 \times \$150{,}000 + 0.4 \times \$75{,}000 = \$120{,}000$. The project will take 1 year to complete and all gains and losses will be realized at the completion of the project. You decide to calculate the expected rate of return on the project by plugging the means into the following formula for rate of return:

$$\text{Rate of Return} = \frac{\text{Contribution} - \text{Investment Cost}}{\text{Investment Cost}}$$
$$= \frac{\$120{,}000 - \$65{,}000}{\$65{,}000} = 0.85$$

Figure 5.17 is a diagram of the uncertainties in the new project. There are four possibilities. Probabilities and rates of return for each outcome are shown. For instance, the probability of having the investment 100 and the contribution 150 is $0.3 \times 0.6 = 0.18$.[1]

**FIGURE 5.17**

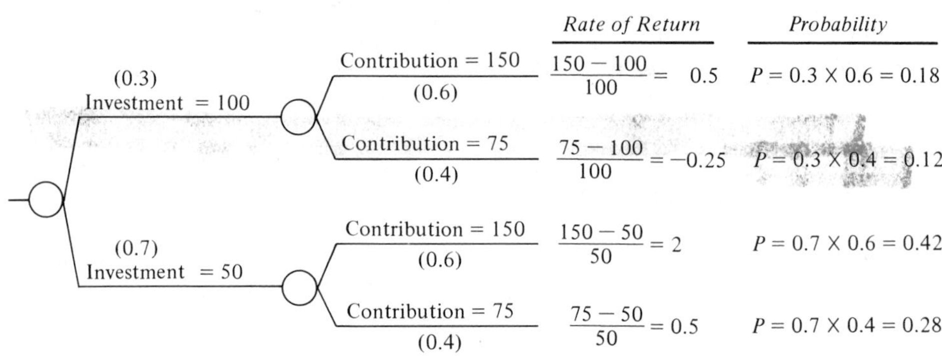


Using these rates of return and probabilities, the expected rate of return is $(0.18)(0.5) + (0.12)(-0.25) + (0.42)(2) + (0.28)(0.5) = 1.04$. The short-cut method gave a value of 0.85. The calculation using the diagram is the correct one. Problems with complicated payoff functions are susceptible to these errors. As a general rule, you should use the entire probability distribution as inputs to expected value calculations.

## MULTISTAGE PROBLEMS

Decision problems with more than a single stage introduce another source of complexity. It is the sequence of decisions and uncertain events that link the initial decision to the consequences. With this added complexity, direct choice among the initial decisions is very difficult. Probability distributions for each initial decision are not available for comparison. Certainty equivalents are equally hard to determine. There are two ways to deal with the problem. Sequential analysis—sometimes called the rollback procedure—is one. Creation of complete strategies is the other. Any of the three methods of making decisions—direct choice, certainty equivalents, or expected values—can be used as part of these procedures.

[1]The condition for this calculation to be valid is called *independence*. It is defined in Chapter 7.

## SEQUENTIAL ANALYSIS OR ROLLBACK

The sequential analysis procedure starts at the end, rather than at the beginning, of the diagram. It works back toward the initial decision.[2] Decisions are made along the way and alternatives discarded. The last step is to choose among the set of initial alternatives. The basic idea is to consider each decision in the sequence separately. We start at the end so that there are no "future decisions" to take into account. As we move backward through the stages, only the consequences for the chosen alternatives are kept. The others are discarded because we know that the alternative that yields these consequences will not be chosen. These ideas will become clear after looking at some examples. First, we state the rollback procedure in general. Read this through *quickly* and then go to the example.

> General Rollback Procedure
>
> 1. Start at the right-hand end points and move backward along any branch until a decision node is reached.
> 2. Choose among the alternatives at this node.
> 3. Eliminate the decision node by crossing out all but the preferred alternative.
> 4. Keep moving backward until the initial decision is reached and treat it like any other decision node.

The rollback procedure is usually used with certainty equivalents or expected values because the decomposition between stages is more complete than with the direct-choice method. However, for completeness, all three options are illustrated using the example below.

**Example 5.6**

In June 1979, Edward Landis, the operations manager of a large supplier of parts to the automobile industry, had been asked if he would take a contract to supply some subassemblies for a demonstration model. The quantity to be ordered was not certain; however, it would be either 20 or 40 and the number would be known in January 1980, 7 months from now. The price was $10,000 per unit. He had to respond by next week and commit his company to delivery of the required number of subassemblies by March 1980.

Landis and his staff had identified three methods of producing the subassemblies. Process 1 would be the cheapest, if it worked satisfactorily. Process 2 was more expensive but sure to work. If process 1 were used, they would know by September 1979 if it worked. If not, there would still be time to use process 2; however, the investment in process 1 would be lost. With either process, however, the lead time and

[2]Actually the procedure has its foundations in Bellman's principle of optimality [R. E. Bellman, *Dynamic Programming* (Princeton, N.J.: Princeton University Press, 1957)].

other work in the company would require that they commit themselves to a fixed production quantity prior to January. A third possibility was to subcontract the work. A reliable subcontractor was available and if the order were placed now the subcontractor would give them a good price and also be able to wait until the production quantity question was resolved. If the orders were placed after August 1979, a higher price would be charged, but as long as the subcontractor had a firm order on the number of units required by January 1980, they could meet the delivery date.

The probability of success with process 1 was assessed by the engineers who would be involved in the work as 0.5. Landis assessed the probability of an order quantity of 40 to be 0.4, after talking with the automobile company. Costs were determined by the engineers and the division accounting staff based on the product design and the processes. The subcontractor's price determined the costs for that alternative.

*Incremental Costs*

| | |
|---|---|
| *Process 1* | |
| Testing process | $20,000 |
| Per unit production cost if successful | 4,000 |
| *Process 2* | |
| Per unit production cost | 6,000 |
| *Subcontracting Costs (per Unit)* | |
| Order placed before August 1, 1979 | 7,000 |
| Order placed after August 1, 1979 | 9,000 |

*Assumptions*

1. If he produces 20 units and 40 are ordered, the remainders are obtained by subcontracting at $9,000 per unit.
2. If he produces 40 units and 20 are ordered, the excess can be disposed of at $2,000 per unit.

Figure 5.18 is a diagram for the problem facing Landis. The costs and revenues are shown in parentheses, the net contributions are placed at each end point, and the probabilities are also in parentheses.

## ●● Rollback Using Direct Choice

**The process.** In step 2 of the general rollback procedure we use direct choice. Referring to Figure 5.18 and starting with the top branch, move past node $G$ to decision node $C$. For purposes of discussion, assume that you are Landis. To make the decision you compare uncertain events $G$ and $H$. On the basis of this comparison, *assume* that you decide on the *produce 20 units* alternative (i.e., you prefer to face uncertain event $H$ to $G$).[3] We can eliminate the *produce 40 units* alternative from decision node $C$.

[3]This is just an assumption to illustrate the procedure. You may, in fact, prefer the other alternative. There is ***no*** reason why you must choose this alternative. Your choice would depend on your attitude toward risk. Throughout this discussion the indicated choices are just examples. Take them as given and concentrate on how they are used.

**FIGURE 5.18**

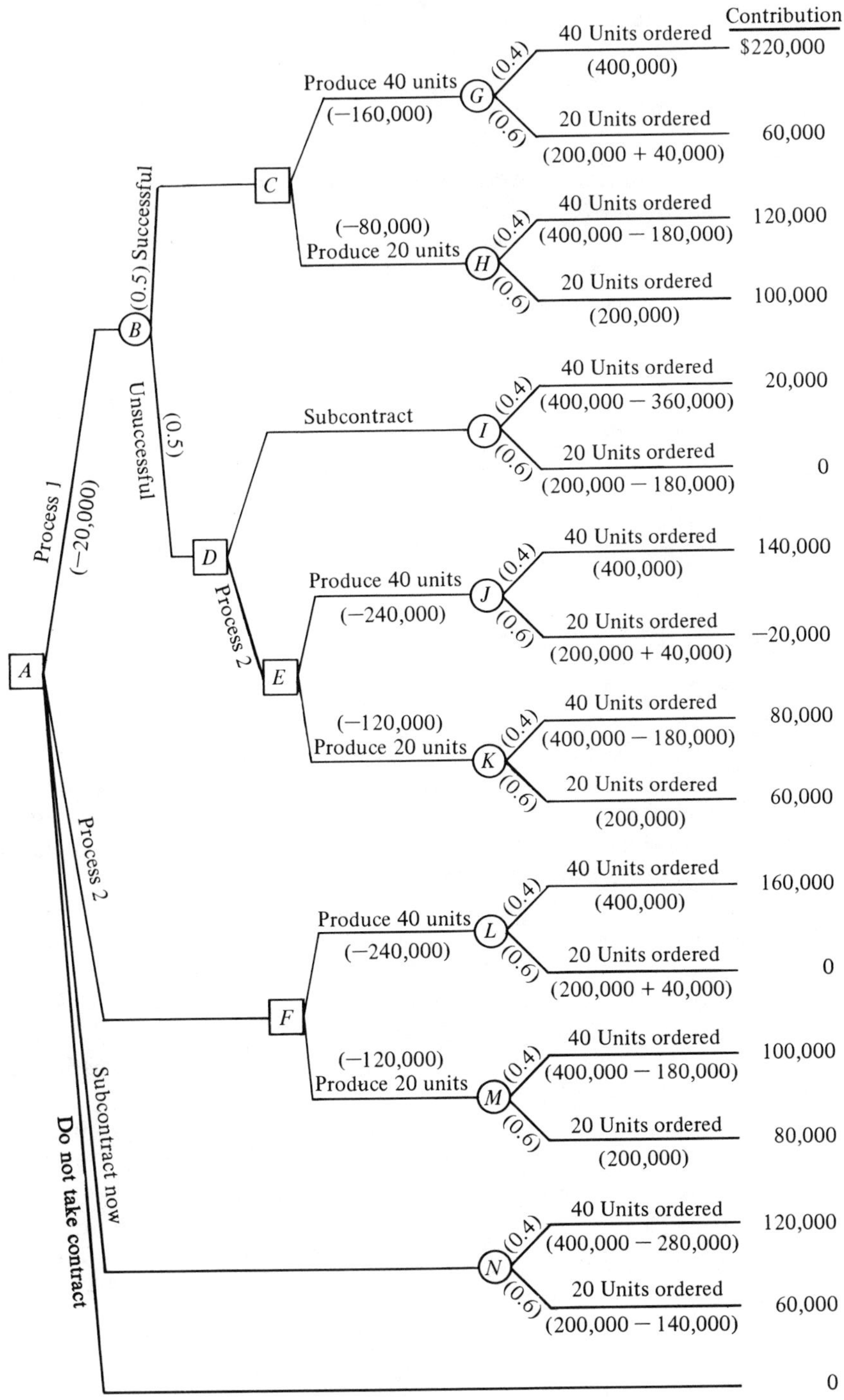
Contribution
A
Process 1
(−20,000)
B
(0.5) Successful
Unsuccessful
(0.5)
C
Produce 40 units
(−160,000)
G
(0.4)
40 Units ordered
(400,000)
$220,000
(0.6)
20 Units ordered
(200,000 + 40,000)
60,000
(−80,000)
Produce 20 units
H
(0.4)
40 Units ordered
(400,000 − 180,000)
120,000
(0.6)
20 Units ordered
(200,000)
100,000
D
Subcontract
I
(0.4)
40 Units ordered
(400,000 − 360,000)
20,000
(0.6)
20 Units ordered
(200,000 − 180,000)
0
Process 2
E
Produce 40 units
(−240,000)
J
(0.4)
40 Units ordered
(400,000)
140,000
(0.6)
20 Units ordered
(200,000 + 40,000)
−20,000
(−120,000)
Produce 20 units
K
(0.4)
40 Units ordered
(400,000 − 180,000)
80,000
(0.6)
20 Units ordered
(200,000)
60,000
Process 2
F
Produce 40 units
(−240,000)
L
(0.4)
40 Units ordered
(400,000)
160,000
(0.6)
20 Units ordered
(200,000 + 40,000)
0
(−120,000)
Produce 20 units
M
(0.4)
40 Units ordered
(400,000 − 180,000)
100,000
(0.6)
20 Units ordered
(200,000)
80,000
Subcontract now
N
(0.4)
40 Units ordered
(400,000 − 280,000)
120,000
(0.6)
20 Units ordered
(200,000 − 140,000)
60,000
Do not take contract
0

**What we are doing.** Think about the process like this. Assume that you reach decision node *C*. This means that you would have chosen *process 1* at decision node *A* and had a *successful* outcome at uncertain event *B*. Which alternative would you choose under these conditions? Of course, these conditions may never occur, either because in the end you do not choose *process 1*, or if you choose *process 1*, the outcome may be *unsuccessful*. But, in order to evaluate the initial decision, we need to consider what you *would* do if you reached decision node *C*. Having decided that if you are faced with the decision at *C* you will choose *produce 20 units*, we can simplify the diagram by eliminating the decision. It is replaced by the consequences of your choice. The revised partial diagram is shown in Figure 5.19.

**FIGURE 5.19**

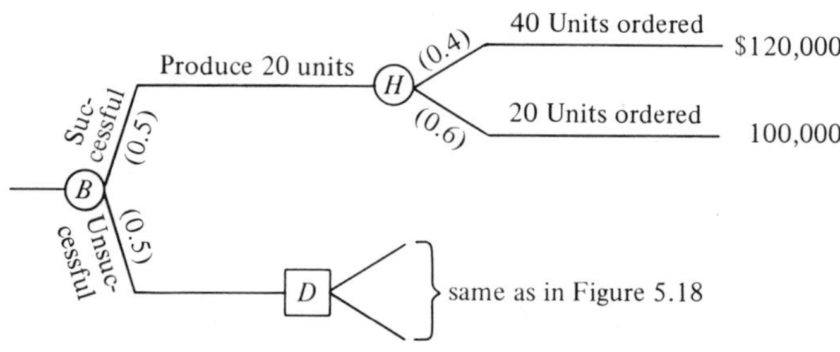


**The process continued.** Stepping down the diagram, we move back past node *I* to decision node *D*. However, since the decision on *E* has not been specified, we consider it first. After comparing the production alternatives and their consequences (uncertain events *J* and *K*), assume that you choose the *produce 20 units* alternative. Decision node *E* is eliminated by crossing out the *produce 40 units* alternative. The choice at decision node *D* can now be made. It is shown in Figure 5.20. The *process 2* alternative at *D* dominates *subcontract*.

Stepping down the diagram to uncertain node *L* and moving backward, we reach decision node *F*. Assume that you choose the *produce 20 units* alternative again. All the intermediate decisions have now been made. The resulting diagram is shown in Figure 5.21.

Although all the intermediate decisions have been eliminated, there are still two stages of uncertain events for the *process 1* alternative. These two uncertain events can be combined using the rules of probability. (The rules are discussed in Chapter 7. For independent events, probabilities are combined by multiplying them together.) The combined events for the *process 1* alternative are shown in Figure 5.22. The four initial alternatives can now be directly compared and a choice made.

**FIGURE 5.20**

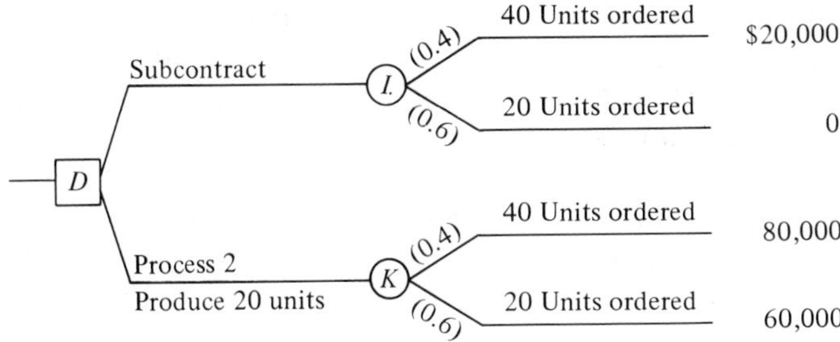


**FIGURE 5.21**

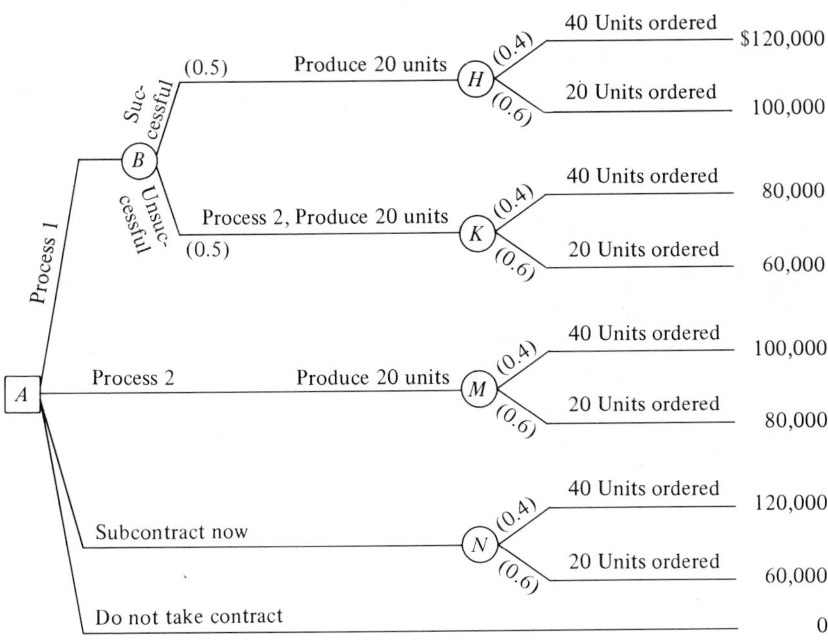


**FIGURE 5.22**

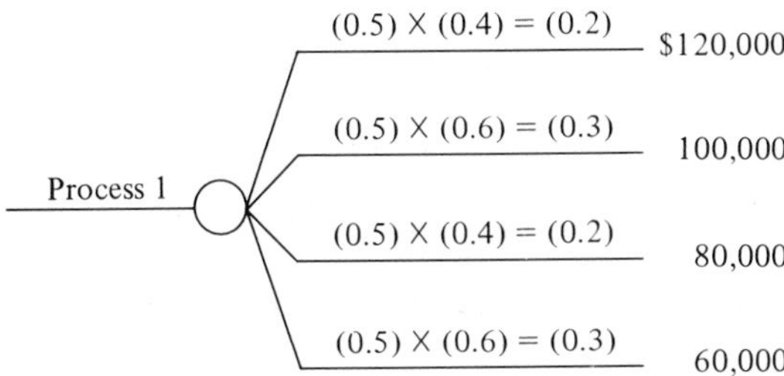

### Rollback Using Certainty Equivalents

**The process.** The decisions at step 2 of the general procedure are based on certainty equivalents. Referring to Figure 5.18 and starting with the top branch, move past node *G* to decision node *C*. Assume that you are Landis. In this procedure you would assess certainty equivalents for uncertain events *G* and *H*. (For purposes of this discussion, do not worry about how you would assess these certainty equivalents. Concentrate on how they are used.) Assume that you decide your certainty equivalent for *G* is $100,000 and for *H* is $105,000.[4] Therefore, you choose *produce 20 units*. Decision node *C* is replaced by $105,000, the certainty equivalent for the *produce 20 units* branch.

**What we are doing.** Think about the process like this. Assume that you reach decision node *C*. This means that you would have chosen *process 1* at decision node *A* and had a *successful* outcome at uncertain event *B*. You would then have to choose between *produce 40 units* and *produce 20 units*. To help make this choice, you decide to assess certainty equivalents for uncertain events *G* and *H*. Of course, you may never have to actually make this decision. You may not choose *process 1*, or, if you do, the outcome may be *unsuccessful*. But, in order to evaluate the initial decision, we need to consider what you *would* do if you ever reached decision node *C*. Based on your certainty equivalents, you would choose *produce 20 units* with a certainty equivalent of $105,000. Since we know what you will do if you reach node *C*, we can eliminate the decision node. In its place we put the certainty equivalent for the uncertain event that follows your choice. That is, decision node *C* is replaced by $105,000. Remember, by definition you are indifferent between the uncertain event and its certainty equivalent, so we can substitute one for the other. The modified partial diagram is shown in Figure 5.23.

**FIGURE 5.23**

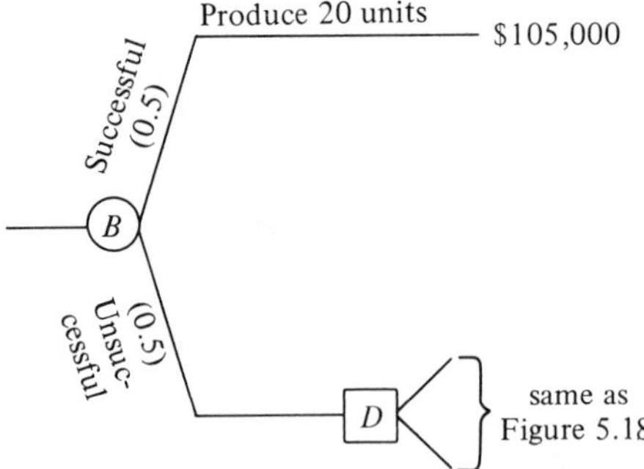


[4]These certainty equivalents and all those used in this discussion are not necessarily the same as those you would assess. They are based on one person's attitude toward risk and there is ***no*** reason to believe that yours or anyone else's would be the same. Do not try to "figure out" where they come from. Just treat them as examples to illustrate the procedure.

**The process continued.** Stepping down the diagram, assume that you assess your certainty equivalents for $I$, $J$, and $K$ as $5,000, $30,000, and $65,000, respectively. This means that you choose *produce 20 units* at decision node $E$ and replace the decision node by $65,000. Decision node $D$ is then shown in Figure 5.24. The choice is *process 2*.

**FIGURE 5.24**

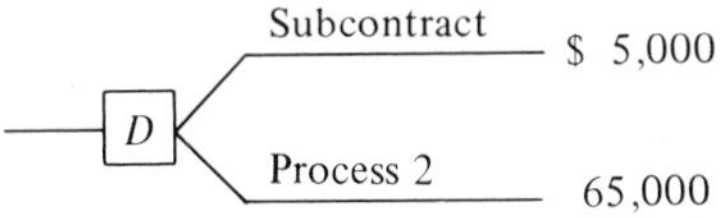

D
Subcontract — $ 5,000
Process 2 — 65,000

Next move backward to the initial choice. Replacing the decision nodes and uncertain events by certainty equivalents, we have the uncertain event shown in Figure 5.25. Assume that you assess a certainty equivalent for uncertain event $B$ as $80,000. This completes the rollback for the *process 1* alternative.

**FIGURE 5.25**

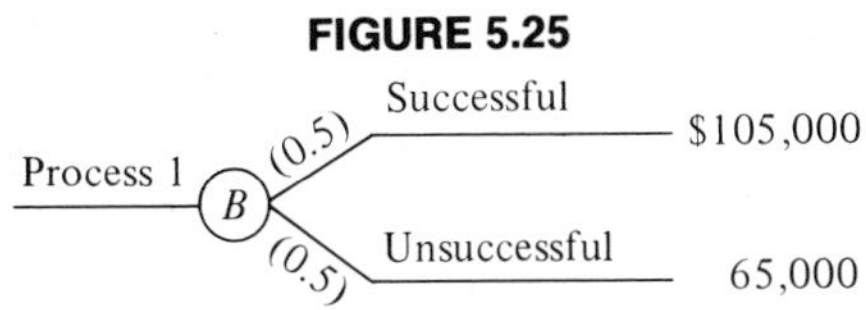


Stepping down the diagram, we reach decision node $F$. Assume that you assess certainty equivalents for uncertain events $L$ and $M$ as $50,000 and $85,000, respectively. You would then choose to *produce 20 units* and decision node $F$ would be replaced by $85,000.

The last certainty equivalent to assess is for uncertain event $N$. Assume you decide that your certainty equivalent is $80,000. The original choice problem has now been reduced to the alternatives and certainty equivalents shown in Figure 5.26. The choice of *process 2* is immediate since each of the alternatives has been evaluated by a certainty equivalent.

**FIGURE 5.26**

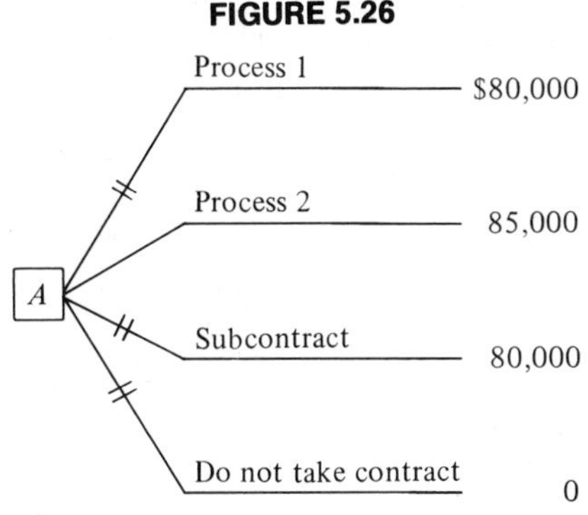

**Summary.** The rollback procedure allowed us to make decisions stage by stage. Certainty equivalents were used to make the choices at each stage. By beginning at the end we never have a "future" decision to worry about when considering choices. After making a decision, we can replace the decision node by the certainty equivalent for the chosen alternative. We know that if we ever reach the decision node, we will make the indicated choice, so it is legitimate to replace it with the certainty equivalent for that choice.

When we reach the initial decision node in the diagram, the choice is obvious. We just choose the alternative with the highest certainty equivalent. The reasoning is that the certainty equivalents are precisely equivalent to the stream of decisions and uncertain events we will face with each alternative. In addition, we know exactly what we will do at all future decision nodes. For instance, in this example we would choose *process 2* and *produce 20 units*.

### Rollback Using Expected Values

**The process.** The rollback using expected values follows the same steps as the rollback using certainty equivalents. The difference is that uncertain events are replaced by their expected values. They are easy to calculate and the rollback can be done mechanically. Figure 5.27 shows the original diagram with the expected values placed in ovals. For instance, starting with the top branch, the expected contribution for node $G$ is $(0.4)\times(\$220{,}000)+(0.6)\times(\$60{,}000)=\$124{,}000$. This value is placed on the diagram in an oval to indicate that the branch leading to the uncertain event is valued at \$124,000 for purposes of comparison. Expected values are calculated for uncertain events $H, I, J, K, L, M, N$ and placed on the diagram. Starting at the top and moving backward, we arrive at the decision node $C$. We compare the \$124,000 expected value for *produce 40 units* with the \$108,000 expected value for *produce 20 units*, and choose *produce 40 units*. The *produce 20 units* alternative is crossed out and the expected value, \$124,000, is transferred to the branch coming into the decision node.

**What we are doing.** The process is exactly like the process using certainty equivalents. We assume that decision node $C$ has been reached (even though we recognize it may never actually be reached) and decide what we would do. Because expected values are being used to make decisions, we would choose *produce 40 units*, with an expected value of \$124,000. Since we are only interested in expected values, the uncertain event can be replaced by its expected value. This eliminates the decision node and allows us to move backward to the next decision.

**The process continued.** Stepping down the diagram to decision node $E$, we choose *produce 20 units*, with an expected value of \$68,000. We cross out *produce 40 units* and move backward to the decision node $D$. Here we choose *process 2* with an expected value of \$68,000 over *subcontracting*.

FIGURE 5.27

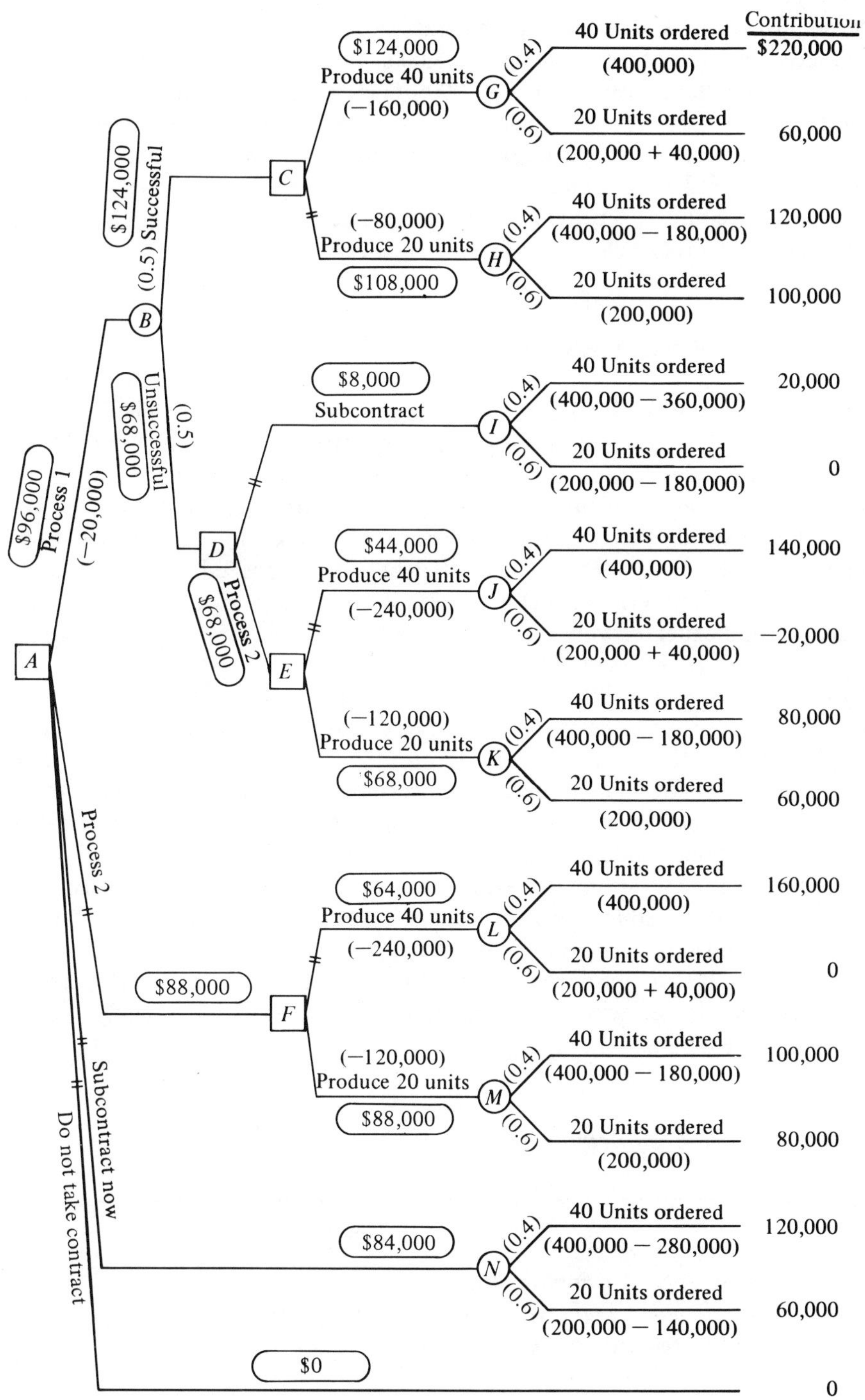

Contribution
$220,000
60,000
120,000
100,000
20,000
0
140,000
−20,000
80,000
60,000
160,000
0
100,000
80,000
120,000
60,000
0
A
Process 1
(−20,000)
$96,000
B
(0.5) Successful
$124,000
(0.5) Unsuccessful
$68,000
C
Produce 40 units
(−160,000)
$124,000
G
(0.4)
(0.6)
40 Units ordered
(400,000)
20 Units ordered
(200,000 + 40,000)
(−80,000)
Produce 20 units
$108,000
H
40 Units ordered
(400,000 − 180,000)
20 Units ordered
(200,000)
D
Subcontract
$8,000
I
40 Units ordered
(400,000 − 360,000)
20 Units ordered
(200,000 − 180,000)
Process 2
$68,000
E
Produce 40 units
(−240,000)
$44,000
J
40 Units ordered
(400,000)
20 Units ordered
(200,000 + 40,000)
(−120,000)
Produce 20 units
$68,000
K
40 Units ordered
(400,000 − 180,000)
20 Units ordered
(200,000)
Process 2
$88,000
F
Produce 40 units
(−240,000)
$64,000
L
40 Units ordered
(400,000)
20 Units ordered
(200,000 + 40,000)
(−120,000)
Produce 20 units
$88,000
M
40 Units ordered
(400,000 − 180,000)
20 Units ordered
(200,000)
Subcontract now
$84,000
N
40 Units ordered
(400,000 − 280,000)
20 Units ordered
(200,000 − 140,000)
Do not take contract
$0

Continuing to move backward, we reach uncertain event *B*. If *successful*, the set of decisions and uncertainties has an expected value of $124,000, and if *unsuccessful*, the expected value is $68,000. Using these values, the expected value of uncertain event *B* is $96,000. This is the expected value of the alternative, *process 1*, given the decisions made at *C*, *D*, and *E*. If *process 1* is used and is successful, we will *produce 40 units.* If it is not successful, we will use *process 2* and *build 20 units.*

The procedure is repeated for the other alternatives. Comparison of the expected values for each alternative leads to choosing *process 1*.

## ●● COMPLETE STRATEGIES

Decision diagrams with multiple stages are strategic models. They involve thinking through the uncertainties and "downstream" decisions required by an initial decision. These diagrams usually represent a large number of *complete strategies*. Sequential analysis does not consider all these strategies explicitly. Instead, the rollback procedure eliminates inferior strategies at each stage. This is usually the most efficient way to proceed. The final result of the rollback is the most preferred complete strategy. For instance, in the analysis using expected values shown in Figure 5.27, the preferred strategy is: choose *process 1*; if it is successful, *produce 40 units*; if it is unsuccessful, use *process 2* and *produce 20 units*. This is a complete strategy because it describes the decisions to be made under every possible contingency. The set of all complete strategies in a multistage problem can be be difficult and time consuming to create. There are no set procedures or formulas for extracting complete strategies from a decision diagram. However, once the concept is clear, some simple guidelines are all that is needed.

Using complete strategies is an alternative to sequential analysis. The idea is to list all possible complete strategies and choose among them. All the necessary decisions are part of the specification of the complete strategy. Therefore, each strategy is characterized by a set of uncertain events. These ideas will be clearer with an example. Read the definition quickly before going to the example.

### ●● Complete Strategy

**Complete Strategy**

***Definition:*** *A* ***complete strategy*** *is a statement describing an initial choice, and a choice for any subsequent decisions that may be required to follow the initial or subsequent choices.*

## ●● Specifying Complete Strategies

To illustrate the process of listing complete strategies, consider the example shown in Figure 5.27. There are four possible initial choices. We will start with the easy ones first.

**Strategy 1: Do not take contract.** This is a complete strategy since there are no follow-on decisions that must be specified if this initial choice is made. The diagram representing this strategy is shown in Figure 5.28.

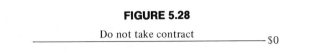

**FIGURE 5.28**

Do not take contract ——— \$0

**Strategy 2: Subcontract work now.** This is also a complete strategy. Its diagram is shown in Figure 5.29.

**FIGURE 5.29**

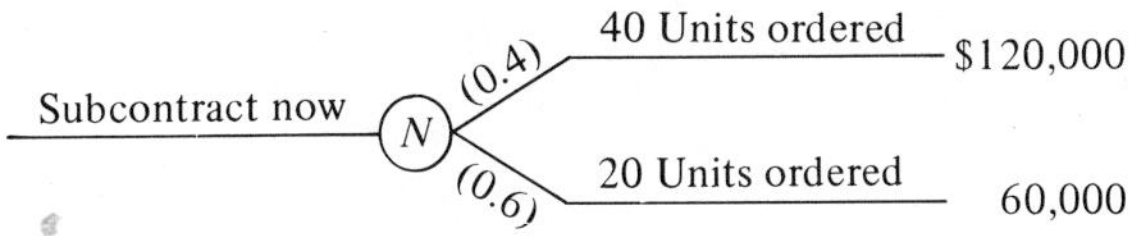


There are two strategies that begin with the initial choice of *process 2*.

**Strategy 3: Process 2 and produce 40 units.** Here we require two choices to be specified: the initial choice and one for decision node *F*. The strategy is complete once these have been specified. This is shown in Figure 5.30.

**FIGURE 5.30**

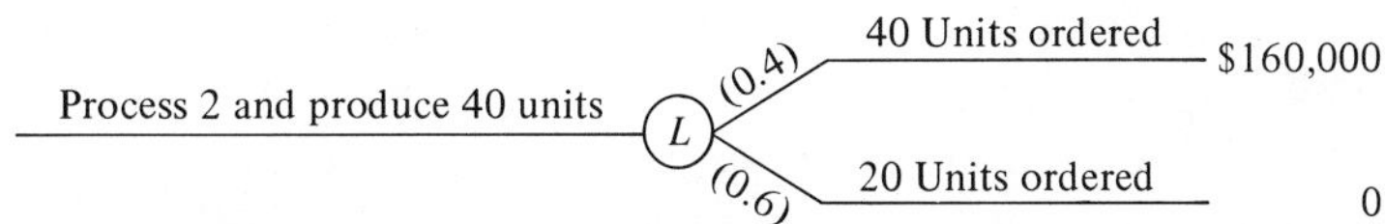


**Strategy 4: Process 2 and produce 20 units.** This is the other possibility if *process 2* is chosen initially. Its diagram is given in Figure 5.31.

**FIGURE 5.31**

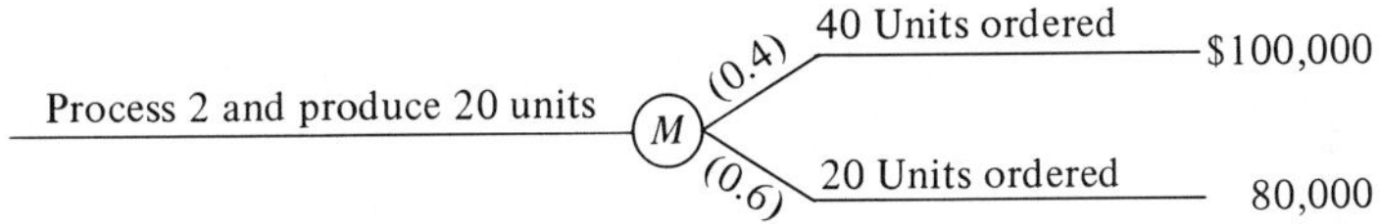

For the initial choice of *process 1* we have six different, complete strategies. (There is no easy rule for determining how many complete strategies flow from an initial decision. It is better to just lay them out one at a time.) These complete strategies are a little harder to visualize. The best thing to keep in mind is that a complete strategy must provide a path through the diagram for all sets of outcomes from uncertain events.

**Strategy 5: Process 1; if successful, produce 40 units; if unsuccessful, subcontract.** Uncertain event *B* has two outcomes. Therefore, a complete strategy must follow each of the two paths. If a decision node is reached, a choice must be specified. In this case, following outcome *successful* we reach decision node *C*. For this strategy we choose *produce 40 units*. There are no more decision nodes along this path. Following outcome *unsuccessful* we reach decision node *D*. For this strategy we choose *subcontract*. There are no more decision nodes along this path and the strategy is complete. It is represented by Figure 5.32.

**FIGURE 5.32**

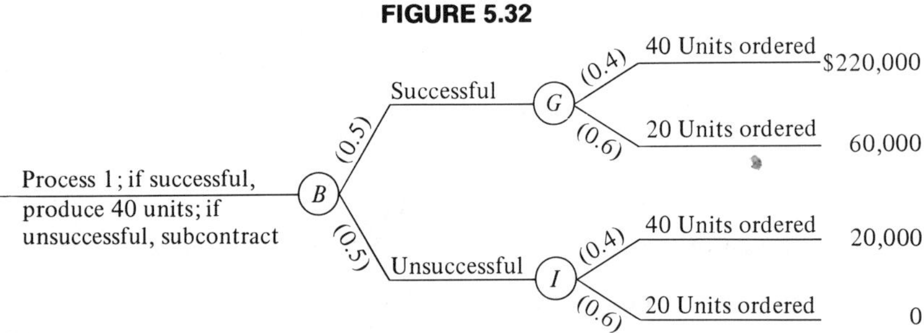


**Strategy 6: Process 1; if successful, produce 40 units; if unsuccessful, process 2 and produce 40 units.** This strategy specifies the same decision, if a successful outcome is obtained, as strategy 5. If an *unsuccessful* outcome is obtained, we reach decision node *D*. In this case we choose *process 2*. Following this path, we reach decision node *E* and specify *produce 40 units*. There are no more decision nodes along this path and the strategy is complete. It is represented by Figure 5.33.

**FIGURE 5.33**

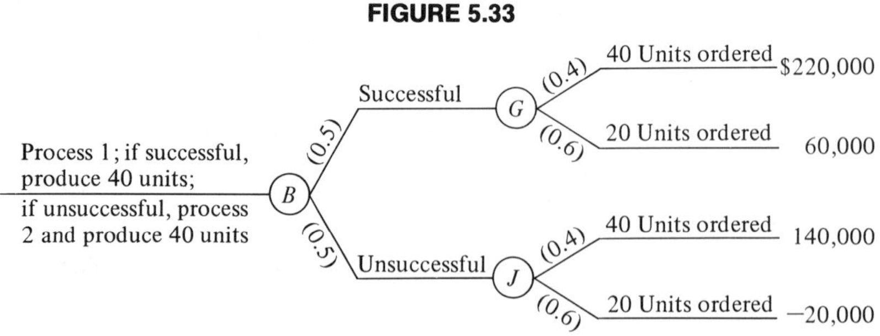

**Strategy 7: Process 1; if successful, produce 40 units; if unsuccessful, process 2 and produce 20 units**

**Strategy 8: Process 1; if successful, produce 20 units; if unsuccessful, subcontract.** This strategy is similar to strategy 5 except 20 units are produced if *process 1* is successful, rather than 40. Strategies 9 and 10 have the same relationship to strategies 6 and 7 as this strategy has to 5.

**Strategy 9: Process 1; if successful, produce 20 units; if unsuccessful, process 2 and produce 40 units**

**Strategy 10: Process 1; if successful, produce 20 units; if unsuccessful, process 2 and produce 20 units.**

The most usual mistake in specifying strategies is to fail to follow the path completely for all possible outcomes from an uncertain event. For instance, *process 1; if successful, produce 40 units* is *not* a complete strategy because it does not specify what to do if the outcome is unsuccessful.

### ●● Choices with Complete Strategies

Once the complete strategies have been delineated, a choice must be made. The decisions can be made using either direct choice, certainty equivalents, or expected values. Often, complete strategies are developed to make it easier to use direct choice. In a presentation to a committee, for instance, it may be best to summarize two or three of the best complete strategies rather than trying to take each person through a sequential analysis.

## SUMMARY

There are three main methods of making choices under uncertainty. Each can be used with single- or multistage problems.

### Direct Choice

Each alternative is described by a probability distribution for its consequences measured by the evaluation units. Checks are made for dominance.

> **Outcome Dominance**
>
> ***Definition:*** *If alternative A is at least as preferred as alternative B for each* ***outcome*** *, and if A is strictly preferred to B for one outcome, then A* ***dominates*** *B.*

**Probabilistic Dominance**

***Definition:*** *If for any values of the evaluation units (in which more is better) the probability of alternative A achieving that value or more is greater than or equal to the probability of alternative B achieving that value or more, then A* ***dominates probabilistically****. The case in which the probabilities are equal for A and B for all values of the evaluation units is an exception. In this case, based on the probability distributions, A and B are equivalent.*

If one alternative does not dominate all others, the choice is made by comparing the probability distributions or some set of *summary measures* from the probability distributions. Looking at the probability of reaching some *aspiration level* is also helpful sometimes.

### Certainty Equivalents

Using certainty equivalents can be easier than making direct choices in some situations. Their assessment can be made easier by the decomposition process described in Chapter 6.

**Certainty Equivalent**

***Definition:*** *The* ***certainty equivalent*** *for an uncertain event is that certain value, in terms of the evaluation units, which a decision maker is just willing to accept in lieu of the gamble represented by the uncertain event.*

### Means or Expected Values

If a decision maker is risk neutral, decisons can be made by comparing expected values. When expected values are used, care must be taken to correctly include the detailed probability distributions in the calculation.

### Multistage Problems

A series of decisions and uncertain events introduces added complexity. There are two ways to deal with these problems.

**Sequential analysis.** Starting at the end and "rolling back" the tree treats each decision sequentially. When a decision node is reached, an alternative is selected and the other alternatives eliminated (crossed out). By moving backward through the diagram, when the initial decision is reached, all other decision nodes have been eliminated from consideration.

**Complete strategies.** A complete strategy is a statement describing an initial choice and a choice for any subsequent decisions that may be required to follow the initial choice. Once the complete strategies have been laid out, any one of the three methods of making choices can be used.

## ASSIGNMENT MATERIAL

**5.1.** Consider the following payoff table, where cell entries are contributions in dollars.

| | *Alternative* | | | |
|---|---|---|---|---|
| *Outcome* | *A* | *B* | *C* | *D* |
| 1 | 7 | 8 | 7 | 5 |
| 2 | 4 | 2 | 3 | 6 |
| 3 | 8 | 9 | 7 | 5 |
| 4 | 12 | 10 | 11 | 6 |

Can any alternatives be eliminated using dominance?

**5.2.** Comment on the statement: "Certainty equivalents provide estimates of the outcomes from uncertain events."

**5.3.** In the example on certainty equivalents an insurance agent played an important role. Is the concept of a certainty equivalent useful if insurance is not available? Why or why not?

**5.4.** Suppose that you have been given the lottery shown in Figure 5.34, where heads and tails will be determined by flipping a *fair* coin. You are in a room with one other person. The coin will be tossed in 5 minutes by an impartial third person. You cannot leave the room or communicate with anyone except the second person in the room prior to the coin flip.

**FIGURE 5.34**

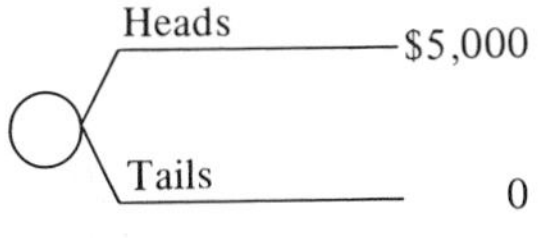

Heads —— $5,000

Tails —— 0

(a) If the other person offered to buy your lottery before the coin flip for $2,500, would you sell?
(b) If the buying offer were $2,400, would you sell?
(c) If the buying offer were $2,200, would you sell?
(d) What is the minimum amount you would accept?

**5.5.** What is your certainty equivalent for the lottery described in problem 5.4?

**5.6. Leslie Electronics, Inc. (B).**
Late in August 1972, Donald Leslie, owner and president of Leslie Electronics, Inc., is trying to decide whether or not to accept a contract from Audio Concepts, Inc., for 100 electronic portasols [see problem 2.7, Leslie Electronics (A)]. Hans Sturdevant, Leslie's plant engineer, is discussing the problem with Leslie.

"I think we should definitely buy the mold, and make the 100 housings ourselves," began Sturdevant. "All of my projected costs show that we will definitely make more money than if we buy the housings."

"The problem I see, Hans," replied Leslie, "is that there is a chance that the mold won't give us a housing that's acceptable to Roth. If this happens, then we're back where we started, purchasing the housings, and we've sunk $17,500 in a useless mold."

"I don't think there's much chance of that," said Sturdevant. "We've had very good luck with this type of casting in the past, and I don't see any reason to doubt that it will work this time. If we go ahead with it, I can give you several sample housings by early next week, and Roth can check them then. True, if Roth doesn't like them we'll have to buy the housings, but as I say, I'm almost sure this won't happen."

*Questions*

1. Draw a decision diagram that accurately portrays Leslie's current decision problem. Be sure to include the financial consequences and any other consequences you feel are relevant.
2. After Sturdevant left the office, Leslie muttered to himself, "If I decide to buy the mold, I would settle for a profit of $22,000 on the whole deal just to be rid of the worry about whether or not the mold will work." What implications does this statement have for Leslie's decision problem?

### 5.7. Leslie Electronics, Inc. (C)

Shortly before Leslie was going to call Roth with his decision regarding the production of electronic portasols [see problems 2.7 and 5.6, Leslie Electronics (A) and (B)], he received a phone call.

"Mr. Leslie, this is Sid Roth," it began. "I have a problem, and it concerns the number of portasols I'm going to need. We spoke earlier of 100, but now, due to the outside possibility of the recording studio being smaller than originally planned, I may need only 50. I won't be able to tell you the quantity for sure for 2 weeks, but I will have to know by tomorrow whether or not you will accept the contract. If you accept and still want me to test a couple of your trial units, I'll be able to let you know if they're OK within a week."

Leslie knew he had little bargaining power with Roth, since Roth would take his portasol contract to Crowe Components, a new, struggling electronics company that was eager for any business it could get. Thus, Leslie knew he had to accept Roth's conditions. Even though Leslie was not happy about this recent turn of events, particularly because he would have to make the decision on the mold prior to learning about the order quantity. Still he felt there was a tidy profit to be made on this contract.

*Questions*

1. Draw a decision diagram for the problem *now* facing Leslie. Be sure to include all the consequences (monetary and nonmonetary) of his decision.
2. Leslie thought, "I know that I must decide *now* whether or not I go with the mold process on the deal, but I just might get Roth to agree to a specific quantity *before* he tests the portasols. I would hate to give him the units for testing not even knowing the quantity he would order." If Roth agrees to do this, how has the problem changed? Diagram the new problem.

3. Regarding the decision problem in question 1, Leslie muttered, "If I buy the mold, I'd give $20,000 to know how many portasols Roth is going to order." What are the implications of this statement for Leslie's decision problem?

**5.8.** Louis Hooper, manager of the Tahoe City street maintenance department must decide about increasing the snow removal equipment. He has identified three mutually exclusive states of weather: no snow, light snow, and heavy snow. He is considering three courses of action: maintain present capacity; contract now for the services of one additional remover at a cost of $10,000; contract now for the services of two additional removers at a cost of $18,000.

If he maintains present capacity and gets light snow or heavy snow, the city will have to buy services from the state at a cost of $12,000 and $27,000, respectively. If he buys one machine and has heavy snow, the city will have to purchase $15,000 worth of service from the state. The probabilities of no snow, light snow, and heavy snow are assessed to be 0.1, 0.5, and 0.4, respectively.

(a) Display in either a diagram or a table the alternatives faced by Hooper.

(b) Plot the probability distributions for costs as (1) density functions; (2) cumulative distributions.

(c) If he were willing to make comparisons on the basis of expected costs, which alternative would he choose?

(d) If you were in Hooper's position which alternative would you choose? Why?

**5.9.** Consider the Computex Corporation problem described in problem 3.2. The probabilities for high quality, medium quality, and low quality given that the radical approach is taken are 0.22, 0.50, and 0.28, respectively.

(a) Diagram the problem faced by Computex.

(b) Plot the probability density function and cumulative distributions for the alternatives.

(c) If Computex were willing to compare based on expected contribution, which alternative would be chosen?

(d) If you were Renap and were convinced that there were no benefits other than those reflected by the possible contribution from this terminal as reflected in the sales manager's estimates, which alternative would you choose?

**5.10.** As the manager of a uranium mining company you are faced with a choice among three exploration strategies. You are uncertain about the true state of the world but have decided one of three things is true: (1) the ore is concentrated in the surface layers; (2) in the middle layers; (3) in deep layers. The exploration strategies available are: (1) purchase equipment that is good for the upper and middle layers but poor in deep layers; (2) purchase equipment that is good in deep layers but only fair for middle and surface layers; (3) purchase equipment that is good at all layers. Considering cost of equipment, the profits for the three strategies (in millions of dollars) are given in the following table:

| | *Strategy* | | |
|---|---|---|---|
| *State of Nature* | $S_1$ | $S_2$ | $S_3$ |
| 1 | 3 | 2 | 2 |
| 2 | 2 | 1 | 2 |
| 3 | 1 | 4 | 2 |

Probability assessments for the three possible states of nature are: $P(1)=0.4$, $P(2)=0.3$, $P(3)=0.3$.

(a) Which strategy would you choose if you were willing to choose based on expected profits?

(b) Which strategy would you choose if your aspiration level is \$3 million?

**5.11.** Consider the decision problem shown in Figure 5.35. Probabilities are given in parentheses and the end points represent the contribution in thousands of dollars.

(a) Formulate the problem in terms of complete strategies.

(b) Plot probability density functions and cumulative distributions for contribution associated with each strategy. (Assume probabilities along a branch are independent and can be multiplied together.)

(c) If expected contribution were used to choose, which strategy should be selected?

(d) Assume that the contributions specified in the problem would accrue to you (i.e., if an outcome of \$−20,000 occurred, you would have to pay \$20,000, and if an outcome of \$90,000 occurred, you would receive the money). Use the probability distributions to make a direct choice of one of the strategies.

(e) Using the same assumptions as in part (d), use the rollback procedure, determining certainty equivalents for each uncertain event. Show your method and choices.

(f) Assume that comparisons based on expected contribution are appropriate. Roll back using expected contribution to determine the choice. Show your method and the expected contributions.

**FIGURE 5.35**

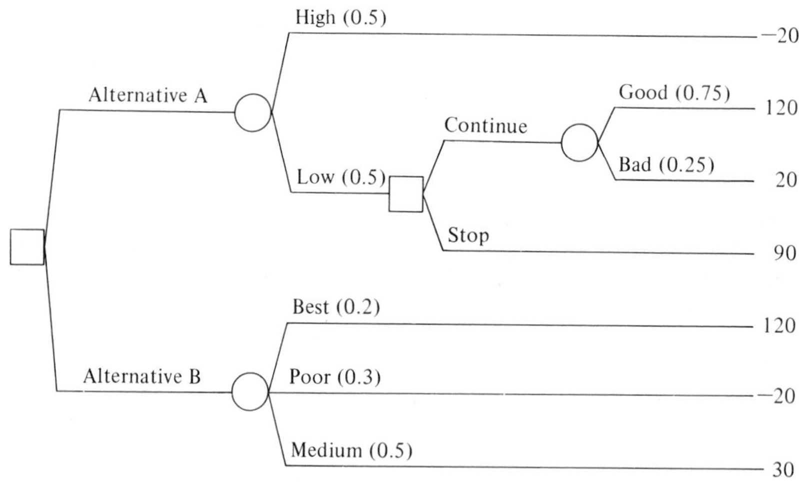


**5.12.** Assume that you face the decision problem shown in Figure 5.36. Probabilities are given in parentheses. The terminal values are in thousands of dollars of net contribution that will accrue to you. All the consequences associated with the decision are completely captured by the dollar contribution figures.

**FIGURE 5.36**

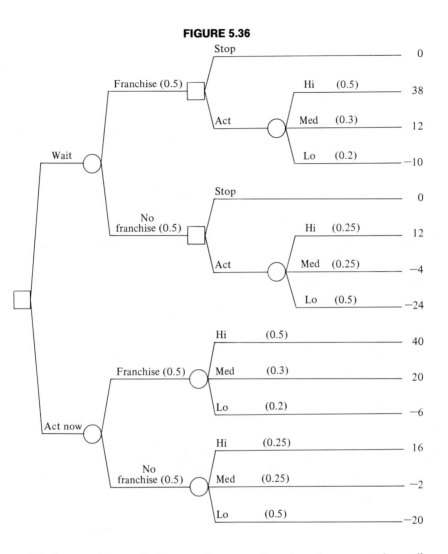

(a) Assume that you decide to make comparisons based on expected contribution. Specify the actions you would take by using the rollback procedure. Show your calculations.

(b) Use the rollback procedure (do not assume comparisons can be made using expected contributions), determining certainty equivalents for each uncertain event. Show your method and choices.

# 6

# Preferences and Calculation of Certainty Equivalents

The options discussed in Chapter 5 for making decisions under uncertainty do not always lead to a clear choice. This is particularly likely to be true for decisions with wide variations in consequences and a lot of uncertainty—decisions that we might describe as very *risky*. This chapter outlines a procedure for decomposing these problems one step further. It allows certainty equivalents to be calculated using *probabilities* and *preferences*. The preferences are encoded in a curve that represents the decision maker's attitude toward risk. The procedure for assessing the curve is based on certainty equivalent decisions for a set of simple, two-outcome gambles. The idea is that risk preferences can be assessed more easily using these simple gambles than in a complicated decision problem. Once the preferences have been encoded in a curve, they can be used to calculate certainty equivalents for the more complicated decision. Besides their use for specific decisions, risk preference curves can be used to explore individual attitudes toward risk and various institutional problems such as risk sharing, syndicate formation, capital markets, and incentive systems.

**FIGURE 6.1**

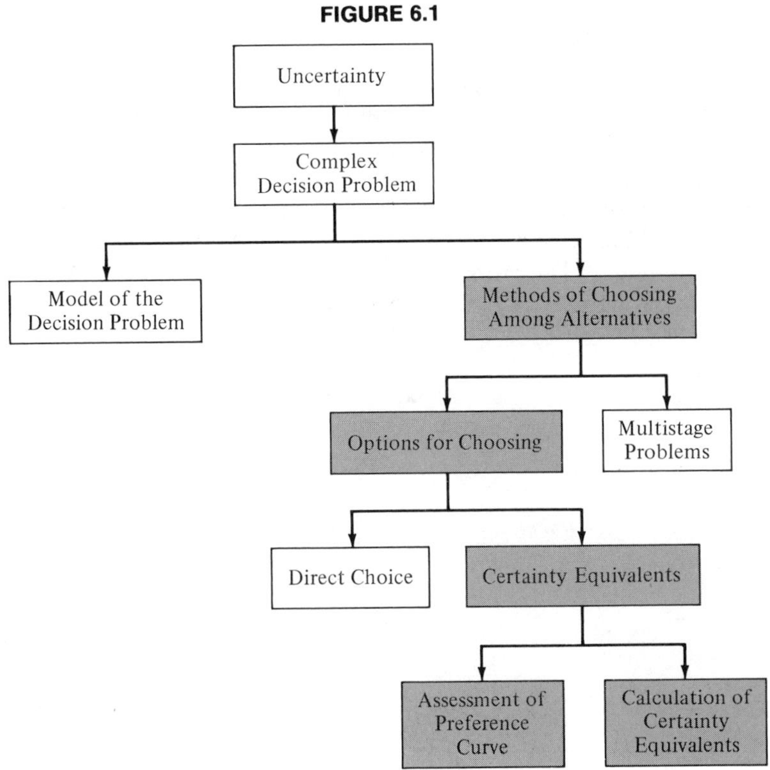

The discussion in this chapter is preliminary in nature. Part III of the book goes into more detail. For instance, questions of risk sharing and the general problems of how risk affects institutions are covered in Part III. In addition, the basic assumptions that lie behind the procedure and the different options for assessing preference curves are not discussed in detail in this chapter. Instead, we rely on plausible arguments and examples. Part III considers these topics in more depth. Figure 6.1 shows how the material relates to other topics.

## BASIC CONCEPTS

The purpose of this chapter is to present the entire certainty equivalent decomposition procedure with a minimum number of technical interruptions. Our goal is a numerical scale, called a *preference scale*, that has two properties: (1) it encodes an individual's attitude toward risk, and (2) it can be used with probabilities to calculate certainty equivalents. This will accomplish the decomposition by allowing probabilities and preferences to be assessed separately and then used to obtain a certainty equivalent. Before presenting the procedure, we define and discuss some important terms.

### The Reference Gamble

We can establish a *reference gamble* for any set of uncertain events. It is a simple two-outcome gamble. One outcome has a payoff greater than or equal to the maximum payoff for any outcome in the events considered. The other outcome has a payoff equal to or less than the minimum payoff for any outcome. For instance, a reference gamble for the decision diagrammed in Figure 6.2 would have payoffs of $100,000 and zero. This reference gamble is shown in Figure 6.3. The probability of winning (getting $100,000) is denoted by $p$, and the probability of losing (getting $0) is denoted by $(1-p)$.

**FIGURE 6.2**

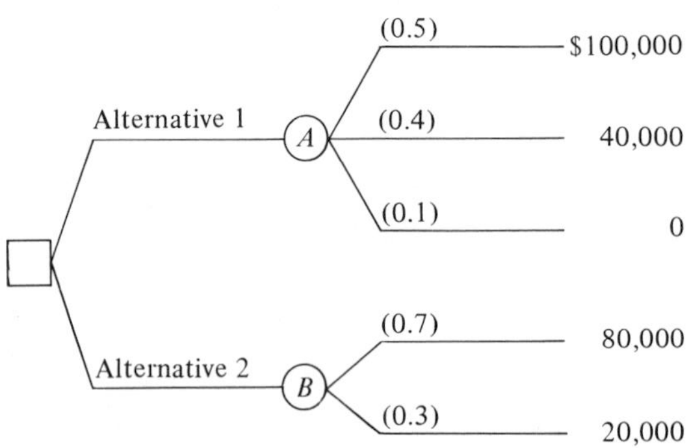

**FIGURE 6.3**
**Reference Gamble**

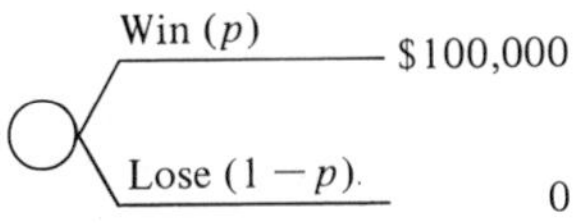

### Preferences

The term "preference" is used in a variety of ways. It refers to a basic relationship among alternatives. If you "prefer" one alternative to another (e.g., $A_1 \succ A_2$), we attribute it to your "preferences." We are primarily interested in preferences for alternatives involving uncertain events. The uncertainty introduces an element we have called *risk*. Accordingly, the term *risk preference* is often used. An individual's risk preference reflects an underlying, or basic, attitude toward uncertain outcomes.

#### Preference Scale

The term *preference scale* is used for a numerical scale that represents an individual's preferences for a set of consequences. Higher numbers are "more preferred" than lower numbers. Preferences for alternatives with uncertain outcomes will be measured by the preference scale.

#### Preference Curve

A *preference curve* is a means for converting from the unit of evaluation used for the consequences (usually dollars measuring contribution) to the preference scale. The conversion is often done by a plotted curve.

#### Utility

*Utility* is another name sometimes used for preference scale. It is used to mean a variety of different things. The usual meaning of *utility* in economics, for instance, is not the same as the preference scale used here. In addition, many people attribute some intuitive meaning to it. Statements are made like "that has no utility." These interpretations are not correct for the preference scale we need. The numbers associated with preference scales or utilities do not correspond directly to any absolute notion of *goodness*. Rather, they are designed to calculate certainty equivalents in specific decision problems.

## BASIC PROCEDURE

The mechanics of a procedure for assessing a preference curve and using it to calculate a certainty equivalent are given in this section. The justification and motivation for the procedure are discussed in the following section.

### Assessing a Preference Curve

The preference curve is obtained from *certainty equivalents* for *reference gambles*. We use a series of reference gambles with different probabilities of winning and ask for certainty equivalents. The certainty equivalents can be obtained by the procedure described in Chapter 5.

> Assessing Preference Curves
>
> 1. Establish the payoffs for a *reference gamble* for the decision problem.
> 2. Specify a value for $p$, the probability of winning the reference gamble, and determine the certainty equivalent for the gamble.
> 3. Record $p$ and the certainty equivalent on a plot with $p$ on the vertical axis and the certainty equivalent on the horizontal axis.
> 4. Repeat steps 2 and 3 by changing $p$ until the plot of $p$ versus certainty equivalents is well defined.
> 5. Draw a curve through the plotted points.

**Example 6.1**

Refer to the decision problem diagrammed in Figure 6.2. Assume that the two alternatives represent products being considered for introduction into a market. The product manager, Sue Jones, must decide between them. As her assistant, you have been asked to help. Because she is uncomfortable with the *risk*, you decide to use a preference curve to calculate a certainty equivalent.

Following the procedure for assessing a preference curve, you establish payoffs of \$100,000 and \$0 for the reference gamble. You turn next to the task of developing the curve. You draw Figure 6.4 to help Jones visualize the reference gambles she must consider.

**FIGURE 6.4**

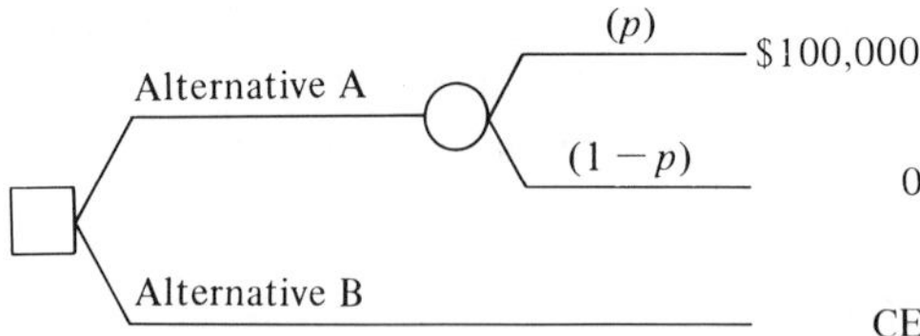


The questioning follows:

You: First we will set $p = 1$ and ask for the value of CE in Figure 6.4 that would make you indifferent between alternatives *A* and *B*.

Jones: That's easy. If $p=1$, then $A$ gives me \$100,000 for sure. Obviously, I wouldn't choose $B$ for anything less than CE=\$100,000.

You: All right. The same reasoning says that if we set $p=0$, you would be indifferent between $A$ and $B$ if CE=\$0.

Jones: Yes. These two points are easy.

You: OK, let's try $p=0.5$. What we need is your certainty equivalent for the reference gamble with $p=0.5$. Using the procedure we've talked about before, would you choose $A$ or $B$ if CE=\$50,000?

Jones: I'd choose $B$.

You: What if CE=\$30,000?

Jones: That's a tough choice. I'm not sure. If it were a flip of a coin on \$100,000 or \$0, what would I do? Looking at it this way, I'd take the \$30,000 for sure, so my answer is $B$.

You: OK. What if CE=\$20,000?

Jones: I would go for $A$.

You: What if I put CE=\$25,000?

Jones: You have me now. I really cannot choose one over the other. I'm indifferent.

You: This is just the point we have been searching for. Your certainty equivalent for the reference gamble with a $p=0.5$ is \$25,000. We can plot this point along with the first two (see Figure 6.5). Now, let's change to $p=0.8$ and repeat the process.

**FIGURE 6.5**

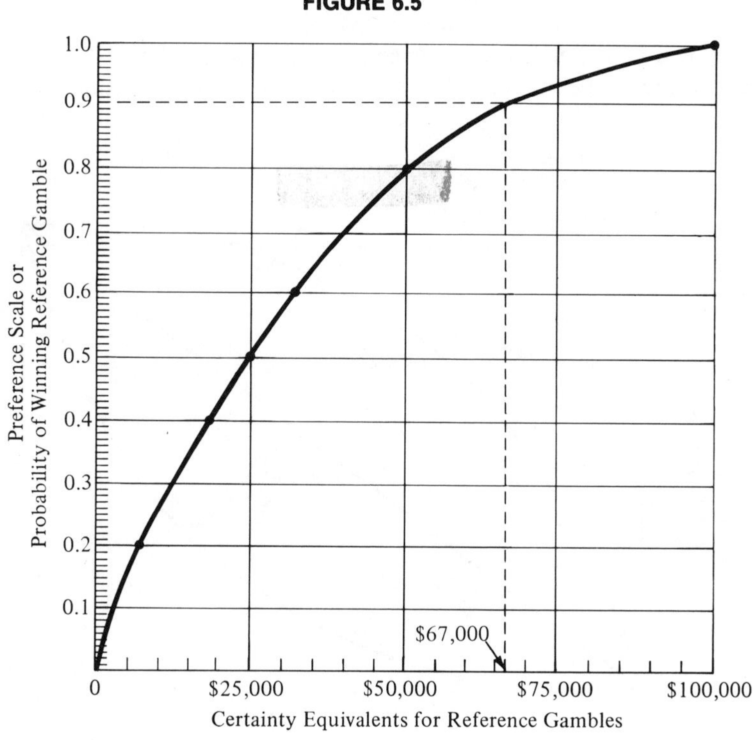

Jones: All right. I am getting the idea. Rather than have you ask a series of questions, let me think about the problem for a minute. How much would I *just* be willing to take rather than face the reference gamble with a 0.8 chance of winning $100,000? $50,000? Yes, if CE=$50,000, I would be indifferent between *A* and *B*.

You: Good. This point can now be added to our plot. What if $p=0.6$?

Jones: Let's see.... My certainty equivalent would be about $33,000. I am not too sure about this number. But as you said, I have to make a decision. If CE= $34,000, I would choose *B*. If CE=$32,000, I would choose *A*. I am indifferent at CE=$33,000.

You: Fine. What is your certainty equivalent for $p=0.4$?

Jones: Using the same reasoning process, it is $18,000.

You: As a last point, what if $p=0.2$?

Jones: My certainty equivalent is $7,000.

### Plotting the Preference Curve

Figure 6.5 is the plot of these responses with a curve drawn through the points. If the shape is not clear, more points can be assessed. This curve establishes *equivalences* between certainty equivalents and probabilities of winning reference gambles. In other words, it provides a means for converting dollar amounts into equivalent reference gambles. The vertical axis is the probability of winning the reference gamble (which is enough to completely specify the reference gamble since the payoffs remain the same). The vertical axis also will be called the preference (or utility) scale. This is the preference curve or, more specifically, Jones' preference curve for this decision. It

**FIGURE 6.6**

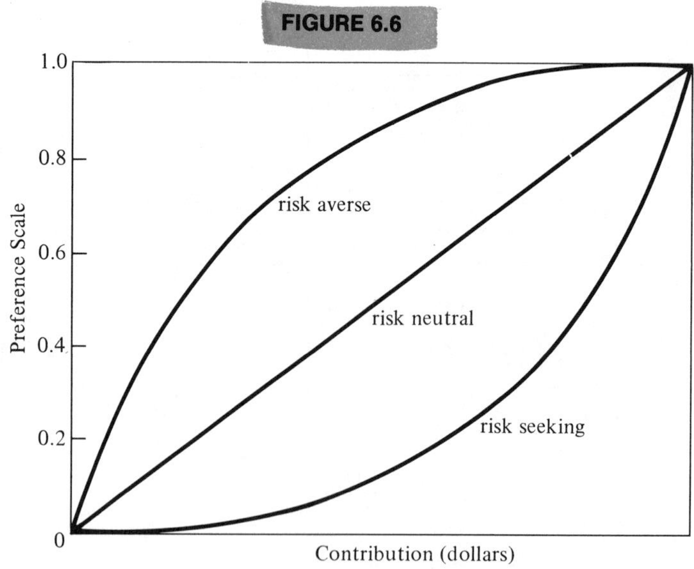

encodes her risk attitude over the range of payoffs $100,000 to $0. Therefore, we can obtain a certainty equivalent for any reference gamble (with outcomes $100,000 and $0) by using Figure 6.5. For example, the reference gamble with $p=0.9$ corresponds to a certainty equivalent of $67,000. Conversely, for any certain dollar amount between $0 and $100,000, we can obtain a reference gamble which is just equivalent to the dollar amount. The curve is the *output* from the preference assessment phase of the certainty equivalent decomposition.

The shape of the preference curve depends on an individual's attitude toward risk. Three general categories of attitudes can be identified: risk averse, risk neutral, and risk seeking. Figure 6.6 shows examples of preference curves for each category. Jones' curve displays the most common of the three attitudes, risk aversion. The curve "bends downward." A risk-neutral curve is a straight line. The curve for a risk seeker "bends upward."[1]

### Calculating Certainty Equivalents

Certainty equivalents for more complicated uncertain events are calculated using preference curves and probabilities. The preference curve takes into account an individual's attitude toward risk. The probabilities take into account the individual's beliefs about the uncertain events. The mechanics of the calculation are:

> Calculating Certainty Equivalents
>
> 1. For each outcome, convert the evaluation units (usually in dollars) to preference scale numbers.
> 2. Calculate the *expected value* of the preference numbers for each uncertain event. Call it $\overline{U}$.
> 3. Use the preference curve to obtain the certainty equivalent corresponding to $\overline{U}$. This is the certainty equivalent for the uncertain event.

As an example, consider calculating Jones' certainty equivalents for the problem shown in Figure 6.2. Figure 6.7 shows the dollar values of each end point and the corresponding preference scale numbers. The preference scale numbers are obtained from Figure 6.5 and shown in ⟨ ⟩'s.

The expected values of the preference numbers are:

Alternative 1: $\overline{U}_1=(0.5)\times(1)+(0.4)\times(0.7)+(0.1)\times(0)=0.780$

Alternative 2: $\overline{U}_2=(0.7)\times(0.95)+(0.3)\times(0.42)=0.791$

[1]The technical name for the shape of the risk-averse curve is *concave*. The risk-seeking curve is *convex*.

**FIGURE 6.7**

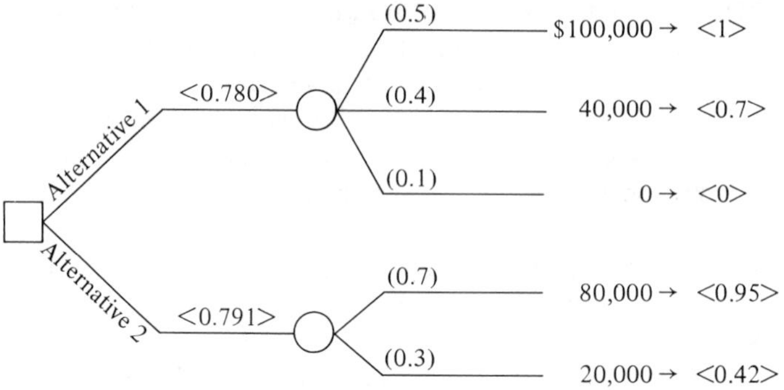

Alternative 1 <0.780>
(0.5) $100,000 → <1>
(0.4) 40,000 → <0.7>
(0.1) 0 → <0>

Alternative 2 <0.791>
(0.7) 80,000 → <0.95>
(0.3) 20,000 → <0.42>

Using Figure 6.5, we find the certainty equivalent for $\overline{U}_1 = 0.780$ to be $48,000 and for $\overline{U}_2 = 0.791$ to be $49,000. Therefore, using this analysis, Jones would choose alternative 2.

### Summary of the Procedure

The potential benefit of the procedure is that certainty equivalent decisions are made on simple two-outcome gambles (the reference gambles) rather than on the more complex uncertain events. The decision maker's attitude toward risk is encoded through these simpler decisions into a preference curve. The preference scale values are then used with probabilities to find an expected preference value for the more complicated uncertain events. This expected preference value is converted into a certainty equivalent by using the preference curve again. If only the choice among alternatives is important, this last step can be eliminated. Alternatives with higher expected preference values will also have higher certainty equivalents (see Figure 6.5).

## BASIS FOR THE PROCEDURE

This discussion is a general explanation of how the procedure works. It uses the example discussed above. Part III contains a thorough treatment of the behavioral assumptions underlying the procedure.

### Substitution of Reference Gambles

For any certain value the preference curve provides an *equivalent* reference gamble. For instance, using Figure 6.5, the reference gamble which Jones considers equivalent to $80,000 has a 0.95 probability of winning. That is, we know that she is indifferent between alternatives *A* and *B* shown in Figure 6.8.

**FIGURE 6.8**

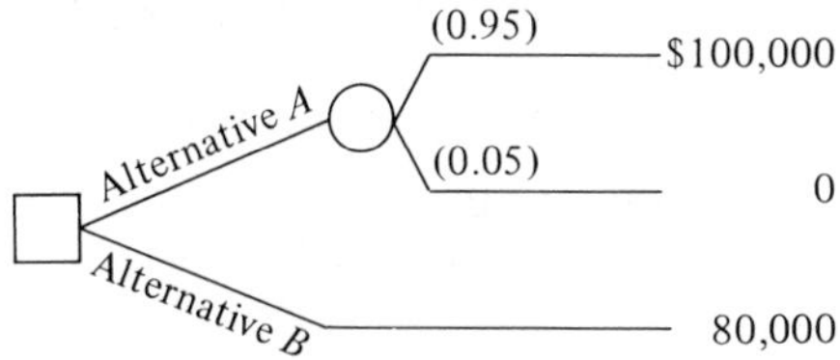


Since she is indifferent between $80,000 and the reference gamble with a 0.95 probability of winning, we can substitute one for the other. If each certain value in the example shown in Figure 6.2 is replaced by the equivalent reference gamble (obtained from Figure 6.5), we have the problem shown in Figure 6.9. As far as Jones is concerned, these two problems are equivalent.

### Reduction to a Single-Stage Gamble

Following "standard" rules of probability, for independent events, the two-stage gambles shown in Figure 6.9 can be reduced to single-stage gambles (Chapter 7 will discuss this in more detail). For instance, if alternative 1 is

**FIGURE 6.9**

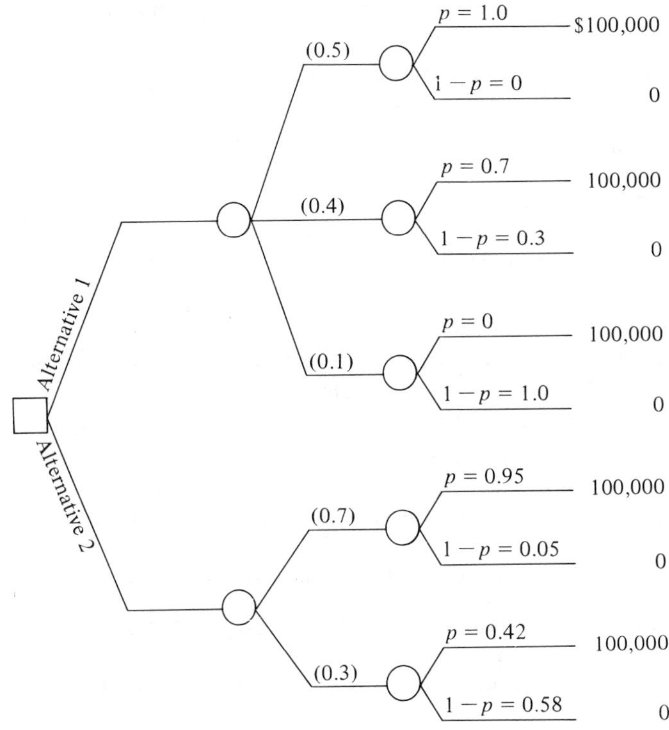

chosen, the probability of obtaining \$100,000 is $(0.5)\times(1.0)+(0.4)\times(0.7)+(0.1)\times(0)=0.780$ and the probability of obtaining \$0 is $(0.5)\times(0)+(0.4)\times(0.3)+(0.1)\times(1)=0.220$. Similarly for alternative 2, the probability of obtaining \$100,000 is $(0.7)\times(0.95)+(0.3)\times(0.42)=0.791$ and the probability of obtaining \$0 is $(0.7)\times(0.05)+(0.3)\times(0.58)=0.209$. Applying these rules, we can replace Figure 6.9 with Figure 6.10. The two-stage gambles have been reduced to *equivalent* single-stage reference gambles.

**FIGURE 6.10**

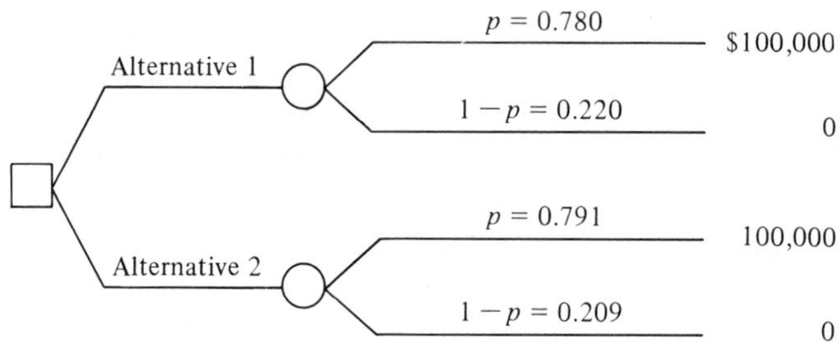


### ●● Justifying the Single-Stage Gamble

There is no question that the technical rules of probability support collapsing the two-stage gambles into single-stage gambles as long as the events are independent. However, there may be a question of whether a decision maker will agree to use them in this situation. Since our objective is to help Jones make a decision, *she* must agree that the original and collapsed versions are equivalent. We can illustrate what collapsing the two-stage gambles means in this case.[2] First, we replace the original uncertain events with draws from a standard urn.[3] For the uncertain event associated with alternative 1, we substitute an urn with 500 red balls, 400 white balls, and 100 blue balls. For the uncertain event associated with alternative 2, we substitute an urn with 700 green balls and 300 yellow balls.

Each of the five reference gambles could also be replaced by a standard urn with the appropriate number of balls labeled *W* for win (\$100,000) and *L* for lose (\$0). If alternative 1 were selected, we would first draw from an urn with 500 red balls, 400 white balls, and 100 blue balls. If the outcome is *white* (this puts us on the middle branch of the uncertain event for alternative 1 in Figure 6.9), we would make a selection from an urn with 700 balls labeled *W* and 300 balls labeled *L*. If the outcome is *red* (top branch), the next selection

[2]Although the discussion does not use the same terminology, it closely follows Chapter 3 in H. Raiffa, *Decision Analysis: Introductory Lectures on Choices Under Uncertainty* (Reading, Mass.: Addison-Wesley, 1968), and Chapter 4 in R. Schlaifer, *Analysis of Decisions Under Uncertainty* (New York: McGraw-Hill, 1969).

[3]A standard urn contains balls with a variety of labels or colors that are all equally likely to be selected on any one draw.

would be from an urn with 1,000 balls labeled *W* and 0 balls labeled *L*. If the outcome is *blue* (bottom branch), the next selection would be from an urn with 0 balls labeled *W* and 1,000 labeled *L*. For each different outcome on the first event, we use the appropriate urn for the second draw. A similar process can be described for alternative 2. The essential thing determined by the draw from the first stage urn is the probability of winning in the second draw.

This two-urn process can be replaced by a single urn that provides exactly the same probability of winning or losing. The balls in the first-stage urn are modified by placing a double label on each ball. For the uncertain event associated with alternative 1 if outcome red occurs, a win occurs with probability 1. Therefore, on each red ball we place a *W* for win. If outcome white occurs, there is a 0.7 probability of winning and a 0.3 probability of losing. Therefore, the 400 white balls are split: $400 \times 0.7 = 280$ labeled *W* and $400 \times 0.3 = 120$ labeled *L*. If outcome blue occurs, the probability of losing is 1, and hence we label all 100 blue balls with an *L*. Figure 6.11 shows the modified urn corresponding to alternative 1. The urn on the right is the same as the one on the left except that the balls with *W* and *L* have been combined regardless of color. If all Jones really cares about is winning and losing (not the color of the ball), there is no need to keep track of the color. We can use the urn on the right to represent the uncertain process associated with alternative 1.

The same thing can be done for alternative 2. If outcome green occurs, there is a 0.95 probability of winning and a 0.05 probability of losing. Therefore, we divide the 700 green balls into $700 \times 0.95 = 665$ labeled *W* and $700 \times 0.05 = 35$ labeled *L*. If outcome yellow occurs, there is a 0.42 probability of winning and a 0.58 probability of losing, and we label $300 \times 0.42 = 126$ with *W* and $300 \times 0.58 = 174$ with *L*. Figure 6.12 shows the urns.

The uncertain events represented by the urns on the right of Figures 6.11 and 6.12 are exactly the same as the uncertain events shown in Figure 6.10. Therefore, if Jones agrees to replace the two urns with the modified single urn, it means she agrees to use the "standard" rules of probability to collapse Figure 6.9 to Figure 6.10.

**FIGURE 6.11**

| *Labels* | *Number of Balls* |
|---|---|
| Red, *W* | 500 |
| Red, *L* | 0 |
| White, *W* | 280 |
| White, *L* | 120 |
| Blue, *W* | 0 |
| Blue, *L* | 100 |
| *Total* | 1,000 |

Urn corresponding to Alternative 1

~

| *Labels* | *Number of Balls* |
|---|---|
| *W* | 780 |
| *L* | 220 |
| *Total* | 1,000 |

Urn corresponding to Alternative 1

FIGURE 6.12

| *Labels* | *Number of Balls* |
|---|---|
| Green, $W$ | 665 |
| Green, $L$ | 35 |
| Yellow, $W$ | 126 |
| Yellow, $L$ | 174 |
| *Total* | 1,000 |

Urn corresponding to Alternative 2

~

| *Labels* | *Number of Balls* |
|---|---|
| $W$ | 791 |
| $L$ | 209 |
| *Total* | 1,000 |

Urn corresponding Alternative 2

### Choice Between Alternatives

The original problem has been converted into the equivalent problem (shown in Figure 6.10), which only involves reference gambles. The choice at this point is not difficult because, presumably, the decision maker would prefer the reference gamble with the highest probability of winning. Therefore, this analysis indicates the decision maker prefers alternative 2.

Certainty equivalents for these reference gambles, and consequently for the original uncertain events, can be obtained from the preference curve. The certain value that is equivalent to a reference gamble with a 0.780 probability of winning is $48,000. For a 0.791 probability of winning, the certainty equivalent is $49,000. Although the motivation for developing the procedure was to calculate certainty equivalents, we see that the choice can be made by just knowing the probabilities for winning the reference gamble. We prefer the reference gamble with the highest probability of winning.

### Relationship to Expected Preference Procedure

The expected preference values calculated on Figure 6.7 are precisely the same as the probabilities of winning the equivalent reference gambles calculated on Figure 6.10. Of course, this is no accident. The reason the values are the same is that the procedure of substituting preference numbers and calculating the expected preference value is numerically the same as calculating the probability of winning the single-stage, equivalent, reference gamble. Since the expected preference values are the same as the probabilities for winning the equivalent reference gambles, the certainty equivalents are the same. This provides the justification for the expected preference procedure.

**• Example 6.2**

This example illustrates how the procedure discussed above is used in a sequential analysis. No attempt is made to describe an actual problem setting. The problem is specified by the decision diagram in Figure 6.13. The preference curve for the decision maker has been obtained and is shown in Figure 6.14. The reference gamble is between $250,000 and $170,000.

FIGURE 6.13

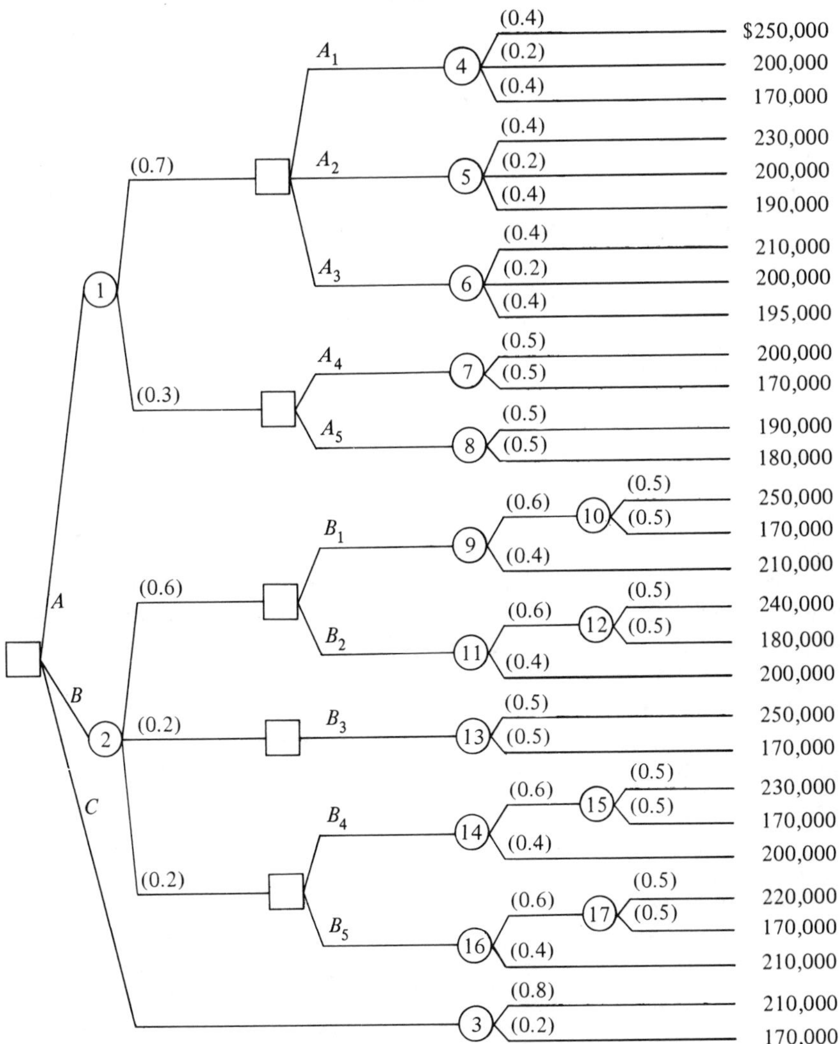


The first step in the analysis is to replace the end values with the preference numbers (probabilities of winning the reference gamble) using Figure 6.14. These preference numbers are shown in ⟨ ⟩'s in Figure 6.15. Next, the expected preference values are calculated for each of the uncertain events 4 through 17. These calculations are shown in Table 6.1 and the results placed in Figure 6.15. Since higher expected preference numbers are preferred to lower ones, the choice at each decision node can be made directly. For instance, in choosing among A1, A2, and A3, the decision maker chooses A2. The certainty equivalent for A1, A2, and A3 could also be determined. But, as we have discussed previously, the decision can be made without going through the conversion. Moving down the diagram, A5

FIGURE 6.14

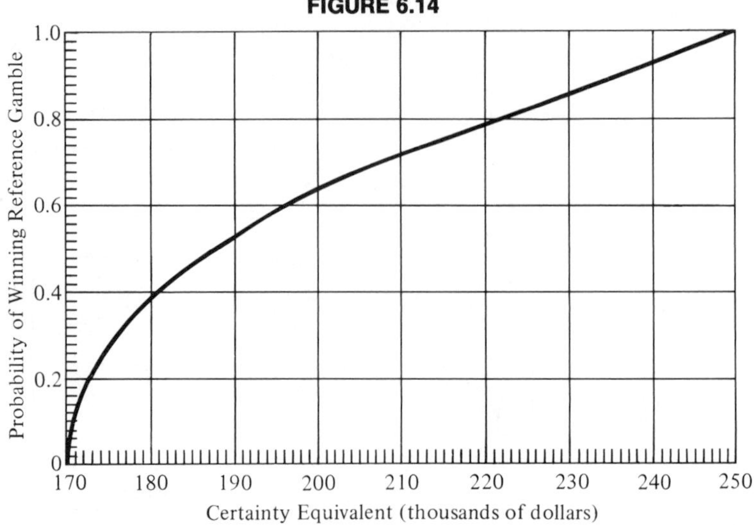


is chosen over A4. Uncertain event 1 has outcomes characterized by preference numbers of 0.684 and 0.455. Continuing the expected preference calculations, alternative *A* has an expected preference value of (0.7)×(0.684)+(0.3)×(0.455)=0.6153. By proceeding in the same way, we calculate expected preference values for alternatives *B* and *C* to be 0.5936 and 0.568, respectively. Therefore, alternative *A* is preferred to alternatives *B* and *C*. Using Figure 6.14, the certainty equivalent for alternative *A* is approximately $197,500.

TABLE 6.1

| *Uncertain Event* | *Calculation of Equivalent Reference Gamble* |
|---|---|
| 4 | (0.4)×(1)+(0.2)×(0.64)+(0.4)×(0)=0.528 |
| 5 | (0.4)×(0.86)+(0.2)×(0.64)+(0.4)×(0.53)=0.684 |
| 6 | (0.4)×(0.71)+(0.2)×(0.64)+(0.4)×(0.59)=0.648 |
| 7 | (0.5)×(0.64)+(0.5)×(0)=0.320 |
| 8 | (0.5)×(0.53)+(0.5)×(0.38)=0.455 |
| 10 | (0.5)×(1)+(0.5)×(0)=0.500 |
| 9 | (0.6)×(0.5)+(0.4)×(0.71)=0.584 |
| 12 | (0.5)×(0.93)+(0.5)×(0.38)=0.655 |
| 11 | (0.6)×(0.655)+(0.4)×(0.64)=0.649 |
| 13 | (0.5)×(1)+(0.5)×(0)=0.500 |
| 15 | (0.5)×(0.86)+(0.5)×(0)=0.430 |
| 14 | (0.6)×(0.43)+(0.4)×(0.64)=0.514 |
| 17 | (0.5)×(0.79)+(0.5)×(0)=0.395 |
| 16 | (0.6)×(0.395)+(0.4)×(0.71)=0.521 |
| 1 | (0.7)×(0.684)+(0.3)×(0.455)=0.6153 |
| 2 | (0.6)×(0.649)+(0.2)×(0.500)+(0.2)×(0.521)=0.5936 |
| 3 | (0.8)×(0.71)+(0.2)×(0)=0.568 |

FIGURE 6.15

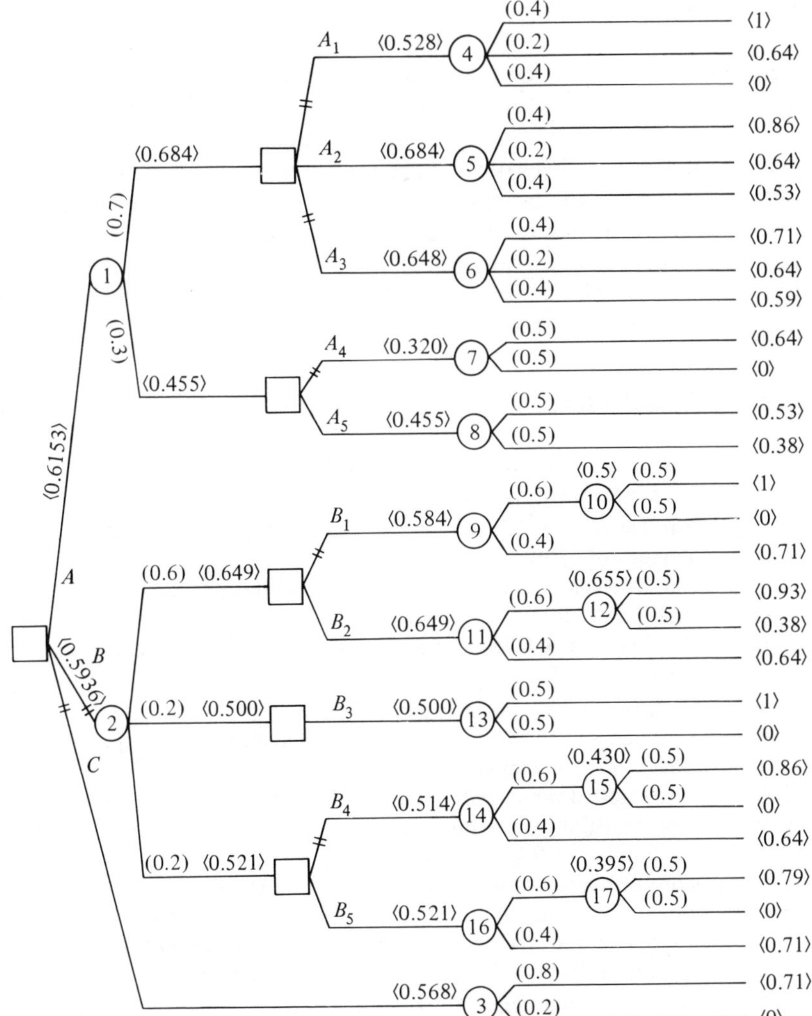


## SUMMARY

*Certainty equivalents* can be calculated using a preference curve and probabilities. Preference curves are assessed using a reference gamble.

A *reference gamble* for a decision problem has two outcomes. One outcome is assigned a payoff greater than or equal to the maximum payoff for any outcome in the decision problem. The other is assigned a payoff equal to or less than the minimum payoff.

A series of probabilities are assigned to winning the reference gamble. A preference curve is assessed by determining certainty equivalents for reference gambles with the different probabilities. The curve is a plot of certainty equivalents versus the probability of winning the reference gamble.

Attitudes toward risk displayed by the preference curve can be categorized as risk averse, risk neutral, and risk seeking. Each has a distinctive shape.

Certainty equivalents for complex uncertain events can be calculated. First, the evaluation units for each outcome are converted into preference numbers using the preference curve. The expected value of these preference numbers is calculated. This expected preference number is reconverted into a certainty equivalent in the evaluation units using the preference curve.

The procedure is based on substituting reference gambles for certain values and reducing compound gambles to a single stage using the standard rules of probability. The alternative with the highest probability of winning the resulting reference gamble is chosen.

## ASSIGNMENT MATERIAL

**6.1.** Suppose that a decision maker assesses the following equivalences, using a reference gamble between $-20K and $120K.

1. Indifferent between a 0.5 chance of winning the reference gamble and a certain amount of $30K.
2. Indifferent between a 0.25 chance of winning the reference gamble and a certain amount of $0.
3. Indifferent between a 0.75 chance of winning the reference gamble and a certain amount of $70K.

(a) Show the three equivalences using diagrams.
(b) Plot the points on a graph of certainty equivalents versus probability of winning the reference gamble.
(c) Connect the plotted points with a smooth line to make a preference curve.
(d) What is the probability of winning the reference gamble that corresponds to a preference number of 0.45 for this problem?
(e) For this problem and decision maker, what is the certain dollar amount that is equivalent to a reference gamble with a probability of winning of 0.3?
(f) For this problem and decision maker, what is the probability of winning the reference gamble that corresponds to a certain dollar value of $50K?

**6.2.** Consider the Pine Mountain Resort, problem 3.1. The following table gives probabilities for various uncertain events faced by Upshaw.

| *Year 1* | *Probability* | *Year 2 Given Year 1* | *Probability* |
|---|---|---|---|
| High demand | 0.3 | High demand | 0.8 |
| | | Medium demand | 0.2 |
| Medium demand | 0.4 | High demand | 0.3 |
| | | Medium demand | 0.6 |
| | | Low demand | 0.1 |
| Low demand | 0.3 | Medium demand | 0.6 |
| | | Low demand | 0.4 |

The state of demand does not depend on any action Upshaw takes. That is, the probabilities are the same regardless of the size of facility he builds.

In considering his problem, Upshaw decided he needed more help in comparing the alternatives. To help, he assessed the following points on a preference curve using a reference gamble between $\$-10$ million and $\$+10$ million.

1. He is indifferent between a reference gamble with a 0.5 chance of winning and $\$-5$ million for certain.
2. He is indifferent between a reference gamble with a 0.75 chance of winning and $0 for certain.
3. He is indifferent between a reference gamble with a 0.92 chance of winning and $5 million for certain.

(a) Plot a preference curve for Upshaw to use on this project using his assessments given above and a smooth curve connecting the points.

(b) Use the preference curve to determine Upshaw's best action. What is the certainty equivalent corresponding to this action?

(c) How does this choice compare with the one Upshaw would have made if he used expected monetary values?

**6.3.** In addition to the questions asked in problem 5.11, do the following:

(a) Determine an appropriate reference gamble.

(b) Using the reference gamble, assess your preference curve.

(c) Assuming that the contributions accrue to you, use the preference curve to determine your choice.

**6.4.** In addition to the questions asked in problem 5.12, do the following:

(a) Determine an appropriate reference gamble.

(b) Using the reference gamble, assess your preference curve.

(c) Use the preference curve to determine your choice.

**6.5. Leslie Electronics, Inc. (D)**

Before Donald Leslie made his decision regarding the electronic portasol contract [see problems 2.7, 5.6, and 5.7, Leslie (A), (B), and (C), respectively], he felt that there was additional information he should consider.

Leslie Electronics was in a fairly critical cash position, and, in fact, its net liquid assets were only $25,000. This meant, by necessity, that Leslie would have to buy many of the materials for the contract on credit, but since this was standard procedure, Leslie was not too worried about this aspect of the problem. He was concerned, however, about the risk associated with this venture. The preference curve shown in Figure 6.16 reflects his attitude toward risk.

Leslie was also concerned that he did not have a better feel for the likelihood of the various outcomes. He called Hans Sturdevant and asked him to come to his office. "Hans," Leslie said, "If we buy the mold, the first thing that we're going to find out is whether or not the housings are acceptable. Can you give me a better idea of how likely it is that we'll be successful?"

"I don't think we have too much to worry about, Mr. Leslie," Sturdevant replied. "As I mentioned before, we've had good luck with this type of casting—I'd say that there's an 80% chance of the mold producing good housings."

After Sturdevant left, Leslie called Audio Concepts, and asked: "Mr. Roth, you said earlier that there's a chance that you won't be needing 100 portasols, but only 50. Can you give me some idea *how* much of a chance there is of that?"

"Well, I don't think there's too much of a chance—the problem is that two of the board members of the recording company think the new San Francisco studio should be a small one, and that their principal studio in Los Angeles should be expanded. The rest of the board members are pretty much convinced that it's in their best interests to build a big showplace of a studio in San Francisco. My best guess at this point in time is that there's about an 85% chance of their building the big studio that would require 100 portasols."

After thanking Roth for his information, Leslie addressed himself to the problem of the value of the mold if he should decide to try manufacturing the housings and if the mold should work. After much consideration he decided to be very conservative and assume that no more housings would be needed. He felt that in the fairly touchy liquid asset position of Leslie Electronics, he should not make any assumptions concerning the future demand for a specialty product such as electric portasols. His best estimate of the salvage value of the $17,500 mold was $500.

(a) Diagram Leslie's decision problem, including all information you think is necessary for him to make a decision.

(b) Determine Leslie's most preferred choice, given his preferences expressed in Figure 6.16.

**FIGURE 6.16**

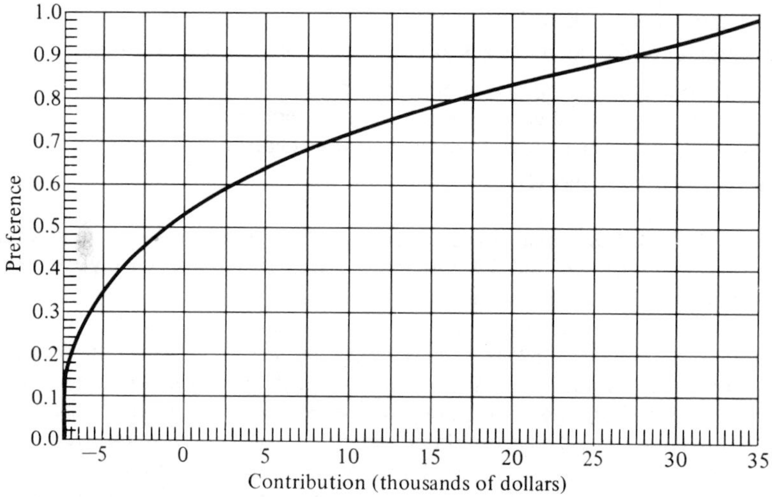

**6.6.** Use the preference curves shown in Figure 6.17 to determine the choices of each board member for the Morris Manufacturing Company case, problem 3.5.

**6.7.** It has just been brought to the attention of a decision maker that he has the opportunity to invest in a certain risky venture. If he is to invest in this venture, however, the necessary capital must be committed within the hour. If the capital is committed and the venture succeeds (the probability of which he estimates to be 1/2), the decision maker will realize a net profit of $8,000 at the end of 3 days. If the venture fails, he will suffer a net loss of $2,000 at the end of 3 days. No other investments are contemplated in this 3-day period.

(a) Assuming that the decision maker's utility for money is given by Figure 6.18, should he make the commitment or not? What is his certainty equivalent for the risky venture?

**FIGURE 6.17**

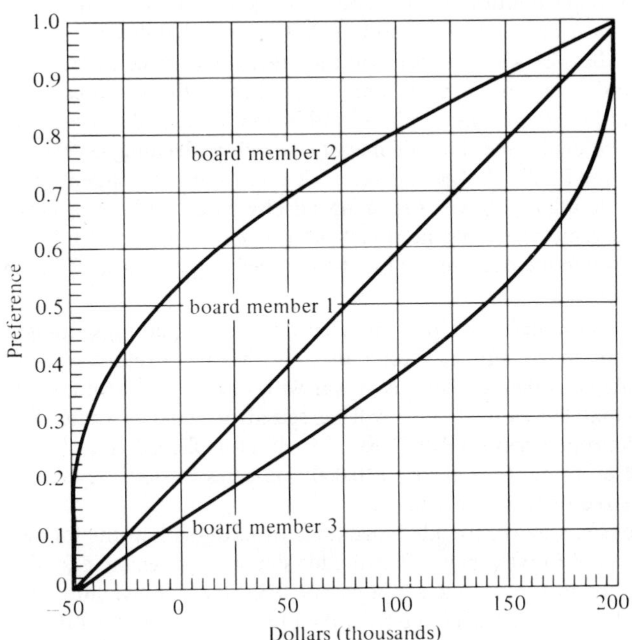


**FIGURE 6.18**

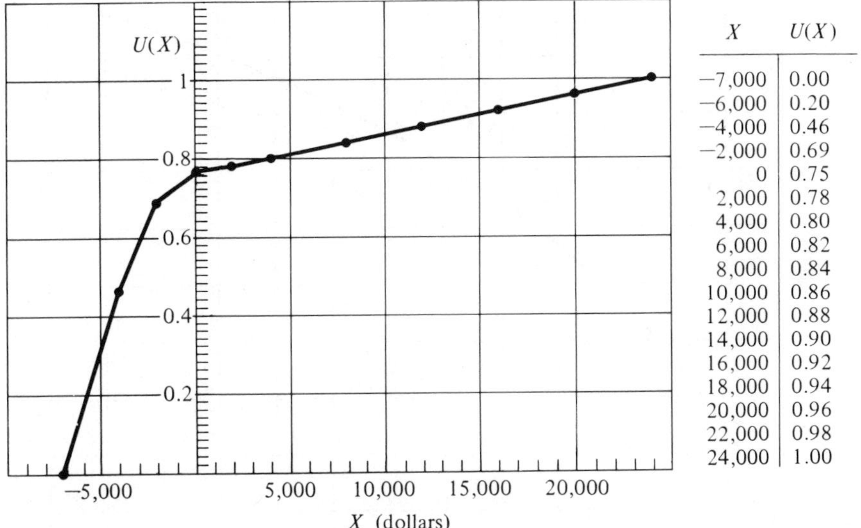


| $X$ | $U(X)$ |
|---|---|
| −7,000 | 0.00 |
| −6,000 | 0.20 |
| −4,000 | 0.46 |
| −2,000 | 0.69 |
| 0 | 0.75 |
| 2,000 | 0.78 |
| 4,000 | 0.80 |
| 6,000 | 0.82 |
| 8,000 | 0.84 |
| 10,000 | 0.86 |
| 12,000 | 0.88 |
| 14,000 | 0.90 |
| 16,000 | 0.92 |
| 18,000 | 0.94 |
| 20,000 | 0.96 |
| 22,000 | 0.98 |
| 24,000 | 1.00 |

(b) Suppose that the decision maker has two identical and independent investment opportunities like those described above. (That is, he has two opportunities *instead* of just one and each has a probability of succeeding of 1/2 regardless of what happens on the other.) Assuming all else to be as before, should he invest in both, one, or neither of the ventures? (*Note:* He must decide on these three options within the hour, and consequently he cannot wait to determine the outcome of one before deciding on the second.)

(c) Suppose finally that he has three identical and independent opportunities like that described above. Assuming all else to be as before, how many of the three ventures should he invest in? (*Note:* As in part (b), he cannot wait to determine the outcome of one before deciding about investing in a second or third.)

6.8. Gordon Cheswicke, Liverpool merchant, is contemplating sending a ship loaded with goods to the British West Indies and having it return with a load of rum. The problem is that England is at war with France and Spain, so there is a good chance that the ship, if sent, will be seized or sunk en route. Should the ship make the round trip safely, Cheswicke will clear £3,000. But if the ship is seized or sunk en route, he will lose £10,000. He assesses that the chances of the ship being seized or sunk are 1 in 10.

Lloyd's, a newly founded insurance firm, offers him the following terms: for a payment of £1,000, they will insure his ship against seizure and all other dangers —if the round-trip voyage is not completed, they will give him £9,000 so that his net will be a loss of £2,000 (he loses the £1,000 premium plus £10,000 on the ship).

**FIGURE 6.19**

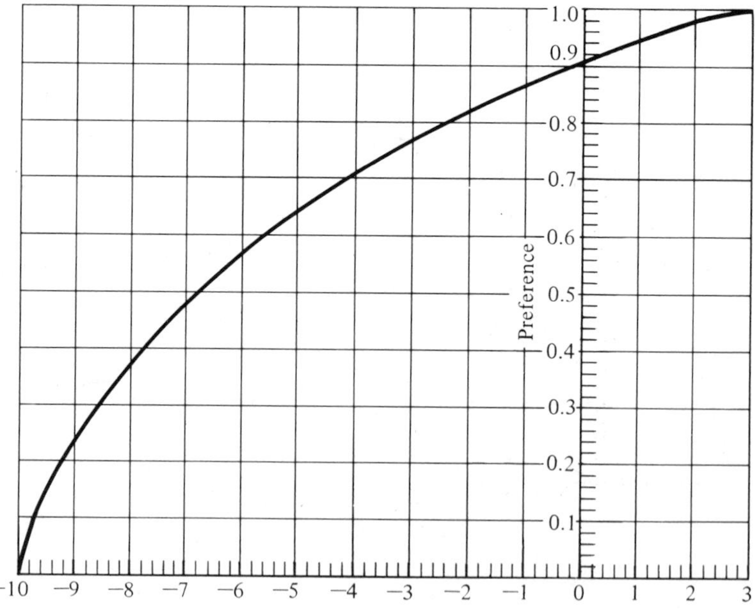

Alternatively, they are willing to insure him for £4,500 for a premium of £475. Cheswicke's preference curve is shown in Figure 6.19.

(a) Diagram the alternatives open to Cheswicke.

(b) Use his preference curve to determine his best course of action.

**6.9** John Barleycorn, a farmer in eastern Washington state, has a decision to make. Barleycorn has under cultivation 1,000 acres of winter wheat, which will be harvested and sold in 2 months. There are two things uncertain about this—Barleycorn does not know how much wheat per acre he will harvest, nor does he know what price he will be able to get for his wheat. Today he has the opportunity to promise to sell some of his wheat for \$3 per bushel rather than taking a chance on what the price will be in 2 months when it is harvested. He is wondering if it might not be a good idea to do this.

This sort of transaction works as follows. Suppose that Barleycorn promises to sell 100K bushels of "future" wheat at this fixed \$3 price.[4] If he harvests 100K bushels of wheat, all of it goes to meet his obligations and he gets \$300K. If he harvests 150K bushels, 100K goes to meet his obligations and the other 50K will be sold at the (currently uncertain) market price that will prevail in 2 months. If this market price is, say, \$4, he will net $\$3 \times 100\text{K} + \$4 \times 50\text{K} = \$500\text{K}$. There is one other possibility—suppose that Barleycorn promised today to sell 150K bushels of "future" wheat for \$3, and that in 2 months his harvest is only 100K bushels. Then to meet his obligations, Barleycorn must obtain another 50K bushels of wheat—he will have to buy those 50K bushels in the market, for the (currently uncertain) market price. If, say, that market price turns out to be \$4, he would net $\$3 \times 150\text{K} - \$4 \times 50\text{K} = \$250\text{K}$. (Carefully note the minus sign!)

The size of Barleycorn's crop depends on the weather in eastern Washington. The weather will be either wet or dry, and Barleycorn assesses probability 0.2 that the weather will be wet. If the weather is wet, Barleycorn will get 100 bushels of

**FIGURE 6.20**

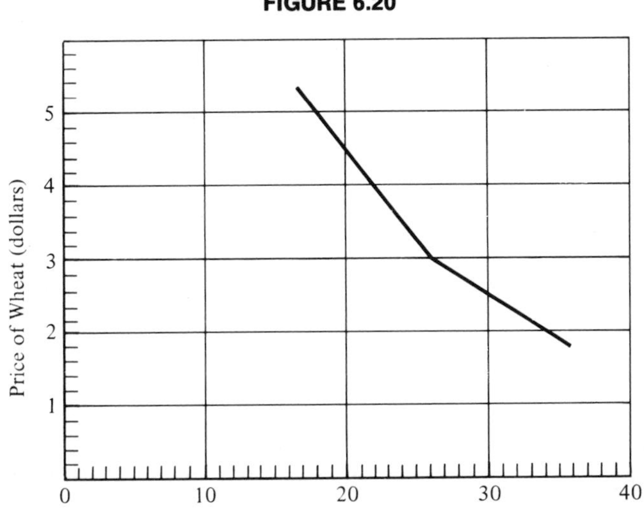


[4]Note that K stands for 1,000. For instance, $100\text{K} = 100{,}000$.

wheat per acre, for a total crop of 100K bushels. If the weather is dry, he will get 150 bushels per acre, for a total of 150K bushels.

The price of wheat in 2 months will be determined by the supply of wheat from two sources, the supply from eastern Washington and the supply from the Prairie Provinces of Canada. Figure 6.20 gives this relationship. The supply of wheat from eastern Washington depends on the weather in eastern Washington—if the weather is wet, the total supply will be 6 million bushels, and if the weather is dry, the total supply will be 10 million bushels. The supply from the Prairie Provinces depends on the weather *there*—if it is wet in the Prairie Provinces, they will supply 12 million bushels, and if it is dry in the Prairie Provinces, they will supply 20 million bushels.

The probability of wet weather in the Prairie Provinces is 0.25. If there is wet weather in eastern Washington, the probability of wet weather in the Prairie Provinces is 1/2.

Barleycorn's attitude toward risk is given by his preference curve in Figure 6.21.

**FIGURE 6.21**

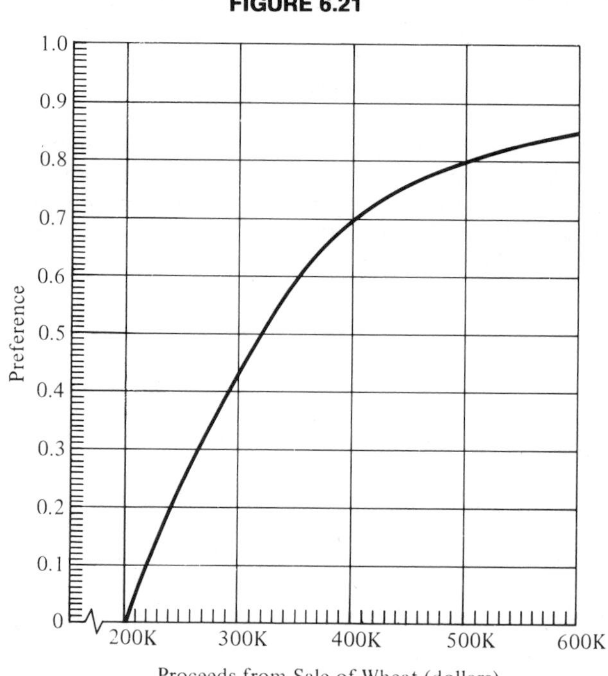


Using the data above, choose among the following three strategies for Barleycorn:

1. Promise to sell 0 bushels of wheat at the fixed price of $3 per bushel.
2. Promise to sell 50K bushels of wheat at the fixed price of $3 per bushel.
3. Promise to sell 150K bushels of wheat at the fixed price of $3 per bushel.

Do *not* try to find the optimal number of bushels for Barleycorn to sell. Just say which of the three strategies is best, which is second best, and which is worst.

# PART 2

# Models and Probability

# 7

# Calculating Probabilities for Compound Events

Basic definitions, concepts, and methods of displaying probabilities were discussed in Chapter 4. These ideas were used to explore the problems of making choices under uncertainty. The probabilities provided information about the uncertain events necessary to complete the model of the decision problem. In this chapter we begin our study of how these probabilities can be obtained for realistic models. Compound events are common in probability models. This chapter discusses compound events and the rules for calculating their probabilities. Figure 7.1 shows how the material fits into the overall discussion.

**FIGURE 7.1**

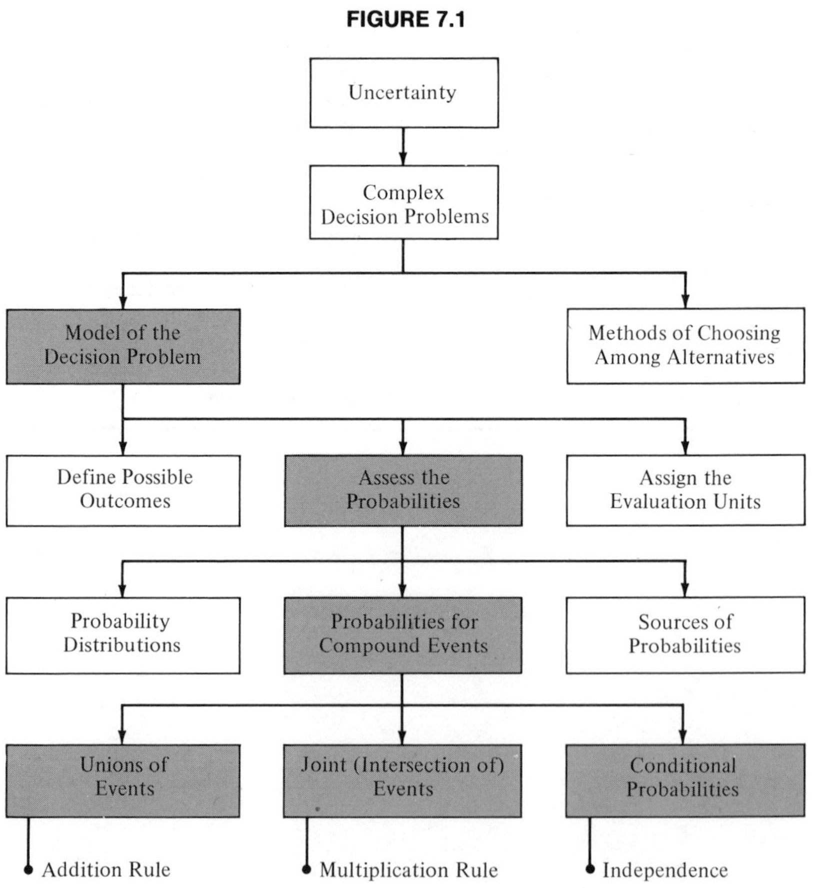

## COMPOUND EVENTS

Two ways events can be compounded are by taking their union and by taking their intersection. Figure 7.2 is a *Venn* diagram showing two events, $H$ and $G$. The compound event formed by their union is written $(H \cup G)$. Figure 7.3 shows two events, $I$ and $J$. The compound event formed by their intersection is written $(I,J)$, (or $(I \cap J)$).

**FIGURE 7.2**

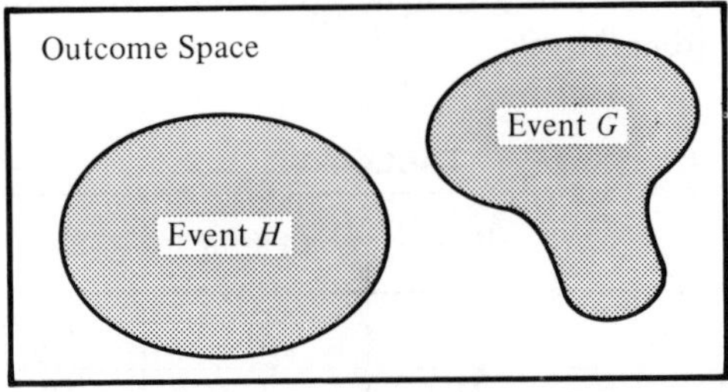


**FIGURE 7.3**

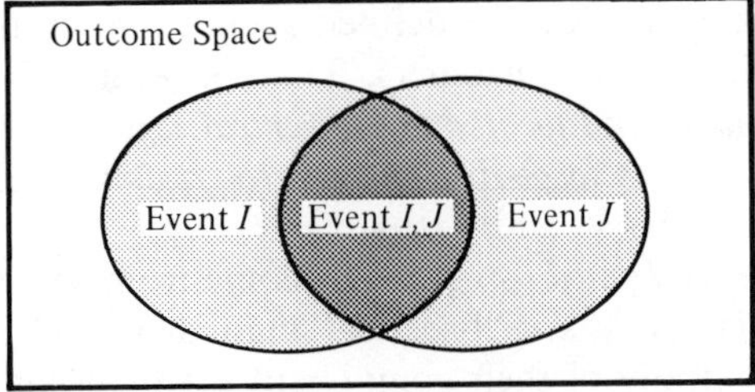


## EXAMPLES OF COMPOUND EVENTS FORMED BY UNIONS

**Example 7.1**

With the urn shown in Figure 7.4, we can draw one of five balls at random. If we define event $A$ as the subset {ball 2} and event $B$ as the subset {ball 3}, then $\{A \cup B\} = \{\text{ball 2, ball 3}\}$.

**FIGURE 7.4**

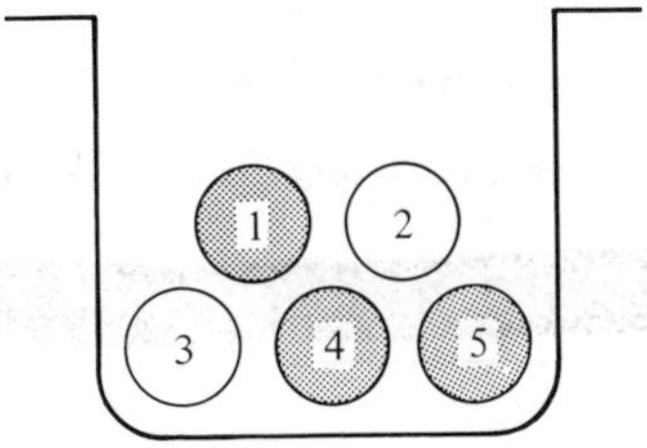

This compound event can also be described as {*light-colored ball*}. (We see from Figure 7.4 that balls 2 and 3 are the only light-colored balls in the urn.) When the collection of a set of separate events forms a natural category (e.g., *light-colored ball*) it can be described either by the category name or as the union of its components.

**Example 7.2**

Assume that you have completed a survey of industrial customers to support a decision on advertising. The customers have been categorized by size and location as shown in Table 7.1. As part of a sampling procedure, you are going to select one customer at random from the set.

**TABLE 7.1**

| | *West* | *Central* | *East* |
|---|---|---|---|
| *Large* | I | II | III |
| *Medium* | IV | V | VI |
| *Small* | VII | VIII | IX |

Each of the nine categories can be defined as an event on the outcome space that includes all industrial customers. That is, event II is the subset of customers that are *large* and *located in the central region*. It is natural to think about the event *customers located in the central region*. This event is defined as the union of events II, V, and VIII.

Compound events *defined using unions* come from some natural aggregation of other events. They are "broader" than their underlying component events. They occur if any of their component events occur. For instance, in Example 7.1, the event *light-colored ball* occurs if either ball 2 *or* ball 3 is drawn.

## THE ADDITION RULE

The addition rule is used to calculate the probability of an event formed by the union of two or more events. It is given below for two events, $A$ and $B$.

**Addition Rule**

***Definition:*** *For two events A and B, the probability of their union is given by*

$$P(A \cup B) = P(A) + P(B) - P(A, B)$$

### Addition Rule for Mutually Exclusive Events

When the events that make up the union are mutually exclusive, the intersection is empty. Therefore, the last term in the rule given above is zero and can be left out. For example the events $G$ and $H$ in Figure 7.2 are mutually exclusive. Therefore, $P(G \cup H) = P(G) + P(H)$.[1]

The events in Example 7.1 are mutually exclusive. If we draw one ball, events $A = \{\text{ball } 2\}$ and $B = \{\text{ball } 3\}$ cannot both occur. Therefore,

$$P(\text{light-colored ball}) = P(A \cup B) = P(A) + P(B)$$

If each ball has an equal chance of being selected, $P(A) = P(B) = \frac{1}{5}$ and $P(\text{light-colored ball}) = \frac{2}{5}$.

The events in Example 7.2 are also mutually exclusive. A customer can only be in one of the nine categories. When surveys such as this are made of populations, the categories are usually designed to be mutually exclusive. To calculate the probability that the customer drawn at random is from the central region, we need to know the probabilities for each category. With these we could use the addition rule and find that

$$P(\text{customer in the central region}) = P(\text{II} \cup \text{V} \cup \text{VIII}) = P(\text{II}) + P(\text{V}) + P(\text{VIII})$$

### Addition Rule for Non-Mutually Exclusive Events

When events are not mutually exclusive, the rule states that the probability of the intersection must be subtracted. Figure 7.3 illustrates a case of two events, $I$ and $J$, that are not mutually exclusive. From the diagram we see that the area represented by the intersection $(I \cap J)$ is included in both $P(I)$ and $P(J)$. It is included twice. Therefore,

$$P(I \cup J) = P(I) + P(J) - P(I,J)$$

which is exactly what the rule states.

A simple example is provided by making a draw from a shuffled deck of cards. Let $A = \{\text{ace}\}$ and $B = \{\text{spade}\}$. The event ace or a spade is $(A \cup B)$. Following the addition rule,

$$P(A \cup B) = P(A) + P(B) - P(A,B)$$

The event $(A,B)$ is both an ace and a spade—the ace of spades. The events $A$ and $B$ are not mutually exclusive. Since $P(A) = \frac{4}{52}$, $P(B) = \frac{13}{52}$, and $P(A,B) = \frac{1}{52}$, $P(A \cup B) = \frac{4}{52} + \frac{13}{52} - \frac{1}{52} = \frac{16}{52}$.

### ●● Addition Rule for More Than Two Events

If the events are mutually exclusive, the addition rule for more than two events is just the simple addition of the probabilities for all events. When events are not mutually exclusive, the rules can become more complicated.

[1]In this form the rule is just one of the three conditions that are given in Chapter 4 as the definition of probability.

For three events, a Venn diagram can be used to derive the rule. For more events this becomes unmanageable. The solution is to combine the events two at a time. This means that you can always use the rule for two events. For instance, assume that you have events $A$, $B$, $C$, and $D$ which are not mutually exclusive, and you are interested in $P(A \cup B \cup C \cup D)$. To illustrate the procedure, we define $L = A \cup B$ and $M = C \cup D$. Therefore, $P(A \cup B \cup C \cup D) = P(L \cup M)$. From the addition rule we have

$$P(L \cup M) = P(L) + P(M) - P(L, M)$$
$$P(L \cup M) = P(A \cup B) + P(C \cup D) - P((A \cup B) \cap (C \cup D))$$

The first two terms can be calculated separately as

$$P(A \cup B) = P(A) + P(B) - P(A, B)$$
$$P(C \cup D) = P(C) + P(D) - P(C, D)$$

The best way to calculate the third term will depend on the information at hand.

## EXAMPLES OF COMPOUND EVENTS FORMED BY INTERSECTIONS

The addition rule for non-mutually exclusive events uses a compound event formed by an intersection. In the card-drawing example, the compound event formed by the intersection was the *ace of spades*. It is described as a compound event because of the original definitions, which were in terms of events $A = \{\text{ace}\}$ and $B = \{\text{spade}\}$. The practice of describing populations by a series of characteristics leads naturally to describing particular outcomes as an intersection. Some examples are given below.

As part of a market survey, assume that you decide two characteristics of potential customers are important: (1) sex, and (2) whether or not they are employed. If we define $F = \{\text{female}\}$ and $E = \{\text{employed}\}$, then the event that a potential customer selected at random is female *and* employed is $(F \cap E)$.

In Example 7.2 (see Table 7.1), categories of interest were company size (large, medium, or small) and location (west, central, or east). The basic events were defined to be I = {large company in the west}, II = {large company in the central region}, III = {large company in the east}, and so on. In this example we formed the event $C = \{$*located in the central region*$\}$. If we define event $L = \{\text{large}\}$, we see that event II can be defined by the intersection of $C$ and $L$. That is, event $\{\text{II}\} = (C \cap L)$. The events I, II, III, and so on, can be defined by intersections of events describing the location and size. Conversely, the events describing location and size can be defined by unions of the events I, II, III, and so on.

Consider tossing two coins. Let $H_1$ be the event heads on coin 1 and $H_2$ the event heads on coin 2. The event that both coins land with heads up is the intersection $H_1 \cap H_2$ (or $H_1, H_2$).

Events *defined using intersections* are a disaggregation of other "broader" events. They occur if *each* of the "broader" categories (events) occur. For instance, event $II = \{C \cap L\}$ described above occurs if the company selected is from the central region *and* it is large.

Events and their probabilities defined as unions and intersections are sometimes given the name *marginal* and *joint*. These terms are widely used and are defined below.

### Marginal Event

**Marginal Event**

***Definition:*** *An event that is modeled by the union of two or more events is sometimes called a* ***marginal event****.*

### Joint Event

**Joint Event**

***Definition:*** *An event that is modeled as the intersection of two or more other events is sometimes called a* ***joint event****.*

## CONDITIONAL PROBABILITIES

Calculation of probabilities for joint events—events defined as the intersection of two or more events—requires an understanding of conditional probabilities.

**Conditional Probability**

***Definition:*** *Given events A and B with P(B) > 0, the* ***conditional probability*** *of event A occurring given that event B has occurred is written P(A|B). It is defined by*

$$P(A|B) = \frac{P(A,B)}{P(B)}$$

A conditional probability is the probability of an event conditioned on the knowledge that some other event has occurred. The notation $P(A|B)$ stands for the probability of event $A$ being true given that event $B$ is true. The "|" should be read "given," meaning "conditioned upon."

### The Concept of Conditional Probability

The following example will be used to explain how we can think about conditional probability.

**Example 7.3**

Assume that we randomly draw two balls from the urn shown in Figure 7.5. The second ball is drawn without replacing the first. Suppose that we are interested in the probability of getting a dark ball on the second draw. Outcome space for the draw is shown in Figure 7.6. Each of the points or simple events in outcome space is equally likely. Therefore, the probability of any event $D_1, D_2, \ldots, D_6$ is $\frac{1}{6}$. Defining $A = \{$dark ball on second draw$\}$, we see $A = \{D_1 \cup D_3 \cup D_5 \cup D_6\}$. Using the addition rule,

$$P(A) = P(D_1) + P(D_3) + P(D_5) + P(D_6) = \tfrac{4}{6}$$

Suppose we are told that the first draw was a dark ball. Now what is the probability that the second ball will be dark?

To illustrate the concept of conditional probability and the formula used to define it, we will go through this calculation three ways.

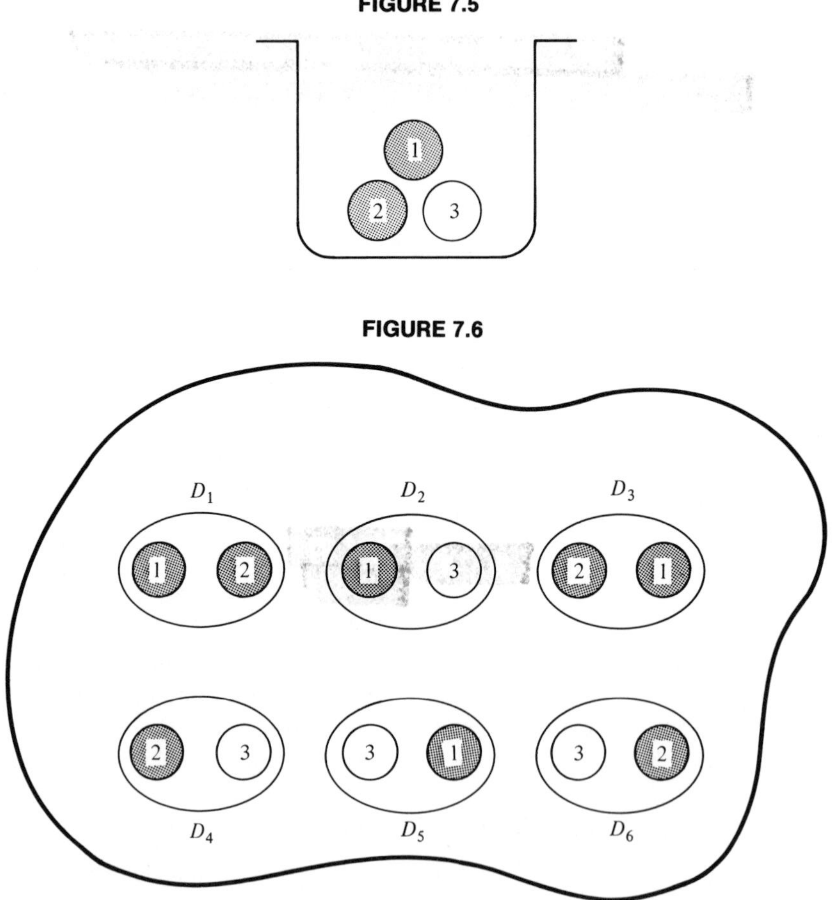


**FIGURE 7.5**

**FIGURE 7.6**

**Approach 1.** If a dark ball has been drawn from the urn we can revise our model of the urn as shown in Figure 7.7. We do not know the number of the dark ball that is left in the urn. But we do not need the number, as long as we are only interested in the probability of drawing a *dark* ball from the modified urn. Using Figure 7.7, we have $P$(dark ball from the modified urn)$=\frac{1}{2}$.

**FIGURE 7.7**

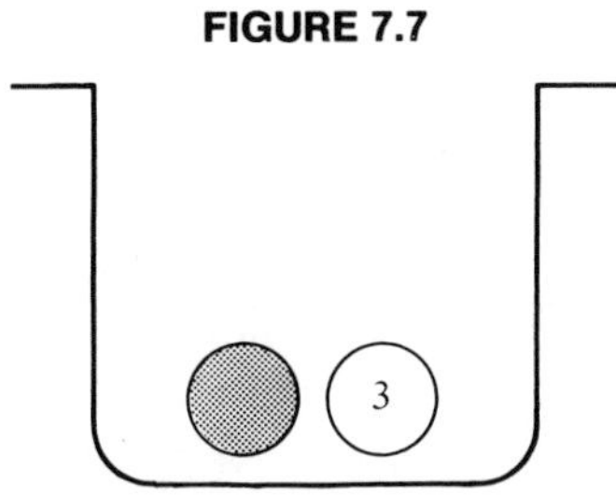


**Approach 2.** Another way to proceed is to recognize that the information on the first draw restricts the available points in the outcome space. Figure 7.8 shows the modified outcome space—all points with a light ball on the first draw have been eliminated. The information that the first draw was *dark* means that the possible outcomes are now $D_1$, $D_2$, $D_3$, and $D_4$. Each of these is still equally likely. But now we only have four possibilities and $P(D_1)=P(D_2)=P(D_3)=P(D_4)=\frac{1}{4}$. The event *dark ball on the second draw with the modified outcome space* is defined as event $C=\{D_1 \cup D_3\}$. Therefore,

$$P(C)=P(D_1)+P(D_3)=\frac{2}{4}=\frac{1}{2}$$

**FIGURE 7.8**

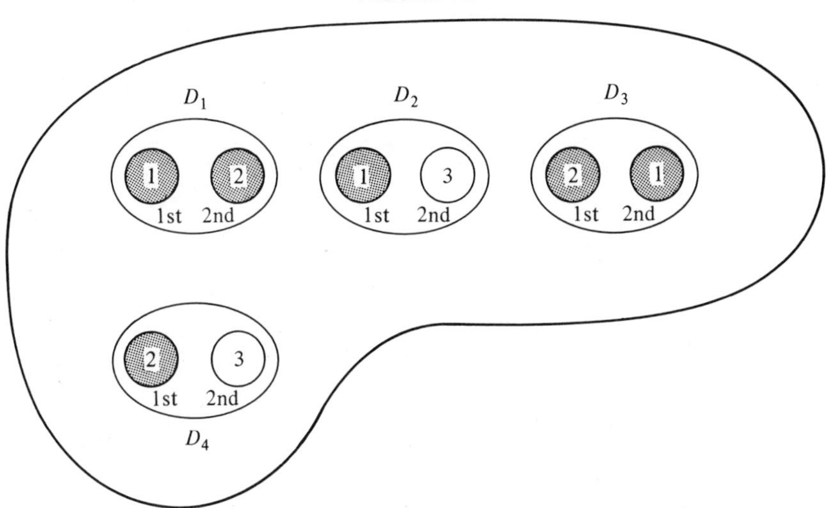

**Approach 3.** We can use the defining formula. Refer again to the complete outcome space (Figure 7.6). Now we define event $B$ to be *dark ball on the first draw*: $B = \{D_1 \cup D_2 \cup D_3 \cup D_4\}$. According to the formula, the probability of *dark ball on the second draw* (event $A$ as defined earlier) given that $B$ has occurred is

$$P(A|B) = \frac{P(A,B)}{P(B)}$$

The joint event $(A, B)$ is defined as $(D_1 \cup D_3 \cup D_5 \cup D_6) \cap (D_1 \cup D_2 \cup D_3 \cup D_4) = (D_1 \cup D_3)$. Therefore,

$$P(A|B) = \frac{P(D_1) + P(D_3)}{P(D_1) + P(D_2) + P(D_3) + P(D_4)} = \frac{\frac{2}{6}}{\frac{4}{6}} = \frac{1}{2}$$

All these approaches give the same, correct, answer for the probability of a dark ball on the second draw if there is a dark ball on the first draw. They are all based on modifying the underlying outcome space by restricting the possible outcomes in light of the information. The first modifies the urn directly. The second restricts the outcome space and determines new probabilities for each outcome. The third does the same thing by taking the ratio of the probabilities that events $A$ and $B$ both occur over the probability that $B$ occurs alone. Another way to look at this third method is by considering the diagram of outcome space shown in Figure 7.9. The information that $B$ has occurred means we are "in" the space enclosed by the light line. The "area" of this space is given by the probability of being in it: $P(B) = \frac{4}{6}$. The shaded part represents the "area" where both $A$ and $B$ occur. This "area" is

**FIGURE 7.9**

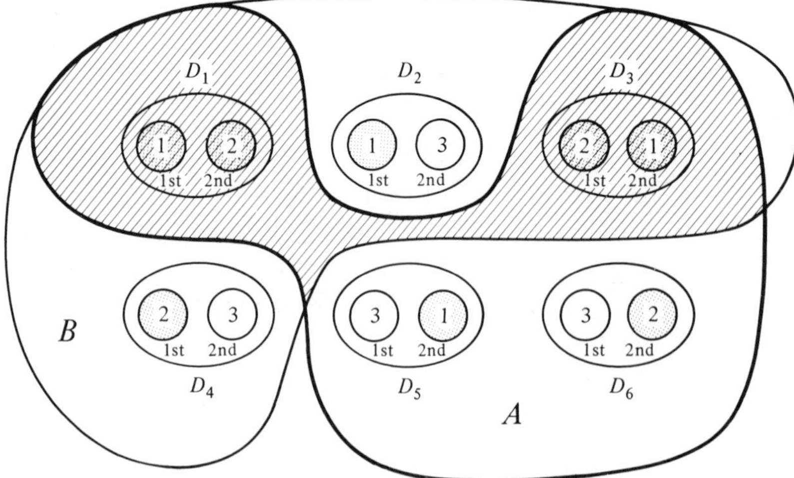

$P(A,B)=\frac{2}{6}$. Now we are told that we are in the space enclosed by the light line with an "area" of $\frac{4}{6}$. What is the probability that we are in the shaded part, with an area of $\frac{2}{6}$? Thinking of the areas as representing probabilities, it is natural to say that the probability of being in the shaded part (i.e., in $(A,B)$) if we know we are in the space enclosed by the light line (i.e., in $B$) is the ratio of the areas. Therefore,

$$P(A|B)=\frac{\frac{2}{6}}{\frac{4}{6}}=\frac{P(A,B)}{P(B)}$$

## Using Tables to Calculate Conditional Probabilities

When calculations involve joint events, tables are often a convenient way to display the information. The next two examples demonstrate how tables can be used to calculate conditional probabilities.

**Example 7.4**

Assume that we have an urn with a total of 100 balls. Twenty-five are red with $W$'s, 20 are red with $L$'s, 35 are green with $W$'s, and 20 are green with $L$'s. The outcome space representing a single draw from the urn is shown in Figure 7.10 (where each square represents one ball).

**FIGURE 7.10**

**Outcome Space for the Urn with 100 Balls (each square represents one ball)**

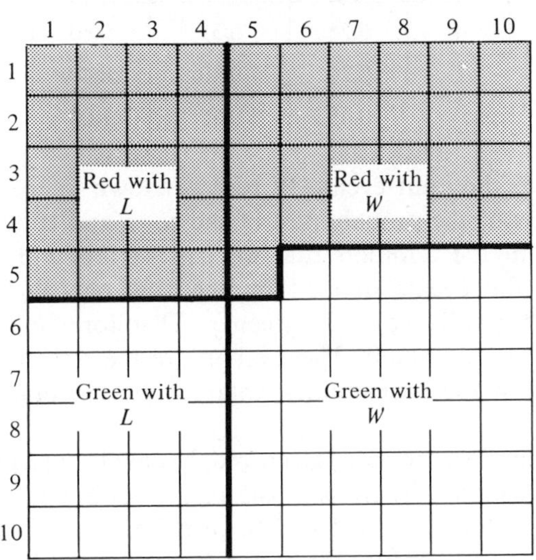


*Outcome Space for the Urn with 100 Balls*
(each square represents one ball)

**TABLE 7.2**

| | Red | Green | |
|---|---|---|---|
| $W$ | 25 | 35 | 60 |
| $L$ | 20 | 20 | 40 |
| | 45 | 55 | 100 |

This outcome space can be summarized using a table. Table 7.2 displays the possible outcomes. For example, the number of red balls with $W$'s is shown in the table entry for row $W$ and column *red* as 25. The row and column totals as well as the grand total are shown in the margin of the table.

Using the table, the conditioning statement, "given red," is interpreted as restricting us to the column labeled red. There are 45 balls in this column. If we are in the red column, we will also be in either row $W$ or $L$. Of the 45 balls in the red column, 25 are in the $W$ row and 20 are in the $L$ row. We can reason that if we are in the red column, the probability of also being in the $W$ row is just $\frac{25}{45}$, or $P(W|\text{red}) = \frac{25}{45} = 0.556$.

A table of *joint probabilities* can also be used to calculate conditonal probabilities. These tables are just like a table that summarizes outcome space. The difference is that *cell* entries are probabilities of the joint event represented by the row and column. Table 7.3 is the table of joint probabilities for this example.

**TABLE 7.3**

| | Red | Green | |
|---|---|---|---|
| $W$ | 0.25 | 0.35 | 0.60 |
| $L$ | 0.20 | 0.20 | 0.40 |
| | 0.45 | 0.55 | 1.00 |

The probability of the joint event $(W, \text{red})$ is shown in the $W$ row and red column. The sums of the probabilities of the rows and columns are given in the margins. From the addition rule we can see that these represent the probabilities for the events defined by the row or column heading. For instance, event $W = \{(W, \text{red}) \cup (W, \text{green})\}$. Therefore, $P(W) = P(W, \text{red}) + P(W, \text{green}) = 0.25 + 0.35 = 0.60$. These tables are the reason the term "marginal" is used to describe probabilities obtained by the union of component events.

The conditioning statement, "given red," is again interpreted as restricting us to the red column. There is a 0.45 chance of being in this column. If we are in the red column, we will also be in either row $W$ or $L$. The chance of being in each row is proportional to the probabilities 0.25 and 0.20. In fact, if we are in the red column, the probability of being in the $W$ row is just $0.25/0.45$, or $P(W|\text{red}) = 0.25/0.45 = 0.556$. We see that this is exactly equivalent to using the formula for conditional probability since $P(W,\text{red})=0.25$ and $P(\text{red})=0.45$.

**Example 7.5**

Consider drawing a single card from a deck of well-shuffled cards. We define two events: event $A$ = card drawn is the ace of spades; event $B$ = card drawn is a spade. Suppose that the drawing has been made and I know the result but you do not. If I tell you event $B$ has occurred (i.e., the card is a spade), what is the probability that event $A$ has occurred? This is a simple conditional probability, $P(A|B)$.

The conditional probability is calculated below using the same two types of tables as used in example 7.4. Table 7.4 is a summary of outcome space for the drawing. Since event $B$ has occurred, we are restricted to row *spade*. The probability of being in column *ace* is $P(A|B)=\frac{1}{13}$.

**TABLE 7.4**

| | *Ace* | *Not Ace* | |
|---|---|---|---|
| *Spade* | 1 | 12 | 13 |
| *Not Spade* | 3 | 36 | 39 |
| | 4 | 48 | 52 |

Table 7.5 is a table of joint probabilities for the drawing. The conditioning statement, "event $B$ has occurred," means we are "in" row *spade*. Therefore,

$$P(A|B)=\frac{\frac{1}{52}}{\frac{13}{52}}=\frac{1}{13}$$

**TABLE 7.5**

| | *Ace* | *Not Ace* | |
|---|---|---|---|
| *Spade* | $\frac{1}{52}$ | $\frac{12}{52}$ | $\frac{13}{52}$ |
| *Not Spade* | $\frac{3}{52}$ | $\frac{36}{52}$ | $\frac{39}{52}$ |
| | $\frac{4}{52}$ | $\frac{48}{52}$ | 1.00 |

## THE MULTIPLICATION RULE

The multiplication rule for calculating probabilities comes directly from the definition of conditional probabilities. The defining formula for the conditional probability of event $A$ given event $B$ is:

$$P(A|B)=\frac{P(A,B)}{P(B)}$$

The multiplication rule is obtained by rearranging the terms of this expression.

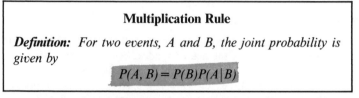

**Multiplication Rule**

***Definition:*** *For two events, A and B, the joint probability is given by*

$$P(A, B) = P(B)P(A|B)$$

The rule specifies that the probability of a joint event $(A,B)$ is the probability of event $B$ multiplied by the conditional probability of event $A$, given $B$. Figure 7.11 displays two events, $A$ and $B$ plus the joint event $(A,B)$. We can interpret the multiplication rule in terms of the areas in the diagram. The probability of $(A,B)$ is represented by the shaded area. This area can be calculated by multiplying the area for event $B$, $P(B)$, by the fraction of the area representing $B$ which also contains $A$, $P(A|B)$. This gives $P(A,B) = P(B)P(A|B)$, which is exactly the multiplication rule.

**FIGURE 7.11**

**Venn Diagram of Two Events A and B**

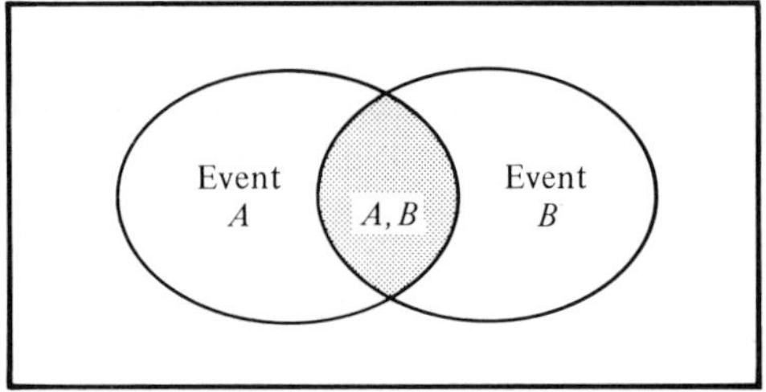


### Reversal of Conditioning

The multiplication rule can be used with either of the events as the *conditioning event*. For two events, $A$ and $B$, we can calculate $P(A,B)$ in either of two ways:

$$P(A,B) = P(B)P(A|B)$$
$$P(A,B) = P(A)P(B|A)$$

**Example 7.6**

Consider a credit manager for a large retail firm. Data indicate that customers fall into three credit categories: good, marginal, and poor. Historically the firm's customers have been 60% good, 30% marginal, and 10% poor. A study has also shown that if a customer is rated good, there is a 90% chance that he pays on time; if a customer is marginal, there is a 50% chance that the payment will be on time; and if a customer is poor, there is only a 20% chance of on-time payment. Suppose that the manager wants to know the probability that a randomly chosen customer will pay on time and be a marginal customer.

Using the multiplication rule, we have

$$P(\text{on time, marginal}) = P(\text{marginal})P(\text{on time}|\text{marginal})$$

From the problem, $P(\text{marginal}) = 0.30$ and $P(\text{on time}|\text{marginal}) = 0.50$. Therefore,

$$P(\text{on time, marginal}) = 0.30 \times 0.50 = 0.15$$

Next consider the probability that a customer chosen at random will be categorized as poor and not pay on time. Using the multiplication rule:

$$P(\text{poor, not on time}) = P(\text{poor})P(\text{not on time}|\text{poor})$$

From the problem, $P(\text{poor}) = 0.10$. The $P(\text{not on time}|\text{poor})$ is not given directly. But we know $P(\text{on time}|\text{poor}) = 0.20$. Since $P(\text{on time}|\text{poor}) + P(\text{not on time}|\text{poor}) = 1.0$ we can calculate $P(\text{not on time}|\text{poor}) = 0.80$. Therefore,

$$P(\text{poor, not on time}) = 0.10 \times 0.80 = 0.08$$

What if the manager wants to know the probability of a customer chosen at random paying on time, regardless of the credit category?

There are three groups such a customer could be in: good, marginal, or poor. Therefore, we can model the event *on time* as the union (on time, good) $\cup$ (on time, marginal) $\cup$ (on time, poor). Using the addition rule, we have

$$P(\text{on time}) = P(\text{on time, good}) + P(\text{on time, marginal}) + P(\text{on time, poor})$$

Using the multiplication rule and the problem information, these joint probabilities are easily calculated.

$$\begin{aligned} \text{P(on time, good)} &= P(\text{good})P(\text{on time}|\text{good}) \\ &= 0.60 \times 0.90 = 0.54 \\ P(\text{on time, marginal}) &= P(\text{marginal})P(\text{on time}|\text{marginal}) \\ &= 0.30 \times 0.50 = 0.15 \\ P(\text{on time, poor}) &= P(\text{poor})P(\text{on time}|\text{poor}) \\ &= 0.10 \times 0.20 = 0.02 \end{aligned}$$

Therefore,

$$\begin{aligned} P(\text{on time}) &= 0.54 + 0.15 + 0.02 \\ &= 0.71 \end{aligned}$$

All these calculations involved joint probabilities. Often, the best approach for these problems is to calculate the table of joint probabilities as the first step. Once this is done, all pertinent questions about probabilities can be answered easily. To illustrate the process for this problem, we start with Table 7.6. The marginal probabilities are given directly in the problem statement and shown in circles.

**TABLE 7.6**

| | *Good* | *Marginal* | *Poor* | |
|---|---|---|---|---|
| *On Time* | | | | |
| *Not on Time* | | | | |
| | 0.60 | 0.30 | 0.10 | 1.00 |

The next step is to fill in enough of the blanks so that the entire table can be completed. Three joint probabilities can be calculated using the multiplication rule and the conditional probabilities, (as we just showed above). These joint probabilities can be added to the table. They are shown circled in Table 7.7. The remaining entries (the numbers not circled in Table 7.7) can be filled in easily since the addition rule requires that the rows and columns must all "add up."

All the questions asked previously can be answered directly from the table. Conditional probabilities also can be calculated. For example, what is the probability that a customer is *good* if he pays *on time*?

$$P(\text{good} \mid \text{on time}) = \frac{P(\text{good, on time})}{P(\text{on time})} = \frac{0.54}{0.71} = 0.76$$

**TABLE 7.7**

| | *Good* | *Marginal* | *Poor* | P(on time) → |
|---|---|---|---|---|
| *On Time* | 0.54 | 0.15 | 0.02 | 0.71 |
| *Not on Time* | 0.06 | 0.15 | 0.08 | 0.29 |
| | 0.60 | 0.30 | 0.10 | 1.00 |

*P*(on time, marginal) → 0.15 (On Time, Marginal)

*P*(poor, not on time) → 0.08 (Not on Time, Poor)

**Example 7.7**

Consider a production manager who wishes to determine if a particular process is under control. The process produces 10% defectives when under control. However, a combination of heat and vibration periodically results in the failure of a sensing device. When this occurs the process produces 30% defectives. Since the sensing device cannot be tested directly, observations of the completed products must be used to determine when the process goes out of control. Testing of the complete process is expensive, so only one unit per batch is tested. If we let $C$ stand for the event *process under control* and $D$ stand for the event *test shows a defective*, the production manager is interested in $P(C|D)$. From past experience we know that the production process is in control 80% of the time.

The problem is to find $P(C|D)$. We know that $P(D|C)=0.10$, $P(D|\sim C)=0.30$, and $P(C)=0.80$. From the definition of conditional probability, we have

$$P(C|D)=\frac{P(C,D)}{P(D)}$$

A table of joint probabilities can be used to calculate the required probabilities. Table 7.8 is the starting point.

**TABLE 7.8**

| | *Control* ($C$) | *Out of Control* ($\sim C$) | |
|---|---|---|---|
| *Defective* ($D$) | | | |
| *Not Defective* ($\sim D$) | | | |
| | 0.80 | 0.20 | 1.00 |

We are told that the probability of a defective when the system is under control is 0.10 and when out of control the probability of a defective is 0.30. Therefore,

$$P(C,D)=P(C)P(D|C)=(0.8)(0.1)=0.08$$

and

$$P(\sim C,D)=P(\sim C)P(D|\sim C)=(0.2)(0.3)=0.06$$

With these two joint probabilities, the table can be completed as shown in Table 7.9.

We can read the inputs to the conditional probability formula directly: $P(C,D)=0.08$, $P(D)=0.14$. Therefore,

$$P(C|D)=\frac{0.08}{0.14}=0.571$$

**TABLE 7.9**

| | *Control* $(C)$ | *Out of Control* $(\sim C)$ | |
|---|---|---|---|
| *Defective* $(D)$ | 0.08 | 0.06 | 0.14 |
| *Not Defective* $(\sim D)$ | 0.72 | 0.14 | 0.86 |
| | 0.80 | 0.20 | 1.00 |

This use of the multiplication rule and conditional probabilities is called Bayes' theorem. An extensive discussion of this method for revising probabilities is given in Chapter 13.

## INDEPENDENCE

The concept of statistical independence is important for building models. It greatly simplifies the calculation of probabilities for joint events. Two events are independent if knowing that one has occurred does not change our assessment of the probability of the other's occurrence.

**Independence**

***Definition:*** *Events A and B are* ***independent,*** *if*

$$P(A|B) = P(A) \quad \text{and} \quad P(B|A) = P(B)$$

*where we assume that* $P(A) > 0$ *and* $P(B) > 0$ *so that the conditional probabilities are well defined.*

This definition applies to two specific *events*. In Chapter 8 we extend the definition to apply to two *uncertain events*. (Remember that an *event* is any subset of outcomes from an *uncertain event*.)

### Example 7.8

An automobile company has compiled the following data concerning cars sold by the company in 1975: among full-size cars, 80% have large engines; 70% of midsize cars sold have small engines; 95% of compacts sold have small engines. Of the cars sold, 20% are full size, 40% are midsize, and 40% are compact. Are the events *a car chosen at random is midsize* and *a car chosen at random has a large engine* independent?

As a first step we construct a table of joint probabilities (Table 7.10). The circled entries are calculated using the conditional probabilities given in the problem and the multiplication rule.

**TABLE 7.10**

| | *Large Engine* | *Small Engine* | |
|---|---|---|---|
| *Full Size* | 0.16 | 0.04 | 0.20 |
| *Midsize* | 0.12 | 0.28 | 0.40 |
| *Compact* | 0.02 | 0.38 | 0.40 |
| | 0.30 | 0.70 | 1.00 |

Let $M = \{\text{a car chosen at random is midsize}\}$ and $L = \{\text{a car chosen at random has a large engine}\}$. If events $M$ and $L$ are independent, $P(M|L) = P(M)$. From Table 7.10, we have

$$P(M|L) = \frac{0.12}{0.30} = 0.40$$
$$P(M) = 0.40$$

Therefore, events $M$ and $L$ are statistically independent.

Are the events $F = \{\text{a car chosen at random is full size}\}$ and $L$ independent? From Table 7.10, we have

$$P(F|L) = \frac{0.16}{0.30} = 0.533$$
$$P(F) = 0.20$$

Therefore, events $F$ and $L$ are *not* statistically independent.

The definition of independence for two events requires that *both* conditional probabilities must equal their unconditional probability. However, when two *events* are being tested for independence, it is only necessary to check one of the conditional probabilities. If one condition holds, the other will also hold.

## MULTIPLICATION RULE FOR INDEPENDENT EVENTS

If two events are known to be independent, the multiplication rule is simplified. Starting with the basic definition, we have $P(A, B) = P(B)P(A|B) = P(B)P(A)$. This is true because independence requires that $P(A|B) = P(A)$.

**Multiplication Rule for Independent Events**

***Definition:*** *If two events A and B are* ***independent,***

$$P(A, B) = P(B)P(A)$$

**Example 7.9**

If we are told that in two tosses of a fair coin, the events *heads on toss 1* and *heads on toss 2* are independent, what is the probability of two heads?

The knowledge that the tosses and events are independent and the coins are *fair* allows us to calculate:

$$\begin{aligned} P(\text{heads on toss 1, heads on toss 2}) &= P(\text{heads on toss 1}) \\ &\quad \times P(\text{heads on toss 2}) \\ &= (0.5) \times (0.5) = 0.25 \end{aligned}$$

## ●● RELATIONSHIP BETWEEN MUTUALLY EXCLUSIVE EVENTS AND INDEPENDENT EVENTS

Two events $A$ and $B$ are mutually exclusive if $A \cap B = \phi$ (i.e., $A$ and $B$ have no elements in common). A question often arises about the relationship between mutually exclusive events and independent events. To illustrate the relationship, consider *mutually exclusive* events $A$ and $B$ with $P(A) > 0$ and $P(B) > 0$, as shown in Figure 7.12. We know that $P(A) > 0$, but $P(A|B) = P(A, B)/P(B) = 0$. Therefore, events $A$ and $B$ are *not* independent if they are mutually exclusive, each with a positive probability of occurring.

If events are *not mutually exclusive*, they can be either independent or dependent. First consider events $C$ and $D$ which are shown in Figure 7.13.

**FIGURE 7.12**

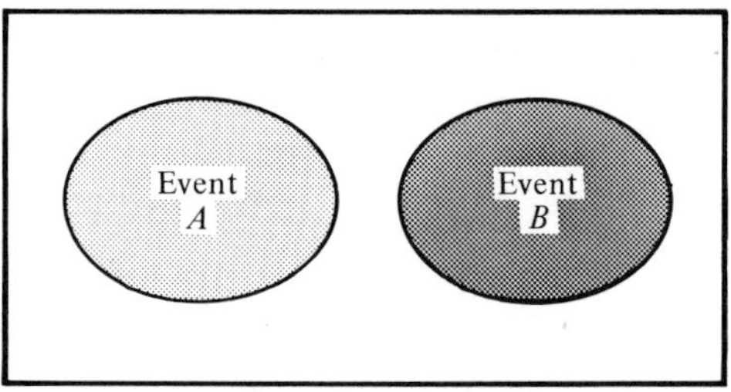


**FIGURE 7.13**

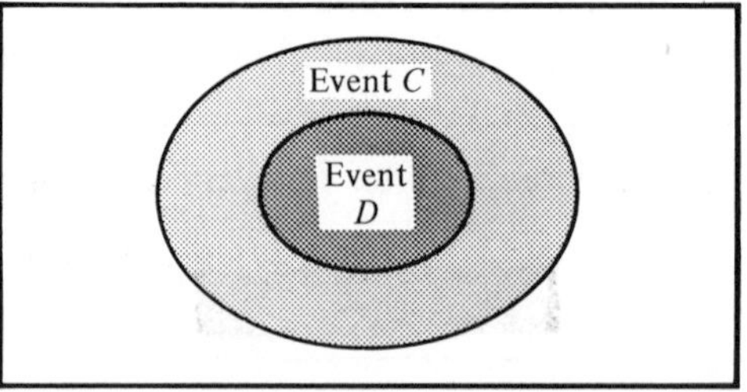

FIGURE 7.14

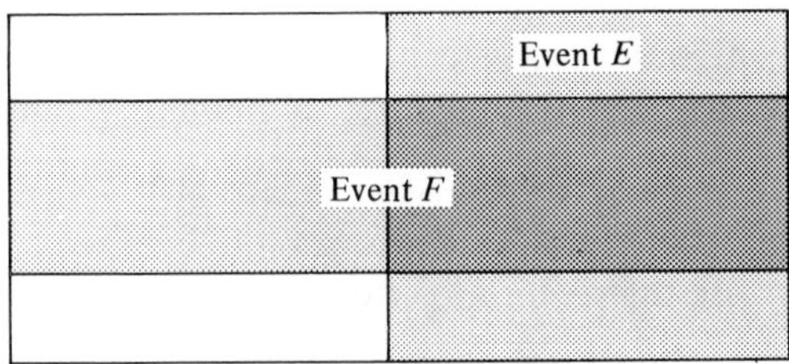


We see that $P(C)<1$ and $P(D)<1$. Since $P(C|D)=1$, events $C$ and $D$ are *not* independent. Next, consider events $E$ and $F$ shown in Figure 7.14. From the figure we have $P(E)=\frac{1}{2}$ and $P(F)=\frac{1}{2}$. Moreover, $P(F|E)=\frac{1}{2}$ and $P(E|F)=\frac{1}{2}$. Therefore

$$P(E)=P(E|F),$$
$$P(F)=P(F|E),$$

making the events $E$ and $F$ statistically independent.

Consider an urn with 100 balls. The makeup is as follows:

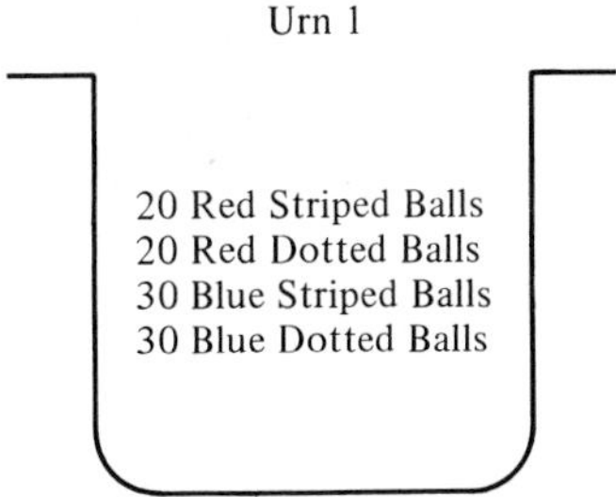


Define

$$R=\text{event ball drawn is red}$$
$$B=\text{event ball drawn is blue}$$
$$S=\text{event ball drawn is striped}$$
$$D=\text{event ball drawn is dotted}$$

Consider the events $R$ and $(R,D)$ (i.e., the events *draw a red ball* and *draw a red dotted ball*). Clearly, $R\cap(R,D)\neq\phi$, and therefore the two events are not mutually exclusive. $P(R)=P(R,S)+P(R,D)=0.20+0.20=0.40$ and $P(R|(R,D))=1$. Therefore, events $R$ and $(R,D)$ are not independent either.

Next, consider events $R$ and $S$ (i.e., the event *a red ball is drawn* and the event *a striped ball is drawn*. Again $R\cap S=(R,S)\neq\phi$, and therefore the two events are not mutually exclusive. In this case we have

$$P(R|S)=\frac{P(R,S)}{P(S)}=\frac{0.20}{0.50}=0.40$$

Therefore, events $R$ and $S$ are independent.

## SUMMARY

Probabilities for compound events can be calculated from the probabilities of the component events. The two types of compound events considered here are:

*Marginal Events:* the union of two or more events.
*Joint Events:* the intersection of two or more events.

The calculations are done using two basic rules: *Addition Rule*, and *Multiplication Rule*.

*Addition Rule:* For two events $A$ and $B$, $P(A \cup B) = P(A) + P(B) - P(A, B)$.

*Addition Rule for Mutually Exclusive Events:* For two mutually exclusive events $A$ and $B$, $P(A \cup B) = P(A) + P(B)$.

The multiplication rule relies on the concept of conditional probability.

*Conditional Probability:* Given two events $A$ and $B$ with $P(B) > 0$, the conditional probability of event $A$ given event $B$ has occurred is written

$$P(A|B) = \frac{P(A,B)}{P(B)}$$

*Multiplication Rule:* For two events $A$ and $B$, $P(A,B) = P(B)P(A|B)$.

A special case of the multiplication rule is used for *independent* events.

*Independent Events:* Two events $A$ and $B$ are *independent* if $P(A|B) = P(A)$.

*Multiplication Rule for Independent Events:* If two events $A$ and $B$ are *independent*, $P(A,B) = P(B)P(A)$.

These rules, definitions, and concepts are helpful in clarifying complex decisions under uncertainty. Their purpose is to provide probabilities for models used in the decision problems. Chapter 8 extends these concepts to more general settings.

## ASSIGNMENT MATERIAL

**7.1.** Consider an outcome space, for tossing two coins, which identifies each possible outcome for the two coins (assume each coin will either land heads or tails). Name the elements in the following:

(a) Event $A$ = *1 or more heads*
(b) Event $B$ = *fewer than two heads*

(c) The *union of A* or $B$ $(A \cup B)$
(d) The *intersection of A* and $B$
(e) The *intersection of A* and $(A \cap B)$
(f) The *union of A* and $(A \cap B)$

**7.2.** The personnel office of J. B. Whickers Company has files for 18,000 employees. Their breakdown by age and sex is as follows:

| | *Sex* | | |
|---|---|---|---|
| *Age* | *Female (F)* | *Male (M)* | *Total* |
| Under 25 | 2,700 | 900 | 3,600 |
| 25–35 | 4,320 | 2,880 | 7,200 |
| Over 35 | 2,160 | 5,040 | 7,200 |
| Total | 9,180 | 8,820 | 18,000 |

If one file is selected at random from the personnel office, what is the probability that it represents:

(a) *An employee 35 years old or under?*
(b) *A female employee 35 or under?*
(c) *Either a male employee or an employee over 35?*
(d) *A male employee over 35?*

**7.3.** A survey of individuals concerning a particular television commercial yielded the following data:

Overall, 12% of the individuals said that they "*recalled the product's name and were favorably impressed by the commercial,*" 28% said that they "*recalled the product's name and were unfavorably impressed,*" and the remaining 60% "*could not recall the product's name.*"

The survey also classified individuals according to their annual income, into categories *high income* (over \$16K per year) and *low income*. Exactly 30% were in the *high income* category. Of this group of high income individuals, 20% *recalled the product's name and were favorably impressed*, 40% *recalled the product's name and were unfavorably impressed*, and 40% *could not recall the product's name*.

Use these data to fill in the following joint probability table for the characteristics of an individual chosen at random from this survey. Be sure to supply the marginal probabilities.

| | *High Income* | *Low Income* | |
|---|---|---|---|
| *Recalled the Product's Name and Was Favorably Impressed* | | | |
| *Recalled the Product's Name and Was Unfavorably Impressed* | | | |
| *Could Not Recall the Product's Name* | | | |
| | | | |

**7.4.** The analysts at Acme Labs have assessed the joint probabilities given in the following table for a new product introduction competition with CB Labs.

| | *Acme Takes* 6 *months* | *Acme Takes* 12 *Months* | *Acme Takes* 18 *Months* | |
|---|---|---|---|---|
| *CB Takes* 6 *Months* | 0.14 | 0.12 | 0.09 | |
| *CB Takes* 12 *Months* | 0.05 | 0.25 | 0.20 | |
| *CB Takes* 18 *Months* | 0.01 | 0.03 | 0.11 | |

(a) What is the probability that Acme takes 12 months and CB takes 18 months?
(b) What is the probability that CB takes 6 months?
(c) What is the probability that CB takes 12 months given that Acme takes 18 months?
(d) Are the events *Acme takes 18 months* and *CB takes 12 months* independent?
(e) What is the probability that CB beats Acme into production by 6 months or more?

**7.5.** Abbott Labs is considering the development of a new product—rotowidgets. The company's main concern is that their arch competitors, Costello Design, is also setting out to develop the rotowidget and might get it into production before Abbott does.

The analysts at Abbott figure that it will take 6 months or 12 months or 18 months for Abbott to get rotowidgets into production, and they assess probabilities 0.2 for 6 months, 0.5 for 12 months, and 0.3 for 18 months.

These analysts also believe that it will take 6 months or 12 months or 18 months for Costello to get rotowidgets into production, but because of Costello's experience with a similar product, rotogizmos, they assess probabilities 0.3, 0.5, and 0.2 for 6 months, 12 months, and 18 months, respectively.

Furthermore, these analysts assess that:

(1) If it takes Abbott 6 months, Costello will surely be in production in either 6 months or 12 months—and each of these is equally likely.
(2) If it takes Abbott 18 months, Costello will take either 12 months or 18 months—and each of these is equally likely.

(a) Write in symbols the probability statements (1) and (2). Use the following notation:

A6 = event that *Abbott takes 6 months*
A12 = event that *Abbott takes 12 months*
A18 = event that *Abbott takes 18 months*
C6 = event that *Costello takes 6 months*
C12 = event that *Costello takes 12 months*
C18 = event that *Costello takes 18 months*

(b) Completely fill in the table of joint probabilities below. Be sure to include the marginal probabilities.

| | *Abbott Takes 6 Months* | *Abbott Takes 12 Months* | *Abbott Takes 18 Months* | |
|---|---|---|---|---|
| *Costello Takes 6 Months* | | | | |
| *Costello Takes 12 Months* | | | | |
| *Costello Takes 18 Months* | | | | |
| | | | | |

**7.6.** A survey research firm is interested in analyzing the market for appliances in a community. There are 250 families broken down according to size of family, ownership of an automatic clothes washer, and home ownership.

| | *Families of 2 Persons or Less* | | *Families of More Than 2 Persons* | |
|---|---|---|---|---|
| | *Has Washer* | *No Washer* | *Has Washer* | *No Washer* |
| *Own Home* | 54 | 40 | 36 | 20 |
| *Don't Own Home* | 36 | 20 | 24 | 20 |

(a) If a family selected at random has more than two persons and does not have a washer, what is the probability that it is a home owner?

(b) Are the events *home ownership* and *ownership of a washer* independent? Why?

**7.7.** A local milk producer is studying the users of its products. A sample of households is selected. In this group, 40% are users of its milk and 30% are users of its yogurt.

(a) Suppose that a household is to be selected at random from the sample group. Further suppose that of the households selected who use the company's milk, 60% use its yogurt. What is the probability that a household selected at random will be a user of both the company's milk and its yogurt?

(b) What is the probability that a household uses neither the milk nor yogurt produced by the company?

**7.8.** A local milk producer classified a sample of households according to the weekly quantity of product used. The results are tabulated below.

|  | More Than 1 Gallon Milk | 1 Gallon Milk | No Milk |
|---|---|---|---|
| More Than 1 Quart Yogurt | 4% | 4% | 2% |
| 1 Quart Yogurt | 10% | 12% | 8% |
| No Yogurt | 16% | 4% | 40% |

(a) If you are told a household selected at random uses 1 quart of the producer's yogurt, what is the probability that it uses 1 or more gallons of the producer's milk?
(b) Are the events *no milk* and *1 quart yogurt* independent?
(c) Are the events *1 or more gallons milk* and *1 quart yogurt* independent?

**7.9.** Westly Salt Company was trying to evaluate a new salt package—the rectangular box. The chief competitor, Thornton Company, was also trying to evaluate the change to a new package. Since the margins are low, production costs are very important to both firms and ultimately important in their overall competitive position. Westly's production manager, Walt Cracker, determined that the cost would be either 5 cents, 10 cents, or 15 cents for the new package with probability 0.2, 0.5, and 0.3, respectively. Based on his knowledge of Thornton's production capabilities, he decided that Thornton's costs would be either 5 cents or 12 cents with probabilities 0.5, 0.5, respectively. If Westly's costs are 5 cents, he felt that Thornton's costs would be 5 cents with probability 0.9. If Westly's costs are 15 cents, he felt that Thornton's costs would be 12 cents with probability 0.8.

(a) What is the probability that Westly's cost is 10 cents and Thornton's cost is 5 cents?
(b) What is the probability that Thornton's cost is 12 cents given that Westly's cost is 10 cents?

**7.10.** A consultant for Westly Salt Company has done a study of the competitive position on production costs compared with Thornton Company. The result is the following table of joint probabilities:

|  |  | Westly's Cost |  |  |
|---|---|---|---|---|
|  |  | 5¢ | 10¢ | 15¢ |
| Thornton's Cost | 5¢ | 0.20 | 0.10 | 0.05 |
|  | 10¢ | 0.05 | 0.25 | 0.05 |
|  | 15¢ | 0.05 | 0.05 | 0.20 |

(a) Complete the table by filling in the marginal probabilities.
(b) Are the events *Westly's cost 5 cents* and *Thornton's cost 5 cents* independent?
(c) What is the probability that Westly's costs are lower than Thornton's?
(d) What is the probability that Westly's costs are lower than Thornton's if Thornton's costs are 15 cents?

# 8

# Discrete Random Variables, Outcome Spaces, and Calculating Probabilities

The three phases of the model building process—*define possible outcomes*, *assess the probabilities*, and *assign the evaluation units*—are interrelated. The main interaction arises because the definition of outcome space affects our ability to complete the other two phases. This chapter discusses the interaction and introduces the concept of a *random variable*. The model-building process can be viewed as defining the random variable of interest and calculating its probability distribution. Figure 8.1 shows how the material fits in with previous chapters. We continue to concentrate on uncertain events that are modeled by a set of discrete outcomes. In Chapter 9 the concepts and ideas are generalized to uncertain events with continuous outcomes.

**FIGURE 8.1**

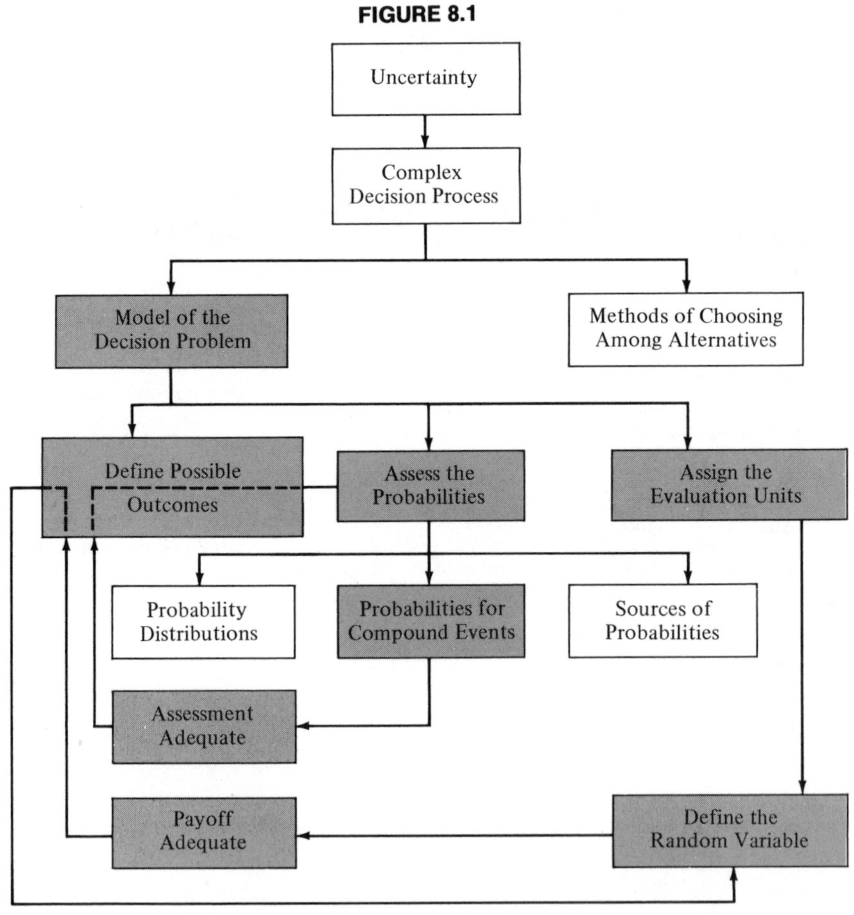

## DEFINING OUTCOME SPACE

The starting point for building a model under uncertainty is specifying outcome space. Diagrams and tables are tools to help in this part of the modeling process. The *decision diagrams*, discussed in Chapter 3, provide the most important tool for defining outcome spaces. The *end points* in a *decision diagram* represent the *outcome space* for the model of the decision problem.

There is usually more than one possible definition of outcome space for an uncertain event. To illustrate the point, consider tossing two coins. Two equally good definitions of outcome space for this uncertain event are:

$\Omega_A = \{$two heads $(2H)$, heads and tails $(HT)$, two tails $(2T)\}$

$\Omega_B = \{$heads on coin 1 and heads on coin 2 $(H_1, H_2)$, heads on coin 1 and tails on coin 2 $(H_1, T_2)$, tails on coin 1 and heads on coin 2 $(T_1, H_2)$, tails on coin 1 and tails on coin 2 $(T_1, T_2)\}$

These two definitions are displayed as points in Figure 8.2. Both definitions are correct. The difference, of course, is that in $\Omega_B$ we kept track of the outcome for each coin, while in $\Omega_A$ we only specified outcomes in terms of the two coins taken together.

**FIGURE 8.2**

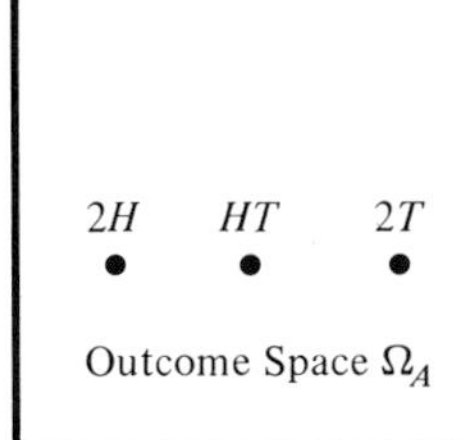


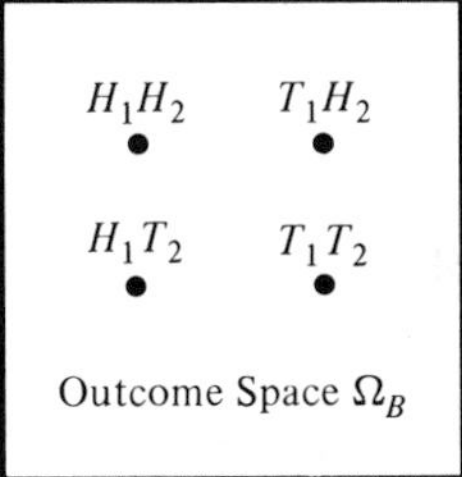


If we were betting on the total number of heads, $\Omega_A$ would be adequate. However, if the payoff depended on which coin (number 1 or number 2) landed with a head, $\Omega_B$ would be required. Outcome space $\Omega_B$ could also be used for betting on the total number of heads. The total number of heads can be determined from $\Omega_B$ as well as $\Omega_A$. In fact, if we know which outcome in $\Omega_B$ occurred, we can always determine the outcome in $\Omega_A$. Formally, we say that $\Omega_B$ is *finer* than $\Omega_A$. When the cost of gathering and processing information is zero, we can prove the intuitive result that you are never worse off using a finer outcome space.[1] This result does not eliminate the problem of

[1]This is a basic result in information economics called Blackwell's theorem. See J. S. Demski, *Information Analysis* (Reading, Mass.: Addison-Wesley 1972), for a discussion of this result and other aspects of information economics.

choosing an outcome space because the costs of gathering and processing information for the finest possible outcome space may be prohibitive. In cases such as tossing two coins, the differential costs between $\Omega_A$ and $\Omega_B$ are trivial. However, in a more complicated problem, information costs often become important.

### Payoff Adequacy

From the perspective of model building, there are two concepts that provide some guidance in deciding on the proper description of outcome space. The first is the concept of *payoff adequacy*.

> **Payoff Adequacy**
>
> ***Definition:*** *An outcome space is* ***payoff-adequate*** *if the elemental description of the points is adequate to determine the payoffs or evaluation units for each point.*

If the payoffs for the two-coin problem were \$1 if coin 1 lands with a head, \$2 if coin 2 lands with a head, and \$0 otherwise, $\Omega_B$ would be payoff-adequate. $\Omega_A$ would not. If the payoff were \$1 per head, then both $\Omega_A$ and $\Omega_B$ would be payoff adequate. The basic idea is that the description of outcome space must be detailed enough so that units of evaluation can be assigned to each point. For example, if the unit to be used for evaluation is contribution, the description of each point in outcome space must allow the price, quantity sold, and cost of production to be determined.

### Assessment Adequacy

The second concept that can be used in developing the description of outcome space is *assessment adequacy*.

> **Assessment Adequacy**
>
> ***Definition:*** *An outcome space is* ***assessment-adequate*** *if the elemental description of the points is adequate for the decision maker to assess probabilities for each point.*

For example, if we want to use the classical definition of probability in the two-coin problem, we cannot use $\Omega_A$, since the outcomes are not equally likely. The elements in $\Omega_B = \{(H_1, H_2), (H_1, T_2), (T_1, H_2)(T_1, T_2)\}$ *are* equally likely, if we assume a fair coin. Therefore, the probability of each point is $\frac{1}{4}$. In $\Omega_A = \{2H, HT, 2T\}$, the outcome $HT$ can occur in two ways, $(H_1, T_2)$ and

$(T_1, H_2)$. Therefore, we cannot directly assess the probabilities for each outcome using the classical definition. In fact, if asked to calculate the probability of $HT$, we would naturally resort to using $\Omega_B$. The basic idea is that the outcome space must be structured so that probabilities can be assessed for each point.

## RANDOM VARIABLES

Because of our emphasis on decisions and models to support choices among alternatives, we have been using random variables all along. The *evaluation units* assigned to the end points of a decision diagram (e.g., contribution) are specific values of a *random variable*. The concept of a random variable is used extensively in probability theory and will make it easier to discuss some aspects of probability. From our perspective a more descriptive term than random variable is *evaluation model for points in outcome space*. Random variables go hand in hand with outcome spaces. Together, they define and place numerical values on all possible outcomes of an uncertain event. The term *random variable* is used because the *actual value* is the result of an uncertain event.

Consider again tossing two coins and the outcome spaces shown in Figure 8.2. There are several bets one could make on the coin tosses. For instance: **Bet 1,** receive $\$-1$ if two heads come up, receive \$0 if a head and a tail come up, receive \$1 if two tails come up; **Bet 2,** receive $\$-1$ if either two heads or two tails come up, receive \$2 if a head and tail come up. The uncertain event, tossing two coins, is identical for both bets. The outcome space, $\Omega_A$, in Figure 8.2 is an adequate and natural way to model the uncertain event. The differences between the two bets is due to the payoffs from the possible outcomes. The points in outcome space are evaluated differently. The bets constitute different random variables defined on the same outcome space. They are "random" because the *value* of the bets depends on the tossing of two coins. Table 8.1 shows the values taken on by the two random variables.

Technically, a random variable defines a number for each point in outcome space (i.e., it is a *rule of correspondence* that assigns numbers to the points in outcome space). Sometimes it is easier to think about the result of

**TABLE 8.1**

| *Outcome Space Description* | *Values of the Random Variable for Bet 1* | *Values of the Random Variable for Bet 2* |
|---|---|---|
| 2H | $\$-1$ | $\$-1$ |
| HT | 0 | 2 |
| 2T | 1 | $-1$ |

the assignment process as the random variable. That is, we may view applying an evaluation formula to the points in outcome space as "creating" a random variable. Strictly speaking, the evaluation formula itself is the random variable. The *results* of applying it to the points in outcome space are the particular values that the random variable can take on. When we use the term *random variable* we mean the overall defining relationship. The specific outcomes are referred to as the *values* of the random variable.

**Random Variable**

***Definition:*** *A* ***random variable*** *is a rule of correspondence between the points in an outcome space and numbers (i.e., it is a function). It is random in the sense that the actual numerical value achieved depends on the outcome. The rule of correspondence is represented by a formula, table, or other procedure that defines the random variable.*

For example, we often use *contribution* to evaluate outcomes. *Contribution* is a random variable defined to be *revenue–variable cost*. Depending on the possibly uncertain outcomes on revenue and cost, we can specify a dollar value for contribution. For instance, if revenue = \$100 and cost = \$60, we say the value of the random variable is \$100 − \$60 = \$40.

**Example 8.1**

A construction job has two components, project $A$ and project $B$. These projects can be undertaken simultaneously. Both projects $A$ and $B$ must be completed to finish the overall job. The outcome space for the possible completion times in weeks for each project is shown in Figure 8.3. What is the probability distribution for job-completion time?

**FIGURE 8.3**

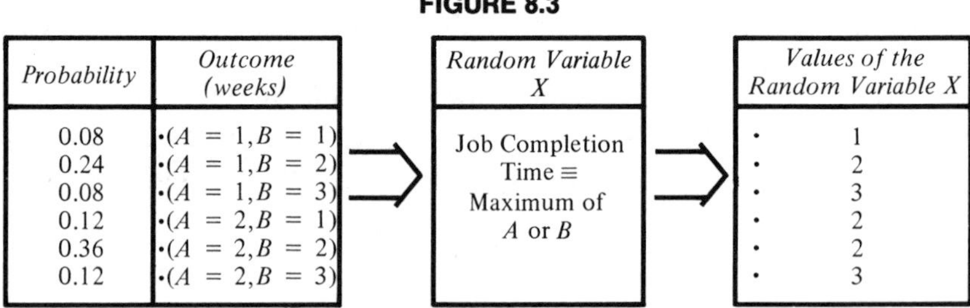

Probability
Outcome (weeks)
0.08 •(A = 1, B = 1)
0.24 •(A = 1, B = 2)
0.08 •(A = 1, B = 3)
0.12 •(A = 2, B = 1)
0.36 •(A = 2, B = 2)
0.12 •(A = 2, B = 3)
Random Variable X
Job Completion Time ≡ Maximum of A or B
Values of the Random Variable X
1
2
3
2
2
3


The random variable in this problem is job-completion time. It is defined as the maximum of completion times for projects $A$ and $B$. If we designate it by $X$, we can formally write

$$X = \text{maximum of the completion times for projects } A \text{ and } B$$

The specific values that the random variable can take on are: 1 week, 2 weeks, and 3 weeks. From Figure 8.3 we see that the probability distribution for the random variable $X$ is

$$P(X=1 \text{ week})=0.08$$
$$P(X=2 \text{ weeks})=0.72$$
$$P(X=3 \text{ weeks})=0.20$$

**Example 8.2**

Consider the same construction job as in Example 8.1. Instead of looking at completion time, what is the distribution of the difference between completion times for projects $A$ and $B$?

The random variable in this case is the difference in completion times. If we designate it by the letter $Y$, we can write

$$Y=|(\text{completion time for } A)-(\text{completion time for } B)|$$

where the | | stands for absolute value. Figure 8.4 shows how the values of $Y$ are determined.

**FIGURE 8.4**

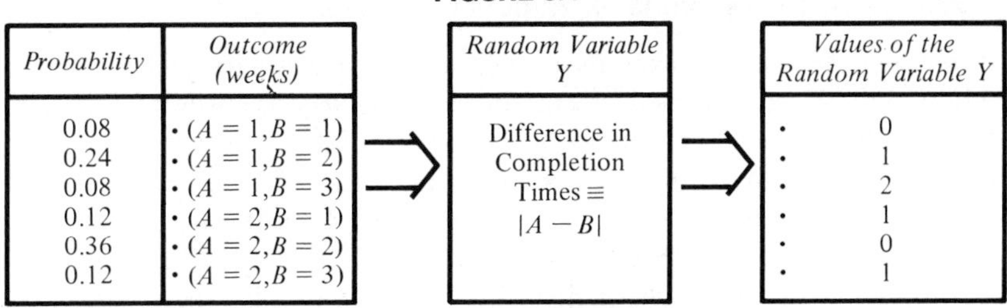


The probability distribution for the random variable $Y$ is

$$P(Y=0)=0.44$$
$$P(Y=1)=0.48$$
$$P(Y=2)=0.08$$

**Example 8.3**

Consider the same construction job as in Example 8.1. Suppose that project $A$ costs \$1000/week for every week it is in progress, and project $B$ costs \$800/week for every week it is in progress. In addition to these charges, there is a cost of \$200/week for every week the overall job is in progress. What is the probability distribution for the total cost of the job?

The random variable of interest in this case is the cost of the job. If we designate it by the letter $Z$, we can write it as

$$Z=\$1000\times(\text{completion time for } A)+\$800\times(\text{completion time for } B)+\$200\times(\text{maximum completion times for } A \text{ and } B)$$

**FIGURE 8.5**

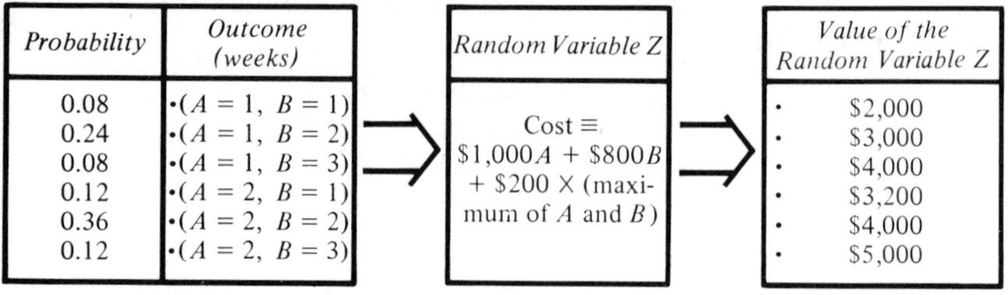


Figure 8.5 shows the values for the random variable $Z$. The probability distribution for the random variable $Z$ is

$$P(Z=\$2000)=0.08$$
$$P(Z=\$3000)=0.24$$
$$P(Z=\$3200)=0.12$$
$$P(Z=\$4000)=0.44$$
$$P(Z=\$5000)=0.12$$

### Probability Distributions for Random Variables

As demonstrated by the examples given above, probability distributions for random variables are defined in exactly the same way as specified in Chapter 4 for uncertain events. For discrete random variables, probability distributions can be given by listing $P(X=x_i)$, $i=1,2,\ldots,n$, where $x_i$ is the $i$th value of the random variable $X$ and $n$ is the number of discrete values taken on by the random variable. The cumulative probability distribution is given by $P(X \leqslant x_i)$, $i=1,2,\ldots,n$. Plots of these distributions can also be given.

### Means of Random Variables

Means of probability distributions or expected values for discrete random variables are also defined in exactly the same way as in Chapter 4.

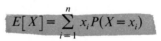

$$E[X]=\sum_{i=1}^{n} x_i P(X=x_i)$$

### Standard Deviations and Variances of Random Variables

The standard deviations and variances of a discrete random variable are calculated using the same formulas as in Chapter 4.

$$\text{Variance}=\sum_{i=1}^{n}(x_i-E[X])^2 P(X=x_i)$$

$$\text{Standard Deviation}=\sqrt{\sum_{i=1}^{n}(x_i-E[X])^2 P(X=x_i)}$$

### Independent Random Variables

The concept of independent *events* was introduced in Chapter 7. Two random variables $X$ and $Y$ may also be independent.

> **Independent Random Variables**
>
> ***Definition:*** *Two random variables X and Y are* ***independent*** *if* $P(X=x_i|Y=y_j)=P(X=x_i)$ *for all values of* $x_i$, $i=1,2,\ldots,n$, *and* $y_j$, $j=1,2,\ldots,m$, *where* $x_i$, $i=1,2,\ldots,n$, *are the values taken on by random variable X and* $y_j$, $j=1,2,\ldots,m$, *are the values taken on by random variable Y.*

For two random variables to be independent, the condition must hold for every combination of $(x,y)$. Independence for *events* only requires the events in question to be independent.

### Calculation of Expected Values for Random Variables

Expected values for random variables are calculated using the standard definition of expected values. There are some properties of expected values that can be helpful in performing calculations. Three of these properties are:

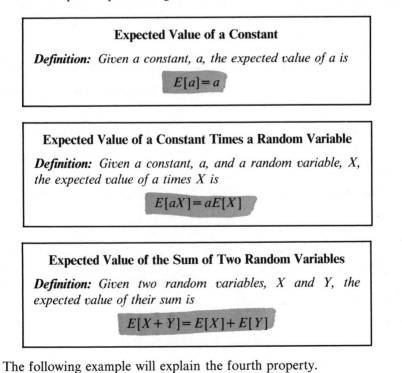

> **Expected Value of a Constant**
>
> ***Definition:*** *Given a constant, a, the expected value of a is*
>
> $$E[a]=a$$

> **Expected Value of a Constant Times a Random Variable**
>
> ***Definition:*** *Given a constant, a, and a random variable, X, the expected value of a times X is*
>
> $$E[aX]=aE[X]$$

> **Expected Value of the Sum of Two Random Variables**
>
> ***Definition:*** *Given two random variables, X and Y, the expected value of their sum is*
>
> $$E[X+Y]=E[X]+E[Y]$$

The following example will explain the fourth property.

**Example 8.4**

Assume that there are two incentive schemes being considered for a sales staff. Under the first scheme, the salesperson receives a fixed proportion of the sale price, say $100 per unit sold. Under the second scheme the payments are as shown in Table 8.2.

**TABLE 8.2**

| *Probability* | 0.07 | 0.31 | 0.30 | 0.19 | 0.13 |
|---|---|---|---|---|---|
| *Sales (units)* | 4 | 5 | 6 | 7 | 8 |
| *Payments / Unit* | $50 | $75 | $110 | $125 | $150 |

We can consider the expected payment under both incentive schemes using the probabilities shown in Table 8.2.

**Incentive scheme 1.** First, we calculate the expected payment using the definition of expected values:

*Method 1*

$$\begin{aligned} E[\text{payment}] &= \$100\times 4\times(0.07)+\$100\times 5\times(0.31)+\$100\times 6\times(0.30) \\ &\quad +\$100\times 7\times(0.19)+\$100\times 8\times(0.13) \\ &= \$600 \end{aligned}$$

Next consider the option of first calculating the expected sales and then multiplying by $100.

*Method 2*

$$E[\text{payment}] = \$100E[\text{sales}] = \$100\times 6 = \$600$$

The two methods result in the same answer as the second rule above indicates that they should.

**Incentive scheme 2.** First, we calculate the expected payment using the definition of expected values:

*Method 1*

$$\begin{aligned} E[\text{payment}] &= \$50\times 4\times(0.07)+\$75\times 5\times(0.31)+\$110\times 6\times(0.30) \\ &\quad +\$125\times 7\times(0.19)+\$150\times 8\times(0.13) \\ &= \$650.50 \end{aligned}$$

Next, consider calculating the expected sales and determining the payment associated with the expected sales. Since expected sales are 6 units (i.e., $E[\text{sales}]=6$) and the payment associated with selling 6 units is $110 per unit, we have

*Method 2*

$$E[\text{payment}] = \$110\times 6 = \$660$$

In this case method 1 and method 2 do *not* result in the same answer. It is important to understand that the expected value of a function of a random variable cannot always be calculated using the expected value of the random variable itself.

> **Expected Values for Nonlinear Functions**
>
> ***Definition:*** *If $X$ is a random variable and $h$ is a nonlinear function, then*
>
> $$E[h(X)] \neq h(E(X))$$

### ●● Random Variables as Functions

A *function* is a rule that specifies a unique element in the *range* (or output) for every element in the *domain* (or input). The rule can be provided in a number of ways, including a machine or "black box" which specifies an output for every input as shown in Figure 8.6.

**FIGURE 8.6**

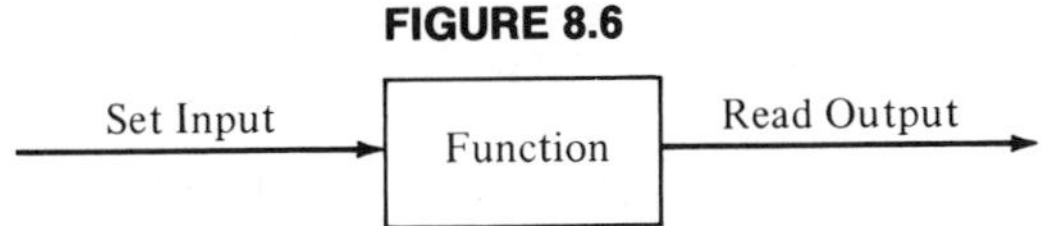


Other methods of specifying the rule or function are illustrated by the following examples.

Assume that a production process is affected by the quality of raw material supplied. Quality can be high, medium, or low. For each of the three qualities, the yield can be specified in units/ton. Table 8.3 represents a function that specifies a unique yield in units/ton (the range) for each quality type (the domain).

**TABLE 8.3**

| *Quality* | High | Medium | Low |
|---|---|---|---|
| *Yield* | 100 | 75 | 50 |

### ●● Notation for Function

> ***Definition:*** *If we let $x$ stand for some element in the domain and $f$ stand for a function, then $f(x)$ is used to denote the range.*

Functions can be represented algebraically or graphically as well as by a table. For instance, we might have $f(x)=5+2x$ as the defining relationship.

FIGURE 8.7

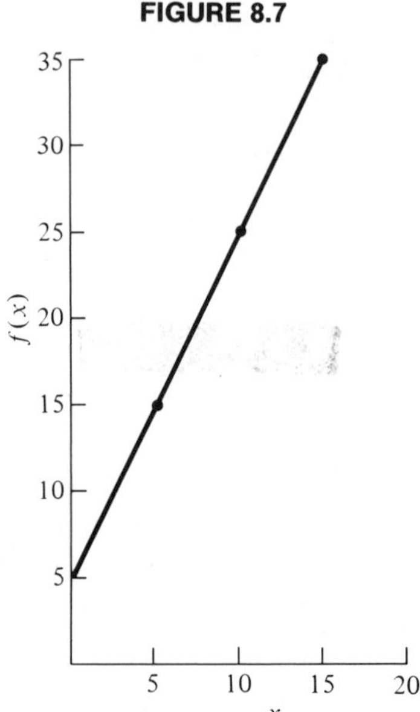


Note that for any value in the domain (i.e., a value for $x$), we can calculate a unique value in the range, $f(x)$. Displaying this same function graphically for nonnegative values of $x$ leads to Figure 8.7.

**Formal Definition of a Random Variable**

***Definition:*** *A* ***random variable*** *is a* ***function*** *that maps the elements of* ***outcome space*** *to the set of real numbers.*

## PROBABILITIES FOR COMPOUND RANDOM VARIABLES

For discrete random variables, *all* the *definitions* and *rules* for compound events *carry over directly*. Each possible value of the random variable is just an event. For example, we can consider the events $X=x$ and $Y=y$. The multiplication and addition rules are directly applicable for calculating the probabilities for compound events. The following examples illustrate these points.

### Example 8.5

Assume that you are interested in the number of gas heating furnaces and gas stoves in your city. A survey shows that 60% of the households have one gas stove and 40% have none; 70% have a gas furnace and 30% have none. Furthermore, you know that

45% have both a gas furnace and a gas stove. What is the probability that a household selected at random will have neither?

First, we consider the random variables of interest. We have two. Let $X = \{\text{number of gas heating furnaces in a household}\}$ and $Y = \{\text{number of gas stoves in a household}\}$. We are interested in the probability that a household has neither. This is written as the joint probability $P(X=0, Y=0)$.

When faced with two random variables and a problem that involves joint probabilities, tables are very useful devices. The rows represent one random variable and the columns the other. For this problem we have Table 8.4. The information given in the problem is circled.

**TABLE 8.4**

| | | *X* Number of Gas Furnaces: 0 | *X* Number of Gas Furnaces: *1* | |
|---|---|---|---|---|
| *Y* Number of Gas Stoves | *0* | 0.15 | 0.25 | (0.40) |
| | *1* | 0.15 | (0.45) | (0.60) |
| | | (0.30) | (0.70) | 1.00 |

The addition rule can be used to fill in the blanks:

$$
\begin{aligned}
1.\ P(X=1, Y=0) + P(X=1, Y=1) &= P(X=1) \\
P(X=1, Y=0) &= 0.70 - 0.45 = \underline{0.25} \\
2.\ P(X=0, Y=1) + P(X=1, Y=1) &= P(Y=1) \\
P(X=0, Y=1) &= 0.60 - 0.45 = \underline{0.15} \\
3.\ P(X=0, Y=0) + P(X=1, Y=0) &= P(Y=0) \\
P(X=0, Y=0) &= 0.40 - 0.25 = \underline{0.15}
\end{aligned}
$$

**Example 8.6**

Suppose that the distribution of lawyers on the Boards of Directors for a certain industry is: 10% have two lawyers, 70% have one, and 20% have none. For the same industry, the distribution of M.B.A.s on the Boards of Directors is: 5% have two, 50% have one, and 45% have none. If the distributions of lawyers and M.B.A.s on the Boards of Directors are independent, what is the probability of having two lawyers and one M.B.A. on a randomly selected Board of Directors?

**TABLE 8.5**

| | | X Number of Lawyers 0 | 1 | 2 | |
|---|---|---|---|---|---|
| Y Number of M.B.A.s | 0 | 0.090 | 0.315 | 0.045 | (0.45) |
| | 1 | 0.100 | 0.350 | 0.050 | (0.50) |
| | 2 | 0.010 | 0.035 | 0.005 | (0.05) |
| | | (0.20) | (0.70) | (0.10) | 1.00 |

The random variables of interest in this problem can be defined: $X$= {number of lawyers on the Board of Directors}, $Y$={number of M.B.A.s on the Board of Directors}. The problem asks for $P(X=2, Y=1)$. The joint probabilities are given in Table 8.5. The information given in the problem is circled.

The multiplication rule for independent random variables is used to calculate the joint probabilities:

1. $P(X=0, Y=0) = P(X=0)P(Y=0) = (0.20)\times(0.45) = \underline{0.090}$
2. $P(X=0, Y=1) = P(X=0P(Y=1) = (0.20)\times(0.50) = \underline{0.100}$
3. $P(X=0, Y=2) = P(X=0)P(Y=2) = (0.20)\times(0.05) = \underline{0.010}$
4. $P(X=1, Y=0) = P(X=1\,P(Y=0) = (0.70)\times(0.45) = \underline{0.315}$
5. $P(X=1, Y=1) = P(X=1)P(Y=1) = (0.70)\times(0.50) = \underline{0.350}$
6. $P(X=1, Y=2) = P(X=1\,P(Y=2) = (0.70)\times(0.05) = \underline{0.035}$
7. $P(X=2, Y=0) = P(X=2\,P(Y=0) = (0.10)\times(0.45) = \underline{0.045}$
8. $P(X=2, Y=1) = P(X=2)P(Y=1) = (0.10)\times(0.50) = \underline{0.050}$
9. $P(X=2, Y=2) = P(X=2)P(Y=2) = (0.10)\times(0.05) = \underline{0.005}$

Of course, in this problem we could have only calculated $P(X=2, Y=1) = 0.05$ rather than fill in the entire table. As a general rule, tables can help you visualize the problem and relationships between probabilities.

## CALCULATING PROBABILITY DISTRIBUTIONS FOR COMPLICATED RANDOM VARIABLES

Probability distributions for random variables that depend on several factors can be difficult to calculate. Probability diagrams are useful tools for these problems. They are just a special case of the decision diagrams described in Chapter 3. They are diagrams that have only event nodes. Two examples are given below.

**Example 8.7**

Assume that you are interested in the number of heads from tossing three fair coins which cannot land on their edges. The probability diagram that represents the outcome space for this problem is shown in Figure 8.8.

**FIGURE 8.8**

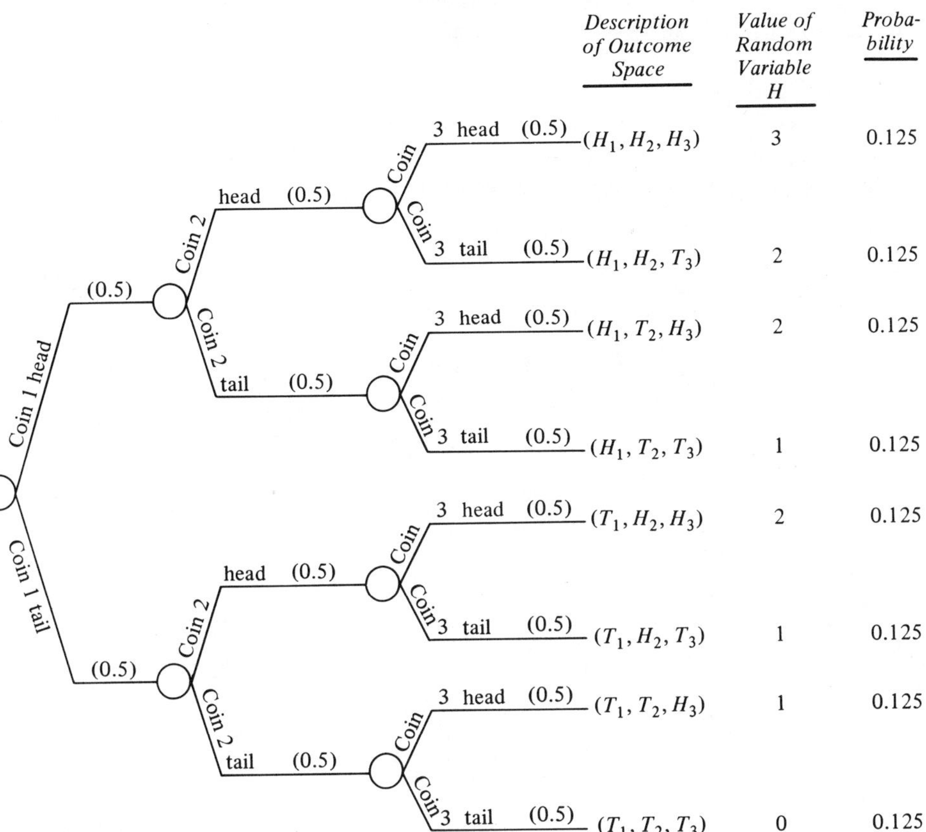

There are three uncertain events, one for each coin toss. We define random variable $H = \{\text{number of heads}\}$. The probabilities for each coin are shown on the diagram. If we assume each toss is independent, then $P(H_1, H_2, H_3) = P(H_1)P(H_2)P(H_3) = (0.5)(0.5)(0.5) = 0.125$. Since the probabilities are the same for each outcome, every point in outcome space has the same probability. The probability distribution for the random variable $H$ is:

$$P(H=0) = P(T_1, T_2, T_3) = 0.125$$
$$P(H=1) = P(H_1, T_2, T_3) + P(T_1, H_2, T_3) + P(T_1, T_2, H_3) = 0.375$$
$$P(H=2) = P(H_1, H_2, T_3) + P(H_1, T_2, H_3) + P(T_1, H_2, H_3) = 0.375$$
$$P(H=3) = P(H_1, H_2, H_3) = 0.125$$

**Example 8.8**

Assume that you are managing a project represented by the network flow diagram in Figure 8.9. The activities are characterized by the completion times shown in Table 8.6. The completion times for each activity are independent of one another. In order to schedule this project with others, you want to obtain a probability distribution for the time needed to finish the project. Work can be done simultaneously on activities in the two separate branches of the flow diagram.

The random variable of interest is project completion time. It is a complicated function of the activity completion times. If we let $t_A$, $t_B$, $t_C$, $t_D$, and $t_E$ represent the completion times for the respective activities, and $T = \{\text{project completion time}\}$, we can write

$$T = t_A + t_E + \max[(t_B + t_C), t_D]$$

To be payoff-adequate (i.e., for us to be able to calculate the value of the

**FIGURE 8.9**

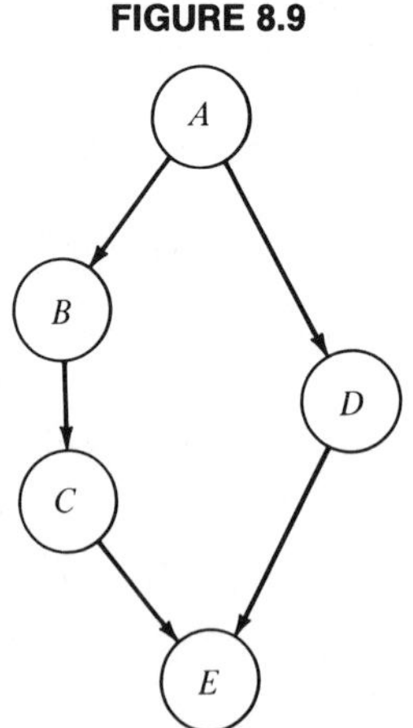

**TABLE 8.6**

| *Activity* | *Completion Time (days)* | *Probability* |
|---|---|---|
| $A$ | 5 | 1.0 |
| $B$ | 2 | 0.4 |
| | 3 | 0.6 |
| $C$ | 1 | 0.7 |
| | 2 | 0.3 |
| $D$ | 3 | 0.5 |
| | 4 | 0.5 |
| $E$ | 2 | 1.0 |

random variable) the points in outcome space must specify values for the completion time of each activity. The natural way to display the outcome space is with the probability diagram shown in Figure 8.10. The value of the random variable $T$ can be calculated for each point. Because the events are independent, the probability for each point in outcome space is also easily calculated and shown in the last column of Figure 8.10.

The probability distribution of $T$ is obtained directly from the diagram and shown below:

$$P(T=10)=0.14$$
$$P(T=11)=0.14+0.06+0.06+0.21+0.21=0.68$$
$$P(T=12)=0.09+0.09=0.18$$

### Assessment-Adequate Diagrams

The examples given above were both payoff- and assessment-adequate. In some cases the natural probability or decision diagram for a problem is not assessment-adequate. Uncertain events that would not ordinarily be included in a diagram are inserted to allow probabilities to be calculated. This procedure is illustrated in the following example.

**Example 8.9**

The Petroil oil exploration company was considering two sites for an exploratory well. Only one could be drilled. The cost of drilling at site number 1 was $100,000. Preliminary geological data indicated that the well would be dry, a low producer, or a high producer. A contract already had been signed with a development company to purchase the site if a successful well is drilled. The purchaser would pay $250,000 for a low producer and $600,000 for a high producer. If the well is dry, Petroil loses the $100,000 drilling cost. The company geologist, Jane Goodwell, was unsure about the

FIGURE 8.10

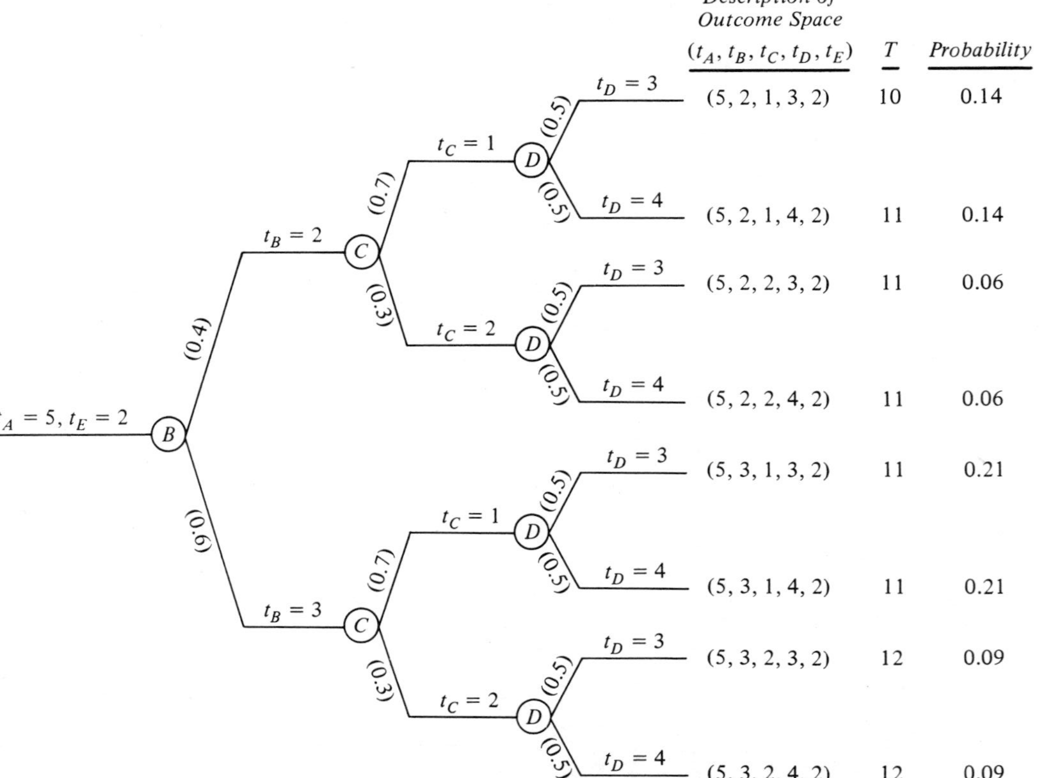


| Description of Outcome Space $(t_A, t_B, t_C, t_D, t_E)$ | $T$ | Probability |
|---|---|---|
| (5, 2, 1, 3, 2) | 10 | 0.14 |
| (5, 2, 1, 4, 2) | 11 | 0.14 |
| (5, 2, 2, 3, 2) | 11 | 0.06 |
| (5, 2, 2, 4, 2) | 11 | 0.06 |
| (5, 3, 1, 3, 2) | 11 | 0.21 |
| (5, 3, 1, 4, 2) | 11 | 0.21 |
| (5, 3, 2, 3, 2) | 12 | 0.09 |
| (5, 3, 2, 4, 2) | 12 | 0.09 |

**TABLE 8.7**

| | *Structure* | |
|---|---|---|
| *Well* | *Dome* | *No Dome* |
| *Dry* | 0.60 | 0.85 |
| *Low* | 0.25 | 0.125 |
| *High* | 0.15 | 0.025 |
| | 1.00 | 1.00 |

existence of a dome structure on this site. She assigned a probability of 0.6 to a dome structure. Her assessments for dry, low-, and high-producing wells were conditioned on the structure. Table 8.7 gives the *conditional* probabilities. She preferred to give the information this way even though, as she said, "We will never know for sure if there is a dome, even if we drill."

Site 2 was quite different. The area had been thoroughly tested using seismic tests and core samples. There was almost certainly oil. The geologist assessed the probability of finding oil to be 0.8. The drawbacks to the site were that the drilling costs were high, $200,000, and that if oil were found, the well would be a low producer. A contract also had been signed with the same developer to buy a low producer on site number 2 for $250,000. To help decide between the two sites, the company president asked for a probability distribution on net contribution for drilling at each site.

A decision diagram can be developed for this problem using the rules given in Chapter 3. Taking the position of specifying the uncertain events that will be revealed based on each decision, we can draw Figure 8.11.

The random variable of interest is net contribution. It can be calculated for each end point. Therefore, the diagram is payoff-adequate. Probabilities

**FIGURE 8.11**

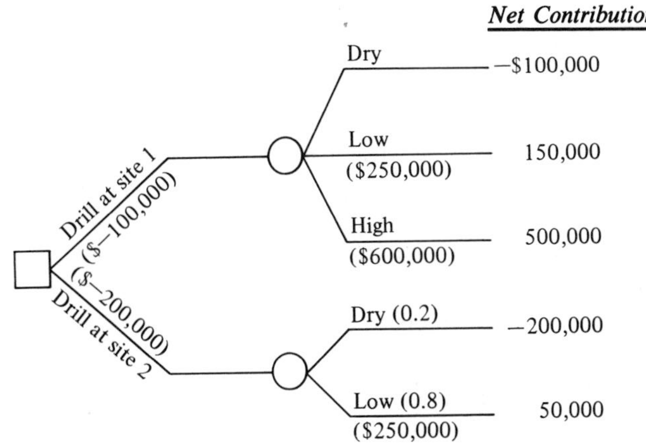

for the uncertain event for the *drill at site 2* alternatives are available and placed on the diagram.

What about the probabilities for the *drill at site 1* alternative? They are not directly available. We only know the probabilities for dry, low, and high if we are told about the structure. The diagram, as it stands, is not assessment-adequate. It can be made assessment-adequate by inserting another uncertain event describing the structure. This is done in Figure 8.12. By including this "extra" node, the description of the outcome space has been expanded beyond that required to calculate the payoffs (we only need dry, low, high to calculate contribution). It now includes the state of the geological structure. With the expanded diagram it is easy to calculate the required probabilities.

**FIGURE 8.12**

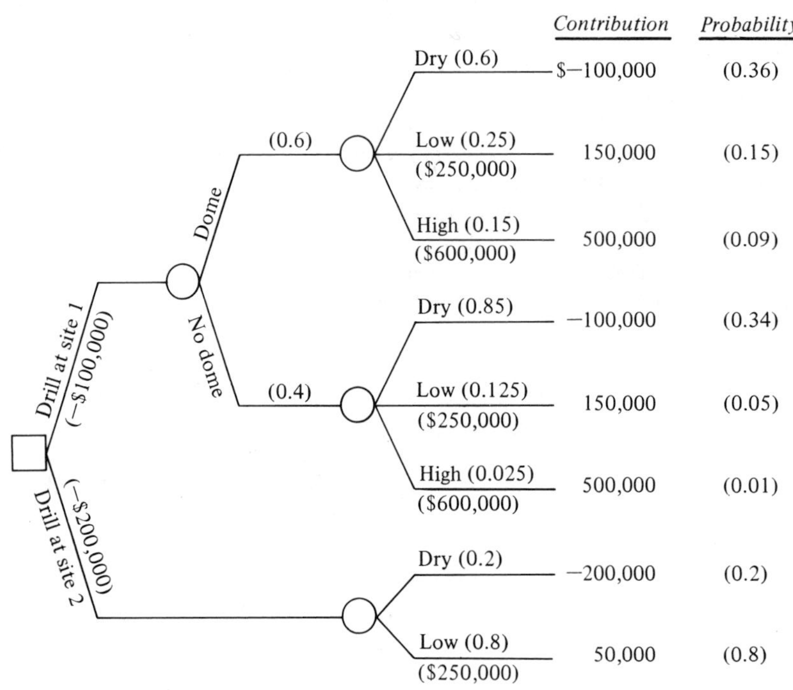


The probability distribution for contribution for *drill at site 1* is:

$$P(\text{contribution} = -\$100{,}000) = 0.7$$
$$P(\text{contribution} = \$150{,}000) \quad = 0.2$$
$$P(\text{contribution} = \$500{,}000) \quad = 0.1$$

In this problem we inserted an "extra" uncertain event so that probabilities could be calculated. The uncertain event did not show up on the original diagram because its outcome would not be observed. All we would find out by drilling is the state of the well, not the state of underlying structure. It is included because the company geologist wanted to use it as the basis for her probability assessments.

These "unobservable" uncertain events are often useful in assessing probabilities. The only *restriction* on their use is that they must *not precede* any decision nodes. If they did, it would imply their outcome is known prior to making a decision. For example, the oil drilling example could not be diagrammed as shown in Figure 8.13.

**FIGURE 8.13**

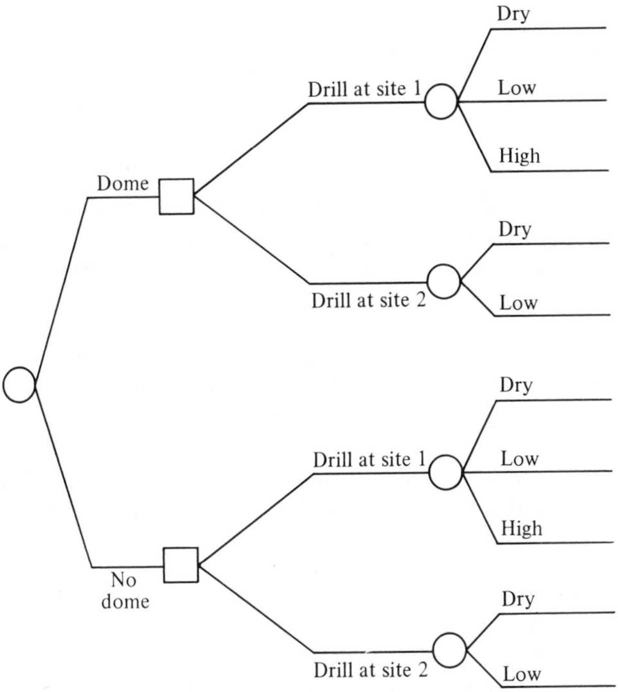

### Using Tables Instead of Inserting "Extra" Uncertain Events into the Diagram

Another way to deal with the problem of obtaining probabilities when the outcome space shown on a diagram is not assessment-adequate is to use a table. The diagram is not modified, and the probabilities are calculated separately. For Example 8.9 we would use the diagram shown in Figure 8.11 and the table of joint probabilities shown in Table 8.8. The probabilities required for Figure 8.11 are given in the right-hand margin.

**TABLE 8.8**

| | *Dome* | *No Dome* | |
|---|---|---|---|
| *Dry* | $P(\text{dry}\mid\text{dome})P(\text{dome})$ $=(0.6)\times(0.6)=0.36$ | $P(\text{dry}\mid\text{no dome})P(\text{no dome})$ $=(0.85)\times(0.4)=0.34$ | 0.70 |
| *Low* | $P(\text{low}\mid\text{dome})P(\text{dome})$ $=(0.25)\times(0.6)=0.15$ | $P(\text{low}\mid\text{no dome})P(\text{no dome})$ $=(0.125)\times(0.4)=0.05$ | 0.20 |
| *High* | $P(\text{high}\mid\text{dome})P(\text{dome})$ $=(0.15)\times(0.6)=0.09$ | $P(\text{high}\mid\text{no dome})P(\text{no dome})$ $=(0.025)\times(0.4)=0.01$ | 0.10 |
| | 0.60 | 0.40 | 1.00 |

## SUMMARY

Defining outcome space is the starting point for building models for decisions under uncertainty. There is usually more than one outcome space consistent with the uncertain events in the problem. Two concepts provide some guidance in developing outcome spaces.

*Payoff-Adequacy:* An outcome space is payoff-adequate if the elemental description of the points is adequate to determine the value of the evaluation units or random variable for each point.

*Assessment-Adequacy:* An outcome space is assessment-adequate if the elemental description of the points is adequate for assessing the probabilities for each point.

We have called the numbers used to evaluate points in outcome space *evaluation units*. A more general term for these numbers is *random variable*. The term "random variable" is widely used and encompasses variables such as time, numerical counts of certain outcomes, distance, and so on, that are not ordinarily used to evaluate decision diagrams.

*Random Variable:* A random variable is a rule of correspondence between the points in an outcome space and numbers.

Probability distributions, means, standard deviations, and expected values for discrete random variables are defined exactly the same way they were in Chapter 4 for uncertain events.

*Independent Random Variables:* Two random variables $X$ and $Y$ are independent if $P(X=x_i\mid Y=y_j)=P(X=x_i)$ for all $i$ and $j$.

Expected values for random variables can be calculated using the following rules:

$$E[a]=a \qquad \text{where } a \text{ is constant}$$
$$E[aX]=aE[X] \qquad \text{where } a \text{ is a constant}$$
$$E[X+Y]=E[X]+E[Y]$$

It is important to recognize that for a nonlinear function, $h(X)$,

$$E(h(X)) \neq h(E[X])$$

Tables of joint probabilities and probability diagrams are useful tools for calculating probability distributions for complicated random variables. The same procedures as described in Chapter 3 are used to create the probability diagrams. When the outcome space defined by these procedures is not payoff-adequate or not assessment-adequate, "extra" uncertain events are included.

## ASSIGNMENT MATERIAL

**8.1.** Describe conditions under which the outcome space $\Omega=\{0 \text{ heads}, 1 \text{ or more heads}\}$ could be payoff-adequate for two tosses of a coin.

**8.2.** If a decision is to be evaluated by the following accounting model, define a payoff-adequate outcome space.

Net Contribution = Revenue − Costs
Revenue = \$3.50 × (Units Sold)
Cost = \$1.50 × (Units Produced) + 0.50 × (Units Sold)
Units Sold = Minimum [(Units Demanded), (5,250 + Units Produced)]

**8.3.** In response to a fire at City Hall, the fire department dispatches two trucks from different locations. From previous studies it is known that truck $A$ will arrive at City Hall in either 1.5 minutes or in 2.1 minutes, the two times being equally likely. There is a 0.3 probability that truck $B$ will take 1.2 minutes, a 0.5 probability that it will take 1.7 minutes, and a 0.2 probability that it will take 2.1 minutes. Assume that the times required for the individual trucks to arrive are independent. What is the probability distribution for the random variable "time elapsed before arrival of the first truck at City Hall"?

**8.4.** A baker is currently deciding how many pies of a certain type he should bake for sale tomorrow. The demand probabilities for this type of pie are known to be the following:

| *n* | *Probability That n Pies Are Demanded Tomorrow* |
|---|---|
| 0 | 0.2 |
| 1 | 0.1 |
| 2 | 0.4 |
| 3 | 0.1 |
| 4 | 0.2 |

The ingredients for one pie cost $0.80 and he will sell the pies fresh (i.e., tomorrow) for $1.00. Any pie not sold tomorrow will be sold (for sure) the following day for $0.60. He considers all other costs (including his own labor) to be either uncontrollable or negligible. He finally decides to make two pies.

(a) Calculate the distribution of the baker's profit from this batch of two pies.
(b) Calculate his expected profit on the batch.
(c) Could you have done the calculation in part (b) knowing only the expected demand (rather than the complete distribution of demand)?

**8.5.** Three firms are bidding for the contract to repair the GSB heating and air-conditioning system. The maintenance director has assessed the probability distributions for each of three firms' bid price. These appear below (assume independence among the bid prices):

| **Firm A** | | **Firm B** | |
|---|---|---|---|
| *Bid Price* | *Probability* | *Bid Price* | *Probability* |
| 6000 | 0.5 | 7000 | 0.4 |
| 8000 | 0.5 | 9000 | 0.6 |

**Firm C**

| *Bid Price* | *Probability* |
|---|---|
| 5500 | 0.3 |
| 7500 | 0.4 |
| 9000 | 0.3 |

(a) Calculate the probability distribution for the winning bid.
(b) Calculate the probability distribution for the difference between the high and low bids.

**8.6.** A construction project consists of four jobs—$A$, $B$, $C$, and $D$. Jobs $B$ and $C$ cannot be begun until $A$ is completed, and $D$ cannot be begun until $C$ is completed. The project is completed when all four jobs are completed. The completion times of the four jobs are uncertain. The completion time of job $A$ is independent of the completion times of $B$, $C$, and $D$, and the completion time of $B$ is independent of the completion times of $A$, $C$, and $D$. The distributions of the completion times of jobs $A$ and $B$ are as follows:

**Job A**

| *Completion Time* | 1 week | 2 weeks |
|---|---|---|
| *Probability* | 0.4 | 0.6 |

**Job B**

| *Completion Time* | 3 weeks | 4 weeks |
|---|---|---|
| *Probability* | 0.5 | 0.5 |

The completion times of jobs $C$ and $D$ are dependent on one another but independent of the completion times for $A$ and $B$. The joint probabilities of these two are given in the following probability table:

| | | *Job C Completion Time* | | |
|---|---|---|---|---|
| | | *1 week* | *2 weeks* | |
| *Job D Completion Time* | *2 Weeks* | 0.2 | 0.4 | |
| | *3 Weeks* | 0 | 0.4 | |
| | | | | |

(a) What is the probability distribution for the total project completion time?

The firm undertaking this project will receive $10K for completing the job, unless it takes more than 5 weeks, in which case they get only $9.5K. Total costs will be $4K + $500 for every week that it takes to complete the project (labor costs) + $500 for every week that it takes to complete job *C* (because *C* requires the rental of machinery).

(b) What is the probability distribution of the firm's net contribution for this project?

**8.7.** Mr. Ralph Meagre, owner of the Potomac Plumbers professional football team, has a decision to make. His team is about to submit a bid for the services of a star running back named O. U. Kidd, who has played out his option with the Niagara Igloos. Kidd has declared that he will play exactly one more season before retiring and that he will play that one season with whatever team will pay him the highest salary. Kidd has instructed each interested team to submit a bid which is an even multiple of $200,000. Kidd has said that if there is a tie for high bid, and if Potomac is one of the high bidders, he will choose to play for Potomac.

Meagre knows that only two other teams, the Boston Brahmins and the Tampa Tadpoles, intend to bid. He assesses their respective bids to be independent random variables with the following distributions. (Bids are in millions of dollars.)

| **Boston** | | **Tampa** | |
|---|---|---|---|
| *Bid* | *Prob.* | *Bid* | *Prob.* |
| 0.6 | 0.2 | 0.8 | 0.3 |
| 0.8 | 0.3 | 1.0 | 0.4 |
| 1.0 | 0.4 | 1.2 | 0.2 |
| 1.2 | 0.1 | 1.4 | 0.1 |

Meagre has also assessed subjective distributions for his team's net profit for the year with and without the services of O. U. Kidd, and he has calculated the means of these distributions. Without the services of Kidd, he assesses a distribution with a mean of $12.6 million. With Kidd's services, he assesses a distribution with a mean of $14.4 million (not including Kidd's salary). If Meagre is willing to choose among alternatives using expected monetary values, what bid should Meagre submit?

**8.8.** Thomas Tipton Travistock "Tip" Tippingwell IV, student at a well-known West Coast business school, has a decision to make. He has just completed all the problems on a take-home midterm exam in Advanced Decision Tree Design. The exam rules read:

> This exam has four problems. All students must complete problems 1 and 2. Each student should choose either 3 or 4 to be graded. Problems 1 and 2 will count 30 points each and problem 3 or 4 will count 40 points.

Tip has completed all four problems, and he must decide whether to have 3 or 4 graded. He has had the professor for this course three times before, so he is able to accurately assess what his scores on the problems will be. He assesses:

1. On 1 he has a perfect score (30).
2. On 2, he'll get either 20, 25, or 30 points, each with probability 0.5, 0.25, and 0.25, respectively.
3. On 3, he'll get either 35 or 40 points, with probabilities 0.5 and 0.5. Moreover, if he gets 30 on 2, he won't get 40 on 3. And if he gets 25 on 2, he'll get 35 on 3 with probability 0.4.
4. On 4, he'll get 30, 35, or 40 points, with probabilities 0.2, 0.4 and 0.4, respectively. Moreover, if he scores 30 on 2, he will score 40 on 4. If he scores 30 on 4, he will score 20 on 2. If he scores 20 on 2, he will not score 40 on 4.

(a) What are the probability distributions of his total score on this exam if he chooses to have 3 graded? If he chooses to have 4 graded?

(b) If Tippingwell wishes to maximize his expected total score, should he have 3 or 4 graded? Be explicit in your reasons—show all calculations.

(c) Before coming to school Tip had made an arrangement with his father concerning performance "bonuses." The incentive scheme stipulated that for exam scores over 95, he would receive $1 for each point scored (i.e., if he scored 98 he would get $98). For scores between 91 and 95, he would receive $0.50 per point, and for scores between 86 and 90, he would receive nothing. For scores less than 86, he must pay $1 for every point *below* 85. Which question should he have graded to maximize his "bonus" on this exam?

**8.9. The Redding Manufacturing Company***

Fred Piesley, newly appointed Treasurer of Redding Manufacturing Company, was reviewing the company's credit policy. He became concerned because he found that credit terms and "risk attitudes" tended to vary among the various divisions of Redding. In part these variations were due to the different businesses that the divisions were in, but some of the variations were caused by the credit managers acting in inconsistent ways. Piesley's goal with respect to credit policy was to get all credit managers to act in a manner that would "maximize profits" for the overall company.

As a beginning, he decided to concentrate on the scale division. The scale division manufactured a single product—a high-accuracy, low-oscillating scale. In general, customers who bought these units rarely required replacement; in a sense, the business was of a no-repeat variety.

The credit manager of the Scale division, Al Sula, explained his current "policy" as follows:

*This case was written by Professor Alex Robichek and included with his permission.

Anytime we get a request for credit we first check the customer's D & B (Dun & Bradstreet) rating. On the basis of the rating we classify customers into three groups: (1) Excellent, (2) Probably Good, and (3) Marginal. In the past, we have extended credit to all "excellent" and "probably good" accounts and rejected the requests of "marginal" accounts. But, because of increased sales competition and some excess capacity, we may have to begin extending credit to "marginal" customers. There are two ways we can do this: (a) extend credit to all "marginal" applicants, or (b) request a special credit report (costing about $30) for each marginal customer and then make the decision based on the analysis of the supplementary information. As yet, we are not sure which way to go—maybe you, Fred, can help us?

In explaining further the subject of "marginal" customers, Sula was able to give Piesley the following additional information:

The price of the scale was $800. Variable costs pertaining to each scale consisted of $320 manufacturing costs and $180 selling and other expenses.

The special supplementary credit reports would permit classification of marginal customers into four subgroups—A, B, C, and D. In Sula's estimation 25 percent of applications would fall in the A group, 30 percent in B, 20 percent in C, and 25 percent in D.

Based on experience in other divisions, Sula had compiled a table indicating likelihood of default (or no default) for the various subgroups:

| *Subgroup* | *Chance of Default* | *Chance of No Default* |
|---|---|---|
| A | .10 | .90 |
| B | .20 | .80 |
| C | .30 | .70 |
| D | .60 | .40 |

He estimated that on credit accounts in default, in 20 percent of the cases the company would recover about $200 (of the $800 billed).

In 30 percent of the cases where credit was not granted, the customers bought the scale anyway on a C.O.D. basis.

1. Diagram the problem facing Redding.
2. If they use expected values to choose among the alternatives, which credit policy would you recommend?

# 9

# Continuous Random Variables, Models, and Calculations

Up to this point we have discussed models for uncertain events that have discrete outcomes. Each uncertain event has been described by a small number of outcomes. In some cases the discrete model is a completely accurate description [e.g., flipping a coin (heads or tails) or the number of defects in a production lot of 10 items $(0, 1, 2, \ldots, 10)$]. In other cases it is a convenient approximation [e.g., possible selling prices for a piece of property ($10,000, $20,000, or $30,000) or number of units of some product sold during a month (1000, 2000, 3000, 4000, 5000)]. Decision diagrams, probability distributions, and probability calculations presented in the preceding chapters have all relied on the discrete formulation. In this chapter we consider methods of modeling for uncertain events that are naturally represented by a

**FIGURE 9.1**

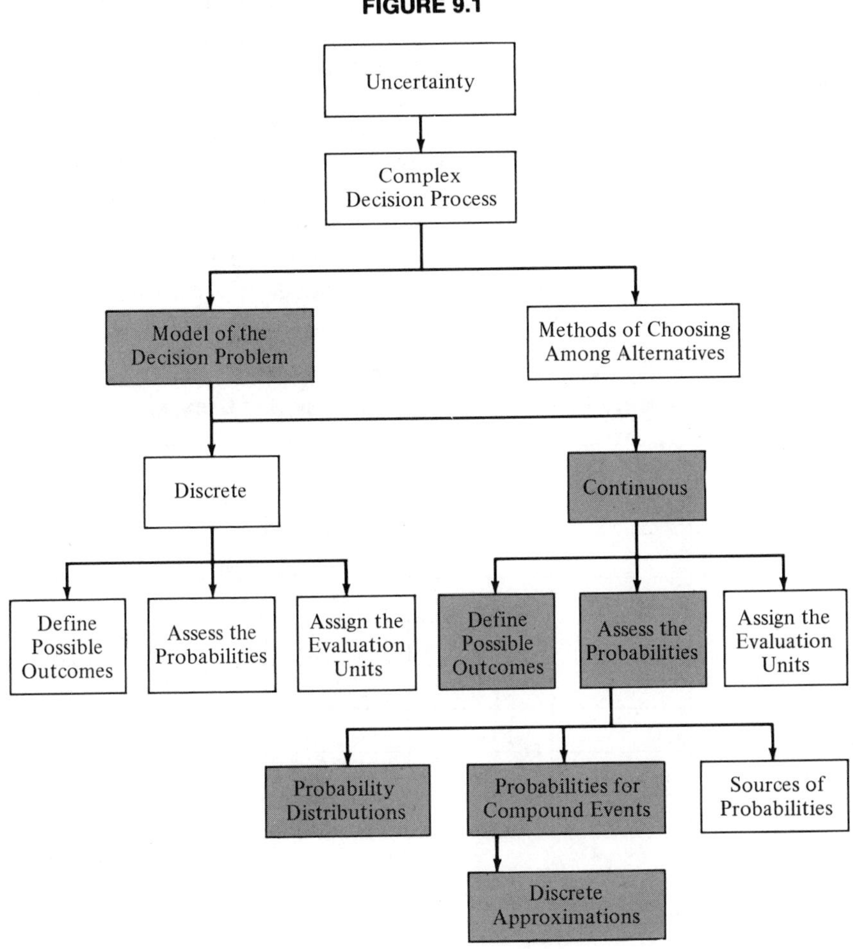

continuous outcome space. A random variable defined on a continuous outcome space is called a *continuous* random variable. Figure 9.1 shows how the material fits into the overall scheme.

## CONTINUOUS VERSUS DISCRETE MODELS

The motivation for using continuous models comes from the problem setting. In some cases, the outcome space is actually continuous, if we neglect limitations due to measurement accuracy. For instance, the volume of oil that can be recovered and the depth of a well required to reach the oil are continuous variables. In other cases the outcome space is *essentially* continuous. For instance, the number of new cars sold in a certain geographic area during a month might cover the range of whole numbers between 1000 and 6000. To provide a completely accurate description of the number of cars sold in a month, the outcome space would have to include each possibility from 1000 to 6000. From a practical point of view it may be impossible to assess separately probabilities for each of the 5001 points required by such a model. A model based on a continuous set of outcomes may be the best approximation available for this essentially continuous outcome space.

The difference between a discrete and continuous probability model can be seen by comparing the cumulative probability distributions in Figures 9.2 and 9.3. Think of the random variable as demand for a product. In Figure 9.2 each unit is treated separately (discretely) and is represented by a step. In Figure 9.3 a continuous approximation is provided. It is easy to see that as

**FIGURE 9.2**

**Cumulative Distribution for Discrete Model of Demand**

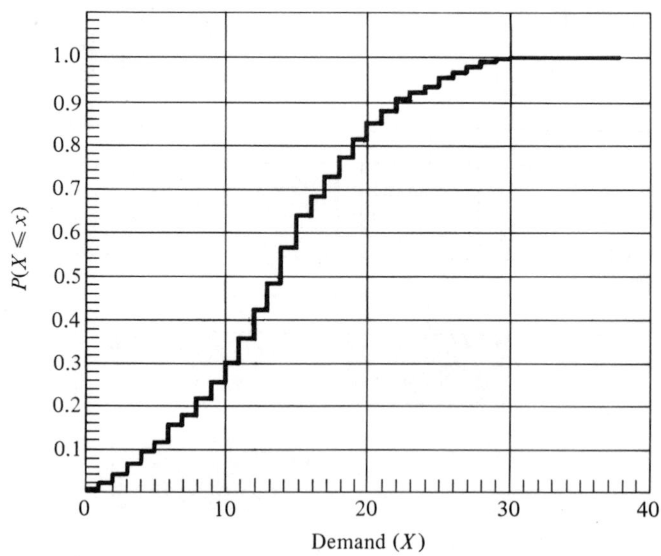

**FIGURE 9.3**

**Cumulative Distribution for Continuous Model of Demand**

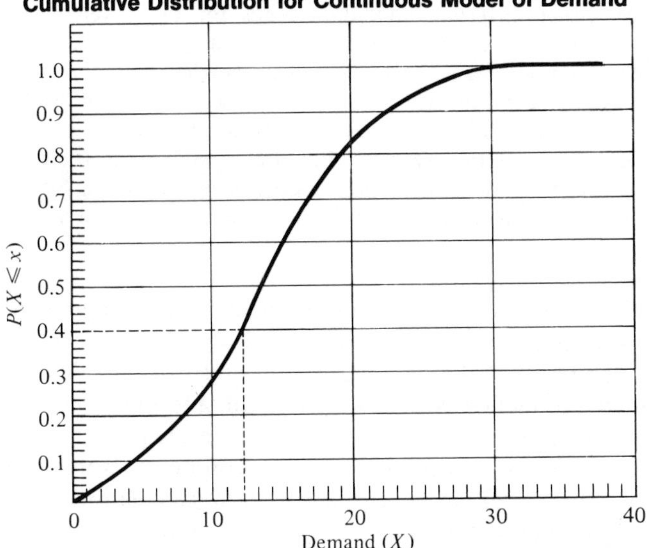


the number of outcomes increases, continuous models rapidly become good approximations for uncertain events that actually have a discrete number of outcomes.

## DIAGRAMS FOR CONTINUOUS MODELS

A diagram for a continuous model does not show individual branches. Instead, event *fans* and alternative *fans* are used. Figure 9.4 shows a hypothetical event fan and a hypothetical alternative fan. The difference between *diagrams* for discrete and continuous uncertain events is that continuous uncertain events are connected only by a representative outcome. Consider the following example.

**FIGURE 9.4**

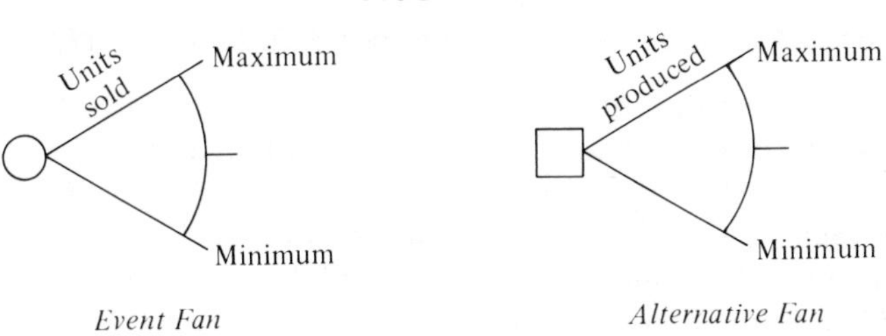

**Example 9.1**

You must decide on investing additional funds for the development of a new consumer product. If you continue development the production cost will be known in 6 months. At this point your production engineers tell you it may be anywhere between $10 and $65 per unit. The price you can charge is $50 and is determined by the market for a close substitute. At this price the demand for the product will range between 2,000 and 10,000 units per year. Because of production efficiencies you must produce the entire lot at one time and before the demand is known. Since the industry is changing rapidly you feel that all benefits from the development will accrue in one year.

The basic structure of this decision problem can be represented by Figure 9.5. The connecting "branches" between fans merely represent typical outcomes. The random variable is contribution and can be calculated for any combination of production cost, units produced, and units demanded. There is no probability information on the diagram or in the problem. To *finish* the model we have to know how to represent continuous probability distributions. To *use* the model we have to know how calculations such as those discussed for discrete distributions can be done with continuous probability distributions.

**FIGURE 9.5**

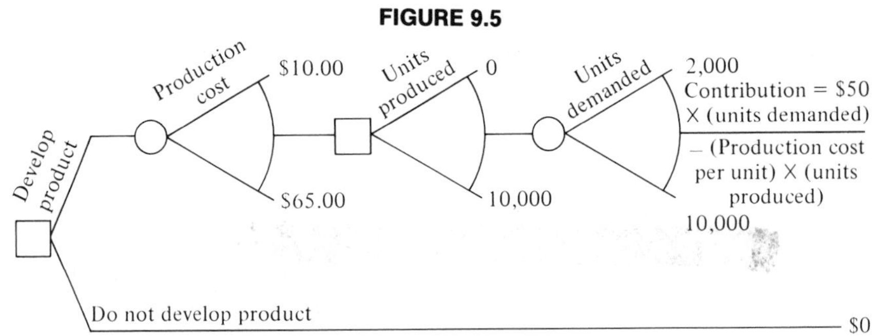


## PROBABILITY DISTRIBUTIONS FOR CONTINUOUS RANDOM VARIABLES

### Cumulative Distributions for Continuous Random Variables

Cumulative distributions have precisely the same interpretation for both continuous and discrete random variables. For instance, in Figure 9.3 we can read off the probability of obtaining a demand value of 12 or less as 0.4. The probability that the random variable $X$ lies between 11.50 and 12.50 can also be determined using the cumulative distribution: $P(11.50 \leqslant X \leqslant 12.50) = P(X \leqslant 12.50) - P(X \leqslant 11.50)$. From Figure 9.3 this equals $0.44 - 0.37 = 0.07$.

FIGURE 9.6
Probability Density Function

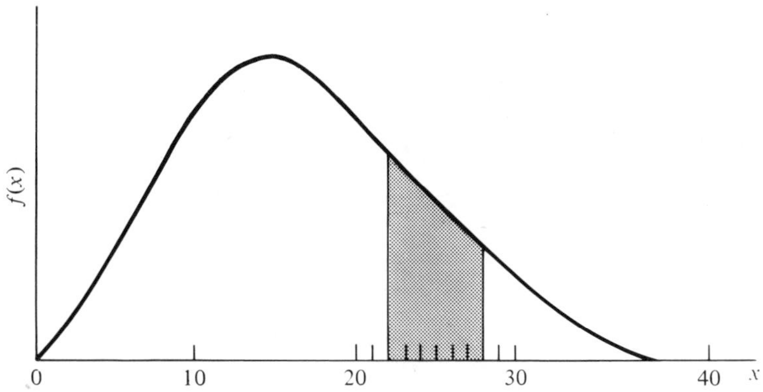


The interpretation of probability *density functions* for continuous random variables and discrete random variables is not the same. Figure 9.6 shows the probability density function for a continuous random variable.

### Requirements on Probability Density Functions for Continuous Random Variables

For a density function, denoted $f(x)$,

1. $f(x) \geqslant 0$ for all values of $x$.
2. The *area* under the curve $f(x)$ and above the $X$-axis is equal to 1.

### Interpretation of Probability Density Functions for Continuous Random Variables

The principal difference between this curve and density functions for discrete random variables is that the height of the curve $f(x)$ does not represent the probability of obtaining a particular value $x$. Instead, the *area* under the curve gives the probability for any interval. For instance, the probability that $22 \leqslant X \leqslant 28$ is given by the *area* under the curve between 22 and 28 (see Figure 9.6). As the interval shrinks to a point, the area goes to zero, which means that the probability of any single point, say 22, is *zero*. Although this seems strange at first, it must be true because there are an infinite number of possible outcomes and if they all had some positive probability of occurring, their sum would exceed 1. When a continuous distribution is used to approximate a discrete distribution, we must remember that a given outcome is modeled by an interval around the outcome. For instance, if the random variable $X$ in Figure 9.6 is really discrete and can only take on integer values, we would calculate the probability that $X=22$ by $P(21.5 \leqslant X \leqslant 22.5)$.

### Relationship Between Cumulative Distributions and Density Functions

There is a direct relationship between cumulative distributions and density functions for continuous random variables. If we had an instrument to measure areas, the cumulative distribution could be plotted from the density function. Using Figure 9.7 as an example, we calculate $P(X \leqslant 1) = P(0 \leqslant X \leqslant 1)$ as the shaded area to the left of $X = 1$. For $P(X \leqslant 2)$ we have the

FIGURE 9.7

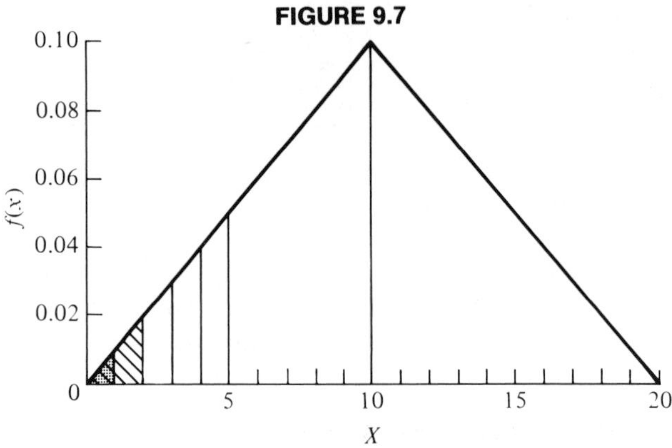


crosshatched area to the left of $X = 2$. Other points on the cumulative curve could be calculated in a similar manner. Because the density function is triangular these areas can be easily calculated as follows:

$$P(X \leqslant 0) = 0$$
$$P(X \leqslant 2) = \tfrac{1}{2}(2) \times (0.02) = 0.02$$
$$P(X \leqslant 4) = \tfrac{1}{2}(4) \times (0.04) = 0.08$$
$$P(X \leqslant 6) = \tfrac{1}{2}(6) \times (0.06) = 0.18$$
$$P(X \leqslant 8) = \tfrac{1}{2}(8) \times (0.08) = 0.32$$
$$P(X \leqslant 10) = \tfrac{1}{2}(10) \times (0.10) = 0.50$$
$$P(X \leqslant 12) = 1.0 - \tfrac{1}{2}(8) \times (0.08) = 1.0 - 0.32 = 0.68$$
$$P(X \leqslant 14) = 1.0 - \tfrac{1}{2}(6) \times (0.06) = 1.0 - 0.18 = 0.82$$
$$P(X \leqslant 16) = 1.0 - \tfrac{1}{2}(4) \times (0.04) = 1.0 - 0.08 = 0.92$$
$$P(X \leqslant 18) = 1.0 - \tfrac{1}{2}(2) \times (0.02) = 1.0 - 0.02 = 0.98$$
$$P(X \leqslant 20) = 1.0 - 0 = 1.0$$

Figure 9.8 shows the cumulative distribution derived from these points. Plotting the density function from the cumulative is more difficult. We will not pursue this here since efficient procedures require an understanding of calculus.

FIGURE 9.8

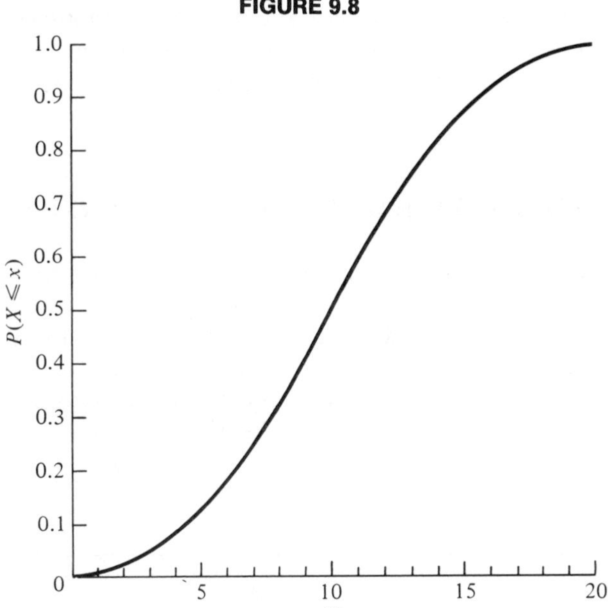


## CALCULATIONS USING CONTINUOUS DISTRIBUTIONS

The definitions and rules for calculating probabilities for discrete random variables have direct analogs for continuous random variables. The difference is that the continuity property requires the use of calculus. Summations are replaced by integrals. An integral can be thought of as the limit of a summation as the number of elements in the summation gets very large. In fact, by definition the shaded area in Figure 9.6 is given by the integral of $f(x)$ from 22 to 28, which is written

$$P(22 \leqslant X \leqslant 28) = \int_{22}^{28} f(x)\,dx$$

Definitions of marginal probabilities, joint probabilities, and conditional probabilities all generalize directly to continuous random variables. Expected values are also defined using integrals:

$$E[X] = \int_{-\infty}^{\infty} x f(x)\,dx$$

If analytical expressions are available for $f(x)$, there are usually methods (in some cases, tables) for evaluating the integrals (i.e., performing desired calculations). Rather than using calculus to calculate probabilities for continuous random variables, we will use two other approaches. These approaches have two advantages. First, they do not require a knowledge of calculus. Second, they can be used for any continuous distribution, even when analytical expressions are not available. Both approaches involve approximations. The first utilizes discrete approximations and is discussed below. The second uses the Monte Carlo method and is discussed in Chapter 15.

## SUMMARY MEASURES FOR CONTINUOUS DISTRIBUTIONS

Expected values (or means), standard deviations, and variances are defined for continuous distributions by replacing the discrete probabilities by continuous density functions and replacing the summations by integrals in the formulas given in Chapter 4. This is illustrated above for expected values. Two other measures of central tendency are often used with continuous distributions. They are the *median* and the *mode*.

### Median

> **Median**
>
> ***Definition:*** *The* ***median*** *is the value of a random variable that divides the area in a density function in half. Therefore, the probability that a random variable is less than or equal to the median is 0.5, and the probability that it is greater than or equal to the median is 0.5*

Medians can be read off directly using cumulative distributions. The value of the random variable corresponding to 0.5 on the cumulative scale is the median. For instance, the median for the probability distribution shown in Figure 9.3 is 13.

### Mode

> **Mode**
>
> ***Definition:*** *The* ***mode*** *is the most likely value of a random variable.*

The mode is easily determined from a graph of the density function since it is just the value of the random variable associated with the highest point on the curve. For instance, the mode for the random variable shown in Figure 9.6 is 15. Both the median and the mode can be used with discrete random variables also (the median may not exist), but are usually used with continuous distributions.

## DISCRETE APPROXIMATIONS

If a continuous probability distribution is approximated by a discrete distribution, we can use all the calculational procedures developed for discrete random variables. The overall modeling strategy is: (1) use *continuous* probability distributions to represent uncertain events with continuous outcomes or a large number of outcomes in order to obtain a *good model*; and (2) *approximate* the continuous probability distributions by *discrete* probability distributions to *facilitate computation*.

In principle, discrete approximations to continuous probability distributions can be made as accurate as desired. The limiting factor is the number of intervals used in the approximation. With the availability of computers, it is feasible to use a large number of intervals.[1] On the other hand, a small number of intervals usually provides an adequate approximation. There are several ways of making the approximation. The essential problem is to capture the important characteristics of a distribution with a few discrete points. A method often used is to divide the random variable scale into equally probable intervals. The number of intervals is increased until a satisfactory approximation is obtained. A detailed step-by-step procedure for this method is given below. Read the steps through quickly and then go over the example that follows before studying them.

### Procedure for Equally Probable Interval Approximation

*Step 1:* Obtain the cumulative distribution function for the continuous random variable.

*Step 2:* Decide on the number of intervals to be used in the approximation for the random variable. Let $n =$ the number of intervals.

*Step 3:* Define the intervals for the random variable by dividing the cumulative probability scale into $n$ equal intervals and obtaining the corresponding intervals for the random variable.

*Step 4:* Select a single point in each random variable interval to represent the entire interval by finding the point that divides the interval into two equally probable intervals.

*Step 5:* Assign probability $1/n$ to each of the points selected in step 4.

Consider the continuous, cumulative distribution shown in Figure 9.9. For purposes of illustration we have chosen five intervals (i.e., $n=5$). Five equal

[1] In fact, integrals performed numerically using computers actually use a large number of discrete points similar to the discrete approximations discussed here.

FIGURE 9.9

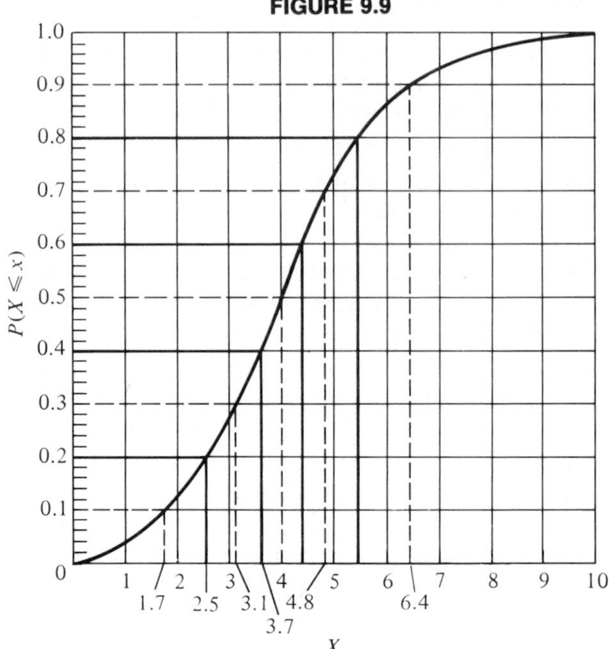


intervals are marked off on the cumulative probability scale (the vertical axis). As shown by the solid lines in Figure 9.9, these intervals are 0 to 0.2, 0.2 to 0.4, 0.4 to 0.6, 0.6 to 0.8, and 0.8 to 1.0. The corresponding intervals for the random variable, $X$, are found by moving horizontally from these points on the vertical axis to the cumulative curve and then vertically downward to the $X$ axis. This is shown by the solid lines in Figure 9.9. The intervals are given in column one of Table 9.1.

Next, a single point on the random variable scale is chosen to represent the entire interval. Using step 4, we choose the point that divides the interval into two equally likely parts. That is, we find a point so that, if the outcome lies in a particular interval, there is a 50–50 chance that it will be on either side of the chosen point. These points are easy to find, since we merely divide the cumulative probability intervals into two equal parts and find the corresponding points on the $X$ axis. These points are shown by the dashed lines in Figure 9.9 and the points are displayed in the second column of Table 9.1.

The probability that the random variable takes on the value in any interval is $1/n$, 0.2 in this case. In a discrete approximation we assign all this probability to the representative point. Figures 9.10 and 9.11 display the cumulative probability distribution and the probability density functions for the discrete approximation. Using this approximation, the expected value can be calculated:

$$
\begin{aligned}
E[X] &= (1.7\times 0.2)+(3.1\times 0.2)+(4.0\times 0.2)+(4.8\times 0.2)+(6.4\times 0.2)\\
&= 4.0
\end{aligned}
$$

**TABLE 9.1**

| *Interval* | *Representative Point* | *Probability* |
|---|---|---|
| $0 \leqslant X \leqslant 2.5$ | $X_1 = 1.7$ | $P(X=1.7)=0.2$ |
| $2.5 \leqslant X \leqslant 3.6$ | $X_2 = 3.1$ | $P(X=3.1)=0.2$ |
| $3.6 \leqslant X \leqslant 4.4$ | $X_3 = 4.0$ | $P(X=4.0)=0.2$ |
| $4.4 \leqslant X \leqslant 5.4$ | $X_4 = 4.8$ | $P(X=4.8)=0.2$ |
| $5.4 \leqslant X \leqslant 10.0$ | $X_5 = 6.4$ | $P(X=6.4)=0.2$ |

**FIGURE 9.10**

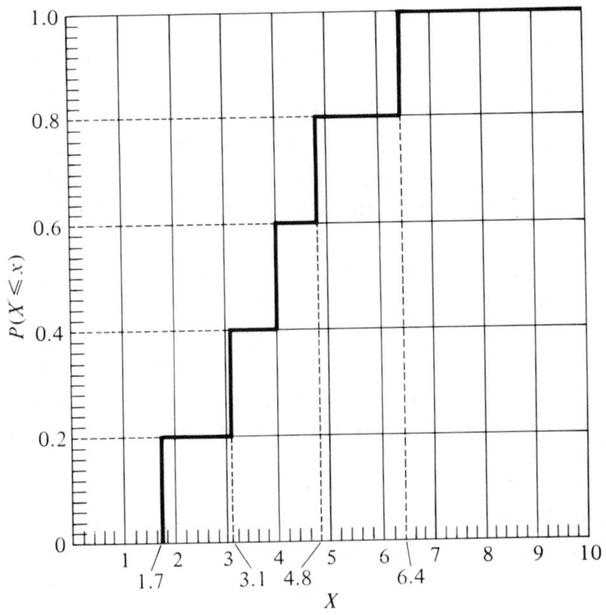


**FIGURE 9.11**

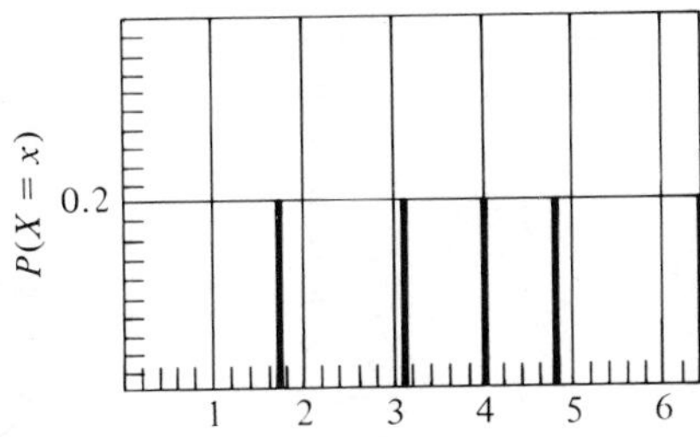

### Procedure for Approximation with Intervals Specified on the Random Variable Axis

In some cases the payoff function or other random variables defined on the outcome space may make it convenient for specific intervals to be defined on the random variable axis, $X$. For instance, you might desire to have intervals spaced so that the integers are the representative points. The steps for obtaining a discrete approximation with intervals specified on the random variable axis are:

> *Step 1:* Obtain the cumulative distribution function for the continuous random variable.
> *Step 2:* Select the intervals to be used in the approximation directly on the axis representing the random variable.
> *Step 3:* Determine the probability associated with each interval using the cumulative distribution function.
> *Step 4:* Select a single point to represent the interval. This can be done either directly in terms of the random variable (e.g., if the intervals are one unit in width, the integers may be chosen to represent the entire interval) or by dividing each interval into equally probable intervals as suggested in step 4 of the first method. If $n$ is small, the choice of the representative point can affect the quality of the approximation. But, as the number of intervals increases, the difference between methods of choosing representative points disappears.

Again using the continuous distribution in Figure 9.9, assume that we desire a discrete approximation in which the representative points are the integers 0 to 10. It is natural to choose intervals equally spaced about these points ($-0.5$

**TABLE 9.2**

| *Interval* | *Representative Point* | *Probability* |
|---|---|---|
| $-0.5 \leqslant X \leqslant 0.5$ | $X_1=0$ | $P(X=0)=0.01$ |
| $0.5 \leqslant X \leqslant 1.5$ | $X_2=1$ | $P(X=1)=0.07$ |
| $1.5 \leqslant X \leqslant 2.5$ | $X_3=2$ | $P(X=2)=0.12$ |
| $2.5 \leqslant X \leqslant 3.5$ | $X_4=3$ | $P(X=3)=0.18$ |
| $3.5 \leqslant X \leqslant 4.5$ | $X_5=4$ | $P(X=4)=0.25$ |
| $4.5 \leqslant X \leqslant 5.5$ | $X_6=5$ | $P(X=5)=0.18$ |
| $5.5 \leqslant X \leqslant 6.5$ | $X_7=6$ | $P(X=6)=0.10$ |
| $6.5 \leqslant X \leqslant 7.5$ | $X_8=7$ | $P(X=7)=0.04$ |
| $7.5 \leqslant X \leqslant 8.5$ | $X_9=8$ | $P(X=8)=0.03$ |
| $8.5 \leqslant X \leqslant 9.5$ | $X_{10}=9$ | $P(X=9)=0.02$ |
| $9.5 \leqslant X \leqslant 10.5$ | $X_{11}=10$ | $P(X=10)=0.0$ |

**FIGURE 9.12**

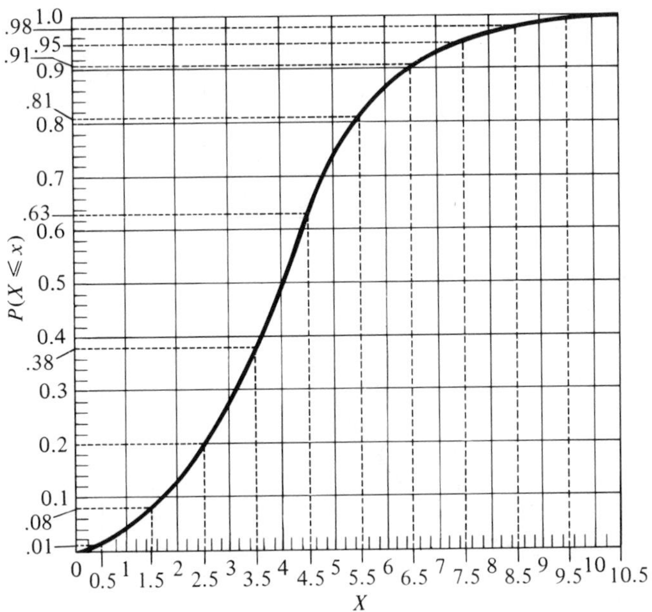


to +0.5, 0.5 to 1.5, 1.5 to 2.5, etc.). Figure 9.12 illustrates the interval choices and probabilities for each interval. The probabilities are tabulated in Table 9.2. Using this approximation, the expected value is

$$E[X] = (0 \times 0.01) + (1 \times 0.07) + (2 \times 0.12) + (3 \times 0.18) + (4 \times 0.25) + (5 \times 0.18) + (6 \times 0.10) + (7 \times 0.04) + (8 \times 0.03) + (9 \times 0.02) + (10 \times 0) = 4.05$$

This compares with an expected value of 4.0 obtained from the first approximation.

## USING DISCRETE APPROXIMATIONS TO SOLVE A PROBLEM

The ability to generate discrete approximations for continuous distributions allows all the definitions and manipulations for discrete random variables to be used for continuous random variables. The following example demonstrates the use of discrete approximations to solve a problem.

**Example 9.2**

Assume that you want to determine the probability distribution for the contribution from sale of a product in which the supply and demand are independent random variables. The probability distributions for these random variables are given in Figures 9.13 and 9.14. Contribution is defined as \$10 times gallons sold minus \$5 times gallons received (i.e., those supplied to you).

FIGURE 9.13

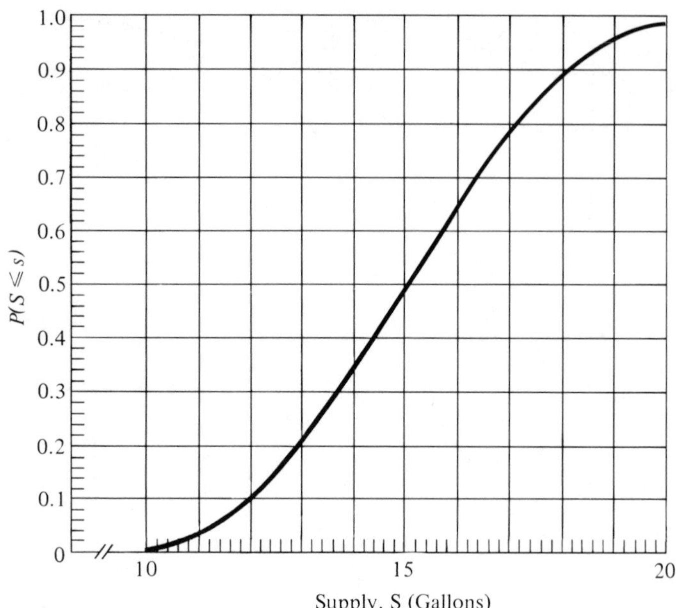


**FIGURE 9.14**

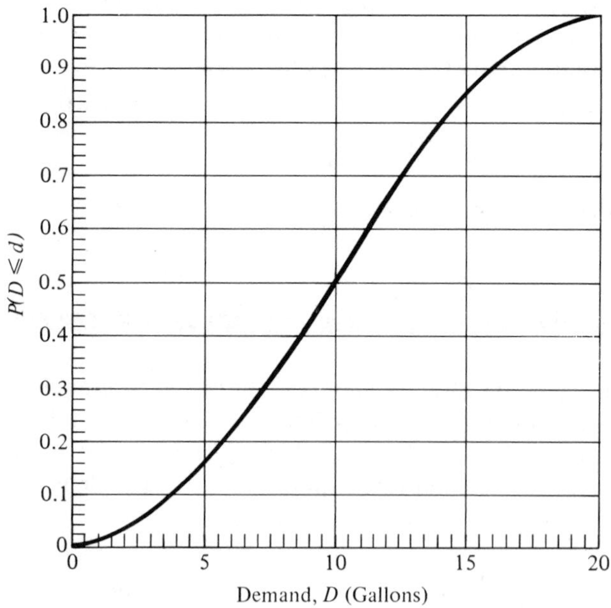

FIGURE 9.15

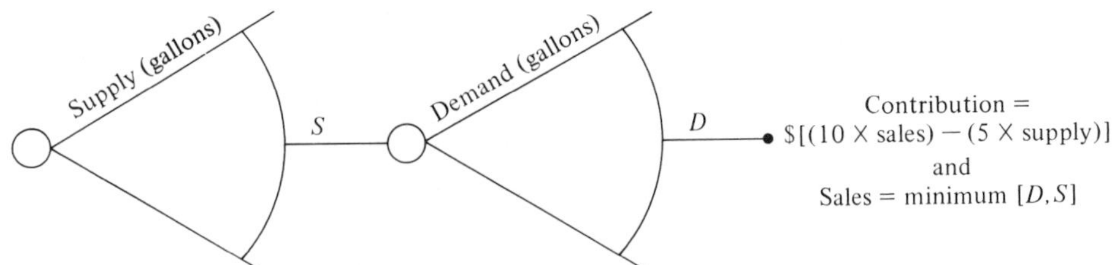


Conceptually, the problem can be diagrammed as shown in Figure 9.15. Assume that we decide to approximate each continuous probability distribution by five equally probable intervals. The approximations are shown in Tables 9.3 and 9.4. The diagram corresponding to this approximation is shown in Figure 9.16. The joint distribution consists of 25 points, each characterized by a supply quantity, $S$, and demand quantity, $D$. The probability of each point is the product of the two independent probabilities, $(0.2)(0.2)=0.04$. The values for the random variable, shown in the diagram, are calculated using the formulas in Figure 9.15. The cumulative probability

**TABLE 9.3**

*Discrete Approximation for Supply*

| |
|---|
| $P(S=12.0)=0.2$ |
| $P(S=13.6)=0.2$ |
| $P(S=15.1)=0.2$ |
| $P(S=16.3)=0.2$ |
| $P(S=18.1)=0.2$ |

**TABLE 9.4**

*Discrete Approximation for Demand*

| |
|---|
| $P(D=3.9)=0.2$ |
| $P(D=7.4)=0.2$ |
| $P(D=10.0)=0.2$ |
| $P(D=12.7)=0.2$ |
| $P(D=16.0)=0.2$ |

distribution for contribution can be calculated by arranging the values shown in Figure 9.16 in increasing order. This is done in Table 9.5 on page 233. Figure 9.17 is a plot of the cumulative distribution for contribution.

## SUMMARY

When the outcomes of an uncertain event are either continuous or consist of a large number of possible outcomes, continuous probability distributions are the most natural models. They represent continuous random variables.

Diagrams for decisions represent these continuous random variables by *fans* and a single representative outcome.

Cumulative distributions for continuous random variables are interpreted in exactly the same way as cumulative distributions for discrete random variables. However, probability density functions for continuous random variables must be interpreted using intervals and the area under the curve.

**FIGURE 9.16**

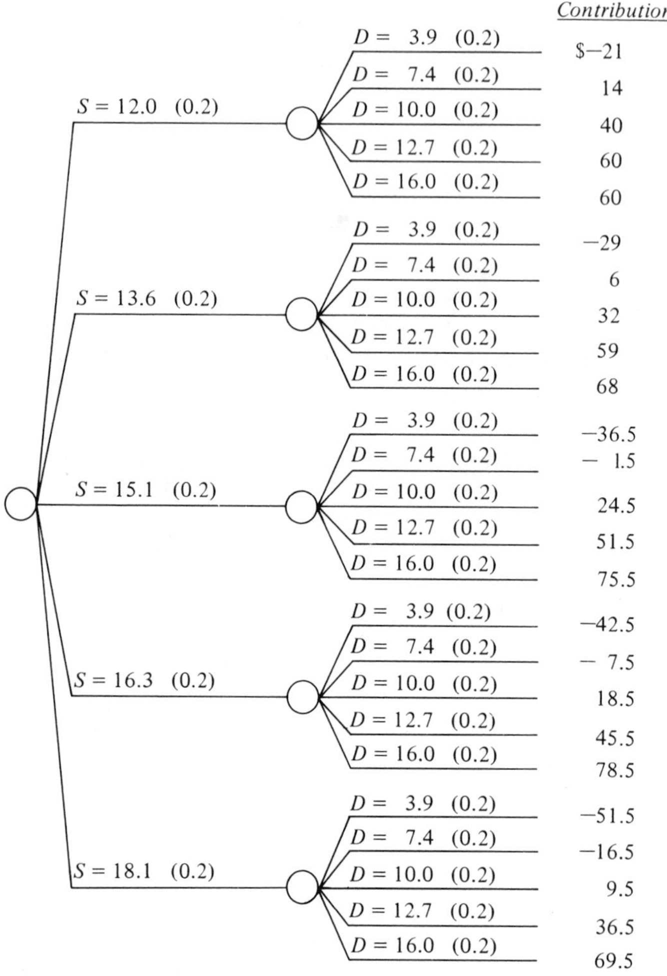


Summary measures are defined as before. Two additional measures of central tendency are:

*Median*: The median is the value of the random variable, $x_m$, such that $P(X \leqslant x_m) = 0.5$.

*Mode*: The most likely value of the random variable.

Calculations with continuous random variables can be done using calculus (if the functions are known) or by using discrete approximations. Discrete approximations are made by representing the random-variable scale by a few specific points and assigning probabilities to these points in a manner that captures the essence of the distribution. For most problems a small number of points provides an adequate approximation.

**TABLE 9.5**

**Probability Distribution for Contribution**

| *Contribution* | *Probability* | *Contribution* | *Probability* |
|---|---|---|---|
| −51.5 | 0.04 | 24.5 | 0.04 |
| −42.5 | 0.04 | 32.0 | 0.04 |
| −36.5 | 0.04 | 36.5 | 0.04 |
| −29.0 | 0.04 | 40.0 | 0.04 |
| −21.0 | 0.04 | 45.5 | 0.04 |
| −16.5 | 0.04 | 51.5 | 0.04 |
| −7.5 | 0.04 | 59 | 0.04 |
| −1.5 | 0.04 | 60 | 0.08 |
| 6.0 | 0.04 | 68 | 0.04 |
| 9.5 | 0.04 | 69.5 | 0.04 |
| 14 | 0.04 | 75.5 | 0.04 |
| 18.5 | 0.04 | 78.5 | 0.04 |

**FIGURE 9.17**

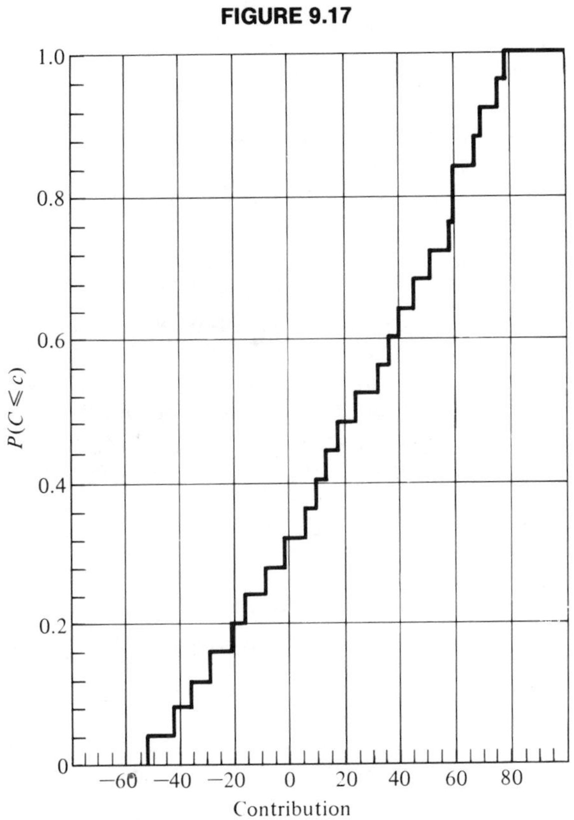

There are two approaches to obtaining a discrete approximation: (1) equally probable intervals, and (2) intervals specified on the random-variable axis.

After a discrete approximation is obtained, the calculations are done using the same methods we have been using throughout for discrete random variables.

## ASSIGNMENT MATERIAL

**9.1.** When should an uncertain event be modeled using a continuous probability distribution?

**9.2.** What is the major conceptual difference between probability density functions for continuous and discrete random variables?

**9.3.** With a discrete random variable we know that the sum of the probabilities must equal 1. What is the corresponding requirement for continuous random variables?

**9.4.** Refer to Figure 9.7. Calculate $P(5 \leqslant X \leqslant 9)$. Show your work.

**9.5.** Refer to Figure 9.8. Calculate $P(5 \leqslant X \leqslant 9)$. Show your work.

**9.6.** Use the equally probable interval method to make a five-interval discrete approximation for the continuous probability distribution shown in Figure 9.8.

**9.7.** Make a 10-interval discrete approximation for the continuous probability distribution shown in Figure 9.8. Use intervals 0–2, 2–4, 4–6, 6–8, 8–10, 10–12, 12–14, 14–16, 16–18, and 18–20.

**9.8.** What is the mean for the continuous probability distribution shown in Figure 9.8 using:

(a) The discrete approximation from problem 9.6?
(b) The discrete approximation from problem 9.7?

**9.9.** The unit contribution from a product depends on which of two prices, $6 or $4, is obtained. For a price of $6, the unit contribution is $3 and for a price of $4, the unit contribution is $1. The total contribution also depends on sales. Sales and price are independent, with the probability distributions shown in Table 9.6 and Figure 9.18. Use a five-point discrete approximation with equally probable intervals for the sales distribution to calculate the probability distribution for total contribution.

**TABLE 9.6**

| *Price* | *Probability* |
|---|---|
| $6 | 0.4 |
| 4 | 0.6 |

FIGURE 9.18

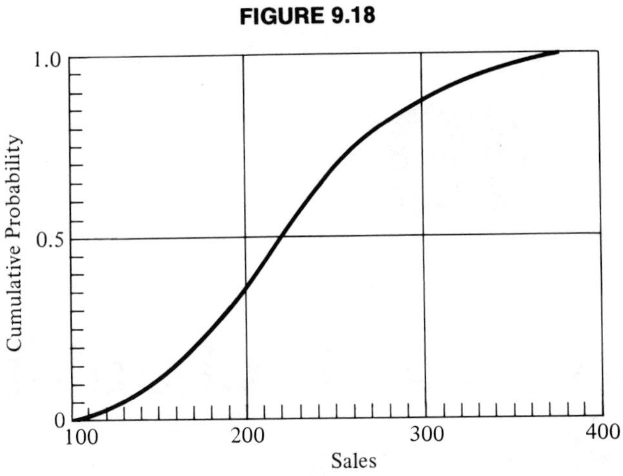

# 10

# Theoretical Probability Distributions

This chapter and the next two discuss three methods of assessing probability distributions for random variables. These methods use the three concepts of probability in different ways. This chapter presents probability distributions that can be obtained *theoretically* once basic probabilities are obtained. Figure 10.1 shows how the material fits into the overall framework. In each case a parameter(s) of the distribution must be obtained using the classical, relative frequency, or subjective approach. From the perspective of model building, there is an advantage to identifying theoretical probability distributions. These distributions represent specific processes. Therefore, we can make judgments on whether the specified conditions for the process are met, instead of making judgments directly in terms of probabilities.

The *binomial* and *Poisson* distributions are presented here for two reasons. First, they represent uncertain events that are commonly found in decisions problems. The ability to recognize the processes represented by these distributions, make the required judgments as to their applicability, and then establish the required probability distributions can be valuable. Second, these distributions serve as examples of a large number of "standard" distributions for discrete random variables. Working with them demonstrates how these other distributions could be used.

**FIGURE 10.1**

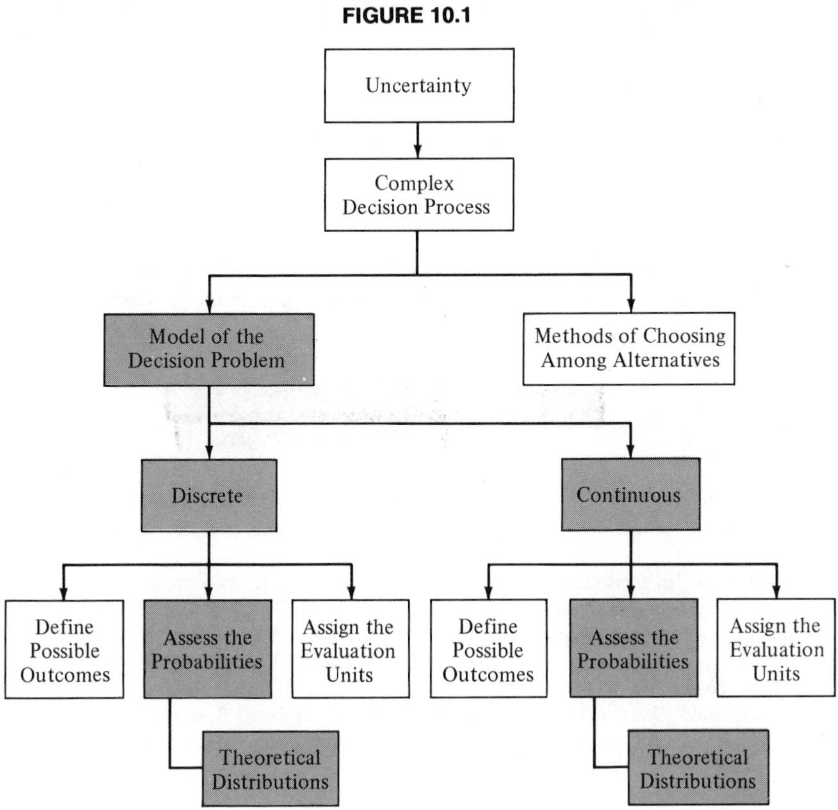

Three theoretical distributions for continuous random variables are included.[1] The *normal* distribution is included because of its wide applicability to problems involving sampling. The *exponential* distribution is included because it is often a good representation for service processes. The *beta* distribution is included because of its convenient properties for updating based on new information.

## BINOMIAL DISTRIBUTION

The *binomial* distribution represents a *Bernoulli* process, named for the man who first described it. As the name "binomial" implies, the process has two outcomes. They are usually referred to as "success" and "failure."

*Characteristics of the Bernoulli Process*

1. Repeated trials, with each trial producing either a success or failure.
2. Constant probability of success at each trial.
3. Each trial is independent in the sense that the sequence of outcomes is independent (i.e., the probability of success at any given trial does not depend on outcomes of other trials).

When these conditions are satisfied, the uncertain event is described by the binomial distribution given by the following formula:

**Binomial Formula**

***Definition:*** *If we let R be the random variable* ***number of successes,*** *n equal the number of trials, and p the probability of success on each trial, the binomial formula for the probability of r successes is*

$$P(R=r|n,p)=\frac{n!}{r!(n-r)!}(p)^r(1-p)^{n-r}$$

*where* $n!$ *stands for* $(n)\times(n-1)\times(n-2)\times\cdots\times(2)\times(1)$. *The term* $n!$ *is called* ***n-factorial,*** *and* $0!$ *is defined to be* $1$.

[1]For a more detailed treatment of probability distributions, see J. Braverman, *Probability, Logic and Management Decisions* (New York: McGraw-Hill, 1972); W. Feller, *An Introduction to Probability Theory and Its Applications*, Vol. 1, 3rd ed. (New York: Wiley, 1968); S. Karlin, *A First Course in Stochastic Processes* (New York: Academic Press, 1966); E. Parzen, *Modern Probability Theory and Its Application* (New York: Wiley, 1960); H. Raiffa and R. Schlaifer, *Applied Statistical Decision Theory*, (Division of Research, Harvard Business School, 1961); and R. L. Winkler, *An Introduction to Bayesian Inference and Decision* (New York: Holt, Rinehart and Winston, 1972).

### Illustration of the Binomial Formula

The appendix at the end of this chapter shows how the binomial formula can be derived. We can illustrate how it works by an example.

**Example 10.1**

Assume that you have an urn with six balls labeled "success" and four labeled "failure." If you make four random draws from this urn (replacing the ball drawn after each draw), what is the probability that you get three successes?

Without knowing anything about the binomial formula, we can develop a model of the uncertain event representing the four draws. The outcome space, probabilities, and values for the random variable number of "success" is shown in Figure 10.2. We are interested in the probability of three successes. The diagram shows that we can get three successes in several ways —four to be exact. Therefore,

$$P(3 \text{ successes}) = P(SSSF) + P(SSFS) + P(SFSS) + P(FSSS)$$

Each of these probabilities can be calculated using the multiplication formula for independent events:

$$P(SSSF) = (0.6)\times(0.6)\times(0.6)\times(0.4) = (0.6)^3\times(0.4) = 0.0864$$
$$P(SSFS) = (0.6)\times(0.6)\times(0.4)\times(0.6) = (0.6)^3\times(0.4) = 0.0864$$
$$P(SFSS) = (0.6)\times(0.4)\times(0.6)\times(0.6) = (0.6)^3\times(0.4) = 0.0864$$
$$P(FSSS) = (0.4)\times(0.6)\times(0.6)\times(0.6) = (0.6)^3\times(0.4) = 0.0864$$

Therefore,

$$P(3 \text{ successes}) = (4)\times(0.6)^3\times(0.4) = 4\times0.0864 = \underline{0.3456}$$

The probability of each of the separate events is the same and is equal to $(p)^r(1-p)^{n-r}$. The number of separate events that yield 3 successes is given by

$$\frac{n!}{r!(n-r)!} = \frac{4\times3\times2\times1}{(3\times2\times1)\times(1)} = 4$$

We see that the binomial formula is just a convenient way to calculate these probabilities.

### The Binomial Distribution

A Bernoulli process with parameters $n$ and $p$ defines a binomial distribution for the number of successes, $R$. For example, with $n=4$ and $p=0.6$, Example 10.1 yields

$$P(R=0) = 0.0256$$
$$P(R=1) = 0.1536$$
$$P(R=2) = 0.3456$$
$$P(R=3) = 0.3456$$
$$P(R=4) = 0.1296$$

**FIGURE 10.2**

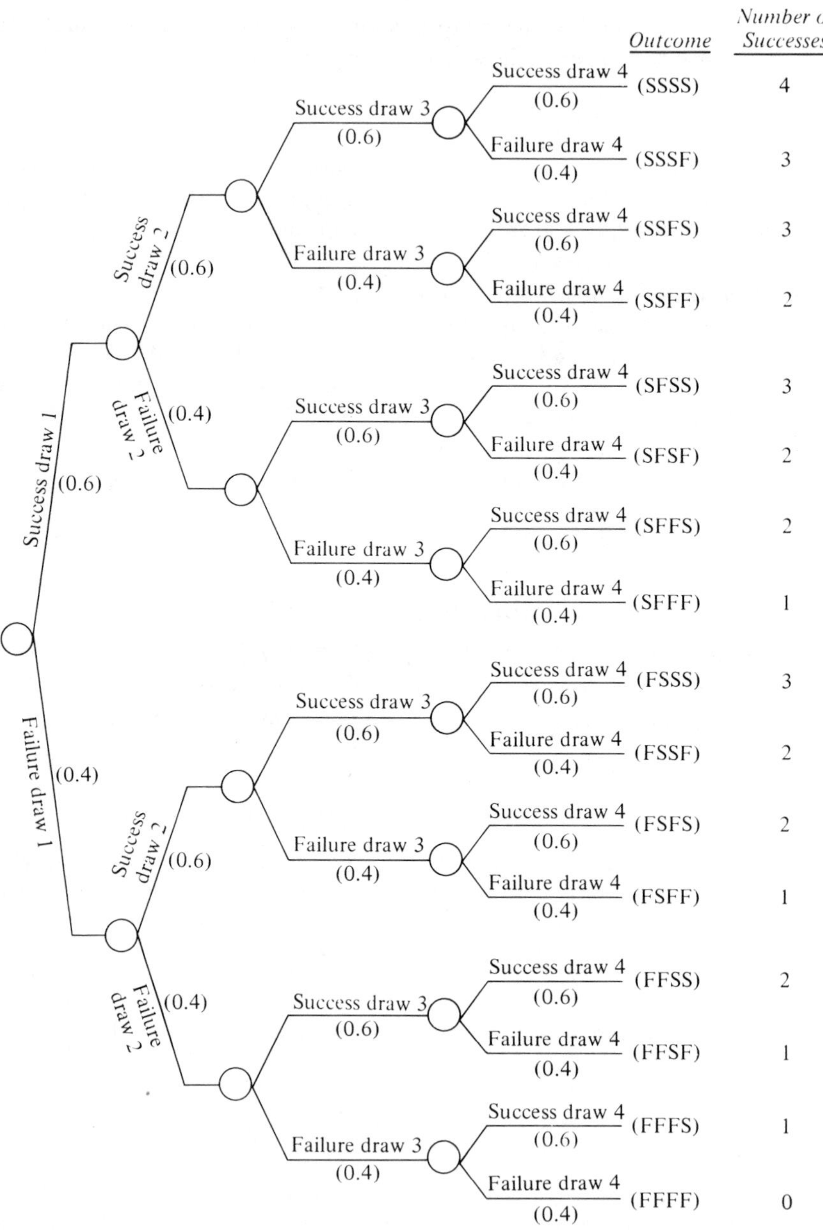

Outcome
Number of Successes
Success draw 1
(0.6)
Failure draw 1
(0.4)
Success draw 2
(0.6)
Failure draw 2
(0.4)
Success draw 2
(0.6)
Failure draw 2
(0.4)
Success draw 3
(0.6)
Failure draw 3
(0.4)
Success draw 4
(0.6)
Failure draw 4
(0.4)
(SSSS) 4
(SSSF) 3
(SSFS) 3
(SSFF) 2
(SFSS) 3
(SFSF) 2
(SFFS) 2
(SFFF) 1
(FSSS) 3
(FSSF) 2
(FSFS) 2
(FSFF) 1
(FFSS) 2
(FFSF) 1
(FFFS) 1
(FFFF) 0

The mean and standard deviation are given by

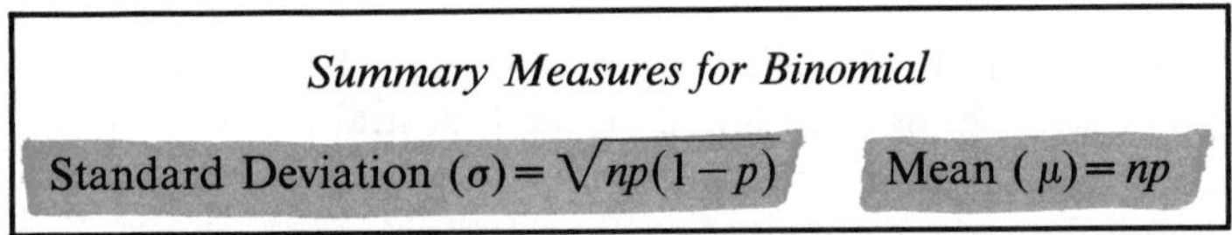

*Summary Measures for Binomial*

Standard Deviation $(\sigma) = \sqrt{np(1-p)}$ Mean $(\mu) = np$

Since the formula for binomial probabilities can be burdensome to calculate, tables have been developed for the probability density functions and cumulative probability distributions. These tables are in Appendices A and B. Their use is described later in the chapter.

### Formulation of Problems Using Binomial Distribution

Some examples of processes that sometimes follow the binomial distribution are:

1. Quality control problems, in which units are either good or bad, or processes are either in control or out of control during a production cycle.
2. Marketing problems, in which customers exhibit preference for brand $X$ or brand $Y$, or sales personnel either make a sale or fail to make a sale.
3. Accounting problems, in which auditors sample clients' accounts to determine if any errors exist. At each trial an error either exists or it does not exist.
4. In public opinion polling, an individual may be for one candidate or the other.

The decision to use a binomial distribution as a model involves verification that the three underlying assumptions hold. Methods of verification are diverse but involve an understanding of the process being modeled.

### Verification of Conditions

Consider, for example, buying hay for feeding cattle. Although a variety of hay types are available, two classifications can be used: alfalfa and grass. The best mixture of the two depends upon the feeding program. Assume that a particular ranch desired 20% grass and 80% alfalfa. Because alfalfa is more expensive, the supplier would provide the minimum amount of alfalfa required by the contract. Therefore, if the supplier complied with the contract, an order of 100 bales would contain 20 bales of grass and 80 of alfalfa. To determine compliance, the rancher might take a sample of 10 bales. Is the sampling process adequately described by the binomial distribution?

There is a series of 10 trials, each producing a grass (success) or an alfalfa (failure) bale, so the first condition is satisfied. The next condition requires the probability of success at each trial to remain constant. Consider two possibilities for sampling:

1. Randomly pick 10 bales in succession;

2. Randomly pick one bale, replace it, randomly pick another, and repeat until 10 bales have been selected.

Under plan 1 the probability of success would *not* be constant each trial. If there actually were 20 bales of grass, on the first trial $P$ (success)$=20/100$. If a grass bale is obtained on the first trial, $P$(success)$=19/99$ for the second trial. If an alfalfa bale is obtained on the first trial, $P$(success)$=20/99$ on the second trial. Under plan 2, however, the probability of success does stay the same for each trial, and therefore satisfies the second condition.

The third condition requires the trials to be independent. Assuming the sampling is done with replacement (plan 2 above), consider two possibilities for selecting the bales: (1) take those on top of the stack, and (2) use a process in which every bale has an equal chance of being selected. In the first case, if the supplier stacks the hay in such a manner that all grass bales are together, independence is not satisfied, because taking the bales from one area means that the probability of grass on trial 2 given grass on trial 1 is higher than the probability of grass on trial 2 given alfalfa on trial 1, and so on. Under the second case, however, the independence assumption is satisfied, and hence a binomial distribution would adequately model the process.

In this example, $p=0.20$ and $n=10$. The outcome space is $\Omega=\{0,1,2,3,4,5,6,7,8,9,10\}$, where the numbers represent the number of successes (grass bales) in a sample of 10.

The problem formulation process involves four steps:

1. Verify that the process satisfies the conditions of a binomial distribution.
2. Determine $p$ and $n$.
3. Specify the outcome space $\Omega=(0,1,\ldots,n)$.
4. Define the events of interest on the outcome space.

Calculation of the appropriate probabilities for the events of interest is done using the formula or tables as demonstrated in the next section.

### Using the Tables

Tables of binomial probability density functions and cumulative probability distributions are convenient for calculating probabilities. Appendix A gives the probability for any single element in outcome space for a range of binomial distributions with $p \leqslant 0.5$ and $n \leqslant 25$. To illustrate the use of this table, consider Example 10.2.

#### Example 10.2

What is the probability of obtaining 5 grass bales in the sample of 10 for the problem described above?

The outcome space in terms of the number of grass bales (a success) is shown in Figure 10.3, where the event *5 grass bales* is shown by the box. The

FIGURE 10.3

| $\Omega$ (number of grass bales) = {0,1,2,3,4,[5],6,7,8,9,10} |
|---|

parameters are $p=0.20$, $n=10$, and the probability of the event *5 grass bales* is

$$P(R=5|n=10,p=0.20)=0.026$$

The value 0.026 can be read directly from the table in Appendix A.

Appendix B gives the cumulative probability of a given number of successes or more. That is, it gives probabilities of the form $P(R \geqslant r|n,p)$. To illustrate, consider Example 10.3.

**Example 10.3**

What is the probability that 3 or more grass bales are obtained in a sample of 10 for the problem described above?

The outcome space remains the same as in Example 10.2. In this case we are interested in the event $R \geqslant 3$. This event is shown by the box in Figure 10.4. The parameters are $n=10$, $p=0.2$, and the probability of the event of interest is

FIGURE 10.4

| $\Omega$ (number of grass bales) = {0, 1, 2, [3,4,5,6,7,8,9,10]} |
|---|

$$P(R \geqslant 3|n=10, p=0.20)=0.322$$

The value 0.322 can be read directly from the table in Appendix B.

Examples 10.4 and 10.5 demonstrate how the tables in Appendixes A and B can be used to obtain probabilities for events not directly tabulated.

**Example 10.4**

What is the probability that 4 or fewer grass bales are obtained in a sample of 10 for the problem described above?

The probability of obtaining a grass bale at each trial remains 0.2. The outcome space and event $R \leqslant 4$ are shown in Figure 10.5.

FIGURE 10.5

| $\Omega$ (number of grass bales) = {[0,1,2,3,4],5,6,7,8,9,10} |
|---|

There are two ways to obtain $P(R \leqslant 4|n=10, p=0.2)$. One way is to use the addition rule and look up the probability of each individual term [i.e., $P(R \leqslant 4)=P(R=0)+P(R=1)+P(R=2)+P(R=3)+P(R=4)=0.966$]. Since the cumulative table is for "greater than or equal to," not "less than or equal to," it cannot be used directly. However, considering the outcome space shown in Figure 10.5, we see that $P(R \leqslant 4|n=10, p=0.2)=1-P(R \geqslant 5|n=10, p=0.2)$. The second expression is in the table. Therefore,

$$P(R \leqslant 4|n=10, p=0.2)=1-0.033=0.967$$

The difference between the two results is due to rounding errors.

**Example 10.5**

What is the probability of obtaining 6 alfalfa bales?

Since we are now interested in the number of alfalfa bales instead of the number of grass bales, the definition of success changes to obtaining an alfalfa bale. The probability of success at each trial becomes 0.8, and the outcome space is defined in terms of the number of alfalfa bales. A minor problem arises because the binomial tables only have probabilities tabulated for $p \leqslant 0.5$. Therefore, we cannot directly look up probabilities for $p=0.8$. However, a slight reformulation allows these tables to be used. As shown in Figure 10.6, each point in outcome space can be described in terms of either successes (alfalfa) or failures (grass). The point in outcome space $R=6$ is the

**FIGURE 10.6**

$\Omega_R$ (number of alfalfa bales) = { 0,1,2,3,4,5,[6],7,8,9,10}

• • • • • • • • • • •

$\Omega_W$ (number of grass bales) = {10,9,8,7,6,5,[4],3,2,1,0 }

same as the point $W=4$, where $R$ stands for success and $W$ stands for failure. Using Appendix A, we have

$$P(R=6|n=10, p=0.8)=P(W=4|n=10, p=0.2)=0.088$$

## POISSON DISTRIBUTION

The binomial distribution describes a process with repeated trials and outcomes that can be described by "success" or "failure." Consider a process where successes (the occurrence of a specified event) can be identified, but where the concept of a trial is not natural. We can determine when an arrival occurs but not the nonoccurrences.

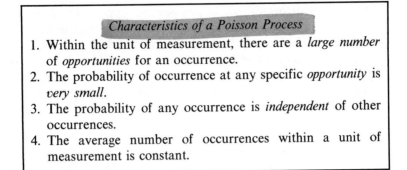

*Characteristics of a Poisson Process*

1. Within the unit of measurement, there are a *large number* of *opportunities* for an occurrence.
2. The probability of occurrence at any specific *opportunity* is *very small.*
3. The probability of any occurrence is *independent* of other occurrences.
4. The average number of occurrences within a unit of measurement is constant.

The first two of these properties are discussed in more detail below.

1. Within the unit of measurement, there are a *large number* of opportunities for an occurrence. For instance, if the unit of measurement is some time interval (say an hour or minute), the amount of time required to complete the arrival process must be small in comparison with the time interval over which you are interested in observing arrivals (see Figure 10.7). If the unit of measurement is an area (say a square yard or square foot), the area associated with an event such as a blemish must be small in comparison with the total area under observation (see Figure 10.8).

**FIGURE 10.7**

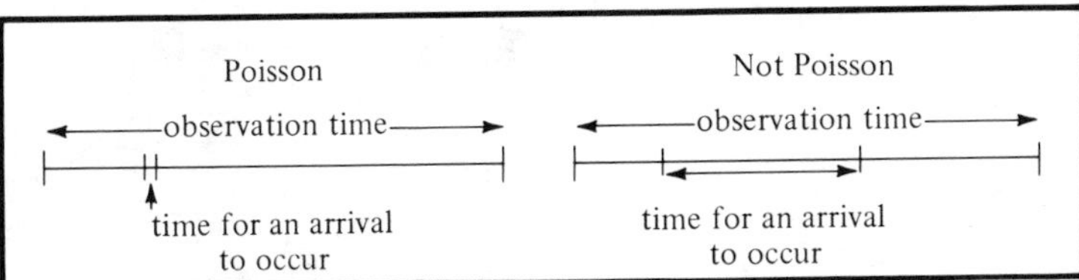


**FIGURE 10.8**

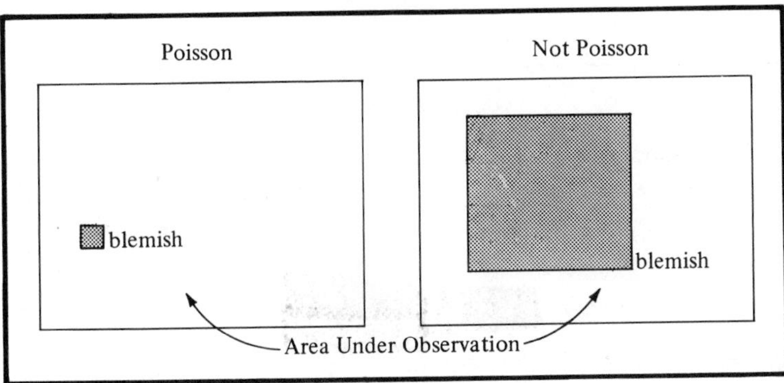

2. The probability of occurrence at any specific opportunity is *very small.* For instance, if an arrival process takes 1 minute to complete, the probability of an arrival during any 1-minute interval must be very small. Therefore, an arrival process like (A) in Figure 10.9 would qualify as Poisson, whereas outcome (B) would not. Similarly, if we observe blemishes on an area, outcome (A) in Figure 10.10 would qualify as Poisson, but outcome (B) would not.

**FIGURE 10.9**

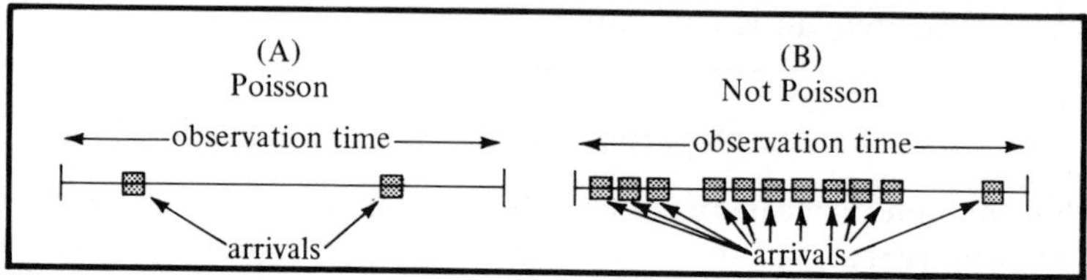


**FIGURE 10.10**

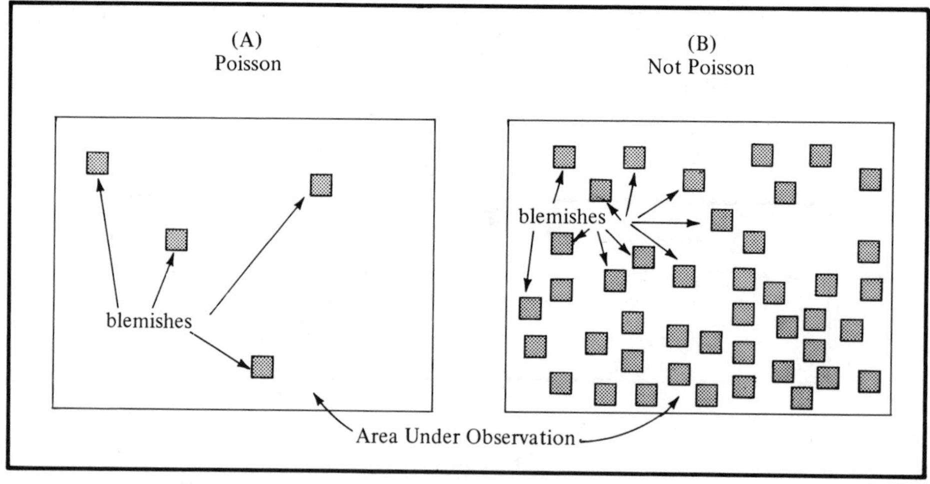


**Poisson Formula**

***Definition:*** *If we let X be the number of occurrences within a measurement interval and m be the average number of occurrences within the measurement interval, the Poisson formula for the probability of X occurrences is*

$$P(X=x)=\frac{e^{-m}m^x}{x!}$$

*where e stands for the constant 2.718.*

### The Poisson Distribution

The parameter $m$ defines a Poisson distribution. The mean and standard deviation are given by

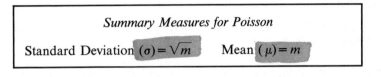

*Summary Measures for Poisson*

Standard Deviation $(\sigma) = \sqrt{m}$ Mean $(\mu) = m$

### Formulation of Problems Using the Poisson Distribution

Some examples of processes that sometimes follow the Poisson distribution are:

1. Arrivals at a service center. For instance, over some periods in a day, the arrivals at an emergency room in a hospital might be represented by a Poisson distribution.
2. Machine breakdowns and equipment failures sometimes follow a Poisson process.
3. The occurrence of defects on finished surfaces may be distributed according to the Poisson distribution.

Exact verification that a Poisson distribution is a good model can be difficult. It may require a substantial amount of investigation and the use of some statistical techniques in any particular instance.

### Using the Tables

The Poisson distribution is tabulated in Appendixes C and D. They contain the probability density functions and cumulative probability distribution for the Poisson distribution with $m \leqslant 10$. The following examples will illustrate how to use the tables.

**Example 10.6**

Assume that an investigation demonstrates that arrivals of jobs at a repair center can be described by the Poisson distribution with an average arrival rate of 2 jobs per hour. What is the probability of exactly three arrivals during the next hour?

From the problem, $m=2$, and the outcome space is shown in Figure 10.11 where the event *3 arrivals* is shown by the box. From the table in

**FIGURE 10.11**

$\Omega$ (arrivals next hour) = $\{0, 1, 2, \boxed{3}, 4, \ldots\}$

Appendix C,

$$P(X=3|m=2)=0.180$$

**Example 10.7**

For the same repair center as described in Example 10.6, what is the probability of three or more arrivals during the next hour?

The average arrival rate is still $m=2$, and the outcome space and event $X \geqslant 3$ are shown in Figure 10.12. From the cumulative table in Appendix D,

$$P(X \geqslant 3|m=2)=0.323$$

**FIGURE 10.12**

Ω (arrivals next hour) = {0,1,2,[3,4,...]}

**Example 10.8**

Again using the repair center in Example 10.6, what is the probability of exactly three arrivals in the next hour and one-half?

In this case, since the time interval of interest has changed, so has the average arrival rate during that period: $m=(2 \text{ per hour}) \times (1.5 \text{ hours})=3$. The outcome space is the same as shown in Figure 10.11. From Appendix C,

$$P(X=3|m=3)=0.224$$

### Poisson Approximation to Binomial

If a process that is described by a binomial distribution has a large $n$ and small $p$, it satisfies the conditions specified for the Poisson distribution. Rules of thumb are that the Poisson can be used to approximate the binomial if any of the following conditions are satisfied:

$$\begin{aligned} n &\geqslant 10 \quad \text{and} \quad p \leqslant 0.01 \\ n &\geqslant 20 \quad \text{and} \quad p \leqslant 0.03 \\ n &\geqslant 50 \quad \text{and} \quad p \leqslant 0.05 \\ n &\geqslant 100 \quad \text{and} \quad p \leqslant 0.08 \end{aligned}$$

**Example 10.9**

For example, suppose you were interested in the probability that there are 10 or more defective parts in a sample of 100 with a defective rate of 5%.

The problem can be formulated as a binomial with the outcome space shown in Figure 10.13. The probability of interest is $P(R \geqslant 10|n=100, p=0.05)$. Appendix B cannot be used because it only has probabilities tabulated

FIGURE 10.13

$\Omega$ (defective) = {0,1,2,...,9,[10,11,...,99,100]}

for $n \leqslant 25$. Rather than use the binomial formula, we could approximate the probability using a Poisson distribution. To use the Poisson we need $m$, the average number of occurrences during the measurement interval. The parameter $m$ is also the mean of the Poisson distribution. For the binomial distribution, the mean number of defectives is $np = 100 \times 0.05 = 5$. To approximate the binomial by a Poisson, we equate their means, $m = np = 5$. From Appendix D,

$$P(X \geqslant 10 | m=5) = 0.032$$

## THE NORMAL DISTRIBUTION

The normal distribution is the well-known "bell-shaped" curve.

**Normal Formula**

***Definition:*** *If f(x) is normally distributed, then*

$$f(x) = \frac{1}{\sigma\sqrt{2\pi}} \exp\left[-\frac{1}{2}\left(\frac{x-\mu}{\sigma}\right)^2\right]$$

This formula represents the curve shown in Figure 10.14.

FIGURE 10.14

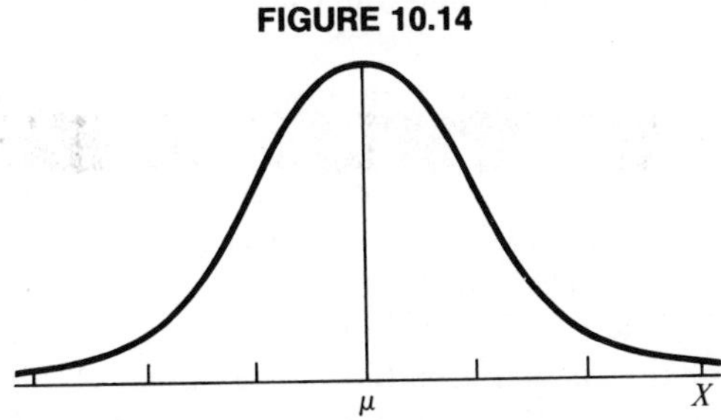


It is widely used in probability and statistics. In many cases its property of symmetry about the expected value seems to fit information available on a random variable. The central limit theorem provides conditions under which a normal distribution represents the outcome from a sampling process.[2]

[2]For a detailed discussion of the central limit theorem and sampling processes, see any text on statistics (e.g., P. G. Hoel, *Introduction to Mathematical Statistics*, 4th ed. (New York: Wiley, 1971) or W. A. Spurr and C. P. Bonini, *Statistical Analysis for Business Decisions*, rev. ed. (Homewood, Ill.: Irwin, 1973).

**Central Limit Theorem**

*Let $f(x)$ be the probability density function for some random variable x, with mean $\mu$ and finite variance $\sigma^2$. Define $\overline{X}_n$ as the mean of a random sample of n values from $f(x)$. Then $\overline{X}_n$ is itself a random variable and, for n sufficiently large, the probability density function for $\overline{X}_n$ is normally distributed, with mean $\mu$ and variance $\sigma^2/n$.*

For practical purposes, as long as $f(x)$ is "reasonable" (i.e., not wildly skewed or multimodal) the probability density function for $\overline{X}_n$ is closely approximated by a normal distribution as long as $n \geqslant 30$.

In addition to the conditions stated in the central limit theorem, both empirical observations and subjective assessment may lead to the use of a normal distribution to represent a random variable. As can be seen from the formula, it is completely specified by two parameters: the mean, $\mu$, and the standard deviation, $\sigma$. Estimates of these parameters can be calculated from empirical observations. Statistical methods are available to test the observations for consistency with a normal distribution.[3]

### Using the Normal Table

Since the normal formula is difficult to use, tables have been developed for the probabilities. Appendix E is the normal table. It gives cumulative probabilities for the standardized normal distribution. This is a normal distribution with a mean of zero and standard deviation of 1. Any normal distribution can be "standardized" to allow the table for the standardized normal distribution to be used.

Given a normally distributed random variable $X$ with mean $\mu$ and standard deviation $\sigma$, a "standardized" random variable $Z=(X-\mu)/\sigma$ can be created. The random variable $Z$ is called the *standard normal deviate*. The tables provide the area under the curve between the mean and some number of standard deviations away from the mean. For instance, consider the density function for the standard normal deviate, $Z$, shown in Figure 10.15. Using Appendix E, the shaded area (i.e., the area between the mean and one standard deviation) is 0.3413. Therefore, $P(0 \leqslant Z \leqslant 1)=0.3413$. To illustrate the use of the tables with other normal distributions, consider the following examples.

[3]A standard method for testing any distribution is the chi-square goodness-of-fit test described in standard statistics tests. Tests designed specifically for the normal distribution are also available. For example, see S. S. Shapiro and M. B. Wilk, "An Analysis of Variance Test for Normality," *Biometrika*, Vol. 52, Nos. 3–4, 1965, and H. W. Lilliefors, "On the Kolmogorov–Smirnov Test for Normality with Mean and Variance Unknown," *Journal of the American Statistical Association*, June 1967.

FIGURE 10.15

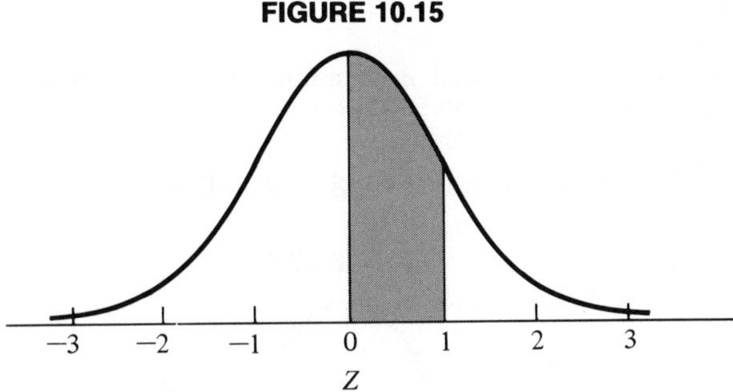


**Example 10.10**

Assume that it has been established that daily demand for a commodity is normal with a mean of 100 units and a standard deviation of 50. What is the probability that demand lies between 100 and 150 units?

Figure 10.16 displays the problem graphically. The horizontal axis represents outcome space and the vertical axis the density function. The $P(100 \leqslant X \leqslant 150)$ is represented by the shaded area. To use the table, the problem is converted to an equivalent problem for the standard normal distribution. This is done by converting to the standard normal deviate, $Z=(X-\mu)/\sigma$. For this problem $\mu=100$ and $\sigma=50$.

$$X_1=100: \quad Z_1=\frac{100-100}{50}=0$$

$$X_2=150: \quad Z_2=\frac{150-100}{50}=1$$

Therefore, using the standard normal curve, the area lies between $0 \leqslant Z \leqslant 1$. This is exactly the same as shown in Figure 10.15. We can formally write the transformation procedure as shown below:

$$P(100 \leqslant X \leqslant 150)=P\left(\frac{100-\mu}{\sigma} \leqslant Z \leqslant \frac{150-\mu}{\sigma}\right)=P(0 \leqslant Z \leqslant 1)=0.3413$$

FIGURE 10.16

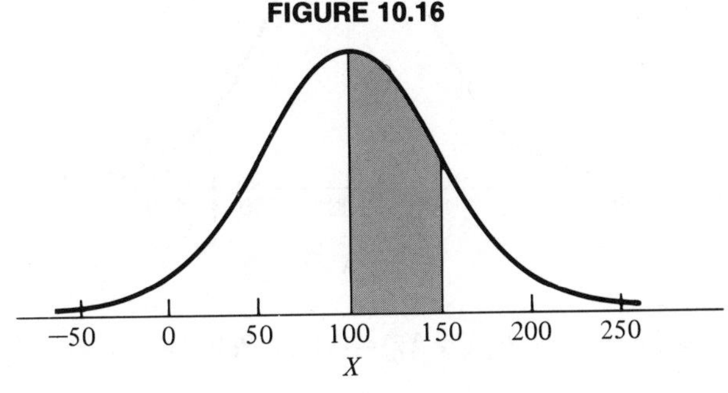

**Example 10.11**

For the same distribution as used in Example 10.10, what is the probability that demand is greater than 175 units?

Figure 10.17 displays the problem graphically.

FIGURE 10.17

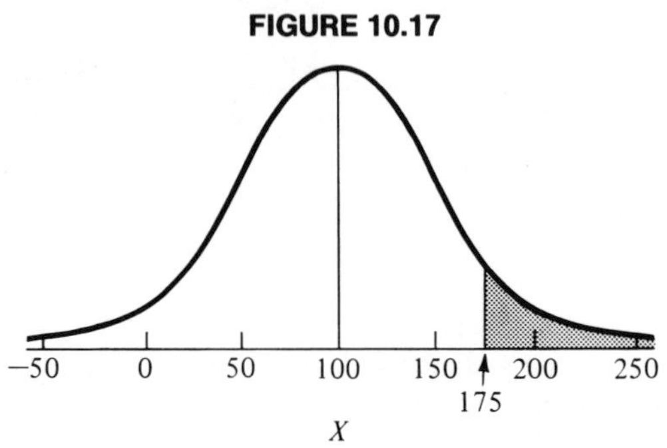


Converting to the standard normal curve, we have $P(X \geqslant 175) = P\left(Z \geqslant \dfrac{175-100}{50}\right) = P(Z \geqslant 1.5)$. Since the normal curve is symmetrical about the mean, we know that $P(Z \geqslant 0) = 0.5$. Therefore, $P(Z \geqslant 1.5) = 0.5 - P(0 \leqslant Z \leqslant 1.5)$. From the table we find that $P(0 \leqslant Z \leqslant 1.5) = 0.4332$ and hence

$$P(Z \geqslant 1.5) = 0.5 - 0.4332 = 0.0668$$

**Example 10.12**

Referring again to the problem statement for Example 10.10, what is the number of units, $X_0$, which must be on hand so that there is only a 10% chance of running out?

Figure 10.18 displays the problem graphically.

FIGURE 10.18

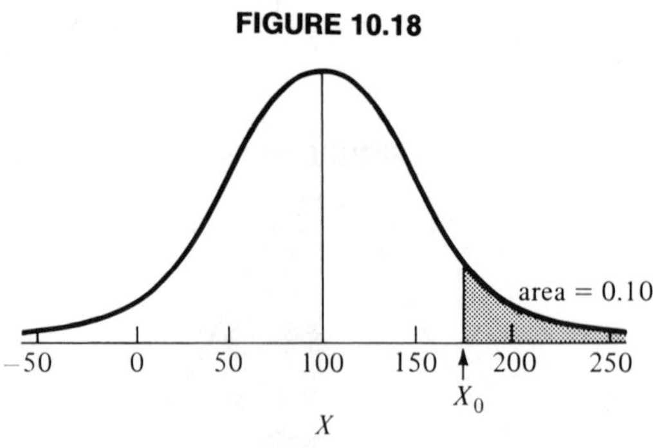


In this case we know that $P(X \geqslant X_0) = 0.1$ or $P(100 \leqslant X \leqslant X_0) = 0.4$. Therefore, using the standard normal distribution we have $P(0 \leqslant Z \leqslant Z_0) = 0.4$. From the body of the table we see that for $Z_0 = 1.28$, $P(0 \leqslant Z \leqslant 1.28) = 0.3997$, which is the closest value to 0.4 in the table. Transforming back to the distribution on demand, we have

$$Z_0 = 1.28 = \frac{X_0 - 100}{50}$$

or

$$X_0 = (1.28) \times (50) + 100 = 164$$

Other areas under the normal curve can be found in a similar fashion. Rules of thumb often used to assess probabilities quickly for normal distributions are:

$$P((\mu - \sigma) \leqslant X \leqslant (\mu + \sigma)) = 0.68$$
$$P((\mu - 2\sigma) \leqslant X \leqslant (\mu + 2\sigma)) = 0.95$$
$$P((\mu - 3\sigma) \leqslant X \leqslant (\mu + 3\sigma)) = 0.99$$

### Normal Approximation to the Binomial

The normal distribution provides a useful approximation to the binomial distribution under some conditions. In general, these conditions require the number of trials, $n$, to be large and the probability of a success on any trial, $p$, to be near 0.5. Guidelines for the use of this approximation are: $np > 5$ and $n(1-p) > 5$. This can be a valuable approximation, since binomial tables may not be available for large $n$, and direct use of the binomial formula can be time consuming. There are two parts to the approximation. The first is to find the appropriate normal distribution. This is done by equating the mean and standard deviation of the binomial and normal approximation. That is, for the normal distribution, set

$$\mu = np \qquad \text{(mean of the binomial)}$$

and

$$\sigma = \sqrt{np(1-p)} \qquad \text{(standard deviation of the binomial)}$$

The second step is to translate the points of interest in the outcome space for the binomial into the outcome space for the normal distribution. The translation must take place because the binomial is a discrete distribution and the normal is a continuous distribution. It is accomplished by assigning a discrete outcome $x$ to the range $x \pm 0.5$. The following example illustrates the procedure.

**Example 10.13**

Consider a manufacturer of complex integrated-circuit components. The defect rate is very high, 60%. The inspection process is costly and time consuming. An engineer is going to take some units to an electronics show, where he will hook them up and test them before they are demonstrated. He needs 30 good units. What is the probability that he will have at least 30 good units if he takes 100?

The normal approximation to the binomial distribution for good units has

$$\mu = np = 100 \times 0.4 = 40$$
$$\sigma = \sqrt{np(1-p)} = \sqrt{100(0.4)(0.6)} = \sqrt{24} = 4.9$$

The discrete formulation is $R \geqslant 30$. Translated to the continuous approximation, we have $X \geqslant 29.5$. The approximations are shown in Figure 10.19. Notice that the outcome, 30 good units, is represented by $29.5 \leqslant X \leqslant 30.5$.

FIGURE 10.19

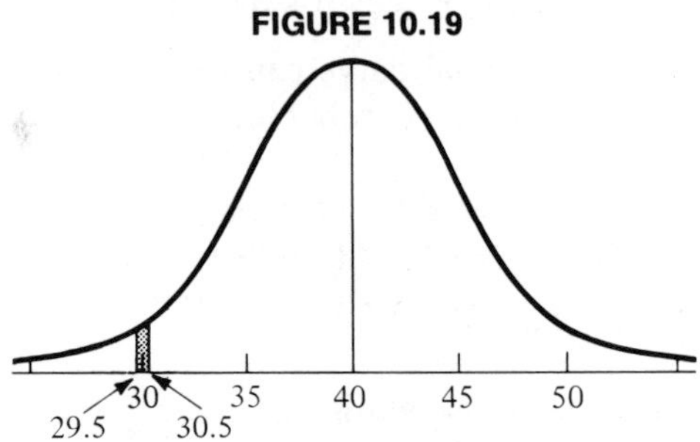


Since we want 30 *or more*, the 30th unit must be included in the outcome space. Therefore, the continuous approximation representation is $X \geqslant 29.5$.

$$\begin{aligned} P(X \geqslant 29.5) &= 0.5 + P(29.5 \leqslant X \leqslant 40) \\ &= 0.5 + P\left(\frac{29.5 - 40}{4.9} \leqslant Z \leqslant 0\right) \\ &= 0.5 + P(-2.14 \leqslant Z \leqslant 0) \\ &= 0.5 + 0.4838 = 0.9839 \end{aligned}$$

## ●● EXPONENTIAL DISTRIBUTION

The exponential distribution often provides a good model for processes in which event times are important. For instance, in designing a service facility, you may be interested in modeling the time between arriving customers or the time required to serve a given customer. In both cases *time* is the random variable of interest, and it is *continuous*.

The conditions under which an exponential distribution provides a good model are precisely the same as those for the Poisson distribution. Consider the arrivals of patients at a hospital emergency room (see Figure 10.20). Assume that we are interested in the number of arrivals in a given time period and that the conditions required for the Poisson distribution are satisfied.

FIGURE 10.20

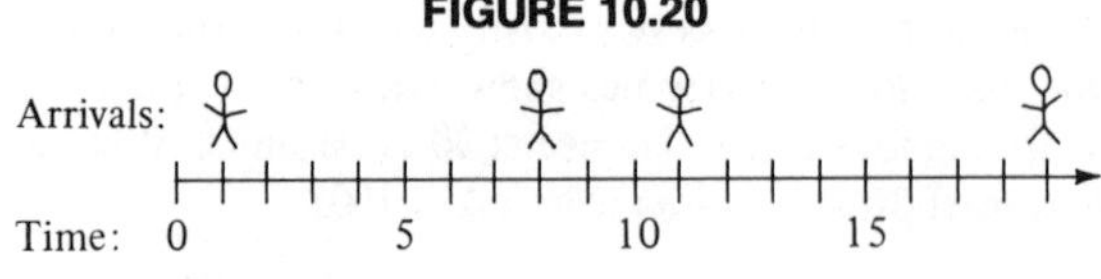

If we are interested in the time between arrivals instead of the number of arrivals in a given time, the exponential distribution provides the appropriate model. It can be derived directly from the Poisson distribution.

### ●● Relationship to Poisson

To illustrate how the exponential distribution is related to the Poisson, assume that arrivals satisfy the conditions for a Poisson distribution with an average of two arrivals per hour. If we are interested in the number of arrivals in some arbitrary time period $t_1$ hours, the mean number of arrivals is $m=2t_1$. The Poisson distribution for arrivals in time period $t_1$ is given by

$$P(X=x)=\frac{(e^{-2t_1})(2t_1)^x}{x!}$$

Now consider the probability that the arrival time, $T$, is less than $t_1$: that is, the probability that one or more arrivals occur during the time period $t_1$. We can calculate the probability that no arrivals occur in the time period $t_1$ as

$$P(T>t_1)=P(X=0|m=2t_1)=e^{-2t_1}$$

Therefore, the probability that an arrival occurs during the time period is

$$P(T\leqslant t_1)=1-P(X=0|m=2t_1)=1-e^{-2t_1}$$

This is just the cumulative distribution for the arrival time.

**Exponential Distribution**

***Definition:*** *If we let λ be the average number of arrivals in some time period t, the cumulative exponential distribution is*

$$P(T\leqslant t)=1-e^{-\lambda t}$$

*The probability density function is*[4]

$$f(t)=\lambda e^{-\lambda t}$$

*It is a one-parameter distribution with mean* $=1/\lambda$ *and standard deviation* $=1/\lambda$.

### ●● The No-Memory Property

An important property of the exponential distribution is that it has no memory. This means that the probability that an arrival will occur in the next time interval is independent of what has happened in previous time intervals.

[4]This can be derived directly from the cumulative distribution by using calculus and differentiating:

$$f(t)=\frac{d}{dt}(1-e^{-\lambda t})=\lambda e^{-\lambda t}$$

For instance, assume we are interested in the probability that an arrival will occur during the next unit interval when $\lambda = 2$ under two different conditions:

1. An arrival has occurred at $t=0$. Therefore, using the cumulative exponential distribution,

$$\begin{aligned}P(0 \leqslant T \leqslant 1) &= P(T \leqslant 1) - P(T \leqslant 0)\\ &= (1-e^{-2(1)}) - (1-e^{-2(0)})\\ &= 1-e^{-2} = 1-0.135 = 0.865\end{aligned}$$

2. An arrival occurred 2 time units ago but no arrivals have occurred since. In this case we want $P(2 \leqslant T \leqslant 3 | T \geqslant 2)$. That is, given no arrivals in $0 \leqslant T \leqslant 2$, what is the probability of an arrival between time units 2 and 3? Again using the cumulative exponential distribution,

$$\begin{aligned}P(2 \leqslant T \leqslant 3 | T \geqslant 2) &= \frac{P((2 \leqslant T \leqslant 3),(T \geqslant 2))}{P(T \geqslant 2)}\\ &= \frac{P(2 \leqslant T \leqslant 3)}{P(T \geqslant 2)}\\ &= \frac{(1-e^{-2(3)}) - (1-e^{-2(2)})}{1-(1-e^{-2(2)})}\\ &= \frac{e^{-2(2)} - e^{-2(3)}}{e^{-2(2)}} = 1 - e^{-2(3-2)}\\ &= 1-e^{-2} = 1-0.135 = 0.865\end{aligned}$$

Therefore, both conditions result in the same probability for arrival in the next time unit and hence the no-memory property. The exponential expression can be evaluated using standard tables, calculators, or slide rules.

## ●● BETA DISTRIBUTION

Another theoretical distribution that may be useful in representing decision models is the beta distribution. Its usefulness stems from two factors: (1) the family of beta distributions is an extremely rich class of functions and can provide good approximations to a wide range of probability distributions; (2) beta distributions can be up-dated easily to include sample information from processes that follow a binomial distribution. This second factor will be discussed in Chapter 13. The first is demonstrated below. The distribution does not arise from an identifiable process. But its variety means that it may provide a good approximation for an uncertain event based on existing empirical and subjective information.[5]

[5]For a detailed discussion of this distribution, see R. L. Winkler, *Introduction to Bayesian Inference and Decision* (New York: Holt, Rinehart and Winston, 1972).

**Beta Distribution**

***Definition:*** *The formula for the distribution is*

$$f(p)=\begin{cases}\dfrac{(n-1)!}{(r-1)!(n-r-1)!}p^{r-1}(1-p)^{n-r-1} & \text{if } 0\leqslant p\leqslant 1\\ 0 & \textit{elsewhere}\end{cases}$$

*where n and r are parameters.*

The shape depends on parameters $n$ and $r$. Samples of probability density functions for the beta distribution are shown in Figures 10.21, 10.22, and 10.23.

Tables providing cumulative distributions for some values of $n$ and $p$ are given in Appendix F.

The values of the random variable in the beta distribution have a range between 0 and 1. As the following example illustrates, the beta distribution is often useful in modeling a Bernoulli process when the probability of success at each iteration is unknown.

**FIGURE 10.21**

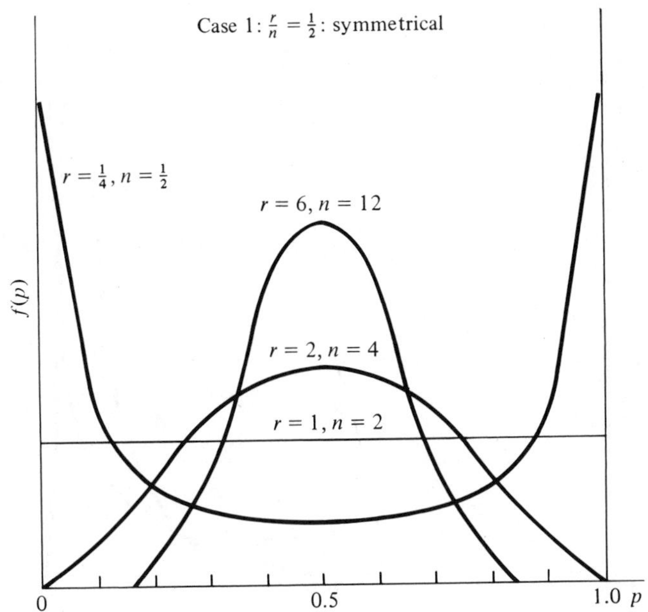

**FIGURE 10.22**

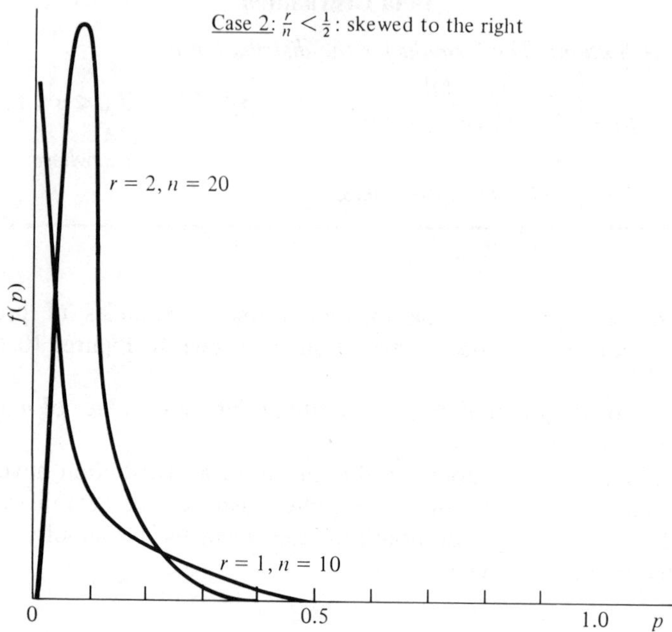


**FIGURE 10.23**

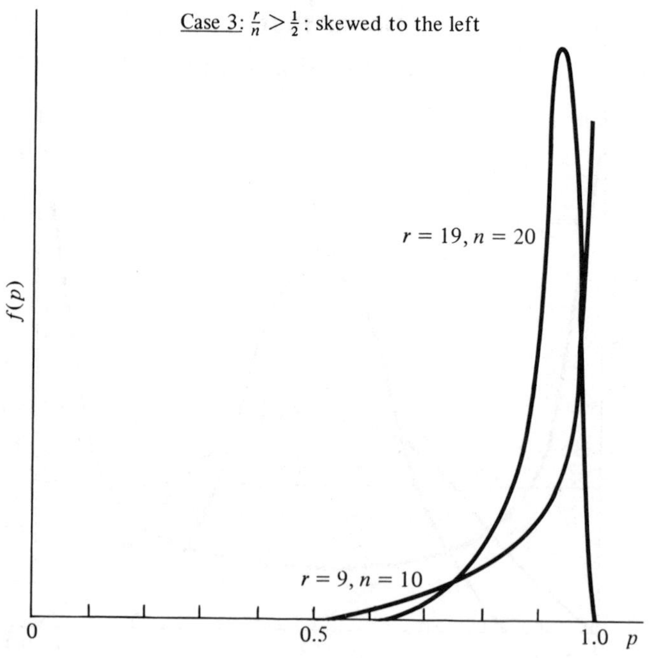

**Example 10.14**

Assume that you are convinced through your own experience and empirical evidence that the proportion of failures, $p$, in a particular process lies between 0.2 and 0.8 with the mean value at 0.5. Furthermore, you believe that the beta distribution with $r=6$ and $n=12$ (see Figure 10.21) provides an adequate assessment of the distribution for this proportion. What is the probability that $p$ is less than 0.4?

From Appendix F we see that

$$P(P \leqslant 0.4016)=0.25$$

## SUMMARY

Theoretical distributions that correspond to identifiable process can be useful in building models of decision process.

**Binomial**

*Conditions:*

*Repeated trials with success or failure*
*Constant probability of success*
*Independent trials*

*Formula:*

$$P(R=r|n,p)=\frac{n!}{r!(n-r)!}(p)^r(1-p)^{n-r}$$

*Mean* $(\mu)=np$

*Standard Deviation* $(\sigma)=\sqrt{np(1-p)}$

**Poisson**

*Conditions:*

*Large number of opportunities for occurrence*
*Small probability of occurrence*
*Occurrences independent*
*Average number occurrences constant*

*Formula:*

$$P(X=x|m)=\frac{e^{-m}m^x}{x!}$$

*Mean* $(\mu)=m$

*Standard Deviation* $(\sigma)=\sqrt{m}$

**Normal**

*Conditions:*

*Sample means from the central limit theorem*
*Other symmetrical process*

*Formula:*

$$f(x)=\frac{1}{\sigma\sqrt{2\pi}}\exp\left[-\frac{1}{2}\left(\frac{x-\mu}{\sigma}\right)^2\right]$$

**Exponential**

*Conditions:*

*Same as Poisson*

*Formula:*

$$f(t)=\lambda e^{-\lambda t}$$

$$\textit{Mean } (\mu)=\frac{1}{\lambda}$$

$$\textit{Standard Deviation } (\sigma)=\frac{1}{\lambda}$$

**Beta**

*Formula:*

$$f(p)=\begin{cases}\dfrac{(n-1)!}{(r-1)!(n-r-1)!}p^{r-1}(1-p)^{n-r-1} & \textit{if } 0\leqslant p\leqslant 1\\ 0 & \textit{elsewhere}\end{cases}$$

These distributions all have tables that can be used to evaluate probabilities.

## ASSIGNMENT MATERIAL

**10.1.** Probability distributions are useful descriptions of processes that involve uncertainty. Describe the important characteristics of a process that is described by:
(a) The binomial distribution.
(b) The Poisson distribution.

**10.2.** A production manager used the following decision rule in inspecting carburetors received from a supplier: Take a sample of 5 items; if any are defective, reject the lot. What is the probability of *accepting* a lot that is actually 20% defective?

**10.3.** Assume that in a very large lot of similar articles produced by a manufacturer, nine-tenths are known to be perfect and one-tenth are known to be defective. If 10 of these articles are selected at random and tested, what is the probability of getting:

(a) Exactly three defectives?
(b) At most three defectives?
(c) At least three defectives?

**10.4.** Jar I contains a large number of marbles, 20% of which are red. Jar II also contains many marbles, 10% of which are red.

(a) If five marbles are taken at random from jar I, what is the probability that exactly two of them will be red?
(b) If ten marbles are taken at random from jar II, what is the probability that exactly two of them will be red?
(c) If seven marbles are taken at random from jar I, what is the probability that less than four will be red?
(d) If eight marbles are taken at random from jar II, what is the probability that four or more will be nonred?

**10.5.** Mary Barnacle, an M.B.A. student, is looking forward to the winter quarter. While Barnacle publicly claims to be eager to commence studying Finance and Marketing, reliable sources have found that she is really anticipating the coming ski season. We are told that she has already scheduled one-day ski trips on 12 separate days throughout the quarter. Presuming that there is a 60% probability of having good ski weather on any given day, what is the chance that Barnacle will enjoy good weather on eight or more of the days on which she goes skiing?

**10.6.** You are the campaign manager for your local congressperson and have just received the latest telephone poll results indicating that 60% of the people in the district favor your candidate. You are somewhat skeptical, so you decide to make a quick check. Selecting 15 names at random from the telephone book, you call and ask for preferences. The results are 6 in favor of your candidate. If the poll is correct, what is the probability of 6 or fewer favorable responses?

**10.7.** The fire chief in Dayton has collected some information on responses to calls in a certain district. There are two fire companies that can respond. A study has shown that the probability of station 1 arriving first is 0.6 and that each call's characteristics are independent of the previous call's characteristics. Conditions over the next few months are expected to be the same as during the time period during which the study was made. You are interested in how often station 1 will arrive first in the next five calls.

(a) Define the outcome space of interest.
(b) Define a probability distribution on the outcome space.
(c) What is the probability that station 1 arrives first in three of the next five calls?
(d) What is the probability that station 1 arrives first at least twice but less than five times in the next five calls?

**10.8.** Calculate the following binomial probabilities:

(a) $P(R \geqslant 2|n=6,p=0.3)$
(b) $P(R<3|n=5,p=0.4)$
(c) $P(R \leqslant 4|n=7,p=0.5)$
(d) $P(0<R \leqslant 3|n=4,p=0.3)$
(e) $P(2 \leqslant R \leqslant 6|n=10,p=0.2)$
(f) $P(R=4|n=7,p=0.7)$
(g) $P(R \geqslant 2|n=5,p=0.8)$
(h) $P(R \leqslant 3|n=6,p=0.6)$

**10.9.** The probability of producing a good part in a production process is 0.8.

(a) What is the probability of producing 9 good parts in a sample of 10?
(b) What is the probability of 7 or more good parts in a sample of 10?

**10.10.** A large company is evaluating 20 cost-reduction proposals voluntarily submitted by employees. None of these proposals are related. Past experience has been that 60% of such proposals are adopted.

(a) What is the probability that exactly 10 proposals will be adopted?
(b) What is the probability that more than 8 will be adopted?

**10.11.** At the local fire department, emergency calls for the fire engine average about one in 2 days. Assuming that calls are independent and come at random, what is the probability of one or more calls in any given day? State your assumptions.

**10.12.** If $X$ is Poisson-distributed with $m=5.3$, what is the probability that $1 \leqslant X \leqslant 5$?

**10.13.** Customers arrive randomly at a bank at the average rate of 24 per hour during the time period between 1:30 P.M. and 2:00 P.M. on a Tuesday. What is the probability that during a 12-minute segment of that time period (a) exactly 5 customers arrive; (b) no customers arrive; (c) 4 or fewer customers arrive? State your assumptions.

**10.14.** Suppose that the average number of accidents to employees working on high-explosive shells over a period of 1 day is 0.16. Assume it has been shown that the number of accidents follows a Poisson distribution.

(a) Find the probability of exactly one accident in a period of 1 week (assume 5 days in a week).
(b) Find the probability of more than one accident in a period of 1 week.
(c) Find the probability of exactly five accidents in a period of 5 weeks.

**10.15.** On the average, 2 out of every 1,000 deaths in the United States are among people from 15 to 24 years of age. What is the probability that among a sample of 500 deaths, none is from this age group?

**10.16.** An urn contains 50 balls: 10 black balls and 40 white balls. You must pay \$1 to play the game. The game consists of three trials. Each trial consists of a ball being drawn randomly from the urn, observed, and then returned to the urn. The number of times a black ball is observed over the three trials is recorded. If that number is one or more, you receive your dollar back plus an additional dollar for each time a black ball was drawn. Otherwise, you receive nothing. For example, if two black balls are drawn, you receive your \$1 back plus \$2. What is the expected gain (loss) from engaging in this gamble?

**10.17. Datanetics**

You are the manager of an electronic instrumentation manufacturing company. You manufacture a component in one department which is used in the final product. You require 100 of the components every day, and have the capacity of producing up to 103 per day. On most days, the number of defective components produced has a binomial distribution with parameters $p = .05$ and $n =$ the number of units that you produce. (That is, the probability that a unit is defective is .05, independent of the other units produced.) But occasionally, for some unknown reason, the machine which produces the components has had a "bad day", and the number of defective units has a binomial distribution with $p = .4$. "Bad days" seem to happen 10% of the time, and the occurrence of a bad day is independent of how long it has been since the last one.

If a defective component is installed, it results in a $5 charge to rework. The units can be reworked before installation, guaranteeing that they won't be defective, at a cost of $1 per unit. One of your engineers has devised a test for whether or not the units are defective, but the test is destructive. You can make 103 units and subject the extra 3 units to his test—this gives you some idea whether or not this is a "bad day", which can be used to decide whether to rework before installation or not. To produce the three extra units and subject them to the test costs $8 per day.

The present quality control policy is to test the extra 3 units. If two or more defectives are found, the units are sent back for rework. The manager of quality control has suggested this policy be tightened up so that a lot is sent back for rework if out of the 3 tested one or more defectives are found.

Compare the present quality control policy with the new policy suggested by the manager of quality control and with the policy of shipping without any inspection. Use expected daily cost as the basis for comparison.

**10.18.** There are 1000 marbles in an urn—650 red, 40 blue, and 310 green. A marble is drawn from the urn 50 times and its color recorded; after each draw the marble is replaced in the urn.

(a) On a single draw, what is the probability of not getting a blue marble?
(b) What is the probability of getting two or more blue marbles in the sample of 50?

**10.19.** If $X$ is normally distributed with mean 15 and standard deviation 8, what is the probability that

(a) $3 \leqslant X \leqslant 13$?
(b) $X \leqslant 17$?
(c) $X > 12$?
(d) $11 \leqslant X \leqslant 18$?

**10.20.** Steven Hufft is a young entrepreneur considering the possibility of opening a retail sales and service outlet for electronic air cleaners in the San Francisco Peninsula area. His potential market contains 100,000 single-family dwelling units. In other parts of the Bay Area the air cleaner has appealed largely to owners of homes valued at $70,000 and above. Hufft wishes to estimate the sales potential for the proposed market area and knows that the value of homes (single-family dwelling units) in the area is normally distributed with a mean of \$60,000 and a standard deviation of \$10,000.

(a) What is the number of homes in the market area having a value of \$70,000 and above?

(b) The manufacturer of the air cleaner has announced a new model that will be appropriate for homes in the \$50,000 to \$70,000 range. How many homes are in the potential market for this new product?

**10.21.** The production manager for Acme Electrical Motors has just received a shipment of 1,000 shafts from an outside supplier. These shafts have been machined to a nominal diameter of 2 inches. He knows from previous experience, however, that the diameters of shafts made by this supplier on a Monday or Friday are normally distributed with mean 2.02 inches and standard deviation 0.03 inch, while the diameters of shafts made any other day of the week are normally distributed with mean 2.01 inches and standard deviation 0.02 inch.

If the diameter of a shaft is between 1.96 and 2.04 inches, it is acceptable for Acme's purposes, but if the diameter lies outside this tolerance interval, the shaft is termed "defective."

(a) What fraction of all shafts made on Mondays and Fridays are defective?

(b) What fraction of the shafts made on other days are defective?

**10.22.** If scores on the GMAT are normally distributed with a mean score of 500 and a standard deviation of 100, what is the probability that two individuals, chosen at random and independently, will both have scores between 400 and 600?

**10.23.** Instead of studying for an exam, Joe takes on Sam in a series of tiddly-winks games. (In the past, Joe has won about 20% of his games against Sam.) If they play 100 games, what is the probability that Joe will win at least 30 of them?

## APPENDIX 10: Compact Counting Techniques and the Binomial Distribution

The classical concept of probability is easy to apply to mutually exclusive and equally likely events if the number of outcomes can be readily counted. In some cases this becomes difficult unless compact counting techniques are used.

**Permutations.** Given $n$ different objects, a selection of $r$ of these objects arranged in a specific order is called a *permutation*.

#### Example

If we have three books colored red (R), yellow (Y), and green (G), how many different ways can we arrange them on a shelf that has room for only two of them?

We could list all six possibilities: RG, GR, RY, YR, GY, YG. Considering the two places on the shelf, we could recognize that we have a choice of any of three for the first slot. Given our first choice, we can then choose one of two for the second. Therefore, we have $3 \times 2 = 6$ possibilities.

In general, we write the number of permutations of $n$ things taken $r$ at a time as ${}_nP_r = n \times (n-1) \times (n-2) \times \cdots \times (n-r+1)$. Introducing the factorial notation, we observe that ${}_nP_r = \dfrac{n!}{(n-r)!}$. [Note that $n! = n \times (n-1) \times (n-2) \times \cdots \times 2 \times 1$, and 0! is defined to be equal to 1.]

**Combinations.** Given $n$ different objects, a selection of $r$ of these objects is called a *combination.*

The difference between combinations and permutations is that a combination is not concerned with order (i.e., RG and GR are the same).

We write ${}_nC_r$ to represent the number of combinations of $n$ things taken $r$ at a time. Consider a combination of $r$ objects. We know that $r$ objects can be arranged in ${}_rP_r = r!$ permutations. Therefore, for each combination we have $r!$ permutations and hence ${}_nC_r r! = {}_nP_r$. Therefore, ${}_nC_r = \dfrac{n!}{r!(n-r)!}$. In our example we have ${}_3C_2 = \dfrac{3!}{2!1!} = 3$.

**Counting when objects are not distinguishable.** Assume that we have 5 books to arrange on a shelf but can only distinguish color. The books consist of 3 red and 2 yellow. How many different arrangements are possible? $RRRYY$, $RYRYR$, and so on.

Considering again the total number of permutations, we have ${}_5P_5 = 5!$. But this includes ${}_3P_3 = 3!$ permutations for every distinguishable arrangement of the red books (i.e., $R_1R_2R_3YY$ is the same as $R_2R_3R_1YY$, etc., since we cannot distinguish among the red books). Similarly for the yellow books, each arrangement can be permuted 2! times. Therefore, if we let $N$ stand for the number of possible arrangements that can be distinguished as different from one another, we have $N3!2! = 5!$ or $N = \dfrac{5!}{3!2!}$. In general, $N = \dfrac{n!}{r!(n-r)!}$ for $n$ objects which can be separated into two groups of $r$ and $n-r$ such that the groups can be distinguished but items within a group are indistinguishable.

Note that this formula is just the same as the combinations formula. To visualize this in terms of combinations, consider the five spaces on the shelf and recognize that each is capable of holding a red book and that after we know which spaces have reds, we automatically know which ones have yellows. Denote the possible position of reds by $R_1R_2R_3R_4R_5$. Now we are interested in the number of different ways in which we can pick 3 of these spaces or the number of combinations of 5 things taken 3 at a time.

$${}_5C_3 = \frac{5!}{3!2!}$$

**Derivation of binomial distribution.** With these counting techniques we can directly develop the binomial distribution in terms of the following example.

A pair of coins is tossed 5 times. What is the probability that exactly 3 of the 5 tries will have double heads?

Let

$$
\begin{aligned}
S &= \text{event } HH \\
F &= \text{event } not\ HH \\
P(S) &= \tfrac{1}{2}\cdot\tfrac{1}{2}=\tfrac{1}{4} \\
P(F) &= 1-P(S)=\tfrac{3}{4}
\end{aligned}
$$

Now consider a 5-toss trial that yields 3 double heads in the following sequence: SFFSS. The probability of this outcome is

$$
\begin{aligned}
P(\text{SFFSS}) &= \left(\tfrac{1}{4}\right)\left(\tfrac{3}{4}\right)\left(\tfrac{3}{4}\right)\left(\tfrac{1}{4}\right)\left(\tfrac{1}{4}\right) \\
&= \left(\tfrac{1}{4}\right)^3\left(\tfrac{3}{4}\right)^2
\end{aligned}
$$

This probability is seen to be the same for any series of 5 tosses which has three $S$'s and two $F$'s. To determine the probability of 3 $S$'s in 5 trials, we just have to add up all different ways in which we can get 3 $S$'s and 2 $F$'s. But this is just ${}_5C_3$, as we saw in the book example above. Therefore, $P(S=3, F=2) = {}_5C_3(\frac{1}{4})^3(\frac{3}{4})^2$.

If we generalize this result to events $S$ and $F$ such that $P(S)=p$, $P(F)=(1-p)$, and $n$ trials with $r$ successes, we have

$$P(S=r|n,p) = {}_nC_r(p)^r(1-p)^{n-r}$$

which is the binomial distribution.

# 11

# Empirical Probability Distributions

Empirical data are widely used as the basis for probability distributions. In some cases the data are used directly with relative frequencies. In others, they are modified to account for additional information. An individual who adopts a probability distribution based on empirical data must make a series of judgments. The uncertain event of interest must be comparable with the one that provided the data. The events that produced the data are generally *assumed* to be *independent*. To be reliable, the *number of observations* must be adequate. Sometimes these judgments can be made with confidence. When this is true, the nature of the judgments can be communicated easily to others. Therefore, the use of empirical data and relative frequencies is often a good method for assessing probability distributions.

Building models based on empirical evidence is an *art*. Modern methods of data analysis provide a large number of tools that can be of assistance.

**FIGURE 11.1**

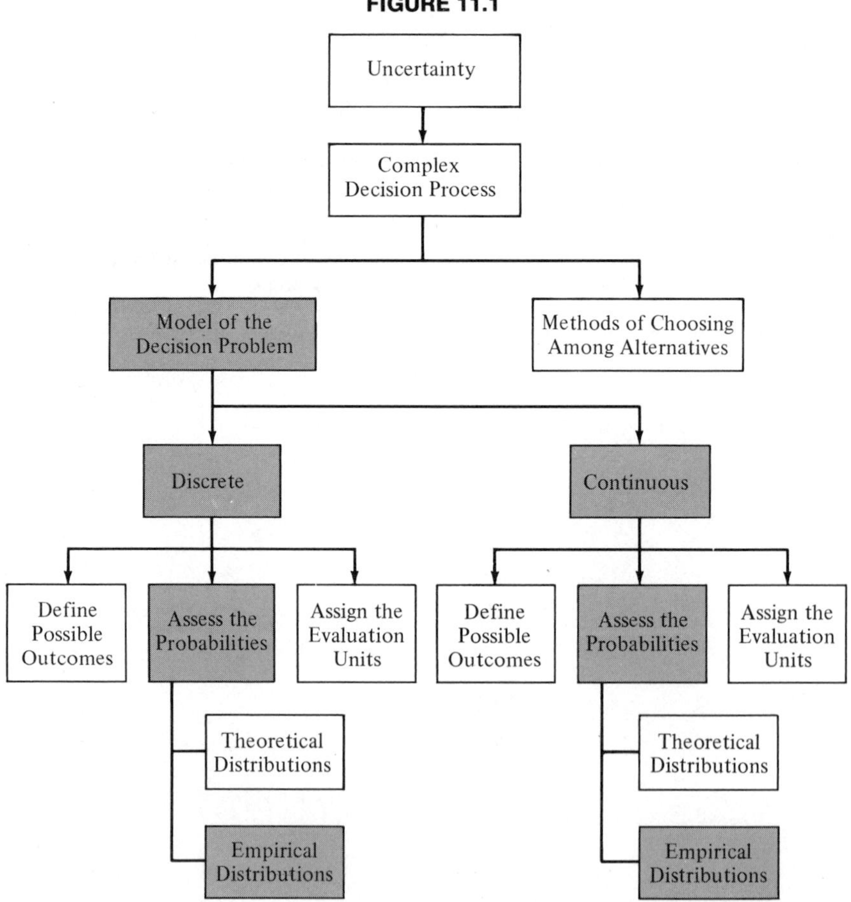

They are based on classical statistics and address some of the judgments mentioned above. These tools are *not* covered here. This material is an introduction to the use of empirical data. It covers the mechanical features of using empirical data, discusses the options available to a model builder, and indicates the linkages to data analysis. Discrete and continuous models are covered. Figure 11.1 shows how the material fits into the overall framework.

## DISCRETE RANDOM VARIABLES

Uncertain events with discrete outcomes can use the definition of relative frequency directly. The mechanics are familiar and easy. Verification of conditions of comparability, independence, and a large number of observations can be more difficult.

### Mechanics of Obtaining the Distribution

If the assumptions required for the relative frequency concept of probability are met, the probability distribution for a discrete random variable, $X$, can be obtained directly as $P(X=x_i)=m_i/m$, where $m$ is the total number of observations and $m_i$ is the number of times $x_i$ occurred.

**Example 11.1**

Assume that you need to know the distribution of quality from a manufacturing process. The manufacturing process has been developed over the last several years and has not varied for six months. The units are categorized into four quality classes, from 1 to 4. A test last week of 10,000 items resulted in the data in Table 11.1. No dependencies are observable or expected.

**TABLE 11.1**

| *Quality* | *Number of Units* |
|---|---|
| 1 | 5,482 |
| 2 | 2,120 |
| 3 | 1,356 |
| 4 | 1,042 |
| Total | 10,000 |

Using relative frequencies, the probability density function is:

$$P(Q=1)=.5482$$
$$P(Q=2)=.2120$$
$$P(Q=3)=.1356$$
$$P(Q=4)=.1042$$

It is plotted in Figure 11.2 and the corresponding cumulative distribution in Figure 11.3.

FIGURE 11.2

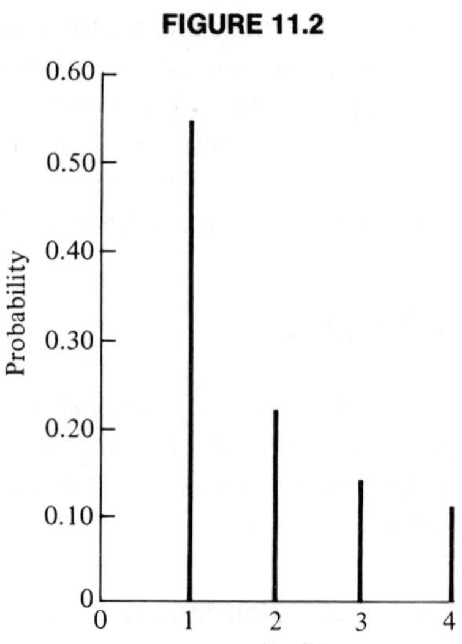


FIGURE 11.3

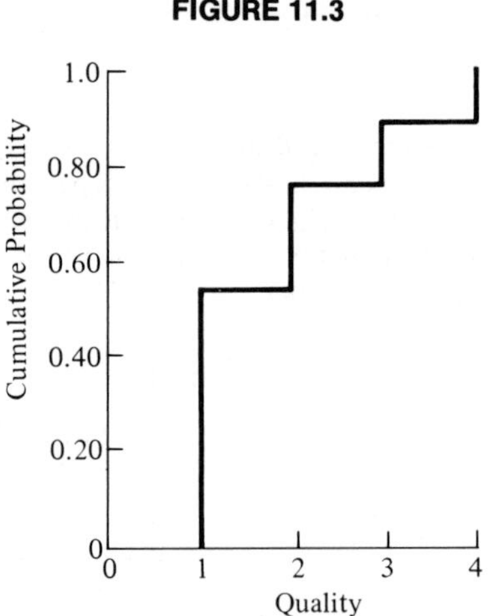


### The Problem with a Small Amount of Data

When we have a large number of observations, the relative frequency concept can be applied with confidence as long as the events are independent and conditions under which the probability distribution will be used are comparable to those used to obtain the data. Strictly speaking, the relative frequency concept of probability requires the number of observations, $m$, to go to infinity. Of course, if $m$ is very large, the error associated with approximating this "limiting frequency" with the "sample frequency" is small. If relatively few observations are available, one of the conditions required for objective probabilities, defined by relative frequencies, is not met. If you adopt relative frequencies as probabilities under these conditions, you are making a judgment that the sample data are adequate.

The error introduced by small samples is called *sampling error*. It arises because a small sample of data from a random process may not be typical. Anyone who has observed play at a gambling casino can recite tales of "peculiar" outcomes. In a simple example, if we flip a fair coin 10 times, we may obtain 7 heads rather than the "expected" 5 heads. We can calculate the probability of getting exactly 5 heads in 10 tosses using the binomial distribution.

$$P(R=5|n=10, p=0.5)=0.246$$

Therefore, the chances are less than 1/4 of obtaining the "expected" number of heads. If we used the relative frequency from a set of 10 tosses to assess the probability of a head, we would be wrong approximately 75% of the time, if the true probability were 0.5.

Classical statistics can help determine the sampling error.[1] The appendix to this chapter has a brief description of how statistics can be used to calculate "confidence intervals" for relative frequencies. To illustrate the problem of dealing with small samples, assume that Table 11.2 represents demand data that have been gathered for a product. You believe daily demand is generated by a stable process, and each day's demand is independent of demand in previous periods.

Using relative frequencies, the probability distribution for the demand is given in Figure 11.4. The small number of observations means there are likely to be sampling errors. The sizes of the errors are calculated in the appendix. But our interest here is not in learning how to calculate sampling

**TABLE 11.2**

| *Daily Demand* | *Number of Times Observed* |
|---|---|
| 0 | 5 |
| 1 | 10 |
| 2 | 20 |
| 3 | 16 |
| 4 | 34 |
| 5 | 15 |
| Total observations | 100 |

[1]See, for example, W. J. Dixon and F. J. Massey, *Introduction to Statistical Analysis*, 3rd ed. (New York: McGraw-Hill, 1969); Hoel, *Introduction to Mathematical Statistics*, 4th ed. (New York: Wiley, 1971); J. Johnston, *Econometric Methods*, 2nd ed. (New York: McGraw-Hill, 1972); A. M. Mood and F. A. Graybill, *Introduction to the Theory of Statistics*, 2nd ed. (New York: McGraw-Hill, 1963); W. A. Spurr and C. P. Bonini, *Statistical Analysis for Business Decisions*, rev. ed. (Homewood, Ill.: Irwin, 1973); R. J. Wonnacott and T. H. Wonnacott, *Introductory Statistics* (New York: Wiley, 1969).

FIGURE 11.4

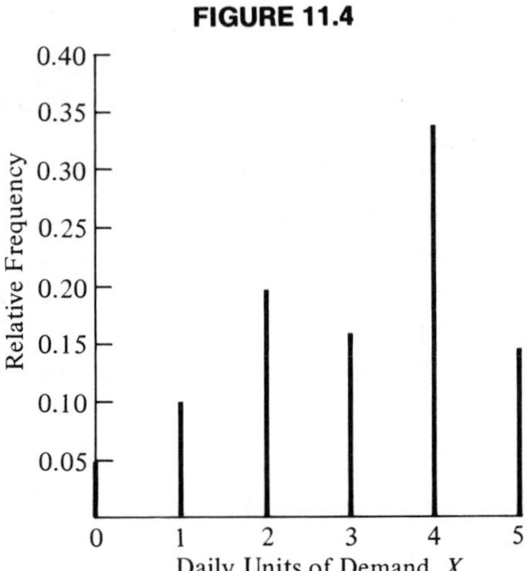


errors. You can learn that by studying statistics. In this problem there is a substantial chance that the relative frequencies deviate from the true probability by as much as $\pm 0.05$. The question is: What can we do under these conditions?

### Options in Dealing with a Small Amount of Data

In the *absence* of any other information, the best assessment for the probabilities is still $P(X = x_i) = m_i / m$. The decision to adopt relative frequencies as probabilities involves both the number of observations and the *other information* an individual might have. For instance, in considering the demand probabilities of Figure 11.4, it may be that you can see no reason for the probability of 3 units to be less than the probability for both 2 and 4 units. Moreover, your experience with similar products may lead you to believe that the distribution should be unimodal (single-peaked) rather than bimodal (double-peaked). Therefore, your "*other information*" says that the relative frequencies are wrong.

Three options are available when empirical evidence is not conclusive. The *first* is to suppress any subjective feelings about the distribution (e.g., about the demand distribution described above) and decide that $m$ is large enough to completely dominate your prior information. This leads to using the relative frequencies directly.

The *second* is to reject the relative frequency data completely. This, of course, means that the probability distributions must be obtained by some other method (building a model so that theoretical distributions can be used, gathering more empirical data, or formally using the subjective assessment methods discussed in Chapter 12).

The *third* is to somehow combine the relative frequency data with prior information.

### Combining Empirical Data with Other Information

There are two ways empirical data are commonly combined with other information. The first is through direct smoothing and the second is through Bayesian revision.

**Direct smoothing.** This is an informal procedure. Your prior beliefs are used to change (smooth) the relative frequencies to conform with your beliefs. For instance, if you believed the demand distribution in Figure 11.4 should have a "smooth" single peak, you might revise the distribution to $P(X=2)=0.16$, $P(X=3)=0.20$. Direct smoothing is an ad hoc way to take into account prior information. No formal process is provided. Instead, the probabilities are directly revised. Because it is ad hoc, no formal guidelines are available. To help in visualizing the probability distributions, they may be plotted as both a density function as shown in Figure 11.4 and as a cumulative distribution.

**Bayesian revision.** This is a formal procedure. It explicitly separates the information into prior information and empirical data. Bayes' theorem is used to revise the prior information based on the new empirical data. This procedure is discussed in Chapter 13.

### Comparability

Ensuring that the uncertain event of interest and the event used to collect the empirical data are comparable is obviously crucial. It may also be difficult. In some cases it may be possible to control the parameters of the process so that the data are representative. For instance, this is the case in the manufacturing process in Example 11.1. Data are taken under the same conditions that the process will use. In other cases control cannot be achieved. For instance, the demand data in Table 11.2 may have been collected during the fall and winter. Should the data be used to predict demand in the summer? The answer will obviously be influenced by the product and other factors such as economic activity. Sometimes a model that "corrects" for different factors can be used. The only general advice is to consider carefully the source of the data and factors that might affect their comparability.

## CONTINUOUS RANDOM VARIABLES

Outcome spaces that are continuous introduce an additional complication. Relative frequencies require categories. For instance, demand of 0, 1, 2, 3, and so on, units, or quality of 1, 2, 3, or 4. With a continuous random variable, these categories are not directly available. They can be created and relative frequencies used. Another option is to plot the data directly as a cumulative probability distribution.

### The Interval-Choice Problem

Categories are created by defining a set of intervals. The choice of the intervals is sometimes obvious. If not, it may be difficult, because the choice can affect the "shape" of the probability distribution. There are no set rules on how intervals should be chosen. The following example illustrates the problem.

**Example 11.2**

The manager of a water district is concerned about the availability of water for the district in the face of a potential drought. A crucial variable is, of course, demand. He has weekly usage data for the last 5 years. He believes that September will be the most difficult month and therefore wants to develop a demand distribution for September based on the available empirical evidence shown in Table 11.3.

One possible choice for the interval is the interval corresponding to the smallest unit that is measured. For instance, if water usage is reported to the nearest 1,000 gallons, the interval is in increments of 1,000 gallons. Using relative frequencies, this choice results in the probability density function shown in Figure 11.5. The distribution assigns a zero probability to all but 19 unit intervals.

**TABLE 11.3**

**Weekly Water Usage for September**

| *Year* | *Week* | *Water Usage (thousands of gallons)* |
|---|---|---|
| 1971 | 1 | 625 |
| | 2 | 705 |
| | 3 | 692 |
| | 4 | 674 |
| 1972 | 1 | 721 |
| | 2 | 695 |
| | 3 | 712 |
| | 4 | 605 |
| 1973 | 1 | 715 |
| | 2 | 792 |
| | 3 | 751 |
| | 4 | 697 |
| 1974 | 1 | 684 |
| | 2 | 774 |
| | 3 | 742 |
| | 4 | 708 |
| 1975 | 1 | 732 |
| | 2 | 688 |
| | 3 | 758 |
| | 4 | 751 |

**FIGURE 11.5**

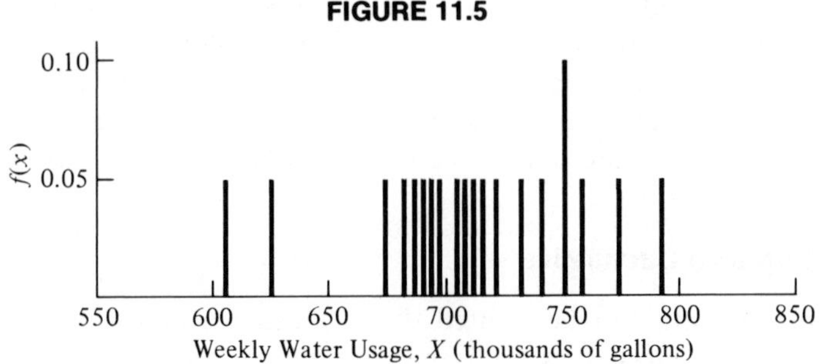


**FIGURE 11.6**

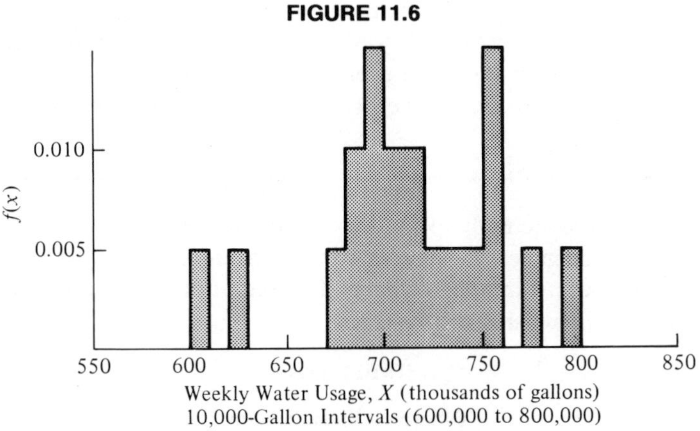


**FIGURE 11.7**

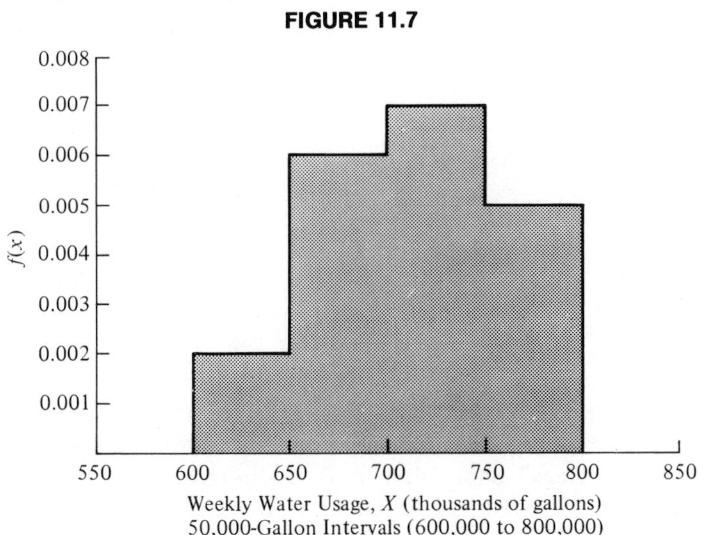

Figures 11.6 and 11.7 show the same data with the choice of the interval width changed to 10,000 gallons and 50,000 gallons, respectively. These distributions are clearly different from Figure 11.5 and from each other.

Rather than deal directly with the choice of an interval, it can be bypassed by plotting the data directly as a cumulative probability distribution.

### Plotting as a Cumulative

The empirical data can be plotted directly using a cumulative probability distribution. The mechanics are simple and illustrated below.

> *Step 1:* Arrange the observations in increasing order.
> *Step 2:* Assign a probability of $1/m$, where $m$ is the number of observations, to each observed outcome.
> *Step 3:* Plot the cumulative probability distribution based on step 2.

This procedure actually provides a cumulative distribution based on using relative frequencies and the smallest measurement unit as the interval. For the water district example we have 20 observations. Table 11.4 shows the data arranged in increasing order.

**TABLE 11.4**

**Observed Water Usage**

| *Water Usage* | *Assigned Probability* | *Water Usage* | *Assigned Probability* |
|---|---|---|---|
| 605 | $\frac{1}{20}$ | 712 | $\frac{1}{20}$ |
| 625 | $\frac{1}{20}$ | 715 | $\frac{1}{20}$ |
| 674 | $\frac{1}{20}$ | 721 | $\frac{1}{20}$ |
| 684 | $\frac{1}{20}$ | 732 | $\frac{1}{20}$ |
| 688 | $\frac{1}{20}$ | 742 | $\frac{1}{20}$ |
| 692 | $\frac{1}{20}$ | 751 | $\frac{2}{20}$ |
| 695 | $\frac{1}{20}$ | 758 | $\frac{1}{20}$ |
| 697 | $\frac{1}{20}$ | 774 | $\frac{1}{20}$ |
| 705 | $\frac{1}{20}$ | 792 | $\frac{1}{20}$ |
| 708 | $\frac{1}{20}$ | | |

Figure 11.8 shows the cumulative probability distribution based on Table 11.4. The "stair steps" show that it is a discrete approximation to the underlying continuous distribution on water usage. The "stair steps" can be eliminated by smoothing the cumulative plot.

FIGURE 11.8

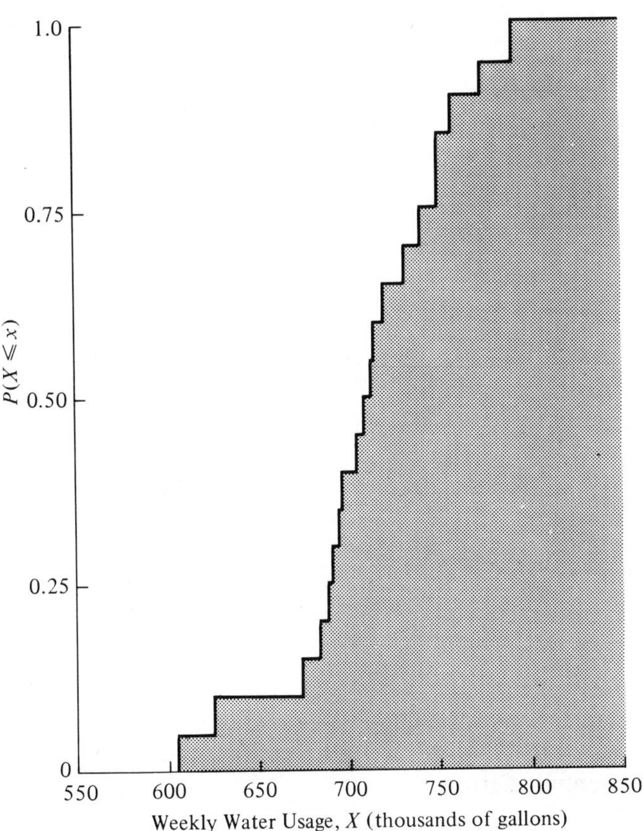


## Direct Smoothing

Direct smoothing to obtain a continuous distribution is an informal, ad hoc procedure just as it is in the discrete case. The *art* associated with building models using empirical data is clearly visible. Two effects can be identified. The first is due to the discrete approximation. The second is due to sampling error.

**Smoothing to eliminate discrete approximation.** To illustrate this problem, we will start backward. Assume that we have the continuous cumulative distribution shown in Figure 11.9. A four-interval, equally probable, discrete approximation is also shown (see Chapter 9 for a discussion of how this discrete approximation is made). Notice that the discrete approximation alternates above and below the actual continuous distribution. Therefore, in going from a "discrete approximation" to a continuous distribution, we could expect the same kind of alternation. In smoothing a cumulative plot based on

FIGURE 11.9

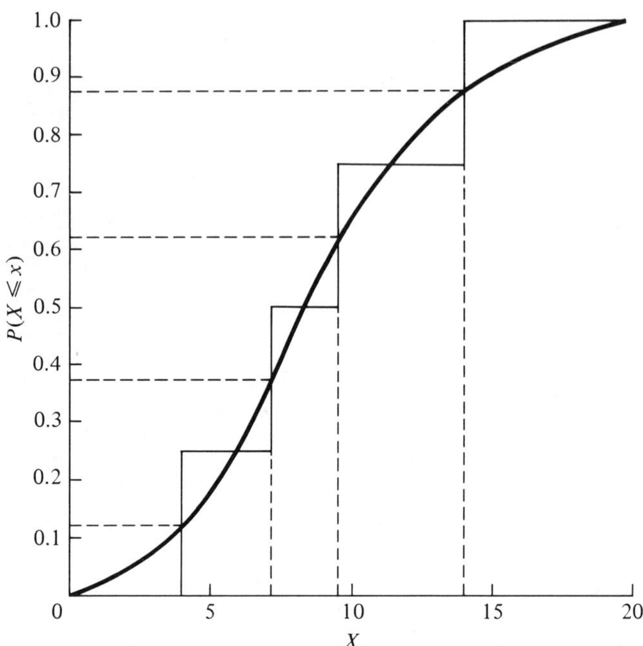


empirical observations for a continuous random variable, we would draw the curve "between" the stair steps. An exception occurs if we are also trying to account for sampling error.

**Smoothing to account for sampling error.** Sampling errors for continuous random variables are just like those for discrete random variables. As discussed with discrete random variables, smoothing can "correct" for these errors *if* you have other information. For example, the smoothed version of Figure 11.8 shown in Figure 11.10 has reduced the probability of outcomes between 600 and 650. Presumably this is based on the belief that the two outcomes in this interval are an overrepresentation of the actual outcomes in this interval. There is, of course, no reason why you would make this judgment unless you had other information. Correcting for sampling error this way is generally very risky business indeed. An expert on data analysis should be consulted for any important problem.

### Comparability

The problem of comparability is no different for continuous random variables than for discrete random variables. Often comparability is made more difficult by a limited amount of data. Sometimes data are available from a general population. But few or no data are available for the exact conditions

**FIGURE 11.10**

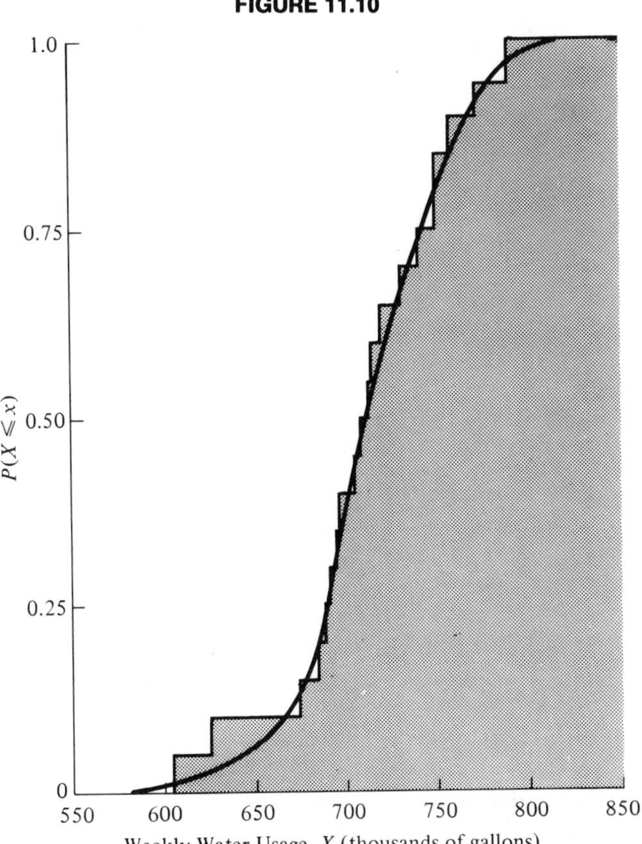


of interest. To illustrate the general problem, consider the water usage problem, Example 11.2. The manager of the water district is interested in a distribution for water demand during the month of September. Assume that he has available weekly data for the past five years. This provides him with a total of $52 \times 5 = 260$ observations. If he were to decide that the comparable population was each week during the last 5 years, he would have 260 observations. The distribution of water usage over these 260 weeks would almost certainly be different than the distribution shown in Figure 11.10 for the weeks in September only. However, restriction to the 20 observations in September is justified on the basis of comparability—since he is interested in September, it makes sense to consider only past data associated with September. The result is a drastic reduction in the number of observations (from 260 to 20). In addition to comparability in month of the year, it would also make sense to consider weather patterns such as Temperature (Hot, Medium, Cool) and Rainfall to Date (Heavy, Light). Those observations that correspond to all the categories we are interested in would be used. For example, assume

**TABLE 11.5**

**Weekly Water Usage for September**

| *Year* | *Week* | *Temperature* | *Rainfall* | *Population* | *Water Usage (thousands of gallons)* |
|---|---|---|---|---|---|
| 1971 | 1 | Hot | Light | 9,500 | 625 |
| | 2 | Hot | Light | 9,500 | 705 |
| | 3* | Medium | Light | 9,500 | 692 |
| | 4 | Hot | Light | 9,500 | 674 |
| 1972 | 1 | Cool | Heavy | 10,100 | 721 |
| | 2 | Medium | Heavy | 10,100 | 695 |
| | 3 | Hot | Heavy | 10,100 | 712 |
| | 4 | Medium | Heavy | 10,100 | 605 |
| 1973 | 1 | Cool | Heavy | 10,800 | 715 |
| | 2 | Medium | Heavy | 10,800 | 792 |
| | 3 | Hot | Heavy | 10,800 | 751 |
| | 4 | Hot | Heavy | 10,800 | 697 |
| 1974 | 1 | Hot | Heavy | 11,200 | 684 |
| | 2 | Medium | Heavy | 11,200 | 774 |
| | 3 | Hot | Heavy | 11,200 | 742 |
| | 4 | Cool | Heavy | 11,200 | 708 |
| 1975 | 1* | Medium | Light | 12,000 | 732 |
| | 2 | Hot | Light | 12,000 | 688 |
| | 3* | Medium | Light | 12,000 | 758 |
| | 4* | Medium | Light | 12,000 | 751 |

that the expanded set of data on water usage shown in Table 11.5 is collected. If temperature is predicted to be medium, and the rainfall has been light this year, we should restrict ourselves to those weeks in September corresponding to a year with light rainfall and medium temperature. These weeks are starred in Table 11.5. The number of observations is now down to four (692, 742, 758, 751).

Another variable to consider is the population of the water district. This year the district has 12,800 people. Using the population variable, we are now without *any* comparable observations. In situations like this, where problems with comparability reduce the number of observations drastically, a model can be used to correct for differences. The idea is that the model determines general relationships between the characteristics that are important to establishing comparability (in the example, month, temperature, rainfall, and population) and the entity of interest (in the example, the water usage per week). In general, these models will not eliminate all the uncertainty associated with a particular event, but they can significantly reduce the uncertainty by improving comparability without drastically lowering the number of observations.

A comprehensive treatment of techniques for building models with empirical data is beyond the scope of this book. The use of regression analysis and econometric methods is treated in many standard texts.[2] The appendix presents an example that is intended to illustrate how these models can be used to help assess probability distributions.

## SUMMARY

Empirical data are one of the most common sources of probabilities. For discrete random variables, the data are used to compute relative frequencies. For both discrete and continuous random variables, we must be concerned with:

*Sampling Error:* When there is only a small amount of data available, sampling errors can be significant.

*Comparability:* The uncertain event being modeled must be comparable to the uncertain event corresponding to the empirical data.

Continuous random variables do not have categories for use with relative frequencies. Categories can be created by choosing intervals. By directly plotting the data on a cumulative curve, the choice of intervals can be avoided.

*Smoothing* is often used to modify the distributions to account for information not included in the empirical observations. This is an informal, ad hoc procedure and should be used with extreme caution. It allows the model builder to "correct" for sampling errors and, for continuous random variables, to turn the discrete observations into a continuous distribution.

## ASSIGNMENT MATERIAL

The following questions refer to data in the table on page 272. These data were gathered by a random sample of customers in a chain of clothing stores.

**11.1.** Use the relative frequency concept to obtain a probability distribution for the sex of the population sampled. Plot both a probability density function and a cumulative probability distribution.

**11.2.** Use the relative frequency concept to obtain a probability distribution of the number of purchases for the population sampled. Plot both a probability density function and a cumulative probability distribution.

**11.3.** If you are interested in the probability distribution for purchases by a male customer, would you use the distribution obtained in problem 11.2? Why or why not? If not, provide a distribution you would use.

[2]See, for example, W. A. Spurr and C. P. Bonini, *Statistical Analysis for Business Decisions*, rev. ed. (Homewood, Ill.: Irwin, 1973), Chapters 16 and 17, and for a more detailed discussion, J. Johnston, *Econometric Methods*, 2nd ed. (New York: McGraw-Hill, 1972).

**11.4.** Use the data to obtain a cumulative probability distribution for the height of the store customers. Treat height as a continuous random variable.

**11.5.** Use the data to obtain a cumulative probability distribution for the weight of the store customers. Treat weight as a continuous random variable.

**11.6.** If you are interested in the probability distribution for the heights of male customers, would you use the cumulative probability distribution described in problem 11.4? If not, what would you use? Treat height as a continuous random variable.

**11.7.** If you are interested in the probability distribution on the weight of female customers who are over 66 inches tall, would you use the distribution described in problem 11.5? Why or why not? If not, provide a distribution you would use. Treat weight as a continuous random variable.

**11.8.** If you are interested in the probability distribution on the weight of male customers who are under 72 inches tall, would you use the distribution plotted in problem 11.5? Why or why not? If not, provide a distribution you would use. Treat weight as a continuous random variable.

| *Customer Number* | *Sex* | *Number of Purchases* | *Height (inches)* | *Weight (pounds)* | *Customer Number* | *Sex* | *Number of Purchases* | *Height (inches)* | *Weight (pounds)* |
|---|---|---|---|---|---|---|---|---|---|
| 1 | M | 1 | 71 | 180 | 26 | F | 4 | 62 | 110 |
| 2 | M | 3 | 70 | 160 | 27 | F | 1 | 63 | 120 |
| 3 | F | 2 | 65 | 110 | 28 | M | 1 | 69 | 150 |
| 4 | M | 1 | 69 | 175 | 29 | F | 2 | 68 | 140 |
| 5 | F | 1 | 62 | 105 | 30 | F | 6 | 66 | 130 |
| 6 | F | 2 | 63 | 120 | 31 | F | 3 | 64 | 120 |
| 7 | M | 1 | 65 | 130 | 32 | M | 1 | 76 | 200 |
| 8 | F | 3 | 62 | 120 | 33 | M | 2 | 70 | 180 |
| 9 | F | 4 | 68 | 140 | 34 | F | 1 | 63 | 120 |
| 10 | F | 2 | 63 | 110 | 35 | M | 1 | 69 | 165 |
| 11 | M | 1 | 74 | 200 | 36 | F | 4 | 61 | 115 |
| 12 | M | 2 | 71 | 190 | 37 | F | 2 | 60 | 110 |
| 13 | M | 1 | 69 | 140 | 38 | F | 1 | 69 | 140 |
| 14 | F | 3 | 60 | 110 | 39 | M | 2 | 74 | 195 |
| 15 | M | 1 | 70 | 140 | 40 | M | 3 | 73 | 180 |
| 16 | F | 4 | 65 | 120 | 41 | F | 1 | 60 | 120 |
| 17 | F | 1 | 62 | 125 | 42 | M | 2 | 70 | 160 |
| 18 | M | 1 | 70 | 145 | 43 | F | 1 | 62 | 120 |
| 19 | F | 2 | 62 | 125 | 44 | F | 1 | 63 | 120 |
| 20 | M | 2 | 71 | 180 | 45 | M | 2 | 69 | 150 |
| 21 | M | 3 | 70 | 190 | 46 | M | 4 | 73 | 170 |
| 22 | F | 5 | 60 | 120 | 47 | F | 1 | 61 | 120 |
| 23 | M | 1 | 73 | 190 | 48 | F | 2 | 67 | 130 |
| 24 | M | 2 | 70 | 160 | 49 | F | 1 | 65 | 110 |
| 25 | M | 6 | 71 | 155 | 50 | M | 3 | 70 | 180 |

## APPENDIX 11.A: Accounting for a Small Amount of Data in Discrete Distributions

For discrete distributions, classical statistics can help address the question of the adequacy of the number of observations. The following result is stated without proof.[3]

Let $x_i$, $i=1,2,\ldots,n$, be values of a random variable defined on a discrete outcome space and let $P(x_i)$, $i=1,2,\ldots,n$, be the true probability distribution for the random variable. Let $\tilde{P}_i = m_i/m$, $i=1,2,\ldots,n$, be the estimates of the $P(x_i)$'s using relative frequencies from $m$ observations, $m_i$ of which yielded $x_i$. As long as $m$ is reasonably large [say $(\tilde{P}_i)m$ and $(1-\tilde{P}_i)m$ are above 5] the distribution of $\tilde{P}_i$ is normal with a standard deviation of $\sqrt{\tilde{P}_i(1-\tilde{P}_i)/m}$.

These results can be used to determine confidence intervals for the relative frequencies. We will use the example in Table 11.2 to demonstrate its use. From Table 11.2 we have $m=100$ and

$$\tilde{P}_1=0.05$$
$$\tilde{P}_2=0.10$$
$$\tilde{P}_3=0.20$$
$$\tilde{P}_4=0.16$$
$$\tilde{P}_5=0.34$$
$$\tilde{P}_6=0.15$$

Since $\tilde{P}_i \times 100$ and $(1-\tilde{P}_i)\times 100$ are 5 or more for all $i$, we can use the results cited above. Table 11.6 gives the standard deviations for each relative frequency. Using these standard deviations and the normal table we can establish confidence levels for each of the relative frequencies.

**TABLE 11.6**

| $i$ | $\sigma_{\tilde{P}_i}$ |
|---|---|
| 1 | 0.0218 |
| 2 | 0.03 |
| 3 | 0.04 |
| 4 | 0.0367 |
| 5 | 0.0474 |
| 6 | 0.0357 |

For instance, if we desire a 95% confidence interval, it will be given approximately by $\tilde{P}_i \pm 2\sigma_{\tilde{P}_i}$. The 95% confidence intervals are displayed on

[3]See, for instance, A. M. Mood and F. A. Graybill, *Introduction to the Theory of Statistics*, 2nd ed. (New York: McGraw-Hill, 1963), p. 237.

FIGURE 11.11

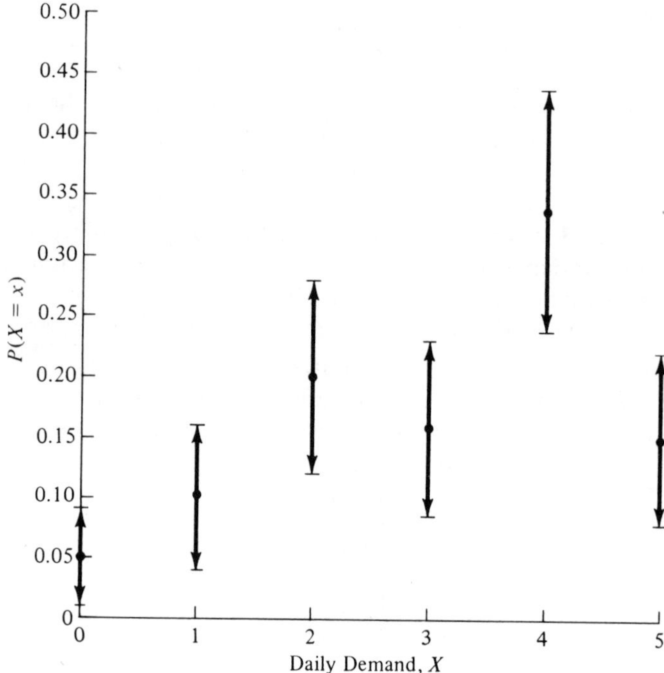


Figure 11.11.[4] We see that even with 100 observations, there is still room for error in assessing the distribution. As the number of points in outcome space increases so that the probability associated with any single point becomes smaller, the number of observations required to maintain the same relative accuracy becomes larger. If we define relative accuracy to be a given percentage, $\gamma$ of the relative frequency, it can be shown that for $\tilde{P}_i \leqslant 0.05$, the number of observations required to maintain the 95% confidence band (i.e., $\pm 2\sigma_{\tilde{P}_i}$ or total length of $4\sigma_{\tilde{P}_i}$) at $\gamma\tilde{P}_i$ or less is[5]

$$m = \frac{16}{\gamma^2 \tilde{P}_i}$$

For instance, if it is desired to obtain a relative accuracy of one-half the assessed value for $\tilde{P}_i$ when $\tilde{P}_i = 0.05$, we have

$$m = \frac{16}{\left(\frac{1}{4}\right)(0.05)} = 1280$$

[4]These confidence intervals apply to each $\tilde{P}_i$ separately.

[5]For $\tilde{P}_i \leqslant 0.05$, $\tilde{P}_i(1-\tilde{P}_i) \approx \tilde{P}_i$. Therefore $4\sigma_{\tilde{P}_i} = 4\sqrt{\tilde{P}_i/m}$. Equating this with $\gamma\tilde{P}_i$, we have $(16/m)\tilde{P}_i = \gamma^2\tilde{P}_i^2$, and solving for $m$, we obtain $m = 16/\gamma^2\tilde{P}_i$.

## APPENDIX 11.B: Improving Comparability with a Model

The following example demonstrates how a model can be used to improve comparability. The method used is a regression model.

The Energy Source Battery Company manufactures batteries for a wide variety of uses. The company's product line ranges from large batteries used to power conventional submarines to miniature batteries that are included in each package of film for a Polaroid camera. One very profitable product line is flashlight batteries. Because of limited production facilities and lead times, the production decision for this product line must be made for the year in late December. Actual production is done during the months of January and February for the entire year. This allows the batteries to be shipped to distributors by early spring—in time for the large summer demand. Owing to other production commitments and large costs involved with converting the plant to flashlight battery production, the entire year's production must be completed during this period. The decision problem faced by the company for this product line is shown in Figure 11.12.

**FIGURE 11.12**

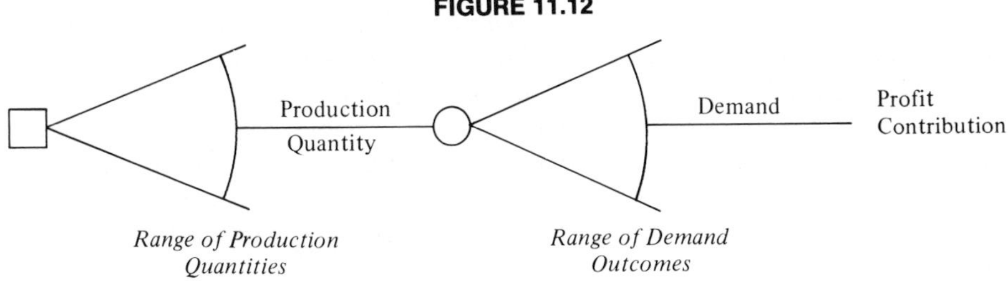


To determine the optimal production quantity, the probability distribution representing the uncertain event "demand" is required. From the records, demand for their product over a number of past years is available. Table 11.7 gives the relevant data for the flashlight battery product line.

**TABLE 11.7**

| *Year* | *Demand (millions of units)* |
|---|---|
| 1968 | 1.7 |
| 1969 | 2.6 |
| 1970 | 2.4 |
| 1971 | 3.0 |
| 1972 | 2.0 |
| 1973 | 2.8 |
| 1974 | 2.2 |
| 1975 | 3.3 |
| 1976 | 2.7 |
| 1977 | 2.9 |

FIGURE 11.13

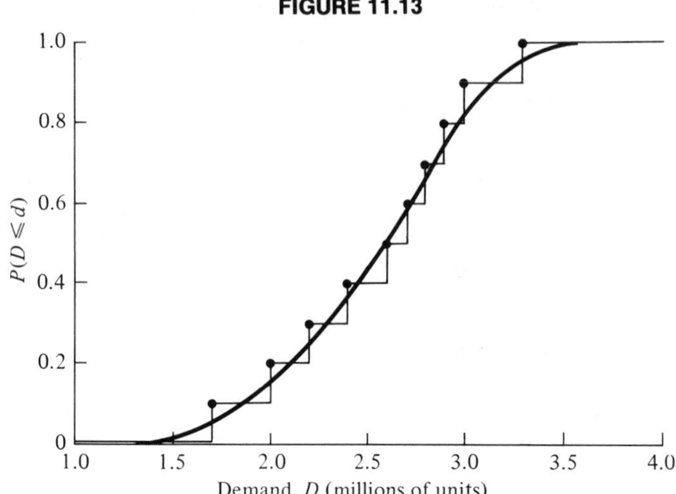


Using the data in Table 11.7 and the methods for determining cumulative distributions discussed in this chapter, we can obtain Figure 11.13. These data on past sales may or may not be applicable to this year's sales. Comparability may involve a number of other variables that affect demand, such as the current state of the economy, competitors' actions, outdoor recreational activity, and so on. These variables are called *independent* variables and are used in a model to help predict a *dependent* variable (in this case demand).

Suppose in this case you believe that a strong relationship should exist between dollar sales of recreational equipment and the demand for flashlight batteries. Demand is strongest during the summer months and many of the uses are related to recreation. Since lead times for other recreational equipment are substantially longer than for batteries, industry estimates for recreational goods are very accurate by the time ESB production decisions must be made. Data on these estimated sales for the 10-year period are given in Table 11.8. These data can be plotted as shown in Figure 11.14. When they are plotted, the general upward slope of demand versus sales suggests that indeed there is a relationship and, moreover, in this case, it appears to be a straight line (or linear) relationship. The line drawn through the points is one of many that could be suggested. It looks reasonable in that half the points lie above it and half below it. Regression analysis provides a tool that can be used to formally determine a model for the relationship. In this case, the model, the equation for the line shown in Figure 11.14, is

$$Y = 0.87 + 0.1X$$

where

$$Y = \text{demand (millions of units)}$$

**TABLE 11.8**

| Year | *Demand for ESB Batteries (millions of units)* | *Recreational Sales Estimates (100 millions \$)* |
|---|---|---|
| 1968 | 1.7 | 8 |
| 1969 | 2.6 | 19 |
| 1970 | 2.4 | 14 |
| 1971 | 3.0 | 17 |
| 1972 | 2.0 | 15 |
| 1973 | 2.8 | 20 |
| 1974 | 2.2 | 16 |
| 1975 | 3.3 | 21 |
| 1976 | 2.7 | 16 |
| 1977 | 2.9 | 22 |
| 1978 | ? | 15 |

and

$X$ = sales estimates for recreational equipment (100 million \$)

As can be seen from Figure 11.14, this model does not explain all the variation in demand. The vertical distance from the line representing the model to the actual observations represents the *residual* variation. If we assume that these residual values are observations from a random variable

**FIGURE 11.14**

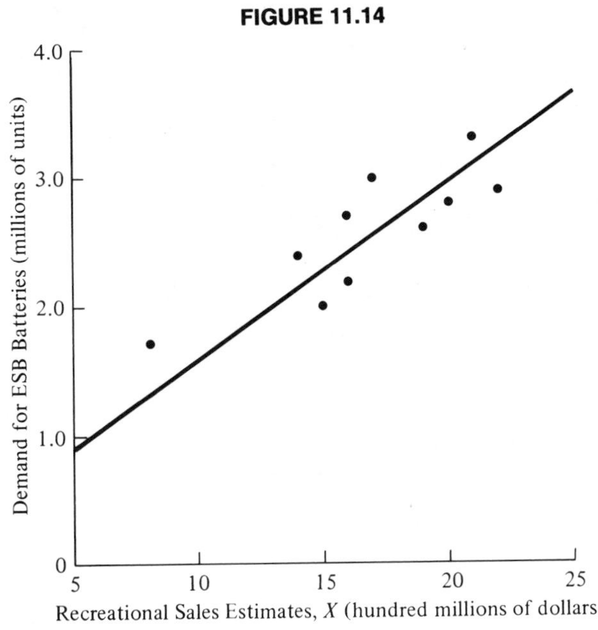

explaining deviations from the model, we can rewrite the model as

$$Y = 0.87 + 0.1X + R$$

where $R$ is a random variable.[6] Under these conditions the residuals (shown in Table 11.9) can be used to assess a probability distribution for $R$. Figure 11.15 shows a cumulative probability distribution for the residuals (obtained by plotting the residuals using the method discussed in this chapter).

**TABLE 11.9**

| *Residuals* (*Vertical Deviations from Regression Line*) |
|---|
| −0.38 |
| −0.28 |
| −0.18 |
| −0.18 |
| −0.08 |
| +0.02 |
| +0.12 |
| +0.22 |
| +0.32 |
| +0.42 |

**FIGURE 11.15**

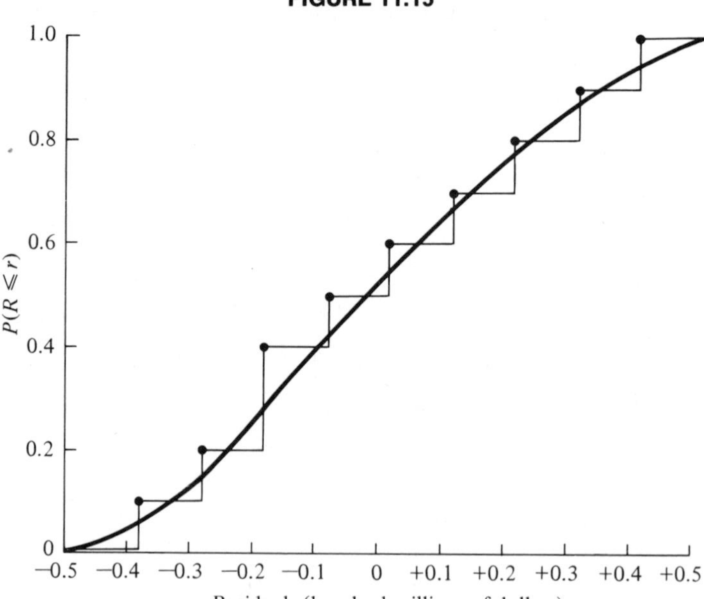


[6]Statistical methods designed to test this assumption are also available and are covered in the references previously cited.

From Table 11.8 we see that the sales estimate for 1978 is \$1,500,000,000. Therefore, using the model, the demand is

$$Y = 0.87 + 0.1 \times 15 = 2.37$$

But we know that this model does not predict sales with certainty. The remaining uncertainty is given by the probability distribution for $R$ shown in Figure 11.15. The scale can be changed to correspond to units of demand rather than residual deviations. The change is made by equating 0 deviations with the demand predicted by the model. In this case the predicted demand is 2.37. Therefore, a residual of $+0.1$ corresponds to a demand of 2.47, and so on. The final demand distribution is plotted in Figure 11.16. By using the model to increase comparability, we can see that the variance or uncertainty has been reduced.

**FIGURE 11.16**

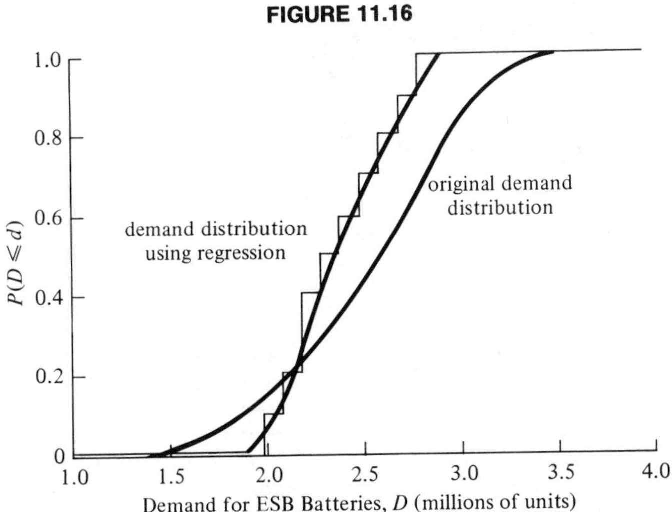

# 12

# Subjective Assessment Of Probability Distributions

In Chapter 4, three views of probability—classical (or theoretical), relative frequency, and subjective—were explained. The first two views are sometimes labeled *objective*. A central issue between the pure objectivist and a subjectivist is whether probabilities are characteristics of physical processes, as the objectivists prefer to assert, or of an individual's state of mind, as the subjectivists believe. Our focus on decisions leads to the adoption of the subjectivist view of probability. This view corresponds to the *practical problem* faced by decision makers who must make *judgments* with *limited information*. It does *not* reject objective evidence, but it recognizes explicitly that use of objective evidence, whether theoretical models or empirical data, requires subjective judgments. These judgments reflect the knowledge of the individual using them.

Using a subjective view of probability raises two issues. One is the obvious question of how these probabilities can be obtained. Making the judgments required to use a theoretical model or empirical data, as described in Chapters 10 and 11, is one procedure. This chapter presents a formal procedure for assessing probabilities subjectively. These procedures are all aimed at determining probabilities that provide a "correct" representation for the uncertain event. When subjective assessments are made that yield numerical values, a second issue arises. Do these numbers qualify as probabilities? That is, even if we are convinced that, conceptually, probabilities represent a state of mind, under what conditions will the numbers obtained directly from individuals qualify as probabilities? Both these issues are discussed in this chapter. Some of the discussion is rather *philosophical*. But the validity of the procedures and the proper use of the analyses depend on these philosophical points. An understanding of these issues can have a *practical* impact on both analyses and decisions. Figure 12.1 shows where the discussion fits into the overall framework.

## SUBJECTIVE JUDGMENTS AND PROBABILITIES

What are the conditions under which subjective judgments will qualify as probabilities? The technical requirements for probabilities have been stated before. But, what if, after agreeing that subjective probabilities should be used, the numbers you assign do not meet the technical requirements? Have you made a mistake? Should you change your assessments? These questions involve the basic nature of human judgments and probabilities.

**FIGURE 12.1**

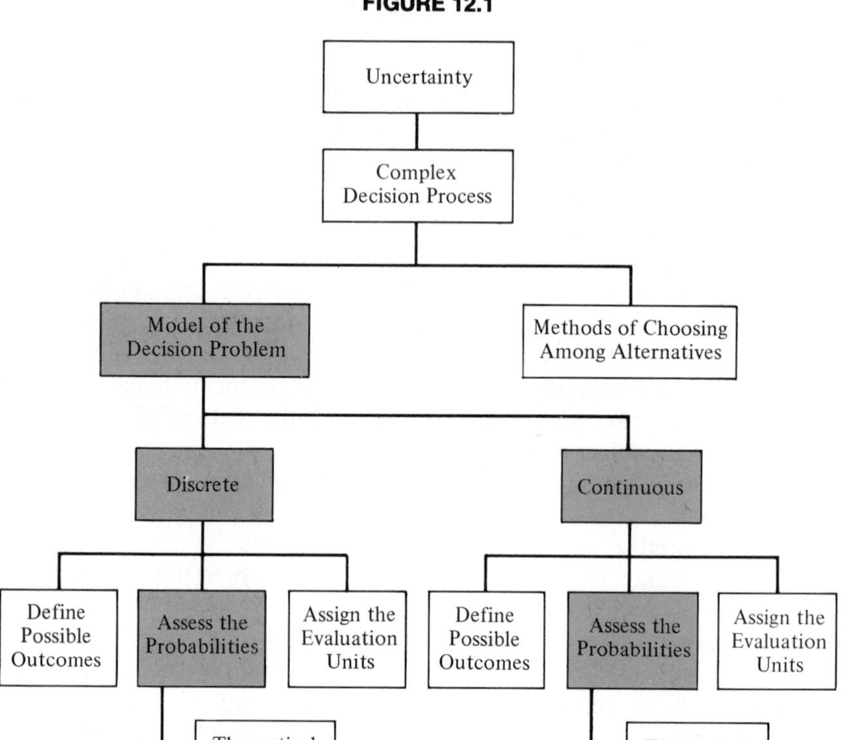

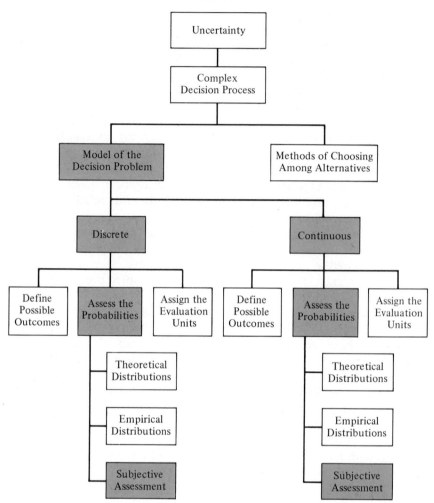

### The Technical Requirements

To qualify as probabilities, the numbers assigned to any two events $A$ and $B$ defined on an outcome space, $\Omega$, must satisfy:

1. $P(A) \geqslant 0$, $P(B) \geqslant 0$.
2. If $A \cap B = \phi$, then $P(A \cup B) = P(A) + P(B)$.
3. $P(\Omega) = 1$.

If the numerical values subjectively assigned to the points in outcome space satisfy these three conditions, they qualify as probabilities and will be described as *coherent assessments*. If the numerical assignments are available, the conditions can be checked directly. For instance, in assessing the success of a new product, a marketing manager might provide the following information:

$$
\begin{aligned}
&P(\textit{highly successful}) &&= 0.2\\
&P(\textit{moderately successful}) &&= 0.5\\
&P(\textit{failure}) &&= 0.3\\
&P(\textit{does not fail}) &&= 0.7
\end{aligned}
$$

Do these numbers qualify as probabilities? The answer is yes, at least as far as we can tell. The first condition is satisfied since all events have nonnegative numbers. If we define the outcome space as $\Omega$ = (highly successful, moderately successful, failure), condition 3 is satisfied. We have one piece of evidence for checking condition 2, namely $P$(highly successful $\cup$ moderately successful) = $P$(does not fail) = $P$(highly successful) + $P$(moderately successful) = 0.7. To completely verify condition 2, we would have to ask about the other combinations of outcomes. However, as a practical matter we often just stipulate that condition 2 holds. Given our knowledge of probabilities, this is certainly a reasonable thing to do.

By checking in this manner, it is possible to identify assessments that qualify as probability distributions and those that do not. One approach to the "qualification" question is merely to *design* all subjective assessments so that the three conditions are satisfied. From a practical point of view this makes sense.

### The Problem

From a more fundamental point of view, the decision to design subjective judgments to satisfy the technical requirements does not address an important question. The subjectivist's view is that probabilities reflect a state of mind and there is no obvious reason why this state of mind must obey the three conditions given above. For instance, the same marketing manager may be asked about a competitor's market share. When pressed by the president he might respond as follows: "I think we will have a good year. In fact, I am confident we will have a larger market share than our competitor. But when you press me for probabilities, I am not sure. For instance, in comparison with a coin flip, in which I know there is a 50–50 chance of heads or tails, I believe I would rather bet on heads than on us having a larger market share. The reason is that there are so many different factors which go into determining market share that I am just more uncertain about it than the coin flip."

Without pressing the marketing manager any further (e.g., asking for specific assessments), we can investigate whether his statements would lead to numerical assessments that satisfy the conditions for probabilities. The outcome space of interest is $\Omega$ = [market share larger ($L$), market share not larger ($NL$)]. From the marketing manager's initial statement we can infer that $P(L) > P(NL)$. From the comparison with coin flip we can infer that

$P(L) < 0.5$. Therefore, we have $P(L) + P(NL) < 1.0$, which violates condition 3. When presented with this evidence the marketing manager may well react saying: "So what? That is the way I feel about it and I see no reason to be concerned about not meeting one of your arbitrary rules."

The question of the conditions under which the numbers assessed subjectively will qualify as probabilities can now be rephrased: What are the underlying behavioral conditions (or axioms) that will prevent assessments like those made by the marketing manager? Or stated slightly differently, what arguments in terms of violation of principles of consistency could be presented to the marketing manager to convince him that he should revise his assessments? The real issue is whether the requirements of probabilities are compatible with other basic conditions when it comes to expressing our feelings about uncertain events.

### Coherence and Axioms

There are a number of sets of behavioral conditions that are consistent with the requirements of probabilities. Behavior that satisfies these conditions is called *coherent*. The appendix in this chapter discusses these conditions or axioms in some detail. The conditions guarantee that subjective judgments which characterize your state of mind concerning any uncertain events will qualify as probabilities. That is, if you conform to these basic conditions, your subjective assessments will satisfy the technical requirements of probabilities.

The conditions are often referred to as conditions for *coherence*. They are rather mild and essentially state that your subjective probabilities are assigned so that a series of bets cannot be arranged to guarantee that you lose. That is, you must be *consistent enough* in your judgments to prevent exploitation. In setting forth these conditions for coherence, deFinetti[1] suggested that the conditions were obviously mild and consistent with the behavior of business people, or else the people would not remain in business very long.

What this means, in terms of the problem raised above, is that you can tell the marketing manager that his statements are inconsistent. This type of behavior would allow the two of you to agree to a series of bets so that he would be sure to lose. If he wants to eliminate this type of inconsistency, he should revise his probability assessments. If he is willing to behave "inconsistently," he does not need to revise his statements.

[1]B. deFinetti, "Foresight: Its Logical Laws, Its Subjective Sources," 1937. English translation in H. E. Kyburg, Jr., and H. E. Smokler (eds.), *Studies in Subjective Probability* (New York: Wiley, 1964). His argument relies on a decision maker trading lotteries for their expected value. This may not be true for large stakes. Other sets of conditions that are equally mild do not rely on this assumption. See L. J. Savage, *The Foundations of Statistics* (New York: Wiley, 1954), and F. J. Anscombe and R. J. Auman, "A Definition of Subjective Probability," *Annals of Mathematical Statistics*, Vol. 34, 1963.

Therefore, if you *want* to be consistent in the sense that no one will be able to exploit you in a series of bets, you will *want* your subjective probability assessments to satisfy the technical requirements. If you *behave* in a "coherent" manner, your probability assessments *will* satisfy the technical requirements. If they do not, it is a signal to you that your behavior is "inconsistent" and you will want to reassess your statements.

If an individual agrees that this condition of coherence is reasonable, it does indeed make sense to use probabilities to describe his or her state of mind about uncertain events. If we are able to behave consistently, our assessments will satisfy the requirements for probabilities. If our assessments fail to meet the requirements for probabilities, as was the case for the marketing manager, we will agree that a mistake has been made and we will want to revise the assessments until they do satisfy the requirements of a probability distribution.

### Maintaining Coherence

Empirical evidence indicates that individuals do not always assess probabilities in a coherent manner.[2] For instance, probabilities sometimes do not add to 1.0. Operationally this means that checks must be included in the assessment process to indicate when assessments are not coherent. Since assessment procedures are open-ended and rely on feedback in a specific setting, a set step-by-step procedure for checking coherence is not used. Condition 1 is easy to keep in mind. Checking that all probabilities sum to 1 is also easy. Condition 2 requires assessment of both events and their union. As indicated earlier, in many cases an individual will just stipulate this condition. This is especially likely if the union of events is complicated so that its assessment is difficult.

## DEFINITION OF SUBJECTIVE PROBABILITY

The *general* definition of subjective probability was given in Chapter 4. Now we need a definition that can be used to assess probabilities. To be *operational*, the definition should include a device for *measuring* probabilities—something like a *yardstick*, except for probabilities. We will not be able to provide anything as satisfactory for probabilities as a yardstick is for measuring length. But we can still try to provide devices that can be compared against uncertain events, just as a *yardstick* is compared against a board to determine the board's length. The problem of providing a measuring device is a difficult one. Basically, we are faced with trying to help people think about probabilities.

[2]See, for instance, C. A. S. Stael von Holstein, *Assessment and Evaluation of Subjective Probability Distributions* (Stockholm: The Economic Research Institute at the Stockholm School of Economics, 1970); or R. L. Winkler, "The Assessment of Prior Distributions in Bayesian Analysis," *Journal of the American Statistical Association*, Vol. 62, December 1967.

### Assessment Lotteries

The device used for measuring probabilities is called an *assessment lottery*. It is intended to provide a concrete example of a random process. The uncertain event in the lottery should be easy to visualize and have *objective* probabilities. A diagram for an assessment lottery is shown in Figure 12.2 Note that *assessment* lotteries and the *reference* gambles used to determine risk preferences are *not* the same (see Chapter 6 for examples of reference gambles). The payoffs for reference gambles are designed for specific uncertain events. Assessment lotteries use some desirable prize $W$ and some less desirable prize $L$ rather than the maximum and minimum payoff. Moreover, the two types of lotteries are aimed at entirely different things. Reference gambles are aimed at measuring an individual's attitude toward risk. Assessment lotteries are aimed at measuring the probability of some event.

The physical realization of an assessment lottery usually takes one of two forms.

1. Drawing a ball randomly from an urn with 100 balls, some fraction $p$ of which are white and some fraction $(1-p)$ of which are red. Drawing a white ball results in a *win* and prize $W$, while drawing a red ball results in a *lose* and prize $L$. This assessment lottery is supposed to allow an individual to visualize the uncertainty through a *mental picture* of an urn (see Figure 12.3).
2. Spinning a reference wheel that is divided into white and red wedge-shaped sections. The fraction of the area (or circumference) that is white is $p$, and the fraction that is red is $(1-p)$. If the spinner lands in the white a *win* results and prize $W$ is obtained; if the spinner lands in the red, a *lose* results and prize $L$ is obtained. These probability wheels are used in practice to provide a strong visual image of the uncertain process (see Figure 12.4).

### Subjective Probability

Using the concept of an assessment lottery, the subjective probability for an uncertain event is defined as:

**Subjective Probability**

***Definition:*** *Your* ***subjective probability*** *for uncertain event E is the setting for the assessment lottery (fraction p) that makes you just indifferent between the assessment lottery (shown in Figure 12.2) and another lottery in which you receive W if event E occurs and L if it does not occur.*

**FIGURE 12.2**

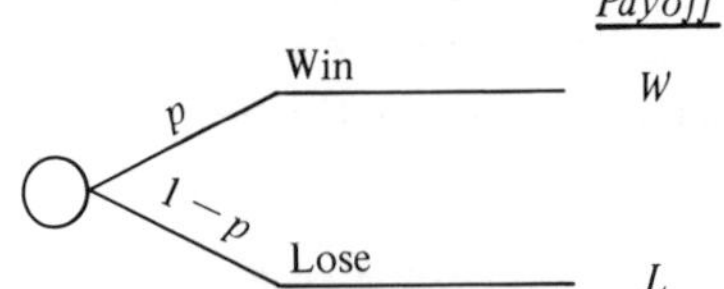


**FIGURE 12.3**

**FIGURE 12.4**

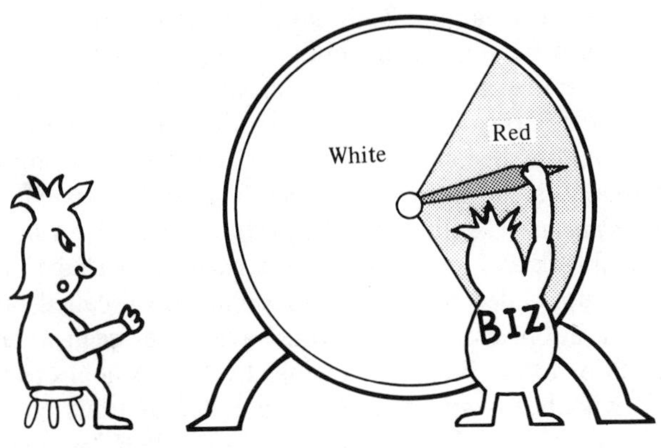

According to the definition, assessment lotteries are compared to an uncertain event, each with the same prizes until a point of indifference is reached. For instance, if after turning in your final exam you were interested in assessing the probability of getting an *honors* grade in a particular course, you would compare the two events shown in Figure 12.5.

**FIGURE 12.5**

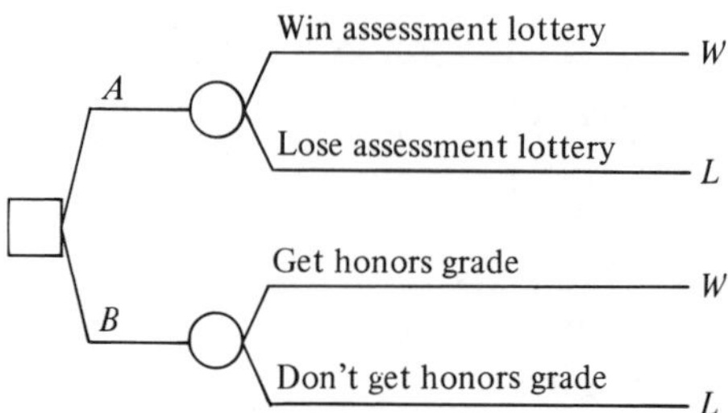


If for some number of red and white balls (or setting on a reference wheel) you agree that alternatives $A$ and $B$ are equivalent, we know that $P$(win assessment lottery) = $P$(get honors grade). By knowing the number of white balls or area of the white wedge, we can directly determine the objective probability of winning the assessment lottery. In this case assume that you are indifferent between $A$ and $B$ with 45 white balls in an assessment lottery. Therefore, we have $P$(honors grade) = 0.45.

Details of the assessment procedure are given later. There are a number of options, including directly providing the probabilities without using assessment lotteries.

## ●● Relationship to Limiting Relative Frequencies

Neither the definition of subjective probability nor any of the behavioral conditions required for assessments to yield probabilities makes any mention of limiting relative frequencies (i.e., the relative frequencies as the number of trials, $m$, becomes very large). Both intuition and a sense of orderliness suggest there should be some connection. From a practical point of view, most people's subjective assessments for probabilities of comparable, independent events will correspond precisely to the relative frequencies as the number of observations becomes very large. However, in trying to make the connection formally, some difficulties arise. The most puzzling involves the concept of *independence*. To illustrate the problem, consider a simple example of tossing a thumbtack and letting it fall on a hard, flat surface. The tack will either land point up, called heads ($H$), or point down, called tails ($T$). For purposes of illustration, assume that you have never seen a tack like this tossed before. Prior to the first toss, a subjective assessment of the probabilities associated with heads and tails for a number of trials could be made. Assume that you make assessments as follows: $P(H_1) = P(H_2) = P(H_3) =$

$P(H_4)=\frac{1}{2}$, where $H_1$ means heads on trial 1, and so on. In fact, assume you are willing to state that as far as you are concerned, based on your current information, the probability of heads on any trial is $\frac{1}{2}$.

As defined in Chapter 7, independence is a probabilistic concept. For instance, if we state that the events *heads on trial* 1 and *heads on trial* 2 are independent, it means that $P(H_2|H_1)=P(H_2)=\frac{1}{2}$. Furthermore, if we stipulate that the sequence of trials with the tack consists of independent events, we have $P(H_n|H_1,H_2,\ldots,H_{n-1})=P(H_n)=\frac{1}{2}$. This means, for example, that if $n=10$, your subjective assessment of heads on the tenth trial, given nine straight heads, is still the same as it was prior to the first toss. More generally, stipulating that events $H_1,H_2,\ldots,H_n$ are independent means that the information obtained from observing the first, say, 50 outcomes must be irrelevant for purposes of subjectively assessing the probability of heads on the fifty-first toss. From the perspective of a subjectivist, this just does not make much sense. It is perfectly obvious that these observations change our state of knowledge and hence may well influence our subjective assessments. A subjectivist will not agree the probabilities are constant and therefore will not agree that the events are independent.

The problem is that independence is the wrong concept. To make the connection between relative frequency and subjective assessment we need to consider a slightly different characteristic of the tack-tossing process. This characteristic is called *exchangeability*. If the trials are exchangeable, it means that they are viewed as physically unrelated.[3] In the tack-tossing example, exchangeability is a reasonable assumption for both subjectivists and objectivists. Each trial is physically unrelated to other trials and therefore everyone would agree that trials could be exchanged (one with another) without changing the problem. With this new condition the connection with limiting relative frequencies can be made. The result is due to deFinetti.[4] He shows that when exchangeability holds, the limiting relative frequency is well defined (i.e., it exists), and furthermore that, given this limiting relative frequency, the only consistent subjective assessment for the individual trials is the limiting relative frequency. *In other words, in the limit as the number of trials goes to infinity, the subjectively assessed probability will equal the relative frequency*. In terms of the tack-tossing examples, if we let $\alpha$ be the limiting relative frequency for heads, it means that $P(H_n|\alpha)=\alpha$. This is, of course, exactly what we need to establish the link between subjective probabilities and relative frequencies. In addition, the concept of exchangeability helps explain a potential dilemma regarding independent events when probabilities are assessed subjectively.

[3]Formally, it means that for any set of $m$ distinct indexes $j_1,j_2,\ldots,j_m$, the probability distributions for the joint events $(H_{j1},H_{j2},\ldots,H_{jm})$ are identical.

[4]B. deFinetti, "La Prevision: Les Logiques, ses Sources Subjectives," *Ann. Inst. Poincaire*, Vol. 7, 1937, pp. 1–68. English translation in H. E. Kyburg and H. E. Smokler (eds.), *Studies in Subjective Probability* (New York: Wiley, 1964), and B. deFinetti, *Theory of Probability*, Vol. I (New York: Wiley, 1974).

## ASSESSMENT PROCEDURES

After accepting the premise that judgments about uncertain events can be expressed as probabilities, we still have the problem of making the assessments. When theoretical models do not fit and relative frequency information is not available or adequate, subjective assessment is the only alternative for obtaining a probability distribution. The absence of a mental "thermometer" that easily reflects an individual's state of mind concerning an uncertain event does not eliminate the need for processing information using probabilities.

The assertion that subjective assessments are less "scientific" than other procedures should be viewed from three perspectives. *First*, if the only other alternative, in the context of a decision, is to pretend that uncertainty does not exist, it is difficult to assign more "scientific validity" to this procedure than using a subjective probability distribution. *Second*, we must not confuse numerical accuracy with scientific validity. A theoretical or empirical distribution may have high numerical accuracy. However, the use of such a distribution involves subjective judgments. Judgments are part of any decision process. They should be made in a manner conducive to accuracy and reliability. In some cases subjective assessment provides the best available alternative. When decision making is the goal, we usually do not have the option of refusing to undertake an analysis until conclusive "scientific" evidence is available. *Third*, there is a question of exactly what is meant by "scientific." If it refers to empirically based observations, it is almost synonymous with limiting relative frequencies. However, if the term implies "logical," "rational," "consistent" processes, the subjective assessment procedures are just as scientific as any other.

### Assessment for Specific Events

There are two basic approaches to assessing the probability of a specific event. The direct approach requires the assessor to provide probability numbers. The indirect approach uses assessment lotteries and allows the assessor to express judgments through choices.

### Direct Assessment for a Specific Event

After a specific event is identified, the assessor makes a direct numerical response.

**Example 12.1**

Suppose that the uncertain event of interest is an athletic event—say a football game with a home team ($H$) and visiting team ($V$). Assume you want to assess the probability that the home team wins, based on the information now available to you. This event is shown in Figure 12.6 and labeled $A$.

**FIGURE 12.6**

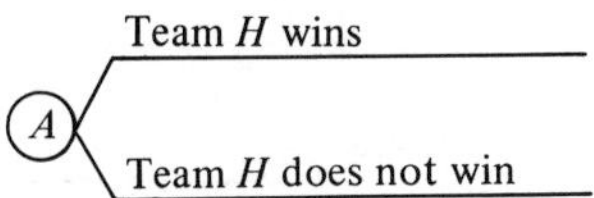


After considering the records of the two teams and any other pertinent information, you merely specify a number that represents your assessment of the probability. There is some evidence that, after an individual becomes an expert on assessing probabilities, this direct approach is effective. However, until a person is trained to think about probabilities, the indirect approach is better.

### Indirect Assessment for a Specific Event

The indirect approach does not require the assessor to state a probability. Instead, it presents a series of choices. Based on the choices, a point of indifference between two alternatives is reached. The probability for the event is obtained from knowing the point of indifference.

Assessment lotteries are used in the indirect approach. They perform the same function as a ruler or scale in measuring length or weight. They are external references against which the item to be measured is compared. The comparison involves determining when the item to be measured is essentially the same as the external reference. For example, when we measure the length of a piece of lumber, a rule is laid next to it and a point is chosen on the rule which makes the rule length and the length of the piece of wood the same (or at least the same as closely as we can tell). We go through a similar procedure with a precision scale in which weights are adjusted until the balance indicates that the item to be weighed and the reference weights are the same. Another way to describe this is that we are indifferent between choosing the reference weights or the item if the only characteristic of interest is their weight. In the indirect-assessment procedure, the assessor is given the choice between an assessment lottery and a lottery involving the event of interest. A statement of indifference means that the probabilities are the same—as closely as the assessor can tell.

The procedure is formalized below. Read it through quickly and then go to the example.

*Indirect Assessment for a Specific Event*

1. A choice is proposed between an alternative, $A$, involving the event of interest—call it $E$—and an alternative, $B$, involving an assessment lottery. A desirable prize, $W$, is obtained if either the event $E$ occurs or the outcome of the assessment lottery is *win*. An undesirable prize, $L$, is obtained if event $E$ does not occur or the outcome of the assessment lottery is *lose*. It is helpful to diagram this choice as shown in Figure 12.7.

**FIGURE 12.7**

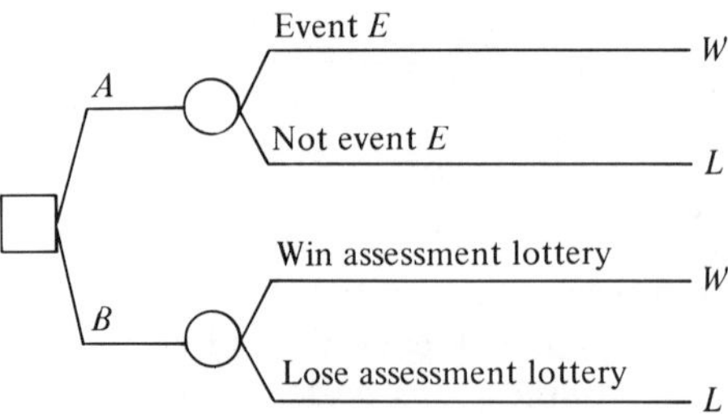


2. An assessment lottery is defined by specifying the number of white balls in an urn or the setting on a reference wheel.
3. The assessor is asked to choose either alternative $A$ or $B$.
4. If $A$ is chosen, the assessment lottery is modified by substituting white balls for red balls or increasing the size of the white wedge on the reference wheel. If $B$ is chosen, the assessment lottery is modified by substituting red balls for white balls, or decreasing the size of the white wedge on the reference wheel. Step 3 is repeated.
5. The process is continued until the assessor is indifferent between $A$ and $B$.
6. The probability of event $E$ is obtained from the percentage of white in the assessment lottery.

To illustrate this procedure consider again the problem in Example 12.1. The event of interest is the home team winning. Assume that you are trying to help your friend Ralph, an ardent sports fan, assess his probability for the home team winning. The conversation might go something like this:

You: The purpose of this exercise is to try to help you *think* about the probability that $H$ wins the game. Presumably you have a lot of information about the teams. But I doubt that it is coded in terms of probabilities.

Because probabilities are an abstract concept, I will try to provide you with some concrete choices. Based on your answers, I will be able to infer your probability for $H$ winning.

To begin with, let me show you this reference wheel (see Figure 12.8). Think of spinning the pointer. If it lands in the white, you will win a desirable prize. Although it does not really matter what the prize is, let's assume it is a new car, just for purposes of discussion. If the pointer lands in the red, you will not get anything.

Now the choices I am going to offer involve this reference wheel and a lottery based on team $H$ winning. The lottery involving team $H$ will also give you a new car if team $H$ wins. If it does not win, you get nothing—just like if the pointer lands in the red. I can summarize the choice by a diagram (see Figure 12.9).

**FIGURE 12.8**
**Reference Wheel**

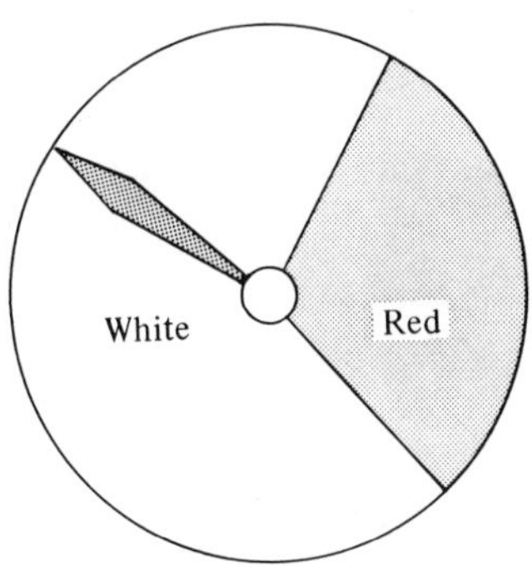


**FIGURE 12.9**

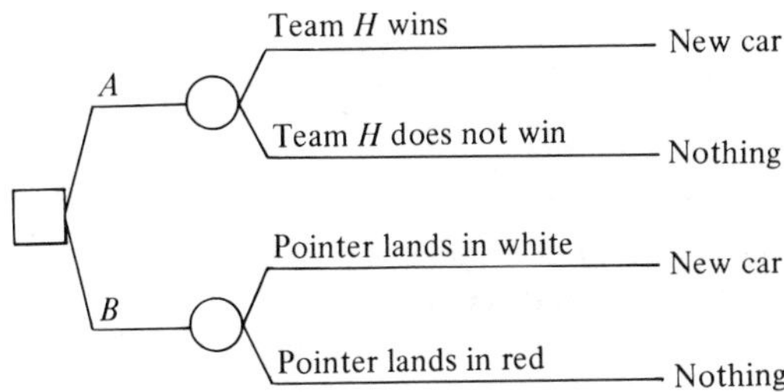


This is all a little complicated to start with, but as we go along you will get the idea. Ready to start?

Ralph: I guess so. You are right about it being a little complicated. What do you want me to do?

You: Look at the reference wheel as I have it set (see Figure 12.10). Thinking about the two alternatives on the diagram, if the reference wheel were set as I have shown you, would you choose *A* or *B*?

**FIGURE 12.10**
**Reference Wheel Setting One**

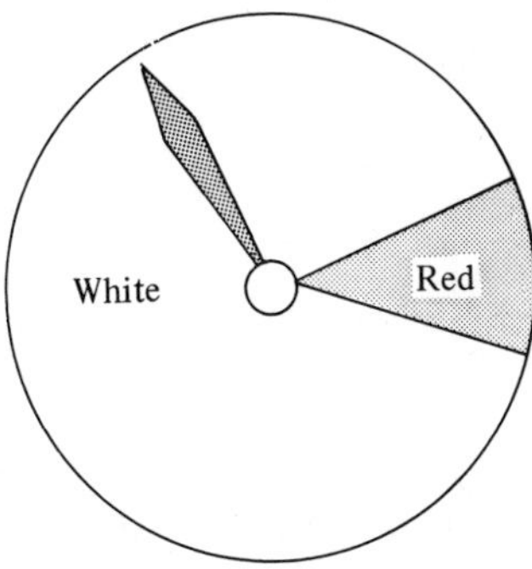

Ralph: That's easy; I'd choose *B*.

You: O.K. Let me reset the wheel (see Figure 12.11). Now, would you choose *A* or *B*?

**FIGURE 12.11**

**Reference Wheel Setting Two**

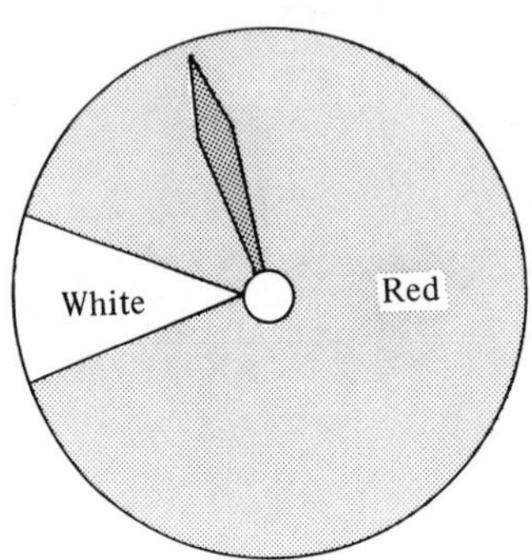


**FIGURE 12.12**

**Reference Wheel Setting Three**

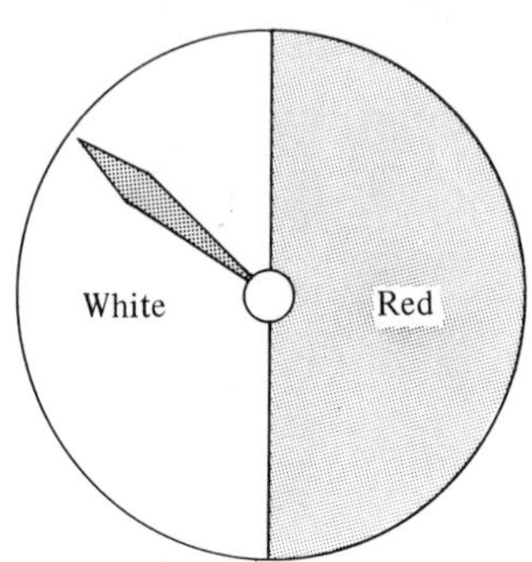


Ralph: Still easy. I'd choose *A*.

You: What about this setting? (See Figure 12.12)

Ralph: I would still choose *A*. I'd rather bet on team *H* winning than the pointer landing in the white with this setting.

You: Let me increase the area a little. How about this setting? (See Figure 12.13.)

**FIGURE 12.13**

**Reference Wheel Setting Four**

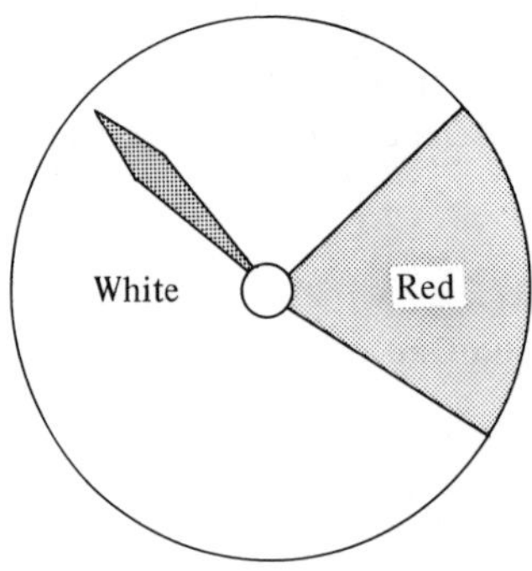


**FIGURE 12.14**

**Reference Wheel Setting Five**

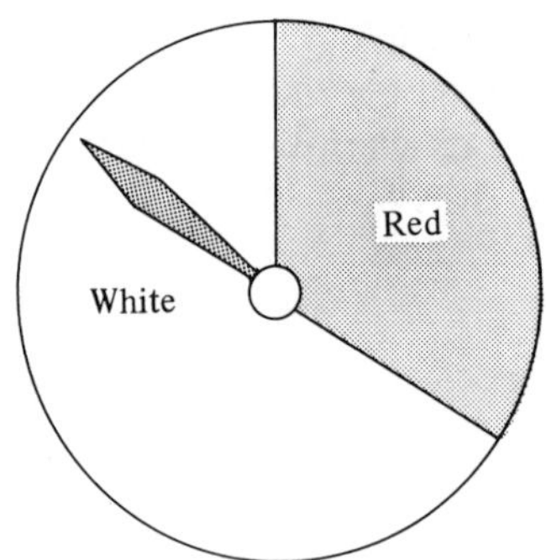


Ralph: This is getting tougher. Let's see, let me try to think out the new setting.... I guess I would choose *B* with this setting.

You: O.K. What is your choice if I use this setting? (See Figure 12.14.)

Ralph: This is really a hard choice. As a matter of fact, I can't make up my mind. The more I think about it, I just can't differentiate the two alternatives.

You: Does this mean you are indifferent between *A* and *B*?

Ralph: Yes, I wouldn't care which of the two I took.

With this information you could infer that Ralph's assessment of the probability that *H* wins is given by the percentage of white in the last setting (about 0.67 in this case).

### Assessment for Continuous Random Variables

Discrete random variables have outcomes that are specific events. Therefore, the procedures described above can be applied to each outcome. Checks for coherence are made and inconsistencies resolved by the assessor. As the number of outcomes increases, the difficulty of assessing the events increases. If there are more than a few outcomes, it is hard to think about each event separately. Random variables with a large number of outcomes are usually assessed as continuous random variables. Procedures for assessing continuous random variables involve an additional step. The events to be assessed must be identified. Once identified, events can be assessed using the methods described above. Another method, the interval technique, can also be used. The overall procedure for assessing probability distributions for continuous random variables is given below. Each step will be discussed in detail.

*Assessment of Continuous Probability Distributions*[5]

*Step* 1: Establish extreme values.
*Step* 2: Begin a cumulative plot.
*Step* 3: Fill out the distribution by establishing events and assessing their probabilities.
*Step* 4: Use the interval technique to find the median and quartiles.
*Step* 5: Visually fit a curve to the cumulative plot.
*Step* 6: Verify the distribution.

### Extreme Values

The first step is to establish the range. Ask for extreme values for the random variable. To test them, ask for a series of events that could lead to outcomes outside these extreme values (e.g., all competitors go out of business and product demand doubles). Assess the probabilities of the following events: (1) outcome greater than or equal to the larger of the identified extreme

[5]The procedure follows one suggested and clinically tested by researchers at Stanford Research Institute. For a more detailed description, see C. S. Spetzler and C. A. S. Stael von Holstein, "Probability Encoding in Decision Analysis," *Management Science*, Vol. 22, No. 3, November 1975.

values; (2) outcome less than or equal to the smaller of the identified extreme values. Both the direct and indirect methods should be used. The statement that they are extreme values is the same as a direct assessment that the probability of these events is zero.

### Cumulative Plot

Plot these extreme values and all others assessed on a cumulative distribution. If the assessment is being conducted by an analyst, do not show the cumulative plot to the individual assessor until assessments have been completed. This will reduce biasing.

### Filling out the Distribution

Next, specify a number of events, such as the *outcome is less than or equal to X units*, where $X$ is less than the larger extreme point and greater than the smaller extreme point. Do not begin by asking about points close to the median to avoid central biasing. There is no set procedure for selecting these events. They generally are chosen to be either the outcomes less than or equal to a point or the outcomes greater than or equal to a point. Assess the probability for each event using either a direct or indirect procedure. Continue until the cumulative plot is well defined.

### Finding the Median and Quartiles

The interval technique can be used as a check and also to help fill out the distribution. It is based on dividing the scale into equally probable ranges. First the median is assessed. A value, $M$, is specified and the two uncertain events shown in Figure 12.15 are formed. Prizes $W$ and $L$ are any desirable and undesirable prize, respectively, just as they are in assessment lotteries. Note that the uncertain events associated with alternatives $A$ and $B$ are the same. The difference between the alternatives is that the prizes have been assigned to different outcomes.

**FIGURE 12.15**

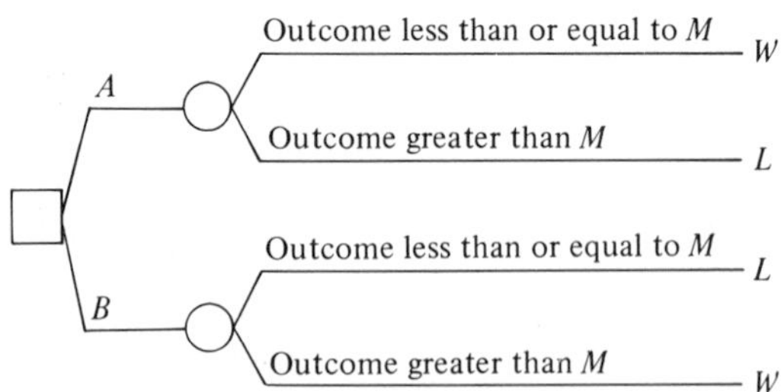

The assessor is asked to choose between $A$ and $B$. If $A$ is chosen, this means the assessor believes it is more likely that the outcome will be less than or equal to $M$ than greater than $M$. Therefore, $M$ is above the median. A lower value of $M$ is selected and the assessor asked to make a choice again. The process continues, with $M$ being changed, until the assessor is indifferent between $A$ or $B$. At this point the probability that the outcome is less than or equal to $M$ is just equal, in the assessor's mind, to the probability that the outcome is greater than $M$. By definition this value of $M$ is the median [i.e., $P(X \leqslant M) = 0.5$].

The quartiles can be obtained in a similar manner. The intervals below and above the median are divided. The lower quartile, $Q_1$, is assessed using the lotteries in Figure 12.16. Again the assessor is asked to choose between $A$ and $B$, and $Q_1$ is varied until the point of indifference is reached. At this point we know that $P(X \leqslant Q_1) = 0.25$. The upper quartile [$P(X \leqslant Q_2) = 0.75$] is assessed in a similar way by choosing a point $Q_2$ greater than $M$. These points are added to the cumulative plot.

**FIGURE 12.16**

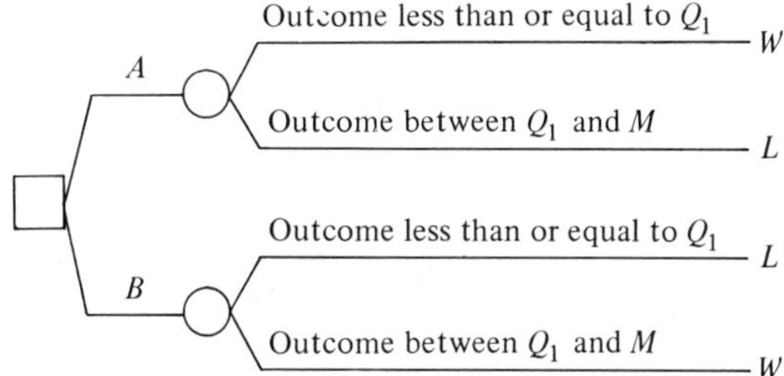


### Visually Fitting Curve

A smooth curve is fit to the points after any obvious inconsistencies are resolved through further questions. There is no set procedure for resolving inconsistencies. The assessor must make the resolution.

### Verification

The curve can be verified through tests to see if the distribution actually represents the assessor's views. The first test is visual inspection of the cumulative graph. Next, a sequence of pairs of bets involving identical payoffs are proposed. They are designed so that, based on the assessed distribution, the probability of winning is equally likely for each bet. If the assessor is not indifferent, modifications are required in the assessed distribution.

## DECOMPOSITION TO AID ASSESSMENT

The method used to decompose or model the uncertain event can be important to obtaining good assessments. If the outcome space is not assessment-adequate, it can be decomposed by adding conditioning events. There is no formula or algorithm for decomposition. The starting point is the random variable of interest. If the assessor wants to condition his or her assessments on some "underlying" events, the diagram can be expanded to add them.

Assume that you are interested in buying stock in XYZ Company. Your question to your stock broker is: "What is the probability the price will increase over the next 6 months?" That is, you are interested in the uncertain event shown in Figure 12.17. Your broker might reply: "Well, it really depends on two things: the first is the company's performance over the next few months, and second is the overall movement of the stock market during the 6-month period." This could be interpreted as meaning that he would like to decompose the problem as shown in Figure 12.18.

Further discussion might reveal that he felt the events *market up / market not up* and *XYZ performance good / XYZ performance not good* were both dependent on the general economic climate (as measured by Gross National

**FIGURE 12.17**

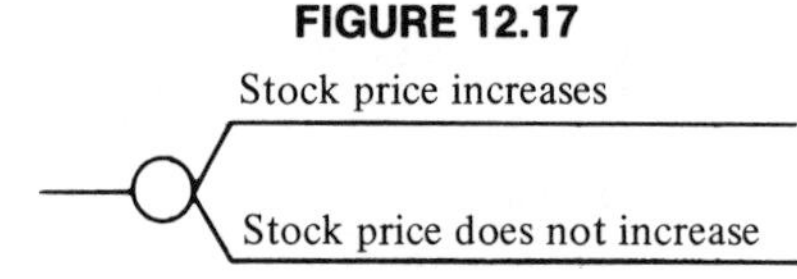


**FIGURE 12.18**

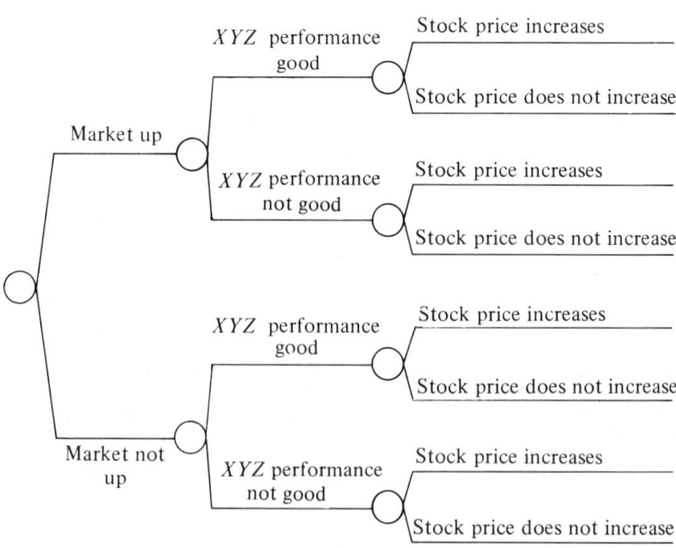

Product, GNP). The overall model to be used for assessment then would be Figure 12.19. The stock price performance is conditioned on XYZ performance, market performance, and GNP movement. Instead of making a single assessment, the broker must now assess probability distributions for each of the uncertain events in Figure 12.19. The advantage is that these assessments can be conditioned on the preceding events. For instance, in assessing the top right-hand event in Figure 12.19, the broker assesses stock

**FIGURE 12.19**

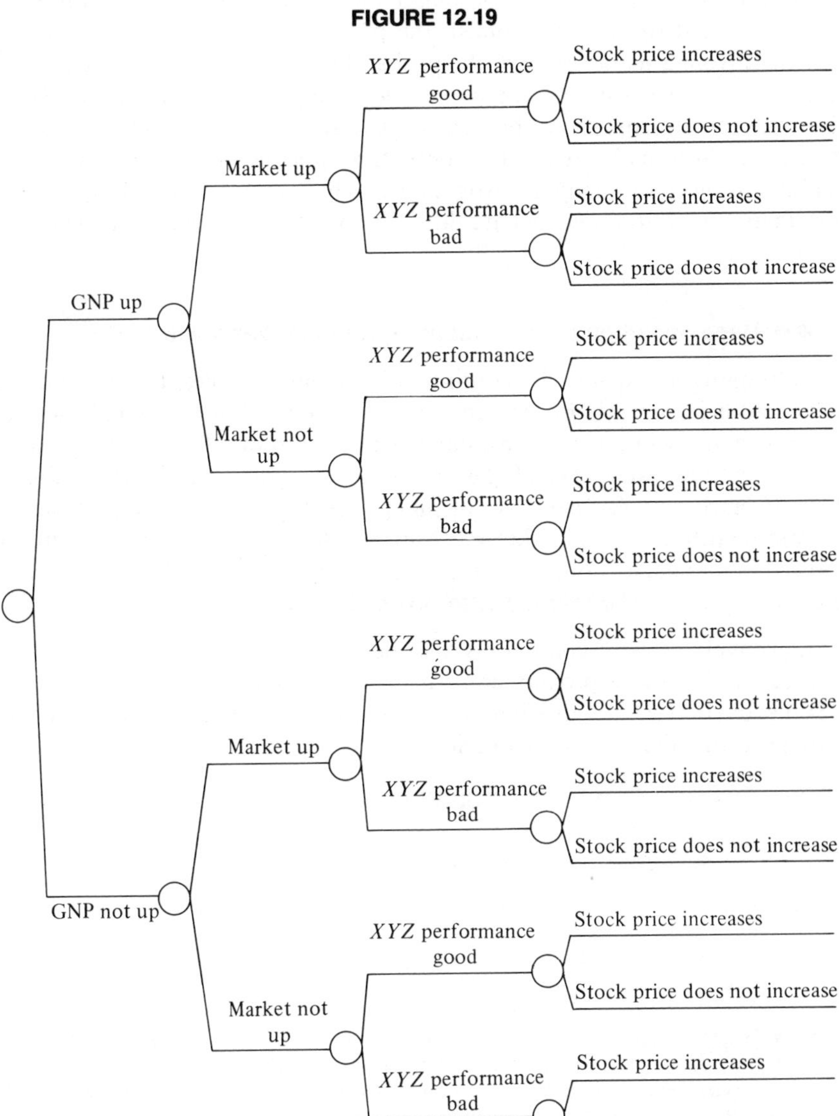

price movement conditioned on *XYZ performance good, market up*, and *GNP up*. There are two advantages of this type of decomposition: (1) it allows judgments to be supplied in the way an expert can best think about them, and (2) it allows more than one expert to be used.

### Using Experts

In the example above you may want to use a separate expert for each type of uncertain event. For instance, you might want to obtain the probabilities on GNP movement from an economist, the probabilities on the overall market movement from a market expert, the probabilities on XYZ performance from someone associated with the company, and finally, the probabilities on stock price movement from your broker. It is also possible to get probability assessments from more than one expert. Group assessment procedures have been the subject of many investigations.[6] The problems posed by having more than one person involved are difficult and still provide a fertile research area.

### ●● Decomposition with Continuous Random Variables

If conditioning is provided by continuous random variables, the sequence of assessment is important. For instance, what if the conditioning event used for economic activity in the above example were *GNP* rather than *GNP up / GNP not up*. The first two stages of the probability diagram are shown in Figure 12.20. If market performance is not independent of GNP, we would have a separate distribution for market performance for every possible outcome of GNP. It is, of course, not practical to assess a different distribution for every outcome of GNP. The solution is to proceed in three steps:

1. Subjectively assess a continuous distribution for GNP.
2. Obtain a discrete approximation for the continuous distribution.
3. Subjectively assess a distribution for market performance for each outcome in the discrete approximation.

**FIGURE 12.20**

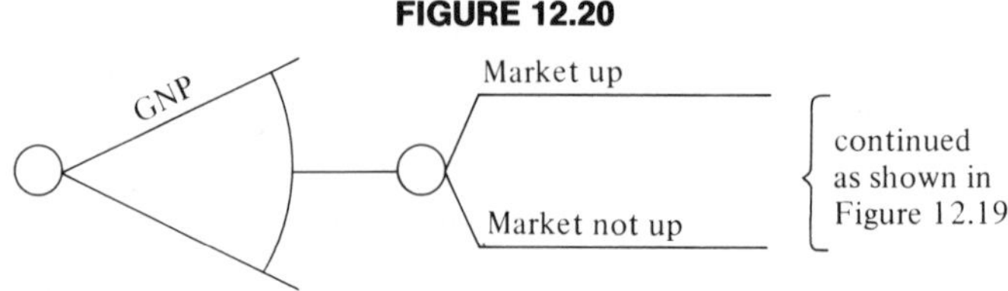


[6]See R. M. Hogarth, "Cognitive Processes and the Assessment of Subjective Probability Distributions," *Journal of the American Statistical Association*, Vol. 70, June 1975; and H. Raiffa, *Decision Analysis, Introductory Lectures on Choices Under Uncertainty* (Reading, Mass.: Addison-Wesley, 1968), for a discussion of some of the problems and results.

## ACCURACY OF SUBJECTIVE ASSESSMENTS

We have discussed behavioral conditions that lead to coherent probability assessments. Procedures have been presented for carrying out the assessments. What about accuracy? Just because we know that *if we are consistent*, the assessments will qualify as probabilities and that certain procedures will yield numbers does not mean they are *accurate*. This is the same problem faced with theoretical and empirical distribution when we tried to establish that a particular distribution represented the uncertain event of interest. In these cases the ultimate authority was the individual decision maker. That is, we argued that individual judgment was required and that if the decision maker judged the objective evidence adequate, the probability distribution should be used. If not, some other method of assessing the distribution should be used.

Following this line of reasoning, if the assessor is the decision maker, once the assessment has been completed and checked for coherence, there is no "higher authority" to turn to for verification. By definition, it represents the decision maker's best judgment, so it makes no sense to talk about accuracy or "goodness" relative to some criterion. On the other hand, we can still think about accuracy in an absolute sense. To pose an extreme example, suppose that the uncertain event of interest was the exact number of acres in a plot of land and the event is uncertain because the surveyor's office is closed. It is clear that when the office opens, a single number will prove to be "correct." A probability distribution that is narrowly peaked around this true but unknown value would seem to be more "accurate" than one that is either peaked about some other value or widely spread out.

It is helpful to think about this assessment accuracy along two dimensions[7]: *substantive* and *procedural*. The first refers to the knowledge of the substantive setting available to the assessor, the second to the assessor's expertise in relating to probability statements. For instance, suppose you are interested in the probability that a particular farm will yield more than 2 tons of hay per acre per year, and there are two people you can talk with about the farm. One is a farmer who has farmed the land for a number of years. The other is a statistician who has driven through the area recently. Let us assume that the farmer has never dealt with probabilities explicitly and the statistician has never grown hay. In one case we can opt for substantive knowledge, and, in the other, for procedural knowledge. The point is that we can think about two different types of knowledge or expertise which bear on the "accuracy" of subjective probability distributions.

We have all had experience in learning about substantive settings. Learning about assessing probabilities is somewhat new. The field of cognitive

[7]See R. L. Winkler, and A. H. Murphy, "Good Probability Assessors," *Journal of Applied Meteorology*, Vol. 7, October 1968.

psychology has studied judgmental processes, thinking, and human information processing in general. Two conclusions are that human beings have limited capacity for information processing, and the strategies used to cope with judgments depend heavily on the task.[8] A significant effort has been devoted to studying human information processing of uncertainty and human abilities as probability assessors. The results suggest that the task is difficult for human beings. When left to their own devices, they will often choose to neglect uncertainty rather than consider it explicitly. Besides the conceptual and intellectual difficulty that human beings experience in dealing with uncertainty, our culture does not generally train individuals to consider uncertainty explicitly:

> The usual tests of language habits of our culture tend to promote confusion between certainty and belief. They encourage both the vice of acting and speaking as though we were certain when we are only fairly sure and that of acting and speaking as though the opinions we do have were worthless when they are not very strong.[9]

Empirically observed limitations include misunderstanding of independence, conservative processing of new information, and difficulty in assessing variability.[10] There are two findings that are encouraging from the standpoint of obtaining and using subjective probability distributions. The first is that procedural experts are able to use a variety of assessment techniques with consistency[11] and the second is that naive subjects (from a procedural perspective) show the ability to gain consistency (learn about assessment) fairly rapidly.[12] In addition, there is an increasing body of knowledge about how individuals process information on uncertainty and clinical research that suggests how this information can be used to obtain probability distributions from substantive experts.

If assessment errors are present, the calculation of probabilities for decomposed events poses a problem. When subjective assessments are made, errors in the "calibration" of the assessor can invalidate the independence assumption.[13]

[8]See A. Newell and H. A. Simon, *Human Problem Solving* (Englewood Cliffs, N.J.: Prentice-Hall, 1972).

[9]L. J. Savage, "Elicitation of Personal Probabilities and Expectations," *Journal of the American Statistical Association*, Vol. 66, December 1971.

[10]See R. J. Hogarth, "Cognitive Processes and the Assessment of Subjective Probability Distribution," *Journal of the American Statistical Association*, Vol. 70, June 1975, for a comprehensive review of these limitations and the empirical research.

[11]R. L. Winkler, "The Assessment of Prior Distributions in Bayesian Analysis," *Journal of the American Statistical Association*, Vol. 62, September 1967.

[12]C. A. S. Stael von Holstein, *Assessment and Evaluation of Subjective Probability Distributions* (Stockholm: The Economic Research Institute at the Stockholm School of Economics, 1970).

[13]See J. M. Harrison, "Independence and Calibration in Decision Analysis," *Management Science*, Vol. 24, No. 3, November 1977.

Accuracy is an important issue with subjective assessments. The best advice is get expert help for important problems; and expertise may be needed along both the substantive and procedural dimensions.

## ●● MODES OF HUMAN JUDGMENTS

Understanding how people think about uncertainty can provide important information on how assessments should be made.[14] As a first step, "motivational" biases should be identified. If an assessor's personal rewards are influenced by a decision, motivational biases may be important. The classic example is asking salespersons to predict sales in their territory for the next year. If these predictions are to be used for setting goals, quotas, and incentive schemes, there may be clear biases that will work to the advantage of the salesperson. When motivational biases exist, the design of incentive systems that control or eliminate the biases can be challenging. One class of incentive schemes that has been studied is scoring rules. A "proper" scoring rule is one with the property that the assessor can maximize his score only by providing judgments consistent with his true beliefs. There are a number of rules that have this property[15]; however, since the problem is part of the more complex organizational incentives problem, we will not pursue it here. Certainly, when the decision maker receives the payoffs there is little incentive for this type of biasing. In other cases, for instance when outside experts are used, recognition of the potential bias may be the most important step.

*Cognitive* biases may be present even when motivational biases have been eliminated. Since these biases may stem from a particular mode of judgment, it can be important to identify the mode of judgment being used to minimize bias. Four different modes are discussed below.

### ●● Availability

Since probabilities are based on information the subject recalls, availability of information or the ease with which relevant information is recalled is important. Information that made a strong impression because of the

[14]The remainder of this section draws heavily on C. S. Spetzler and C. A. S. Stael von Holstein, "Probability Encoding in Decision Analysis," *Management Science*, Vol. 22, No. 3, November 1975. They, in turn, have relied on the research of Kahneman and Tversky: D. Kahneman and A. Tversky, "Subjective Probability: A Judgment of Representativeness," *Cognitive Psychology*, Vol. 3, 1972; Kahneman and Tversky, "On the Psychology of Prediction," *Psychological Review*, Vol. 80, 1973; Tversky and Kahneman, "Availability: A Heuristic for Judging Frequency and Probability," *Cognitive Psychology*, Vol. 5, 1973; and Tversky and Kahneman, "Judgment Under Uncertainty: Heuristics and Biases," *Science*, Vol. 185, 1974.

[15]See, for example, J. E. Matheson and R. L. Winkler, "Scoring Rules for Continuous Probability Distributions," *Management Science*, Vol. 22, No. 10, June 1976; A. H. Murphy and R. L. Winkler, "Scoring Rules in Probability Assessment and Evaluation," *Acta Psychologia*, Vol. 34, 1970; and L. J. Savage, "Elicitation of Personal Probabilities and Expectations," *Journal of American Statistical Association*, Vol. 66, December 1971.

consequences associated with it and recent information are examples of information that is readily available and hence often given too much weight. Deliberate attempts to make available competing information by asking about past outcomes can reduce this bias.

### ●● Adjustment and Anchoring

Often subjects pick a starting point and adjust from it. In some instances, adjustment from the initial point is insufficient. Anchoring results when subsequent points on a distribution are not processed independently from the starting point. An experimental result often observed is that subjects who are first asked for a median or most likely point fail to adjust adequately. The result is a central bias.

### ●● Representativeness

Comparability among events is an important consideration in subjective assessment just as it was when using empirical data. However, if overdone, general knowledge will be underutilized. For example, suppose that a production manager is trying to evaluate a new process. A test indicates poor performance. Although this same process has not been used before, experience with other similar processes indicates that it should work. Furthermore, initial tests often provide spurious results. There is a tendency to rely excessively on the poor test results with the specific process (i.e., the most representative information) rather than including the more general information. This type of bias can often be reduced by structuring the assessment problem to explicitly include assessment of prior probabilities using the general information followed by the use of Bayesian revision to take into account new information (see Chapter 13).

### ●● Unstated Assumptions

Responses are typically conditioned on a set of assumptions. When unexpected outcomes occur, assessors sometimes "explain" them by pointing to some underlying assumption that was violated. For example, in assessing the sales for a new product an individual may make a series of implicit assumptions about the economy, competitors, and the production capability of his own organization. Good assessment practice makes explicit the important assumptions on which the probabilities are conditioned.

## SUMMARY

When theoretical models or empirical evidence is not available, probabilities can be assessed subjectively. Two questions arise: What are the conditions under which subjective knowledge about uncertain events can be expressed as probabilities? How can the accuracy of subjective assessments be improved? The first question leads to a set of behavioral conditions which guarantee that assessments will satisfy the technical requirements of probability distributions. The conditions are quite weak and essentially specify enough consistency so that a series of bets cannot be arranged against you that will guarantee a loss.

The answer to the second question involves the psychology of human information processing. Procedures for assessment of specific events can be classified as *direct* and *indirect*. In *direct* assessment the assessor supplies the numerical probability for the event. Empirical evidence shows that, after a person is trained to think about probabilities, this can be an efficient assessment procedure.

*Indirect* assessment only requires an assessor to make choices among lotteries. An *assessment lottery* is introduced to provide a physical process that can be compared against the event to be assessed. Assessment lotteries are used in much the same manner as any other measuring device (e.g., a ruler or balance scale). When comparison indicates that the object to be measured and the measuring device are equivalent, the unit of measurement is read from the scale. By choosing between a series of assessment lotteries and a lottery based on the uncertain event of interest, a point of indifference is reached. The probability of winning the assessment lottery is then assigned to the uncertain event.

**Subjective Probability**

***Definition:*** *Your **subjective probability** for uncertain event E is the setting for the assessment lottery (fraction p) that makes you just indifferent between the assessment lottery and another lottery in which you receive W if event E occurs and L if it does not occur.*

Assessment of probabilities for continuous random variables requires an additional step. Series of events must be identified. These events are selected to fill out a cumulative distribution for the continuous random variable.

Decomposition is a powerful tool in subjective assessment. It allows judgments to be based on conditioning statements. It also provides a means for using different experts for each condition that is important for assessing a random variable.

## ASSIGNMENT MATERIAL

**12.1.** Briefly describe why there is a question about the legitimacy of subjective probabilities. How is the question answered?

**12.2.** What role is played by an assessment lottery in subjective assessment?

**12.3.** Differentiate between substantive and procedural expertise.

**12.4.** Give an example of a potential motivational bias.

**12.5.** Without using an assessment lottery, assess probabilities for the following uncertain events:

(a) The next President of the United States is a Republican/Democrat/other.
(b) A team of your choice wins/loses its next game.
(c) You come down with the flu during the next month.
(d) A woman is elected President of the United States during the next 10 years.
(e) The Dow Jones industrial average is higher/the same/lower 1 week from today.

**12.6.** Set up and use assessment lotteries to assess probabilities for the events in problem 12.5. Comment on your perception of the "benefits" and "costs" of using this procedure over direct assessment.

**12.7.** Treat the Dow Jones industrial average 1 week from today as a continuous random variable. Use the procedure suggested in the text to assess a cumulative distribution.

**12.8.** Treat the area in square miles of the state (country) you now reside in as a continuous random variable. Without looking at an atlas, assess a cumulative distribution for its area.

## APPENDIX 12: Axiom Systems for Subjective Probabilities

Three different axiom systems are given here. The first, by Savage,[16] is a set that establishes the existence of a probability measure if the stated conditions are satisfied. It is a nonconstructive system in that it does not specify how the probability assessments are to be made; however, the conditions constitute a set of consistency requirements which guarantee that expressions regarding an individual's state of mind concerning an uncertain event are compatible with the requirements of a probability measure. The conditions are based on a choice setting in which an individual expresses preferences directly in terms of actions.

### Notation

Acts are represented by lowercase letters, such as $f$, $g$.
Consequences are represented by greek letters, such as $\beta$, $\gamma$.
Outcome space is represented by $\Omega$.
Events on outcome space are represented by capital letters, such as $A$, $B$.
($\sim B$ is the complement of $B$ and read "not $B$")

Savage proves that given:

Pl: If for any two acts $f$ and $g$, either $f$ is not preferred to $g$, $g$ is not preferred

[16]L. J. Savage, *The Foundation of Statistics* (New York: Wiley, 1954).

to $f$, or both; and, if $f$ is not preferred to $g$, and $g$ is not preferred to $h$, then $f$ is not preferred to $h$.

P2: If outcome space is partitioned into $B$, $\sim B$ and $f$, $g$ and $f'$, $g'$ are such that:

1. in $\sim B$, $f$ and $g$ result in the same consequences (i.e., $f$ and $g$ agree), and $f'$ and $g'$ result in the same consequences (i.e., $f'$ and $g'$ agree);
2. in $B$, $f$ and $f'$ result in the same consequences (i.e., $f$ and $f'$ agree), and $g$ and $g'$ result in the same consequences (i.e., $g$ and $g'$ agree);
3. $f$ is not preferred to $g$ then $f'$ is not preferred to $g'$.

P3: If act $f$ yields consequence $\gamma$ and act $f'$ yields consequence $\gamma'$ over the entire outcome space (i.e., no matter what state of nature is revealed), $f$ is not preferred to $f'$ given some subset of outcome space, $B$, implies that $\gamma$ is not preferred to $\gamma'$. Conversely, if $\gamma$ is not preferred to $\gamma'$, $f$ is not preferred to $f'$ given any subset of outcome space $B$.

P4: Which of two events an individual chooses to bet on does not depend upon the size of the bet.

P5: There is at least one pair of consequences $\gamma$, $\gamma'$ such that $\gamma'$ is not preferred to $\gamma$.

P6: If $f$ is strictly not preferred to $g$ and if $\gamma$ is any consequence, there exists a partition of outcome space $\Omega$ such that if $f$ or $g$ is modified on any single element of outcome space so that it takes on consequence $\gamma$ for this element, the other values remaining the same, the modified $f$ is still strictly less preferred than the modified $g$.

then there exists a unique probability measure which agrees with the individual's state of mind regarding the uncertain events as expressed by his or her preferences.

From the point of view of the value of subjective probability as a concept, it is important to evaluate how restrictive the conditions are. As always, when a set of behavioral axioms is proposed, they can be viewed in two different lights. On the one hand, they can be compared with a description of how people actually behave. Thus, the evaluation could take the form of behavioral research aimed at verifying the axioms as descriptions of human behavior. On the other hand, the axioms can be considered as normative. That is, they provide a definition of the way individuals should behave. In this instance the evaluation proceeds by examining the axioms and asking the question: Given a choice, would I prefer to act in accordance with the proposed axiom? If the answer is yes, the conditions can be put forth as normative in the sense that we agree we should act in accordance with them. There is, of course, a potential dilemma if we agree that we prefer to act in accordance with a set of conditions that are inconsistent with our actual behavior. If when confronted with evidence of noncompliance we can modify our behavior, the dilemma is easily resolved. On the other hand, if we are incapable of modifying our behavior, the normative theory is of little practical value.

With this in mind, consider the conditions proposed above. Condition P1 is a combination of the two conditions that are fundamental to any theory of choice. They amount to the assumption that a decision maker has a set of preferences for the acts of interest and that these preferences are transitive (for more discussion of these assumptions, see Chapter 18). Condition P2 is more complicated, but it essentially says that preference among acts only involves subsets of outcome space in which the acts differ and in these subsets preferences are the same as those assessed for other acts which have identical consequences in the area of difference.

Condition P3 amounts to a statement that there is a consistent relationship between preferences for acts and their consequences. P4 requires that in choosing between two possible uncertain events for placing a bet (say $A_1$=rain tomorrow and $A_2$=sunny next Wednesday), the choice does not depend on the size of the bet. (For example, if you would choose to bet on $A_1$ rather than $A_2$ when the payoff for winning is \$1, you would make the same choice if the payoff were \$1,000.) Condition P5 and P6 are technical assumptions that involve ensuring that the setting in which the choices are made is sufficiently rich; therefore, these are not restrictions on an individual's behavior.

On the basis of this discussion the conditions appear to be mild. The implication is that most people behave (or desire to behave) in a manner such that subjective assessments of uncertain events will qualify as probabilities.

Although these conditions ensure the existence of a set of assessments that qualify as probabilities, since they do not include a means for obtaining them, we consider another set of conditions suggested by deFinetti. In his original exposition,[17] deFinetti assumed that the stakes to be used in the assessment procedure were small enough that certainty equivalents for simple lotteries are expected monetary values. This limitation should be kept in mind when considering the conditions stated below. DeFinetti shows that if:

1. For any set of events $E_1, E_2, \ldots, E_i, \ldots$ and lotteries shown in Figure 12.21, an individual specifies the amount for which he/she is willing to trade the lottery, call it $C_i$, then $P_i = C_i/S$ is defined as the subjective probability for event $E_i$.

**FIGURE 12.21**

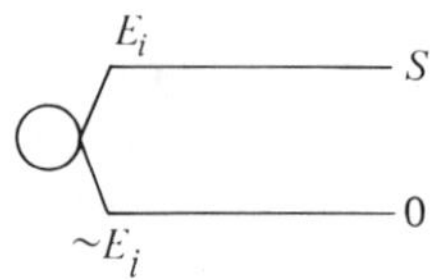


[17]B. deFinetti, "Foresight: Its Logical Laws, Its Subjective Sources," 1937. English translation in H. E. Kyburg, Jr., and H. E. Smokler (eds.), *Studies in Subjective Probability* (New York: Wiley, 1964).

2. The probabilities are assigned to events in a manner so that if the individual will trade for the specified $C_i$'s, it is not possible to arrange a series of bets against the individual so that he/she is assured of losing.

then, the set $P_i$ satisfies the conditions for probabilities.

The method for assessing the probabilities suggested by deFinetti is less than ideal. Certainty equivalents do not have to be expected monetary values and the certainty equivalent decisions not only may include components of risk but be more difficult to make than other assessments. However, it does provide us with an explicit definition of subjective probability and a condition, called *coherence* by deFinetti (condition 2), which guarantees that these assessed values qualify as probabilities. DeFinetti's position was that the coherence condition was not only desirable, since failure to meet it for an individual in a business setting would leave open the possibility of exploitation, but, since this exploitation was not taking place, business managers were generally acting in accordance with the condition. From our perspective it provides additional evidence that many individuals will want to make subjective assessments that qualify as probabilities.

The last set of conditions will only be discussed in general here and presented in more detail in Chapter 18. Anscombe and Auman[18] have shown that if the two conditions specified below are appended to the axioms presented in Chapter 18, the subjective assessments defined below qualify as probabilities.

**FIGURE 12.22**

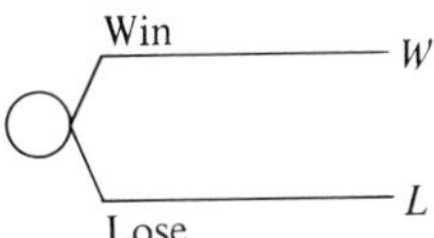


Consider an assessment lottery as shown in Figure 12.22, where $W$ represents some desirable prize and $L$ some not so desirable prize. Your subjective probability for event $E$ is defined as the setting for the assessment lottery (fraction $p$) which makes you just indifferent between the assessment lottery and another lottery in which you receive $W$ if event $E$ occurs and $L$ if it does not occur.

### Conditions

1. If two lotteries are identical except for the prizes associated with one outcome, your preferences for the lotteries will be the same as your preferences for the prizes associated with that outcome.

[18]F. J. Anscombe, and R. J. Auman, "A Definition of Subjective Probability," *Annals of Mathematical Statistics*, Vol. 34, 1963.

2. If the prize you receive depends upon both an assessment lottery and a lottery that is not an assessment lottery, it is immaterial to you which lottery is performed first.

Each of these three sets of conditions defines consistency requirements in behavior which are sufficient to ensure that subjective assessments which reflect your state of mind or knowledge about an uncertain event are consistent with the requirements of a probability distribution. Therefore, if you subscribe to them, you would not be satisfied with a set of assessments that did not constitute a probability distribution.

# 13

# Bayesian Revision of Probabilities

Bayesian revision is the name given to a method for integrating empirical data, or *observations*, with information known *prior* to the empirical observations. The prior information is encoded as a probability distribution using any of the methods of assessment previously discussed. The revision process calculates a conditional probability distribution based on both the prior information and the empirical observations. We have two random

**FIGURE 13.1**

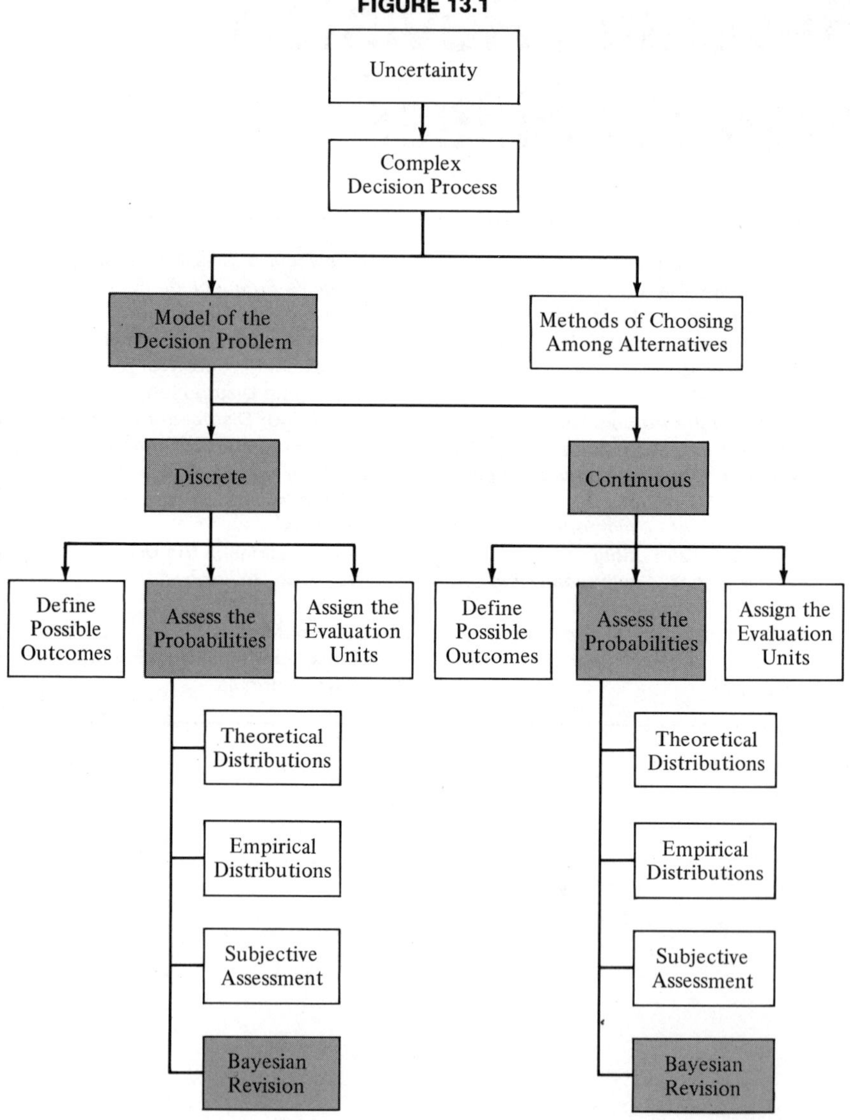

variables. One is associated with the event of interest, and the other is associated with the empirical observations. The two random variables are related through a set of conditional probabilities called *likelihoods*. The probability distribution that is assessed for the random variable of interest before obtaining the empirical observations is called the *prior* distribution. The result of the revision is called the *posterior* distribution. The mechanics of the calculations are the *same* as used in Chapter 7 for determining conditional probabilities. The new material in this chapter is the interpretation of the revision process and its application in more complicated settings. Figure 13.1 shows how the material fits into the overall framework.

## THE REVISION PROCESS FOR DISCRETE RANDOM VARIABLES

In this section we discuss the basic mechanics of the revision process when the prior distributions are discrete. If priors are continuous, we have two options. We may use a discrete approximation, or for continuous distributions with a special property (called *conjugate distributions*), revisions can be made easily without resorting to a discrete approximation. These distributions are discussed later in the chapter. The mechanics of the revision calculation *are the same as* the procedure presented in Chapter 7 for calculating conditional probabilities. A more formal presentation is given in the appendix to this chapter.

### Basic Revision Calculations

To illustrate the basic revision calculations, consider the following example.

**Example 13.1**

Suppose that we have a production lot of 100 items. The number of defectives in the lot is 10 or 20, depending on which of two processes was used in the production. The probability is 50–50 that either process was used. One unit is inspected and found *not* to be defective. What is the probability that the lot has 10 defectives, given that the sample was not defective? What is the probability that the lot has 20 defectives, given that the sample was not defective?

We are after conditional probabilities. The random variables can be defined as $A \equiv \{\text{the number of defectives in the lot}\}$, $B \equiv \{\text{the number of defectives in the sample}\}$. We want to find $P(A=10|B=0)$ and $P(A=20|B=0)$. Since we have two random variables, a table will be useful. Table 13.1 shows that before the sample $P(A=10)=P(A=20)=0.5$. The data given directly by the problem are circled. To calculate the remaining entries, we recognize that $P(B=0|A=10)=\frac{90}{100}=0.9$ and $P(B=0|A=20)=\frac{80}{100}=0.8$. All entries are not required since only the revisions corresponding to $B=0$ were asked for. With the table completed, it is easy to see that $P(A=10|B=0)=0.45/0.85$ and $P(A=20|B=0)=0.40/0.85$.

**TABLE 13.1**

| | $A=10$ | $A=20$ | |
|---|---|---|---|
| $B=0$ | (0.9) $\times 0.5=0.45$ | (0.8) $\times 0.5=0.40$ | 0.85 |
| $B=1$ | 0.05 | 0.10 | 0.15 |
| | (0.5) | (0.5) | 1.00 |

The mechanics of this calculation are straightforward and have been used before. To emphasize the revision procedure, names are given to the probabilities used in the calculations.

**Prior probability distribution**

$$P(A=10)=0.5, \qquad P(A=20)=0.5$$

**Likelihoods**

$$P(B=0|A=10)=0.9, \qquad P(B=0|A=20)=0.8$$

**Posterior probability distribution**

$$P(A=10|B=0)=\frac{0.45}{0.85}=0.53, \qquad P(A=20|B=0)=\frac{0.40}{0.85}=0.47$$

By tracing through the calculations in the table, we can see that

$$P(A=10|B=0)=\frac{P(A=10, B=0)}{P(B=0)}$$

$$=\frac{P(B=0|A=10)P(A=10)}{P(B=0|A=10)P(A=10)+P(B=0|A=20)P(A=20)}$$

$$=\frac{(0.9)(0.5)}{(0.9)(0.5)+(0.8)(0.5)}$$

$$=\frac{0.45}{0.85}=0.53$$

$$P(A=20|B=0)=\frac{P(A=20, B=0)}{P(B=0)}$$

$$=\frac{P(B=0|A=20)P(A=20)}{P(B=0|A=10)P(A=10)+P(B=0|A=20)P(A=20)}$$

$$=\frac{(0.8)(0.5)}{(0.9)(0.5)+(0.8)(0.5)}$$

$$=\frac{0.40}{0.85}=0.47$$

The generalization of these calculations is called *Bayes' theorem.* It can be written as[1]

$$P(A=a|B=b)=\frac{P(B=b|A=a)}{P(B=b)}\times P(A=a)$$

### Interpretation of the Revision Process

The first thing to notice about the revision process is the role played by the empirical observations. Using the notation above, these empirical observations are represented by the random variable $B$. The *likelihood* $P(B=b|A=a)$ is just the probability that the empirical result is obtained ($B=b$) given the specified value of the random variable of interest ($A=a$). This likelihood is divided by the overall probability of obtaining the empirical result ($B=b$). This ratio, $P(B=b|A=a)/P(B=b)$, is used to modify directly the prior probability for the random variable of interest, $P(A=a)$. The revision process allows the overall assessment process to be *decomposed.* First, an assessment is made using information available before receiving the empirical evidence. Any of the assessment procedures previously discussed can be used at this stage. Second, the likelihoods are assessed for the empirical evidence. Again, any of the assessment procedures can be used. Finally, Bayes' theorem is used to combine these two assessments.

The examples below are designed to illustrate the method of calculation and to point out properties of the revision process.

**Example 13.2**

Suppose there are two types of urns, each with 10 balls, as shown in Figure 13.2. Urn 1 has 2 white balls, 3 black balls, and 5 red balls, and urn 2 has 3 white balls, 2 black

**FIGURE 13.2**

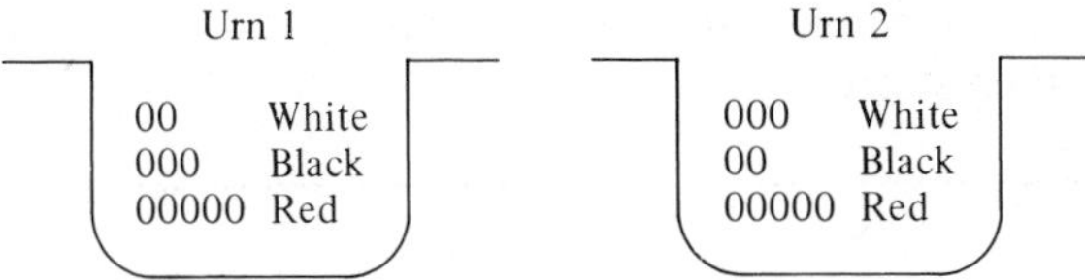


[1]The validity of the expression can be observed directly from the definition of conditional probabilities. By definition,

$$P(A=a|B=b)=\frac{P(A=a,B=b)}{P(B=b)}$$

and

$$P(A=a,B=b)=P(B=b|A=a)P(A=a)$$

Therefore,

$$P(A=a|B=b)=\frac{P(B=b|A=a)P(A=a)}{P(B=b)}$$

balls, and 5 red balls. Further, assume that there are 2 urns of type 1 and 8 urns of type 2. An urn is selected at random from the set of 10 but placed so that we cannot observe it. Next, a ball is selected at random from the urn and is observed to be black. What is the probability that the selected urn is type 1?

Table 13.2 is a table of joint probabilities based on the problem information.

**TABLE 13.2**

| | *Urn Type 1* | *Urn Type 2* | |
|---|---|---|---|
| *White* | (0.2)(0.2)=0.04 | (0.3)(0.8)=0.24 | 0.28 |
| *Black* | (0.3)(0.2)=0.06 | (0.2)(0.8)=0.16 | 0.22 |
| *Red* | (0.5)(0.2)=0.10 | (0.5)(0.8)=0.40 | 0.50 |
| | 0.2 | 0.8 | 1.00 |

If we define $U=1$ to be urn type 1 and $U=2$ to be urn type 2, then prior to drawing the sample we have:

*Prior Distribution*

$$P(U=1)=\tfrac{2}{10}=0.2$$
$$P(U=2)=\tfrac{8}{10}=0.8$$

What we are interested in is $P(U=1|\text{sample ball is black})$, or the posterior probability of $U=1$ given the sample result. If we let $S$ stand for the sample observation, with possible outcomes $w$=white, $b$=black, and $r$=red, the likelihoods of interest are:

*Likelihoods*

$$P(S=b|U=1)=\tfrac{3}{10}=0.3$$
$$P(S=b|U=2)=\tfrac{2}{10}=0.2$$

Using these likelihoods and those for white and red balls, Table 13.2 is completed. From Table 13.2 we can obtain the posterior distribution as conditional probabilities. Since the sample was black, we restrict ourselves to the middle row and find:

*Posterior Distribution*

$$P(U=1|S=b)=\tfrac{0.06}{0.22}=0.273$$
$$P(U=2|S=b)=\tfrac{0.16}{0.22}=0.727$$

The posterior distribution can be found using Bayes' theorem without using the table. The calculations are the *same* but not carried out with a table of joint probabilities.

*Posterior Distribution*

$$P(U=1|S=b)=\frac{P(S=b|U=1)P(U=1)}{P(S=b|U=1)P(U=1)+P(S=b|U=2)P(U=2)}$$

$$P(U=2|S=b)=\frac{P(S=b|U=2)P(U=2)}{P(S=b|U=1)P(U=1)+P(S=b|U=2)P(U=2)}$$

$$P(U=1|S=b)=\frac{0.3\times0.2}{(0.3\times0.2)+(0.2\times0.8)}$$
$$=\frac{0.3}{0.22}\times0.2=0.273$$

$$P(U=2|S=b)=\frac{0.2\times0.8}{(0.3\times0.2)+(0.2\times0.8)}=\frac{0.2}{0.22}\times0.8=0.727$$

As expected, drawing a black ball is not conclusive; but the probability that the urn is a type 1 is increased.

**FIGURE 13.3**

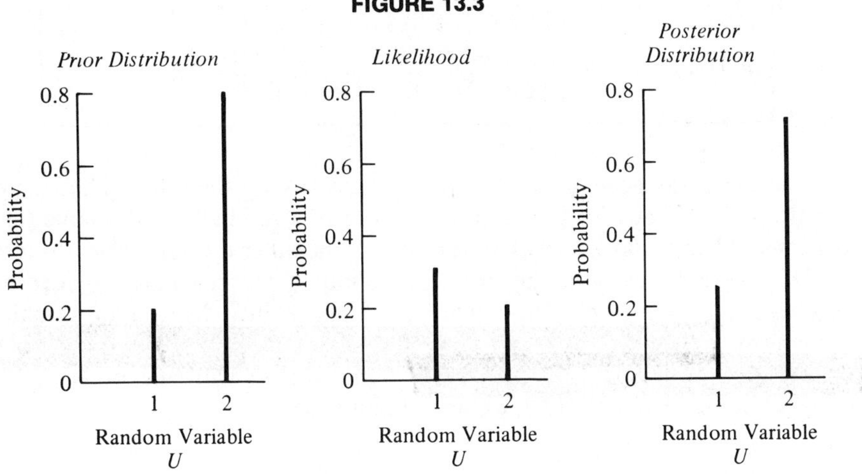

Figure 13.3 plots the probabilities of interest. (Note that the likelihoods are probabilities but do not form a probability distribution since each is conditioned on a separate value of $U$.)

### Equal Likelihoods

**Example 13.3**

Consider the same set of urns as Example 13.2, but assume that the sample outcome is a *red* ball instead of a *black* ball.

The analysis follows the same steps as in Example 13.2, this time without using a table.

*Prior Distribution*

$$P(U=1)=0.2$$
$$P(U=2)=0.8$$

*Likelihoods*

$$P(S=r|U=1)=0.5$$
$$P(S=r|U=2)=0.5$$

*Posterior Distribution*

$$P(U=1|S=r)=\frac{0.5\times 0.2}{(0.5\times 0.2)+(0.5\times 0.8)}=\frac{0.10}{0.50}=0.2$$
$$P(U=2|S=r)=\frac{0.5\times 0.8}{(0.5\times 0.2)+(0.5\times 0.8)}=\frac{0.40}{0.50}=0.8$$

Therefore, the posterior and prior distributions are the same. The reason is that the likelihoods for the sample outcome of a red ball are the same (i.e., it is equally likely that the red ball is drawn from either urn type 1 or urn type 2). This corresponds with the intuitive notion that a red ball provides no information in this case. Consequently, the probability distribution remains unchanged. Whenever the likelihoods are equal, the prior and posterior probability distributions are the same. Summarizing with the plots of the probabilities for Example 13.3, we have Figure 13.4.

**FIGURE 13.4**

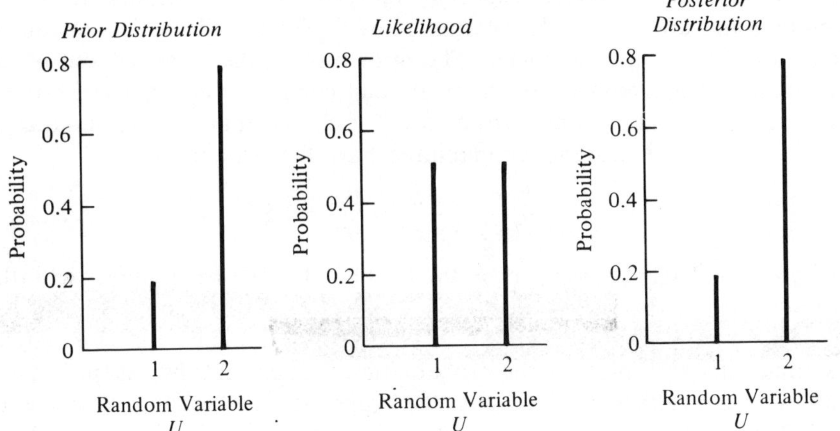


## Equal Priors

**Example 13.4**

Assume that instead of two type 1 urns and eight type 2 urns as in Example 13.2, we have five type 1 urns and five type 2 urns. If the sample from a randomly selected urn is a black ball, what is the probability that the urn selected is type 1?

The analysis again follows the same steps.

*Prior Distribution*

$P(U=1)=0.5$
$P(U=2)=0.5$

*Likelihoods*

$P(S=b|U=1)=0.3$
$P(S=b|U=2)=0.2$

*Posterior Distribution*

$$P(U=1|S=b)=\frac{0.3\times\cancel{0.5}}{(0.3\times\cancel{0.5})+(0.2\times\cancel{0.5})}=\frac{0.3}{0.3+0.2}=0.6$$

$$P(U=2|S=b)=\frac{0.2\times\cancel{0.5}}{(0.3\times\cancel{0.5})+(0.2\times\cancel{0.5})}=\frac{0.2}{0.3+0.2}=0.4$$

In this example the prior probabilities for each value of the random variable are equally likely. Inspecting the posterior probabilities, it can be seen that they are completely determined by the likelihoods (which, of course, depend on the sample outcome). The prior probabilities "cancel" out of the calculation. The likelihood of the black ball coming from urn 1 is 1.5 times the likelihood that it comes from urn 2 (i.e., the ratio of probabilities is $0.3/0.2 = 1.5$). The posterior probabilities have the same ratio,

$$\frac{P(U=1|S=b)}{P(U=2|S=b)} = \frac{0.6}{0.4} = 1.5$$

and are completely determined by the likelihoods. The result agrees with the intuitive notion that if all prior states are judged to be equally likely, any differentiation must come from the sample outcome. Figure 13.5 summarizes Example 13.4 with plots of the probabilities. Notice that the "shape" of the plot of the likelihoods is exactly the same as the "shape" of posterior probabilities. The only difference is that the posterior probabilities have been scaled up so that they sum to 1.

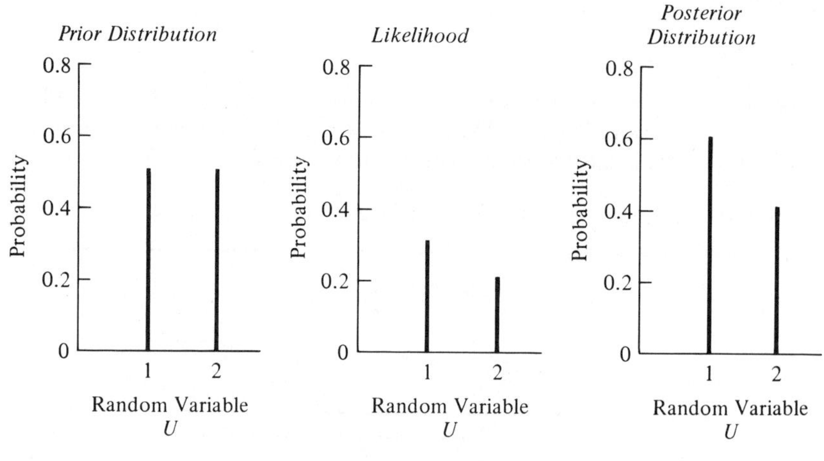


**FIGURE 13.5**

### Increasing the Amount of Evidence

To see how the *amount* of empirical data can affect the posterior probabilities, we consider two more examples.

**Example 13.5**

Consider the two types of urns shown in Figure 13.6. Assume that we have five type 1 urns and five type 2 urns and that one urn is picked at random and sampled. Instead of sampling the urn only once, assume that it is sampled with replacement 10 times and 3 red balls are drawn. What is the probability that the samples come from a type 1 urn?

**FIGURE 13.6**

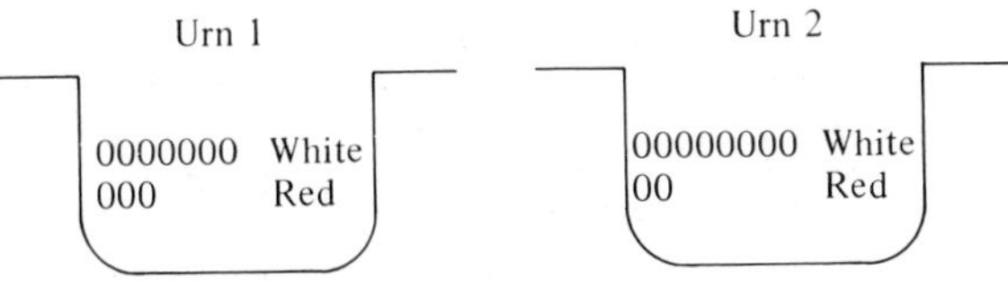


Proceeding as before:

*Prior Distribution*

$P(U=1)=0.5$
$P(U=2)=0.5$

*Likelihoods*

The likelihoods are given by a binomial distribution with $n=10$ and $r=3$. For $U=1$, the probability of success is $p=0.3$, and for $U=2$, the probability of success is $p=0.2$.

$P(3 \text{ red balls in 10 trials} | U=1) = P(r=3|n=10, p=0.3) = 0.267$
$P(3 \text{ red balls in 10 trials} | U=2) = P(r=3|n=10, p=0.2) = 0.201$

*Posterior Distribution*

$$P(U=1|r=3, n=10) = \frac{0.267 \times 0.5}{(0.267 \times 0.5) + (0.201 \times 0.5)} = \frac{0.1335}{0.2340} = 0.571$$

$$P(U=2|r=3, n=10) = \frac{0.201 \times 0.5}{(0.267 \times 0.5) + (0.201 \times 0.5)} = \frac{0.1005}{0.2340} = 0.429$$

A table could also be used for the calculations in this example. However, only a small fraction of the information required to fill in the table is needed, so it is not an efficient way to do the calculations (see Table 13.3).

**TABLE 13.3**

| | Number of Red Balls Drawn | | | | | | | | | | | |
|---|---|---|---|---|---|---|---|---|---|---|---|---|
| | 0 | 1 | 2 | 3 | 4 | 5 | 6 | 7 | 8 | 9 | 10 | |
| *Urn Type 1* | | | | 0.267×.5 =0.1335 | | | | | | | | 0.5 |
| *Urn Type 2* | | | | 0.201×.5 =0.1005 | | | | | | | | 0.5 |
| | | | | 0.2340 | | | | | | | | 1.0 |

The probability plots are given in Figure 13.7.

**FIGURE 13.7**

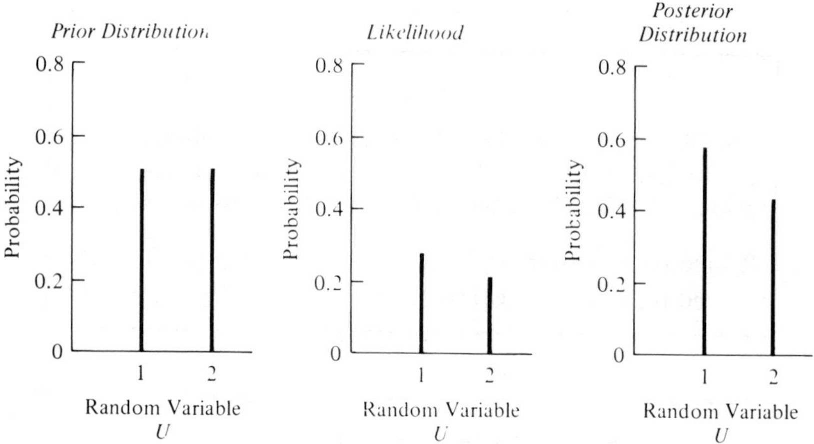


**Example 13.6**

Consider the same situation as Example 13.5 except that instead of 10 trials, 20 trials were made and six red balls drawn. This keeps the proportion of red balls in the sample the same but increases the sample size.

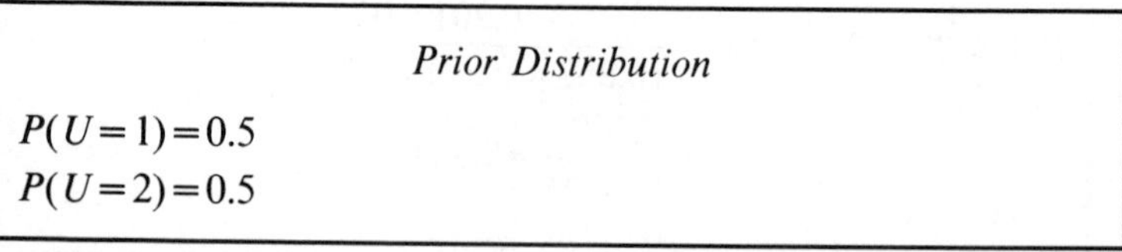

*Prior Distribution*

$P(U=1)=0.5$
$P(U=2)=0.5$

*Likelihoods*

$P(6 \text{ red balls in 20 trials}|U=1)=P(r=6|n=20,p=0.3)=0.192$
$P(6 \text{ red balls in 20 trials}|U=2)=P(r=6|n=20,p=0.2)=0.109$

*Posterior Distribution*

$$P(U=1|r=6,n=20)=\frac{0.192\times0.5}{(0.192\times0.5)+(0.109\times0.5)}$$
$$=\frac{0.096}{0.1505}=0.638$$
$$P(U=2|r=6,n=20)=\frac{0.109\times0.5}{(0.192\times0.5)+(0.109\times0.5)}$$
$$=\frac{0.0545}{0.1505}=0.362$$

The results are summarized in Figure 13.8.

**FIGURE 13.8**

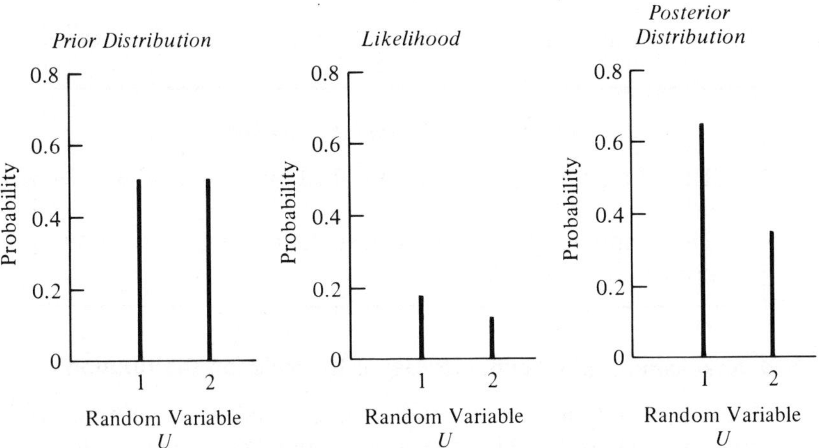


Comparison of the results for Examples 13.5 and 13.6 demonstrates that as the amount of empirical information increases, everything else remaining the same, the posterior distributions become more peaked. In this case the proportion of red balls was the same for both examples and consistent with the long-run average for urn 1. The increase in sample size changed the posterior probability for urn 1 from 0.57 to 0.64. This phenomenon agrees with the intuitive feeling that as the sample evidence increases it should "swamp" the prior beliefs. When the sample size is large enough, the prior information is not important.

## ASSESSMENT OF LIKELIHOODS

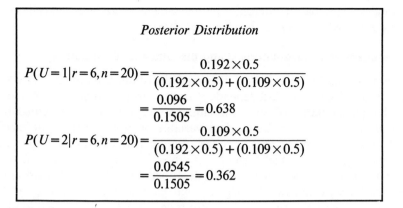

The crucial aspect in the use of Bayesian revision is identification of the likelihoods. They are the key to relating the empirical data to the random variable of interest. The likelihoods depend on both the empirical data and the random variable of interest. The assessment procedures concentrate on the *process* used to *generate* the *empirical data*.

### Assessment of Likelihoods Using the Binomial Distribution

As described in Chapter 10, the binomial distribution represents a process characterized by repeated, independent trials with the probability of success at each trial constant. When the data-gathering process is represented by a *binomial distribution* and the random variable of interest can be defined in terms of the *probability* of *success*, $p$, the likelihoods can be determined directly using the binomial formula or tables. Examples 13.5 and 13.6 are data-gathering processes that can be described by a binomial distribution. The samples were drawn with replacement from a single urn. The random variable of interest $U$ represented the urn type. ($U=1$ corresponded to urn 1, $U=2$ corresponded to urn 2.) Each urn type had a different probability of drawing a red ball (a success). Therefore, the likelihoods could be calculated directly using the binomial. For example,

$$P(3 \text{ red balls in } 10 \text{ trials} | U=1) = P(r=3 | n=10, p=0.3) = 0.267$$

*Conditions for Binomial Likelihoods*

1. The data-gathering process described by a binomial distribution.
2. The random variable of interest defined in terms of the probability of success, $p$.

### ●● Assessment of Likelihoods Using the Poisson Distribution

The Poisson distribution is sometimes characterized as describing the occurrence of rare events in which the average number of events per unit of measurement is constant and occurrences are independent (see Chapter 10 for a more detailed description). If the data-gathering process can be characterized as a *Poisson* process and the random variable of interest defined in terms of the *average number of events per unit of measurement*, the likelihoods can be calculated using a Poisson distribution.

For instance, if the random variable of interest were the average number of arrivals per hour at a hospital emergency room and it could take on values of 1, 2, or 3 for a certain period of the day, the likelihoods for a data-gathering process that observed a single arrival (defined as $A=1$) in 1 hour are

$$P(A=1 | m=1) = 0.368$$
$$P(A=1 | m=2) = 0.271$$
$$P(A=1 | m=3) = 0.149$$

The numbers are obtained using the Poisson distribution in Appendix C.

*Conditions for Poisson Likelihoods*

1. The data-gathering process described by a Poisson distribution.
2. The random variable of interest defined in terms of the average number of events per unit of measurement.

### ●● Assessment of Likelihoods Using the Normal Distribution

When samples are taken from any distribution, the central limit theorem describes conditions for the distribution of the means of the sample to be normally distributed.[2] The mean value of the distribution of sample means equals the true mean. The standard deviation is equal to $\sigma/\sqrt{n}$, where $\sigma$ is the population standard deviation and $n$ the sample size. A data-gathering process that involves an observation from a normal distribution is called a *normal process*. If the random variable of interest can be defined in terms of the mean of a normal data-gathering process, and if the process standard deviation is assumed to be known, the likelihoods are readily available. The following example demonstrates the procedure.

**Example 13.7**

Assume the data-gathering process yields a sample mean $\overline{X}=50$ from a sample with 25 observations, and the random variable of interest is the mean of the population from which the sample was drawn. With this sampling process, we assume that the distribution of $\overline{X}$ is normal with $\sigma_{\overline{X}}=\sigma/\sqrt{25}$. From prior information, assume that the population standard deviation is $\sigma=25$ and the mean is either $\mu_1=45$ or $\mu_2=60$.

The likelihoods can be calculated by assigning the range 49.5 to 50.5 to represent 50 (because the normal distribution is a continuous distribution) and using the normal distribution:

$$P\left(\overline{X}=50 \mid \mu_1=45, \sigma_{\overline{X}}=\frac{25}{\sqrt{25}}\right)=P\left(49.5 \leqslant \overline{X} \leqslant 50.5 \mid \mu_1=45, \sigma_{\overline{X}}=\frac{25}{\sqrt{25}}\right)=0.0484$$

$$P\left(\overline{X}=50 \mid \mu_2=60, \sigma_{\overline{X}}=\frac{25}{\sqrt{25}}\right)=P\left(49.5 \leqslant \overline{X} \leqslant 50.5 \mid \mu_2=60, \sigma_{\overline{X}}=\frac{25}{\sqrt{25}}\right)=0.0108$$

These probabilities were obtained using the normal table in Appendix E and are shown graphically in Figure 13.9.

[2]The sample size required before the normal distribution provides a good approximation to the distribution of the sample means depends on the underlying population. But for "reasonable" populations (i.e., those that are not wildly skewed or multimodal), the approximation is very good for $n \geqslant 20$.

**FIGURE 13.9**

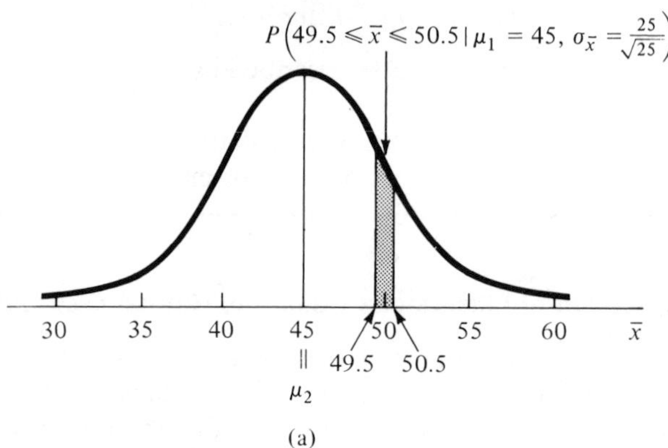


(a)

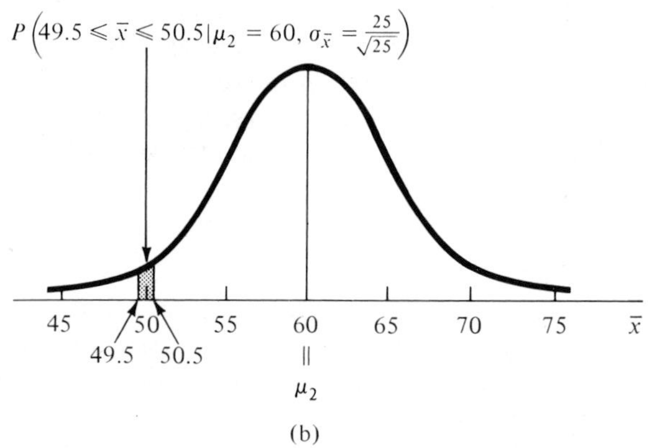


(b)

> *Conditions for Normal Likelihoods*
>
> 1. The data-gathering process yields a sample mean from some probability distribution whose standard deviation is assumed to be known *or* from other information we know that the observation came from a normal distribution.
> 2. The random variables of interest defined in terms of the mean for the probability distribution from which the sample was taken.

## ●● Assessment of Likelihoods Using Theoretical Distributions in General

At this point the procedure for calculating likelihoods using a parameterized theoretical distribution can be stated in general. *First*, a *data-generation* process must be found that is described by the *theoretical* distribution.

*Second*, the *random variable* of interest must involve one or more of the *parameters* of the theoretical distribution, and all other parameters of the distribution must be known. When these conditions are met, likelihoods can be calculated using the theoretical distribution.

### Assessment of Likelihoods Using Relative Frequencies

Many data-generation processes can be characterized as tests devised to determine some particular property. For example, credit checks on customers are devised to reveal their credit worthiness, seismic tests on potential oil-bearing properties are designed to reveal the geological structure, and medical tests are aimed at diagnosing specific medical problems. Often, the tests are calibrated by trying them on particular populations and obtaining relative frequency information. In some cases, these data can be used to calculate likelihoods.

To illustrate the use of relative frequency data for assessing likelihoods, consider a simplified example that is typical of this class of problems.

**Example 13.8**

Assume that you are interested in knowing if a given customer will default on a purchase or make the full payment required. Let $D$ = event default and $\sim D$ = event no default. Assume that a credit rating service is available which will classify the customer into two categories, $A$ = good risk and $B$ = poor risk. We are interested in knowing about *defaulting*, and we can observe the *classification* $A$ or $B$.

As shown in Figure 13.10, if we obtain the classification from a credit agency, we need to know the probabilities $P(D|A)$, $P(\sim D|A)$, $P(D|B)$, and $P(\sim D|B)$.

If data are available on the frequency of defaults from groups $A$ and $B$, these probabilities can be assessed directly. If no data are available, they could be collected. In some cases you may have prior experience on the probability of defaulting [i.e., the prior probabilities $P(D)$ and $P(\sim D)$ are well established] but no information on credit categories. Relative frequency data could be collected to assess the *likelihoods* $P(A|D)$, $P(B|D)$, $P(A|\sim D)$,

**FIGURE 13.10**

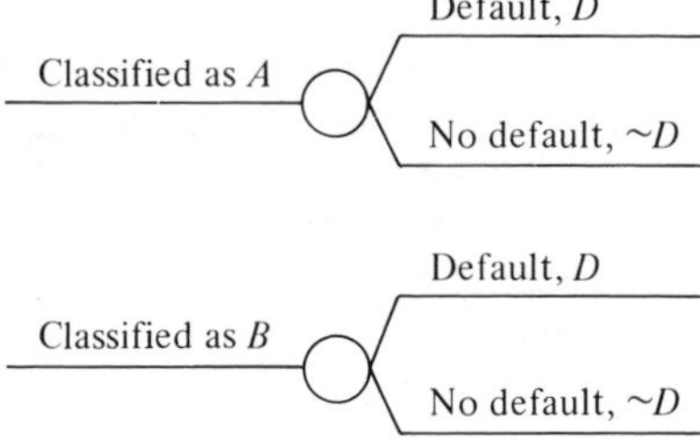

and $P(B|\sim D)$ by sampling customers who have defaulted and not defaulted. With this information the desired probabilities can be calculated using Bayes' theorem:

$$P(D|A)=\frac{P(A|D)}{P(A)}P(D), \qquad \text{etc.}$$

In some cases tests are naturally calibrated to provide data for assessing likelihoods. Assume that you have developed a new seismic test for detecting underground geological structures and are interested in its accuracy. Denote the structures as favorable, $S_f$, and unfavorable, $S_u$. Several sites may be available where the structures are known with certainty because of extensive exploration programs. To determine the accuracy of the new procedure, you could go to each location and run a series of tests recording the outcomes as test favorable, $T_f$, or test unfavorable, $T_u$. The result would be relative frequencies that could be used to assess $P(T_f|S_f)$, $P(T_u|S_f)$, $P(T_f|S_u)$, and $P(T_u|S_u)$. The test could be run a large number of times, resulting in a very good assessment of the likelihoods. If the test is used at any particular site, an observation $T_f$ or $T_u$ is obtained. To calculate the probabilities of a favorable or unfavorable structure, the likelihoods are used with the prior probabilities on the structure. For instance,

$$P(S_f|T_f)=\frac{P(T_f|S_f)}{P(T_f)}P(S_f), \qquad \text{etc.}$$

As illustrated in these two examples, the advantage of using relative frequencies to calculate likelihoods (which are then used to determine posterior distributions) is that the relative frequency information on the likelihoods may be obtained separately from the information on the prior probabilities. In the seismic test, for example, the tests could be calibrated (likelihoods assessed) at one site and then used at another site.

## ●● Assessment of Likelihoods Using a Subjective Approach

If neither theoretical models nor relative frequencies are available for assessing likelihoods, they can, of course, be assessed subjectively. The usefulness of a procedure that uses subjectively assessed likelihoods depends on the way the assessor prefers to think about the uncertainty.

**Example 13.9**

Assume that you are interested in a competitor's plans for a new product. Your marketing strategy would change if you knew the competitor would introduce a new design. The only information at hand is that the competitor's order placed for a particular raw material is substantially more than the previous year's order. The increase could be due to a number of factors—higher expected demand with the old design, a new design that used more of this material, or just inventory accumulation. Figure 13.11 displays the assessment problem.

**FIGURE 13.11**

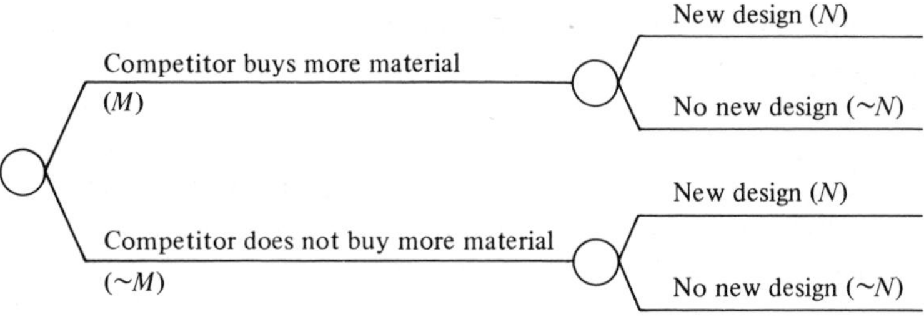


Two options for assessment are available. The first is to directly assess $P(N|M)$. The second is to assess the prior probabilities, $P(N)$ and $P(\sim N)$, and the likelihoods $P(M|N)$ and $P(M|\sim N)$.

There are more assessments required by the second method, but it is possible that the assessor may be more confident in the judgments on the likelihoods and priors than the posterior directly. It is not even necessary to completely assess the likelihoods. All that is required is the ratio of the likelihoods:

$$P(N|M) = \frac{P(M|N)P(N)}{P(M|N)P(N) + P(M|\sim N)P(\sim N)}$$

Dividing by $P(M|N)$,

$$P(N|M) = \frac{P(N)}{P(N) + \left[\dfrac{P(M|\sim N)}{P(M|N)}\right]P(\sim N)}$$

Therefore, assessments can be made by considering the odds that more material would be ordered if no new design were being proposed versus more material if a new design existed. That is, an assessor might like to think directly in terms of the odds that more material would be ordered under the two conditions. If the assessor stated that he considered it twice as likely that more material would be ordered if a new design existed than if it did not exist, then

$$\frac{P(M|\sim N)}{P(M|N)} = \frac{1}{2}$$

If, in addition, assessments are that $P(N)=0.6$, $P(\sim N)=0.4$, we have

$$P(N|M) = \frac{0.6}{0.6 + \frac{1}{2} \times 0.4} = \frac{0.6}{0.8} = 0.75$$

This procedure is an alternative to thinking directly about the probability that a new design exists given more material ordered.

## ●● THE REVISION PROCESS FOR CONJUGATE DISTRIBUTIONS

If a prior probability distribution is *conjugate* with respect to some data-gathering process, the posterior distribution is the same type as the prior distribution. The normal distribution is conjugate with respect to a normal data-gathering process and the beta distribution is conjugate with respect to a data-gathering process that is described by a binomial distribution. For these cases, even though the prior distributions are continuous, the revised or posterior distributions can be determined easily using simple formulas.

### ●● Normal Prior Distributions with a Normal Data-Gathering Process

Normal data-gathering processes were discussed previously. If the prior distribution for some random variable of interest is normal and the data-gathering process is normal, the posterior distribution is also normal. That is, a normal distribution is conjugate with respect to a normal data-gathering process. When this is true, the posterior distribution can be determined by using simple formulas for the parameters.

To illustrate, let $\mu$ be the random variable of interest. Assume that the prior probability distribution on $\mu$ is normal with mean $m$ and standard deviation $\sigma$. The data-gathering process is normally distributed with an unknown mean $u$, which is the random variable of interest (i.e., the mean of the data-gathering process is given by the random variable $\mu$), and a standard deviation, $\sigma'$. Assume that the observation from the data-gathering process is $m'$. The posterior distribution for the random variable of interest, $\mu$, is normally distributed with parameters mean $= m''$ and standard deviation $= \sigma''$, given by the following formulas:

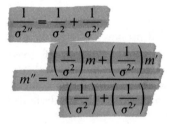

$$\frac{1}{\sigma^{2''}} = \frac{1}{\sigma^2} + \frac{1}{\sigma^{2'}}$$

$$m'' = \frac{\left(\dfrac{1}{\sigma^2}\right)m + \left(\dfrac{1}{\sigma^{2'}}\right)m'}{\left(\dfrac{1}{\sigma^2}\right) + \left(\dfrac{1}{\sigma^{2'}}\right)}$$

The most obvious example of this type of revision or updating of a probability distribution is a sampling process with a normal prior distribution on the population mean.

**Example 13.10**

Assume that you needed to know the *mean* sales for a given product for purposes of choosing an order quantity. Based on your prior information, you assess the probability distribution for the unknown mean sales to be normal with a mean $m = 100$ equivalent units per day (where the equivalence factor accounts for variations due to the day of the week and any seasonality in sales) and a standard deviation $\sigma = 20$. You decide to gather some data and take a sample of 25 days, which yields a mean value of $m'=90$ equivalent units per day and a population standard deviation of $\sigma_p=30$. What is the revised probability distribution on mean sales?

From the central limit theorem, we know the distribution for our sample $m'=90$ is normal with a standard deviation of $\sigma_p/\sqrt{25} = \frac{30}{5}=6$. With this information the posterior distribution is known to be normal with parameters:

$$\frac{1}{\sigma^{2\prime\prime}} = \frac{1}{20^2} + \frac{1}{6^2} = \frac{109}{3{,}600}$$

$$\sigma^{2\prime\prime} = \frac{3{,}600}{109} = 33$$

$$\sigma'' = \underline{5.75}$$

$$m'' = \frac{\left(\frac{1}{20^2}\right)100 + \left(\frac{1}{6^2}\right)90}{\left(\frac{1}{20^2}\right) + \left(\frac{1}{6^2}\right)}$$

$$= \frac{\frac{100}{400} + \frac{90}{36}}{\frac{109}{3{,}600}}$$

$$= 8.26 + 82.57 = \underline{90.83}$$

## ●● Beta Prior Distributions with a Binomial Data-Gathering Process

If the random variable of interest is represented by the beta distribution, and the data-gathering process is represented by a binomial distribution with the probabilities of success dependent on the random variable of interest, the posterior distribution for the random variable of interest is a beta distribution. Another way of stating these conditions is that the beta distribution is conjugate with respect to a binomial data-gathering process. Under these conditions the posterior distribution can be easily determined using simple formulas for the parameters.

Let the prior distribution for the random variable of interest, $p$, be a beta distribution with parameters $r$ and $n$. If the data-gathering process follows a binomial distribution with a probability of success given by the random variable, $p$, and if $r'$ successes are obtained in $n'$ trials, the posterior distribution for the random variable of interest, $p$, is a beta distribution with parameters

$$r'' = r + r'$$

$$n'' = n + n'$$

**Example 13.11**

Suppose that you are interested in the defective rate in a production process and that you assess your prior distribution on the proportion of defectives to be a beta distribution with $r=6$, $n=120$. To aid in your assessment, you take a sample of 30 and find 2 defectives. What is the posterior distribution on the defective rate?

With this information the posterior distribution on the proportion of defectives is a beta distribution with $r=6+2=8$ and $n=120+30=150$.

## SOME ILLUSTRATIONS OF THE USE OF BAYESIAN REVISION

The illustrations given below are examples of how Bayesian revision can be applied to different classes of problems. They demonstrate how the mechanics of the revision process can be undertaken in three different settings.

**Example 13.12**

Assume that you are the operations manager for a manufacturing plant. An important decision regarding equipment replacement must be made. A new model for a machine tool has just been introduced. It is similar to the machine tools you have used previously but has several new features. The old models are still available. One of the most important considerations in your analysis of the new equipment is the defect rate for the new model when used in your specific application. Because of your prior

FIGURE 13.12

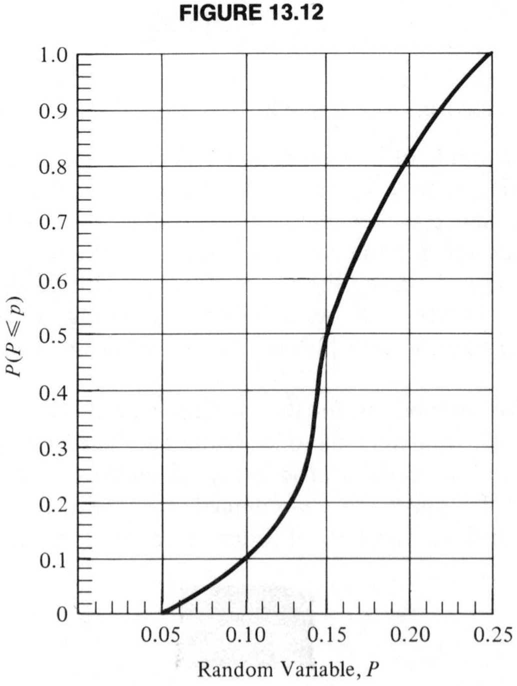

experience with similar machines, you have some feeling for what the defect rate will be and have assessed the prior distribution shown in Figure 13.12. You also have arranged to have one of your employees test a new model on a sample of 20 items. The results showed two defectives. What is the posterior distribution for the defect rate?

The random variable of interest in this problem is the defect rate or proportion of defectives, $p$. One option available is to use the empirical results to directly estimate the proportion as $p = \frac{2}{20} = 0.1$, and this value could be used in subsequent analyses. Another option is to combine the sample data with the prior experience using Bayes' theorem. The prior distribution shown in Figure 13.12 could have been assessed using previous data (e.g., you might assume that the distribution of defectives would be the same as old models on which data are available) or using subjective methods that indirectly consider previous data on old models as well as other information such as the manufacturer's reputation, performance claims for the new model, and the design of the equipment. Using the prior distribution for defect rate shown in Figure 13.12, and following the standard procedure from Chapter 9, we can form the discrete approximation shown in Table 13.4.

**TABLE 13.4**

| *Value of P* | *Probability* |
|---|---|
| $p=0.10$ | 0.2 |
| $p=0.14$ | 0.2 |
| $p=0.15$ | 0.2 |
| $p=0.18$ | 0.2 |
| $p=0.22$ | 0.2 |

The data-generation process can be represented by a binomial distribution with $n=20$ and $r=2$. The assumption is that the process and machine remained the same over the 20 trials so that the trials were independent and the rate of defectives constant for each trial (e.g., we assume that the machine did not come out of adjustment and the operator did not undergo any significant learning). On this basis the likelihoods can be obtained directly from the binomial tables. The calculations are shown in Table 13.5.

The first column specifies the possible values for the random variable $P$, the proportion defectives, based on the discrete approximation of the prior distribution on $P$. Column (2) contains the prior probabilities assigned to each value of the random variable. The third column contains the likelihoods. They are calculated using the binomial tables. For instance, the entry in the first row is $P(r=2|n=20, p=0.10)=0.285$. The other row entries are found in the same way, with $P$ taking on the values 0.14, 0.15, 0.18, and 0.22. Column (4) is the product of columns (2) and (3). It represents the joint probability that the specified value of the random variable and the sample outcome 2 defectives in 20 trials occur. It is just the numerator in Bayes'

**TABLE 13.5**

| (1) *Value of the Random Variable P* | (2) *Prior Probability* | (3) *Likelihood of 2 Defectives in 20 Trials Given P* | (4) *Product of (2)×(3)* | (5) *Posterior Probability* |
|---|---|---|---|---|
| $p=0.10$ | 0.2 | 0.285 | 0.0570 | 0.2744 |
| $p=0.14$ | 0.2 | 0.247 | 0.0494 | 0.2377 |
| $p=0.15$ | 0.2 | 0.229 | 0.0458 | 0.2204 |
| $p=0.18$ | 0.2 | 0.173 | 0.0346 | 0.1665 |
| $p=0.22$ | 0.2 | 0.105 | 0.0210 | 0.1010 |
| | Total = 1.0 | | Total = 0.2078 | |

↑ overall probability of obtaining 2 defectives in 20 trials

formula. By summing all these joint probabilities, we obtain the overall probability of obtaining 2 defectives in 20 trials or the denominator in the Bayes' formula. Therefore, the posterior probabilities can be calculated by dividing the value in column (4) by the sum of column (4). These values appear in column (5).

Once the posterior distribution is found, it can be used in the decision process. For instance, if only the expected value of the defective rate is required, it can be calculated ($E[P]=0.10\times0.2744+0.14\times0.2377+0.15\times0.2204+0.18\times0.1665+0.22\times0.1010=0.146$).

### ●● Example 13.13

Assume that you have been given the task of advising the President on the allocation of party campaign funds to various geographic areas. Previous work has led you to believe that the allocation scheme should depend on voter interest on particular topics. You have rather arbitrarily created three categories of interest. The measure of interest you have established is the rate at which calls come into party headquarters when new issues are raised. Since funds must be allocated quickly when new issues arise, you are interested in knowing quickly which of the interest categories a group falls into for a particular issue. Historical data give you prior information. An issue of interest to the southwest has recently come into prominence. From the Los Angeles section you have received three inquiries in the last day. Prior experience indicates that there is a 30% chance the section falls into category 1, with an average call rate of 1 per day; a 40% chance the section falls into category 2 with an average call rate of 5 per day; and a 30% chance the section falls into category 3 with an average call rate of 10 per day. Based on this information, what are the chances the Los Angeles section is responding as a category 1, 2, and 3?

If we assume that the *data-generating process* is a Poisson process, the calculations are straightforward and contained in Table 13.6. The evidence strongly supports the hypothesis that the section is responding with a category 2 interest to this particular issue.

**TABLE 13.6**

| (1) Category and Response Rate | (2) Prior Probability | (3) Likelihood of 3 Inquiries Given $m$ | (4) Product of (2)×(3) | (5) Posterior Probability |
|---|---|---|---|---|
| $1, m=1$ | 0.3 | 0.061 | 0.0183 | 0.239 |
| $2, m=5$ | 0.4 | 0.140 | 0.0560 | 0.730 |
| $3, m=10$ | 0.3 | 0.008 | 0.0024 | 0.031 |
| | Total = 1.00 | | Total = 0.0767 | |

**●● Example 13.14**

Assume that your company is in the process of establishing franchises in various parts of the country. Prior to letting the franchise, a market survey is taken to determine the expected sales. The results of this survey are used for making long-range production and material purchasing plans. Once the franchise is operating it is important to quickly determine how accurate the expected sales figures are, because changes in long-range plans must be made as rapidly as possible. The market research results for the latest franchise indicate that the seasonally adjusted expected sales are given by the distribution shown in Figure 13.13. Table 13.7 provides a discrete approximation. Regardless of what the mean sales are, the survey indicates the standard deviation of the daily sales figure will be approximately \$200. Plans were made on the basis of expected sales of \$1,000 per day. The first month's adjusted sales after the franchise

**FIGURE 13.13**

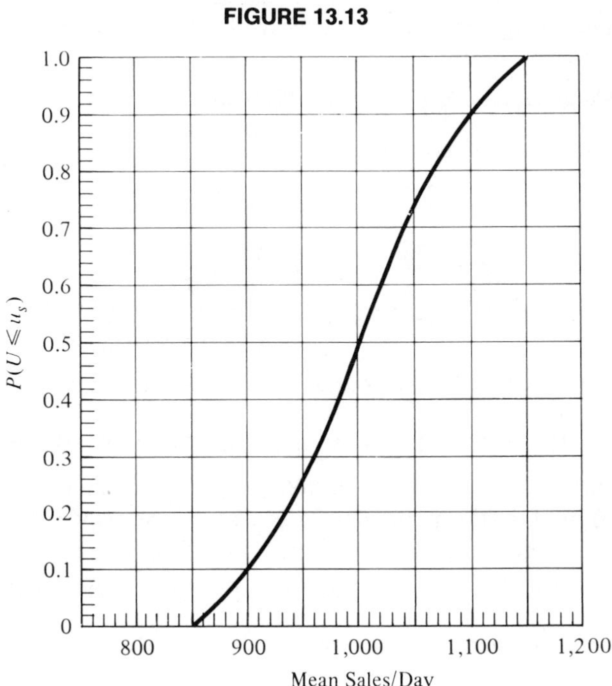

**TABLE 13.7**

| *Mean Sales / Day* ($\mu_s$) | *Probability* |
|---|---|
| $\mu_s = 900$ | 0.2 |
| $\mu_s = 960$ | 0.2 |
| $\mu_s = 1000$ | 0.2 |
| $\mu_s = 1040$ | 0.2 |
| $\mu_s = 1100$ | 0.2 |

had operated long enough to overcome any initial startup effects showed an average of \$900/day based on 25 days. The president has asked for some information on the sales picture in light of the first month's results.

The data-gathering process in this instance involves making 25 observations on adjusted daily sales and calculating the mean sales per day. According to the problem, the standard deviation of daily sales is known to be \$200. If we define $\overline{X}$ to be the random variable representing the outcome of the sampling process, we know from the central limit theorem that $\overline{X}$ is normally distributed with a standard deviation of $200/\sqrt{25}$ ($\sigma_{\overline{X}} = 200/\sqrt{25} = 40$). The mean of the sampling distribution (i.e., the distribution of $\overline{X}$) is the same as the mean of the underlying distribution (i.e., the actual distribution of sales). This is represented by the prior distribution on $\mu_s$ given in Figure 13.13 and Table 13.7.

The likelihoods for the discrete values of $\mu_s$ are illustrated by the vertical lines in Figure 13.14 for $\mu_s = 900$, $\mu_s = 960$, and $\mu_s = 1{,}000$. These likelihoods are calculated using the interval 899.5 to 900.5 and the normal tables. For instance:

$$P(\overline{X} = 900 | \text{given } \mu_s = 900, \sigma_{\overline{X}} = 40) = P(899.5 \leqslant \overline{X} \leqslant 900.5 | \mu_s = 900, \sigma_{\overline{X}} = 40)$$

Converting to standard normal deviates,

$$Z_1 = \frac{899.5 - 900}{40} = \frac{-0.5}{40} = -0.0125$$

$$Z_2 = \frac{900.5 - 900}{40} = \frac{0.5}{40} = +0.0125$$

$$P(-0.0125 \leqslant Z \leqslant 0.0125) = 2 \times P(0 \leqslant Z \leqslant 0.0125)$$
$$= 2 \times 0.0050 = 0.010$$

The $P(0 \leqslant Z \leqslant 0.0125)$ is found using Appendix E and extrapolating between

$$P(0 \leqslant Z \leqslant 0.01) = 0.004 \text{ and } P(0 \leqslant Z \leqslant 0.02) = 0.008.$$

The difference $(0.008 - 0.004)$ multiplied by the fraction $0.0025/0.010$ is $(0.004)(0.25) = 0.001$ (the point 0.0125 is 25% of the way between 0.01 and 0.02 and the difference is allocated proportionally). Therefore,

$$P(0 \leqslant Z \leqslant 0.0125) = 0.004 + (0.008 - 0.004)(0.25) = 0.004 + 0.001 = 0.005,$$

and the likelihood that $\overline{X} = 900$ given $\mu_s = 900$ is 0.010.[3] Similar calculations

[3]If values of the normal density function are available, the height for $\overline{X} = 900$ could be used instead of the 0.010 as calculated here.

**FIGURE 13.14**

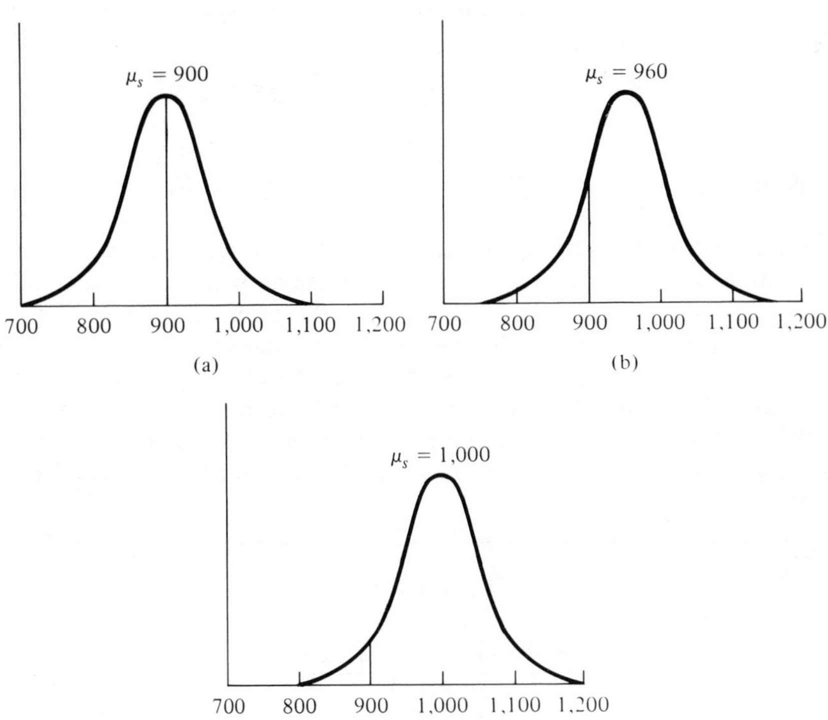


**TABLE 13.8**

| *(1)* *Value of Random Variable* $\mu_s$ | *(2)* *Prior Probability* | *(3)* *Likelihood of* $\bar{X} = 900$ *Given Value for* $\mu_s$ | *(4)* *Product of* $(2) \times (3)$ | *(5)* *Posterior Probability* |
|---|---|---|---|---|
| $\mu_s = 900$ | 0.2 | 0.010000 | 0.002000 | 0.720 |
| $\mu_s = 960$ | 0.2 | 0.003200 | 0.000640 | 0.231 |
| $\mu_s = 1,000$ | 0.2 | 0.000675 | 0.000135 | 0.049 |
| $\mu_s = 1,040$ | 0.2 | 0 | 0 | 0 |
| $\mu_s = 1,100$ | 0.2 | 0 | 0 | 0 |
| | Total = 1.0 | | Total = 0.002775 | 1.000 |

provide the other likelihoods in Table 13.8. With these likelihoods the posterior probabilities are calculated in Table 13.8. The expected daily adjusted sales for the franchise is

$$E[\mu_s] = (900)(0.720) + (960)(0.231) + (1{,}000)(0.049) = 919$$

## SUMMARY

Bayesian revision or updating provides a mechanism for incorporating new information in the form of empirical observations with prior information about a random variable. The link between the prior information (as embodied in a prior probability distribution) and the empirical data is provided by *likelihoods* which are also probabilities. The result is a posterior distribution that reflects both the empirical data and the prior information. This posterior distribution is just a conditional probability distribution, where the conditioning is provided by the empirical data. It can be calculated using Bayes' theorem.

*Bayes' Theorem*

$$P(A=a|B=b) = \frac{P(B=b|A=a)P(A=a)}{P(B=b)}$$

There are two broad categories of applications for this procedure. The first involves a random variable that represents a characteristic of some population which is unknown simply because not enough data have been gathered. That is, there is some true but unknown value that could be observed with any desired precision through increasing the number of observations. For example, the characteristic might be the proportion of defectives generated by a production process. The problem is that only a few observations are available and more may be costly. Previous experience with similar processes might provide some information. This previous experience and the observations available can be combined to obtain a posterior distribution for the random variable.

A second broad area involves determining from which of a specified set of populations or categories a particular observation or set of observations has been obtained. That is, several populations and their exact characteristics may have been previously identified. The problem is to determine the population that corresponds to the observations at hand. For example, a production process may be known to have two different modes of operation. When the process is in control, the proportion of defectives is 0.1, and when it is out of control, the proportion of defectives is 0.4. Bayesian revision can be used to assess the *probability* that the process is in control or out of control given a set of observations. The motivation is to know which of the two is responsible for a particular observation. In some cases it is not possible to identify the population or category with certainty through continued sampling. Consider a credit manager who is interested in knowing whether or not a customer will default. The manager cannot know for certain until the customer either defaults or pays. Data gathering possibilities are limited. The manager may be able to run a credit check. On the basis of the credit check the probabilities of defaulting can be revised, but no matter how many additional credit checks are run, the probability of default and no default may both be substantial.

The assessment of likelihoods depends on the data-gathering process. Processes corresponding to *binomial*, *Poisson*, and *normal* distributions can be identified. In other cases relative frequency data or subjective assessments must be made.

The revision process can be accomplished with both discrete and continuous prior distributions. *Normal* and *beta* prior distribution are *conjugate* with respect to normal and binomial data-gathering processes, respectively. When continuous prior distributions are not conjugate for the data-gathering process, discrete approximations can be used.

## ASSIGNMENT MATERIAL

**13.1.** Several minutes ago a fair coin was flipped. You do not know the result of that flip, but you do know that if a head were observed, a sample of five marbles was to be taken from jar I, and if a tail were observed, a sample of 10 marbles was to be taken from jar II. Jar I contains 20% red marbles and jar 2 contains 10% red marbles. The sampling is done with replacement. You are told only that the sample taken contained two red marbles. Given this information, what is the probability that the coin flip resulted in a head?

**13.2.** You are confronted with a large jar filled with many marbles. You know that this is either jar type *A* or jar type *B*, their salient characteristics being as follows:

| *Type* | *Mean Marble Diameter (inches)* | *Standard Deviation of Marble Diameters (inches)* |
|---|---|---|
| A | 0.36 | 0.10 |
| B | 0.39 | 0.05 |

You assess the probability that this is actually jar type *A* to be 0.7. A sample of 25 marbles is drawn at random from the jar, and it is reported to you that the average diameter of these 25 marbles is between 0.375 and 0.385 inch. What is the probability that this is jar type *A*?

**13.3.** Assume that you purchase semiconductors for a retail product from a single manufacturer. Past experience has allowed you to collect data on the semiconductors you receive and you have found they fall into two groups. Group 1 has 20% defectives and group 2 has 40% defectives. Your experience is that 80% of the time you have been receiving units falling into group 1. In discussions with the manufacturer you find that the difference is caused by two different sources of raw materials. Furthermore, the manufacturer feels that both sources must be maintained and refuses to differentiate among the end products either in terms of price or by just identifying the material source, claiming it would impose too large a burden on the production staff. Since the economics of your production process are sensitive to the defect rate of the input, it is important to know which group you are working with before the process starts. Testing prior to the manufacturing process is expensive; therefore, only a small sample can be taken. In fact, current policy is to take a sample of 10 from each batch of 1,000. Given two defectives in a sample, what is the probability that the batch is from group 1?

**13.4.** A new company, Modex Engineering, is setting up a number of sales representatives for its product line. The sales representatives also handle a series of products from manufacturers other than Modex. The company faces a rather delicate problem in providing the proper incentive for the sales representatives. Obviously, the representatives will place more effort on lines that are more profitable to them. Profitability depends on the discount allowed. The larger the discount, the larger the margin to the sales representative for a given price to the customer. From Modex's point of view, however, the per unit margin decreases as the discount is increased. To decide on the proper discount policy the company would like to discover the relationship between discount and the rate of orders from sales representatives. Given the expected order rates, an expected profit can be calculated. In order to gather some information, several different discount policies are designed and tried initially in some similar sales areas. The "test" discounts cannot be kept in place too long because after 2 months it will be difficult to make changes without upsetting the representatives. Based on past experience, the market manager has established a distribution for order rates (average orders per month) for a variety of discount policies. For discount policy 1, the distribution is given in Table 13.9. During the 2-month test, four orders were received. In light of these data, what is the expected order rate using discount policy 1? Assume that the data-gathering process is represented by a Poisson distribution.

**TABLE 13.9**

| *Average Orders per Month* | *Prior Probability* |
|---|---|
| 1 | 0.1 |
| 2 | 0.2 |
| 3 | 0.3 |
| 4 | 0.3 |
| 5 | 0.1 |

**13.5.** The following payoff table for marketing choices for a new film has been determined by the management of a motion picture studio (the amounts are in thousands of dollars).

| *Box Office Result* | *Distribute as "A" Feature* | *Sell to TV Network* | *Distribute as "B" Feature* |
|---|---|---|---|
| Success | $ 5,000 | $1,000 | $ 3,000 |
| Failure | $−2,000 | $1,000 | $−1,000 |

The prior probability of a box office success has been judged at 0.3. The studio plans a series of sneak previews. Historically, it has been found that favorable previews have been obtained for 70% of all successful films previewed, while unfavorable previews have resulted from 80% of the box office failures subjected to such experimentation.

(a) What are the posterior probabilities for box office success and failure, given that the sneak preview is favorable?
(b) What are the posterior probabilities for box office success and failure, given that the sneak preview is unfavorable?
(c) If a sneak preview results in a net cost of $10,000, would you recommend it be taken? (Assume that choices are based on expected values.)

### 13.6 Haggard Productions, Inc.[4]

Ferlin Haggard, patron of the arts and fast-buck promoter, is considering backing a Broadway play for the upcoming season. The list of prospective plays has been narrowed to the following two: *Cabernet*, a musical adaptation of *The Grapes of Wrath*, and *How to Succeed in Business Without Dying*, a melodrama based on *The Godfather*.

From back issues of *Variety*, Haggard has determined that musicals of the Cabernet type are *hits* (or successful) 20% of the time and *flops* (or failures) 80% of the time. He similarly learned that melodramas are hits 30% of the time.

Haggard's current financial resources are quite limited; his net liquid assets amount to only $750,000. As a result, he can afford to produce only one play for the coming season. However, Haggard does have the option of previewing *one* of the plays in New Haven before deciding which, if any, play he would like to produce for the Broadway (New York) stage. Since the time before the season begins is too short to allow Haggard to preview both plays in New Haven, he does have the option of previewing one play and producing the other for Broadway.

The costs and revenues associated with the two plays are given below. Net costs are given for New Haven (i.e., cost–revenues).

| | *Net Cost of New Haven Preview* | *Additional Cost of New York Opening (with New Haven Preview)* | *Cost of Opening in New York (Bypassing New Haven)* | *Revenue if Hit* | *Revenue if Flop* |
|---|---|---|---|---|---|
| *Cabernet* | $200,000 | $500,000 | $600,000 | $4,000,000 | $300,000 |
| *How to Succeed* | 75,000 | 275,000 | 325,000 | 1,000,000 | 100,000 |

[4]The basic decision diagram for this problem is asked for in problem 3.3.

Haggard has observed that of the *hit* musicals on Broadway that were previewed in New Haven, 80% were hits in New Haven; of the musicals that flopped in New York and were previewed in New Haven, 40% were hits in New Haven. Of the hit melodramas in New York that were previewed, 90% were hits in New Haven; 60% of the previewed melodramas that flopped in New York were hits in New Haven. While Haggard may find preview results useful, he feels the accuracy of this kind of test is not high enough to compel him in all cases to act in accordance with the preview result. If Haggard is willing to act on the basis of expected values, what action would you recommend?

**13.7 Datanetics Revisited**

Consider the Datanetics quality control problem in Chapter 10 (problem 10.17). Assume you have decided to make 103 units and subject 3 units to the test. With which test results should you rework all units before installation, and with which should you install the units and only rework those found to be defective after installation?

## APPENDIX 13: Formal Notation and Bayes Formula

$$P(X=x_i|Y=y_j)=\frac{P(Y=y_j|X=x_i)P(X=x_i)}{\sum_{k=1}^{n} P(Y=y_j|X=x_k)P(X=x_k)}$$

where

$P(X=x_i)$ is the "prior" probability for the outcome $X=x_i$ and the entire set $P(X=x_i)$, $i=1,2,\ldots,n$, represents the prior probability distribution for the random variable $X$.

$P(Y=y_j|X=x_i)$, $i=1,2,\ldots,n$, are the "likelihoods" or the conditional probabilities of the empirical result $Y=y_j$ given each of the possible values of the random variable of interest.

$\sum_{k=1}^{n} P(Y=y_j|X=x_k)P(X=x_k)$ is just the marginal probability of the result $Y=y_j$ under all the possible states of the random variable $X$. That is, it is equal to $P(Y=y_j)$. This can be seen by recognizing that each term in the summation is the probability of the joint random variable $(Y=y_j, X=x_k)$ $[P(Y=y_j, X=x_k)=P(Y=y_j|X=x_k)P(X=x_k)]$, and that by summing over all possible values of the random variable $X$ we obtain $P(Y=y_j)$.

$P(X=x_i|Y=y_j)$ is the "posterior" probability of $X=x_i$ and the entire set $P(X=x_i|Y=y_j)$, $i=1,2,\ldots,n$ is the "posterior" distribution for the random variable $X$ given the empirical observation $Y=y_j$.

# 14

# Information and Its Value

Information is some form of communication that contributes to an individual's knowledge. The communication itself is often referred to as a *signal*. The *content* of the signal can be measured in a number of ways. Communication engineers concentrate on the number of *bits* of information in a signal. From the perspective of an individual decision maker, the appropriate measures involve probabilities and preferences. If the content of a signal does not change an individual's state of knowledge, it does not qualify as information. This means that the concept of information is tied to uncertainty. If a signal does not change an individual's action, it has no value (in the context of the decision at hand). This means the value of information depends on the decision problem and the decision maker's preferences. This chapter discusses the concept of information and how to evaluate an alternative to obtain new information. Figure 14.1 indicates where the topic fits into the overall scheme of the material presented.

## CONCEPT OF INFORMATION

The concept of information is tied directly to uncertainty. Unless there is a lack of knowledge prior to the receipt of the signal, we do not regard the communication as providing information. This lack of knowledge reflects uncertainty on the part of the individual and can be modeled by a probability distribution. You may not know last year's reported earnings of Company XYZ or you may not know the outcome of a future court decision. In both cases the lack of knowledge can be represented by a probability distribution.

The *beliefs* of a person are changed by receiving a signal with information in it. For instance, by obtaining a copy of the financial statement for Company XYZ, you could obtain perfect information on last year's reported earnings of Company XYZ. All the uncertainty would be resolved. In the court decision example, perfect information is not available prior to the actual court ruling. However, a legal expert may provide significant information relating to the outcome and, thus, change your beliefs. Assume that before discussing the case with a legal expert, your state of knowledge regarding a court decision is reflected by the assessment of a 0.5 chance of winning and a 0.5 chance of losing. Your beliefs are modeled in terms of a probability distribution because of the uncertainty. The information you receive from a lawyer may cause you to revise your beliefs. They may now be represented by a 0.8 chance of winning and a 0.2 chance of losing. A formal model for revising probabilities in light of new information is provided by Bayes' theorem. This revision technique (discussed in Chapter 13) provides a basis for our discussion of information.

**FIGURE 14.1**

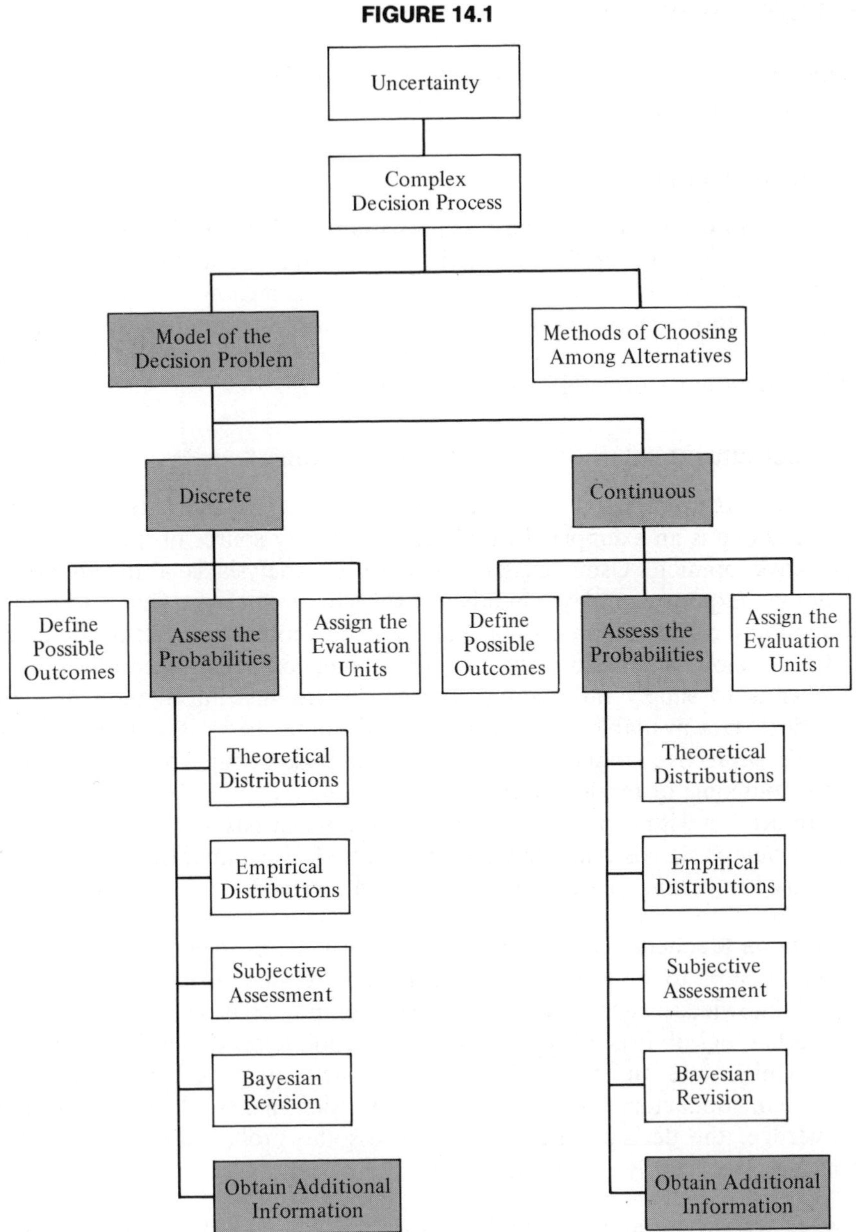
Uncertainty
Complex Decision Process
Model of the Decision Problem
Methods of Choosing Among Alternatives
Discrete
Continuous
Define Possible Outcomes
Assess the Probabilities
Assign the Evaluation Units
Define Possible Outcomes
Assess the Probabilities
Assign the Evaluation Units
Theoretical Distributions
Empirical Distributions
Subjective Assessment
Bayesian Revision
Obtain Additional Information
Theoretical Distributions
Empirical Distributions
Subjective Assessment
Bayesian Revision
Obtain Additional Information

## SOURCES OF INFORMATION

Information sources can conveniently be classified into empirical data and subjective opinion.

### Empirical Data

Empirical data can be used to assess probability distributions directly. In this case prior beliefs are used to verify that the relative frequencies represent the "correct" probabilities, or to "smooth" them somehow so that they do represent the decision maker's assessment of the probabilities (see Chapter 11). Empirical data can also be used with *prior* distributions and *likelihoods* to obtain *posterior* probability distributions.

### Subjective Opinion—Types of Information from Experts

In many cases empirical data are not available. The court decision mentioned above is an example. In these cases the only source of information is subjective opinion. Using *experts* to assist in analysis is a time-honored tradition. Experts can play a number of roles in an analysis. One is to create and guide the analytic process or the "study." Another is to act in the place of the decision maker and make a choice among competing alternatives. Still another is to supply information. In some cases this information may be empirical data available to the expert, but in other cases it will involve the expert's subjective opinion—or beliefs—about some uncertain event (unknown outcome or random variable).

In dealing with expert opinion, a decision maker has a choice of both the *information* or signals requested (i.e., the method of communication), and the *method of processing* or using the information received.

**Experts as teachers.** One extreme is to discuss the problem with the expert in an attempt to become an expert. That is, obtain essentially the same overall knowledge as the expert. For instance, in a decision that depends on the technological feasibility of a new semiconductor device, the decision maker might use an expert as a teacher. The expert's general knowledge about semiconductors is transferred to the decision maker. Based on this new knowledge, the decision maker could assess the probability of the device working satisfactorily and make a choice.

**Use of expert judgments.** Another possibility is to ask for the expert's judgment on the particular uncertain event in question. That is, no attempt is made to understand the problem at the same depth as the expert. Rather, the decision maker asks for a judgment from the expert. There are several options open on how the judgments can be elicited.

One option can be characterized as a *point estimate* or single value representing a most likely outcome. For instance, in the semiconductor example, the expert would be asked: "Give me your judgment as to whether the device will work or not." If the uncertain event involved the sales for a given product, the expert might be asked: "Give me your judgment regarding the sales level for product *A*."

If more information is desired, and the information relates to a problem with a range of outcomes, the decision maker could ask for the *worst* and *best* cases (or maximum and minimum values of the random variable).

Having the information on the range of outcomes, the decision maker might want to know how sure the expert was of his/her statements. If this part of the information-gathering process is to go beyond the "oh, pretty sure," "not too sure," or "very sure" stage, it leads to *probability statements* by the expert. Probability distributions provide the ultimate language for communication of judgments from experts to decision makers. A probability distribution provides all the information an expert can possibly supply about his judgment on a particular problem.

### Processing Expert Judgments

A decision maker is still faced with processing the information supplied by an expert. The revised beliefs are $P(\text{outcome of interest}|\text{signal from expert})$. Using Bayes' theorem, we can write

$$P(\text{outcome of interest}|\text{signal from expert}) = \frac{P(\text{signal from expert}|\text{outcome of interest}) \times P(\text{outcome of interest})}{P(\text{signal from expert})}$$

Even if never actually used to revise beliefs, this model highlights an important consideration in using experts. The likelihood $P(\text{signal from expert}$ $|\text{outcome of interest})$ is essentially a measure of the expert's *credibility*. If the expert were perfectly credible, the likelihood would reflect it. For example, with the semiconductor expert, assume you originally believed that there was a 0.30 chance that the device would work and the expert's statement was that it would work.

$$P(\text{device works}|\text{expert says it will work}) = \frac{P(\text{expert says it will work}|\text{device works}) \times P(\text{device works})}{P(\text{expert says it will work})}$$

If you believe the expert to be perfectly reliable, then $P(\text{expert says it will work}|\text{device works}) = 1.0$. The denominator can be calculated as

$$\begin{aligned} P(\text{expert says it will work}) &= P(\text{expert says it will work}|\text{device works}) \times P(\text{device works}) \\ &\quad + P(\text{expert says it will work}|\text{device doesn't work}) \\ &\quad \times P(\text{device doesn't work}) \\ &= (1.0)(0.3) + (0)(0.7) = 0.3 \end{aligned}$$

Therefore, we obtain the expected result:

$$P(\text{device works}|\text{expert says it will work}) = \frac{(1.0)(0.3)}{0.3} = 1.0$$

If you believe the expert is not completely reliable, presumably you would assign a probability less than 1.0 to the likelihood.

The point this serves to emphasize is that the expert's credibility is crucial to the way the signals supplied are processed by the decision maker. When experts have an incentive to bias their opinion, this obviously reduces their *credibility*, and if formal revision procedures were used, it would be reflected in the likelihoods assessed for the signal received. The difficulty, of course, is that the individual's beliefs cannot be directly observed—only the outcomes of the events for which probabilities have been assessed. When this is true, we say that a problem of moral hazard exists. The potential for a conflict in incentives should be recognized by a decision maker and the revision process (either formally or informally) should take the incentives into consideration.[1]

**More than one expert.** How should the beliefs of two or more experts be combined? There are a number of ideas that are appealing for their simplicity, such as "taking the average" or "weighted average." However, on closer scrutiny these schemes do not hold up.[2] Allowing the experts to communicate and identify any differences in opinion is often the most effective procedure. Basically, you let *them* do the combining. This is consistent with the idea that differences in assessments are due to different sets of information held by each expert. If the differences can be identified, the experts may reach agreement. In a procedure like this, there may be effects due to group dynamics that influence the agreements. By carefully designing the setting, these effects can be minimized.

**Letting experts make choices.** As a last point it is clear that if experts are allowed to make choices, not only their *beliefs* but also their *preferences* are involved. If the decision maker and the expert have different preferences, the result may not be the choice preferred by the decision maker.

## VALUE OF INFORMATION

What is the value of information in a particular setting? The basic principle is that *information only has value in a decision problem if it results in a change in some action to be taken by a decision maker*. Even though some data or statements from an expert provide new knowledge, it may not have any value in the context of a particular decision problem.

[1]For an analysis of this problem, see J. S. Demski, and G. Feltham, *Cost Determination: A Conceptual Approach* (Ames, Iowa: Iowa State Press, 1976).

[2]See H. Raiffa, *Decision Analysis, Introductory Lectures on Decisions Under Uncertainty* (Reading, Mass.: Addison-Wesley, 1968).

The value of information can be calculated using the techniques already developed. An *information alternative* is created and included in the decision diagram like any other alternative. The *cost* that makes the information alternative equivalent to the *best alternative without information* is called the *value* of the information.

Two cases are usually considered:

**Expected Value of Perfect Information**

***Definition:*** *The **Expected Value of Perfect Information (EVPI)** =*

*(expected value if perfect information could be obtained) −(expected value of the best alternative without information)*

**Expected Value of Sample Information**

***Definition:*** *The **Expected Value of Imperfect or Sample Information (EVSI)** =*

*(expected value of the information alternative)−*

*(expected value of the best alternative without information)*

Information alternatives are treated like any other alternative on a decision diagram. In determining the EVPI or EVSI, no information costs are included on the diagram. After rolling back the tree, the difference between the information alternative and the best alternative without information is directly available.

Some calculational short cuts and interpretations are demonstrated by the examples that follow.

### Expected Value of Perfect Information (EVPI)

Perfect information about a given event means complete elimination of all uncertainty about the event's outcomes. That is, *after* receiving the information, you will know exactly which outcome will occur. In some cases perfect information *is* obtainable. For instance, if the uncertain event involved the decision of a customer to let a contract, it might be possible to find out what the decision is by offering the customer an incentive for telling you. In other cases perfect information is not possible but is a useful concept. It is useful because it provides an *upper bound* on the value of information in a particular decision, and because the calculations usually can be done easily.

There are several ways to visualize and calculate the EVPI. To illustrate the methods, consider the following example.

**Example 14.1**

A construction contract must be completed prior to June 1, 1978 to avoid a significant penalty. There are three different plans that can be used for the construction. The plans differ primarily in their ability to provide flexibility in the face of varying weather conditions. Plan 1 will be the most profitable if good weather exists during the construction period; however, it is the worst under other conditions. Plan 2 is adequate under all conditions. Plan 3 is good under two weather types but poor under the other two possible weather types. The plans and their net contribution in thousands of dollars for the four possible weather types are shown in Table 14.1 along with the assessed probabilities for the weather possibilities.

**TABLE 14.1**

**Net Contribution**

| *Weather* | *Plan* 1 | *Plan* 2 | *Plan* 3 | *Probability* |
|---|---|---|---|---|
| Type $n_1$ | 48 | 24 | 40 | 0.4 |
| Type $n_2$ | 16 | 24 | 16 | 0.2 |
| Type $n_3$ | 16 | 32 | 24 | 0.2 |
| Type $n_4$ | 16 | 24 | 16 | 0.2 |
| EMV | 28.8 | 25.6 | 27.2 | 1.00 |

Alternatives involving information can be included just like any other alternative on a decision diagram. In this example, if we include the option of obtaining perfect information we have the diagram shown in Figure 14.2. From the diagram we see that the expected monetary value of the alternative *perfect information* is $35,200. Note that the decision to obtain perfect information does *not* eliminate all uncertainty. You are still (until the perfect information is received) uncertain about what the information will reveal. Without perfect information plan 1 will yield the maximum expected monetary value of $28,800. Therefore, the value of the perfect information must be the difference between $35,200 and $28,800, or $6,400.

This calculation can also be done using tables. Table 14.1 provides the expected monetary value for the best plan without perfect information. The expected monetary value with perfect information can be calculated using Table 14.2.

## • Other Ways to Calculate EVPI

Another way to look at EVPI is by considering opportunity losses. An opportunity loss is the difference between the highest payoff available for a given outcome (in this case, weather type) and the payoff associated with a particular plan. For instance, if the weather type is $n_1$, the highest possible payoff is $48,000, and hence the opportunity loss associated with plan 3 is

**FIGURE 14.2**

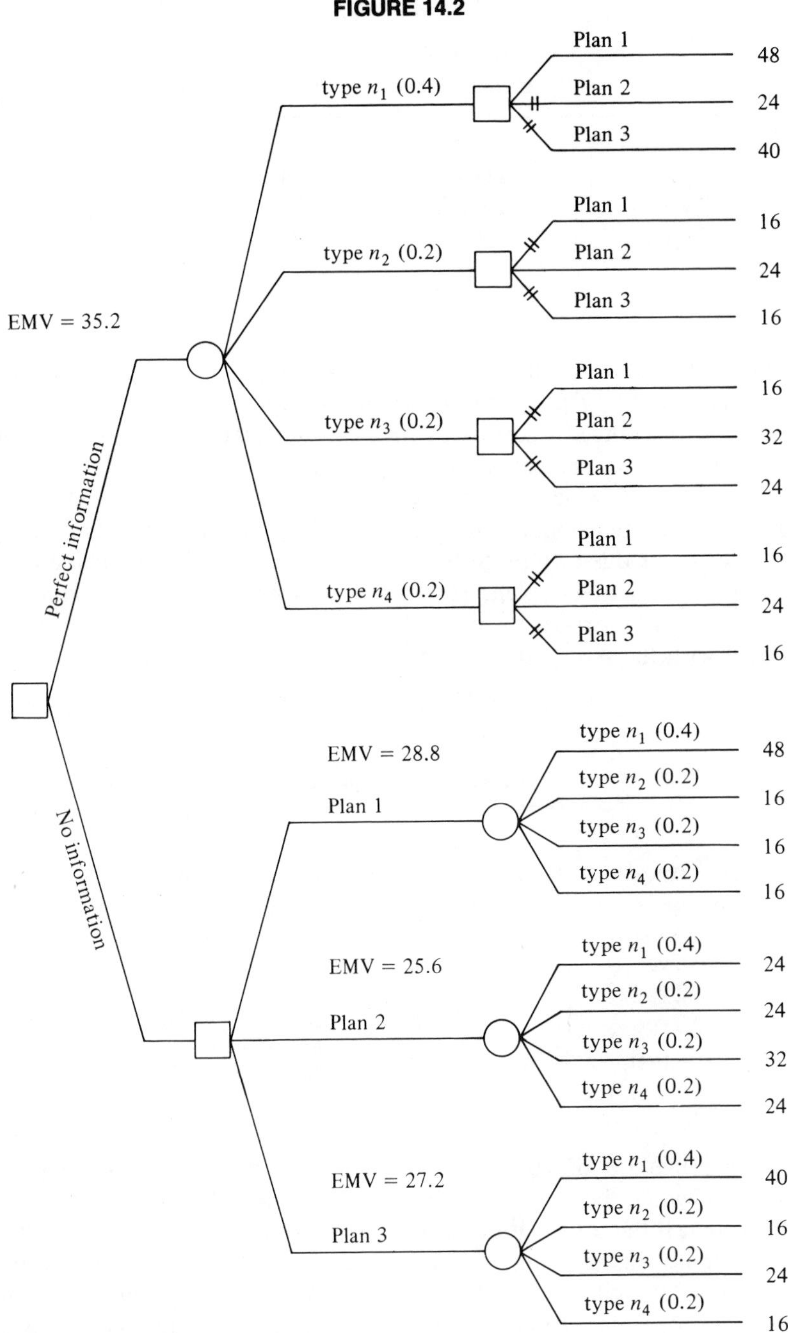

EMV = 35.2
Perfect information
type $n_1$ (0.4)
Plan 1
48
Plan 2
24
Plan 3
40
type $n_2$ (0.2)
Plan 1
16
Plan 2
24
Plan 3
16
type $n_3$ (0.2)
Plan 1
16
Plan 2
32
Plan 3
24
type $n_4$ (0.2)
Plan 1
16
Plan 2
24
Plan 3
16
No information
EMV = 28.8
Plan 1
type $n_1$ (0.4)
48
type $n_2$ (0.2)
16
type $n_3$ (0.2)
16
type $n_4$ (0.2)
16
EMV = 25.6
Plan 2
type $n_1$ (0.4)
24
type $n_2$ (0.2)
24
type $n_3$ (0.2)
32
type $n_4$ (0.2)
24
EMV = 27.2
Plan 3
type $n_1$ (0.4)
40
type $n_2$ (0.2)
16
type $n_3$ (0.2)
24
type $n_4$ (0.2)
16

**TABLE 14.2**

| *Weather* | *Choice with Perfect Information* | *Payoff* | *Probability* |
|---|---|---|---|
| Type $n_1$ | Plan 1 | 48 | 0.4 |
| Type $n_2$ | Plan 2 | 24 | 0.2 |
| Type $n_3$ | Plan 2 | 32 | 0.2 |
| Type $n_4$ | Plan 2 | 24 | 0.2 |
| | EMV | 35.2 | |

($48,000 − $40,000) = $8,000. Table 14.3 shows the opportunity losses for the plans in Table 14.1. The minimum expected opportunity loss is $6,400 for plan 1. This, of course, is consistent with the fact that plan 1 has the highest expected payoff. No matter what you do, because of the uncertainty, you may choose a plan which is not best for the type of weather that actually occurs. The expected opportunity loss of the best action available is just the expected value of this difference between the best possible outcome and that associated with a given plan. If perfect information were available, this difference could be driven to zero. Therefore, the expected opportunity loss associated with the best plan is just the EVPI.

**TABLE 14.3**

**Opportunity Losses**

| *Weather* | *Plan* 1 | 2 | 3 | *Probability* |
|---|---|---|---|---|
| Type $n_1$ | 0 | 24 | 8 | 0.4 |
| Type $n_2$ | 8 | 0 | 8 | 0.2 |
| Type $n_3$ | 16 | 0 | 8 | 0.2 |
| Type $n_4$ | 8 | 0 | 8 | 0.2 |
| EOL | 6.4 | 9.6 | 8.0 | 1.00 |

Another method of visualizing EVPI is to consider how much perfect information would be worth to you for each possible weather state. For instance, what if the information transmitted were that weather type $n_1$ would occur? Without this information you would choose Plan 1. With this information you would still choose plan 1. Therefore, the information *weather type* $n_1$ would result in no change in your choice and it would not be worth anything to you. However, if the signal were *weather type* $n_2$ you would switch to plan 2, increasing your payoff by $24,000 − $16,000 = $8,000.

**TABLE 14.4**

| *Weather* | *Current Choice* | *Choice if Information Specified Given Weather State* | *Change in Payoff* | *Probability* |
|---|---|---|---|---|
| Type $n_1$ | Plan 1 | Plan 1 | 0 | 0.4 |
| Type $n_2$ | Plan 1 | Plan 2 | 8 | 0.2 |
| Type $n_3$ | Plan 1 | Plan 2 | 16 | 0.2 |
| Type $n_4$ | Plan 1 | Plan 2 | 8 | 0.2 |

Table 14.4 displays your actions and the difference in payoff for each state of weather.

Now place yourself back at a point in time before the information on which weather state will occur has been transmitted, and ask: "How much would I be willing to pay for the information?" The amount clearly depends upon which signal (i.e., weather type) is transmitted. All you have available are the probabilities of various weather types, and therefore you can calculate the EVPI as $(0 \times 0.4) + (\$8{,}000 \times 0.2) + (\$16{,}000 \times 0.2) + (\$8{,}000 \times 0.2) = \$6{,}400$.

### Expected Value of Imperfect or Sample Information

When the information available is not perfect but still offers the potential for reducing the uncertainty associated with a decision problem, its expected value can sometimes be calculated. Information from sampling often falls into this category. When a model of the information-gathering process is available, Bayes' theorem can be used to calculate the required distributions. To illustrate, consider the following example.

**Example 14.2**

Referring to Example 14.1, assume you have determined that the weather will be either type $n_1$ or type $n_2$. The probability of type $n_1$ is 0.4 and the probability of type $n_2$ is 0.6. All other data are the same as in Example 14.1. Additional information is available from a weather service. It is not always reliable. If the weather is type $n_1$, the service predicts it 80% of the time and predicts type $n_2$ 20% of the time. If the weather is type $n_2$, the service predicts type $n_2$ 70% of the time, but predicts type $n_1$ 30% of the time. What is the expected value of the weather service information?

This problem can be diagrammed as shown in Figure 14.3. The difference between this problem and an analysis under perfect information is that uncertainty remains *after* the signal is received. The probabilities based on this information are calculated using Bayes' theorem from the joint probabilities in Table 14.5. They are summarized in Table 14.6.

FIGURE 14.3

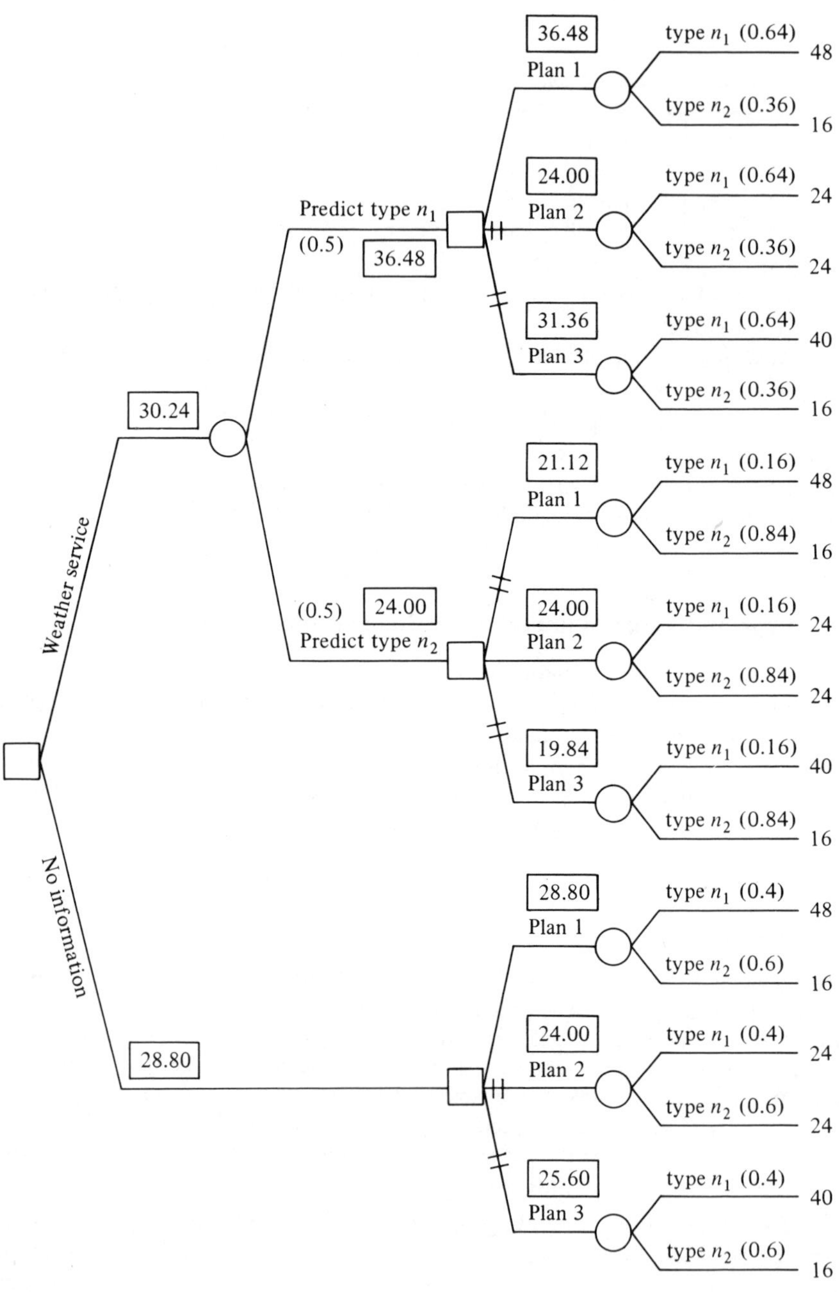

Weather service
No information
30.24
28.80
Predict type $n_1$
(0.5)
36.48
(0.5)
24.00
Predict type $n_2$
36.48
Plan 1
24.00
Plan 2
31.36
Plan 3
21.12
Plan 1
24.00
Plan 2
19.84
Plan 3
28.80
Plan 1
24.00
Plan 2
25.60
Plan 3
type $n_1$ (0.64)
type $n_2$ (0.36)
type $n_1$ (0.16)
type $n_2$ (0.84)
type $n_1$ (0.4)
type $n_2$ (0.6)
48
16
24
24
40
16

**TABLE 14.5**

| | *Predict Type* $n_1$ | *Predict Type* $n_2$ | |
|---|---|---|---|
| *Type* $n_1$ | $(0.8)\times(0.4)=0.32$ | $(0.2)\times(0.4)=0.08$ | 0.4 |
| *Type* $n_2$ | $(0.3)\times(0.6)=0.18$ | $(0.7)\times(0.6)=0.42$ | 0.6 |
| | 0.50 | 0.50 | 1.00 |

**TABLE 14.6**

$$P(\text{type } n_1|\text{predict type } n_1)=\frac{0.32}{0.50}=0.64$$

$$P(\text{type } n_2|\text{predict type } n_1)=\frac{0.18}{0.50}=0.36$$

$$P(\text{type } n_1|\text{predict type } n_2)=\frac{0.08}{0.50}=0.16$$

$$P(\text{type } n_2|\text{predict type } n_2)=\frac{0.42}{0.50}=0.84$$

By rolling back the diagram with these probabilities, we see that the difference between the *weather service* alternative and the *no information* alternative is $30,240 − $28,800 = $1,440. This is the expected value of sample information, EVSI, for this example.

### • EVSI Without Bayes' Theorem

There is no requirement that Bayes' theorem be used in calculations of the value of imperfect information. The following example illustrates an EVSI calculation without Bayes' theorem.

**Example 14.3**

Faced with a difficult technological problem, the manager of an engineering and development laboratory was considering bringing in an outside expert to help determine whether the process under development would be a technological success. It was impossible to know for sure if the process would be a success until the research was completed. However, the expert he had in mind was more knowledgeable than anyone on his staff on the crucial part of the project. If the process turns out to be a success, the payoffs will be large--approximately $10,000,000. On the other hand, a failure will result in a substantial loss, estimated to be $5,000,000. The manager currently assesses the chances of success at only 30%. When considering the expert, he feels confident the assessment provided after the investigation will be a probability of success of 60%, 40%, 20%, or 0%. Moreover, he feels that each possibility is equally likely. As a matter of fact, this assessment on the expert's response, which corresponds to an overall probability of success of 30% $[(0.25)\times(0.60)+(0.25)\times(0.40)+(0.25)\times(20)+(0.25)\times(0)=0.30]$, just confirms his opinion about the success of the project. Nevertheless, since it is a potentially profitable project, he still wants to consider the possibility of hiring the expert.

**FIGURE 14.4**

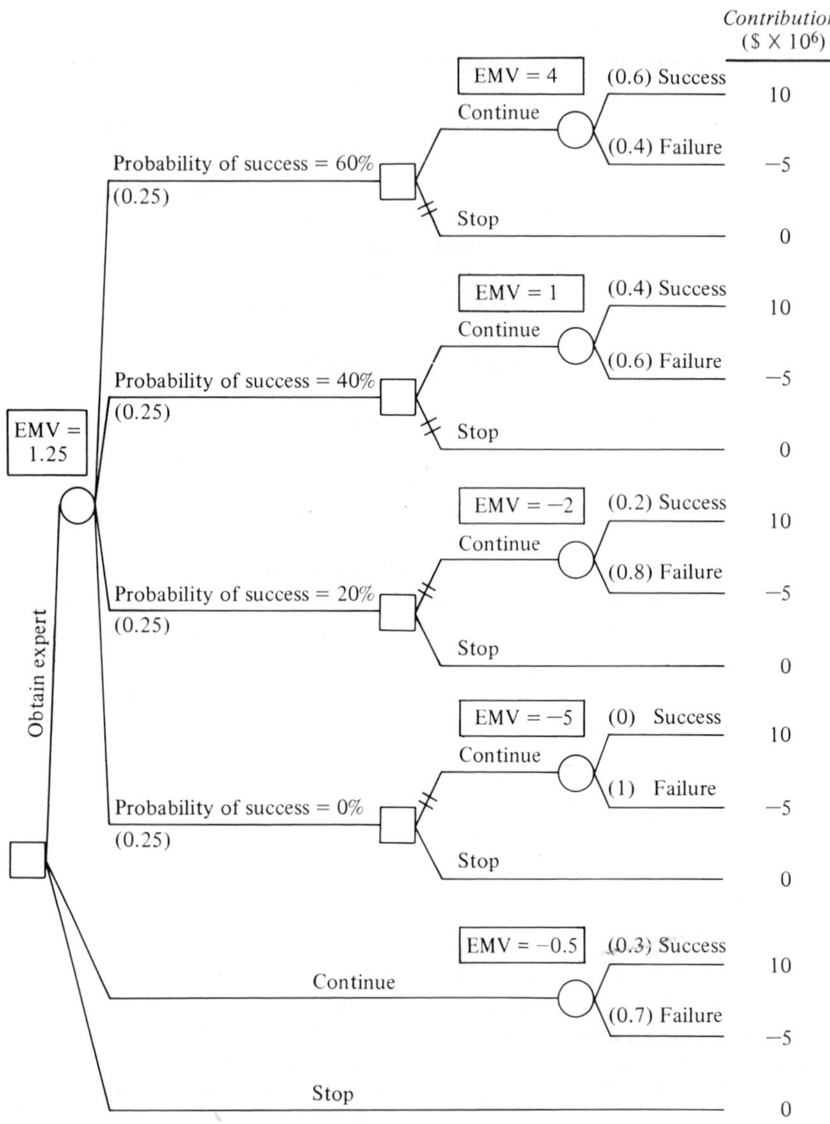


The diagram facing the manager is shown in Figure 14.4. The *obtain expert* alternative has the highest expected monetary value. The next best alternative based on expected contribution is to stop, which yields a contribution of \$0. Therefore, without the expert's help, the project will be stopped with an expected incremental contribution of \$0. Consequently, the expected value of the expert's information is \$1.25 − \$0 = \$1.25 million.

## • The Relationship Between Value of Information and Amount of Uncertainty

The value of information depends on both the amount of uncertainty (or the prior knowledge available) and the payoffs. To demonstrate, consider the following simplified example.

**Example 14.4**

As an investor you are convinced that XYZ Company's earnings have an equal chance to be either $2 per share or $2.50 per share for last year. Furthermore you believe the stock price will be 10 times last year's earnings per share (EPS) in either case. The stock is now selling for $22 per share and the earnings are to be reported in 1 month. Your cash flow position allows you to invest for only 2 months (assume that there are no market effects and no transaction charges). You now own no XYZ stock and if you buy you will buy 1,000 shares. Furthermore, assume that you decide to make your decision based on expected contribution. Although you are not sure if you can obtain "perfect" information, you realize that it would be possible to get close to perfect information by talking with company officials. Since this would be a time-consuming and expensive process, you want to get a feel for the value of the information. Figure 14.5 shows your problem, assuming you could obtain perfect information.

**FIGURE 14.5**

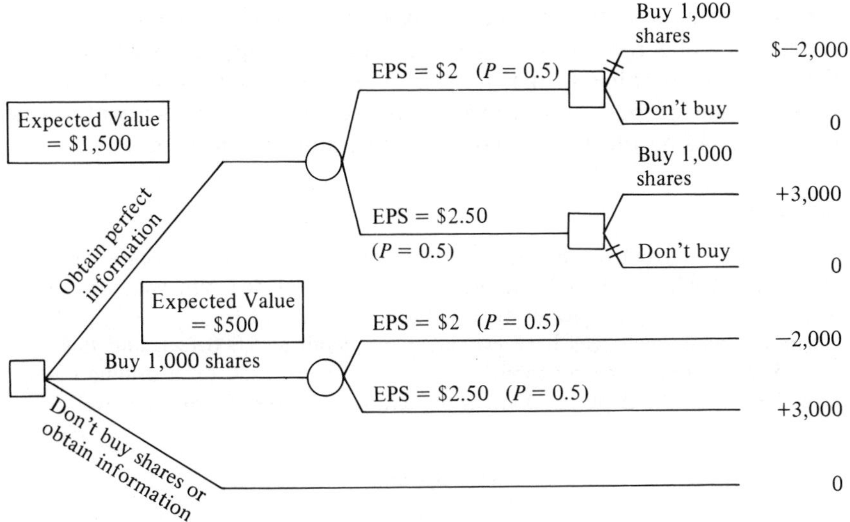


The EVPI is $1,500 − $500 = $1,000. This value is based on the prior assessment $P(\text{EPS}=\$2)=0.5$, $P(\text{EPS}=\$2.50)=0.5$. If the prior probabilities were changed from 0.5, the EVPI would change. Figure 14.6 displays how EVPI changes for this particular problem as $P(\text{EPS}=\$2.50)$ varies from 0 to

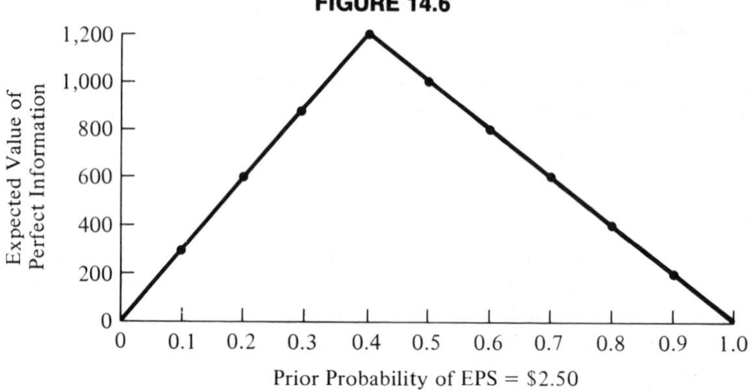


1.0. At either extreme the EVPI is low because the *amount* of uncertainty is not great. In the middle ranges the additional uncertainty is reflected in a higher EVPI.

## SENSITIVITY ANALYSIS

Sensitivity analysis provides a simple but powerful tool for investigating the value of information. If the decision maker's actions are the same for any possible value of a random variable, then even knowing the exact value that will occur has no value to the decision maker. Under these conditions the expected value of perfect information is seen to be zero without further calculations. As an illustration, consider the following problem.

### Example 14.5

The president of a petroleum exploration company is trying to decide whether a wildcat well should be drilled. His geologists have provided him with assessments relating to the likely quantities of oil, as shown in Figure 14.7.

The company geologists have estimated the depth at 5,000 feet, and this figure was used to determine the contribution shown in Figure 14.7. (The drilling costs, of course, depend on the depth, and are estimated to be $100 per foot.) The well will be

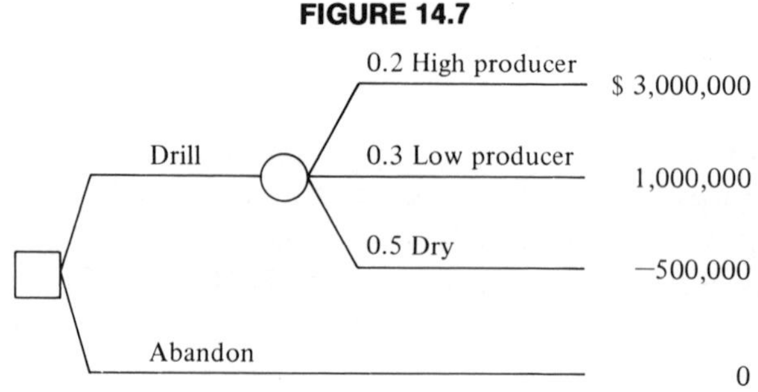

sold if successful. The expected revenue is $3,500,000 for a high producer, $1,500,000 for a low producer, and zero for a dry well. Past experience indicates that estimates of drilling depth can be seriously in error. Therefore, when offered the chance to purchase some exploration data previously obtained on the site, the president was reluctant to turn it down. However, he was not sure if it would be worth the price.

Sensitivity analysis can be used to analyze the president's problem. Assume that the president will choose the alternative with the highest expected value. The expected contribution can be written in terms of well depth as follows.[3]

$$\begin{aligned}\text{Expected Contribution for Drill} = & \ (3{,}500{,}000 - 100 \times \text{depth}) \times 0.2 \\ & + (1{,}500{,}000 - 100 \times \text{depth}) \times 0.3 \\ & + (-100 \times \text{depth}) \times 0.5 \\ = & \ 1{,}150{,}000 - 100 \times \text{depth}\end{aligned}$$

For the estimated depth level of 5,000 feet, the expected contribution for drill is $650,000. The relationship between expected contribution and depth is shown in Figure 14.8. From the curve we see that the decision will not change as long as the depth is believed to be less than 11,500 feet. Therefore, although the expected contribution may be sensitive to depth, the decision in this case is not particularly sensitive. If the president asked the geologists for a maximum depth figure and was given 10,000 feet, he would know that the exploration data would be of no value to him for this particular decision.

**FIGURE 14.8**

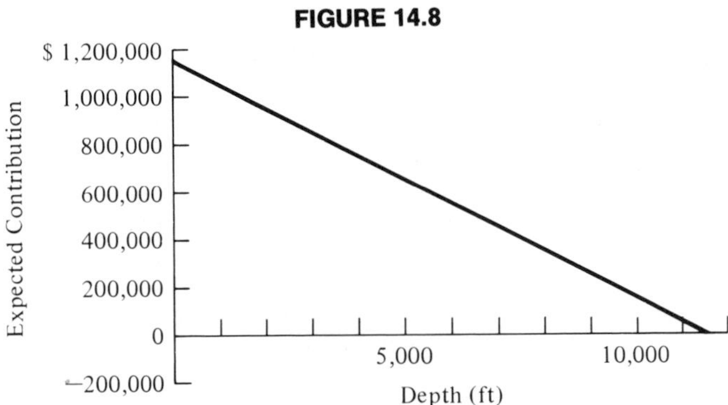


## ●● VALUE OF INFORMATION WITH DIFFERENT RISK ATTITUDES

The analyses shown above all use expected monetary values for evaluating alternatives. Under these conditions the expected value of information is easy to determine. The difference between the expected monetary value with the

[3]A similar analysis can be done when risk preference is considered. However, because of the nonlinearity of the preference curves, it often must be done using trial and error. Value of information with different attitudes toward risk is discussed in the next section.

information and the expected monetary value of the best alternative without information is precisely the information cost that would bring the expected monetary value of the information alternative down to the same value as the best alternative without information. When a decision maker is not risk-neutral, the procedure for determining the value of information is slightly more complicated. A trial-and-error procedure is used to determine the information cost that makes the *information alternative* and the *best alternative without information* equivalent. When preference curves are used, this means making the expected preference for both alternatives equal. Returning to Example 14.1, we calculate the value of the perfect information if the decision maker were risk-averse with the preference curve for net contribution shown in Figure 14.9.

**FIGURE 14.9**

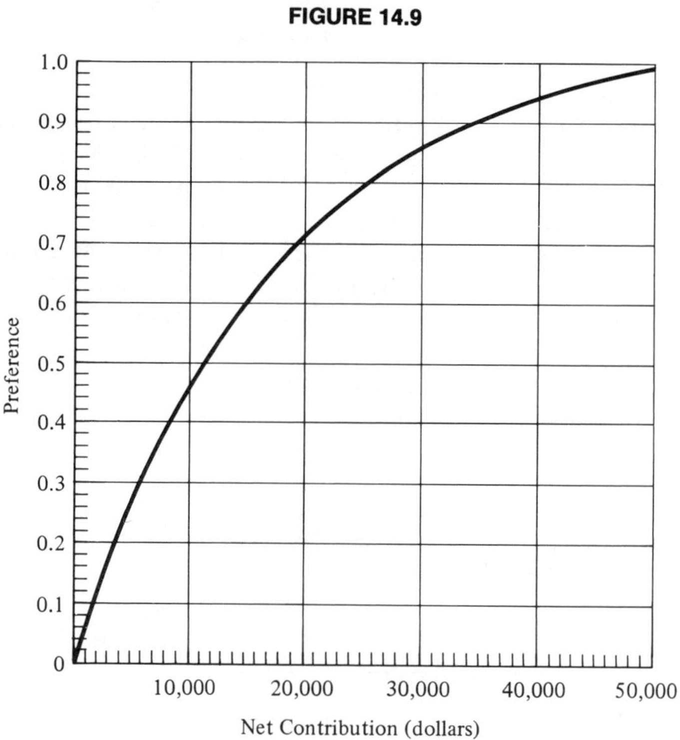


Table 14.7 shows the expected utility for each plan. Table 14.8 shows the trial-and-error calculation for the cost that equates the expected utility of the perfect information alternative with the expected utility of plan 2 (the most preferred alternative based on Table 14.7). Since the decision maker is risk-averse, he will be willing to pay more than the EVPI. In this problem, after trying the EVPI = \$6,400 and then \$10,000, the value of \$7,000 was tried. The expected utility of 0.792 is very close to the expected utility for plan 2. Therefore, the value of the information to the decision maker is approximately \$7,000.

**TABLE 14.7**

| Weather | | Plan 1 | Plan 2 | Plan 3 | Probability |
|---|---|---|---|---|---|
| | Type $n_1$ | 0.97 | 0.77 | 0.93 | 0.4 |
| | Type $n_2$ | 0.62 | 0.77 | 0.62 | 0.2 |
| | Type $n_3$ | 0.62 | 0.87 | 0.77 | 0.2 |
| | Type $n_4$ | 0.62 | 0.77 | 0.62 | 0.2 |
| Expected Utility | | 0.760 | 0.790 | 0.774 | 1.00 |
| Certainty Equivalent | | 23,000 | 25,000 | 24,200 | |

**TABLE 14.8**

| | | *Net Contribution—Information Cost and Corresponding Utilities* | | | | | | | |
|---|---|---|---|---|---|---|---|---|---|
| | | *Cost* = 0 | | *Cost* = \$6,400 | | *Cost* = \$10,000 | | *Cost* = \$7,000 | |
| *Weather* | *Choice with Perfect Information* | *Payoff* | *Utility* | *Payoff* | *Utility* | *Payoff* | *Utility* | *Payoff* | *Utility* |
| Type $n_1$ | Plan 1 | 48 | 0.970 | 41.6 | 0.950 | 38 | 0.930 | 41 | 0.940 |
| Type $n_2$ | Plan 2 | 24 | 0.770 | 17.6 | 0.660 | 14 | 0.580 | 17 | 0.645 |
| Type $n_3$ | Plan 2 | 32 | 0.870 | 25.6 | 0.800 | 22 | 0.750 | 25 | 0.790 |
| Type $n_4$ | Plan 2 | 24 | 0.770 | 17.6 | 0.660 | 14 | 0.580 | 17 | 0.645 |
| Expected Utility | | | 0.870 | | 0.804 | | 0.754 | | 0.792 |
| Certainty Equivalent | | 31,000 | | 25,800 | | 22,200 | | 25,200 | |

This trial-and-error procedure can be used to find the value of information in any problem, including the value of imperfect information. In some special cases the value of information can be calculated more easily.

## SUMMARY

Information *changes* an individual's *knowledge*. Since a precondition to changing an individual's knowledge is *uncertainty on the part of the individual*, information is tied directly to uncertainty and probabilities. Sources of information are *empirical data* and *other individuals*. In seeking information from an individual, we generally turn to "experts." The procedure for processing the information signals involves revision of beliefs or probabilities. Bayes' theorem provides a normative procedure for this process.

The *value of the information* depends on whether this revision of beliefs *changes* the decision maker's *actions*. If no change takes place, the information has zero value in the context of the decision problem under investigation. If a change does take place, the value of the information can be calculated by evaluating the information alternative, along with the alternatives without information. For a risk-neutral individual, the difference between the expected value of the information alternative and the expected value of the best alternatives without information is the expected value of the information.

Expected Value of Perfect Information (EVPI)

$$\equiv\text{(expected value if perfect information could be obtained)}$$
$$-\text{(expected value of the best alternative without information)}$$

Expected Value of Imperfect or Sample Information (EVSI)

$$\equiv\text{(expected value of the information alternative)}$$
$$-\text{(expected value of the best alternative without information)}$$

For individuals who are not risk-neutral, the *value of information* is equal to the cost that makes the information alternative equivalent to the best alternative without information. In general, a trial-and-error procedure is required to find this cost.

## ASSIGNMENT MATERIAL

**14.1.** The owner of a clothing store must decide how many men's shirts to order for the new season. For a particular type of shirt, he must order in lots of 100 shirts. If he orders 100 shirts, his cost is $10 per shirt; if he orders 200 shirts, his cost is $9 per shirt; and if he orders 300 or more shirts his cost is $8 per shirt. His selling price is $12 but any left over at the end of the season will be sold at half-price. For simplicity he is willing to assume demand will be either 100, 150, 200, 250, or 300 shirts and that he will suffer no loss of goodwill among his customers if he runs out of shirts. He must place his entire order for the season now, with no chance of reordering. He decides that probabilities for demand are: $P(D=100)=0.1$, $P(D=150)=0.2$, $P(D=200)=0.3$, $P(D=250)=0.2$, $P(D=300)=0.2$.

(a) Use a payoff table to determine the order quantity that will maximize expected contribution. (Consider only order quantities of 100, 200, and 300 shirts.)

(b) Calculate the expected value of perfect information.

**14.2.** Stan Stellar, a risk-neutral decision maker, is trying to decide between selling his 10,000 shares of ADZ, Inc., now and holding them until after the earnings are reported in 2 weeks. He knows he can keep them no longer than 2 weeks and believes the price will be either $9, $10, $11, or $12 *per share* at the end of the 2 weeks. He thinks that the *current* price of $10 will not change until after the announcement on earnings. His probability assessments for the price in 2 weeks are shown in the following table:

| | *Price Per Share* | | | |
|---|---|---|---|---|
| | $9 | $10 | $11 | $12 |
| *Probability* | 0.3 | 0.3 | 0.2 | 0.2 |

(a) What is the expected value of perfect information for Stan?

(b) Stan has an opportunity to gather some information on the stock price movement by talking with a friend, Ray Resurch, who follows the company. Ray is generally reliable but not infallible. Moreover, he will only state his opinion as to whether the stock price will go "up" or "down." Based on his long acquaintance with Ray, Stan assesses the following probabilities. If the price goes down to $9, Ray will forecast down with probability 0.6. If the price stays the same, he will forecast down with probability 0.4. If the price goes up to $11, he will forecast up with probability 0.7; and if the price goes up to $12, he will forecast up with probability 0.8. What is the expected value of Ray's information?

**14.3.** Mark Harris, Production Manager of Medical Electronics, Inc., is preparing for the delivery of one of his company's new blood analyzers to the Stanford Medical Center. All that remains to be done is to subject the analyzer to a testing procedure to determine if the equipment meets its design specifications.

Medical Specialties will earn a profit of $3,100 if the analyzer produced for Stanford satisfies its specifications. If testing reveals a failure to meet specifications, the equipment will be completely reworked before delivery, thereby *guaranteeing* that the analyzer will be satisfactory. In the event that rework is done, the profit will be only $1,600. Should it happen that the analyzer passes the testing, is delivered to Stanford, and is *then* found to be unsatisfactory, rework costs and a heavy penalty clause in the sales contract will force Medical Electronics to take a $900 loss on the deal. Harris will always act in accordance with a test result—deliver if the unit passes the test and rework if it fails the test.

Harris' problem is that he must choose which of two testing procedures he should use. Both tests cost $100 (test costs are *not* reflected in the profit figures above) and differ only in their accuracy.

If the unit actually meets specifications, test 1 will indicate the analyzer to be "satisfactory" 80% of the time. Under these conditions, test 2 will give a "satisfactory" result 60% of the time. When the analyzer fails to meet specifications, test 1 will indicate "satisfactory" result 30% of the time while for test 2, this figure is 10%.

Compute the expected value of sample information for each of the two tests if Harris assesses a prior probability of 60% that the unit meets specifications.

**14.4.** Reggie Pomfret, president of the British conglomerate General Specific Ltd., is currently trying to decide whether his Regipom Cosmetics Division should introduce a new product called Prom Balm. Reggie is uncertain about both the potential market for this new product and the unit cost of producing it. The net profit earned by the new product depends upon these two uncertain factors in the following manner. (Profit is expressed in millions of pounds.)

| | | *Unit Production Cost* | | |
|---|---|---|---|---|
| | | *1.0* | *1.5* | *2.0* |
| *Market* | *Large* | 10 | 6 | 2 |
| *Size* | *Small* | 2 | −2 | −4 |

Reggie must decide within the next week (half fortnight) whether or not to go into production with Prom Balm. If he decides against the introduction of the new product, the assets of General Specific will remain exactly as they are today. Reggie's best technical experts view the market size and production cost as independent random variables and have assessed the following distributions for them:

| *Market Size* | *Probability* | *Production Cost* | *Probability* |
|---|---|---|---|
| Large | 0.6 | 1.0 | 0.2 |
| Small | 0.4 | 1.5 | 0.3 |
| | | 2.0 | 0.5 |

In answering the following questions, assume risk neutrality.

(a) Given his current state of information, what should Reggie do?

(b) Suppose that, before making his decision, Reggie could obtain perfect information concerning both the market size and the production cost. What is the most that he would be wiliing to pay for such information?

(c) What is the most that he would be willing to pay for perfect information about the market size alone?

(d) Harriet Vane of the Regipom marketing department says that in the next week she could conduct a QSMS (quick and sloppy market survey) at only a modest expense. A QSMS is quite crude and results simply in either a positive result or a negative result. Based upon past experience, she assesses a probability of 0.7 that the survey result will be positive if the actual potential market is large, and a probability of 0.2 that it will be positive if the market is small. What is the most that Reggie would be willing to pay for a QSMS?

**14.5.** As director of marketing you are interested in the proportion of the population who will buy a new convenience food. You realize that the market is limited and decide that you can approximate the possible proportions by ($P_B=0.05$, $P_B=0.10$, and $P_B=0.15$). Your feelings are that there is a 0.5 chance that $P_B=0.05$, a 0.3 chance that $P_B=0.10$, and a 0.2 chance that $P_B=0.15$. Before making a final decision on marketing the project, you are considering using a consumer panel to test the product. The available panel is made up of five individuals selected randomly from the market you will be entering. Each member will independently consider the product and either buy or not buy. Your estimates indicate that profitability of the product will be as follows:

| *Proportion of Buyers* | *Profitability* |
|---|---|
| $P_B=0.05$ | $\$-1{,}000{,}000$ |
| $P_B=0.10$ | 1,000,000 |
| $P_B=0.15$ | 2,000,000 |

The alternatives available are to market without a test, decide to abandon the product, or to use the consumer panel. What is the expected value of the information provided by the consumer panel?

## 14.6. Ramirez Farms (A)

Diego Ramirez, owner of Ramirez Farms, located in the San Joaquin Valley near the small town of Hidalgo, California, pondered a difficult decision late in August 1972. Diego raises Thompson Seedless grapes, and his problem concerned what to do with his "left-over" grapes.

The Thompson Seedless grape is a multiple-use variety that can be utilized for canning, fresh table consumption, wine production, or for sun-drying into raisins. The acreage of canning and table grapes is invariably contracted for at the beginning of the season, and then the remainder of the crop may be shifted late in the season to either wine grapes or to raisins. This is known as "going wet" or "going dry," respectively.

This decision is usually made in August, near the end of the season, and once it has been made, it is irrevocable. The weather conditions after the decision is made are critical, and they are difficult to predict. Raisins in Hidalgo are sun-dried completely in the open, and rain during this time can inflict heavy losses on a farmer who is going dry. If the farmer is going wet, the grapes remain on the vines for several weeks longer, and rain does not do as much damage.

Diego Ramirez has 100 acres of "uncommitted" grapes and wishes to consider three alternatives: (1) allocate all his acreage to raisins, (2) allocate all of the acreage to wine grapes, or (3) allocate approximately half of the acreage to each use. As for the weather, he feels that he can simplify his problem by assuming that the rainfall situation will either be none at all, light, or heavy. Diego has available the past 20 years of weather records, and has listed the rainfall information in the following table.

| *Year* | *Rainfall* | *Year* | *Rainfall* |
|---|---|---|---|
| 1952 | None | 1962 | None |
| 1953 | Light | 1963 | Heavy |
| 1954 | Heavy | 1964 | None |
| 1955 | Light | 1965 | None |
| 1956 | None | 1966 | Light |
| 1957 | Light | 1967 | Light |
| 1958 | None | 1968 | None |
| 1959 | Heavy | 1969 | None |
| 1960 | None | 1970 | Heavy |
| 1961 | None | 1971 | Light |

He has constructed the table below to show his expected dollar profit per acre under the various acreage alternatives and weather conditions.

| *Weather* | *Acreage Allocation* | | |
|---|---|---|---|
| *Conditions* | *Raisins* | *Wine* | *Both* |
| Dry | 60 | 40 | 50 |
| Light | 50 | 30 | 40 |
| Heavy | −20 | 20 | 10 |

Which alternative course of action would you suggest that Ramirez take?

**14.7. Ramirez Farms (B)**

Diego Ramirez, a grape grower in the San Joaquin Valley of California, faces an important decision regarding the allocation of his remaining grape crop [see Ramirez Farms (A)]. Every year many grape growers are faced with the same problem, and as a result, several weather-forecasting "enterprises" have come into existence.

As he is pondering his decision, a Joseph Barnes arrives at his door, introduces himself as an Elements Prognosticator, and makes the following claim:

"Mr. Ramirez," he began, "I know that the possibility of rain is a crucial aspect of your decision, and I think I can help you. I have devised an elaborate weather test, and although it's not perfect, it gives a pretty good indication of whether or not the period of time in question will have no rain, light rain, or heavy rain.

"Unfortunately, my test is not perfect. In the case of a dry end of season, the test will indicate dry 70% of the time. But it will also indicate that the rainfall will be light 20% of the time, and heavy 10% of the time. If the end of season has light rainfall, my test will correctly indicate that situation 50% of the time. Unfortunately, it will also indicate dry 20% of the time, and heavy 30% of the time. In the case of heavy rainfall, the test is accurate 60% of the time, but it indicates dry 20% of the time, and light 20% of the time.

"Now I'm the first to realize that my test isn't perfect, and just for that reason it's not excessively expensive. But let's not talk price right away. I'll leave you this brochure that summarizes what I've told you, and I'll come back tomorrow and we can talk prices."

This was really a lot for Ramirez to swallow. At first glance it looked like Barnes' information couldn't be worth anything, since it seemed to be so uncertain. As he began to analyze his new problem, there was another knock at his door.

"Hello, Mr. Ramirez," the stranger said. "My name is Phil Jonik. I just saw Joe Barnes driving away, and I'm pretty sure I know what he offered you. He's a well-meaning fellow, but he's pretty new to the Elements Prognostication business, and hasn't developed very good tests yet.

"I'm an old hand at this game, and although I haven't been in Hidalgo before, I am very well acquainted with the San Joaquin Valley and all of its weather pattern peculiarities. Let me come straight to the point. I can offer you a test that will tell you whether the weather during the time period in which you are interested will have no rain, light rain, or heavy rain. And my test is correct 100% of the time.

"Now, of course, my test costs more, but you can be 100% confident of its results. I'll leave you this brochure, and I'll return tomorrow so we can talk about what my test will cost you."

Diego Ramirez raised his eyes searchingly for a moment, then swiftly strode to the kitchen. He grabbed a box of raisins and a bottle of wine, and, moving quickly to his desk, he resumed analyzing his problem.

(a) What benefit, if any, would Ramirez receive if he uses Barnes' test? Jonik's test?
(b) How much should Ramirez be willing to pay for Barnes' test? Jonik's test?

# 15

# Monte Carlo Methods

Computational difficulties with models using continuous random variables led to the use of discrete approximations in Chapter 9. A sampling technique, called Monte Carlo, provides another method for making calculations with continuous distributions. The technique is also useful in analyzing systems with discrete random variables where arrivals, departures, and waiting times are important. Monte Carlo is the basis for widely used computer simulation programs.[1] As the name implies, the technique relies on randomly

**FIGURE 15.1**

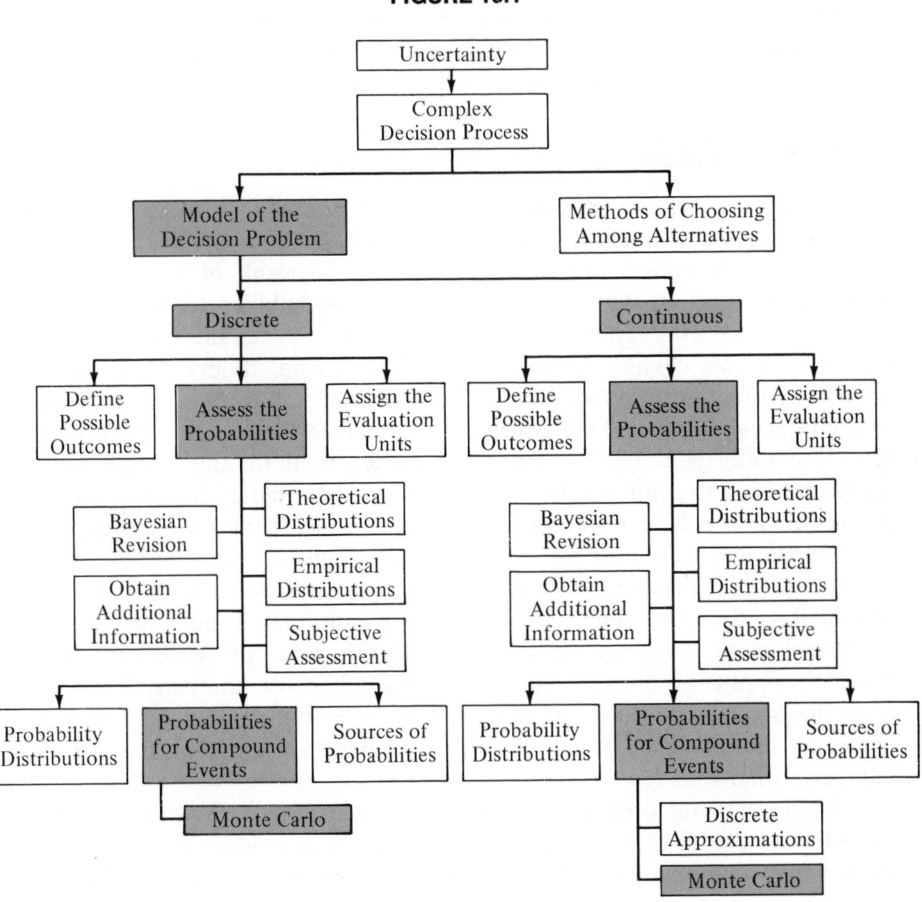


[1]For a detailed discussion of the specialized techniques which are available, see, for example, G. Gordon, *System Simulation* (Englewood Cliffs, N. J.: Prentice-Hall, 1969), or T. Naylor et al., *Computer Simulation Techniques* (New York: Wiley, 1966).

generated outcomes similar in nature, if not purpose, to those used in gambling casinos. This chapter presents the mechanics of the technique and discusses its applications in models under uncertainty. Figure 15.1 shows how this material relates to other topics.

## SAMPLING FROM DISCRETE PROBABILITY DISTRIBUTIONS

The Monte Carlo method is basically an experimental procedure. It can be used to develop *relative frequencies* for *compound events*. This is accomplished by sampling the component probability distributions using random numbers. Monte Carlo models are typically implemented on a computer. The sampling error can often be made quite small by using a large number of observations. The idea is a simple one. However, carrying out a complicated simulation analysis using Monte Carlo techniques can be very challenging. A basic input to any Monte Carlo sampling procedure is a set of *random numbers*.

### Random Numbers

A set of *random numbers* provides a sequence of digits in which the probability of any digit, or sequence of digits, is *equally likely*. For the digits 0 to 9, a set of random numbers can be thought of as the result of a sequence of independent trials in which each digit had a probability of 0.1 of being selected on each trial. The key point is that any number in the set of possible numbers has an equally likely chance of occurring at any place in the sequence. Random numbers can be obtained from tables (see Appendix G) or from specially designed computer programs called random-number generators. If a table is used, the specific sequence used in any Monte Carlo calculation will depend on the starting point in the table, and the rule for proceeding along the rows and columns of the table. Tables are designed so that any starting point and any consistent rule (such as, "go along rows from left to right until reaching the last column, then move down to the next row and begin in the first column") which is not conditional on outcomes (e.g., it is not legitimate to change directions whenever a series of "good" or "bad" outcomes is obtained) will yield a random sequence of numbers. If two or more digits are desired (e.g., 00 to 99 or 0000 to 9999), the tables are used in the same manner except that a single "number" consists of the desired number of digits.

When computer programs are used, at each "draw" a random number (sometimes called a *pseudo random number* since most random-number generators have some small nonrandomness) of a specified number of digits is supplied. In many cases the user must include a program for selecting the required number of digits.

### Monte Carlo Sampling—Coin Example

As a simple example, suppose that you and a friend end up on the proverbial desert island without so much as a coin to flip or die to toss to help pass the time. However, by a stroke of luck, you have a table of random numbers. As a first game you want to bet on heads or tails in a coin flip. The random-number table is used to *simulate* a coin flip by assigning one-half of the digits to the outcome *heads* (the probability of heads is 0.5) and the other half of the digits to the outcome *tails*. One such assignment is shown in Table 15.1.

**TABLE 15.1**

| *Outcome* | *Probability* | *Random Number Assignment* |
|---|---|---|
| Head | 0.5 | 0–4 |
| Tail | 0.5 | 5–9 |

Here the numbers chosen are the single digits 0 through 9. Since each digit is equally likely to appear on every trial, and heads and tails each have five digits assigned to them, heads and tails have an equal chance of occurring on each trial. If the sequence of one-digit random numbers from a table is 3, 6, 4, 6, 1, 8, 3, 4, 9, 4, the corresponding outcomes are $H$, $T$, $H$, $T$, $H$, $T$, $H$, $H$, $T$, $H$.

### Monte Carlo Sampling—Die Example

As a second game, suppose that you decide to simulate rolling a die. The probability of any number between 1 and 6 is one-sixth for a fair die. Therefore, all we need to do is assign one-sixth of the digits to each outcome. Because 10 (or 100, 1,000, etc., for that matter) cannot be divided into six equal groups, we just neglect some of the numbers. For instance, the assignment shown in Table 15.2 could be used.

**TABLE 15.2**

| *Outcome* | *Probability* | *Random Number Assignment* |
|---|---|---|
| 1 | $\frac{1}{6}$ | 1 |
| 2 | $\frac{1}{6}$ | 2 |
| 3 | $\frac{1}{6}$ | 3 |
| 4 | $\frac{1}{6}$ | 4 |
| 5 | $\frac{1}{6}$ | 5 |
| 6 | $\frac{1}{6}$ | 6 |

Two things are important to notice about this assignment. The first is that there is no significance, other than ease of identification, to assigning number 1 to outcome 1, and so on. We could have just as easily assigned number 9 to outcome 1. The second is that numbers 0, 7, 8, and 9 have not been assigned. We just disregard these numbers when they appear. Even though on each "trial" there is only a 0.1 probability of any digit, if we only consider trials in which one of the six specified numbers occurs, the conditional probability of any outcome given a random number in the range 1 to 6 is $\frac{1}{6}$. Moreover, the relative frequencies of the outcomes (neglecting numbers 0, 7, 8, and 9) should approach $\frac{1}{6}$ as the number of trials becomes large. For the sequence of random numbers 4, 4, 2, 6, 8, 7, 9, 3, 2, 9, 7, 7, 0, 9, 6, 1, 6, 7, 8, 4, 0, the simulated die outcomes are 4, 4, 2, 6, 3, 2, 6, 1, 6, 4.

At this point it should be clear that it is not the specific random numbers that are assigned to an outcome that is important, but the percentage of the numbers assigned to each outcome. For instance, the assignment in the die example could have just as well been that shown in Table 15.3. With this assignment the sequence of random numbers presented above must be reinterpreted as three-digit numbers instead of one digit numbers. Therefore, the sequence is rewritten: 442, 687, 932, 977, 096, 167, 840. The simulated die outcomes are 5, 1, 2.

**TABLE 15.3**

| *Outcome* | *Probability* | *Random Number Assignment* |
|---|---|---|
| 1 | $\frac{1}{6}$ | 000–099 |
| 2 | $\frac{1}{6}$ | 100–199 |
| 3 | $\frac{1}{6}$ | 200–299 |
| 4 | $\frac{1}{6}$ | 300–399 |
| 5 | $\frac{1}{6}$ | 400–499 |
| 6 | $\frac{1}{6}$ | 500–599 |

### Use of Cumulative Distributions

Rather than using tables for the assignment of random numbers to outcomes, a cumulative distribution can be used. The procedure can be illustrated by returning to the coin-flipping example. The cumulative distribution function for the random variable, $X$=number of tails (i.e., outcome head, $X=0$; outcome tail, $X=1$) is shown in Figure 15.2.

Assuming that we choose to use three-digit random numbers, we can assign 000 to 499 to outcome *heads* ($X=0$) and 500 to 999 to outcome *tails* ($X=1$). Figure 15.2 can be used directly. By interpreting the height of the jump at $X=0$ as 0 to 0.499 and the height at $X=1$ as 0.500 to 0.999, a three-digit random number can be used to enter Figure 15.2 on the vertical axis (see, for example, the random number 281 in Figure 15.2). A horizontal

**FIGURE 15.2**

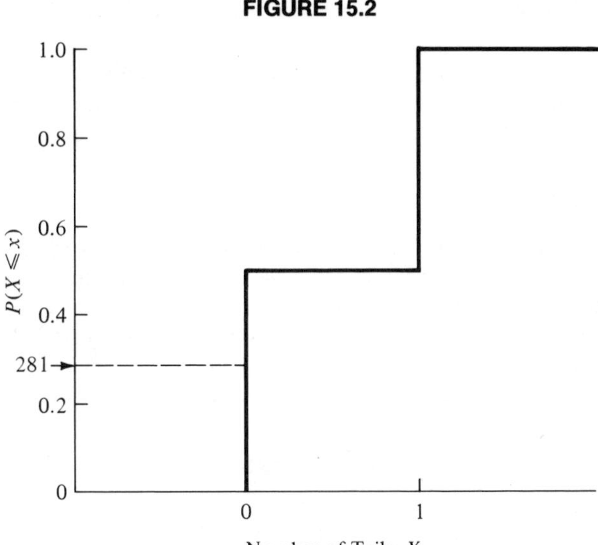


line will hit the jump associated with either $X=0$ or $X=1$ and therefore by drawing the horizontal line across until it hits a vertical jump, the outcome can be established. For complicated probability distributions, direct use of cumulative distributions simplifies the Monte Carlo sampling procedure.

### Summary of Monte Carlo Sampling Procedure

Sampling from a probability distribution using the Monte Carlo method involves the following steps:

1. Obtain cumulative distributions for the random variables that are components of the model.
2. Choose the number of digits to be included in the random number. The number of digits should be appropriate for the accuracy and scale of the cumulative distribution.
3. Obtain a sequence of random numbers from a table or computer program.
4. Enter the cumulative probability scale (vertical axis of the cumulative probability distribution) with each random number. Move horizontally across the graph to intersect the cumulative curve and record the coordinate of the horizontal axis for the intersection. This value is the sample outcome corresponding to the random number.

## ● CALCULATING A PROBABILITY DISTRIBUTION USING MONTE CARLO

This example illustrates how the Monte Carlo method can be used to calculate a distribution for a random variable that depends on three separate events.

### Example 15.1[2]

Assume that you are managing a project represented by the network flow diagram in Figure 15.3. The activities are characterized by the completion times shown in Table 15.4 and the completion times for each activity are independent of one another. In order to schedule this project with others, you want to obtain a probability distribution for the time needed to finish the project. Work can be done simultaneously on activities in the two separate branches of the flow diagram.

**FIGURE 15.3**

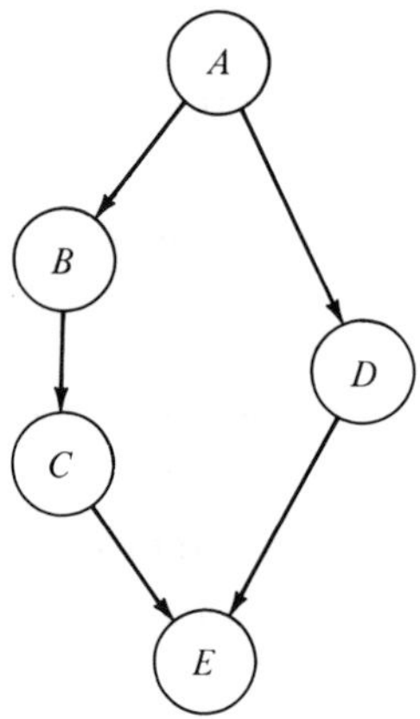


**TABLE 15.4**

| *Activity* | *Completion Time (Days)* | *Probability* |
|---|---|---|
| *A* | 5 | 1.0 |
| *B* | 2 | 0.4 |
| | 3 | 0.6 |
| *C* | 1 | 0.7 |
| | 2 | 0.3 |
| *D* | 3 | 0.5 |
| | 4 | 0.5 |
| *E* | 2 | 1.0 |

[2]This problem was done using a probability diagram in Example 8.8.

The random variable of interest is project completion time, which is a complicated function of the activity completion times. If we let $t_A$, $t_B$, $t_C$, $t_D$, and $t_E$ represent the completion times for the respective activities, and $T = \{\text{project completion time}\}$, we can write

$$T = t_A + t_E + \max[t_B + t_C, t_D]$$

Therefore, the outcome space of interest is the set of points that specifies all possible combinations of the activity completion times. The Monte Carlo technique samples these points in outcome space and allows us to build up a probability distribution for $T$ based on the sample outcomes. The cumulative distributions for the completion times of activities $B$, $C$, and $D$ are plotted as shown in Figures 15.4, 15.5, and 15.6. Each experiment involves simulating the actual completion of the project. The procedure for a few random numbers is shown in Table 15.5. If we continue sampling, we would obtain frequency data for the possible outcomes of $T$. For instance, we *might* obtain the frequencies shown in Table 15.6. The probability distribution for completion time based on these data is

$$P(T=10)=0.15,$$
$$P(T=11)=0.66,$$
$$P(T=12)=0.19.$$

By repeating the experiment a large number of times, the relative frequency data will come arbitrarily close to the actual probability distribution. For a small, discrete random variable case such as this, probability diagrams as described in Chapter 8 are clearly superior to the Monte Carlo method, since no sampling error is introduced and the computation involved is trivial.

**FIGURE 15.4**

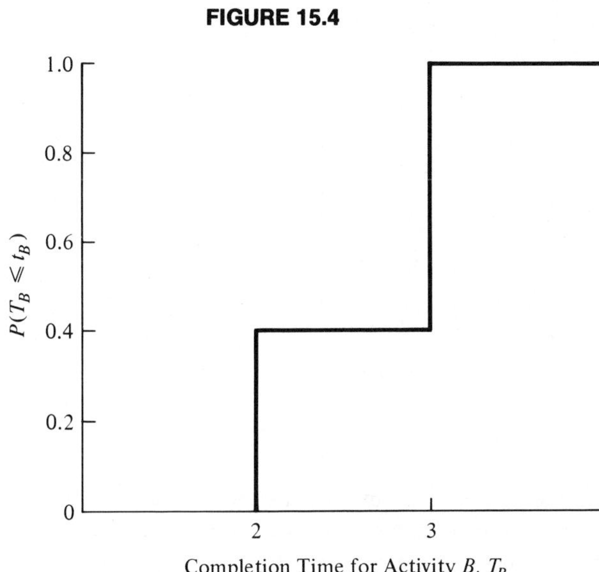

**FIGURE 15.5**

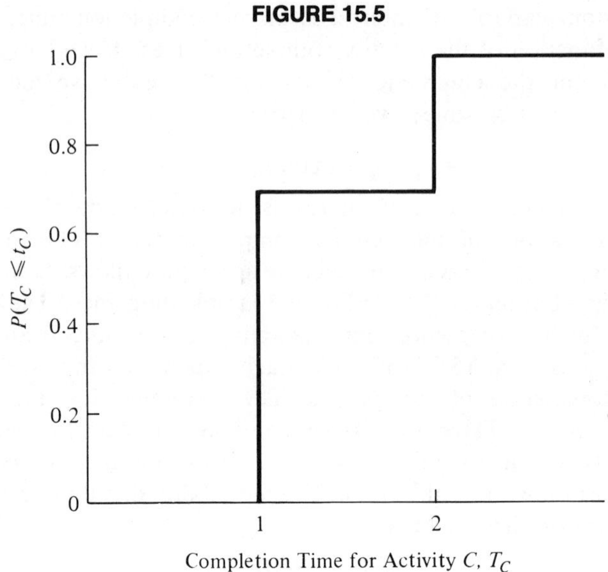


**FIGURE 15.6**

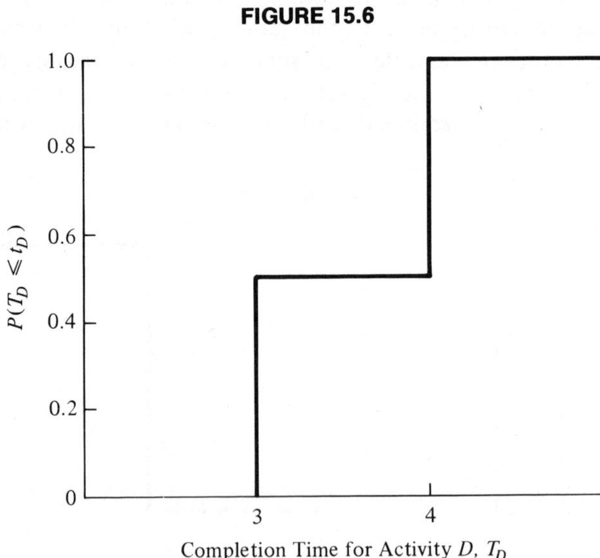


However, if the completion time distributions for each activity were continuous, or if the random variable were more complex, a sampling procedure like this may be the most efficient method.

**TABLE 15.5**

| *Random Numbers* | *Activity B Time* | *Activity C Time* | *Activity D Time* | *Project Completion Time* |
|---|---|---|---|---|
| 396, 536, 637 | $t_B = 2$ | $t_C = 1$ | $t_D = 4$ | $T = 11$ |
| 077, 458, 550 | $t_B = 2$ | $t_C = 1$ | $t_D = 4$ | $T = 11$ |
| 517, 413, 393 | $t_B = 3$ | $t_C = 1$ | $t_D = 3$ | $T = 11$ |
| 522, 305, 336 | $t_B = 3$ | $t_C = 1$ | $t_D = 3$ | $T = 11$ |
| 029, 549, 348 | $t_B = 2$ | $t_C = 1$ | $t_D = 3$ | $T = 10$ |
| etc. | | | | |

**TABLE 15.6**

| *Completion Time* | *Frequency* |
|---|---|
| $T = 10$ | 15 |
| $T = 11$ | 66 |
| $T = 12$ | 19 |
| Total | 100 |

## ●● EVENT-ORIENTED (QUEUING) PROBLEMS

There are some problems where Monte Carlo techniques provide the only viable approach. These problems often involve systems whose state at any particular time is contingent on one or more events occurring. Queuing problems provide a prime example. To demonstrate the problem and how Monte Carlo can be used, consider the following example problem.

**Example 15.2**

Assume that you are trying to evaluate alternative staffing policies for a service center. At the present you have one person manning the center. The arrivals at the center are given by the distribution shown in Figure 15.7 and the service time by the distribution shown in Figure 15.8. As part of your analysis you want to know the waiting-time distribution for customers.

The problem is complicated because the waiting time for a customer depends on how many others are waiting and how long they take to be serviced. For instance, during the time the first customer is being served, anywhere between 0 and 4 new customers can arrive. Each of these customers is served in 1, 2, 3, or 4 minutes, during which time new customers may or may not arrive, and so forth. The number of points in a payoff and assessment adequate outcome space is hard to think about even for this relatively simple problem. On the other hand, a Monte Carlo model can be

FIGURE 15.7

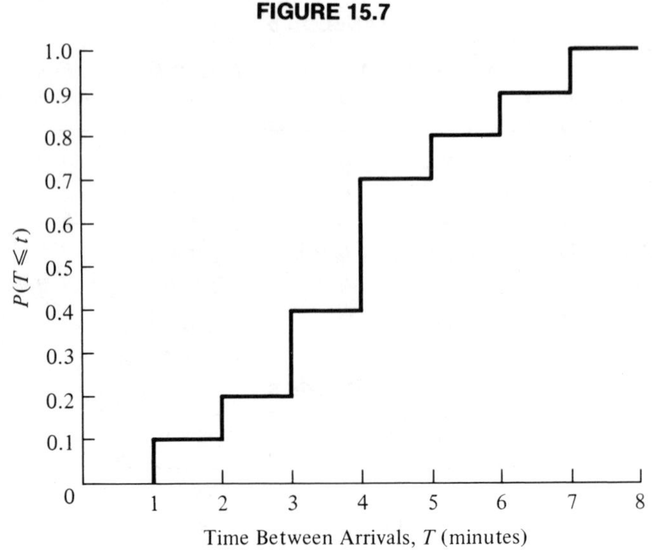


FIGURE 15.8

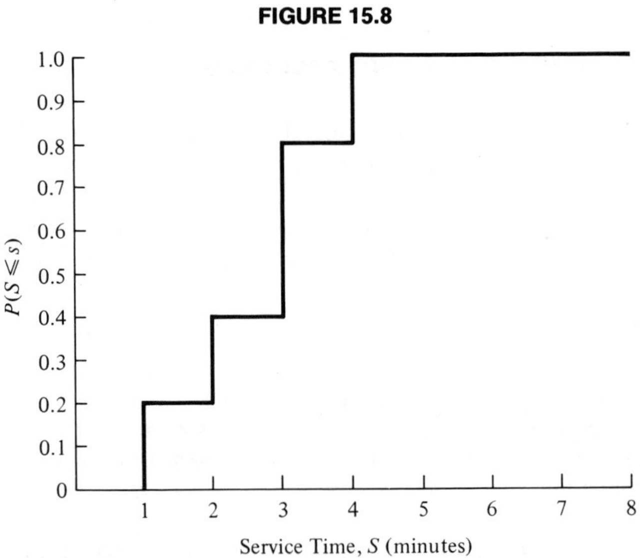


built easily. First, the arrivals are simulated by sampling from the interarrival time distribution (see Table 15.7). Each one of the arrivals is then tracked through the system and its waiting time recorded as shown in the last column of Table 15.7. By continuing this simulation (increasing the number of samples) we can build up the desired customer-waiting-time distribution. Table 15.7 traces customers through the system for the first 20 minutes.

**TABLE 15.7**

| Time (1) | Arrival: Random Number (2) | Arrival: Interarrival Time (3) | Arrival: Actual Time (4) | Service: Random Number (5) | Service: Service Time (6) | Service: Service Period (7) | Waiting Time (8) |
|---|---|---|---|---|---|---|---|
| 0 | 22 | 3 | | | | | |
| 1 | | | | | | | |
| 2 | | | | | | | |
| 3 | 17 | 2 | $T_1=3$ | 43 | 3 | ↑ | $W_1=0$ |
| 4 | | | | | | $S_1$ | |
| 5 | 42 | 4 | $T_2=5$ | 78 | 3 | ↓ | $W_2=1$ |
| 6 | | | | | | ↑ | |
| 7 | | | | | | $S_2$ | |
| 8 | | | | | | ↓ | |
| 9 | 73 | 5 | $T_3=9$ | 21 | 2 | $S_3$ | $W_3=0$ |
| 10 | | | | | | ↓ | |
| 11 | | | | | | | |
| 12 | | | | | | | |
| 13 | | | | | | | |
| 14 | 08 | 1 | $T_4=14$ | 91 | 4 | ↑ | $W_4=0$ |
| 15 | 35 | 3 | $T_5=15$ | 64 | 3 | | $W_5=3$ |
| 16 | | | | | | $S_4$ | |
| 17 | | | | | | ↓ | |
| 18 | 84 | 6 | $T_6=18$ | 14 | 1 | ↑ | $W_6=3$ |
| 19 | | | | | | $S_5$ | |
| 20 | | | | | | ↓ | |
| etc. | | | | | | | |

Column 1 is the clock time. Column 2 displays the random number used to determine the interarrival times. For instance, at time 0 the random number 22 was used with Figure 15.7 to determine that the first customer arrives at time 3. The result of the random draw is shown by the arrow to $T_1=3$. For each arrival, the service time is determined using Figure 15.8 by the random number shown in column 5. In the case of the first customer, the service time is 3 minutes. Since the system is empty, the service is started immediately on arrival at time equals 3 minutes as shown in column 7. At time equals 3 the first customer arrives and another random number is picked to determine the arrival time for customer 2. In this case the random number 17 used with Figure 15.7 indicates that the next arrival is 2 minutes after the first arrival. This is translated to the actual arrival time in column 4 and corresponds to a clock time of 5 minutes. The second customer also has a service time of 3 minutes (see column 6), but the service period must be delayed until customer 1 finishes at a clock time of 6 minutes. Therefore, customer 2 has a waiting time of 1 minute as shown in column 8.

## MONTE CARLO SAMPLING FROM CONTINUOUS PROBABILITY DISTRIBUTIONS

When the probability distributions are continuous, sampling can be done using cumulative distributions in the same way as with discrete distributions. Random numbers are used to enter the vertical axis of the cumulative distribution and the corresponding value of the random variable is read from the horizontal axis. To illustrate the procedure with continuous distributions, assume that you need to know the distribution of revenue (price × sales) for a product in which price and sales are the continuous random variables shown in Figure 15.9 and 15.10. If we use three-digit random numbers, the procedure (which usually would be undertaken on a computer) is illustrated in Table 15.8. The mechanics are the same as those illustrated for discrete

**FIGURE 15.9**

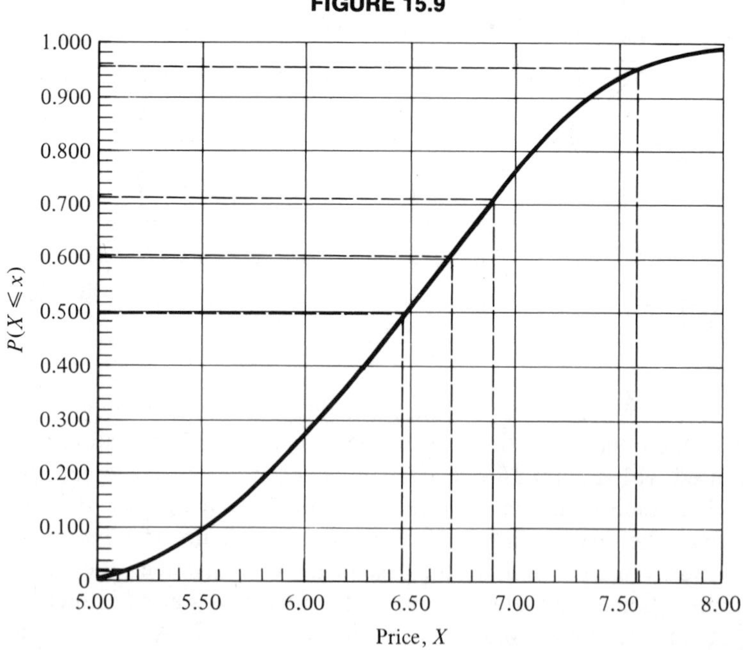

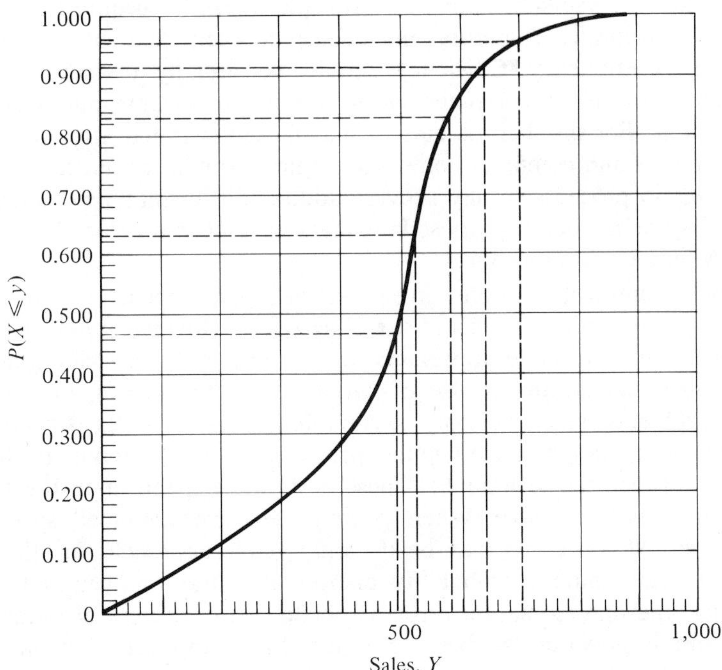


distributions. By continuing the procedure, the number of samples can be increased, and the techniques for plotting distributions from empirical data used to obtain a probability distribution for contribution (see Chapter 11).

**TABLE 15.8**

| *Random Number* | *Price* | *Random Number* | *Sales* | *Revenue = Price × Sales* |
|---|---|---|---|---|
| 714 | 6.90 | 630 | 520 | 3,588 |
| 498 | 6.46 | 917 | 640 | 4,134 |
| 958 | 7.59 | 829 | 580 | 4,402 |
| 023 | 5.15 | 956 | 700 | 3,605 |
| 603 | 6.70 | 469 | 490 | 3,283 |

## ●● COMPARISON OF DISCRETE APPROXIMATIONS AND MONTE CARLO

Mechanically the Monte Carlo procedure is straightforward and relatively easy to implement on a computer. The discrete approximation procedure for continuous random variables, discussed in Chapter 9, also can be implemented on a computer. In both cases when problems become complex, with many uncertain events, some of which are dependent, the computational burden can become substantial. In principle, either procedure can be made arbitrarily accurate. Therefore, the choice between them boils down to a question of efficiency. Efficiency should be broadly defined to include preparation of inputs, computer codes, computational time, and accuracy of the solution. For simple problems such as those illustrated here, the preparation of inputs and computer codes should be of similar complexity, although Monte Carlo procedures may provide additional flexibility. For more complicated systems, special-purpose languages have been developed to facilitate using Monte Carlo procedures.

The accuracy of solutions, given a set of inputs, depends on two types of errors: approximation errors and sampling errors. *Approximation errors* result from the use of discrete approximations to probability distributions. *Sampling errors* arise from the use of Monte Carlo techniques. For relatively simple problems, which will only be run a few times, the costs associated with preparation of inputs and computer programs probably dominate the comparison between the techniques. These costs will depend upon the software and individuals available. When complicated, event-oriented systems are considered, Monte Carlo may be the only viable approach. In other cases, with relatively smooth probability distributions and well-behaved random variables, the approximation error associated with discrete diagramming is small and it provides the best approach. For complicated problems with substantial dependencies, technical details beyond the scope of this discussion are important and expert help may be required.

## SUMMARY

Monte Carlo provides an alternative computational procedure for probability models. It is based on sampling from the component probability distributions using random numbers. The data from the samples are used to assess probability distributions for the random variable of interest using relative frequencies. For some systems such as those that are contingent on the timing of events (e.g., arrivals in a queuing system), it may provide the only viable method for computing desired probabilities. For models based on continuous probability distributions, Monte Carlo provides an alternative to the use of discrete approximations. The choice between the two computational methods is influenced by the size of the approximation and sampling errors, as well as the cost of building the models.

The sampling procedure consists of four steps:

1. Obtain cumulative distributions for random variables that are components of the model.
2. Choose the number of digits to be included in the random number.
3. Obtain a sequence of random numbers.
4. Use the random numbers to sample from the cumulative distributions.

## ASSIGNMENT MATERIAL

**15.1.** Describe how to use the Monte Carlo procedure to sample from the following probability distribution:

| $X$ | $P(X)$ |
|---|---|
| 5 | 0.25 |
| 10 | 0.11 |
| 15 | 0.64 |

**15.2.** As part of a study, you develop the continuous probability distribution shown in Figure 15.11.

**FIGURE 15.11**

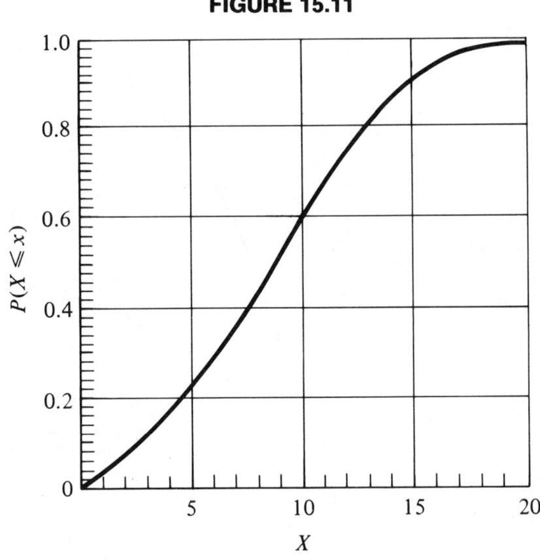


(a) Calculate the expected value of $X$ by converting the distribution into a discrete distribution with five outcomes.

(b) Obtain 10 samples using the Monte Carlo method. Describe your method in detail.

(c) What is your estimate of the expected value of $X$ based on the Monte Carlo sample?

(d) Discuss the errors associated with each of the methods above.

**15.3.** A manager is attempting to estimate the total cost of operating the plant next month. There are two major sources of uncertainty: labor rates and demand for the product. The labor contract is now being negotiated, and the manager assesses the following probabilities for the labor cost per hour:

| *Rate* | *Probability* |
|---|---|
| \$5.00/hour | 0.40 |
| 5.50/hour | 0.30 |
| 6.00/hour | 0.30 |

These rates apply to regular time. There are 1,000 regular time hours available next month. Any labor used above 1,000 hours will be paid at time-and-a-half (i.e., 150% of regular rate).

The demand for the product is also unknown and independent of the labor cost per hour. The manager assesses the cumulative distribution for demand shown in Figure 15.12. The plant will produce enough to satisfy demand, working overtime if necessary. It takes exactly 1 labor hour to produce each unit of product. Describe how to use the Monte Carlo method to obtain a probability distribution for total labor costs. Demonstrate your procedure by making five trials.

**FIGURE 15.12**

**Cumulative Probability Distribution for Demand**

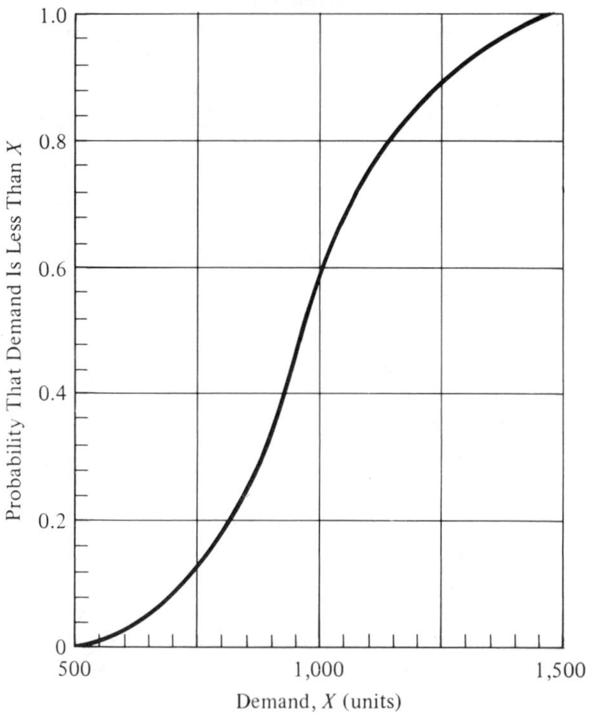


**15.4.** A chemicals firm must decide whether to try to develop a new process that its research division has suggested. There are two uncertainties involved—the production cost is random, and the size of the market for the product is random. The decision tree facing the firm is shown in Figure 15.13. The firm's evaluation units are net profit and the accounting model is as follows:

**FIGURE 15.13**

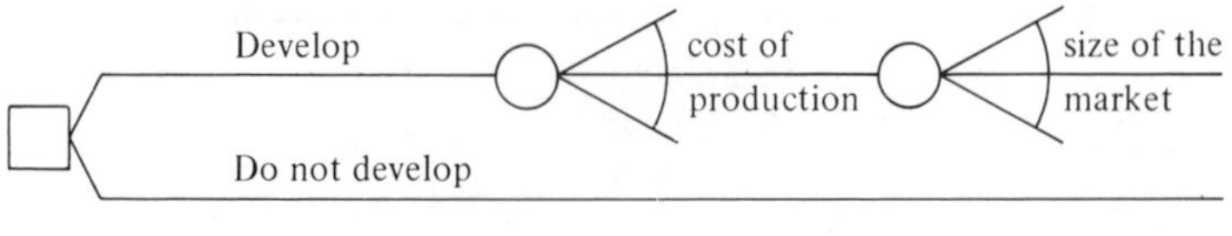

Develop

cost of production

size of the market

Do not develop

1. If they choose not to develop, net profit is \$0.
2. If they develop, $C$ is the cost of production and $X$ is the size of the market, their net profit is $\$(4-C)\cdot X-20{,}000$.

The firm assesses probabilities for production costs and market size as shown in Figures 15.14 and 15.15.

The firm decides to determine the probability distribution for net profit associated with the "develop" decision. The method they chose to use is Monte Carlo. Explain concisely how the Monte Carlo method can be used to determine the desired probability distribution. As part of this explanation, demonstrate how the process works using two-digit random numbers and five trials.

**FIGURE 15.14**

**Distribution Function of the Cost of Production**

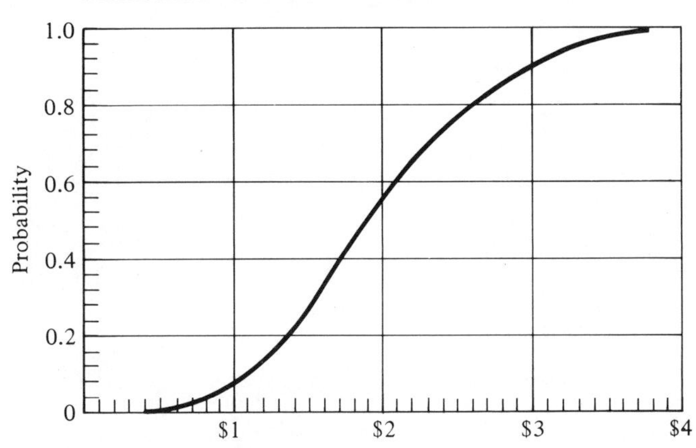


**FIGURE 15.15**

**Distribution Function of the Size of the Markets**

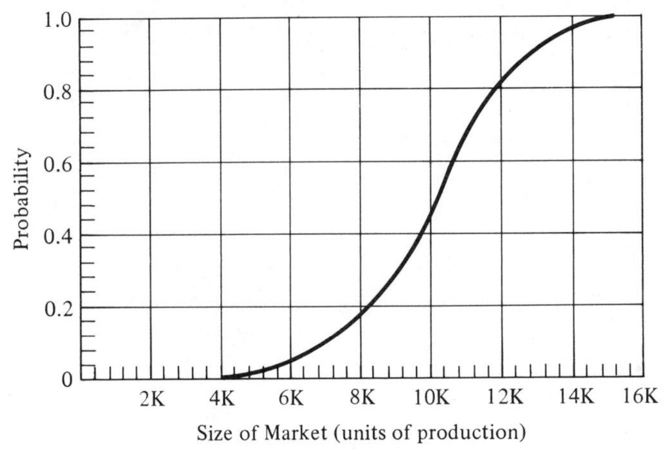

# PART 3

# Choices and Preferences

# 16

# Attitudes Toward Risk and the Choice Process

Chapter 5 presented the basic options for choosing under uncertainty. Direct choice, certainty equivalents, and expected values were discussed. The decomposition of certainty equivalent decisions using preferences and probabilities was discussed in Chapter 6. The choice process that is most useful depends on both the problem and the individual. Basic attitudes toward risk, such as risk aversion, risk neutrality, and risk-seeking attitudes, have important implications for the choice process. Even within the class of risk-averse individuals, characteristics such as constant risk aversion can affect the process used to make a choice. In this chapter we briefly review the options on choosing among alternatives, discuss attitudes toward risk and their implications for the choice process, and present some empirical evidence. Figure 16.1 shows how the material fits into the overall scheme.

**FIGURE 16.1**

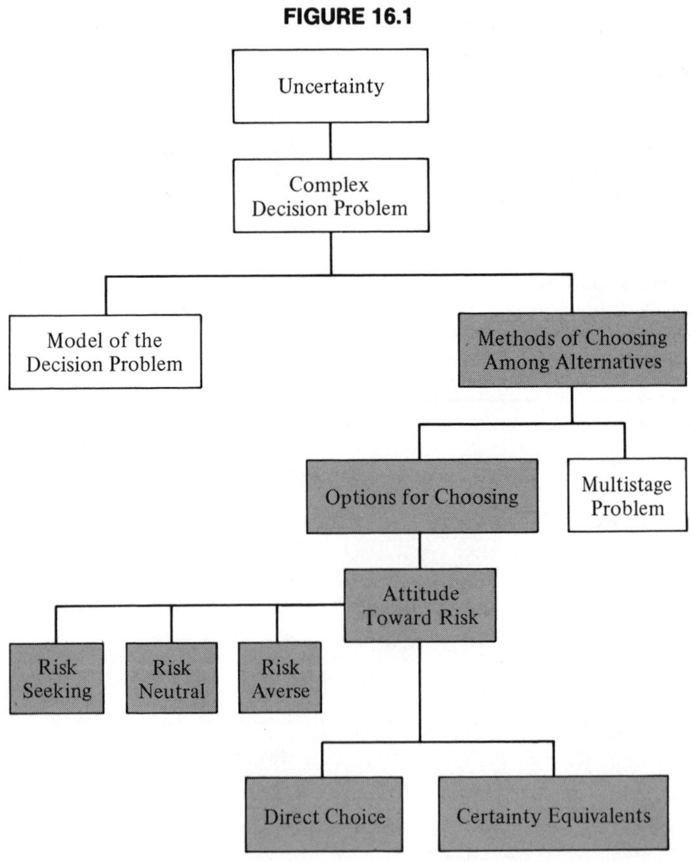

## REVIEW OF OPTIONS FOR CHOOSING

### Direct Choice

Direct choice does not rely on any decomposition in the choice process. The output from the model is used to choose among the alternatives. Outcome dominance and probabilistic dominance are used when they are applicable. The probability distributions for the random variables associated with each alternative are compared to evaluate the risk. In some cases summary measures—means, standard deviations, and so on—for these distributions are used in the comparison. The decision maker must process this information to understand the uncertainty and evaluate the risk. The result is a direct decision among the alternatives.

### Certainty Equivalents

Certainty equivalents establish an equivalence between uncertain events and a certain value. Once the equivalence is obtained, the choice is easy, since the uncertainty has been removed. The process for determining a certainty equivalent can be decomposed. A preference curve is assessed to encode a decision maker's attitude toward risk. This curve is used with the probability distributions for the random variables to *calculate* a certainty equivalent.

Expected monetary values also are used to make choices under some conditions. We discuss these conditions and other special attitudes toward risk below.

## RISK AVERSION

An individual with a certainty equivalent for an uncertain event that is less than the expected value of the payoff (or evaluation units) is called *risk-averse*. This attitude toward risk is prevalent among decision makers when the "stakes" are high. The difference between the expected payoff value and the certainty equivalent is called the *risk premium*.

**Risk Premium**

***Definition:* *Risk Premium*** *= Expected Payoff Value − Certainty Equivalent*

Risk-averse individuals have a positive risk premium. The size of the risk premium depends upon (1) the degree of risk aversion, (2) the values taken on by the random variable of interest, and (3) the probability distribution for the

**FIGURE 16.2**

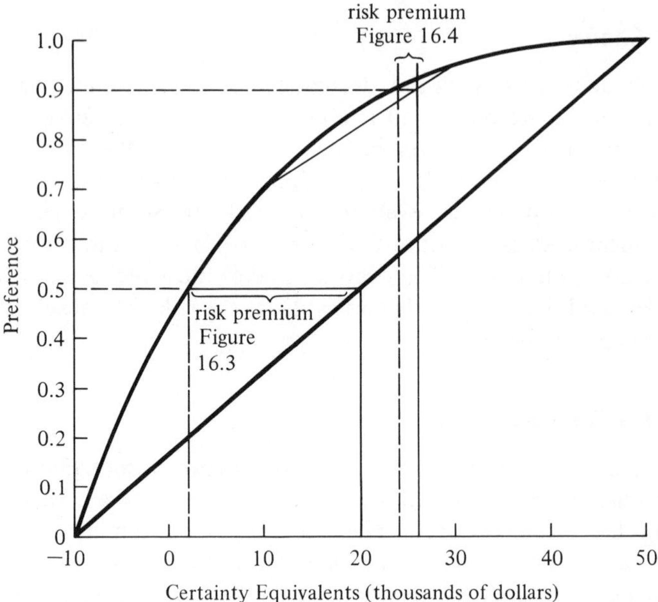


random variable of interest. Knowing that a positive risk premium exists restricts the shape of the preference curve. To understand the implications of risk aversion on the shape of the preference curve, consider the curve shown in Figure 16.2. For a gamble with a 0.5 chance at \$50,000 and a 0.5 chance at \$ − 10,000, the certainty equivalent is calculated as shown in Figure 16.3.

The certainty equivalent of \$2,000 is displayed on Figure 16.2 by the dashed line. The straight line connecting the end points of the curve is just the risk-neutral preference curve. For this gamble the expected value is (0.5)(\$50,000) + (0.5)(\$ − 10,000) = \$20,000. Therefore, the risk premium is \$20,000 − \$2,000 = \$18,000. It is shown on Figure 16.2 by the horizontal distance between the risk-neutral curve and the preference curve. As another example, consider the gamble shown in Figure 16.4.

The certainty equivalent is \$24,000 (see Figure 16.2). The expected monetary value is (0.8)(\$30,000) + (0.2)(\$10,000) = \$26,000, resulting in a risk premium of \$26,000 − \$24,000 = \$2,000. This risk premium is shown on Fig-

**FIGURE 16.3**

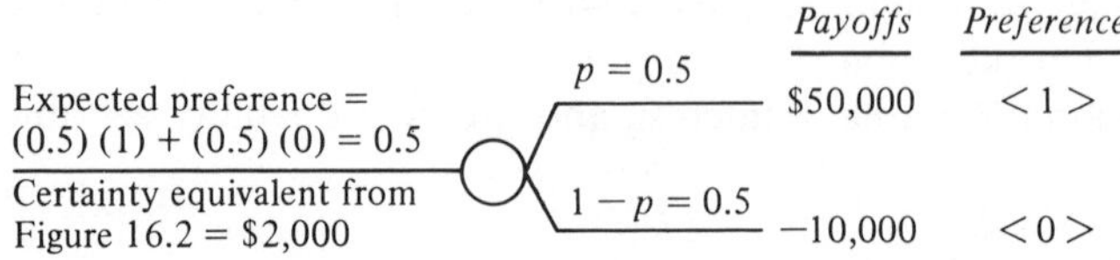

**FIGURE 16.4**

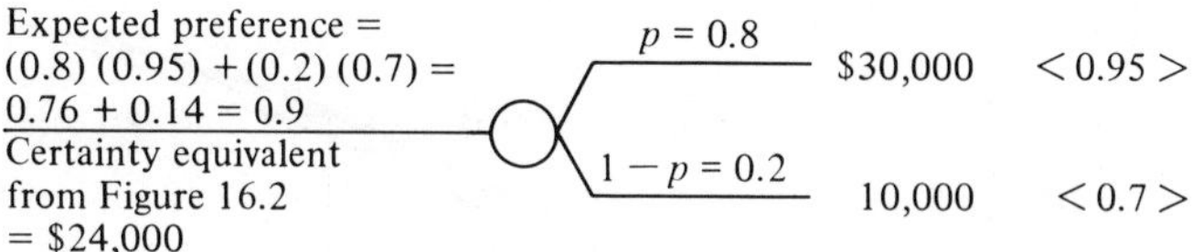


ure 16.2 as the horizontal distance between the straight line connecting the points corresponding to $10,000 and $30,000 on the preference curve and the preference curve itself. Since a risk-averse individual has a positive risk premium, the preference curve will always lie to the left or *above* the risk-neutral curve.[1] This means that the curve must be relatively smooth and never "flatten out" to the point that it is straight.

## ●● Decreasing Risk Aversion

One special case of risk aversion is decreasing risk aversion. This condition implies that the degree of risk aversion decreases as the payoffs increase. To be more precise, the risk premium decreases for gambles that are identical except for adding the same constant to each payoff. For instance, consider the series of gambles specified by Figure 16.5. They are the same except that in moving from (1) to (2), (2) to (3), and (3) to (4), $10,000 has been added to both payoffs. The range between payoffs, and the probabilities for each outcome, are the same. These gambles, and examples of certainty equivalents and risk premiums consistent with decreasing risk aversion, are summarized in Table 16.1 and displayed in Figure 16.6.

**FIGURE 16.5**

| | (1) | (2) | (3) | (4) |
|---|---|---|---|---|
| $p = 0.5$ | $20,000 | $30,000 | $40,000 | $50,000 |
| $1 - p = 0.5$ | $−10,000 | $0 | $10,000 | $20,000 |

**TABLE 16.1**

| 50–50 *Gamble* | *Expected Monetary Value* | *Certainty Equivalent* | *Risk Premium* |
|---|---|---|---|
| $ − 10,000, $20,000 | $ 5,000 | $ −2,000 | $7,000 |
| $0, $30,000 | 15,000 | 10,500 | 4,500 |
| $10,000, $40,000 | 25,000 | 21,000 | 4,000 |
| $20,000, $50,000 | 35,000 | 32,000 | 3,000 |

[1]The technical term for this condition is that the preference curve is *concave*.

FIGURE 16.6

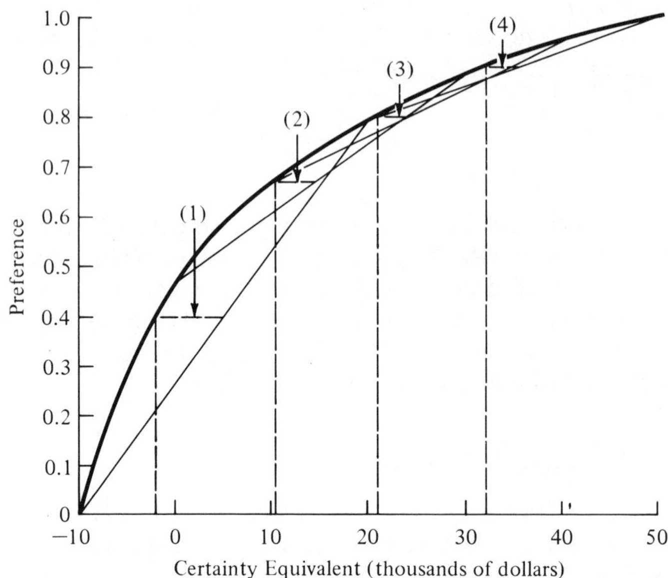


The rationale for such an attitude toward risk is that, as the minimum payoff increases, an individual becomes less risk averse. If an individual specifies that he desires to be decreasingly risk averse, the shape of the preference curves is severely restricted. In fact, ensuring that a curve is consistent with such a condition is not a trivial matter. Computer programs have been written to help in the assessment of preference curves with these and other conditions.

### Constant Risk Aversion

Another special case is constant risk aversion. This condition implies that the risk premium is the same for gambles that are identical except for adding the same constant to each payoff. One case of constant risk aversion is a linear preference function. In this case the risk premium is constant at zero. The other possibility is a preference function with an exponential form.

**Constant Risk Aversion**

***Definition:*** ***Constant risk aversion*** *corresponds to an exponential preference function of the form*

$$U(X) = a - be^{-\lambda X}$$

*where* $e = 2.718$, $\lambda$ *is a constant that determines the degree of risk aversion, and* $a$ *and* $b$ *are scaling constants. These scaling constants can be used to make the preference function lie between 0 and 1 over the range of interest.*

Constant risk aversion means that the risk premium depends on the difference between the outcomes but not the absolute values of the outcomes. Therefore, if an individual were faced with the gambles indicated in Figure 16.7, the risk premium for all of them would be identical. If the certainty equivalent for the first gamble is $4,000, the risk premium is (0.5)($10,000) +

**FIGURE 16.7**

| | (1) | (2) | (3) |
|---|---|---|---|
| $p = 0.5$ | $10,000 | $12,000 | $15,000 |
| $1 - p = 0.5$ | $0 | $ 2,000 | $ 5,000 |

(0.5)(0) − $4,000 = $5,000 − $4,000 = $1,000. Constant risk aversion implies that the certainty equivalent for gambles 2 and 3 are $6,000 and $9,000, respectively.

Methods of assessing a preference function with constant risk aversion are discussed in Chapter 17.[2]

## CHOICES UNDER RISK AVERSION

Knowledge that a decision maker is risk averse means that the certainty equivalent is less than the expected payoff value. This is usually not enough information to choose between alternatives.[3] Direct choice and certainty equivalents can be used to make decisions.

The following problem does *not* present new information on these methods but serves as an example showing both methods. It provides a review of these procedures, complete strategies, and the use of discrete approximations. If you do not need to review these procedures, skip this example.

### Example 16.1

Consider the problem in Figure 16.8. It describes a pricing choice on a product that will be phased out after one more year. Assume that the probability of the competition following a price increase is 0.4. The probability distribution for market share is assessed to be independent of the total market but dependent on the relative prices. If the price for brand $X$ is not changed or the competition follows a price increase, the probability distribution assessed for market share is given by Figure 16.9(a) and its

[2]For computer programming, see M. R. Middleton, "Computer Programs for Elementary Decision Analysis," Technical Report No. 25, Graduate School of Business, Stanford University, May 1973.

[3]The exception is when one alternative has no uncertainty and a payoff greater than or equal to the expected value of a second alternative. In this case, knowledge of risk aversion is sufficient to eliminate the second alternative.

**FIGURE 16.8**

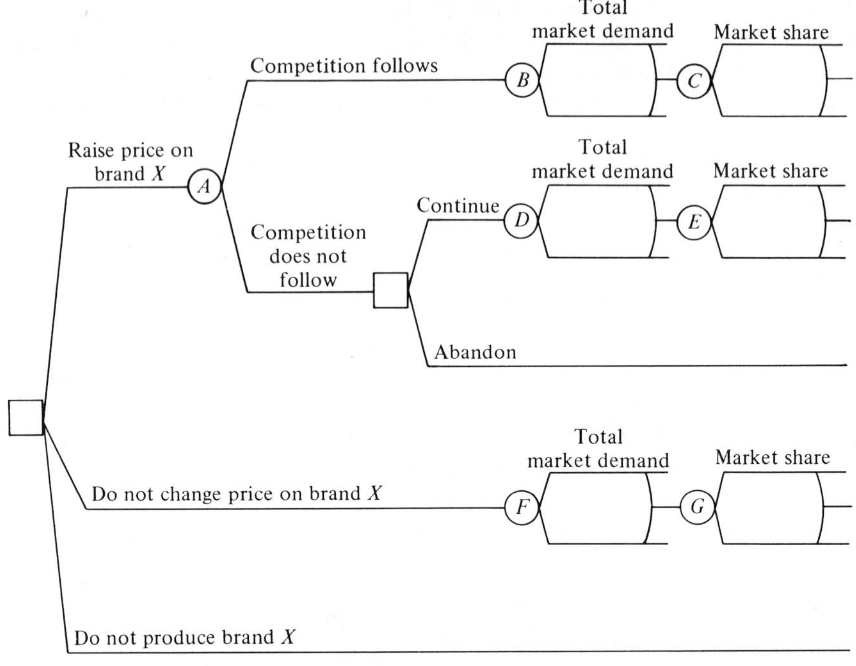

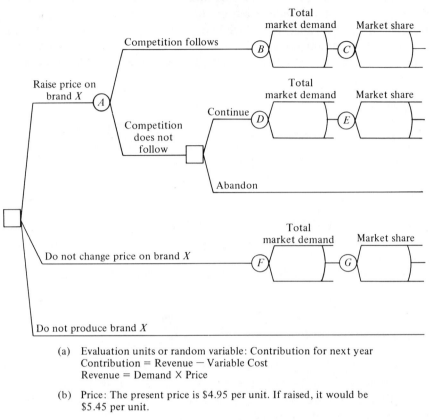

(a) Evaluation units or random variable: Contribution for next year
Contribution = Revenue − Variable Cost
Revenue = Demand × Price

(b) Price: The present price is \$4.95 per unit. If raised, it would be \$5.45 per unit.

(c) Variable cost: If the price is not changed, variable production costs are \$3.95 per unit + marketing costs of \$270,000. If the price is changed, variable production costs are \$3.95 per unit + marketing costs of \$350,000.

discrete approximation by Figure 16.9(b). If the price on brand *X* is raised and the competition does not follow, the probability distribution assessed for market share is given in Figure 16.9(c) and its discrete approximation in Figure 16.9(d). The total market demand is dependent on the lowest market price. The assessed distributions are shown in Figure 16.10.

### • Using Direct Choice with Complete Strategies

The decision maker can identify four complete strategies (see Chapter 5 for discussion of complete strategies).

Strategy 1. Raise price on brand *X* and if competition does not follow, continue.

**FIGURE 16.9**

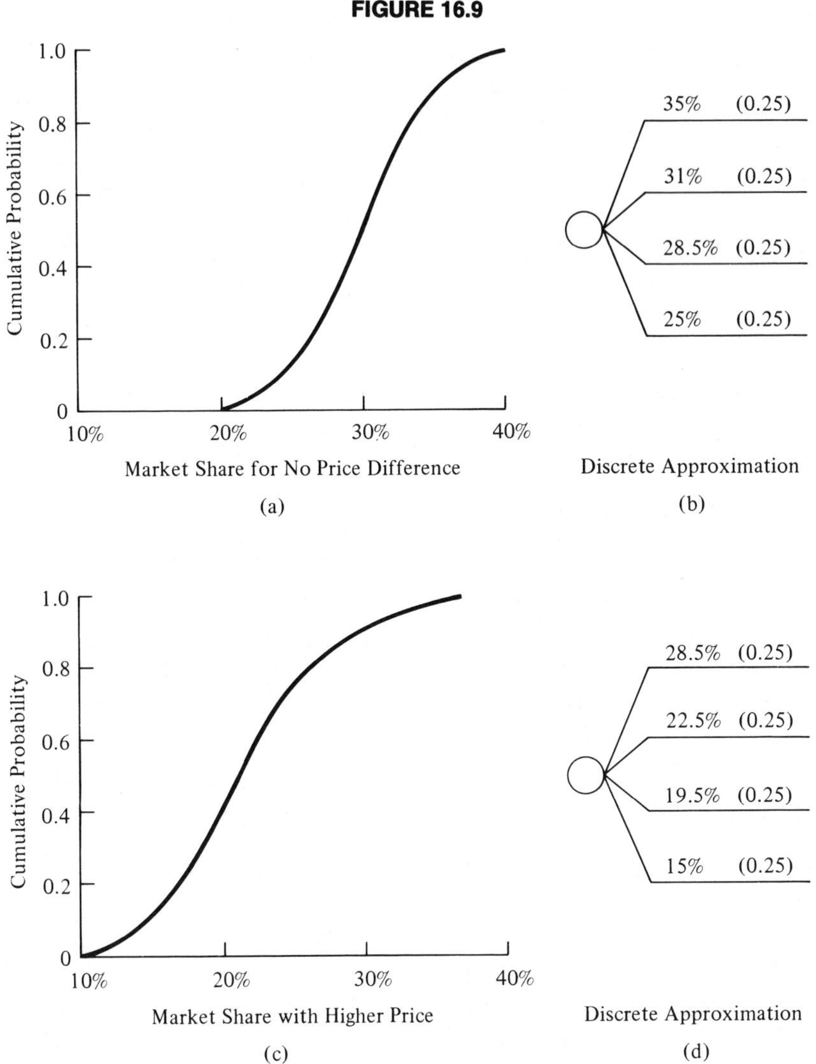


Strategy 2. Raise price on brand $X$ and if competition does not follow, abandon this year with zero contribution.
Strategy 3. Do not change price on brand $X$.
Strategy 4. Do not produce brand $X$.

Diagrams for the uncertain events associated with strategies 1, 2, and 3 are shown in Figures 16.11, 16.12, and 16.13.

The smoothed probability distribution for each of the strategies is plotted in Figure 16.14. (These were obtained by plotting the discrete cumulative

FIGURE 16.10

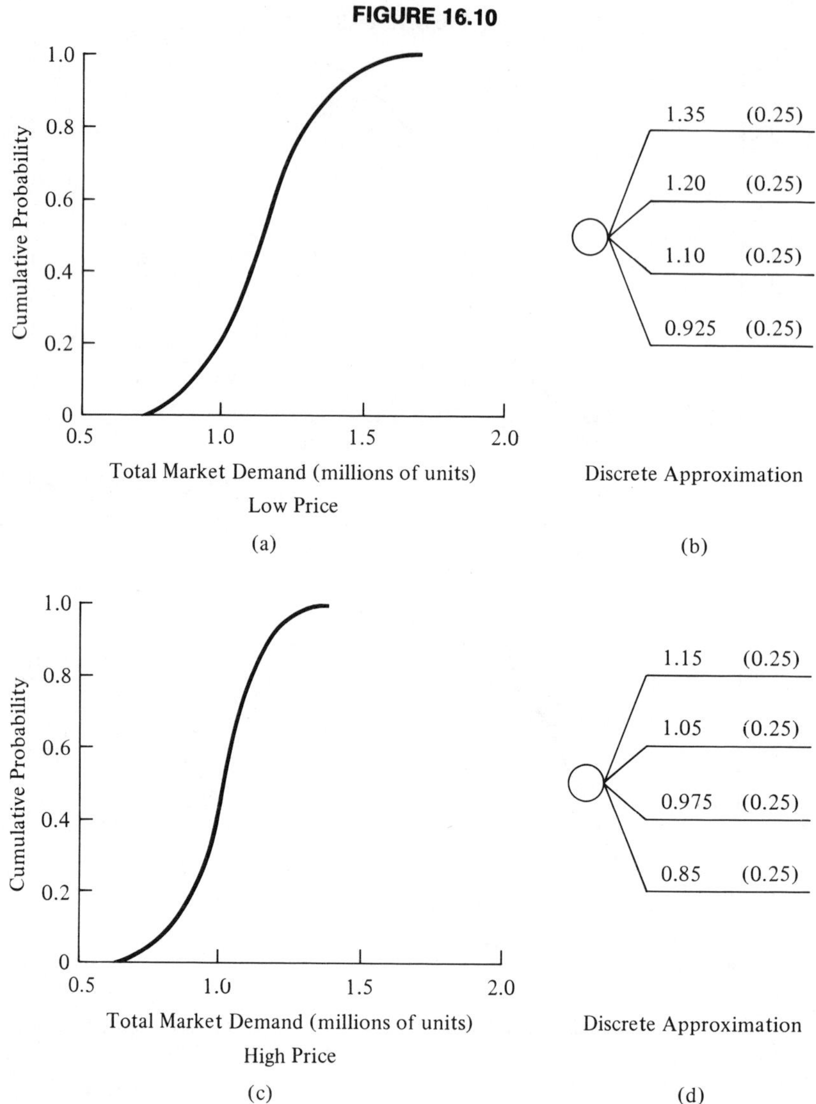


distributions calculated from each of the probability diagrams and then "smoothing" them.)

If direct choice is used, the decision maker uses these probability distributions on contribution to determine the most preferred alternative. Although not shown, strategy 4 will provide a guaranteed contribution of zero. Summary measures could also be used to compare the alternatives as shown in Table 16.2.

**FIGURE 16.11**

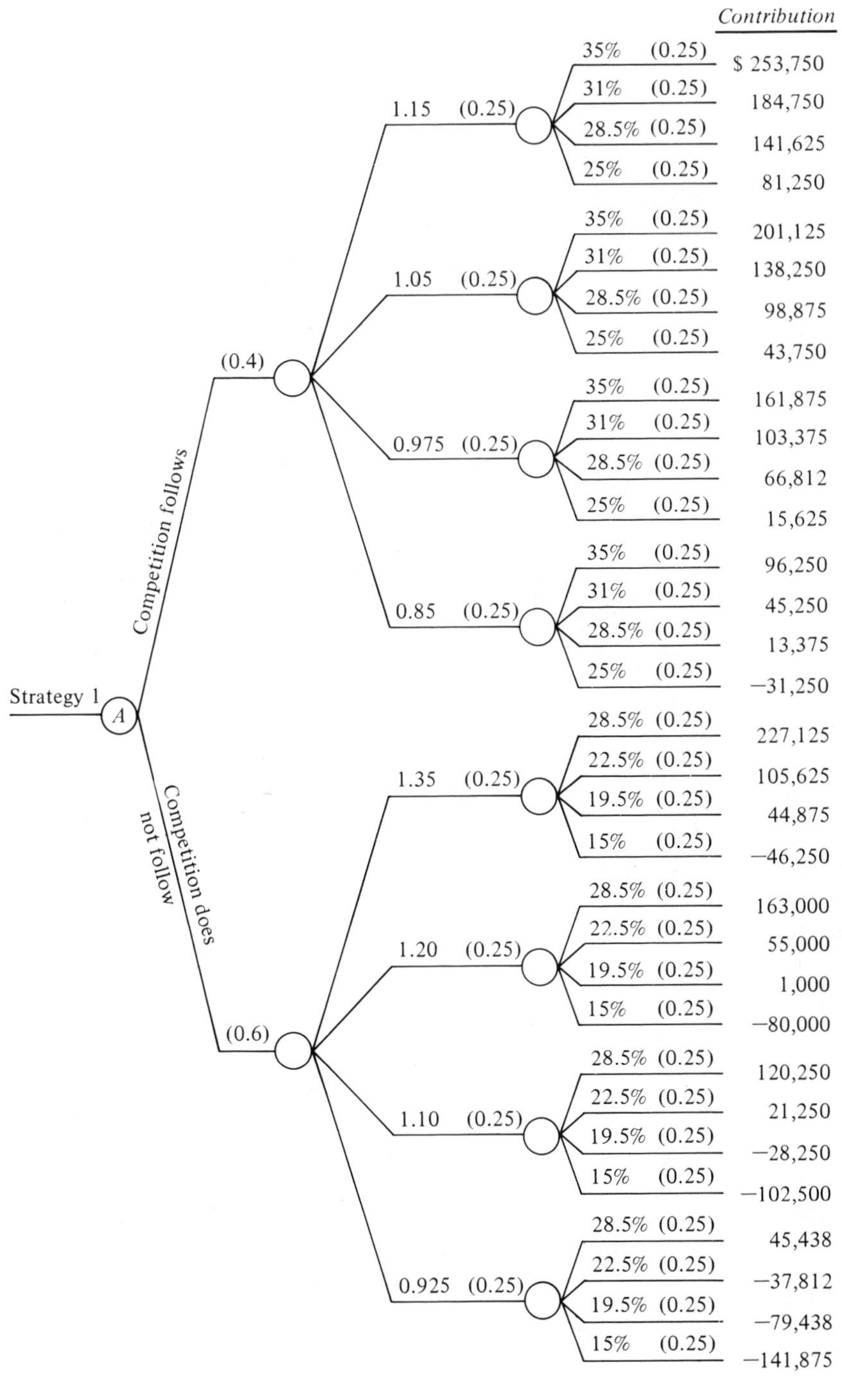

Contribution
Strategy 1
A
Competition follows
(0.4)
1.15 (0.25)
35% (0.25)
31% (0.25)
28.5% (0.25)
25% (0.25)
$ 253,750
184,750
141,625
81,250
1.05 (0.25)
35% (0.25)
31% (0.25)
28.5% (0.25)
25% (0.25)
201,125
138,250
98,875
43,750
0.975 (0.25)
35% (0.25)
31% (0.25)
28.5% (0.25)
25% (0.25)
161,875
103,375
66,812
15,625
0.85 (0.25)
35% (0.25)
31% (0.25)
28.5% (0.25)
25% (0.25)
96,250
45,250
13,375
−31,250
Competition does not follow
(0.6)
1.35 (0.25)
28.5% (0.25)
22.5% (0.25)
19.5% (0.25)
15% (0.25)
227,125
105,625
44,875
−46,250
1.20 (0.25)
28.5% (0.25)
22.5% (0.25)
19.5% (0.25)
15% (0.25)
163,000
55,000
1,000
−80,000
1.10 (0.25)
28.5% (0.25)
22.5% (0.25)
19.5% (0.25)
15% (0.25)
120,250
21,250
−28,250
−102,500
0.925 (0.25)
28.5% (0.25)
22.5% (0.25)
19.5% (0.25)
15% (0.25)
45,438
−37,812
−79,438
−141,875

**FIGURE 16.12**

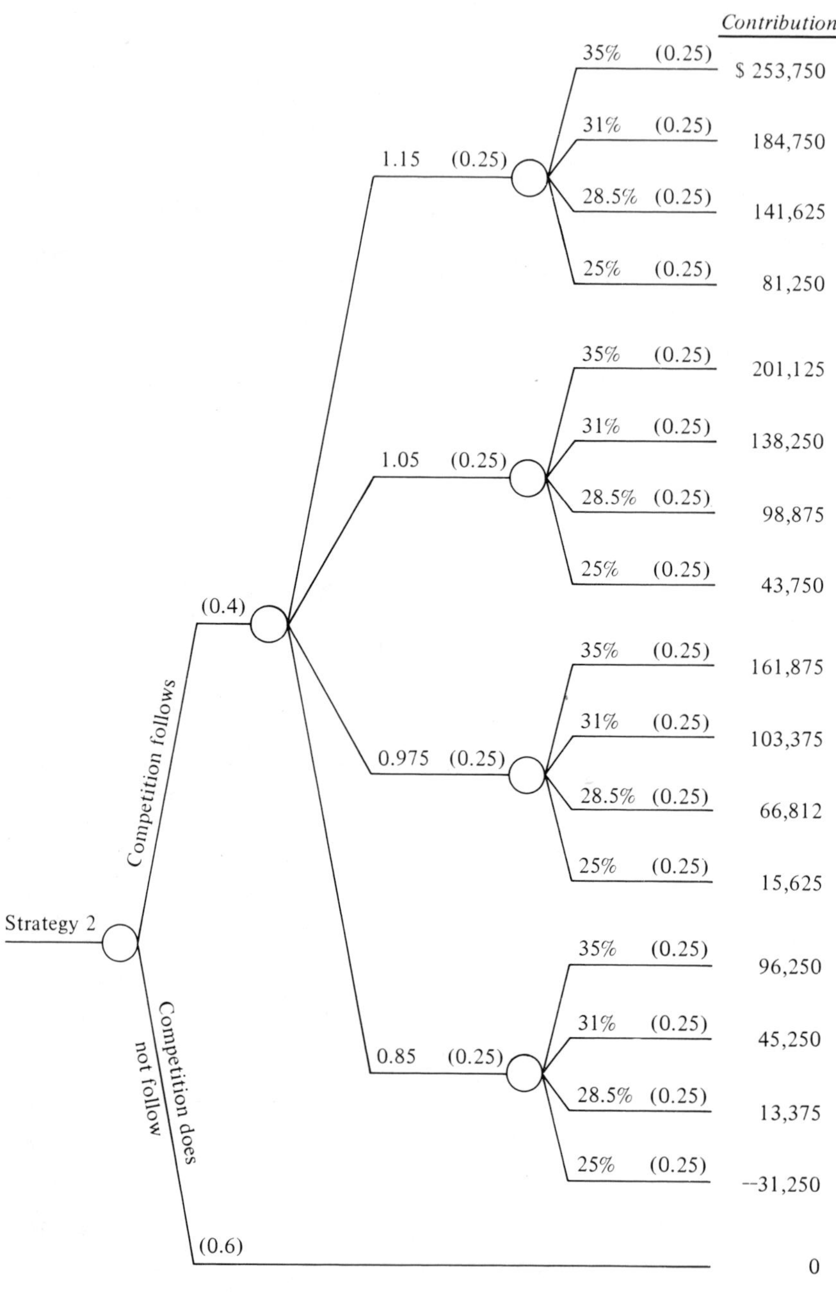

Contribution
Strategy 2
Competition follows
(0.4)
Competition does not follow
(0.6)
1.15 (0.25)
35% (0.25)
$ 253,750
31% (0.25)
184,750
28.5% (0.25)
141,625
25% (0.25)
81,250
1.05 (0.25)
35% (0.25)
201,125
31% (0.25)
138,250
28.5% (0.25)
98,875
25% (0.25)
43,750
0.975 (0.25)
35% (0.25)
161,875
31% (0.25)
103,375
28.5% (0.25)
66,812
25% (0.25)
15,625
0.85 (0.25)
35% (0.25)
96,250
31% (0.25)
45,250
28.5% (0.25)
13,375
25% (0.25)
--31,250
0

**FIGURE 16.13**

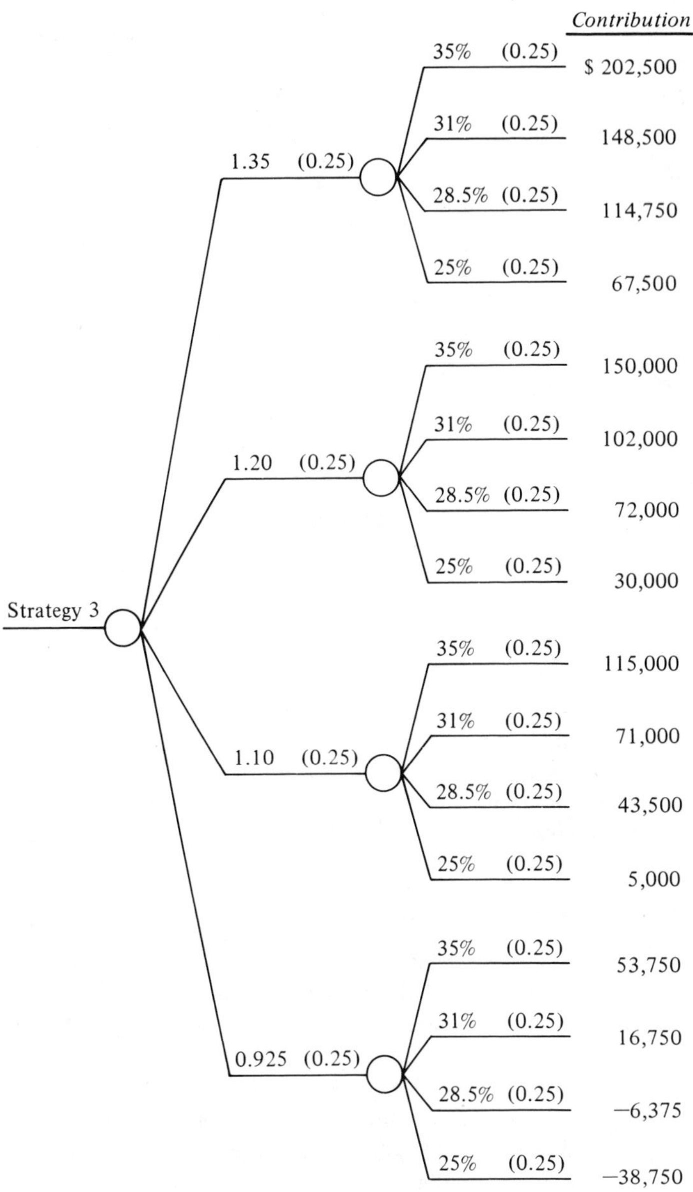

Contribution
Strategy 3
1.35 (0.25)
35% (0.25)
$ 202,500
31% (0.25)
148,500
28.5% (0.25)
114,750
25% (0.25)
67,500
1.20 (0.25)
35% (0.25)
150,000
31% (0.25)
102,000
28.5% (0.25)
72,000
25% (0.25)
30,000
1.10 (0.25)
35% (0.25)
115,000
31% (0.25)
71,000
28.5% (0.25)
43,500
25% (0.25)
5,000
0.925 (0.25)
35% (0.25)
53,750
31% (0.25)
16,750
28.5% (0.25)
−6,375
25% (0.25)
−38,750

FIGURE 16.14

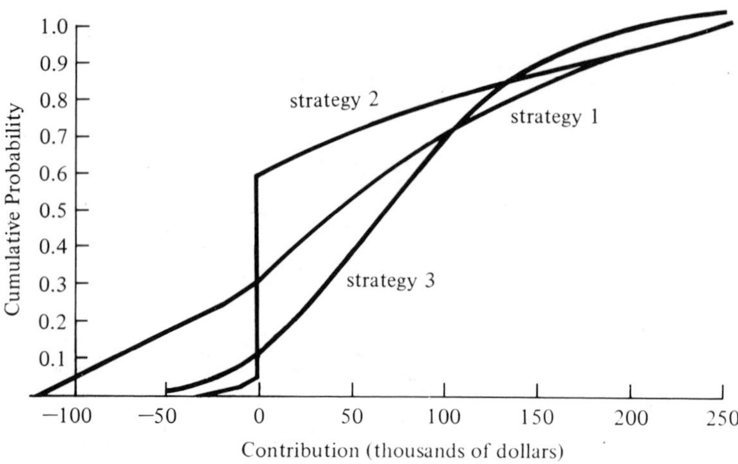


TABLE 16.2

| | *Strategy 1* | *Strategy 2* | *Strategy 3* |
|---|---|---|---|
| Mean | \$50,396 | \$40,367 | \$71,695 |
| Standard deviation | \$98,421 | \$68,066 | \$63,877 |
| Minimum contribution | \$−141,875 | \$−31,250 | \$−38,750 |
| Probability contribution 0 or less | 0.30 | 0.60 | 0.10 |
| Probability contribution 20 or less | 0.40 | 0.66 | 0.22 |
| Probability contribution 100 or more | 0.30 | 0.20 | 0.32 |
| Probability contribution 150 or more | 0.17 | 0.13 | 0.10 |
| Maximum contribution | \$253,750 | \$253,750 | \$202,500 |

### ● Using Certainty Equivalents

Certainty equivalents can be calculated using a preference curve as described in Chapter 6. If we assume that the preference curve shown in Figure 16.15 has been assessed for this problem, the decision can be made by taking the expected value of the preference numbers (utilities) as shown in Figure 16.16. The results indicate that a decision maker with these preferences prefers to produce brand *X* but not change the price. The certainty equivalent for this choice, which is strategy 3, is \$65,000. The mechanics of this procedure are easy once the preference curve has been assessed.

#### Minimizing Variance for Risk-Averse Decision Makers

Risk aversion means that less *risk* is preferred to more risk. The intuitive notion of risk is clear by now. It involves both uncertainty and the magnitude of the evaluation units. But we do not have a precise definition of risk

**FIGURE 16.15**

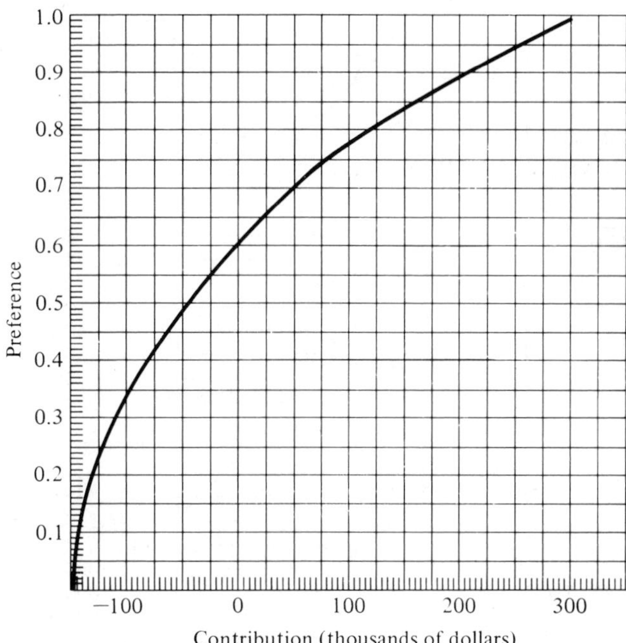


that can be used to calculate a value or *magnitude of risk*. If we did, a risk-averse individual would want to minimize this value, *everything else being equal*. An often-used surrogate for risk is the *variance* (or standard deviation) of the probability distribution for the random variable of interest (e.g., contribution). Since the variance is a measure of dispersion, it can be thought of as describing the *amount of uncertainty*, and, consequently, it captures an important part of the notion of risk. Following this line of reasoning, a risk-averse individual would want to minimize the variance, *everything else being equal*. This leads to the following rules of thumb for choosing between two alternatives with evaluation units $X$:

1. Alternative 1 is preferred to alternative 2 if

   $E[X_1] \geqslant E[X_2]$ and $\sigma^2_{X_1} < \sigma^2_{X_2}$

2. Alternative 1 is preferred to alternative 2 if

   $\sigma^2_{X_1} \leqslant \sigma^2_{X_2}$ and $E[X_1] > E[X_2]$

   where $\sigma^2_{X_1}$ and $\sigma^2_{X_2}$ denote the variances for the probability distributions associated with alternatives 1 and 2.

## FIGURE 16.16

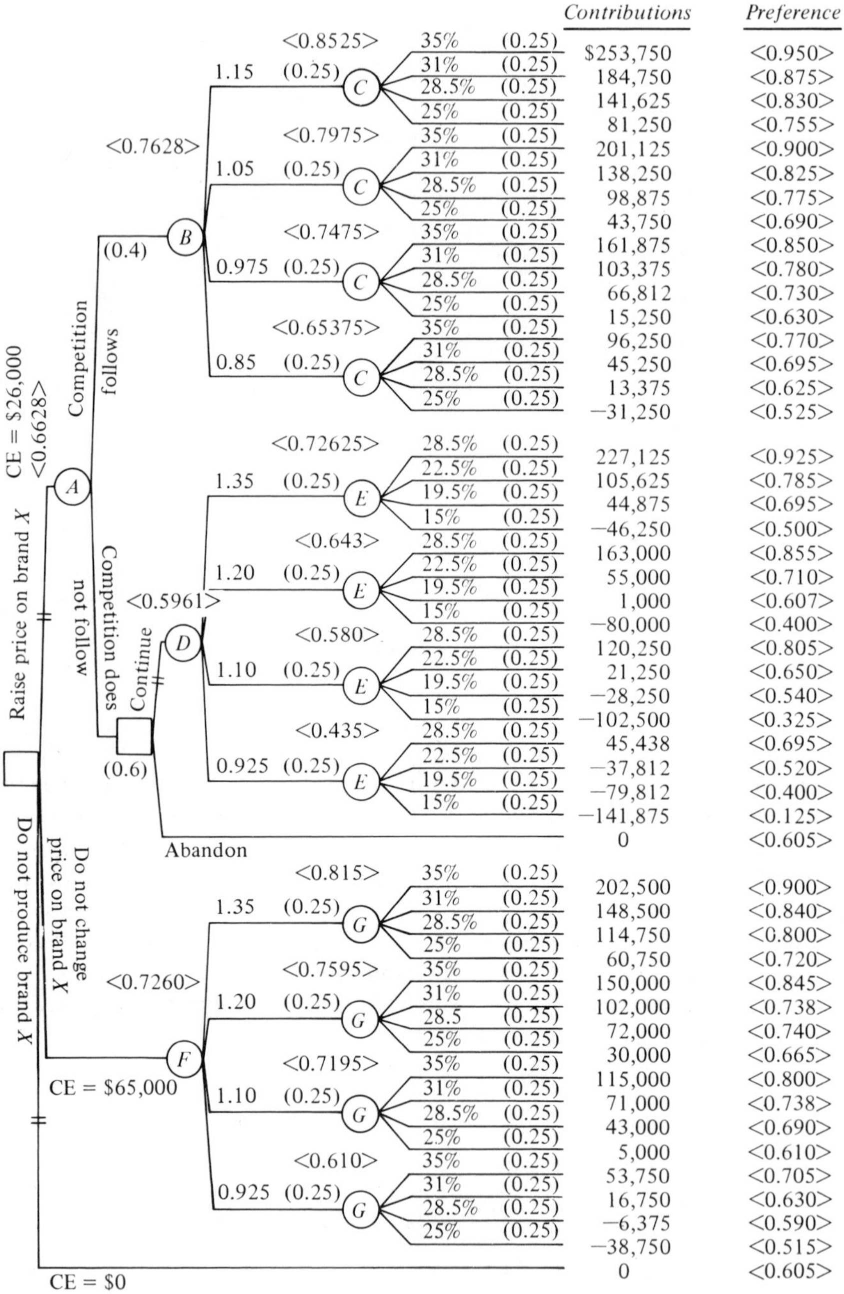

Raise price on brand $X$ CE = \$26,000 <0.6628>

(A)

Competition follows (0.4) (B) <0.7628>

1.15 (0.25) (C) <0.8525> 35% (0.25) 31% (0.25) 28.5% (0.25) 25% (0.25)

1.05 (0.25) (C) <0.7975> 35% (0.25) 31% (0.25) 28.5% (0.25) 25% (0.25)

0.975 (0.25) (C) <0.7475> 35% (0.25) 31% (0.25) 28.5% (0.25) 25% (0.25)

0.85 (0.25) (C) <0.65375> 35% (0.25) 31% (0.25) 28.5% (0.25) 25% (0.25)

Competition does not follow (0.6) Continue (D) <0.5961>

1.35 (0.25) (E) <0.72625> 28.5% (0.25) 22.5% (0.25) 19.5% (0.25) 15% (0.25)

1.20 (0.25) (E) <0.643> 28.5% (0.25) 22.5% (0.25) 19.5% (0.25) 15% (0.25)

1.10 (0.25) (E) <0.580> 28.5% (0.25) 22.5% (0.25) 19.5% (0.25) 15% (0.25)

0.925 (0.25) (E) <0.435> 28.5% (0.25) 22.5% (0.25) 19.5% (0.25) 15% (0.25)

Abandon

Do not change price on brand $X$ (F) CE = \$65,000 <0.7260>

1.35 (0.25) (G) <0.815> 35% (0.25) 31% (0.25) 28.5% (0.25) 25% (0.25)

1.20 (0.25) (G) <0.7595> 35% (0.25) 31% (0.25) 28.5 (0.25) 25% (0.25)

1.10 (0.25) (G) <0.7195> 35% (0.25) 31% (0.25) 28.5% (0.25) 25% (0.25)

0.925 (0.25) (G) <0.610> 35% (0.25) 31% (0.25) 28.5% (0.25) 25% (0.25)

Do not produce brand $X$ CE = \$0

| *Contributions* | *Preference* |
|---|---|
| \$253,750 | <0.950> |
| 184,750 | <0.875> |
| 141,625 | <0.830> |
| 81,250 | <0.755> |
| 201,125 | <0.900> |
| 138,250 | <0.825> |
| 98,875 | <0.775> |
| 43,750 | <0.690> |
| 161,875 | <0.850> |
| 103,375 | <0.780> |
| 66,812 | <0.730> |
| 15,250 | <0.630> |
| 96,250 | <0.770> |
| 45,250 | <0.695> |
| 13,375 | <0.625> |
| −31,250 | <0.525> |
| 227,125 | <0.925> |
| 105,625 | <0.785> |
| 44,875 | <0.695> |
| −46,250 | <0.500> |
| 163,000 | <0.855> |
| 55,000 | <0.710> |
| 1,000 | <0.607> |
| −80,000 | <0.400> |
| 120,250 | <0.805> |
| 21,250 | <0.650> |
| −28,250 | <0.540> |
| −102,500 | <0.325> |
| 45,438 | <0.695> |
| −37,812 | <0.520> |
| −79,812 | <0.400> |
| −141,875 | <0.125> |
| 0 | <0.605> |
| 202,500 | <0.900> |
| 148,500 | <0.840> |
| 114,750 | <0.800> |
| 60,750 | <0.720> |
| 150,000 | <0.845> |
| 102,000 | <0.738> |
| 72,000 | <0.740> |
| 30,000 | <0.665> |
| 115,000 | <0.800> |
| 71,000 | <0.738> |
| 43,000 | <0.690> |
| 5,000 | <0.610> |
| 53,750 | <0.705> |
| 16,750 | <0.630> |
| −6,375 | <0.590> |
| −38,750 | <0.515> |
| 0 | <0.605> |

In other words, the decision maker prefers to maximize the expected value and minimize the variance. When one alternative has an expected value that is equal to or greater than another, and a lower variance than the others, it is chosen. Or, if one has a variance that is less than or equal to another and a higher expected value, it is chosen. In the example summarized in Table 16.2, we see that this reasoning would lead to a choice of strategy 3. If one alternative has a higher expected value but also a higher variance, these rules of thumb do not provide any help.

The intuitive reasoning behind these rules is clear; however, they do not always work. If the probability distributions for $X_1$ and $X_2$ are *reasonably symmetrical*, the rules hold for a risk-averse decision maker. If the distributions are not symmetrical, then a more detailed analysis may be required.

### Separability with Constant Risk Aversion

When *constant risk aversion* holds and events are *independent*, an important simplification can be made. Multiple projects can be treated separately. In general, if you are evaluating a series of projects, the complete portfolio and all possible combinations must be considered. To illustrate this problem and the simplification possible under constant risk aversion, consider the following example.

**Example 16.2**

Suppose that you have two projects which can be funded. Both are risky but well within your normal scope of business. The projects involve uncertain events and payoffs that are independent of each other. Project *A* has a 70% chance of making a contribution of $10,000 and a 30% chance of $−3,000. Project *B* has a 20% chance of $30,000 and an 80% chance of $−7,000. Either project or both projects can be undertaken.

The complete decision diagram is shown in Figure 16.17. It represents all combinations: *accept A and B*, *accept A only*, *accept B only*, and *accept neither*. Using a general preference curve shown in Figure 16.18, we obtain the results shown in Figure 16.17 in the ovals. We see that *accept A only* has a certainty equivalent of $6,500. *Accept B only* has a certainty equivalent of $−1,000. *Accept both A and B* has a certainty equivalent of $5,000. Therefore, the certainty equivalent for *accept both A and B* is less than the sum of the certainty equivalents for each project taken separately ($5,000 versus $6,500−$1,000=$5,500).

The results using constant risk aversion are shown on Figure 16.17 in the boxes. The degree of risk aversion used to calculate the certainty equivalents was consistent with a risk premium of $8,000 on a 50–50 gamble between $−10,000 and $50,000 (i.e., a certainty equivalent of $12,000). The optimal strategy in this case is the same as with the general risk preference curve: *accept A only*. The point to notice is that the certainty equivalent for *accept*

**FIGURE 16.17**

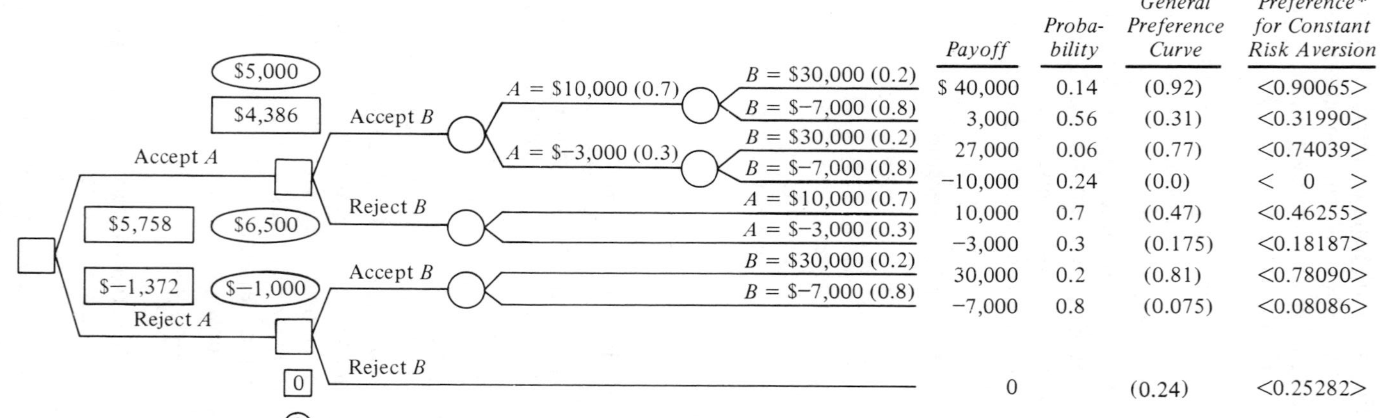


*The preference function is $U(X) = 1.48368 - 1.23087e^{-0.00001868X}$.

FIGURE 16.18

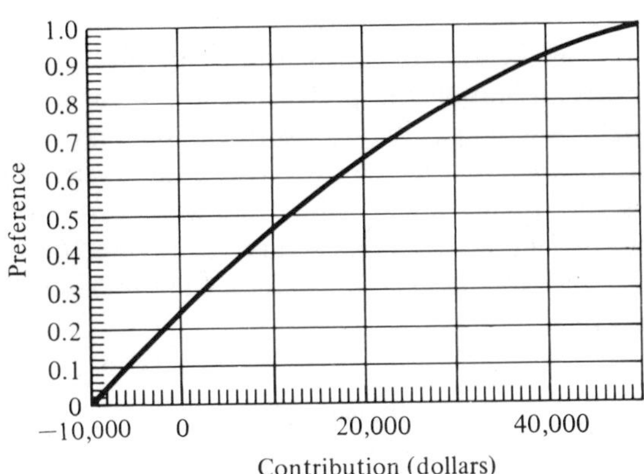


*both A and B*, \$4,386, is the sum of the certainty equivalents of the two projects taken separately, \$5,758 − \$1,372 = \$4,386. Therefore, under conditions of constant risk aversion, each alternative *can be considered separately*. (Of course, the assumption of independence for the probabilities of the uncertain events associated with each alternative must hold.) In *general*, risk aversion requires all alternatives to be considered together.

## ●● More Properties with Constant Risk Aversion

Another property which can be illustrated using constant risk aversion is that risk premiums approach zero for "small" gambles. Even when substantial risk premiums exist for large gambles, a preference function with constant risk aversion results in certainty equivalents for small gambles which are essentially the same as those from a risk-neutral curve. To illustrate, assume that we have constant risk aversion with the certainty equivalent for a 50–50 gamble between \$ − 10,000 and \$50,000 equal to \$12,000. The risk premium for this gamble is \$8,000. The risk premiums for a series of gambles are shown in Table 16.3. Although the risk aversion is rather severe, the risk premium is still negligible for small gambles.

TABLE 16.3

| 50–50 *Gamble* | *Expected Monetary Value* | *Certainty Equivalent* | *Risk Premium* | *% Gamble Range* |
|---|---|---|---|---|
| \$ − 10,000, \$50,000 | \$20,000 | \$12,000 | \$8,000 | 13.3 |
| \$0, \$40,000 | 20,000 | 16,348 | 3,652 | 9.1 |
| \$10,000, \$30,000 | 20,000 | 19,071 | 929 | 4.6 |
| \$15,000, \$25,000 | 20,000 | 19,767 | 233 | 2.3 |
| \$18,000, \$22,000 | 20,000 | 19,963 | 37 | 0.9 |
| \$19,000, \$21,000 | 20,000 | 19,991 | 9 | 0.4 |

## RISK NEUTRALITY

The assumption or specification of risk neutrality defines a unique shape for a preference curve. By definition the preference curve for a risk-neutral individual is a straight line (e.g., Figure 16.19). When risk neutrality exists, certainty equivalents are equal to the expected value of the payoff. Consider the gamble shown in Figure 16.20, which shows a certainty equivalent of \$20,000 using the risk-neutral preference curve in Figure 16.19. The expected monetary value is just (0.5)(\$30,000) + (0.5)(\$10,000) = \$20,000, the same as the certainty equivalent.[4]

**FIGURE 16.19**

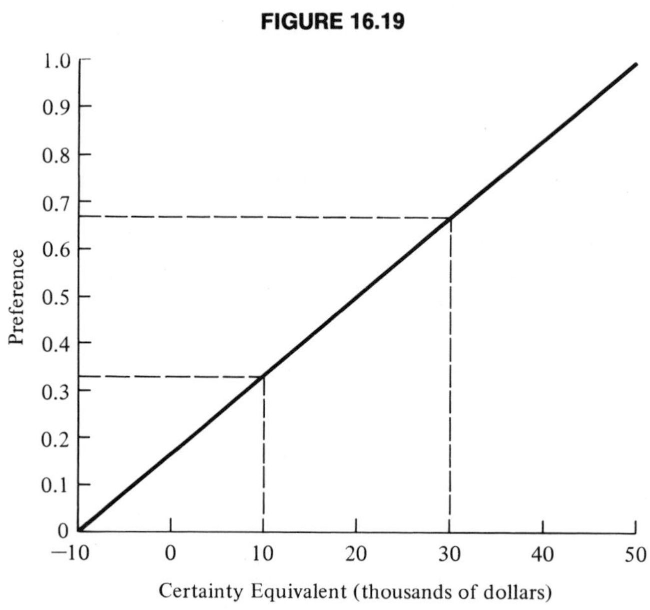


**FIGURE 16.20**

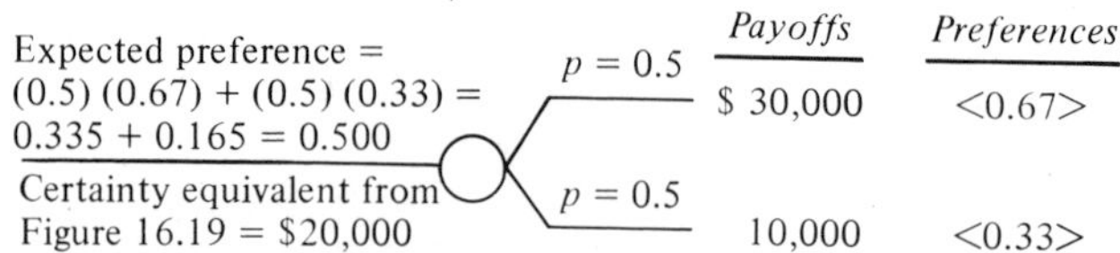


[4]A general demonstration of this property follows from the fact that a linear preference curve can be described as $U(X) = bX$, where $X$ is the random variable of interest. The expected preference for any gamble is $E[U] = \Sigma_i p_i(bx_i)$. For any preference value $U$ the certainty equivalent is $x = U/b$. Therefore, the certainty equivalent for the gamble is $x = \Sigma_i p_i(bx_i)/b = \Sigma_i p_i x_i = E[X]$.

## CHOICES UNDER RISK NEUTRALITY

There are two important simplifications in the choice process under risk neutrality. The first, demonstrated above, is that certainty equivalents can be calculated without using a preference curve. This simplifies the calculations and eliminates the requirement for assessing a preference curve.

**Example 16.3**

Assume risk neutrality in Example 16.1. Use sequential analysis to determine the best choice.

The diagram is shown in Figure 16.21. The expected values are given in the ovals. The best choice is *do not change price on brand X*.

### Separability with Risk Neutrality

Risk neutrality is a special case of constant risk aversion. Therefore, options can be analyzed separately.

**Example 16.4**

Consider the problem specified in Example 16.2. Use sequential analysis to determine the best choice under conditions of risk neutrality.

Figure 16.22 shows the diagram and the analysis for the problem. Expected values are shown in the ovals. Note that the expected value for *accept both A and B* is just equal to the expected value of *accept A only* plus the expected value of *accept B only* ($6,100 + $400) = $6,500. This demonstrates the separability feature. When a large number of projects is being considered, this simplification can be important.

## RISK SEEKING

Risk-seeking behavior is the opposite of risk-averse behavior in that the certainty equivalent for a gamble is greater than the expected value of the payoff. Risk premiums are negative. Figure 16.23 illustrates a preference function for a risk seeker. Knowing that the risk premium is negative means that the curve must lie *below* every straight line connecting any two points on the curve. As is the case with risk aversion, this requirement significantly restricts the shape of the preference curve. The risk premium for a 50–50 chance at $ − 10,000 and $50,000 is shown in Figure 16.23. Since the certainty equivalent is $37,000 and the expected value is $20,000, the risk premium is $ − 17,000.

**FIGURE 16.21**

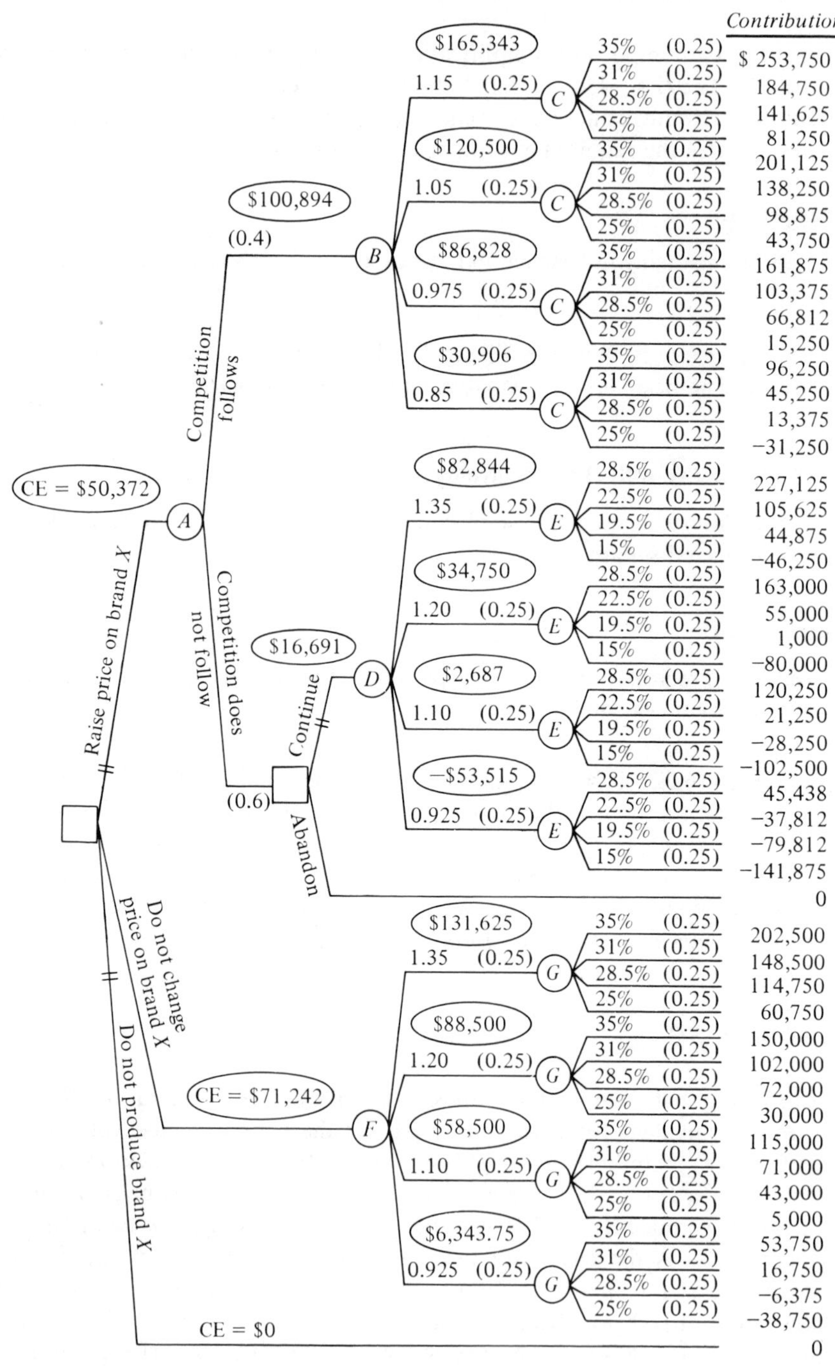

Contribution
CE = $50,372
Raise price on brand X
A
Competition follows
(0.4)
$100,894
B
$165,343
1.15 (0.25)
$120,500
1.05 (0.25)
$86,828
0.975 (0.25)
$30,906
0.85 (0.25)
C
35% (0.25)
31% (0.25)
28.5% (0.25)
25% (0.25)
$ 253,750
184,750
141,625
81,250
201,125
138,250
98,875
43,750
161,875
103,375
66,812
15,250
96,250
45,250
13,375
−31,250
Competition does not follow
(0.6)
Continue
Abandon
$16,691
D
$82,844
1.35 (0.25)
$34,750
1.20 (0.25)
$2,687
1.10 (0.25)
−$53,515
0.925 (0.25)
E
28.5% (0.25)
22.5% (0.25)
19.5% (0.25)
15% (0.25)
227,125
105,625
44,875
−46,250
163,000
55,000
1,000
−80,000
120,250
21,250
−28,250
−102,500
45,438
−37,812
−79,812
−141,875
0
Do not change price on brand X
CE = $71,242
F
$131,625
1.35 (0.25)
$88,500
1.20 (0.25)
$58,500
1.10 (0.25)
$6,343.75
0.925 (0.25)
G
202,500
148,500
114,750
60,750
150,000
102,000
72,000
30,000
115,000
71,000
43,000
5,000
53,750
16,750
−6,375
−38,750
Do not produce brand X
CE = $0
0

FIGURE 16.22

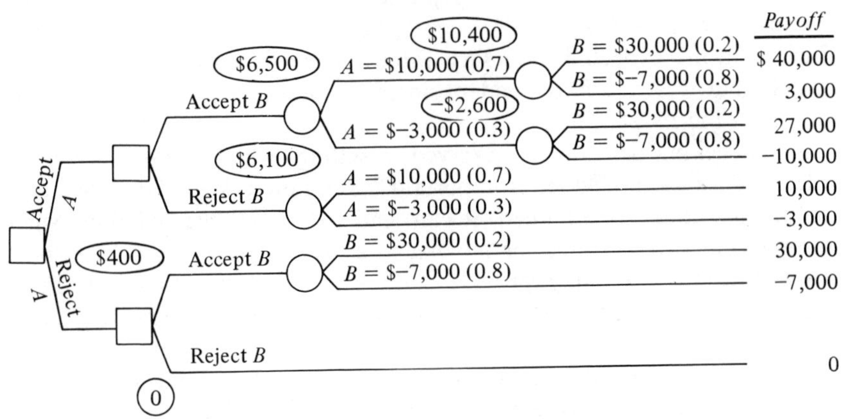


FIGURE 16.23

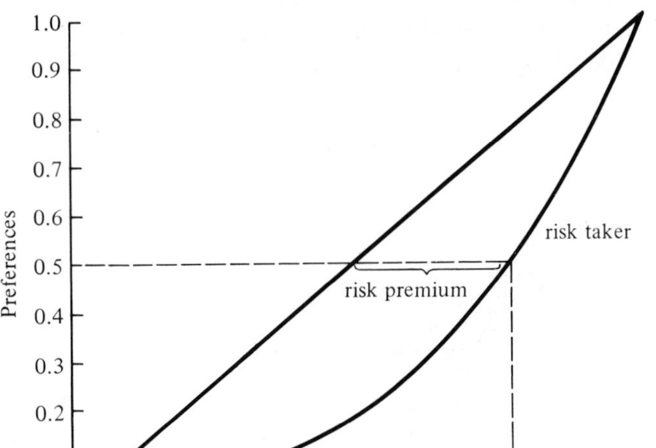


## EMPIRICAL EVIDENCE

The empirical evidence on risk-taking behavior comes from a variety of studies, including some undertaken in organizational settings.[5] The studies show different attitudes; however, there are some general results.

[5]See, for example, R. O. Swalm, "Utility Theory—Insights into Risk Taking," *Harvard Business Review*, November–December 1966.

For "small" gambles that are repetitive, individuals are often risk-neutral. For instance, in a firm, quality control policies and inventory policies are often set using expected monetary values. There is no precise definition of "small," but it is clearly dependent on the resources available to the individual taking the risk.

Risk-seeking behavior is observed in settings where there is a threshold, or level of aspiration, which is important.[6] The rationale is that once a certain amount of money is obtained, it can lead to a new "way of life," such as starting your own business or moving to a larger house. Outcomes short of this aspiration level may provide some additional benefits, but they are essentially more of the same thing rather than something new and different that is highly valued.

An observation that is consistent with the threshold theory is that individuals are risk seeking for gambles with a negative expected monetary value. With the choices presented in Figure 16.24, many individuals will select $A$ over $B$ (note that $B$ pays the expected monetary value of the gamble in $A$). The reasoning is that the consequences of losing $1,000 are not that much worse than losing $500, whereas "if I can break even I will get back to the status quo, which is important to me."

**FIGURE 16.24**

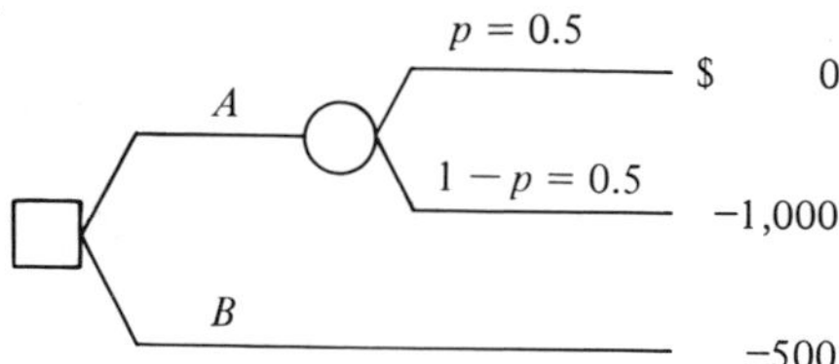


Risk aversion is the most generally observed attitude toward risk for uncertain events whose consequences are significant. The existence of insurance markets attests to this behavior. Decisions within organizations also display a significant degree of risk aversion. The curves shown in Figure 16.25 were obtained from decision makers in a large industrial organization.[7] The overall attitudes are strongly risk-averse. For negative outcomes, a slight degree of risk-seeking behavior is implied. However, the steep downward

[6]See M. Friedman and L. J. Savage, "The Utility Analysis of Choices Involving Risk," *Journal of Political Economy*, April 1948, pp. 279–304; F. Mosteller and P. Nogee, "An Empirical Measurement of Utility," *Journal of Political Economy*, Vol. 59, October 1951, pp. 371–404; S. Siegel, "Level of Aspiration and Decision Making," *Psychological Review*, Vol. 64, 1957, pp. 253–262; and C. J. Grayson, *Decisions Under Uncertainty*, Boston: Harvard Business School, 1960.

[7]Source: Ralph O. Swalm, "Utility Theory—Insights into Risk Taking," *Harvard Business Review*, Nov.–Dec. 1966. Reprinted by permission of the publisher. 

FIGURE 16.25

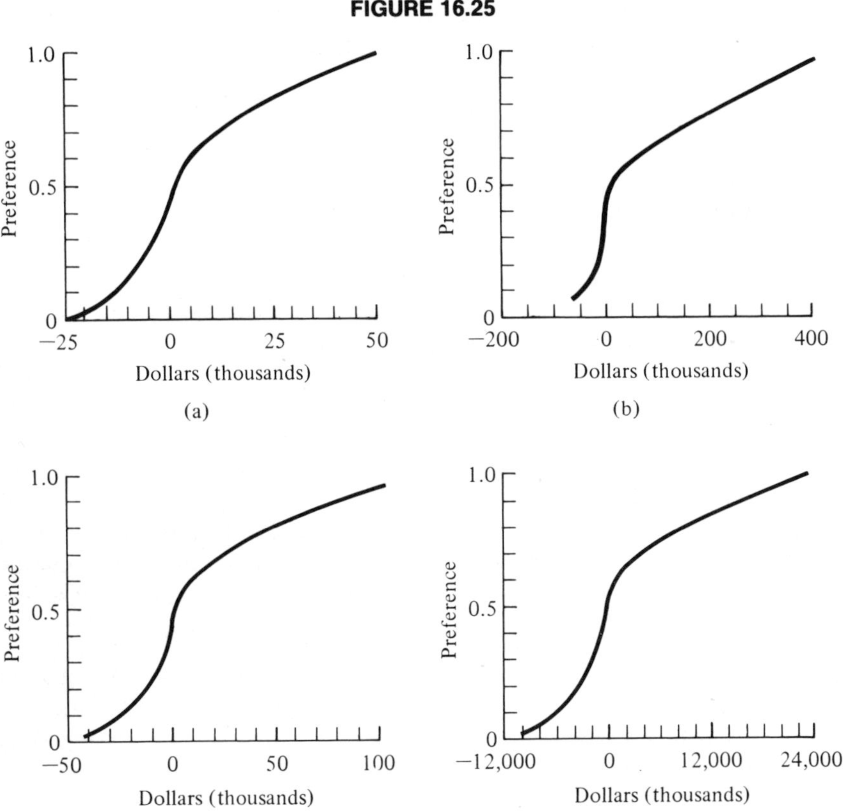


slope of the curves for negative outcomes means that most gambles have a positive risk premium. That is, if a straight line is used to connect two points, the preference curve lies above the line in most cases.

The shapes of the curves are very similar. But notice that the scales for the horizontal axes are different. The curves have been standardized for the amount of money the individuals normally control. This implies that attitudes toward risk are a function of the planning horizon of each individual rather than the financial position of the company. Decision makers at different levels are making decisions with different risk attitudes. This means a lack of consistency among managers. For instance, when faced with the identical gamble (0.5 chance at 0 and 0.5 chance at $100,000), manager *B* would assess a certainty equivalent of $35,000 while manager *C*'s certainty equivalent would be $20,000. The overall degree of risk aversion also raises the question of whether any of the managers are acting in the best interests of the company. The question of what constitutes the "company" and how the market for stock in a publicly held company affects the "best interests" is a complicated one and will not be pursued here. For our purposes we merely recognize that a company's policy toward risk taking may well be less risk-averse than a manager's over the range of responsibility of the individual manager.

## SUMMARY

Three basic attitudes toward risk can be identified: risk aversion, risk neutrality, and risk seeking. The choice process is affected by these attitudes.

*Risk aversion* corresponds to positive risk premiums.

The *risk premium* for a gamble is defined to be the (expected payoff value) − (certainty equivalent).

Within the class of risk-averse individuals, we can distinguish those with *decreasing risk aversion* and *constant risk aversion*. For constant risk aversion, the preference function is given by $U(X) = a + be^{-\lambda X}$.

Choices under risk aversion can be made by direct choice or certainty equivalents—usually obtained by decomposition using preference curves. For two alternatives with "well-behaved" symmetrical probability distributions for the random variable of interest, a risk-averse individual will prefer:

1. The alternative with the lower variance if the expected values are equal, or if the alternative with the lower variance has a higher expected value.
2. The alternative with the higher expected value if the variances are equal, or if the alternative with the higher expected value has a lower variance.

Under these conditions, if one alternative has the highest expected value and lowest variance, it is obviously preferred. The intuitive rationale for these rules is that variance is a measure of the amount of uncertainty—hence risk—and risk-averse individuals want to minimize risk.

With constant risk aversion, multiple projects can be analyzed separately, providing an important simplification for the choice process when a portfolio of projects must be evaluated.

*Risk neutrality* corresponds to a zero risk premium. The preference curve is a straight line. There are two simplifications in the choice process when risk neutrality holds. First, certainty equivalents are equal to expected payoffs, so there is no need to use a preference curve. Second, projects can be analyzed separately because risk neutrality is a special case of constant risk aversion.

*Risk seeking* corresponds to a negative risk premium.

Empirical evidence indicates that individuals are risk neutral when the "stakes" are low. The most usual reaction when the "stakes" are high is risk aversion, although in special cases, including gambles with negative expected values, some individuals display risk-seeking characteristics. In general, it appears that decision makers in large companies are quite risk-averse.

## ASSIGNMENT MATERIAL

**16.1.** Use the preference curve shown in Figure 16.26 to answer the following questions.

**FIGURE 16.26**

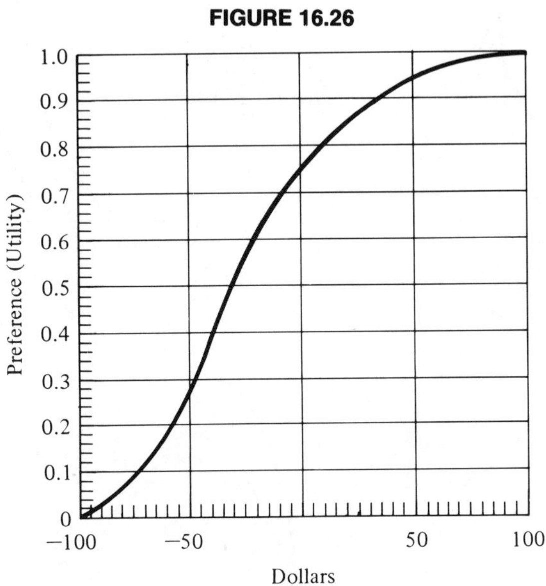


(a) Consider a 50–50 gamble between $\$-100$ and $\$-30$. What is the individual's certainty equivalent? Is she/he exhibiting risk-seeking, risk-neutral, or risk-averse behavior?

(b) Consider a 50–50 gamble between \$0 and \$100. What is the individual's certainty equivalent? Is she/he exhibiting risk-seeking, risk-neutral, or risk-averse behavior?

(c) Consider a 50–50 gamble between $\$-100$ and \$100. What is the individual's certainty equivalent? Is she/he exhibiting risk-seeking, risk-neutral, or risk-averse behavior?

(d) Consider a 50–50 gamble between $\$-100$ and \$30. What is the individual's certainty equivalent? Is she/he exhibiting risk-seeking, risk-neutral, or risk-averse behavior?

**16.2.** Consider the distributions shown in Figure 16.27. Assume that the distributions in each figure represent payoffs associated with two mutually exclusive projects. The expected monetary values of the projects are as follows:

| *Project* | *Expected Monetary Value* | *Project* | *Expected Monetary Value* |
|---|---|---|---|
| *A* | 20 | *D* | 35 |
| *B* | 20 | *E* | 19 |
| *C* | 26 | *F* | 22 |

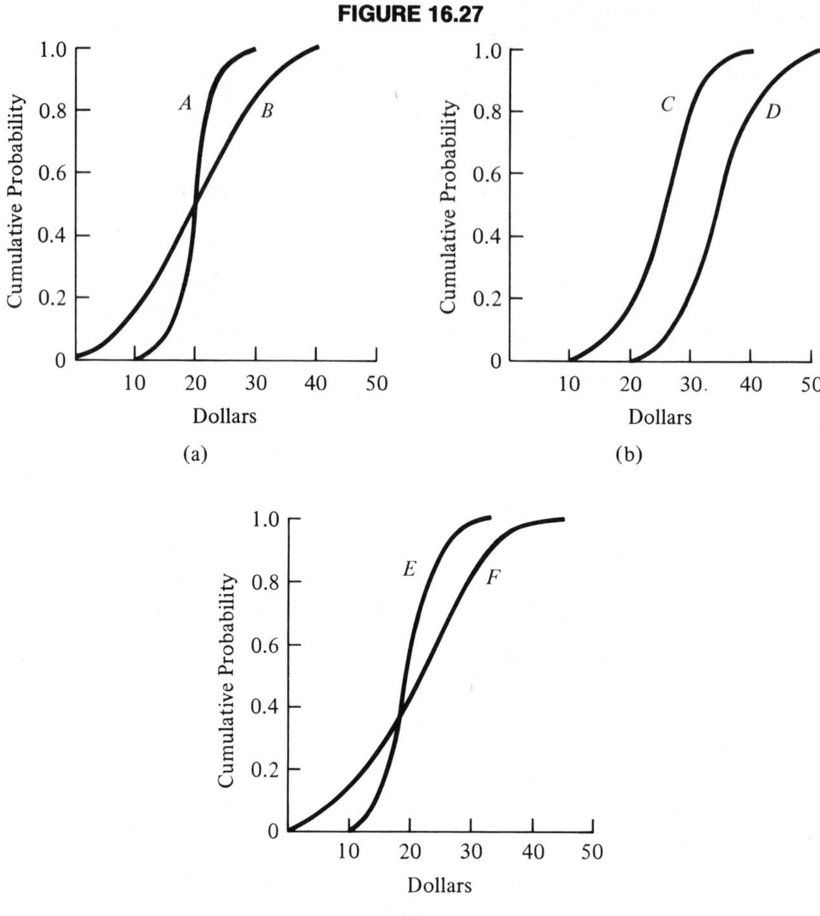


(a) Consider Figure 16.27(a). Suppose that an individual is risk-neutral. Which project *A* or *B* would he/she prefer? Which project would an individual prefer if he/she is risk-averse? Which project would be preferred by a risk-seeking individual?
(b) Answer the same question as in part (a) for projects *C* and *D* depicted in Figure 16.27(b).
(c) Can you tell which of the projects, *E* and *F*, in Figure 16.27(c) would be preferred by a risk-averse individual? Why or why not?

**16.3.** It has just been brought to the attention of a decision maker that he has the opportunity to invest in a certain risky venture. If he is to invest in this venture, however, the necessary capital must be committed within the hour. If the capital is commited and the venture succeeds (the probability of which he assesses to be $\frac{1}{2}$), the decision maker will realize a net profit of $8,000 at the end of 3 days. If the venture fails, he will suffer a net loss of $2,000 at the end of three days. No other investments are contemplated in this 3-day period.

(a) Assuming that the decision maker is risk neutral, should he make the commitment or not? What is his certainty equivalent for the risky venture?

(b) Suppose that the risk-neutral decision maker has two identical and independent investment opportunities like that described above. (That is, he has two opportunites *instead* of just one.) Should he invest in both, one, or neither of the ventures? (*Note*: He must decide on these options within the hour; consequently, he cannot wait to determine the outcome of one before deciding on the second.)

(c) If he has three such ventures, all identical and independent, how many of the three should he invest in?

**16.4.** Assume that a decision maker is risk-averse, with constant risk aversion and a risk premium for a 50–50 gamble between \$8,000 and \$ −2,000 of \$1,500.

(a) Should he make a commitment for the single investment opportunity described in problem 16.3?

(b) Suppose that the constantly risk-averse decision maker described above has two identical and independent opportunities such as those described above. Should he invest in both, one, or neither? (*Note*: He must decide on these options within the hour; consequently, he cannot wait to determine the outcome of one before deciding on the second.)

(c) If he has three such ventures, all identical and independent, how many of the three should he invest in?

**16.5.** Assume that a decision maker is risk-averse with the preference curve shown in Figure 16.28.

**FIGURE 16.28**

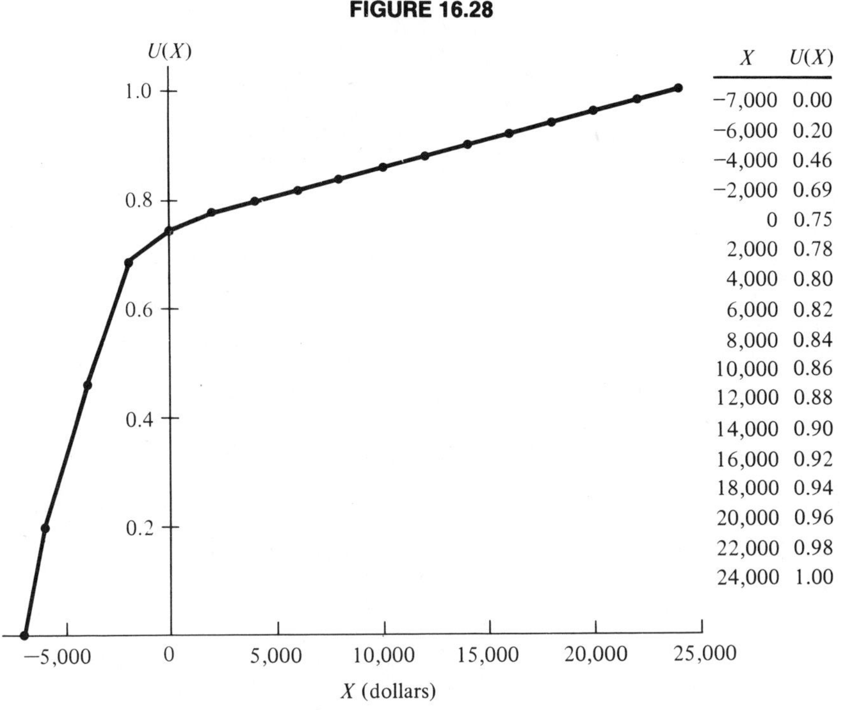


| $X$ | $U(X)$ |
|---|---|
| −7,000 | 0.00 |
| −6,000 | 0.20 |
| −4,000 | 0.46 |
| −2,000 | 0.69 |
| 0 | 0.75 |
| 2,000 | 0.78 |
| 4,000 | 0.80 |
| 6,000 | 0.82 |
| 8,000 | 0.84 |
| 10,000 | 0.86 |
| 12,000 | 0.88 |
| 14,000 | 0.90 |
| 16,000 | 0.92 |
| 18,000 | 0.94 |
| 20,000 | 0.96 |
| 22,000 | 0.98 |
| 24,000 | 1.00 |

(a) Should he make a commitment for the single investment opportunity described in problem 16.3?

(b) Suppose that he has two identical and independent opportunities like that described above. (*Note*: He must decide on these options within the hour; consequently, he cannot wait to determine the outcome of one before deciding on the second.) Should he invest in both, one, or neither?

(c) If he has three such ventures, all identical and independent, how many of the three should he invest in? (*Note*: This problem is the same as Problem 6.7.)

**16.6.** An individual is risk-averse with constant risk aversion. Certainty equivalents for a series of 50–50 gambles are as follows:

| *Gamble* | *Lose* | *Win* | *Expected Gain* | *Certainty Equivalent Gain* |
|---|---|---|---|---|
| 1 | 0 | 10 | $ 5 | $ 4.88 |
| 2 | 0 | 20 | 10 | 9.50 |
| 3 | 0 | 30 | 15 | 13.88 |
| 4 | 0 | 40 | 20 | 18.01 |
| 5 | 0 | 50 | 25 | 21.91 |

What is the individual's certainty equivalent for the gamble shown in Figure 16.29?

**FIGURE 16.29**

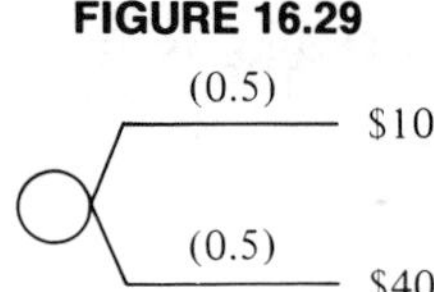

# 17

# Preference Assessment Procedures

One method for assessing a preference curve using reference gambles was presented in Chapter 6. In this chapter we consider the assessment problem in general and describe other assessment procedures. The question of resolution of inconsistencies is explored and procedures for special risk attitudes are discussed. Figure 17.1 shows how the material fits into the overall framework.

**FIGURE 17.1**

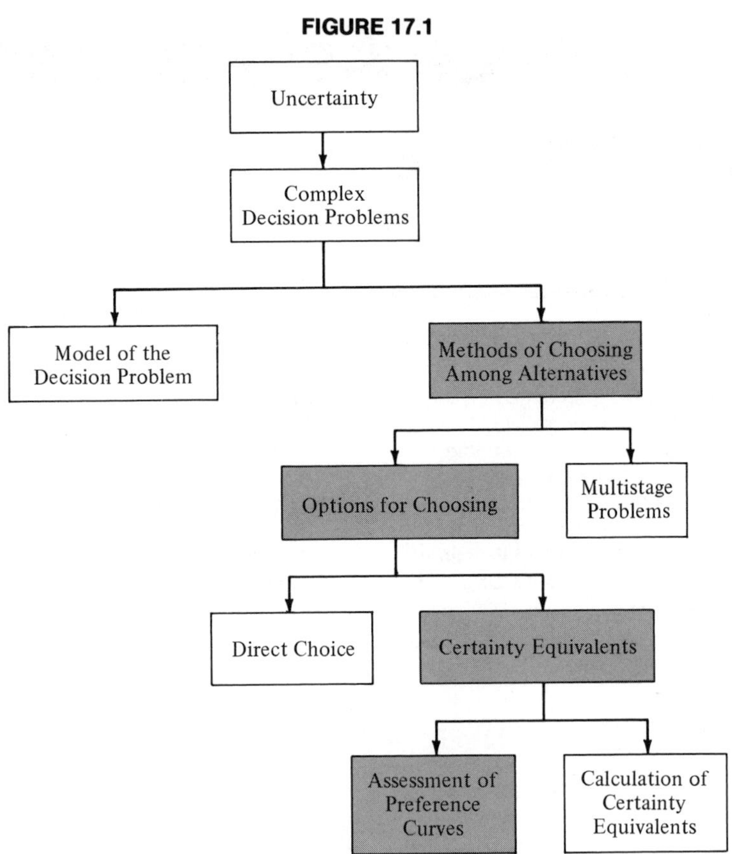


## THE PREFERENCE ASSESSMENT PROBLEM IN GENERAL

At the outset we need to be clear on the objectives and possible benefits from using a preference assessment procedure. The only reason for undertaking a preference analysis is that complexity due to uncertainty associated with the alternatives is so great that the decision maker feels unsure of which choice to make. That is, the decision maker realizes that the choice revolves around his preferences as they relate to taking risks, that his feelings toward risk are not entirely clear in his own mind, and that he cannot informally apply his feelings using direct choice. From this perspective the objective of using preference analysis is to help an individual clarify a difficult choice. The potential benefit is to make a decision that is consistent with his attitude toward risk.

Since the purpose of assessing a preference curve is to help a decision maker be more consistent, we will concentrate on procedures that are designed to provide the most help for a decision maker. We will not spend an excessive amount of time discussing whether or not consistency is ensured over a variety of conditions. Instead, we recognize that inconsistencies exist and, in fact, constitute the only reason for undertaking the analysis in the first place. The objective is to create settings that minimize the inconsistencies.

The preference assessment procedure is done after completing a model consisting of the uncertain events, probabilities, and evaluation units for the decision. We assume that a single, numerical evaluation unit is used. This measure must be meaningful in the sense that it is adequate for a decision maker to choose among alternatives. For instance, rate of return (ROR) as a measure for choosing among capital budgeting projects would not likely qualify. The reason is that preferences may depend on both the return and the amount invested (i.e., before choosing between project $A$ with an ROR = 50% and project $B$ with an ROR = 40%, it would be important to know that project $A$ requires a \$1,000,000 investment while project $B$ requires a \$10,000,000 investment).

Everything else that is important to a decision maker's attitude toward risk is considered part of a *base position*. The base position is the same for all alternatives. It is sometimes argued that some parts of the base position should be displayed explicitly on the diagram. For instance, the base net liquid asset position is sometimes displayed. The idea is that the liquid asset position plays a major role in determining attitudes toward risk. The reason for explicitly displaying it is to remind the decision maker of this position when the assessment is being made. The issue is not whether the liquid asset position affects an individual's attitude toward risk, but rather, if it does, whether it is useful to display it explicitly (our convention has been not to display it as part of the assessment procedure). What is important is for the decision makers to have clearly in mind all the factors that influence their attitudes toward risk.

### Choice of the Range of Payoff Values (Evaluation Units)

The only firm requirement on the range of payoff values encompassed by the preference curve is that the minimum and maximum values for the problem at hand are included. However, following the guideline that we want to make it as easy as possible for the assessor to be consistent, the range of payoff values considered for the assessment procedure should be close to the range of payoff values in the problem under consideration. For instance, if a decision involves payoffs between $\$-100,000$ and $500,000, asking for preference assessments over the range $\$-1,000,000$ to $10,000,000 may not allow the decision maker to think consistently about his attitude toward risk over the narrower range of interest. If an individual were *perfectly consistent* and *equally able to conceptualize the risks* over both the larger and smaller range, then, theoretically, it would not make any difference which range is used. Since individuals are not perfectly consistent and since some risks are more meaningful than others, as a general rule, it makes sense to use the range that corresponds to the problem at hand. This is the range that is important to the decision maker, and the one he is most likely to be able to relate to in a consistent manner.

## PREFERENCE ASSESSMENT USING THE BASIC REFERENCE GAMBLE

We can divide the methods for obtaining preference curves into two categories. The first uses the basic reference gamble directly and was described in Chapter 6. The second method uses a variety of 50–50 gambles. This section reviews the procedure described in Chapter 6 and explains a variation of it.

### The Basic Reference Gamble

The *reference gamble* is an uncertain event with two outcomes. The outcome described as *win* has a payoff equal to the top end of the preference scale range. The outcome described as *lose* has a payoff equal to the bottom end of the range. The probability of winning varies and is denoted by $p$ [consequently, the probability of losing is $(1-p)$]. If we desire a preference curve over the range of payoffs $\$-10,000$ to $50,000, the basic reference gamble is shown in Figure 17.2.

### The Basic Reference Gamble Assessment Procedure

The procedure for assessing preferences using reference gambles is given below. This is a repeat of the procedure presented in Chapter 6.

*The Reference Gamble Procedure*

1. Establish the payoffs for a *reference gamble* for the decision problem.
2. Specify a value for $p$, the probability of winning the reference gamble, and determine the certainty equivalent for the gamble.
3. Record $p$ and the certainty equivalent on a plot with $p$ on the vertical axis and the certainty equivalent on the horizontal axis.
4. Repeat steps 2 and 3 by changing $p$ until the plot of $p$ versus certainty equivalents is well defined.
5. Draw a curve through the plotted points.

**FIGURE 17.2**
**Reference Gamble**

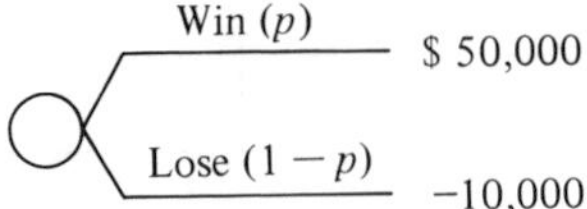


The procedure is implemented using a diagram such as the one shown in Figure 17.3. The values of $p$ are varied and certain values determined so that the decision maker is indifferent between alternatives $A$ and $B$. For $p=1$, everyone will agree that the certainty equivalent is $50,000. Similarly for $p=0$, the certainty equivalent is $−10,000. Assume that for the specified probabilities your certainty equivalents are given in Table 17.1.[1] Figure 17.4 shows a preference curve based on these assessments.

**FIGURE 17.3**

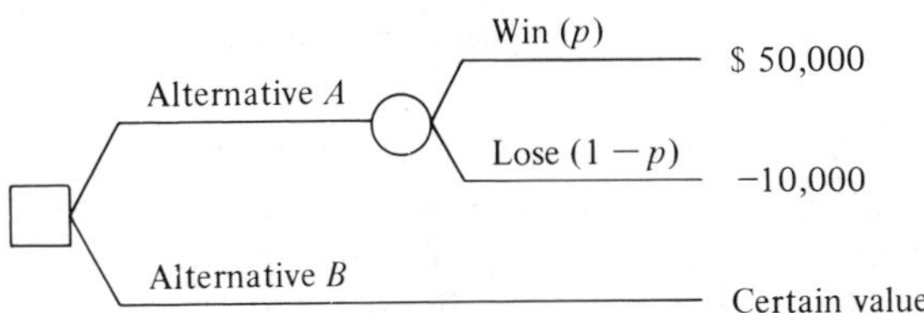


**TABLE 17.1**

| *Probability of Winning the Reference Gamble* | *Certainty Equivalent* |
|---|---|
| 1.0 | $50,000 |
| 0.8 | 34,000 |
| 0.6 | 18,000 |
| 0.5 | 10,000 |
| 0.4 | 6,000 |
| 0.2 | −2,000 |
| 0 | −10,000 |

### ●● A Variation on the Reference Gamble Assessment Procedure

Reference gambles can be used in a slightly different way to assess preference curves. The procedure is essentially the same except that certain values are specified for the gamble (see Figure 17.3), and then probabilities are determined for the reference gamble so that the decision maker is indifferent

[1]Of course, here and throughout the discussion, there is no reason why your *actual* certainty equivalents will be those assumed.

FIGURE 17.4

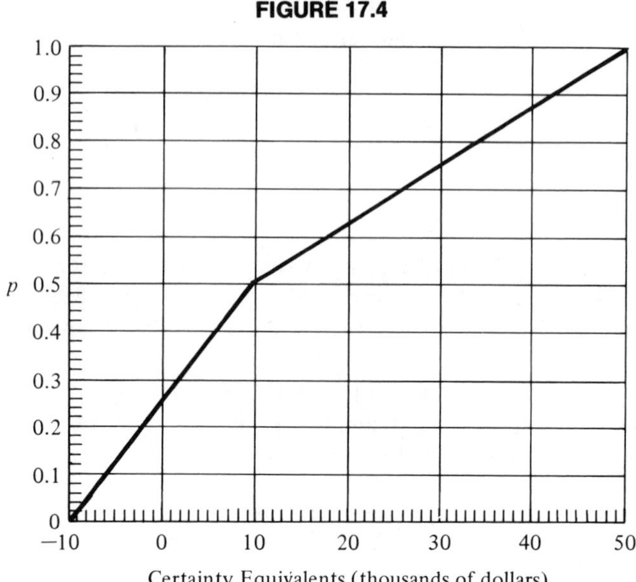


between alternatives $A$ and $B$. The correspondence between \$50,000 and $p=1$, and \$−10,000 and $p=0$ are the same. The questions specify a certain value, say \$40,000, and ask for the probability $p$ that results in indifference between $A$ and $B$ (see, for instance, Figure 17.5). Using this procedure you might obtain Table 17.2 and a preference curve such as Figure 17.6. The two

FIGURE 17.5

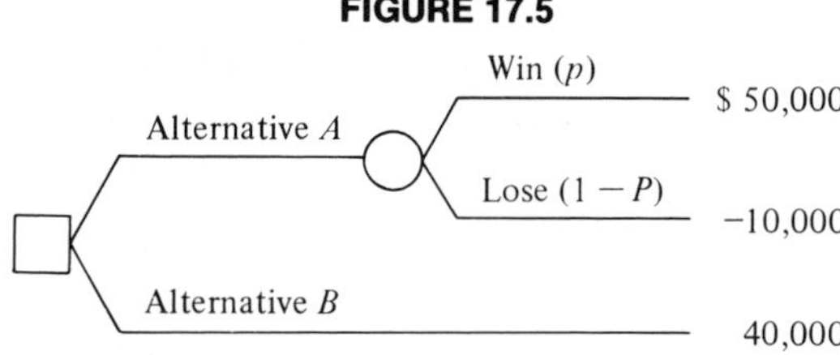


TABLE 17.2

| *Probability of Winning the Reference Gamble* | *Certainty Equivalent* |
|---|---|
| 1.0 | \$50,000 |
| 0.90 | 40,000 |
| 0.78 | 30,000 |
| 0.65 | 20,000 |
| 0.50 | 10,000 |
| 0.30 | 0 |
| 0 | −10,000 |

**FIGURE 17.6**

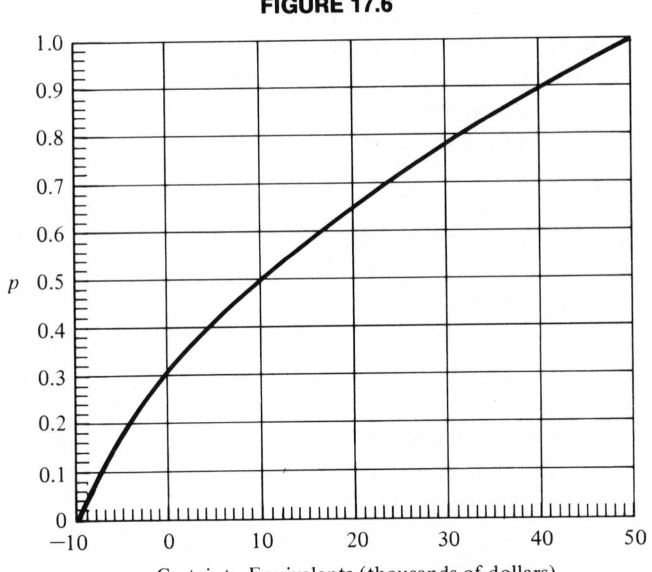


preference curves, Figures 17.4 and 17.6, are not precisely the same, although they are close. The differences are not surprising, since the two methods presented slightly different problems to the decision maker.

## PREFERENCE ASSESSMENT USING 50–50 GAMBLES

The preference assessment procedure using 50–50 gambles begins with the basic reference gamble. Certainty equivalents are obtained for $p=1$, $p=0$ and $p=0.5$. From this point on the gambles depend on the certainty equivalents specified at each step. Figure 17.7 shows an example of the gambles. Read the following procedure quickly and then go to the example that follows.

**FIGURE 17.7**

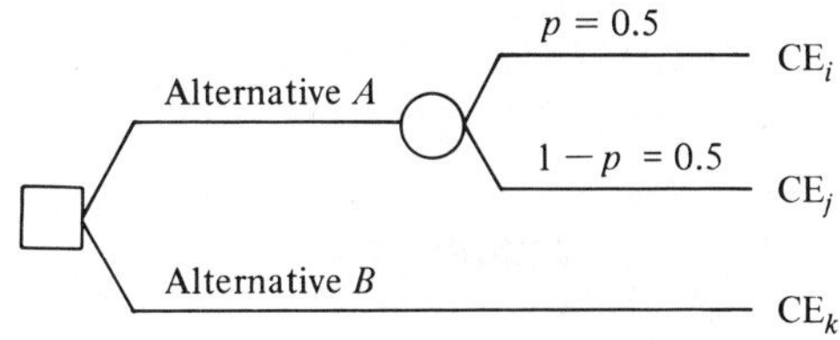


*The 50–50 Gamble Procedure*

1. Establish the payoffs for a *reference gamble* for the decision problem.

2. Determine certainty equivalents $CE_1$, $CE_2$, and $CE_3$ for the reference gamble with $p=1$, $p=0$, and $p=0.5$, respectively. Record them on a plot with $p$ on the vertical axis and the certainty equivalent on the horizontal axis. This establishes $U(CE_1)=1.0$, $U(CE_2)=0$, and $U(CE_3)=0.5$ as the preferences for these certainty equivalents.
3. Create a sequence of new gambles, each with a probability of winning of $p=0.5$. The payoffs $CE_i$ and $CE_j$ are varied and restricted to values of certainty equivalents previously specified (see Figure 17.7).
4. Determine certainty equivalents, $CE_k$, for each gamble.
5. For each gamble calculate the expected preference for alternatives $A$ and $B$. For alternative $A$: $E[U_A]=(0.5)U(CE_i)+(0.5)U(CE_j)$. For alternative $B$: $E[U_B]=(1)U(CE_k)$. Indifference between $A$ and $B$ means that $E[U_A]=E[U_B]$ or $U(CE_k)=(0.5)U(CE_i)+(0.5)U(CE_j)$.
6. Plot each $[CE_k, U(CE_k)]$ pair with $CE_k$ on the horizontal axis and $U(CE_k)$ on the vertical axis.
7. Repeat steps 3, 4, 5, and 6 until the plot is well defined.
8. Draw a curve through the plotted points.

The following discussion illustrates the procedure. Assume that we begin with the same reference gamble as shown in Figure 17.3. For $p=1$, $CE_1=$ \$50,000, and for $p=0$, $CE_2=\$-10{,}000$. Therefore, we have $U(\$50{,}000)=1.0$, and $U(\$-10{,}000)=0$.

Next, we assess a certainty equivalent for the reference gamble with $p=0.5$. Assume that your certainty equivalent is \$10,000. This means that $U(\$10{,}000)=(0.5)U(\$50{,}000)+(0.5)U(\$-10{,}000)$, or $U(\$10{,}000)=0.5$. We now have three points on the preference curve. Following step 3 we create a sequence of new gambles. For instance, form the 50–50 gamble shown in Figure 17.8. Assume that your certainty equivalent is \$26,000. The preference values $U(\$50{,}000)$ and $U(\$10{,}000)$ previously obtained are shown on the diagram. The expected preference for alternative $A$ is

$$\begin{aligned}E[U_A]&=(0.5)U(\$50{,}000)+(0.5)U(\$10{,}000)\\&=(0.5)(1)+(0.5)(0.5)=0.75\end{aligned}$$

**FIGURE 17.8**

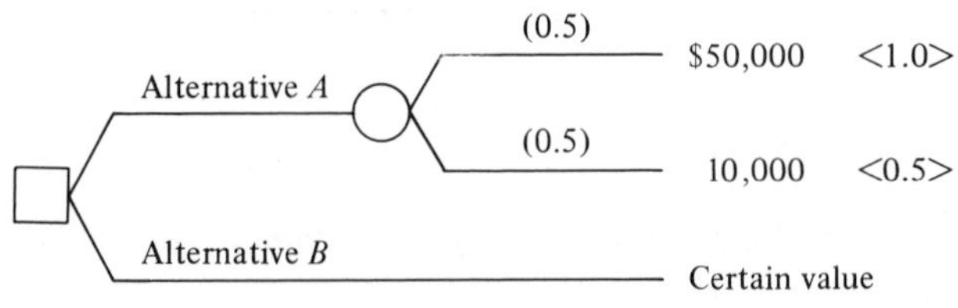

Since you are indifferent between $A$ and $B$, $E[U_A]=E[U_B]$. Therefore, $U(\$26{,}000)=0.75$. This point can be added to our plot. We can now form any gamble using payoffs for which we already have preference numbers, and repeat the process. Assume that we form the 50–50 gamble shown in Figure 17.9 and that your certainty equivalent is $\$-1{,}000$.

**FIGURE 17.9**

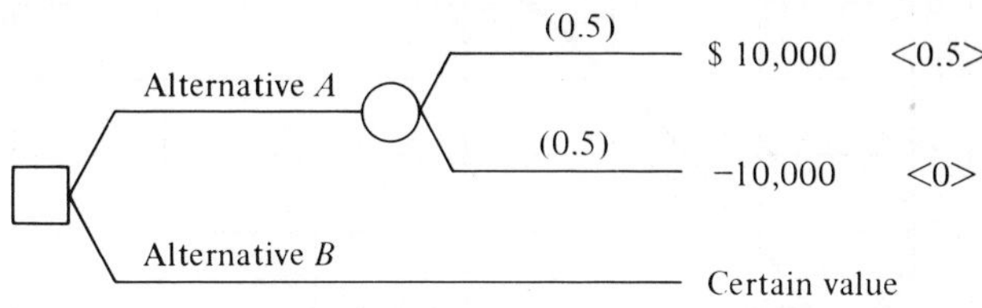


The expected preference for alternative $A$ is

$$E[U_A]=(0.5)(0.5)+(0.5)(0)=0.25$$

Therefore, $E[U_B]=U(\$-1{,}000)=E[U_A]=0.25$, and we have another point on the preference curve.

This procedure can be continued by specifying new 50–50 gambles, with payoffs for which we have the preference values, until the desired number of points have been obtained. With the assessments made above, we have Table 17.3. Figure 17.10 can be drawn. Notice that again the preference curve is very similar to curves assessed using the other methods (see Figures 17.4 and 17.6). The question is, which of the methods is the best?

**TABLE 17.3**

| *Preference Numbers or Utility* | *Certainty Equivalent* |
|---|---|
| 1.00 | $50,000 |
| 0.75 | 26,000 |
| 0.50 | 10,000 |
| 0.25 | −1,000 |
| 0 | −10,000 |

## COMPARISONS OF METHODS FOR ASSESSING PREFERENCE CURVES

The choice among the procedures should be based on ease of use by the decision maker. Which one presents settings that are the easiest for a decision maker to think about and understand? Presumably a procedure that is easier to think about will result in assessments that are more consistent and in which

FIGURE 17.10

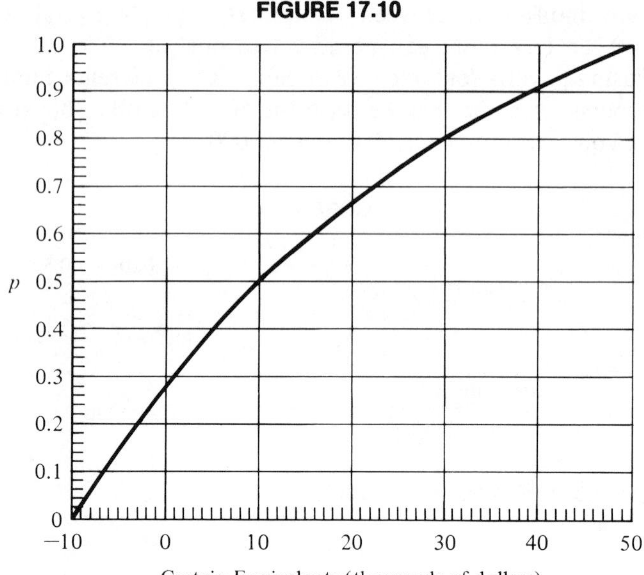


the decision maker will have more confidence. Since probabilities are difficult to conceptualize, particularly when small differences or small probabilities are being considered, the 50–50 method is often recommended. The argument is that a 50–50 gamble is the simplest of all settings that include uncertainty and therefore is the best setting to use for assessing preferences. If we accept this reasoning, the method using the basic reference gamble is mainly of conceptual value. Recall that this method was used to establish the relationship between preference numbers and probabilities of winning the reference gamble. This relationship provides the rationale for the computational procedure used to obtain the preference curve with 50–50 gambles (i.e., the expected preference calculation).

There is another issue regarding assessment of preference information. It is the exact method by which a decision maker determines certainty equivalents. One method is direct assessment. As the decision maker you would be asked to directly specify a certain value which makes you indifferent between alternatives *A* and *B* shown in Figure 17.11. The indirect method

FIGURE 17.11

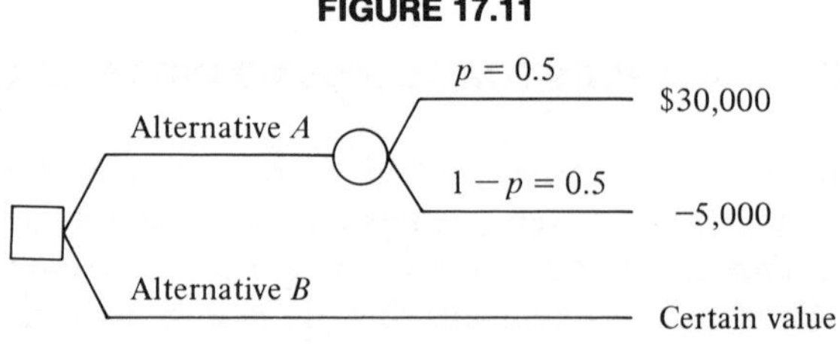

(described in Chapter 6) presents a series of choices in which the decision maker merely chooses between alternative $A$ and alternative $B$. For instance, the certain value might be specified to be \$−4,000. In this case the decision maker would almost certainly choose $A$. If the certain value were raised to \$20,000, the decision maker would almost certainly choose $B$. For a certain value of \$10,000, the choice of $A$ over $B$ would depend upon the decision maker. The strategy for the indirect method is to present a series of choices to determine the point of indifference. For instance, if the choice is $A$ for \$10,000 but $B$ for \$11,000, we know that the decision maker's certainty equivalent lies between \$10,000 and \$11,000. The choice between the direct method and indirect method may again depend upon the decision maker. The indirect method makes clear that a certainty equivalent is a decision and it provides the most basic means of obtaining the certainty equivalent.

## ASSESSMENT FOR SPECIAL RISK ATTITUDES

If special attitudes toward risk are identified, the preference curve may be assessed with fewer points.

### Risk Neutrality

Risk neutrality is the simplest case. The preference curve is a straight line. Since certainty equivalents are equal to expected values, the curve is not required for evaluating decisions.

### Risk Aversion

If a decision maker is risk-averse over the entire range of interest, the preference curve must be relatively smooth. In particular, it must lie above any straight line connecting two points.[2] This means that it can never "dip" or even "flatten out" to the point that it is straight. These requirements mean that a few assessments rapidly restrict the shape of the preference curve.

For example, consider the five points on Figure 17.12. The smooth curves that are consistent with risk aversion over the entire range lie within the shaded area. As points are added, the differences between curves rapidly become smaller. Under these conditions a decision maker can have some confidence in drawing a preference curve with relatively few points.

### ●● Constant Risk Aversion

Constant risk aversion implies a preference curve of the form $U(X)=a-be^{-\lambda X}$, where $X$ is the random variable measured in terms of the evaluation units. If we require $U(X_{min})=0$, $U(X_{max})=1.0$, where $X_{min}$ is the lowest value

[2]The curve must be concave.

**FIGURE 17.12**

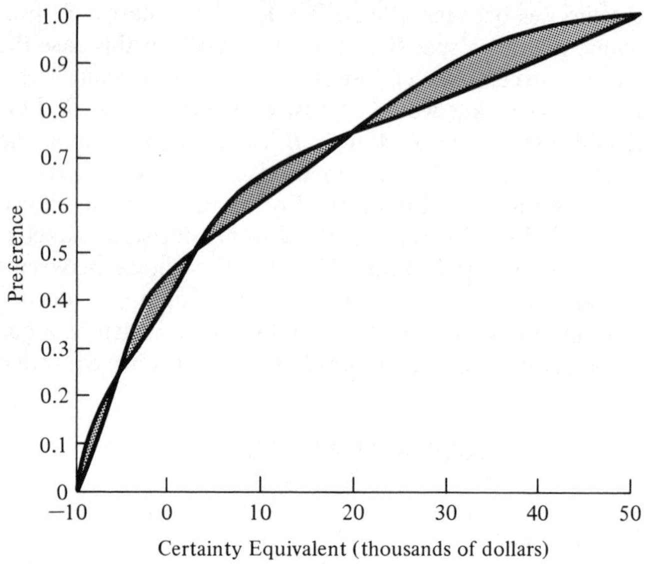

for the preference scale and $X_{max}$ is the highest, only one more equation is needed to find the values for parameters $a$, $b$, and $\lambda$. This means that a single certainty equivalent assessment is all that is required to specify completely the preference curve. If we use the 50–50 gamble shown in Figure 17.13, we have

**FIGURE 17.13**

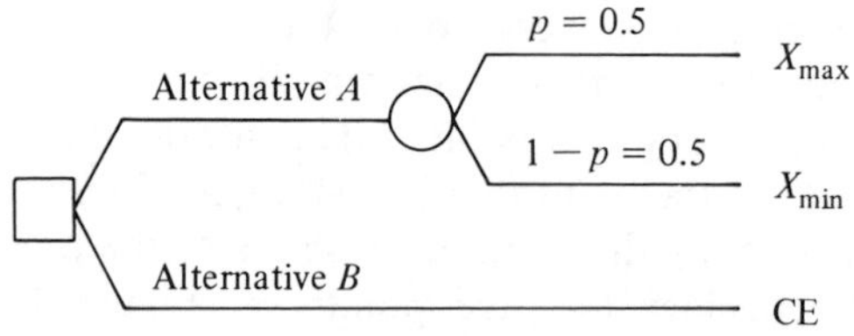


$0.5\,U(X_{max}) + 0.5\,U(X_{min}) = U(\text{CE})$. From this and the requirements that $U(X_{min}) = 0$ and $U(X_{max}) = 1.0$, we can establish:

1. $e^{-\lambda(\text{CE})} = 0.5(e^{-\lambda(X_{min})} + e^{-\lambda(X_{max})})$.
2. $a = \dfrac{e^{-\lambda(X_{min})}}{e^{-\lambda(X_{min})} - e^{-\lambda(X_{max})}}$.
3. $b = \dfrac{1}{e^{-\lambda(X_{min})} - e^{-\lambda(X_{max})}}$.

For any values of CE, $X_{min}$, and $X_{max}$, 1 can be solved for $\lambda$. This can be done by trial and error or by means of a sophisticated search procedure on a computer. Equations 2 and 3 can then be evaluated directly.

### Risk-Seeking

The same type of regularity conditions that apply for risk-averse curves also apply for risk-seeking curves. In this case the curve must lie *below* any straight line. It can never "peak" or even "flatten out" to the point that it is straight. If it does, it will not be risk-seeking over some range.

## RESOLUTION OF INCONSISTENCIES

As discussed above, conditions on the general shape of a preference curve can be inferred from assumptions on risk-taking behavior. Identifying these conditions reduces the number of assessments required to specify the curve. The assumptions on behavior, such as risk aversion, are global or overall statements on how an individual feels about risk. In many cases assumptions such as risk aversion over a particular range can be made rather easily. The more special conditions such as constant risk aversion may be more difficult to identify.

Even though these conditions cut down the number of assessments required, the problem of inconsistencies still exists. For instance, what if a particular assessment is inconsistent with an overall assumption? In these cases the only option is to turn to the individual making the assessments and point out the inconsistency. The decision on whether to modify the assessments or the assumptions must be faced and resolved. As part of the process, a series of assessments can be used and an effort made to help the assessor think clearly about various gambles. However, ultimately each individual must decide for himself how to resolve inconsistencies.

## ●● SCALE VALUES FOR PREFERENCES OR UTILITIES

Up to this point we have been consistent in allowing the scale values for the preference curves to be interpreted in terms of probabilities of winning the basic reference gamble. This is the natural scale to use and allows a specific physical interpretation. However, any scale can be used. Although the scale loses its interpretation in terms of probabilities of winning a basic reference gamble, the mechanics of the procedure still work.[3] The expected preference or utility calculations will work and the curve generated will have the same shape. It is the shape of the preference curve, not the absolute values

[3]The formal condition is that the scale is unique up to a positive linear transformation.

associated with it, that is important. Curves with the same shapes but different scales will have different expected preference values but will yield the same certainty equivalents.

## SUMMARY

Assessment procedures for preferences are designed to help a decision maker who is unsure of which choice to make when uncertainty complicates a decision. They are designed to help *clarify* attitudes toward risk by using a series of simple gambles. The objective is to allow a decision maker to be *more consistent* with his *own* risk preferences.

Preference scales must encompass the *maximum* and *minimum* values of the evaluation units assigned to all the outcomes of the alternatives under consideration. To enhance consistency the scale should not be significantly wider than this range.

There are two basic procedures for assessing preference curves:

*Basic Reference Gamble Method:* A basic reference gamble has a probability $p$ of winning, which yields the top of the preference scale range, and a probability of $(1-p)$ of losing, which yields the bottom of the preference scale range. Values for $p$ are varied and certainty equivalents recorded for the reference gambles. A plot is made of $p$ versus the certainty equivalents. When the plot is well defined, a smooth curve is drawn through the points.

*50–50 Gamble Method:* In this method the probabilities of winning and losing are fixed at $p=(1-p)=0.5$. The payoffs for winning and losing are changed and certainty equivalents for the resulting gambles assessed. Preference numbers are obtained by equating the expected preference of the gamble with the preference of the certainty equivalent. The preferences are plotted versus the certainty equivalents and a smooth curve drawn through the points. The 50–50 method has the advantage of using a gamble with probabilities that are easy to understand.

For either method the certainty equivalents can be assessed directly or by using a series of choices as described in Chapter 6. When special attitudes toward risk can be identified, the preference curve can be assessed with fewer points.

## ASSIGNMENT MATERIAL

**17.1.** Comment on the following statements.

(a) Preference curves are useful because they eliminate the requirement for explicitly considering your attitude for risk.

(b) The purpose behind assessing a preference curve is to reduce inconsistencies.

(c) Assessing preference curves may help make decisions because it eliminates the necessity of making certainty equivalent assessments.

(d) Certainty equivalents are subjective estimates of the outcome of an uncertain event.

(e) Preference analysis provides a means for explicitly including an individual's attitude toward risk, whether he/she is risk-averse, risk-neutral, or risk-seeking.

**17.2.** What is the argument for using assessment procedures based on 50–50 gambles as opposed to assessment procedures based on using reference gambles?

**17.3.** Explain why identification of special attitudes toward risk can simplify the assessment process.

**17.4.** Given the following information, plot four points on the individual's preference curve. The maximum payoff is \$1,000. The minimum payoff is \$0. The certainty equivalent for a 50–50 gamble between \$1,000 and \$0 is \$400. The certainty equivalent for a 50–50 gamble between \$400 and \$0 is \$100.

**17.5.** As part of a decision analysis, George Larson provided the following information.

(a) Larson indicated he was indifferent between a 50–50 chance at \$+10 million and \$−10 million and \$−5 million for certain.

(b) His certainty equivalent for a lottery offering a 0.5 chance at \$−5 million and a 0.5 chance at \$+10 million was \$0.

(c) Larson was indifferent between a lottery with a 0.7 chance at \$+10 million and a 0.3 chance at \$0 and \$+5 million for certain.

Sketch a preference curve for Larson based on this information.

**17.6.** Refer to Figure 17.10.

(a) Specify a reference gamble that is equivalent (based on this curve) to the certain amount \$30,000.

(b) Specify a 50–50 gamble that is equivalent (based on this curve) to the certain amount \$30,000.

**17.7.** Thomas Bayes had long been promised a graduation present of \$10,000 by his father, to be received on graduation day, 3 months hence. His father had recently offered an alternative gift, and Bayes was trying to decide between the two gifts, since his father had asked for a decision by the following day. The alternative gift would be 1000 shares of stock in Satisficing Systems, Inc., a consulting firm with which Bayes was slightly acquainted. On the day he was trying to decide, the stock was selling for \$12 per share. Thus, it looked to Bayes as if he would be wise to take the stock, since its present value was \$12,000. He would not receive the stock until graduation day, however, and he recognized that the stock price 3 months in the future was uncertain. He also recognized that his utility for money was not linear, and that his risk aversion would therefore influence his decision. With these facts in mind, Bayes reached the following conclusions:

1. He felt that the stock price was more likely to rise than fall in the intervening 3 months, and that it was as likely to be above \$14 per share as below that figure when he would receive the stock.

2. He felt that there was only 1 chance in 100 that the stock price would drop to less than $6 per share, and an equal chance that the price would be more than twice its current price on graduation day.
3. He also thought that there was only 1 chance in 5 that the price would be below $10, and that there was 1 chance in 4 that it would be above $16 when he received it.

In considering his preferences, Bayes reached the following conclusions:

1. That his certainty equivalent for a lottery offering a 50–50 chance at zero and $25,000 was $9,000.
2. That his certainty equivalent for a lottery offering a 0.2 chance at $25,000 and a 0.8 chance at zero was $3,000.
3. That his certainty equivalent for a lottery offering a 50–50 chance at $3,000 or $25,000 was $12,000.
4. That his certainty equivalent for a lottery offering a 50–50 chance at $12,000 or $25,000 was $17,000.

Determine the cumulative probability distribution that Bayes has assigned to the stock price.

Calculate Bayes' certainty equivalent for the gift of the stock.

**17.8. International Vending Company (A)**

The International Vending Company (IVC) provides complete vending and concession services for professional athletic events around the world. They have been highly successful over the last five years and have contracts to provide food, drinks, souvenirs and programs to over 500 events in this next year.

Because of this recent growth and the large number of events to be covered, last year they decentralized their operations through a type of franchising. IVC has twenty-five separate operational centers which are responsible for carrying out the detailed planning and providing services in a geographical area. These centers have only limited authority which allows them to hire personnel and make day-of-the-game modifications regarding order levels within the policy guidelines set down by IVC. Franchise owners are paid 60% of the net profits.

Executives in IVC have established tight controls on the franchises as a result of some very bad experiences in the early stages of the company's operations. They feel these controls are required to ensure the requisite quality of service and assign a large measure of their recent success to the controls.

IVC's success has not been limited to increasing sales. They have also established good profit margins. Here they feel their decentralization program combined with strong controls and good planning has provided the conditions which allow them to maintain good profits. Each year the staff considers a wide range of alternative plans for selling in each locality and for each game. They, of course, utilize inputs from the local operators but they set the final plans based on extensive reviews of markets, buying behavior and the economies available to them from purchasing on a large scale and selling standard items.

At the beginning of each year the staff identifies five alternative plans which can be utilized at any game. The profitability of each plan depends mainly on weather conditions on the day of the game and the popularity of the teams which are playing. They have found from past experience that popularity of teams can be forecast quite accurately by two weeks before a game when they have to make a final choice on which of the five plans they will utilize for the game at hand. The weather, however, is a different story. Because of the uncertainty in the weather they develop profit forecasts for each plan based on four different states of weather:

$n_1$ = warm, no rain
$n_2$ = warm, rain
$n_3$ = cold, no rain
$n_4$ = cold, rain

Although most of their franchises handle at least ten events per year, this year IVC has set up a special franchise, on a trial basis, which will only take care of the Super Bowl. Because of the special nature of this franchise, the owner will receive 40% of the net profits. IVC planners have worked out estimates of net profit for each of their five plans under each of the weather conditions as follows:

| | | | Plan* | | |
|---|---|---|---|---|---|
| *Weather* | $P_1$ | $P_2$ | $P_3$ | $P_4$ | $P_5$ |
| 1. Warm, no rain | 12 | 20 | 24 | 16 | 12 |
| 2. Warm, rain | 12 | 8 | 8 | 12 | 12 |
| 3. Cold, no rain | 16 | 12 | 8 | 12 | 12 |
| 4. Cold, rain | 12 | 8 | 8 | 12 | 8 |

*Figures are in units of $10,000

The staff in consultation with the weather bureau has also obtained probabilities reflecting the chances of each type of weather:

| *Weather* | *Probability* |
|---|---|
| Warm, no rain | .4 |
| Warm, rain | .2 |
| Cold, no rain | .2 |
| Cold, rain | .2 |

1. What plan would you utilize if you were president of IVC and were risk neutral?
2. How much would the president be willing to pay to learn which of the four possible weather states would actually occur?
3. Place yourself in the position of the franchise owner. Assess a preference curve and use it to determine your choice among the plans.

# 18

# Behavioral Assumptions and Limitations of Decision Analysis

The procedures for undertaking analyses of decisions under uncertainty have been discussed. In this chapter we consider the question: When does this type of analysis makes sense? Or, put slightly differently, what are the conditions under which the suggested decomposition will yield the "correct" choice? There are two parts to this question. One part involves the *choice process* once the alternatives have been completely specified through a model. The other involves the validity of the *model* as a representation of the decision problem. Figure 18.1 shows which parts of the process are considered in this chapter.

**FIGURE 18.1**

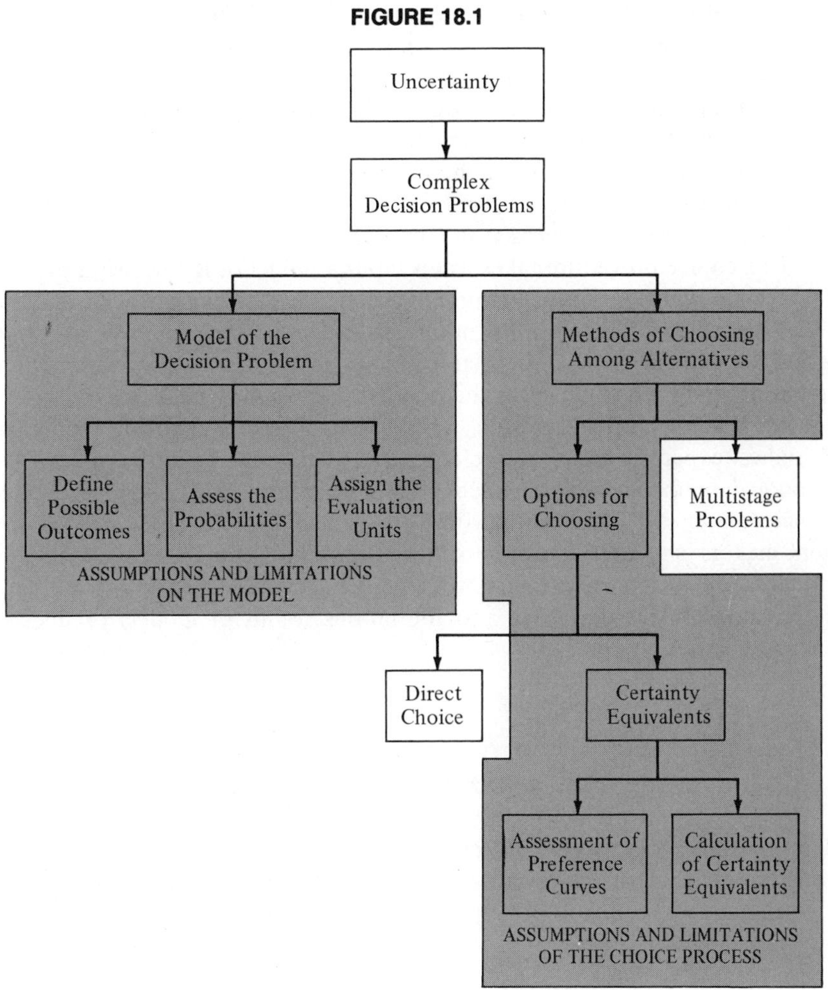

## THE BASIC IDEAS

The mechanics of calculating certainty equivalents from probability distributions and preference curves are familiar by now. In developing them we relied on a set of plausible arguments. To complete our understanding of making choices using preference analysis, we need to explore these arguments in more detail. The purpose is to understand when these arguments are valid. The approach is to establish a set of assumptions, relating to the behavior of a decision maker, that guarantee the validity of the arguments (and hence the procedure). If these assumptions (sometimes called axioms) hold, the decomposition of the choice process by calculating certainty equivalents using probability distributions and preference curves is a valid procedure for choosing among alternatives.

In evaluating the behavioral assumptions, you should focus on whether you agree they are *reasonable*. You may agree for either of two reasons: (1) you believe they are true in the sense that they characterize individual behavior, or (2) regardless of whether they describe how people in general behave, they represent patterns you would personally like to satisfy. If you accept the assumptions, using expected preferences as a guide for action is legitimate. These results ensure the *existence* of a set of preferences that can be used to choose among alternatives. The operational problem of finding these preferences was discussed in Chapter 17.

This choice procedure takes as an input a model of the decision problem. We assume that the characterization of each alternative in terms of uncertain events and payoffs is a faithful model of the actual problem. We know that in all but the simplest settings, the model will be an approximation of the actual problem. In some cases the approximations may be so severe that any detailed analysis is of little value. The statements about choosing on the basis of highest expected preference refer to the approximation of the real problem embodied in the model to which preference theory is applied. Even when choices are made without resorting to a complete preference analysis, decision makers should be aware of the assumptions and limitations of the models used to represent their problems. This chapter discusses some of the more important assumptions and limitations found in models of decisions under uncertainty.

## THE BEHAVIORAL ASSUMPTIONS OR AXIOMS FOR CHOICE

Below we describe five behavioral assumptions or axioms. If these assumptions are satisfied by a decision maker, there exists a set of preferences such that the decision maker prefers the alternative with the highest expected preference value.

**Assumption 1 (Ordering of Outcomes and Transitivity)**
*A decision maker can order (establish preference or indifference) any two alternatives and the ordering is transitive. For example, given any alternatives* $A_1, A_2, A_3$, *either* $A_1 \succ A_2, A_2 \succ A_1$, *or* $A_1 \sim A_2$, and if $A_1 \succsim A_2, A_2 \succsim A_3$, *then* $A_1 \succsim A_3$.

The assumption has two parts. The first provides the technical assurance that the decision maker's preferences exist over a complete set of alternatives. It also seems to pose a dilemma which appears to preclude any analytical assistance with the choice problem. The assumption seems to say that a condition for using the decomposition procedure to provide help in choosing between two alternatives is to state a preference between them. In other words, the procedure can only provide help on making choices *when it is not necessary*—a rather limiting condition for a procedure designed to help in decision making. The situation is not quite so bleak. What the assumption requires is a basic set of tastes or preferences over all alternatives. However, these preferences do not need to be explicitly available. It means that if the decision maker contemplated long enough and hard enough, these preferences would emerge. Of course, this is exactly where some assistance may be helpful. The whole idea of the assistance is that preferences for complex alternatives can be obtained through the expression of preferences over simple alternatives. What the assumption does make perfectly clear is that the *decision maker* must supply the preferences. No analytical technique can do that.

The technical name for the second part of this assumption is transitivity. It ensures a degree of consistency in the decision maker's preferences. Assume that you have an opportunity to invest in one of three alternatives: an *oil well*, a *shopping center*, and an *apartment house*. This assumption says that if you prefer the *shopping center* to the *apartment house*, and the *apartment house* to the *oil drilling*, you must prefer the *shopping center* to the *oil drilling*.

**Assumption 2 (Reduction of Compound Uncertain Events)**

*You are indifferent between a compound uncertain event and the simple uncertain event determined by reduction using standard probability manipulations.*

For example, you are indifferent between the two uncertain events shown in Figure 18.2.

**FIGURE 18.2**

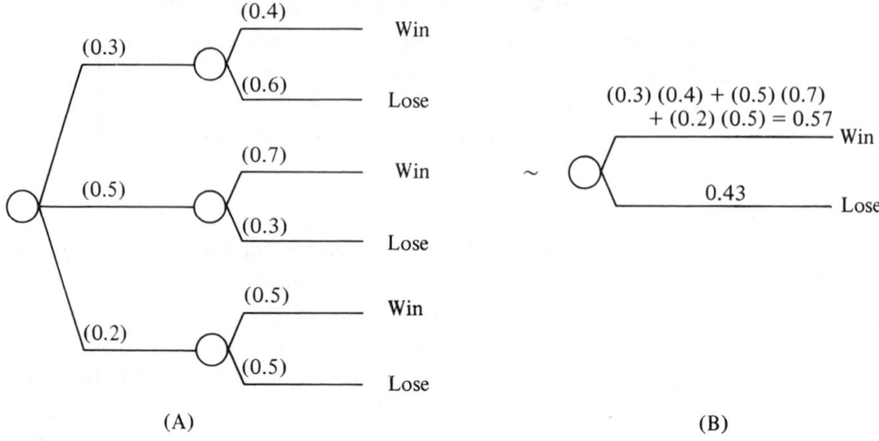


This is sometimes referred to as the "no fun in gambling" assumption. Uncertain event ($B$) is obtained from ($A$) by using standard probability manipulations to determine the probabilities of *win* and *lose*.

> **Assumption 3 (Continuity)**
>
> *You are indifferent between each outcome, A (e.g., win $100) and some uncertain event involving only two "basic" outcomes—$A_1$, which is better than A, and $A_2$, which is worse than A.*

This assumption asserts that you can always find $p$, the probability of obtaining $A_1$ in Figure 18.3, such that you are indifferent between $a_1$ and $a_2$.

**FIGURE 18.3**

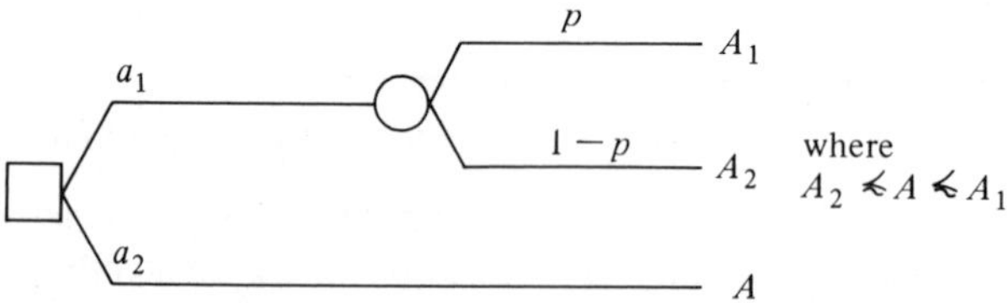


In cases in which one of the outcomes is very bad, this assumption may be difficult to verify. But in general the argument is that if $p=1$, $a_1$ is at least as preferred as $a_2$, and when $p=0$, $a_2$ is at least as preferred as $a_1$. Therefore, as $p$ varies from 1 to 0, there must be some point of indifference.

**Assumption 4 (Substitutibility)**

*You are indifferent between any original uncertain event and one formed by substituting, for some outcome A, an uncertain event that you have judged to be equivalent to the outcome A.*

That is, if you are indifferent between some certain outcome $A$ and some uncertain event when the two are considered separately, you are also indifferent between them when substituted into some uncertain event.

**Assumption 5 (Monotonicity)**

*Uncertain event $L_1$ in Figure 18.4 is preferred to $L_2$ if and only if $p_1 > p_2$, where $A_1 \succ A_2$.*

**FIGURE 18.4**

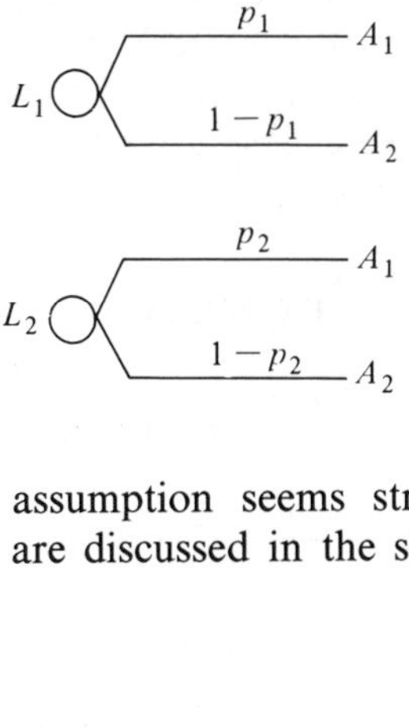

On the surface this assumption seems straightforward. Situations in which it may be violated are discussed in the section on limitations of the behavioral assumption.

## IMPLICATIONS OF THE ASSUMPTIONS

The implications of the assumptions are given in the following proposition.

**Proposition**

*Given any two uncertain events $B_1$ and $B_2$, if assumptions 1 through 5 hold, there are numbers, $U_1, U_2, \ldots$, representing preferences (or utilities) associated with payoffs for outcomes, such that the overall preference between the uncertain events is reflected by the expected values of the U's for each event.*

FIGURE 18.5

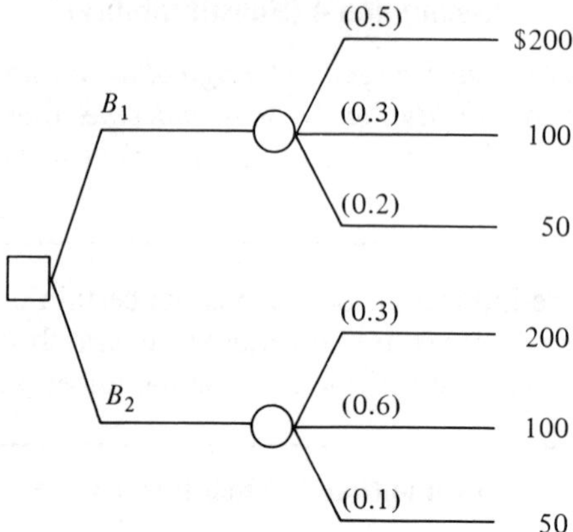


Rather than a formal proof, an example will be given to show how the assumptions lead to the conclusion stated in the proposition.

Consider the uncertain events in Figure 18.5.

1. By assumption 3 (continuity), we can find equivalent reference gambles, for each certain amount in Figure 18.5, in which the best outcome is at least \$200 and the worst is less than or equal to \$50. For purposes of illustration, assume that we choose a reference gamble between \$500 and zero, and that the equivalences are those shown in Figure 18.6.

FIGURE 18.6

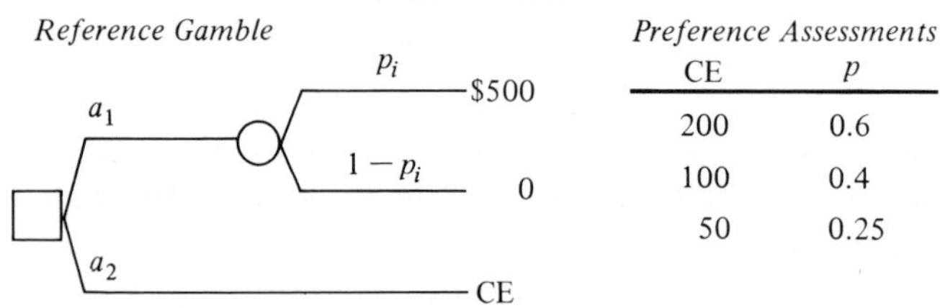


*Preference Assessments*

| CE | $p$ |
|---|---|
| 200 | 0.6 |
| 100 | 0.4 |
| 50 | 0.25 |

2. By assumption 4 (substitutability), the reference gambles determined at step 1 can be substituted into $B_1$ and $B_2$, forming the equivalent uncertain events $B_1'$ and $B_2'$ shown in Figure 18.7.
3. By assumption 2 (reduction of compound uncertain events), we are indifferent between $B_1'$ and $\overline{B}_1$ and $B_2'$ and $\overline{B}_2$, shown in Figure 18.8.
4. By assumption 1 (transitivity), since $B_1 \sim B_1'$ and $B_1' \sim \overline{B}_1$, then $B_1 \sim \overline{B}_1$. Similarly, since $B_2 \sim B_2'$ and $B_2' \sim \overline{B}_2$, then $B_2 \sim \overline{B}_2$. In other words, we are indifferent between the two lotteries shown in Figure 18.8 and the corresponding lotteries shown in Figure 18.5.
5. By assumption 5 (monotonicity), we have $\overline{B}_1 \succ \overline{B}_2$ since $0.470 > 0.445$.

**FIGURE 18.7**

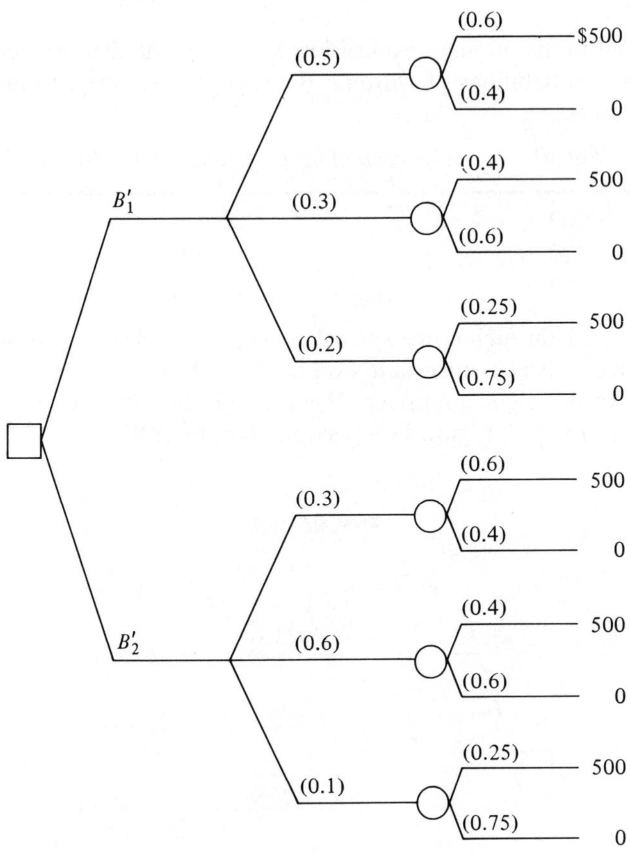


**FIGURE 18.8**

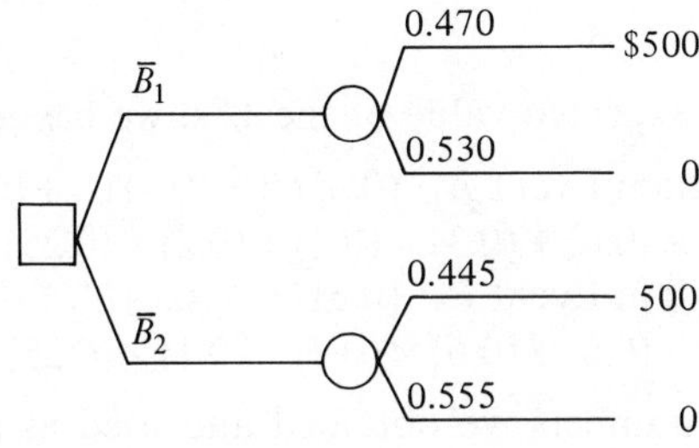


where (0.5) (0.6) + (0.3) (0.4) + (0.2) (0.25) = 0.470
and (0.3) (0.6) + (0.6) (0.4) + (0.1) (0.25) = 0.445

6. By assumption 1 (transitivity), we have $B_1 \sim \bar{B}_1 > \bar{B}_2 \sim B_2$ and hence $B_1 > B_2$.
7. Returning to the original proposition we can define the numbers $U_1, U_2, \ldots$ to be the probabilities of winning the reference gambles shown in Figure 18.6. That is:

| *Payoff* | *Corresponding Preference or Utility Number* |
|---|---|
| 200 | $U_1 = 0.6$ |
| 100 | $U_2 = 0.4$ |
| 50 | $U_3 = 0.25$ |

8. From steps 1 through 6, we know that numbers 0.470 and 0.445 reflect the preference between uncertain events $B_1$ and $B_2$. That is, we prefer the event with the highest number. If we assign the values of $U_1$, $U_2$, and $U_3$ as shown in step 7, Figure 18.5 becomes Figure 18.9.

**FIGURE 18.9**

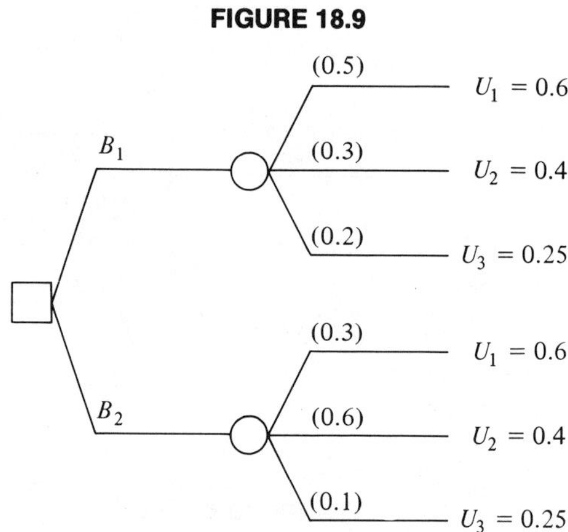


If we calculate the expected value of the $U$'s, we have:

$$\text{Uncertain Event } B_1\text{: } (0.5)\,U_1 + (0.3)\,U_2 + (0.2)\,U_3$$
$$= (0.5) \times (0.6) + (0.3) \times (0.4) + (0.2) \times (0.25) = 0.470$$
$$\text{Uncertain Event } B_2\text{: } (0.3)\,U_1 + (0.6)\,U_2 + (0.1)\,U_3$$
$$= (0.3) \times (0.6) + (0.6) \times (0.4) + (0.1) \times (0.25) = 0.445$$

These are just the numbers we obtained and used as a basis for $B_1 > B_2$. Therefore, we have demonstrated that there exist numbers $U_1$, $U_2$, and $U_3$ whose expected value reflects the preferences of an individual between the two uncertain events.

These numbers are the preferences or utilities that result from the preference assessment procedures discussed in Chapter 17. Therefore, if the behavioral assumptions are satisfied, the procedure of choosing based on the highest expected preference is legitimate and will result in the most preferred choice.

## LIMITATIONS IMPOSED BY THE BEHAVIORAL ASSUMPTIONS

The extent to which these behavioral assumptions limit the application of the preference analysis procedure depends on the frequency with which they are violated. Below we discuss some conditions under which the assumptions may be violated.

### Transitivity for Individuals

There is evidence which suggests that transitivity is often violated by decision makers.[1] Explanations of *why* transitivity does not hold range from a basic belief that people are inconsistent to the suggestion that behavior that is apparently intransitive can be explained by considering a richer set of attributes or measures associated with each outcome. For example, an individual may state that he prefers a meal of *steak and wine* to a meal of *cheese and wine* and prefers a meal of *cheese and wine* to a meal of *sausage and beer*. But, on entering a restaurant where *steak and wine* and *sausage and beer* are available, the individual may choose *sausage and beer* over *steak and wine*. One explanation is that there are important attributes that are not displayed, such as cost or time of day, which explain the behavior. For example, the individual actually prefers *sausage and beer at \$1 for a noon meal* to *steak and wine at \$10 for a noon meal*.

However, for our purposes, the most appropriate question is not whether individuals exhibit intransitive behavior. As noted before, if everyone always displayed completely consistent behavior, there would be no need for decision aids to help with consistency. The question that is most important to us is: Given the choice, do decision makers (or do you) prefer to act transitively? For example, suppose that in discussing a new personnel policy with the president of a company, we were told that he preferred the *current plan* to an *affirmative action plan*. However, he believes the *affirmative action plan* is better than *no plan* at all, and *no plan* at all is better than the *current plan*. If we pointed out that preference of *no plan* at all to the *current plan* was "inconsistent" with his first two choices, would he then feel obliged to go back and reassess his preferences to obtain "consistency?" In most cases, when given the chance, decision makers are interested in achieving this type

[1]See, for example, J. R. Miller III, "The Effect of Clarification on Intransitive Preferences," Graduate School of Business, Stanford University, Research Paper No. 2, 1971; W. Edwards, "Probability-Preferences in Gambling," *American Journal of Psychology*, Vol. 66, 1953, pp. 349–364; J. M. Davis, "The Transitivity of Preference," *Behavioral Science*, Vol. 3, 1958, pp. 26–33.

of consistency. The question is: Do you feel sufficiently convinced of the benefits to try to act in accordance with the assumption and suggest that others should also? Circumstances may exist when some people would decide against satisfying this assumption. However, there are large classes of problems, including those associated with organizations, where the assumption is valid.

### Existence of Preferences for Groups

We have stressed throughout that preference analysis as presented here applies to an individual decision maker. When groups make decisions, a conceptual problem arises. Even if each individual is willing to subscribe to the assumptions, is there such a thing as a preference function for the group? If so, what are its properties and how can it be determined? Unfortunately, there is no satisfactory operational answer to these questions.[2] Even if we assume that a group preference function *should* be found, the group may not exhibit transitive behavior, or even be able to order the outcomes.[3]

On the other hand, it can be argued that the transitivity and ordering assumption should apply equally well to groups as individuals. Just as we suggested in the face of empirical evidence of intransitivity for individuals, the question is: Does the group desire to act in a transitive manner? The argument in favor of transitivity for a group seems to be just as compelling as the argument for individuals.

The assumption that is harder to justify for a group is substitutibility. A problem arises when we have members with different beliefs as to the probabilities of the outcomes as well as different preferences. The idea is that the uncertainty and differing beliefs as to the probabilities can lead to bargaining that results in a group preferring a different set of prizes in the context of the uncertain event than when each prize is considered separately.

All of these complications stem from substantial differences in preferences and beliefs among group members. When groups are relatively homogeneous in their preferences and beliefs, these complications may not arise. A group may be able to agree on a preference function and its use in the normal way to help decide on complicated problems.

### Continuity Assumption with Extreme Outcomes

The continuity assumption specifies that for any prize $W$ that is "worse" than a prize $W_1$ and "better" than a prize $W_2$, we can find a probability $p$ so that an individual is indifferent between the prize $W$ and an uncertain event with probability $p$ of winning $W_1$ and $(1-p)$ of getting $W_2$. When outcomes are

[2]See H. Raiffa, *Decision Analysis, Introductory Lectures on Choices and Uncertainty* (Reading, Mass.: Addison-Wesley, 1968).

[3]See K. J. Arrow, *Social Choice and Individual Values* (New York: Wiley, 1951).

**FIGURE 18.10**

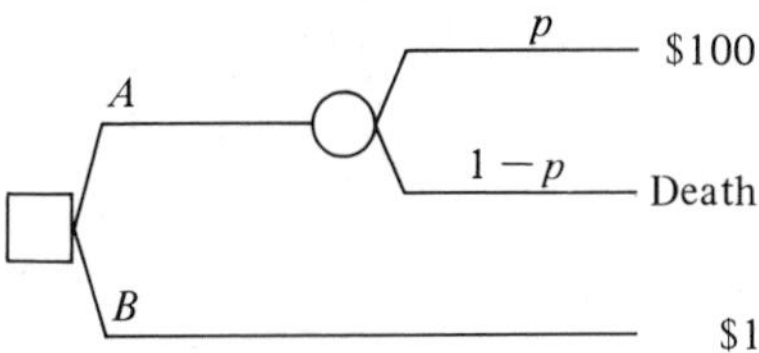


*very* bad, it is sometimes argued that this assumption breaks down. For instance, consider the two alternatives shown in Figure 18.10.

Some people argue that the only condition under which they would accept $A$ over $B$ is if $p = 1.0$. That is, there is no condition under which $A \sim B$. $B$ is strictly preferred to $A$ unless $p = 1.0$, and if $p = 1.0$, $A$ is strictly preferred to $B$. This violates the continuity assumption. Perhaps you would agree with this analysis. If so, consider how you would respond to the following proposition. There is an envelope with your name on it and a $100 bill inside at the toll plaza of the Golden Gate Bridge. If you arrive within the next 2 hours, the money is yours. Assume that you are located 30 miles south of the toll plaza and must drive there on a freeway to collect your envelope. If you decide not to go, I will give you $1 (and go myself to collect the money). Assuming that you had a car and the time, would you go? As anyone who has driven on a California freeway can attest, there is a small but positive probability of an accident each time you venture on one. Therefore, if you decide to go after the envelope, the implication is that you will choose $A$ over $B$ when $p$ is less than 1.0. Once you have started down this path, I could try to specify some probability $p$ such that you are just indifferent between $A$ and $B$. Therefore, even in such an extreme case as this, it may be possible to establish continuity. Fortunately, most decision problems do not include such extreme outcomes.

### Monotonicity Assumption with Differences in the Time at Which Uncertainty Is Resolved

The monotonicity assumption implies that, for two uncertain events with identical payoffs, an individual's preference will depend only on the probability of winning. Therefore, an individual would be indifferent between the two uncertain events shown in Figure 18.11. Now suppose that $C$ represents a flip of a coin *today* with a payoff in *1 year*, and $D$ represents a flip of the same coin *1 year* from now with the payoff to be received immediately after the coin is flipped. Would you still be indifferent? Many people would now prefer $C$ to $D$ because the uncertainty is resolved sooner. The idea is that even though you will not receive the payoff until next year, it may change your behavior during the next year if you find out which outcome you will receive now. Notice that a preference analysis would assign the same expected utility to both $C$ and $D$. Therefore, it does not reflect how your

**FIGURE 18.11**

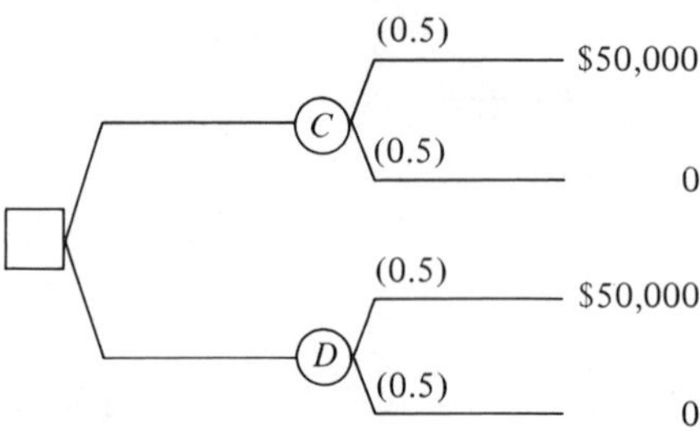


preferences are affected by the time at which the uncertainty is resolved.[4] This means that the procedures presented here are restricted to problems with alternatives in which there is no substantial difference in the time at which uncertainty is resolved—or for problems in which the decision maker has no preference for early resolution of uncertainty.

## ASSUMPTIONS AND LIMITATIONS ON THE MODEL

Models are approximations of the real decision problem. Their usefulness depends on how well they represent the actual decision. Difficulties in each of the three areas of model building that can lead to invalid results are discussed below.

### Defining Possible Outcomes

If decision diagrams become too large, they are difficult to handle. This means the process of limiting them to only those events and alternatives that are relevant to the decision under consideration is important. In Chapter 16 we pointed out that risk-averse or risk-seeking attitudes preclude treating decisions on projects separately except under conditions of constant risk aversion. Even when risk attitudes do not preclude separation, dependence among the uncertain events can prevent treating decisions separately. For instance, if you were a producer of swimming pool equipment, the evaluation of a new product line for outdoor redwood tubs could not be separated from the old products as long as their demand is correlated. In this case both sets of products are likely to be directly dependent on weather and the availability of water. Therefore, the probabilities of good and poor sales outcomes for both lines are dependent.

[4]See D. Kreps and E. Porteus, "Temporal Resolution of Uncertainty and Dynamic Choice Theory," *Econometrica* Vol. 46, 185–200 (1978).

**Example 18.1**

As the president of a swimming pool equipment manufacturing company, you decide that the demand for a swimming pool line can be represented by the outcomes *good year* and *poor year*. The profitability in a good year is \$40,000 and in a bad year is \$10,000. For a new line of redwood tubs, the demand can also be represented by outcomes *good year* and *poor year*. The profitability on a good year is \$10,000 and in a poor year is \$−7,000. Assume that demand for the products is perfectly correlated. Therefore, *P*(good year swimming pools|good year redwood tubs) = 1.0, and so on. Assume that the probability for a good year in swimming pools is 0.5. Furthermore, assume that you are constantly risk-averse over the range \$−10,000 to \$50,000 and that you have assessed your preference function to be $U(X) = 1.48368 - 1.23087e^{-0.00001868X}$. Should you take on the new line?

Consider your choice if you treat the new line by itself. Figure 18.12 shows the alternatives. The preferences are shown in brackets and the analysis indicates you should take on the new line.

**FIGURE 18.12**

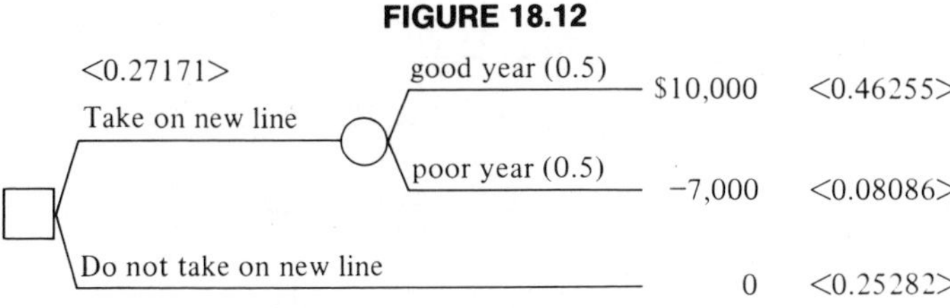


If the new line and the old swimming pool line are considered together, we have the diagram shown in Figure 18.13. Note that the payoffs are the sums of the payoffs from the swimming pool line and the alternative chosen for the new line. This analysis indicates you should not take on the new line. Therefore, treating the new line separately does not give the correct answer, even though the risk-preference function displays constant risk aversion. The reason is that the outcomes for the swimming pool line and the new line are not independent. The problem is that the overall risk faced by the individual

**FIGURE 18.13**

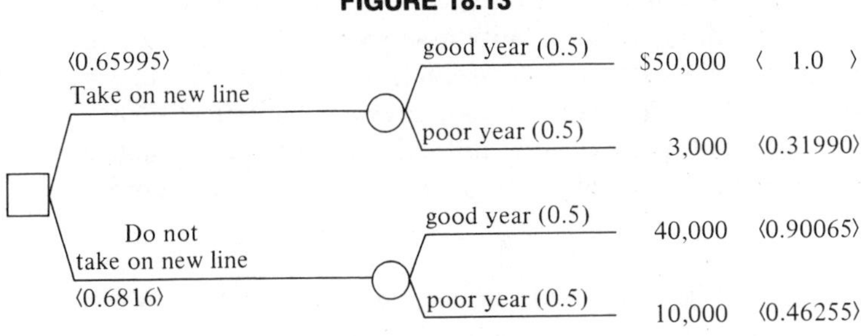

is due to a "portfolio" of dependent products. The stock market provides the best examples of portfolio problems. If individuals are risk-averse, the entire portfolio must be considered when evaluating risk.

### Subjective Assessment of Probability for Independent Uncertain Events

When probabilities are obtained by subjectively assessing a series of independent uncertain events, calibration error may limit our ability to assess the probabilities separately. The problem can be illustrated by considering a control system (say for a spacecraft). Assume that we have two completely separate systems (i.e., physically, electrically, and mechanically independent) and we want to determine the probability of failure. The events are shown in Figure 18.14.

**FIGURE 18.14**

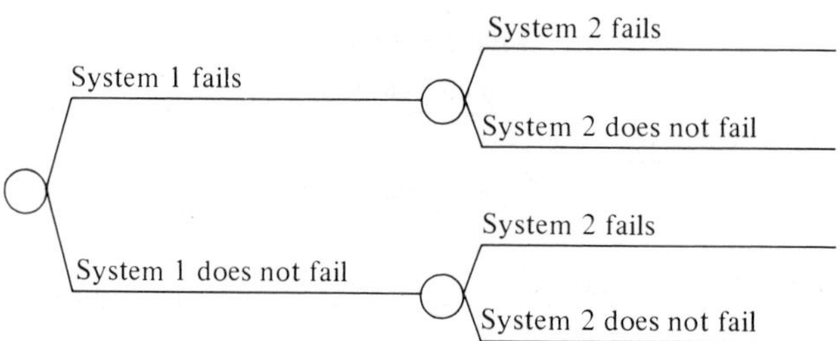


Since the events are physically identical, we may assess them both to have the same probability of failure. Assume that our subjective assessment is $P(\text{failure}) = .001$. Because of the "independence," we would calculate $P(\text{system 1 fails, system 2 fails}) = P(\text{system 1 fails}) \times P(\text{system 2 fails}) = (0.001) \times (0.001) = 0.000001$. The problem with this reasoning is that even though the two systems are physically independent, they may be statistically dependent through the assessment procedure. The probability of failure was assessed to be 0.001, but our assessment may be "wrong" or we may be miscalibrated. The occurrence of a failure in system 1 provides some evidence that the original assessment was in error (at least that is a possibility). The remedy for this is to use conditional probability assessments to calculate the probability of both failing. We calculate $P(\text{system 1 fails, system 2 fails}) = P(\text{system 2 fails} | \text{system 1 fails}) \times P(\text{system 1 fails})$. From a theoretical point of view, this approach does not present any difficulties. However, practically, it may substantially increase the difficulty of the assessment problem.[5]

[5]See J. M. Harrison, "Independence and Calibration in Decision Analysis," *Management Science*, Vol. 24, No. 3, November 1977, for additional discussion.

### Assigning Evaluation Units When Payoffs Occur Over an Extended Time Horizon

When the consequences of an action result in payoffs (costs and revenue) that occur over an extended time horizon, a problem arises over the proper way to evaluate risks. Revenues in different time periods actually constitute a multiattribute problem $(R_1, R_2, \ldots, R_n)$ where $R_1$ is net revenue in time period 1, and so on. Since money *now* is generally considered more valuable than money next year (at the very least it can be invested in a savings account), discounting techniques have been developed to determine the present value of a future stream of revenue or costs. This method of reducing the multiattribute problem to a single attribute, net present value, is a familiar technique in financial analysis. Its use requires choice of a discount rate ($r$) [the formula is $\text{NPV} = \Sigma_{i=1}^{n} R_i/(1+r)^i$] and it is this choice that introduces a problem. If there is no uncertainty, the "risk-free" discount rate can be used. This rate is usually taken to be the interest rate available on government securities. The risk-free rate represents the market cost of delaying consumption for 1 year.

Suppose that you have an investment that will yield either a 3-year stream of \$10,000, \$12,000, \$14,000, or a 3-year stream of \$−10,000, \$−8,000, \$−6,000, each with a probability of 0.5. The uncertain event is shown in Figure 18.15. Assume that none of the other problems discussed in this section is present. The streams associated with outcomes $A$ and $B$ are deterministic. Therefore, their net present value can be calculated using the risk-free rate. If we assume that the risk-free rate is 6%, we have:

$$\text{NPV}_A = \frac{\$10{,}000}{1.06} + \frac{\$12{,}000}{(1.06)^2} + \frac{\$14{,}000}{(1.06)^3}$$
$$= \$9{,}434 + \$10{,}680 + \$11{,}755 = \$31{,}869$$
$$\text{NPV}_B = \frac{\$-10{,}000}{1.06} - \frac{\$8{,}000}{(1.06)^2} - \frac{\$6{,}000}{(1.06)^3}$$
$$= \$-9{,}434 - \$7{,}120 - \$5{,}038 = \$-21{,}592$$

**FIGURE 18.15**

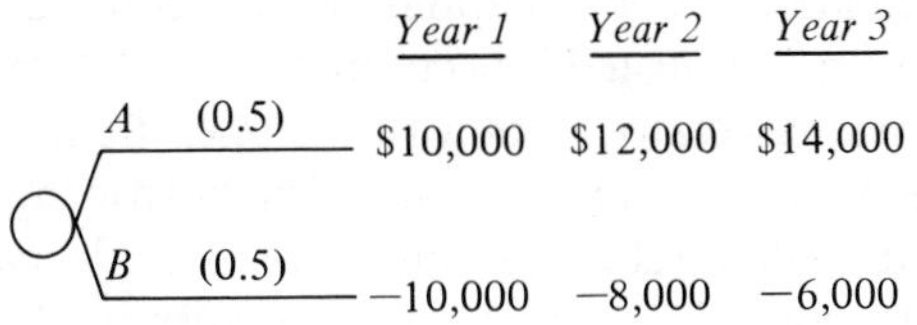

| | | *Year 1* | *Year 2* | *Year 3* |
|---|---|---|---|---|
| $A$ | (0.5) | \$10,000 | \$12,000 | \$14,000 |
| $B$ | (0.5) | −10,000 | −8,000 | −6,000 |

This means that we can replace the 3-year streams with an *equivalent* present value. As we will discuss in Chapter 20, this equivalence may not hold for all individuals. But if we are interested only in the income streams in terms of what we could obtain by investing them in a riskless security, it is reasonable to replace the 3-year streams by the net present values calculated using the risk-free rate (see Figure 18.16). The expected value of this net present value is $5,138.50. Risk could be considered by calculating a certainty equivalent using a risk preference curve as we have done throughout the book. Using the preference curve in Figure 18.17, we have the certainty equivalent shown in Figure 18.16.

**FIGURE 18.16**

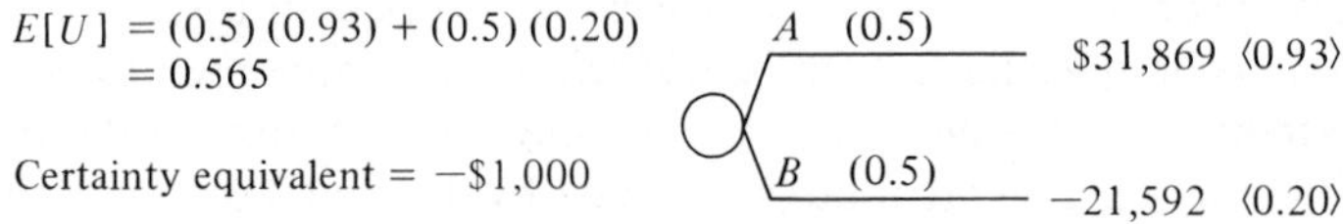


**FIGURE 18.17**

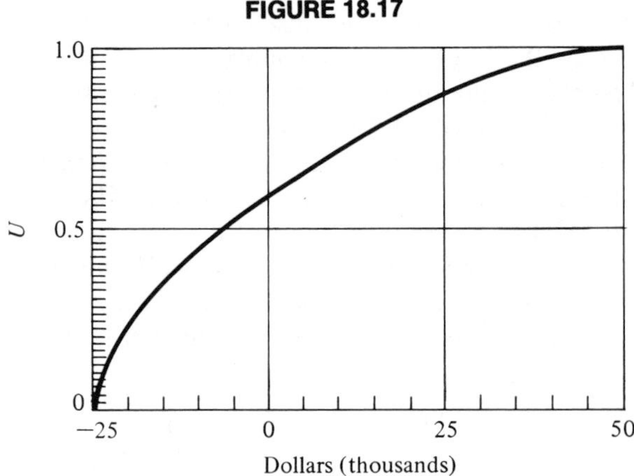


Financial theory suggests another way to take risk into account.[6] It is done by increasing the discount rate to account for the risk. The more risk, the higher the discount rate.

The choice of this discount rate is a difficult problem. For a firm, it may be possible to calculate a "cost of capital" or a "required rate of return" that could be used as a "risk-adjusted" discount rate to determine the net present value. The more risk associated with a firm's operation, the higher its cost of capital—either because it is charged more for borrowing money or because investors require a higher return in order to provide capital for the firm. Therefore, when the cost of capital is used to determine the net present value, some of the discounting takes into account risk and some is due to the delayed consumption. If the cost of capital accounts for all the risk, then presumably projects should be evaluated using expected net present value. Assume that the required rate of return is determined to be 15% for the

[6]J. C. Van Horne, *Financial Management and Policy*, 4th ed. (Englewood Cliffs, N. J.: Prentice-Hall, 1977).

investment shown in Figure 18.15. Using this discount rate, we have:

$$\text{NPV}_A = \frac{\$10{,}000}{1.15} + \frac{\$12{,}000}{(1.15)^2} + \frac{\$14{,}000}{(1.15)^3}$$

$$= \$8{,}696 + \$9{,}074 + \$9{,}205 = \$26{,}975$$

$$\text{NPV}_B = \frac{\$-10{,}000}{1.15} - \frac{\$8{,}000}{(1.15)^2} - \frac{\$6{,}000}{(1.15)^3}$$

$$= \$-8{,}696 - \$6{,}049 - \$3{,}945 = \$-18{,}690$$

The expected net present value using this discount rate is $4,142.50, compared to $5,138.80 using the risk-free rate. Therefore, we see that increasing the discount rate to account for risk can lower the expected net present value. The reduction is similar to the reduction obtained using a risk-averse preference function. When complications because of portfolio effects and reinvestment of income make the use of preference curves difficult or inappropriate, this approach can provide some help on choosing among alternatives for a firm.

Since the cost of capital is a market-determined value, any market imperfection will result in an imperfect evaluation of the risk. For individuals, it is particularly likely that market discount rates will not properly account for risk.

## SUMMARY

The preference analysis method is valid if certain assumptions are satisfied. A preference curve and expected preferences can be used if the model is an appropriate approximation of the real decision and the five behavioral assumptions are satisfied. These assumptions are:

1. *Ordering of outcomes and transitivity.*
2. *Reduction of compound uncertain events.*
3. *Continuity.*
4. *Substitutibility.*
5. *Monotonicity.*

**Proposition**

*If these assumptions are satisfied, there exist preference numbers so that preferences for alternatives can be determined by calculating expected preferences.*

There are a number of instances where these assumptions are observed to be violated. *Transitivity* is often violated, but generally individuals will strive to satisfy it. There is a question as to whether *groups* can or should satisfy *transitivity* and *substitutibility*. When *extreme outcomes* are present, the *continuity* assumption may be violated. *Differences* in the time at which uncertainty is *resolved* affects the *monotonicity assumption*.

The overall assumption that the model is a valid representation of the choice problem may not be valid under some circumstances. Some conditions are particularly difficult to deal with. *Defining outcomes* can require excessive detail when *dependencies* exist among uncertain events. This leads to a *portfolio* effect. Calibration errors make the subjective assessment of "independent" events difficult. Assigning a single evaluation unit to each outcome raises a number of problems when payoffs are received over an extended time horizon.

## ASSIGNMENT MATERIAL

**18.1.** Comment on the following statement: Preference theory establishes that expected preferences should be used to choose among alternatives.

**18.2.** John Dixon was interested in buying a new car. He had decided that three attributes were important: warranty, style, and cost. He looked at three cars, which we will describe as *A*, *B*, and *C*. Car *A* had a 5-year, 50,000-mile warranty and cost $12,000. He rated its style as moderately good. Car *B* had a 3-year, 30,000-mile warranty, cost $5,000, and he rated the style as marginal. Car *C* had the best style, cost $7,500, and had a 1-year, 10,000-mile warranty. In trying to decide among the three cars, Dixon decided to compare them two at a time and choose the car that was preferred on the most attributes.

(a) Use this rule to compare car *C* with car *B*; car *B* with car *A*; and car *A* with car *C*.

(b) Comment on Dixon's consistency if he uses the suggested rule.

**18.3.** Having just been certified as a qualified "decision maker" by the School of Preference and Decision Theory and taken your first consulting job, you discover a client who is intransitive. Being a dedicated disciple, you want to convince him to change his behavior. Do you have any valid lines of reasoning to use? Explain your answer.

**18.4.** After subjecting a client to over an hour of questions, you obtain a preference curve which you feel happy with and tell the client that you can now analyze his problem and advise him which course of action he should take. Thinking that everything is going better than expected, you turn to leave, only to be stopped by: "Wait a minute! What do you mean that *you* can now analyze *my* problem? I thought you were an expert at using quantitative methods of analysis. All I have been doing for the last hour is making subjective decisions about problems involving uncertainty. If I still have to make all the judgmental decisions, what good can you or your quantitative methods be to me?" Somewhat taken aback, but never at a loss for words, you reply:

**18.5.** As a consultant, you have just completed a full-blown decision analysis of a complex problem, including development and use of your client's preference curve. The probabilities used were objective (obtained from well-established theoretical and empirical models) and noncontroversial. The results indicate that the two alternatives had expected utilities of 0.85 and 0.65, respectively.

You tell the client he should choose the alternative with expected utility of 0.85; that is, you prescribe a course of action for him. Describe briefly the sense in which the action you recommend is "best" and any conditions required for your recommendation to be valid.

**18.6.** After undertaking a preference (utility) analysis using a risk-averse preference curve, you determine that two lotteries *A* and *B* have exactly the same expected preference (utility) of 0.65. You also note that the standard deviation of dollar payoffs for lottery *A* is $55 and that for lottery *B* is $75. If your choice between the lotteries is based on the principles of decision theory, what is your preference?

# 19

# Risk Sharing and Incentive

The procedures we have developed for studying decisions under uncertainty can be used to study a variety of organizational problems. One set of problems comes under the heading of *risk sharing*—partnerships, syndicates, and corporations are forms of organizations that are created to allow risk sharing. Financial markets and insurance markets exist to facilitate risk sharing. *Diversification* and *hedging* are strategies designed to take advantage of the effects of risk sharing. Another set of problems that can be studied are *incentive systems* within an organization. Delegation of decision-making authority can create a problem when decision makers have different attitudes toward risk. This chapter discusses both sets of problems. The purpose is to demonstrate how the models can be used to gain insights into these settings. Figure 19.1 shows how the chapter relates to other material.

**FIGURE 19.1**

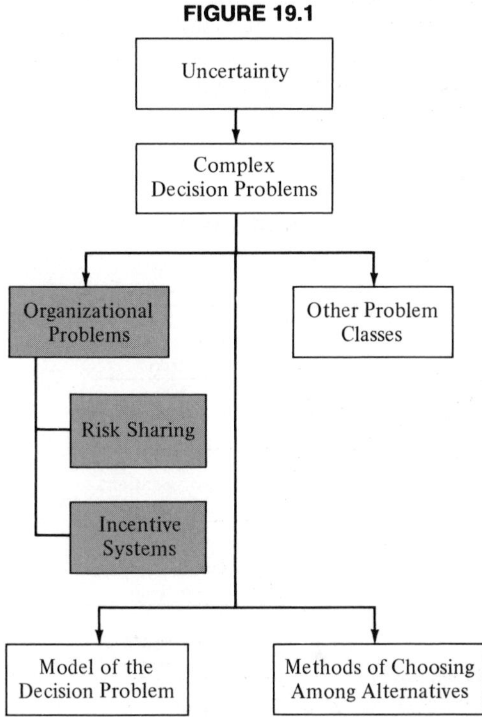


## RISK SHARING

Risk sharing is the motivating force for many institutional arrangements and markets. Ventures with substantial risk lead to joint ownership arrangements in order to share the risk. Examples are drilling for oil, developing a particular piece of land, or starting a company. In the first two examples, risk sharing is typically accomplished through formation of a syndicate, while in the last example risk sharing often takes place by issuing stock. The basic ideas will be illustrated by an example.

**Example 19.1**

Assume that you are the sole proprietor of a real estate development firm that has the option to undertake the development of a new shopping center. The project is similar to others in which you have been involved in the past, with the exception of the size. The total investment in this project is several times as large as in other projects. This is your only project and your plans are to develop the shopping center, including obtaining the clients for each store. Once the development phase is completed, you will sell the project to a group of investors. The two uncertainties are the weather and the possibility of a strike by the building trades union. If you undertake the project, you have the option of taking out strike insurance. For a $100,000 premium you will receive a $150,000 payment if there is a strike and nothing if there is no strike. Your options and the probabilities are shown in Figure 19.2.

You have an outside investor who is willing to put up as much as 70% of the investment for this project on the basis that contribution is shared in direct proportion to the percentage of investment. You have enough resources to undertake the entire project yourself, but are interested in pursuing the possibility of forming a partnership to share the risk. To help in the analysis, assume that you assess the preference curve shown in Figure 19.3.

**FIGURE 19.2**

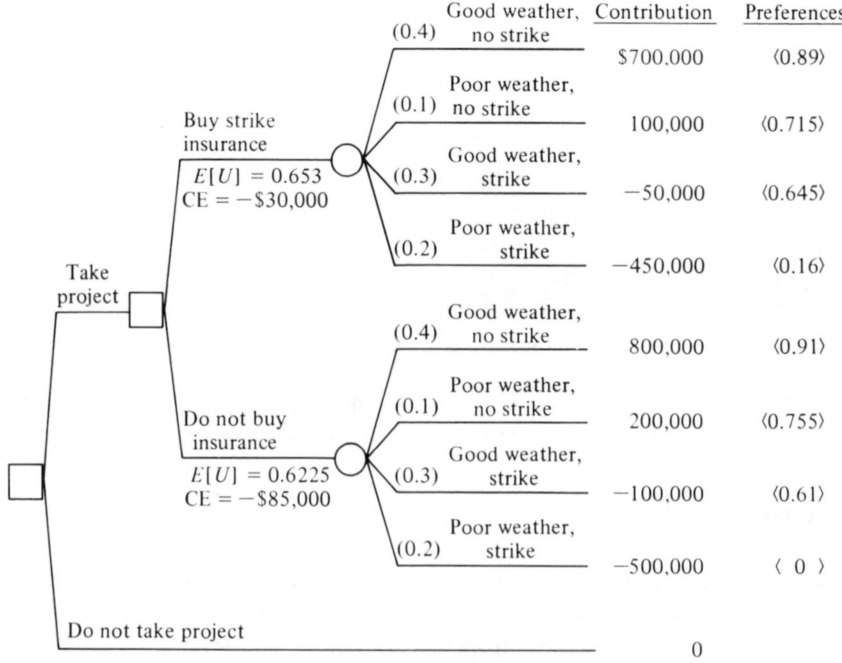

FIGURE 19.3

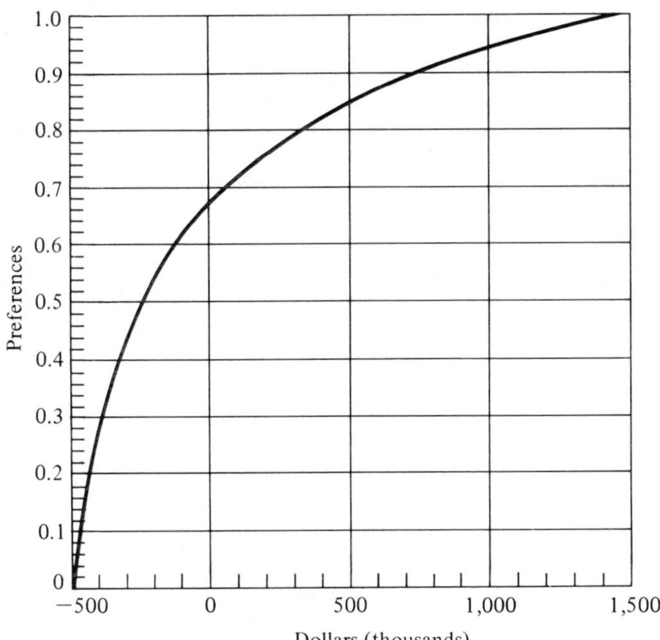


Your choice, assuming no outside investor, can be analyzed as shown on Figure 19.2. It indicates that your best strategy, if you undertake the project, is to buy the insurance. But this option has a certainty equivalent of $\$-30{,}000$. Therefore, you would not want to develop the project under these conditions.

We can investigate the possibility of forming a partnership by evaluating the development options for a range of sharing interests. Tables 19.1 and 19.2 show these calculations for several different shares. Note that your contribution is just the share percentage times the overall contribution. Figure 19.4 shows a plot of share versus certainty equivalent for the two options.

The analysis shows that the certainty equivalents for both options increase substantially when the project is shared with an outside investor. This increase is due to the reduction in risk accomplished by the straight sharing arrangement. The ability to share the risk turns an undesirable alternative into a desirable one.

The best arrangement in this case is a 50–50 sharing agreement. Under this arrangement you would undertake the project and not buy the insurance. The general shape of these plots of certainty equivalents versus share depends on both the preference function and the project.

**TABLE 19.1**

**Analysis for Do Not Buy Insurance Alternative**

| | | *80% Project* | | *50% Project* | | *30% Project* | |
|---|---|---|---|---|---|---|---|
| *State* | *Probability* | *Contribution* | *Preference* | *Contribution* | *Preference* | *Contribution* | *Preference* |
| Good weather, no strike | 0.4 | $640,000 | 0.88 | $400,000 | 0.82 | $240,000 | 0.77 |
| Poor weather, no strike | 0.1 | 160,000 | 0.74 | 100,000 | 0.715 | 60,000 | 0.70 |
| Good weather, strike | 0.3 | −80,000 | 0.625 | −50,000 | 0.645 | −30,000 | 0.655 |
| Poor weather, strike | 0.2 | −400,000 | 0.27 | −250,000 | 0.50 | −150,000 | 0.575 |
| Expected values | | 168,000 | 0.6675 | 105,000 | 0.693 | 63,000 | 0.6895 |
| Certainty equivalents | | | $−5,000 | | $50,000 | | $40,000 |

**TABLE 19.2**

**Analysis for Buy Insurance Alternative**

| | | *80% Project* | | *50% Project* | | *30% Project* | |
|---|---|---|---|---|---|---|---|
| *State* | *Probability* | *Contribution* | *Preference* | *Contribution* | *Preference* | *Contribution* | *Preference* |
| Good weather, no strike | 0.4 | $560,000 | 0.86 | $350,000 | 0.803 | $210,000 | 0.76 |
| Poor weather, no strike | 0.1 | 80,000 | 0.705 | 50,000 | 0.695 | 30,000 | 0.685 |
| Good weather, strike | 0.3 | −40,000 | 0.65 | −25,000 | 0.657 | −15,000 | 0.662 |
| Poor weather, strike | 0.2 | −360,000 | 0.355 | −225,000 | 0.52 | −135,000 | 0.590 |
| Expected values | | 148,000 | 0.6805 | 92,500 | 0.6918 | 55,500 | 0.6891 |
| Certainty equivalents | | | $20,000 | | $45,000 | | $38,000 |

The curves also show that the *buy insurance* alternative is preferred for high project shares. But as more of the risk is transferred to your partner, the insurance becomes less attractive. Finally, at about 62%, you prefer to proceed without any insurance.

Now let us see what your answer to the offer from the outside investor would be if you were risk-neutral. The expected monetary values for the 100% case are:

FIGURE 19.4

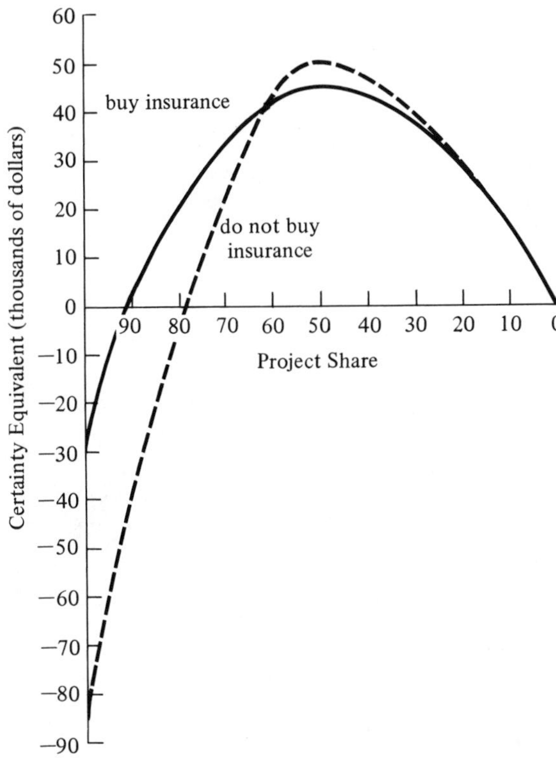


**Buy insurance**

$$\text{EMV} = (0.4)(\$700{,}000) + (0.1)(\$100{,}000) + (0.3)(\$-50{,}000) + (0.2)(\$-450{,}000)$$
$$= \$185{,}000$$

**Do not buy insurance**

$$\text{EMV} = (0.4)(\$800{,}000) + (0.1)(\$200{,}000) + (0.3)(\$-100{,}000) + (0.2)(\$-500{,}000)$$
$$= \$210{,}000$$

Therefore, if you held 100%, you would undertake the project without any insurance. From Tables 19.1 and 19.2 we have the EMV's for several other shares. These data are plotted in Figure 19.5. The shape of these curves (a straight line between the 100% value and zero) is the same for all risk-neutral preference curves. Under these conditions we would never observe risk sharing, since the certainty equivalents fall off continuously as shares are given up.

The general result is that a risk-averse individual will benefit from spreading the risk. The sharing in this example was done by giving up part of the project. A closely related strategy for risk sharing is *diversification.*

FIGURE 19.5

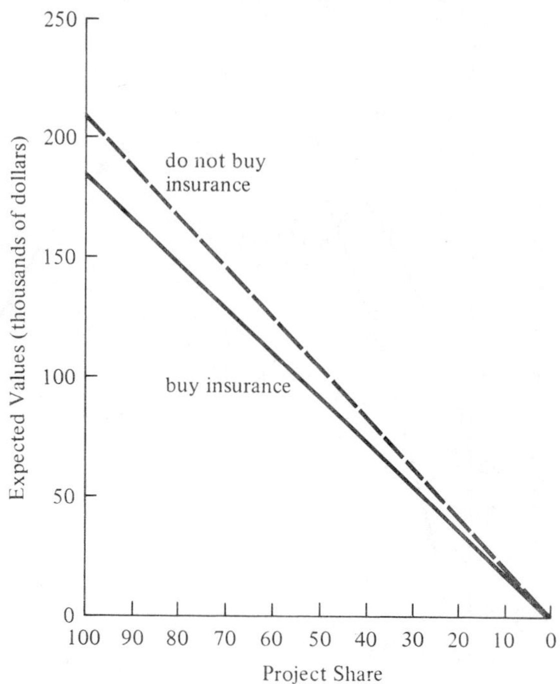


## DIVERSIFICATION

Rather than just take a smaller share of a single project, an individual can take shares of several investments. This *diversification* can lead to sharing risks on a number of projects. With a high degree of diversification no single investment represents a substantial risk.

### Diversification with Independent Investments

As a first case, we consider diversification by investing in a set of independent projects. The effect of this diversification for a risk-averse individual is demonstrated by the following example.

**Example 19.2**

Consider a single individual with the option to invest in one, two, or three wildcat oil wells. To keep things easy to understand, assume that each project will be either a success or failure. In all cases the wells will be sold if they are successful and the profit will be $900,000 if the investor has 100% interest. If the well is a failure, the cost will be $300,000 for a 100% interest. Further assume that the investor believes that the probabilities associated with each investment are *independent* and exactly the same: probability of success = 0.4, and probability of failure = 0.6. In this case we assume that the investor has $300,000 to invest which can be used to purchase any of the following:

*A*: 100% of one project (since all projects are perceived to be the same it does not matter which he chooses).
*B*: 50% of two projects.
*C*: $33\frac{1}{3}$% of three projects.

These alternatives are diagrammed in Figure 19.6. The expected monetary value of all three alternatives is the same, $180,000. If the preference function shown in Figure 19.3 is used, the certainty equivalents are as shown in Figure 19.6. They demonstrate the value of diversification because the certainty equivalent for the most highly diversified alternative is the highest. We see that a risk-neutral individual has no incentive to diversify, because the expected values are the same for all three alternatives. An individual with the preference function shown in Figure 19.3 increases his certainty equivalent from $ – 60,000 to $80,000 by diversifying over three identical projects.

**FIGURE 19.6**

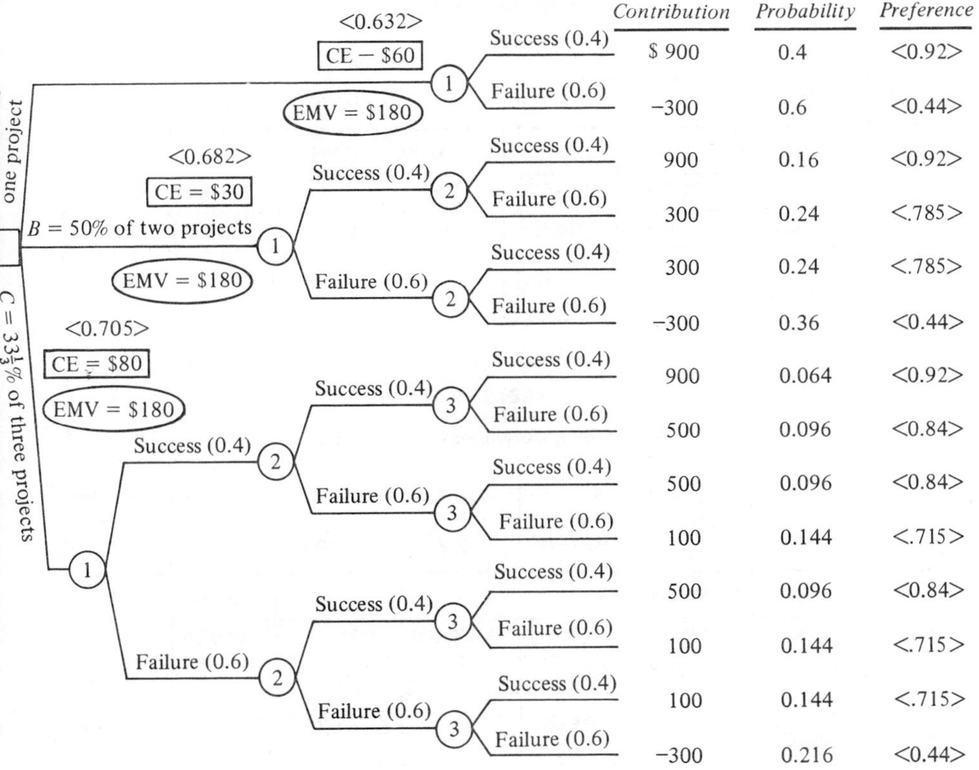

### Diversification with Dependent Investments

Another type of diversification, called *hedging*, reduces risk by utilizing investments with payoffs that are dependent. For instance, assume that a farmer can plant two crops, wheat and rice, and, for purposes of illustration, that both crops are dependent on the weather as shown by the payoffs in Table 19.3. Using the preference curve shown in Figure 19.3 again, neither planting wheat (certainty equivalent=$-15,000) nor rice (certainty equivalent=$-40,000) is attractive. Together, however, they allow the farmer to hedge against either type of weather. If he plants both, the payoff for wet weather is zero and for dry weather is $100,000. The certainty equivalent for this combined investment is $48,000, making it attractive to plant both. When investment opportunities are dependent, we cannot assume that diversification will be beneficial, making a combination more desirable than any single investment. Instead of creating a hedge, the opposite can occur. For instance, if the farmer were to consider wheat and corn and the payoff were as shown in Table 19.4, he would *not* be better off to diversify and plant both wheat and corn.

**TABLE 19.3**

**Hedging Example**

| | | *Wheat Only* | | *Rice Only* | | *Both Wheat and Rice* | |
|---|---|---|---|---|---|---|---|
| *State* | *Probability* | *Payoff* | *Preference* | *Payoff* | *Preference* | *Payoff* | *Preference* |
| Wet | 0.5 | $-200,000 | 0.54 | $ 200,000 | 0.755 | 0 | 0.67 |
| Dry | 0.5 | 300,000 | 0.785 | -200,000 | 0.54 | $100,000 | 0.715 |
| Expected values | | 50,000 | 0.6625 | 0 | 0.6475 | 50,000 | 0.6925 |
| Certainty equivalents | | | $-15,000 | | $-40,000 | | $48,000 |

**TABLE 19.4**

**Reinforcing Dependent Investments**

| | | *Wheat Only* | | *Corn Only* | | *Both Wheat and Corn* | |
|---|---|---|---|---|---|---|---|
| *State* | *Probability* | *Payoff* | *Preference* | *Payoff* | *Preference* | *Payoff* | *Preference* |
| Wet | 0.5 | $-200,000 | 0.54 | $-200,000 | 0.54 | $-400,000 | 0.27 |
| Dry | 0.5 | 300,000 | 0.785 | 200,000 | 0.755 | 500,000 | 0.84 |
| Expected values | | 50,000 | 0.6625 | 0 | 0.6475 | 50,000 | 0.555 |
| Certainty equivalents | | | $-15,000 | | $-40,000 | | $-180,000 |

### Diversification and Financial Markets

The benefits of spreading risk implies that individuals should never hold a significant share of any "risky" asset. Financial markets have been created to allow this type of diversification. An investor can hold stock in many corporations as well as invest in other projects. Yet, we still observe individuals holding a large share of their investments in one asset. The most obvious example is an individual entrepreneur. There are several reasons for this. One is that there are often nonpecuniary benefits associated with holding a large share of an asset. If you are the sole owner, you have control over the disposition of the resources, as well as your level of participation. There may be additional psychological benefits to managing your own company. Other reasons involve differential information and incentives, discussed below.

## RISK SHARING WITH DIFFERENTIAL INFORMATION

To this point we have only considered risk sharing from the perspective of one individual. Clearly, to *share* risk there must be more than one person involved. With more than one person, there is an opportunity for both different preferences and different beliefs as well as differential information about these preferences and beliefs.

### Agreements with the Same Preferences and Beliefs

Consider again Example 19.1. If the outside investor had exactly the same preference function as yours and exactly the same beliefs as specified by the probability distribution, would you agree on the optimal shares to hold?

Under these conditions, the outside investor's curve of certainty equivalents is exactly the same as yours over the range 0 to 70%. This means that both of you agree that 50% is the optimal share. If we change the participants' preferences slightly, the problem becomes more complicated. Assume that the results of the analyses of optimal project share with a different preference function are as shown in Figure 19.7. If both participants have the same preference function and beliefs, they would both prefer 70%. But, both would participate with less than 70%. This situation is common and must be resolved through some type of bargaining process. The problem gets a little more complicated if we consider the issue of control over the project. Let us return to Example 19.1 and consider two cases.

**Case 1: Complete information.** Assume that both of you know each other's preferences and beliefs. That is, you know that both certainty equivalent plots are given by Figure 19.4. Under this condition—at least for the decision on buying insurance—you do not care who has control (i.e., who makes the decision). Both of you would choose *do not buy insurance*.

FIGURE 19.7

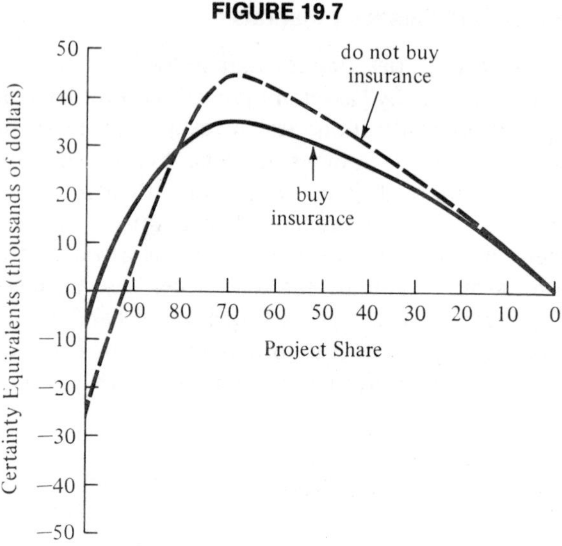


**Case 2: Differential information.** Assume neither knows the other's preferences or beliefs. All you know is that the other party has agreed to a 50–50 sharing arrangement. If you give up control, the decision diagram is changed (see Figure 19.8). The difference is that the choice node on buying insurance is replaced by an uncertain event. The decision is no longer yours to make. If you do not know the outside investor's preferences and beliefs, you can only model his actions with a probability distribution. Of course, in this simple example you might include the insurance decision as part of the agreement, but, in general, the actions of the other person may not be known.

In this example, there is presumably a high degree of cooperation between the participants. You can appreciate that noncooperative or competitive settings make the assessment of the probable actions of others very difficult. This is the subject of game theory and is not covered here.

### Agreement with Different Preferences and Beliefs

When preferences and beliefs differ, the opportunities for agreement change. A less-risk-averse individual will place a higher value on a risky asset than a more-risk-averse individual will. Opportunities for agreement depend on who is buying and who is selling.

The most common form of differential information leads to differences in beliefs. Two individuals with different information will likely hold different beliefs, resulting in different probability distributions. In Example 19.1, for instance, it is likely that you would have more information than the outside investor. In general, we can think of this as having your probability distribution more tightly peaked than his. This difference in beliefs may contribute

**FIGURE 19.8**

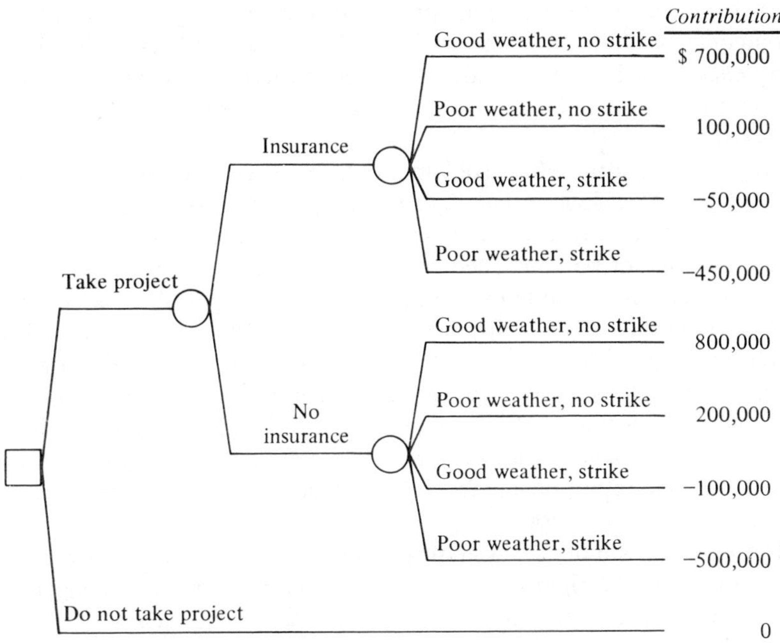


toward individuals holding more of a single asset than would be predicted by the diversification argument. Their certainty equivalents may be higher than that placed on the asset by a less-well-informed market.

## INCENTIVE SYSTEMS

An effect of differential information within organizations is the delegation of decision-making authority. The fact that individuals at lower levels in an organization have more detailed knowledge of certain processes, markets, and so on, coupled with the cost of transferring this information, leads to delegation. For instance, the president of a company may delegate a subset of decisions to a division manager. A division manager will often delegate decisions to a project manager, and so on. The general hierarchical arrangement is described by a principal–agent relationship.

Delegation creates an *incentives* problem. The purpose of delegation is to take advantage of efficiencies and better information at lower levels in an organization. However, subordinates may not make the same decisions as their superiors because of different preferences. Incentive systems are designed to overcome these differences.

The empirical evidence presented in Chapter 16 for managers in a large company indicates a rather severe degree of risk aversion. An explanation for this is that subordinates view the consequences of the outcomes differently than those higher up in the company. From the company's point of view, a bad outcome resulting in a loss of \$100,000 may be of very little financial consequence. On the other hand, the project manager may well see such an outcome as detrimental to his own career. The result is a difference in attitudes toward risk.

One way to address this problem would be to evaluate managers on the quality of their decisions rather than on the particular outcomes. If there is truly uncertainty and risk associated with a particular decision, it means that the outcome cannot be controlled by the manager, in which case evaluation based on outcomes amounts to holding a manager responsible for something out of his control. On the other hand, the quality of decisions may also be difficult to judge, since subjective judgments in the form of probability assessments as well as preferences may enter the problem. Ensuring unbiased inputs and judging the reliability of a manager's expert opinion is a difficult problem. The framework for decomposition presented here provides a starting point for separating beliefs from preferences and laying out the assumptions that go into a decision.

The other possibility is to eliminate the differences in attitudes toward risk by obtaining the right combination of incentives for the managers who will be delegated decision-making power. A variety of methods, including stock options and sharing rules, can be designed to induce subordinates to make decisions that are consistent with those a superior would make under the same circumstances. We cannot calculate incentive plans that are *optimal* in general because it requires a match between individual attitudes toward risk and specific plans. However, the basic characteristics of different plans can be analyzed.

To illustrate how sharing rules can influence decisions taken by subordinates, consider a franchise sales operation in which local managers are responsible for choosing the product mix as well as the sales campaign for their own area. Assume that a "typical" set of alternatives and outcomes is shown in Figure 19.9. Plan $A$ is a high-risk, high-reward plan, while plan $B$ is much more conservative. Assume that risk preferences for the local manager are shown by the preference curve in Figure 19.10 and that the overall franchise owner (headquarters) is risk-neutral. If the local manager is on a straight salary and perceives poor outcomes to be detrimental to his career, plan $B$ is more attractive, since it has a lower probability of a poor outcome. Moreover, the financial consequences of a poor outcome are much less severe under plan $B$. On the other hand, headquarters prefers plan $A$ [expected contribution $=(200{,}000)\times(0.5)+(100{,}000)\times(0.3)-(50{,}000)\times(0.2)=\$120{,}000$] over plan $B$ [expected contribution $=(120{,}000)\times(0.5)+(80{,}000)\times(0.4)-(10{,}000)\times(0.1)=\$91{,}000$]. To induce the local managers to make choices more in line with those preferred by headquarters, a variety of incentives schemes could be postulated. Below we consider the effect of two options that involve sharing rules.

**FIGURE 19.9**

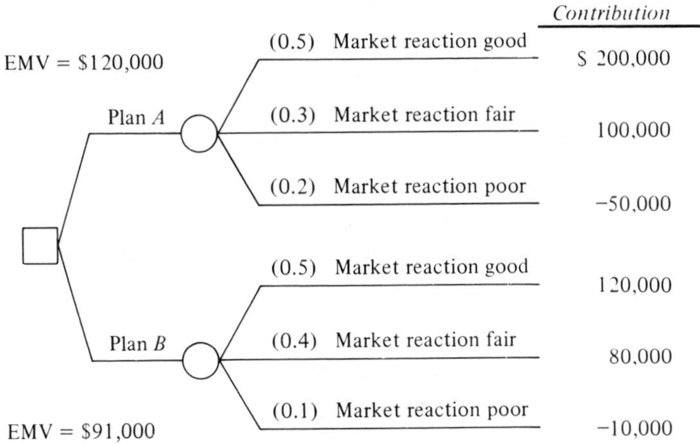


**FIGURE 19.10**

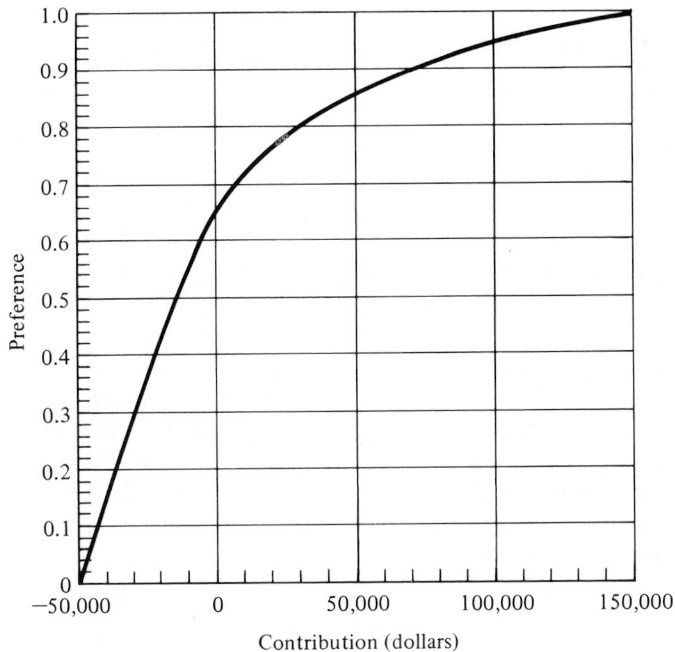

**Sharing Rule 1**

*A straight percentage of contribution is used as a compensation scheme rather than a fixed salary. In this case, assume that headquarters uses a 50–50 sharing rule.*

From the local manager's point of view, the alternatives and payoffs are as shown in Table 19.5. Therefore, even with a profit-sharing plan, the local manager prefers plan *B*. Headquarters, of course, still prefers plan *A*, which now has an expected contribution to them of $60,000 versus $45,500 with plan *B*.

**TABLE 19.5**
**Sharing Rule 1**

| *Plan A* | | | *Plan B* | | |
|---|---|---|---|---|---|
| *Probability* | *Manager's Contribution* | *Preference* | *Probability* | *Manager's Contribution* | *Preference* |
| 0.5 | $100,000 | 0.95 | 0.5 | $60,000 | 0.88 |
| 0.3 | 50,000 | 0.85 | 0.4 | 40,000 | 0.83 |
| 0.2 | −25,000 | 0.35 | 0.1 | −5,000 | 0.61 |
| Expected preference: | | 0.800 | Expected preference: | | 0.833 |
| Certainty equivalent: | | $32,000 | Certainty equivalent: | | $42,000 |

Assume that the local manager's salary under the old plan was $40,000. Under these conditions, the local manager prefers the new sharing rule to the old salary, but headquarters does not. Headquarters' expected contribution under the new plan is $45,500 from plan *B* while under the old plan it was $91,000 (the expected contribution from plan *B*) minus $40,000 (the manager's salary), or $51,000. Headquarters has not changed the manager's choice of plans from *B* to *A*, which was the original intent of the sharing plan. What is needed is some method of reducing the risk as perceived by the manager when the 50–50 sharing rule is used, without eliminating the incentive based on participating in the profits.

**Sharing Rule 2**

*A rule that combines a fixed payment with a share of the contribution is used to allocate risk between the local manager and headquarters. In this case assume that the manager receives a lump-sum payment of $20,000 plus 25% of the contribution.*

Compensations under the two sharing rules as well as the fixed salary are shown in Figure 19.11. The analysis of the two plans under rule 2 is shown in Table 19.6. Under rule 2 the local manager prefers plan $A$, with a certainty equivalent of \$45,000. We also see that the local manager prefers sharing rule 2 over the other compensation plans because the \$45,000 is higher than his best certainty equivalent from the other plans. From the point of view of headquarters, the expected contribution under sharing rule 2 for plan $A$ is \$90,000 (75% of the \$120,000 expected contribution from plan $A$) minus the \$20,000 lump-sum payment, or \$70,000, and for plan $B$ it is (0.75)×(\$91,000) − \$20,000 = \$48,250. Therefore, under sharing rule 2, both the local manager and headquarters prefer plan $A$. Moreover, they both prefer sharing rule 2 to the other methods of compensation discussed because it results in the highest certainty equivalent value for both of them. Of course, this example does not

**FIGURE 19.11**

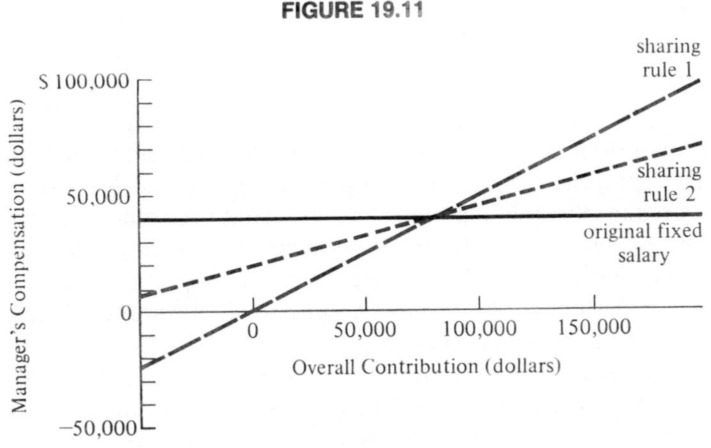


**TABLE 19.6**

**Sharing Rule 2**

| Plan A | | | Plan B | | |
|---|---|---|---|---|---|
| *Probability* | *Manager's Contribution* | *Preference* | *Probability* | *Manager's Contribution* | *Preference* |
| 0.5 | \$20,000 + 50,000 = 70,000 | 0.9 | 0.5 | \$20,000 + 30,000 = 50,000 | 0.85 |
| 0.3 | \$20,000 + 25,000 = 45,000 | 0.84 | 0.4 | \$20,000 + 20,000 = 40,000 | 0.83 |
| 0.2 | \$20,000 − 12,500 = 7,500 | 0.7 | 0.1 | \$20,000 − 2,500 = 17,500 | 0.75 |
| Expected preference: | | 0.842 | Expected preference: | | 0.832 |
| Certainty equivalent: | | \$45,000 | Certainty equivalent: | | \$41,000 |

mean that such a sharing rule will always result in a plan that headquarters prefers being chosen. Clearly, the results depend upon the alternatives and risks involved.

There are a large number of sharing rules that could be proposed and evaluated. In general, the calculation of optimal incentives plans may be impossible because of lack of information. However, the issues and options may become clearer when considered in terms of the uncertainties and attitudes toward taking risk of the managers involved.

The incentive problem provides another reason that individuals hold more of a risky asset than would be predicted. Investors in a small company may require that managers have enough stock so that they will have an incentive to act in the stockholders' best interests. Insurance companies may require that a firm carry more self-insurance than would be optimal from a risk-sharing perspective to ensure that they have an adequate incentive to prevent claims.

## SUMMARY

Risk sharing and incentive systems are examples of organizational problems that can be approached using expected preference analysis. Risk-averse individuals can reduce the risk in a project by sharing it with others. Partnerships and syndicates are common forms of organizations developed to share risk among a few individuals. Corporations are an organizational form that allows a wider sharing of risk through issuing stock. Insurance and financial markets exist to facilitate risk sharing.

Giving up some share of a project can increase its value to a risk-averse individual (i.e., its certainty equivalent increases). A risk-neutral individual does not have any incentive to share risk. (In some cases a risk-neutral individual may give up part of a project because of a constraint on resources. But, if the constraint were removed, the individual would prefer to keep it all —assuming a positive expected monetary value.)

*Diversification* is a means of risk sharing by holding small shares of many different projects. For independent projects or investments, and risk-averse individuals, diversification will increase the certainty equivalent for a portfolio as long as the projects are equally attractive on an individual basis. Diversification with dependent projects can either increase or decrease the risk. The use of dependent projects to reduce the risk is called *hedging*.

Differential information presents a number of problems. If there are decisions that must be made after the risk-sharing agreement is completed, outside investors must treat these as uncertain events unless they know the preferences and beliefs of the individual in control. Even for individuals with decision-making authority (principals) a problem can arise. Those lower in an organization (agents) may have better information about certain processes or markets. If the cost of transferring this information to the principal is high, decision-making authority is delegated to the agent. The agent's preferences may be quite different from the principal's, depending on the incentive scheme used.

Incentive systems using stock options and profit sharing are examples of schemes designed to make the decisions of the principals and agent coincide.

## ASSIGNMENT MATERIAL

**19.1.** Describe why a risk-averse individual may desire to give up part of a project.

**19.2.** Would a risk-neutral individual ever prefer to give up *part* of a project?

**19.3.** Diversification is a form of risk sharing. The benefits of risk sharing suggest that risk-averse individuals will want to spread their holdings as widely as possible across a set of independent investments. Discuss three reasons why a risk-averse individual may end up holding more of a single risky asset than would be predicted by this phenomenon.

**19.4.** Describe how hedging can reduce risk.

**19.5.** Discuss two ways to deal with the empirically observed fact that subordinates are more risk-averse than superiors.

**19.6. International Vending Company (B)**
As the franchise owner for the Super Bowl (see International Vending Company (A), Chapter 17, problem 17.8), assume you have the risk preference curve shown in Figure 19.12.

**FIGURE 19.12**

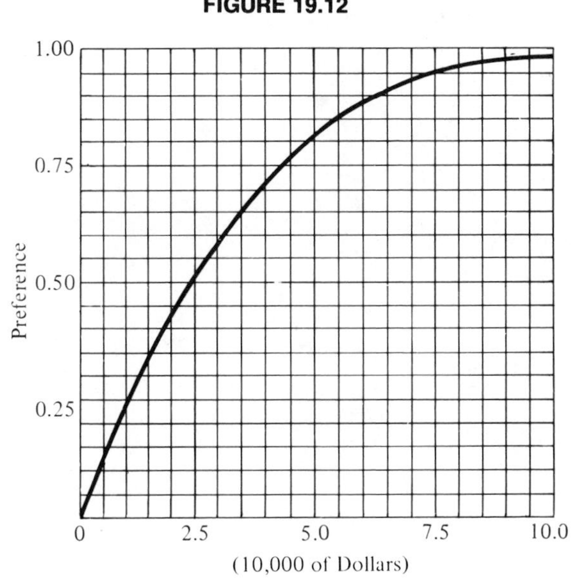

(a) Under the sharing arrangement described in the (A) case, which plan do you prefer?
(b) If the company offered to pay you a lump sum of $27,000 plus 20% of the net profits, which plan would you choose?

**19.7. International Vending Company (C)**

Assume that as the franchise owner for the Super Bowl the company has told you that you must implement plan $P_3$ as described in International Vending Company (A) [Chapter 17, problem 17.8]. Further assume that your risk preference curve is given by Figure 19.12.

(a) If one of your associates offered to share the risk with you on a straight percentage basis (e.g., if you shared on a 50–50 basis, you would get 50% of the net profits and your associate would get 50%), would you be interested? If so, at what percentage?
(b) If your associate offered to purchase 50% of your interest in this year's Super Bowl, what is the minimum price in which you would be interested?

# 20

# Choices with Multiple Attitudes

If a single evaluation unit is not adequate to describe the outcome of a decision, we have a multiple attribute problem. Choosing among alternatives with multiple attributes can be difficult. This chapter introduces the problem and discusses several approaches to making choices with multiple attributes. They can be classified as descriptive procedures and trade-off procedures. Figure 20.1 shows how this material fits into the overall framework of the book.

**FIGURE 20.1**

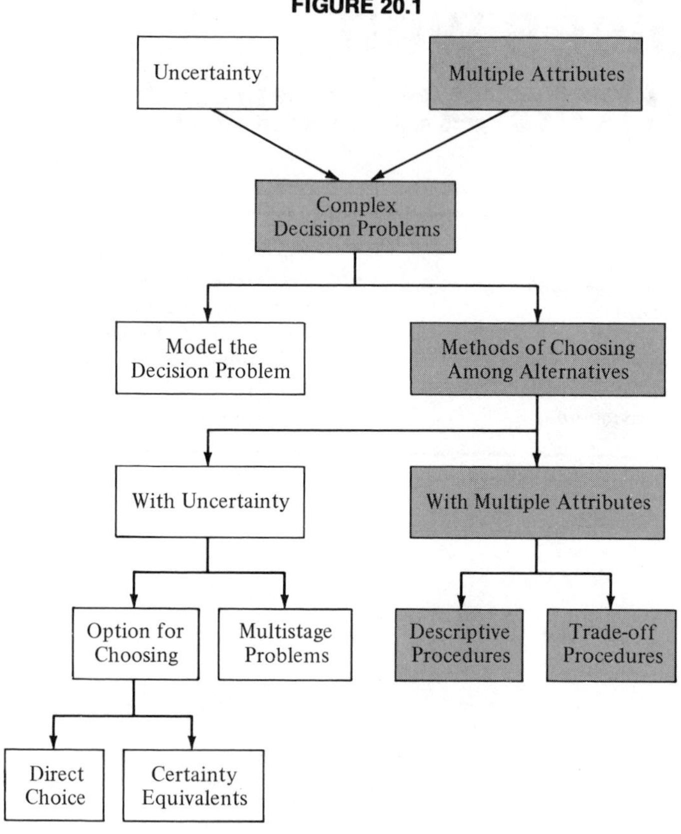


## THE PROBLEM

The problem of choosing when decisions are characterized by more than a single attribute can be illustrated by an example.

**Example 20.1**

The owner of a small market research firm has been offered a contract to determine the most important issues in the minds of the voters for the coming statewide election. The work would be done for a Republican candidate for the legislature. The firm has considerable expertise in development of instruments for sampling opinions on new products, questionnaires, and interview techniques, but has never done any work in the political arena. The contract itself is not very lucrative; in fact, the firm will undoubtedly lose money. In spite of the fact that this contract would not be profitable, the firm's owner knows that some of his competitors have made money on this type of work in the past.

The firm's regular business is slow, reflecting a downturn in general business activity. As a matter of fact, if the contract is not accepted, the owner would be required to lay off three full-time staff members. After considerable thought about the important aspects of the decision, the owner has come up with Table 20.1.

**TABLE 20.1**

| *Attribute* | *Take Contract* | *Don't Take Contract* |
|---|---|---|
| Contribution | \$ −5,000 | 0 |
| Layoffs | 0 | 3 |
| New capability | Yes | No |

A simple expression of preferences on each attribute separately is not enough to determine a choice between the two alternatives. Assume that higher contribution is preferred to lower contribution; fewer layoffs to more layoffs; and new capability to no new capability. With these preferences, the alternative *take contract* is preferred for attributes *layoffs* and *new capability*, but *don't take contract* is preferred for the attribute *contribution*. To make a choice, some means is required to either consider all the attributes at the same time or to decompose the problem so that they are considered sequentially. Making the necessary *trade-offs* remains one of the most difficult problems faced by decision makers.

## DESCRIPTIVE PROCEDURES

Decision makers deal with multiple attribute problems all the time. They have developed procedures to simplify the choice process. In this section we describe four such procedures. In some cases the only virtue of these procedures is their simplicity. The assumptions required to ensure that the procedures provide choices consistent with a decision maker's preferences may be quite severe.

## Dominance

When one alternative dominates the others the choice is easy. The procedure is simple and requires alternatives to be compared on each attribute. Unfortunately, it only works in special cases.

**Dominance**

***Definition:*** *If alternative A is at least as preferred as alternative B on all attributes and strictly preferred on at least one attribute, we say that alternative A dominates alternative B.*

**Example 20.2**

Assume that Example 20.1 is changed so that the *contribution* for the alternative *take contract* is zero. Which alternative should be selected?

Using the assumptions that more contribution is preferred to less, fewer layoffs to more, and new capability to no new capability, we have the following comparisons:

| *Attribute* | *Preferred Alternative* |
|---|---|
| Contribution | Indifferent |
| Layoffs | Take contract |
| New capability | Take contract |

Therefore, *take contract* dominates *don't take contract.*

## Satisficing

The satisficing procedure suggests that multiple attribute problems be processed by setting an acceptable or *satisfactory* level for each attribute. The attributes for each alternative are compared with these satisfactory levels. Alternatives with attribute levels that are not satisfactory are discarded and all alternatives that meet the satisficing levels are kept.

**Example 20.3**

Assume that you are trying to choose one of four sites for a new building. The attributes of interest to you are cost, size, location, and transportation cost. Table 20.2 shows how each alternative rates on these four attributes.

Using these levels of satisficing we see that site 1 is not acceptable on the attribute *size* and is therefore eliminated. Site 2 and site 3 meet all the

**TABLE 20.2**

| *Attribute* | *Site* 1 | *Site* 2 | *Site* 3 | *Site* 4 | *Satisficing Level* |
|---|---|---|---|---|---|
| Cost | $75,000 | $80,000 | $100,000 | $60,000 | $100,000 or less |
| Size | 4.5 | 5.0 | 8.4 | 6.7 | 5 acres or more |
| Location | Good | Medium | Good | Poor | Medium or better |
| Transportation | $150,000 | $200,000 | $250,000 | $300,000 | $250,000/year or less |

required levels. Site 4 fails to meet the acceptable level on *location* and *transportation*. Therefore, using these levels of satisficing we have a tie between sites 2 and 3.

From an operational standpoint, two features deserve comment. First, the procedure may not find a unique solution. Second, no guidance is given on how the satisficing levels are picked initially. Advocates of the procedure suggest that levels can be varied until a unique solution is found. But, the question of how they should be varied is not addressed. On the positive side, the procedure is simple once the satisficing levels are reached.

From a more fundamental perspective, the procedure makes strong assumption on the independence of the attributes. This is required because they are treated separately. For instance, site 1 has been eliminated even though it is better than site 2 on three of the four attributes. Although it misses the size requirement by only 0.5 acre, there is no way that this deficiency can be made up by superior performance on the other attributes.

### Lexicographic Procedure

The lexicographic procedure requires the attributes to be ranked and the alternatives compared one attribute at a time, starting with the highest ranked attribute, until a choice is made. Using Example 20.3, assume that the decision maker ranks the attributes in terms of importance: location, cost, transportation, and size. Using the lexicographic procedure, we first compare the alternatives on the attribute location. Sites 1 and 3 are tied and preferred to sites 2 and 4 on this attribute. Therefore, sites 2 and 4 are eliminated and we move to the next most important attribute, cost. We compare sites 1 and 3 on cost and see that site 1 is preferred. Since we have a unique solution, the procedure terminates.

Operationally, the procedure requires a comparison among the attributes through the ranking procedure. However, once this is completed, the alternatives are considered one attribute at a time. Notice that only two of the four attributes were considered. The procedure often considers only one or two attributes before a choice is reached.

From a fundamental standpoint, this procedure also makes severe independence assumptions and lacks the ability to allow a poor performance on one attribute to be made up by superior performance on others.

### Combination Procedure

The suggestion is made that the three procedures discussed be used in combination. First, dominance is used to eliminate any dominated alternatives. Next, satisficing is used to eliminate alternatives that are not adequate on one or more of the attributes. Those alternatives that survive both the dominance and satisficing procedures are subjected to the lexicographic procedure.

There is some intuitive appeal to this combination. Especially if the satisficing procedure can identify levels that are truly minimum (or maximum) acceptable levels for each attribute. However, this procedure relies on very strong independence assumptions.[1]

## TRADE-OFF PROCEDURES

To overcome some of the limitations of the descriptive procedures discussed above, procedures that allow trade-offs to be made have been developed. These procedures allow a poor performance on one attribute to be compensated by a superior performance on another. Also, they do not rely on preference independence assumptions.

The procedure is designed to find alternatives that are equivalent to the original set and that only differ in the scale level of one attribute.[2] That is, all but one of the attribute levels are made the same. The attributes that are driven to the same level are called the *base set* and their measures are called the *base levels*. For convenience, we will call the single attribute which is not included in the base the *surviving* attribute. Once these equivalent alternatives have been established, the decision is easy, because it can be made by choosing the alternative with the most preferred value on the surviving attribute. In the private sector and many times in the public sector, the choice for the surviving attribute is dollars.

[1]See K. R. MacCrimmon, "Decision-Making Among Multiple-Attribute Alternatives: A Survey and Consolidated Approach," The RAND Corporation, RM-4823-ARPN, 1968, for an overview of descriptive procedures. A more detailed analysis is found in R. Keeney and H. Raiffa, *Decisions with Multiple Objectives: Preferences and Value Trade-offs* (New York: Wiley, 1976).

[2]The scale characteristics of measures for attributes can differ. *Numerical* scales are the most familiar (e.g., dollars, height, weight, and elapsed time). These examples of numerical scales are also *ratio* scales, meaning they have a natural origin; for example, regardless of the unit (inches, meters, etc.) zero height means the same thing. (There are technical definitions of each type of scale that are not given here.) Numerical scales which have arbitrary origins, such as temperature, are called *interval* scales (note that the zero point is different for the Fahrenheit and centigrade scales). Besides numerical scales, there are also *ordinal* and *nominal* scales. Ordinal scales only provide rankings (e.g., in rating the comfort of various transportation systems as "excellent," "good," "fair" or "poor"). In this case no information is given as to how much better "good" is than "fair." Nominal measures only categorize. Geographic attributes are often measured using nominal scales (e.g., East, South, Midwest, West).

### The Trade-off Procedure

The method illustrated here for dealing with the multiattribute problem can be summarized as shown below. Read this through quickly before going on to the example.

> Trade-Off Procedure
>
> *Step 1:* Choose a surviving attribute. Where monetary considerations are the most important, contribution in dollars is often a good choice.
>
> *Step 2:* Choose a base level for the remaining attributes. It reduces the number of trade-offs required if the levels chosen correspond to one of the levels in an actual alternative.
>
> *Step 3:* Devise alternatives that are equivalent to the existing set but with the attributes other than the surviving attribute changed to the base level.
>
> *Step 4:* Compare the surviving attributes to select the preferred alternative.

The basic procedure will be illustrated by a simple example.

**Example 20.4**

Consider Example 20.1, modified so that the only attributes of interest are contribution and layoffs. With this assumption, the alternatives can be summarized by:

*Alternative 1 (Take contract):* (contribution = \$ − 5,000; layoffs = 0)
*Alternative 2 (Don't take contract):* (contribution = 0; layoffs = 3)

The first step is to choose the surviving attribute and the base level. In this case we will choose contribution measured in dollars as the surviving attribute and 3 layoffs as the base. In theory, either attribute could be chosen as the survivor and any level of the other attribute as the base level. From a practical point of view it makes sense to choose the base level to correspond to the level(s) in some alternative.

Next, the procedure requires that we find an alternative that is just equivalent to alternative 1 but with the base level of 3 layoffs (i.e., we must determine the amount of money which must be added to just offset the addition of 3 layoffs). Many things may influence this amount of money but, for purposes of illustration, assume we decide that under these conditions we would be indifferent between *no layoffs* and *3 layoffs plus \$3,000*. That is, changing from 0 to 3 layoffs is just offset by the addition of \$3,000. If this is true, we know that the following alternatives are equivalent:

*Alternative 1:* (contribution = \$ − 5,000; layoffs = 0)
*Alternative 1A:* (contribution = \$ − 5,000 + \$3,000 = \$ − 2,000; layoffs = 3)

In terms of preference and indifference relationships we have:

*Alternative 1:* (contribution = \$ − 5,000; layoff = 0) ~ *Alternative 1A:* (contribution = \$ − 2,000; layoffs = 3)

The comparison between alternatives 1A and 2 is easy since both have 3 layoffs, but alternative 1A has a \$ − 2,000 contribution and alternative 2 has a contribution of 0. This means that we have the following preference relationship:

*Alternative 2:* (contribution = 0; layoffs = 3) ≻ *Alternative 1A:* (contribution = \$ − 2,000; layoffs = 3)

Since alternative 2 is preferred to alternative 1A and we are indifferent between alternative 1A and alternative 1, it is obvious that alternative 2 is preferred to alternative 1.[3]

Unfortunately, there is no mechanism that can automatically generate equivalent alternatives. In some cases the existence of markets for the attributes that make up the base can be useful. For example, one alternative may require the acquisition of a machine that is *left over* after the project is completed. If we were not interested in using the machine for other purposes, we could substitute the salvage market value for the machine. If we need the machine for other projects, we might use the replacement value.

In other cases, costs associated with changes may be helpful. For instance, if the primary considerations in the layoffs were severance pay and rehiring costs, we could use them to determine "cost" of changing from 0 to 3 people laid off. Neither market values nor costs necessarily provide the required trade-off since individual circumstances and preferences may result in some individuals placing a lower or higher value (cost) on a particular change.

## Indifference Curves

The trade-off procedure just discussed can also be illustrated in terms of indifference curves. Figure 20.2 shows the comparison problem graphically.

Alternative 1 is represented by point 1 and alternative 2 by point 2. By selecting the base as (layoffs = 3), we are restricting the space of comparisons to the vertical line through (layoffs = 3). The development of alternative 1A, which is just equivalent in the mind of the decision maker, is the same as finding where the indifference curve through 1 crosses the (layoffs = 3) line. In our example it crossed at (contribution = \$ − 2,000) and the indifference curve might look like the solid line in Figure 20.2.

A number of other methods of making the trade-off are possible. For instance, if the base level for layoffs were chosen as zero, our task would be

[3]Note the reasoning that allows the conclusion that alternative 2 is preferred to alternative 1 assumes transitivity.

FIGURE 20.2

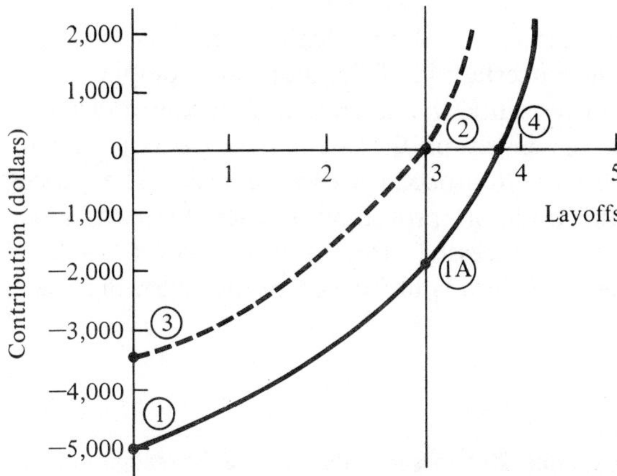


to find point 3 on the indifference curve for alternative 2 (the dashed line). Another option is to choose layoffs as the surviving attribute with base level zero on contribution. In this case we would have had to determine point 4 on the indifference curve for alternative 1.

### More than Two Dimensions

If we put the attribute *new capability* back into our example, the problem becomes slightly more complex and the trade-off procedure may be done in two steps.

*Alternative 1:* (contribution = \$ − 5,000; layoff = 0; new capability = yes)
*Alternative 2:* (contribution = \$0; layoff = 3; new capability = no)

If the original trade-off were made assuming (new capability = yes), we can use its results to specify:

*Alternative 1* $\sim$ *Alternative 1A:* (contribution = \$ − 2,000; layoff = 3; new capability = yes)

If we maintain contribution as the surviving attribute and pick the base level as (new capability = no), the next trade-off required is the amount of money that just compensates for changing to (new capability = no) in alternative 1A. If we decide that the change from (new capability = yes) to (new capability = no) is just compensated by \$4,000, we have

*Alternative 1A* $\sim$ *Alternative 1B:* (contribution = \$ − 2,000 + \$4,000 = \$ + 2,000; layoffs = 3; new capability = no)

Alternative 1B can now be directly compared with alternative 2 on the surviving attribute since their base attributes, layoff and new capability, are the same. We see that *Alternative 2* $\prec$ *Alternative 1* when the new capability is taken into consideration.

## MULTIPLE ATTRIBUTE PROBLEMS WITH UNCERTAINTY

The procedures discussed above dealt with decisions involving multiple attributes, but no uncertainty. If decisions are complicated by both multiple attributes and uncertainty, the *descriptive* procedures discussed above cannot be used, since the levels of the attributes are not known with certainty. However, the *trade-off* procedure can be used. The process involves two stages. First, the trade-off procedure is used for each outcome. Second, a preference curve is assessed using the base-level levels of the trade-off procedure. The procedure is illustrated in the following example.

### Example 20.5

Expanding on Example 20.1, assume that further investigation shows that there is uncertainty as to the contribution if the firm takes the contract. The owner feels there is a 0.3 chance that they can actually break even and a 0.7 chance that they lose $5,000. If they do not take the contract, there is also the possibility (0.6 chance) that a small job will be available at a break-even level so that no layoffs would be required.

The new problem can be diagrammed as shown in Figure 20.3. For the trade-off analysis we need to pick a surviving attribute and a base level. Assume that we choose contribution as the surviving attribute and the base as (layoffs = 3) and (new capability = no), as done in Example 20.4. We now treat each outcome in the decision diagram separately and use the trade-off procedure to obtain an equivalent outcome with the base level. Starting at the top of the diagram, we have the following (note that the trade-offs are

**FIGURE 20.3**

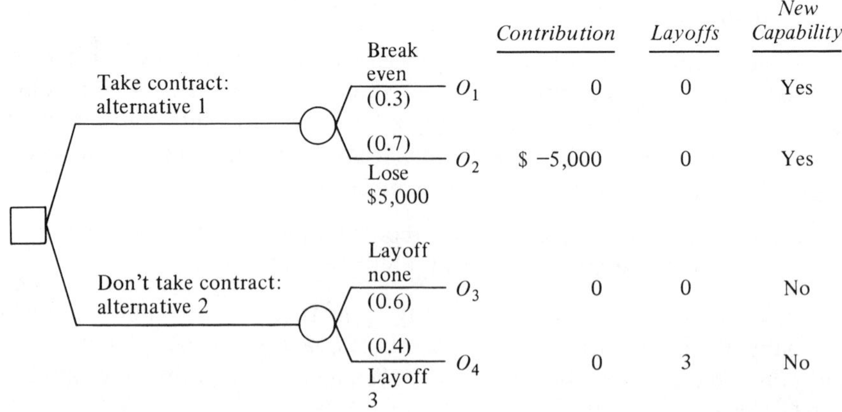

made arbitrarily for purposes of the example):

| | | |
|---|---|---|
| *Original* ⇒ | $O_1$: | contribution = \$0; layoffs = 0; new capability = yes ~ |
| *Trade-off to base case on layoffs* ⇒ | $O_{1A}$: | contribution = \$0 + \$3,000; layoffs = 3; new capability = yes ~ |
| *Trade-off to base case on capability* ⇒ | $O_{1B}$: | contribution = \$3,000 + \$4,000 = \$7,000; layoffs = 3; new capability = no |

| | | |
|---|---|---|
| *Original* ⇒ | $O_2$: | contribution = \$ − 5,000; layoffs = 0; new capability = yes ~ |
| *Trade-off to base case on layoffs* ⇒ | $O_{2A}$: | contribution = \$ − 5,000 + \$3,000; layoff = 3; new capability = yes ~ |
| *Trade-off to base case on capability* ⇒ | $O_{2B}$: | contribution = \$ − 2,000 + \$4,000 = \$2,000; layoffs = 3; new capability = no |

| | | |
|---|---|---|
| *Original* ⇒ | $O_3$: | contribution = \$0; layoff = 0; new capability = no ~ |
| *Trade-off to base case on layoffs* ⇒ | $O_{3A}$: | contribution = \$3,000; layoffs = 3; new capability = no |

| | | |
|---|---|---|
| *Original* ⇒ | $O_4$: | contribution = \$0; layoffs = 3; new capability = no |

Note that the trade-offs moving from 0 to 3 layoffs were the same in each setting. This is not a necessary condition. It would be perfectly proper for this trade-off to change based on the levels of contribution and new capability. The trade-off procedure does not assume these trade-offs are independent of the levels of other attributes.

This trade-off procedure has devised a set of equivalent outcomes with a base level of (layoffs = 3) and (new capability = no). If we substitute these in the diagram, we have Figure 20.4. The next step is to assess a preference function over the surviving attribute, contribution, given the base level of (layoffs = 3) and (new capability = no). That is, in assessing the preference curve, the owner must place himself in the hypothetical position of having laid off 3 workers and having no new capability. The preference curve must measure his attitude toward risk under these conditions. Internalizing this hypothetical situation may be difficult, and if it cannot be done with confidence, the decision maker should resort to direct choice. For purposes of illustration, assume that the owner agrees to assess the preference curve under these conditions, and that the curve is shown in Figure 20.5.

**FIGURE 20.4**

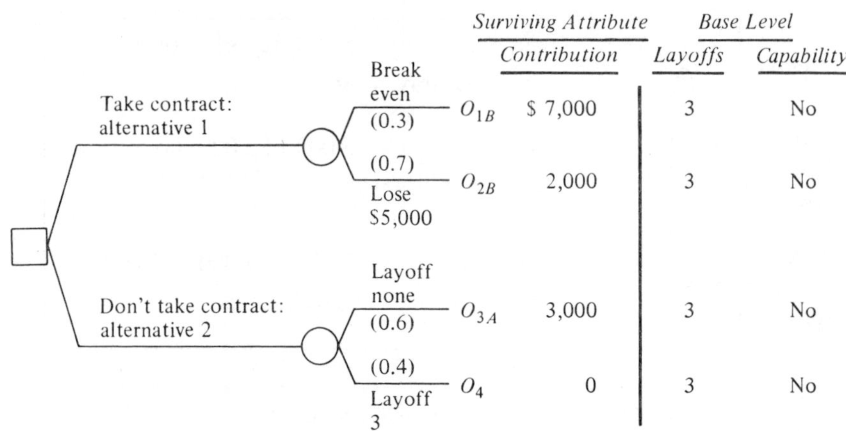


**FIGURE 20.5**

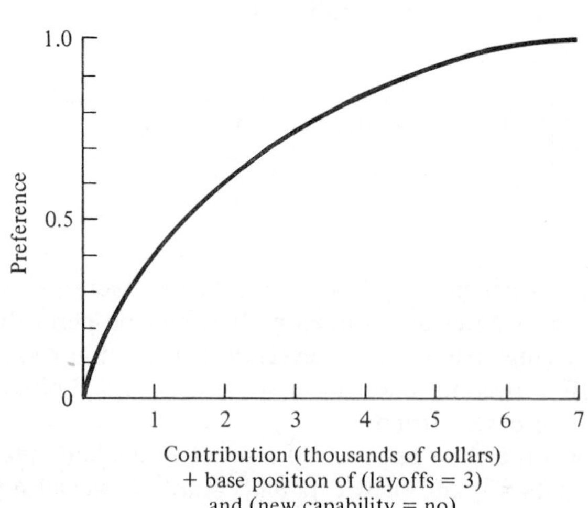

With this curve we have $U(O_{1B})=1.0$, $U(O_{2B})=0.6$, $U(O_{3A})=0.75$, and $U(O_4)=0$. Therefore, expected preferences for the two alternatives are:

| | |
|---|---|
| *Alternative 1:* | $(0.3)(1)+(0.7)(0.6)=0.72$ |
| *Alternative 2:* | $(0.6)(0.75)+(0.4)(0)=0.45$ |

The choice based on this analysis is clearly alternative 1.

The complexity of decomposition procedures increases rapidly when both multiple attributes and uncertainty are present. The trade-off procedure presented above is fundamentally sound *if* the required preferences can be assessed. Other models can also be used. Additive models are the most popular, but multiplicative models are also proposed. These models require stringent independence assumptions on preferences over the attributes. A discussion of these more complex procedures is beyond the scope of this book.[4]

## SUMMARY

When decisions are complicated by multiple attributes, decision makers often require help. Descriptive procedures are used, although, with the exception of the dominance procedure, they require severe independence assumptions.

*Dominance:* Compare alternatives attribute by attribute. An alternative that is at least as good as a second alternative on every attribute and strictly better on at least one attribute is said to dominate the second alternative.

*Satisficing:* Satisfactory levels are set for each separate attribute. Any alternative that is at least as good as these levels for every attribute is kept. Others are ruled out.

*Lexicographic:* Attributes are ranked in order of importance. Alternatives are compared on one attribute at a time, starting with the highest-ranked attribute. Lower-ranked attributes are used until they are exhausted or until a unique choice is made.

Combinations of these procedures are sometimes suggested.

Trade-off procedures do not require independence assumptions. But they also place more of a burden on the individual for processing. They use a *surviving* attribute and base levels for the remaining attributes. Indifference relations are used to create equivalent alternatives with the base attributes all at the same levels.

[4]A thorough treatment of multiple attribute problems can be found in R. Keeney and H. Raiffa, *Decisions with Multiple Objectives: Preferences and Value Trade-offs* (New York: Wiley, 1976).

When uncertainty is also present, the trade-off procedures can be combined with a preference assessment over the surviving attribute. This assessment must be done taking into account the levels of the base set of attributes.

## ASSIGNMENT MATERIAL

**20.1.** Describe why multiple attributes complicate a decision problem.

**20.2.** Consider the following set of alternatives and attributes. All scales go from 0 to 10 with 10 being the most preferred. Are any of the alternatives dominated?

| | *Alternative* | | | | |
|---|---|---|---|---|---|
| *Attribute* | 1 | 2 | 3 | 4 | 5 |
| 1 | 8 | 5 | 9 | 9 | 8 |
| 2 | 6 | 6 | 6 | 0 | 3 |
| 3 | 3 | 7 | 6 | 9 | 5 |
| 4 | 2 | 4 | 9 | 2 | 2 |
| 5 | 4 | 4 | 4 | 3 | 6 |
| 6 | 1 | 6 | 1 | 6 | 0 |

**20.3.** If satisficing levels are set as follows, which alternatives are not eliminated?

| *Attribute* | *Satisficing Level* |
|---|---|
| 1 | 6 |
| 2 | 4 |
| 3 | 5 |
| 4 | 2 |
| 5 | 4 |
| 6 | 1 |

**20.4.** If the attributes are ranked 2, 5, 3, 1, 4, 6, which one would be chosen by a lexicographic procedure?

**20.5. Tetons Area Rapid Transit (A)**

You are the manager of TART (Tetons Area Rapid Transit) with the charge of bringing first class transportation to the Grand Tetons National Park. Initial work has created a goal fabric for your comparison between alternatives which is given in Figure 20.6. That is, you have decided that the two things which are important for you are the system cost and the travel time. You have two alternative systems that have been proposed. System *A* is projected to cost $100 million and is designed to make a round trip in 90 minutes. System *B* cost is estimated at $80 million but the round trip will average 100 minutes. Both systems are proposed by the same firm, so no difference in estimating capabilities are included. Because of the high quality of the firm and its experience, you feel that these are "hard" numbers (i.e., there is no need to consider uncertainty).

Assume the role of the TART manager and decide which system you prefer. Discuss your methodology.

**FIGURE 20.6**

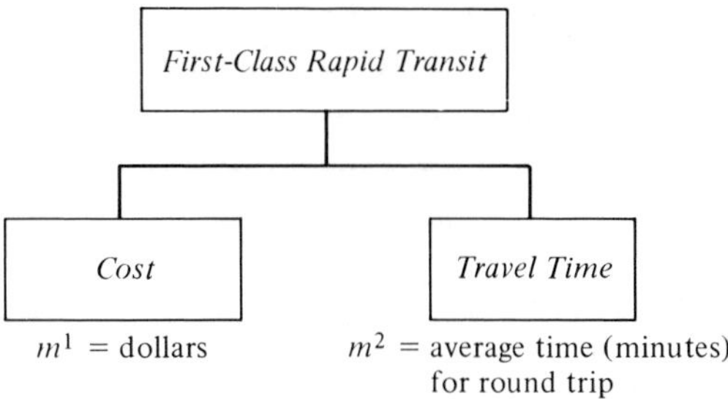


**20.6. Tetons Area Rapid Transit (B)**

Even though you felt fairly comfortable making the decision between systems *A* and *B* in the TART (A) case and were even prepared to develop a model for general use, you decided that some outside help on evaluation would be desirable. A quick search turned up a well-regarded consulting firm PubSeC (Public Sector Consulting). Your PubSeC consultant looked over the "model" you had developed and immediately suggested an expansion of the number of attributes which you should consider. The goal hierarchy suggested is shown in Figure 20.7.

**FIGURE 20.7**

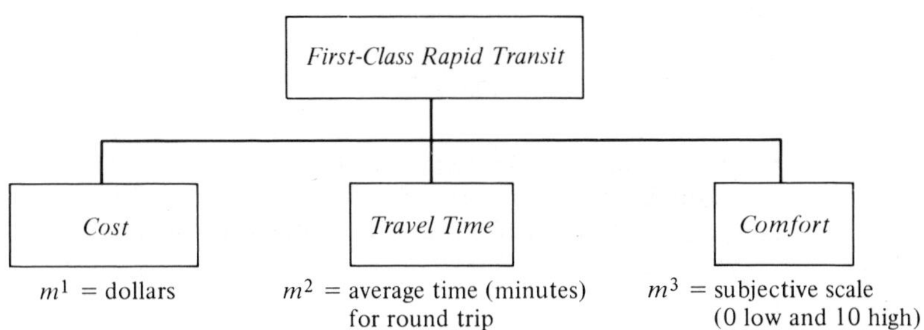


The inclusion of comfort as a factor seemed like a good idea, but the use of a subjective scale seemed a little arbitrary. The consultant said that he thought comfort could be meaningfully described in terms of a scale. Zero would be equivalent to sitting on the floor of a truck bed and 10 would correspond to riding in a new Cadillac (or Lincoln Continental). A standard Greyhound bus would rate 6, the New York subway 3, and a Boeing 747 would rate 8.

With this new hierarchy you set out to determine your preferences again. After consultation with the firm, you determined $m^3=7$ for system *A* and $m^3=5$ for system *B*.

Assume the role of the TART manager and decide between systems *A* and *B*.

**20.7. Tetons Area Rapid Transit (C)**

After some false starts and some guidance with which you feel less than comfortable from your PubSeC consultant, as manager of TART you decide that there are important uncertainties involved in the alternatives so far developed. You decide to revert to the criterion hierarchy shown in Figure 20.8.

**FIGURE 20.8**

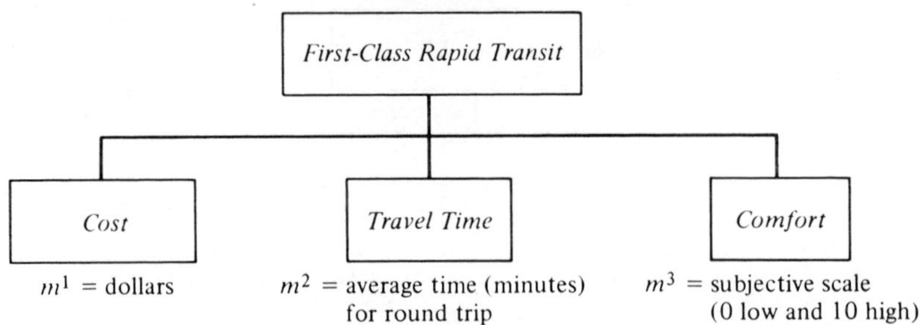


You feel that the uncertainty arises in two places: the cost estimates and the travel-time estimates. In fact, after discussion with your engineers, you have developed the following information on your two leading alternatives:

| *Alternative* | *Outcome* | *Probability* |
|---|---|---|
| $A_1$: | $m^1=80$; $m^2=80$; $m^3=7$ | 0.5 |
| $A_2$: | $m^1=110$; $m^2=90$; $m^3=7$ | 0.5 |

| *Alternative* | *Outcome* | *Probability* |
|---|---|---|
| $B_1$: | $m^1=70$; $m^2=80$; $m^3=8$ | 0.6 |
| $B_2$: | $m^1=120$; $m^2=95$; $m^3=8$ | 0.4 |

Undaunted by this complication, your PubSec consultant says that he can handle this easily if you will just answer a few more questions for him.

Assume the role of the manager and determine which alternative you prefer.

# Appendices

# A

# Binomial Distribution – Individual Terms

THE TABLE presents individual binomial probabilities for the number of successes, $r$, in $n$ trials, for selected values of $p$, the probability of a success on any one trial.

$$P(r) = {}_nC_r\, p^r q^{n-r}$$

| n | r | .01 | .02 | .04 | .05 | .06 | .08 | .10 | .12 | .14 | .15 | p .16 | .18 | .20 | .22 | .24 | .25 | .30 | .35 | .40 | .45 | .50 | r |
|---|---|---|---|---|---|---|---|---|---|---|---|---|---|---|---|---|---|---|---|---|---|---|---|
| 2 | 0 | 980 | 960 | 922 | 902 | 884 | 846 | 810 | 774 | 740 | 722 | 706 | 672 | 640 | 608 | 578 | 562 | 490 | 422 | 360 | 302 | 250 | 0 |
| | 1 | 020 | 039 | 077 | 095 | 113 | 147 | 180 | 211 | 241 | 255 | 269 | 295 | 320 | 343 | 365 | 375 | 420 | 455 | 480 | 495 | 500 | 1 |
| | 2 | 0+ | 0+ | 002 | 002 | 004 | 006 | 010 | 014 | 020 | 022 | 026 | 032 | 040 | 048 | 058 | 062 | 090 | 122 | 160 | 202 | 250 | 2 |
| 3 | 0 | 970 | 941 | 885 | 857 | 831 | 779 | 729 | 681 | 636 | 614 | 593 | 551 | 512 | 475 | 439 | 422 | 343 | 275 | 216 | 166 | 125 | 0 |
| | 1 | 029 | 058 | 111 | 135 | 159 | 203 | 243 | 279 | 311 | 325 | 339 | 363 | 384 | 402 | 416 | 422 | 441 | 444 | 432 | 408 | 375 | 1 |
| | 2 | 0+ | 001 | 005 | 007 | 010 | 018 | 027 | 038 | 051 | 057 | 065 | 080 | 096 | 113 | 131 | 141 | 189 | 239 | 288 | 334 | 375 | 2 |
| | 3 | 0+ | 0+ | 0+ | 0+ | 0+ | 001 | 001 | 002 | 003 | 003 | 004 | 006 | 008 | 011 | 014 | 016 | 027 | 043 | 064 | 091 | 125 | 3 |
| 4 | 0 | 961 | 922 | 849 | 815 | 781 | 716 | 656 | 600 | 547 | 522 | 498 | 452 | 410 | 370 | 334 | 316 | 240 | 179 | 130 | 092 | 063 | 0 |
| | 1 | 039 | 075 | 142 | 171 | 199 | 249 | 292 | 327 | 356 | 368 | 379 | 397 | 410 | 418 | 421 | 422 | 412 | 384 | 346 | 299 | 250 | 1 |
| | 2 | 001 | 002 | 009 | 014 | 019 | 033 | 049 | 067 | 087 | 098 | 108 | 131 | 154 | 177 | 200 | 211 | 265 | 311 | 346 | 368 | 375 | 2 |
| | 3 | 0+ | 0+ | 0+ | 0+ | 001 | 002 | 004 | 006 | 009 | 011 | 014 | 019 | 026 | 033 | 042 | 047 | 076 | 111 | 154 | 200 | 250 | 3 |
| | 4 | 0+ | 0+ | 0+ | 0+ | 0+ | 0+ | 0+ | 0+ | 0+ | 001 | 001 | 001 | 002 | 002 | 003 | 004 | 008 | 015 | 026 | 041 | 062 | 4 |
| 5 | 0 | 951 | 904 | 815 | 774 | 734 | 659 | 590 | 528 | 470 | 444 | 418 | 371 | 328 | 289 | 254 | 237 | 168 | 116 | 078 | 050 | 031 | 0 |
| | 1 | 048 | 092 | 170 | 204 | 234 | 287 | 328 | 360 | 383 | 392 | 398 | 407 | 410 | 407 | 400 | 396 | 360 | 312 | 259 | 206 | 156 | 1 |
| | 2 | 001 | 004 | 014 | 021 | 030 | 050 | 073 | 098 | 125 | 138 | 152 | 179 | 205 | 230 | 253 | 264 | 309 | 336 | 346 | 337 | 312 | 2 |
| | 3 | 0+ | 0+ | 001 | 001 | 002 | 004 | 008 | 013 | 020 | 024 | 029 | 039 | 051 | 065 | 080 | 088 | 132 | 181 | 230 | 276 | 312 | 3 |
| | 4 | 0+ | 0+ | 0+ | 0+ | 0+ | 0+ | 0+ | 001 | 002 | 002 | 003 | 004 | 006 | 009 | 013 | 015 | 028 | 049 | 077 | 113 | 156 | 4 |
| | 5 | 0+ | 0+ | 0+ | 0+ | 0+ | 0+ | 0+ | 0+ | 0+ | 0+ | 0+ | 0+ | 0+ | 001 | 001 | 001 | 002 | 005 | 010 | 018 | 031 | 5 |
| 6 | 0 | 941 | 886 | 783 | 735 | 690 | 606 | 531 | 464 | 405 | 377 | 351 | 304 | 262 | 225 | 193 | 178 | 118 | 075 | 047 | 028 | 016 | 0 |
| | 1 | 057 | 108 | 196 | 232 | 264 | 316 | 354 | 380 | 395 | 399 | 401 | 400 | 393 | 381 | 365 | 356 | 303 | 244 | 187 | 136 | 094 | 1 |
| | 2 | 001 | 006 | 020 | 031 | 042 | 069 | 098 | 130 | 161 | 176 | 191 | 220 | 246 | 269 | 288 | 297 | 324 | 328 | 311 | 278 | 234 | 2 |
| | 3 | 0+ | 0+ | 001 | 002 | 004 | 008 | 015 | 024 | 035 | 041 | 049 | 064 | 082 | 101 | 121 | 132 | 185 | 235 | 276 | 303 | 312 | 3 |
| | 4 | 0+ | 0+ | 0+ | 0+ | 0+ | 001 | 001 | 002 | 004 | 005 | 007 | 011 | 015 | 021 | 029 | 033 | 060 | 095 | 138 | 186 | 234 | 4 |
| | 5 | 0+ | 0+ | 0+ | 0+ | 0+ | 0+ | 0+ | 0+ | 0+ | 0+ | 001 | 001 | 002 | 002 | 004 | 004 | 010 | 020 | 037 | 061 | 094 | 5 |
| | 6 | 0+ | 0+ | 0+ | 0+ | 0+ | 0+ | 0+ | 0+ | 0+ | 0+ | 0+ | 0+ | 0+ | 0+ | 0+ | 0+ | 001 | 002 | 004 | 008 | 016 | 6 |
| 7 | 0 | 932 | 868 | 751 | 698 | 648 | 558 | 478 | 409 | 348 | 321 | 295 | 249 | 210 | 176 | 146 | 133 | 082 | 049 | 028 | 015 | 008 | 0 |
| | 1 | 066 | 124 | 219 | 257 | 290 | 340 | 372 | 390 | 396 | 396 | 393 | 383 | 367 | 347 | 324 | 311 | 247 | 185 | 131 | 087 | 055 | 1 |
| | 2 | 002 | 008 | 027 | 041 | 055 | 089 | 124 | 160 | 194 | 210 | 225 | 252 | 275 | 293 | 307 | 311 | 318 | 298 | 261 | 214 | 164 | 2 |
| | 3 | 0+ | 0+ | 002 | 004 | 006 | 013 | 023 | 036 | 053 | 062 | 071 | 092 | 115 | 138 | 161 | 173 | 227 | 268 | 290 | 292 | 273 | 3 |
| | 4 | 0+ | 0+ | 0+ | 0+ | 0+ | 001 | 003 | 005 | 009 | 011 | 014 | 020 | 029 | 039 | 051 | 058 | 097 | 144 | 194 | 239 | 273 | 4 |
| | 5 | 0+ | 0+ | 0+ | 0+ | 0+ | 0+ | 0+ | 0+ | 001 | 001 | 002 | 003 | 004 | 007 | 010 | 012 | 025 | 047 | 077 | 117 | 164 | 5 |
| | 6 | 0+ | 0+ | 0+ | 0+ | 0+ | 0+ | 0+ | 0+ | 0+ | 0+ | 0+ | 0+ | 0+ | 001 | 001 | 001 | 004 | 008 | 017 | 032 | 055 | 6 |
| | 7 | 0+ | 0+ | 0+ | 0+ | 0+ | 0+ | 0+ | 0+ | 0+ | 0+ | 0+ | 0+ | 0+ | 0+ | 0+ | 0+ | 0+ | 001 | 002 | 004 | 008 | 7 |
| 8 | 0 | 923 | 851 | 721 | 663 | 610 | 513 | 430 | 360 | 299 | 272 | 248 | 204 | 168 | 137 | 111 | 100 | 058 | 032 | 017 | 008 | 004 | 0 |
| | 1 | 075 | 139 | 240 | 279 | 311 | 357 | 383 | 392 | 390 | 385 | 378 | 359 | 336 | 309 | 281 | 267 | 198 | 137 | 090 | 055 | 031 | 1 |
| | 2 | 003 | 010 | 035 | 051 | 070 | 109 | 149 | 187 | 222 | 238 | 252 | 276 | 294 | 305 | 311 | 311 | 296 | 259 | 209 | 157 | 109 | 2 |
| | 3 | 0+ | 0+ | 003 | 005 | 009 | 019 | 033 | 051 | 072 | 084 | 096 | 121 | 147 | 172 | 196 | 208 | 254 | 279 | 279 | 257 | 219 | 3 |
| | 4 | 0+ | 0+ | 0+ | 0+ | 001 | 002 | 005 | 009 | 015 | 018 | 023 | 033 | 046 | 061 | 077 | 087 | 136 | 188 | 232 | 263 | 273 | 4 |
| | 5 | 0+ | 0+ | 0+ | 0+ | 0+ | 0+ | 0+ | 001 | 002 | 003 | 003 | 006 | 009 | 014 | 020 | 023 | 047 | 081 | 124 | 172 | 219 | 5 |
| | 6 | 0+ | 0+ | 0+ | 0+ | 0+ | 0+ | 0+ | 0+ | 0+ | 0+ | 0+ | 001 | 001 | 002 | 003 | 004 | 010 | 022 | 041 | 070 | 109 | 6 |
| | 7 | 0+ | 0+ | 0+ | 0+ | 0+ | 0+ | 0+ | 0+ | 0+ | 0+ | 0+ | 0+ | 0+ | 0+ | 0+ | 0+ | 001 | 003 | 008 | 016 | 031 | 7 |
| | 8 | 0+ | 0+ | 0+ | 0+ | 0+ | 0+ | 0+ | 0+ | 0+ | 0+ | 0+ | 0+ | 0+ | 0+ | 0+ | 0+ | 0+ | 0+ | 001 | 002 | 004 | 8 |
| 9 | 0 | 914 | 834 | 693 | 630 | 573 | 472 | 387 | 316 | 257 | 232 | 208 | 168 | 134 | 107 | 085 | 075 | 040 | 021 | 010 | 005 | 002 | 0 |
| | 1 | 083 | 153 | 260 | 299 | 329 | 370 | 387 | 388 | 377 | 368 | 357 | 331 | 302 | 271 | 240 | 225 | 156 | 100 | 060 | 034 | 018 | 1 |
| | 2 | 003 | 013 | 043 | 063 | 084 | 129 | 172 | 212 | 245 | 260 | 272 | 291 | 302 | 306 | 304 | 300 | 267 | 216 | 161 | 111 | 070 | 2 |
| | 3 | 0+ | 001 | 004 | 008 | 013 | 026 | 045 | 067 | 093 | 107 | 121 | 149 | 176 | 201 | 224 | 234 | 267 | 272 | 251 | 212 | 164 | 3 |
| | 4 | 0+ | 0+ | 0+ | 001 | 001 | 003 | 007 | 014 | 023 | 028 | 035 | 049 | 066 | 085 | 106 | 117 | 172 | 219 | 251 | 260 | 246 | 4 |
| | 5 | 0+ | 0+ | 0+ | 0+ | 0+ | 0+ | 001 | 002 | 004 | 005 | 007 | 011 | 017 | 024 | 033 | 039 | 074 | 118 | 167 | 213 | 246 | 5 |
| | 6 | 0+ | 0+ | 0+ | 0+ | 0+ | 0+ | 0+ | 0+ | 0+ | 001 | 001 | 002 | 003 | 005 | 007 | 009 | 021 | 042 | 074 | 116 | 164 | 6 |
| | 7 | 0+ | 0+ | 0+ | 0+ | 0+ | 0+ | 0+ | 0+ | 0+ | 0+ | 0+ | 0+ | 0+ | 001 | 001 | 001 | 004 | 010 | 021 | 041 | 070 | 7 |
| | 8 | 0+ | 0+ | 0+ | 0+ | 0+ | 0+ | 0+ | 0+ | 0+ | 0+ | 0+ | 0+ | 0+ | 0+ | 0+ | 0+ | 0+ | 001 | 004 | 009 | 018 | 8 |
| | 9 | 0+ | 0+ | 0+ | 0+ | 0+ | 0+ | 0+ | 0+ | 0+ | 0+ | 0+ | 0+ | 0+ | 0+ | 0+ | 0+ | 0+ | 0+ | 0+ | 001 | 002 | 9 |
| 10 | 0 | 904 | 817 | 665 | 599 | 539 | 434 | 349 | 279 | 221 | 197 | 175 | 137 | 107 | 083 | 064 | 056 | 028 | 013 | 006 | 003 | 001 | 0 |
| | 1 | 091 | 167 | 277 | 315 | 344 | 378 | 387 | 380 | 360 | 347 | 333 | 302 | 268 | 235 | 203 | 188 | 121 | 072 | 040 | 021 | 010 | 1 |
| | 2 | 004 | 015 | 052 | 075 | 099 | 148 | 194 | 233 | 264 | 276 | 286 | 298 | 302 | 298 | 288 | 282 | 233 | 176 | 121 | 076 | 044 | 2 |
| | 3 | 0+ | 001 | 006 | 010 | 017 | 034 | 057 | 085 | 115 | 130 | 145 | 174 | 201 | 224 | 243 | 250 | 267 | 252 | 215 | 166 | 117 | 3 |
| | 4 | 0+ | 0+ | 0+ | 001 | 002 | 005 | 011 | 020 | 033 | 040 | 048 | 067 | 088 | 111 | 134 | 146 | 200 | 238 | 251 | 238 | 205 | 4 |
| | 5 | 0+ | 0+ | 0+ | 0+ | 0+ | 001 | 001 | 003 | 006 | 008 | 011 | 018 | 026 | 037 | 051 | 058 | 103 | 154 | 201 | 234 | 246 | 5 |
| | 6 | 0+ | 0+ | 0+ | 0+ | 0+ | 0+ | 0+ | 0+ | 001 | 001 | 002 | 003 | 006 | 009 | 013 | 016 | 037 | 069 | 111 | 160 | 205 | 6 |
| | 7 | 0+ | 0+ | 0+ | 0+ | 0+ | 0+ | 0+ | 0+ | 0+ | 0+ | 0+ | 0+ | 001 | 001 | 002 | 003 | 009 | 021 | 042 | 075 | 117 | 7 |
| | 8 | 0+ | 0+ | 0+ | 0+ | 0+ | 0+ | 0+ | 0+ | 0+ | 0+ | 0+ | 0+ | 0+ | 0+ | 0+ | 0+ | 001 | 004 | 011 | 023 | 044 | 8 |
| | 9 | 0+ | 0+ | 0+ | 0+ | 0+ | 0+ | 0+ | 0+ | 0+ | 0+ | 0+ | 0+ | 0+ | 0+ | 0+ | 0+ | 0+ | 001 | 002 | 004 | 010 | 9 |

Source: William A. Spurr and Charles P. Bonini, *Statistical Analysis for Business Decisions*, rev. ed. (Homewood, Ill.: Richard D. Irwin, 1973) © 1973 by Richard D. Irwin, Inc., pp. 683–88.

$$P(r) = {}_nC_r\, p^r q^{n-r}$$

| n | r | .01 | .02 | .04 | .05 | .06 | .08 | .10 | .12 | .14 | .15 | .16 | .18 | .20 | .22 | .24 | .25 | .30 | .35 | .40 | .45 | .50 | r |
|---|---|---|---|---|---|---|---|---|---|---|---|---|---|---|---|---|---|---|---|---|---|---|---|
| | | | | | | | | | | | | p | | | | | | | | | | | |
| 10 | 10 | 0+ | 0+ | 0+ | 0+ | 0+ | 0+ | 0+ | 0+ | 0+ | 0+ | 0+ | 0+ | 0+ | 0+ | 0+ | 0+ | 0+ | 0+ | 0+ | 0+ | 001 | 10 |
| 11 | 0 | 895 | 801 | 638 | 569 | 506 | 400 | 314 | 245 | 190 | 167 | 147 | 113 | 086 | 065 | 049 | 042 | 020 | 009 | 004 | 001 | 0+ | 0 |
| | 1 | 099 | 180 | 293 | 329 | 355 | 382 | 384 | 368 | 341 | 325 | 308 | 272 | 236 | 202 | 170 | 155 | 093 | 052 | 027 | 013 | 005 | 1 |
| | 2 | 005 | 018 | 061 | 087 | 113 | 166 | 213 | 251 | 277 | 287 | 293 | 299 | 295 | 284 | 268 | 258 | 200 | 140 | 089 | 051 | 027 | 2 |
| | 3 | 0+ | 001 | 008 | 014 | 022 | 043 | 071 | 103 | 135 | 152 | 168 | 197 | 221 | 241 | 254 | 258 | 257 | 225 | 177 | 126 | 081 | 3 |
| | 4 | 0+ | 0+ | 001 | 001 | 003 | 008 | 016 | 028 | 044 | 054 | 064 | 086 | 111 | 136 | 160 | 172 | 220 | 243 | 236 | 206 | 161 | 4 |
| | 5 | 0+ | 0+ | 0+ | 0+ | 0+ | 001 | 002 | 005 | 010 | 013 | 017 | 027 | 039 | 054 | 071 | 080 | 132 | 183 | 221 | 236 | 226 | 5 |
| | 6 | 0+ | 0+ | 0+ | 0+ | 0+ | 0+ | 0+ | 001 | 002 | 002 | 003 | 006 | 010 | 015 | 022 | 027 | 057 | 099 | 147 | 193 | 226 | 6 |
| | 7 | 0+ | 0+ | 0+ | 0+ | 0+ | 0+ | 0+ | 0+ | 0+ | 0+ | 0+ | 001 | 002 | 003 | 005 | 006 | 017 | 038 | 070 | 113 | 161 | 7 |
| | 8 | 0+ | 0+ | 0+ | 0+ | 0+ | 0+ | 0+ | 0+ | 0+ | 0+ | 0+ | 0+ | 0+ | 0+ | 001 | 001 | 004 | 010 | 023 | 046 | 081 | 8 |
| | 9 | 0+ | 0+ | 0+ | 0+ | 0+ | 0+ | 0+ | 0+ | 0+ | C+ | 0+ | 0+ | 0+ | 0+ | 0+ | 0+ | 001 | 002 | 005 | 013 | 027 | 9 |
| | 10 | 0+ | 0+ | 0+ | 0+ | 0+ | 0+ | 0+ | 0+ | 0+ | 0+ | 0+ | 0+ | 0+ | 0+ | 0+ | 0+ | 0+ | 0+ | 001 | 002 | 005 | 10 |
| | 11 | 0+ | 0+ | 0+ | 0+ | 0+ | 0+ | 0+ | 0+ | 0+ | 0+ | 0+ | 0+ | 0+ | 0+ | 0+ | 0+ | 0+ | 0+ | 0+ | 0+ | 0+ | 11 |
| 12 | 0 | 886 | 785 | 613 | 540 | 476 | 368 | 282 | 216 | 164 | 142 | 123 | 092 | 069 | 051 | 037 | 032 | 014 | 006 | 002 | 001 | 0+ | 0 |
| | 1 | 107 | 192 | 306 | 341 | 365 | 384 | 377 | 353 | 320 | 301 | 282 | 243 | 206 | 172 | 141 | 127 | 071 | 037 | 017 | 008 | 003 | 1 |
| | 2 | 006 | 022 | 070 | 099 | 128 | 183 | 230 | 265 | 286 | 292 | 296 | 294 | 283 | 266 | 244 | 232 | 168 | 109 | 064 | 034 | 016 | 2 |
| | 3 | 0+ | 001 | 010 | 017 | 027 | 053 | 085 | 120 | 155 | 172 | 188 | 215 | 236 | 250 | 257 | 258 | 240 | 195 | 142 | 092 | 054 | 3 |
| | 4 | 0+ | 0+ | 001 | 002 | 004 | 010 | 021 | 037 | 057 | 068 | 080 | 106 | 133 | 159 | 183 | 194 | 231 | 237 | 213 | 170 | 121 | 4 |
| | 5 | 0+ | 0+ | 0+ | 0+ | 0+ | 001 | 004 | 008 | 015 | 019 | 025 | 037 | 053 | 072 | 092 | 103 | 158 | 204 | 227 | 222 | 193 | 5 |
| | 6 | 0+ | 0+ | 0+ | 0+ | 0+ | 0+ | 0+ | 001 | 003 | 004 | 005 | 010 | 016 | 024 | 034 | 040 | 079 | 128 | 177 | 212 | 226 | 6 |
| | 7 | 0+ | 0+ | 0+ | 0+ | 0+ | 0+ | 0+ | 0+ | 0+ | 001 | 001 | 002 | 003 | 006 | 009 | 011 | 029 | 059 | 101 | 149 | 193 | 7 |
| | 8 | 0+ | 0+ | 0+ | 0+ | 0+ | 0+ | 0+ | 0+ | 0+ | 0+ | 0+ | 0+ | 001 | 001 | 002 | 002 | 008 | 020 | 042 | 076 | 121 | 8 |
| | 9 | 0+ | 0+ | 0+ | 0+ | 0+ | 0+ | 0+ | 0+ | 0+ | 0+ | 0+ | 0+ | 0+ | 0+ | 0+ | 0+ | 001 | 005 | 012 | 028 | 054 | 9 |
| | 10 | 0+ | 0+ | 0+ | 0+ | 0+ | 0+ | 0+ | 0+ | 0+ | 0+ | 0+ | 0+ | 0+ | 0+ | 0+ | 0+ | 0+ | 001 | 002 | 007 | 016 | 10 |
| | 11 | 0+ | 0+ | 0+ | 0+ | 0+ | 0+ | 0+ | 0+ | 0+ | 0+ | 0+ | 0+ | 0+ | 0+ | 0+ | 0+ | 0+ | 0+ | 0+ | 001 | 003 | 11 |
| | 12 | 0+ | 0+ | 0+ | 0+ | 0+ | 0+ | 0+ | 0+ | 0+ | 0+ | 0+ | 0+ | 0+ | 0+ | 0+ | 0+ | 0+ | 0+ | 0+ | 0+ | 0+ | 12 |
| 13 | 0 | 878 | 769 | 588 | 513 | 447 | 338 | 254 | 190 | 141 | 121 | 104 | 076 | 055 | 040 | 028 | 024 | 010 | 004 | 001 | 0+ | 0+ | 0 |
| | 1 | 115 | 204 | 319 | 351 | 371 | 382 | 367 | 336 | 298 | 277 | 257 | 216 | 179 | 145 | 116 | 103 | 054 | 026 | 011 | 004 | 002 | 1 |
| | 2 | 007 | 025 | 080 | 111 | 142 | 199 | 245 | 275 | 291 | 294 | 293 | 285 | 268 | 245 | 220 | 206 | 139 | 084 | 045 | 022 | 010 | 2 |
| | 3 | 0+ | 002 | 012 | 021 | 033 | 064 | 100 | 138 | 174 | 190 | 205 | 229 | 246 | 254 | 254 | 252 | 218 | 165 | 111 | 066 | 035 | 3 |
| | 4 | 0+ | 0+ | 001 | 003 | 005 | 014 | 028 | 047 | 071 | 084 | 098 | 126 | 154 | 179 | 201 | 210 | 234 | 222 | 184 | 135 | 087 | 4 |
| | 5 | 0+ | 0+ | 0+ | 0+ | 001, | 002 | 006 | 012 | 021 | 027 | 033 | 050 | 069 | 091 | 114 | 126 | 180 | 215 | 221 | 199 | 157 | 5 |
| | 6 | 0+ | 0+ | 0+ | 0+ | 0+ | 0+ | 001 | 002 | 004 | 006 | 008 | 015 | 023 | 034 | 048 | 056 | 103 | 155 | 197 | 217 | 209 | 6 |
| | 7 | 0+ | 0+ | 0+ | 0+ | 0+ | 0+ | 0+ | 0+ | 001 | 001 | 002 | 003 | 006 | 010 | 015 | 019 | 044 | 083 | 131 | 177 | 209 | 7 |
| | 8 | 0+ | 0+ | 0+ | 0+ | 0+ | 0+ | 0+ | 0+ | 0+ | 0+ | 0+ | 001 | 001 | 002 | 004 | 005 | 014 | 034 | 066 | 109 | 157 | 8 |
| | 9 | 0+ | 0+ | 0+ | 0+ | 0+ | 0+ | 0+ | 0+ | 0+ | 0+ | 0+ | 0+ | 0+ | 0+ | 001 | 001 | 003 | 010 | 024 | 050 | 087 | 9 |
| | 10 | 0+ | 0+ | 0+ | 0+ | 0+ | 0+ | 0+ | 0+ | 0+ | 0+ | 0+ | 0+ | 0+ | 0+ | 0+ | 0+ | 001 | 002 | 006 | 016 | 035 | 10 |
| | 11 | 0+ | 0+ | 0+ | 0+ | 0+ | 0+ | 0+ | 0+ | 0+ | 0+ | 0+ | 0+ | 0+ | 0+ | 0+ | 0+ | 0+ | 0+ | 001 | 004 | 010 | 11 |
| | 12 | 0+ | 0+ | 0+ | 0+ | 0+ | 0+ | 0+ | 0+ | 0+ | 0+ | 0+ | 0+ | 0+ | 0+ | 0+ | 0+ | 0+ | 0+ | 0+ | 0+ | 002 | 12 |
| | 13 | 0+ | 0+ | 0+ | 0+ | 0+ | 0+ | 0+ | 0+ | 0+ | 0+ | 0+ | 0+ | 0+ | 0+ | 0+ | 0+ | 0+ | 0+ | 0+ | 0+ | 0+ | 13 |
| 14 | 0 | 869 | 754 | 565 | 488 | 421 | 311 | 229 | 167 | 121 | 103 | 087 | 062 | 044 | 031 | 021 | 018 | 007 | 002 | 001 | 0+ | 0+ | 0 |
| | 1 | 123 | 215 | 329 | 359 | 376 | 379 | 356 | 319 | 276 | 254 | 232 | 191 | 154 | 122 | 095 | 083 | 041 | 018 | 007 | 003 | 001 | 1 |
| | 2 | 008 | 029 | 089 | 123 | 156 | 214 | 257 | 283 | 292 | 291 | 287 | 272 | 250 | 223 | 195 | 180 | 113 | 063 | 032 | 014 | 006 | 2 |
| | 3 | 0+ | 002 | 015 | 026 | 040 | 074 | 114 | 154 | 190 | 206 | 219 | 239 | 250 | 252 | 246 | 240 | 194 | 137 | 085 | 046 | 022 | 3 |
| | 4 | 0+ | 0+ | 002 | 004 | 007 | 018 | 035 | 058 | 085 | 100 | 115 | 144 | 172 | 195 | 214 | 220 | 229 | 202 | 155 | 104 | 061 | 4 |
| | 5 | 0+ | 0+ | 0+ | 0+ | 001 | 003 | 008 | 016 | 028 | 035 | 044 | 063 | 086 | 110 | 135 | 147 | 196 | 218 | 207 | 170 | 122 | 5 |
| | 6 | 0+ | 0+ | 0+ | 0+ | 0+ | 0+ | 001 | 003 | 007 | 009 | 012 | 021 | 032 | 047 | 064 | 073 | 126 | 176 | 207 | 209 | 183 | 6 |
| | 7 | 0+ | 0+ | 0+ | 0+ | 0+ | 0+ | 0+ | 001 | 001 | 002 | 003 | 005 | 009 | 015 | 023 | 028 | 062 | 108 | 157 | 195 | 209 | 7 |
| | 8 | 0+ | 0+ | 0+ | 0+ | 0+ | 0+ | 0+ | 0+ | 0+ | 0+ | 0+ | 001 | 002 | 004 | 006 | 008 | 023 | 051 | 092 | 140 | 183 | 8 |
| | 9 | 0+ | 0+ | 0+ | 0+ | 0+ | 0+ | 0+ | 0+ | 0+ | 0+ | 0+ | 0+ | 0+ | 001 | 001 | 002 | 007 | 018 | 041 | 076 | 122 | 9 |
| | 10 | 0+ | 0+ | 0+ | 0+ | 0+ | 0+ | 0+ | 0+ | 0+ | 0+ | 0+ | 0+ | 0+ | 0+ | 0+ | 0+ | 001 | 005 | 014 | 031 | 061 | 10 |
| | 11 | 0+ | 0+ | 0+ | 0+ | 0+ | 0+ | 0+ | 0+ | 0+ | 0+ | 0+ | 0+ | 0+ | 0+ | 0+ | 0+ | 0+ | 001 | 003 | 009 | 022 | 11 |
| | 12 | 0+ | 0+ | 0+ | 0+ | 0+ | 0+ | 0+ | 0+ | 0+ | 0+ | 0+ | 0+ | 0+ | 0+ | 0+ | 0+ | 0+ | 0+ | 001 | 002 | 006 | 12 |
| | 13 | 0+ | 0+ | 0+ | 0+ | 0+ | 0+ | 0+ | 0+ | 0+ | 0+ | 0+ | 0+ | 0+ | 0+ | 0+ | 0+ | 0+ | 0+ | 0+ | 0+ | 001 | 13 |
| | 14 | 0+ | 0+ | 0+ | 0+ | 0+ | 0+ | 0+ | 0+ | 0+ | 0+ | 0+ | 0+ | 0+ | 0+ | 0+ | 0+ | 0+ | 0+ | 0+ | 0+ | 0+ | 14 |
| 15 | 0 | 860 | 739 | 542 | 463 | 395 | 286 | 206 | 147 | 104 | 087 | 073 | 051 | 035 | 024 | 016 | 013 | 005 | 002 | 0+ | 0+ | 0+ | 0 |
| | 1 | 130 | 226 | 339 | 366 | 378 | 373 | 343 | 301 | 254 | 231 | 209 | 168 | 132 | 102 | 077 | 067 | 031 | 013 | 005 | 002 | 0+ | 1 |
| | 2 | 009 | 032 | 099 | 135 | 169 | 227 | 267 | 287 | 290 | 286 | 279 | 258 | 231 | 201 | 171 | 156 | 092 | 048 | 022 | 009 | 003 | 2 |
| | 3 | 0+ | 003 | 018 | 031 | 047 | 086 | 129 | 170 | 204 | 218 | 230 | 245 | 250 | 246 | 234 | 225 | 170 | 111 | 063 | 032 | 014 | 3 |
| | 4 | 0+ | 0+ | 002 | 005 | 009 | 022 | 043 | 069 | 100 | 116 | 131 | 162 | 188 | 208 | 221 | 225 | 219 | 179 | 127 | 078 | 042 | 4 |

$$P(r) = {}_nC_r\, p^r q^{n-r}$$

| n | r | p | | | | | | | | | | | | | | | | | | | | | r |
|---|---|---|---|---|---|---|---|---|---|---|---|---|---|---|---|---|---|---|---|---|---|---|---|
| | | .01 | .02 | .04 | .05 | .06 | .08 | .10 | .12 | .14 | .15 | .16 | .18 | .20 | .22 | .24 | .25 | .30 | .35 | .40 | .45 | .50 | |
| 15 | 5 | 0+ | 0+ | 0+ | 001 | 001 | 004 | 010 | 021 | 036 | 045 | 055 | 078 | 103 | 129 | 154 | 165 | 206 | 212 | 186 | 140 | 092 | 5 |
| | 6 | 0+ | 0+ | 0+ | 0+ | 0+ | 001 | 002 | 005 | 010 | 013 | 017 | 029 | 043 | 061 | 081 | 092 | 147 | 191 | 207 | 191 | 153 | 6 |
| | 7 | 0+ | 0+ | 0+ | 0+ | 0+ | 0+ | 0+ | 001 | 002 | 003 | 004 | 008 | 014 | 022 | 033 | 039 | 081 | 132 | 177 | 201 | 196 | 7 |
| | 8 | 0+ | 0+ | 0+ | 0+ | 0+ | 0+ | 0+ | 0+ | 0+ | 001 | 001 | 002 | 003 | 006 | 010 | 013 | 035 | 071 | 118 | 165 | 196 | 8 |
| | 9 | 0+ | 0+ | 0+ | 0+ | 0+ | 0+ | 0+ | 0+ | 0+ | 0+ | 0+ | 0+ | 001 | 001 | 003 | 003 | 012 | 030 | 061 | 105 | 153 | 9 |
| | 10 | 0+ | 0+ | 0+ | 0+ | 0+ | 0+ | 0+ | 0+ | 0+ | 0+ | 0+ | 0+ | 0+ | 0+ | 0+ | 001 | 003 | 010 | 024 | 051 | 092 | 10 |
| | 11 | 0+ | 0+ | 0+ | 0+ | 0+ | 0+ | 0+ | 0+ | 0+ | 0+ | 0+ | 0+ | 0+ | 0+ | 0+ | 0+ | 001 | 002 | 007 | 019 | 042 | 11 |
| | 12 | 0+ | 0+ | 0+ | 0+ | 0+ | 0+ | 0+ | 0+ | 0+ | 0+ | 0+ | 0+ | 0+ | 0+ | 0+ | 0+ | 0+ | 0+ | 002 | 005 | 014 | 12 |
| | 13 | 0+ | 0+ | 0+ | 0+ | 0+ | 0+ | 0+ | 0+ | 0+ | 0+ | 0+ | 0+ | 0+ | 0+ | 0+ | 0+ | 0+ | 0+ | 0+ | 001 | 003 | 13 |
| | 14 | 0+ | 0+ | 0+ | 0+ | 0+ | 0+ | 0+ | 0+ | 0+ | 0+ | 0+ | 0+ | 0+ | 0+ | 0+ | 0+ | 0+ | 0+ | 0+ | 0+ | 0+ | 14 |
| | 15 | 0+ | 0+ | 0+ | 0+ | 0+ | 0+ | 0+ | 0+ | 0+ | 0+ | 0+ | 0+ | 0+ | 0+ | 0+ | 0+ | 0+ | 0+ | 0+ | 0+ | 0+ | 15 |
| 16 | 0 | 851 | 724 | 520 | 440 | 372 | 263 | 185 | 129 | 090 | 074 | 061 | 042 | 028 | 019 | 012 | 010 | 003 | 001 | 0+ | 0+ | 0+ | 0 |
| | 1 | 138 | 236 | 347 | 371 | 379 | 366 | 329 | 282 | 233 | 210 | 187 | 147 | 113 | 085 | 063 | 053 | 023 | 009 | 003 | 001 | 0+ | 1 |
| | 2 | 010 | 036 | 108 | 146 | 182 | 239 | 275 | 289 | 285 | 277 | 268 | 242 | 211 | 179 | 148 | 134 | 073 | 035 | 015 | 006 | 002 | 2 |
| | 3 | 0+ | 003 | 021 | 036 | 054 | 097 | 142 | 184 | 216 | 229 | 238 | 248 | 246 | 236 | 218 | 208 | 146 | 089 | 047 | 022 | 009 | 3 |
| | 4 | 0+ | 0+ | 003 | 006 | 011 | 027 | 051 | 081 | 114 | 131 | 147 | 177 | 200 | 216 | 224 | 225 | 204 | 155 | 101 | 057 | 028 | 4 |
| | 5 | 0+ | 0+ | 0+ | 001 | 002 | 006 | 014 | 027 | 045 | 056 | 067 | 093 | 120 | 146 | 170 | 180 | 210 | 201 | 162 | 112 | 067 | 5 |
| | 6 | 0+ | 0+ | 0+ | 0+ | 0+ | 001 | 003 | 007 | 013 | 018 | 023 | 037 | 055 | 076 | 098 | 110 | 165 | 198 | 198 | 168 | 122 | 6 |
| | 7 | 0+ | 0+ | 0+ | 0+ | 0+ | 0+ | 0+ | 001 | 003 | 005 | 006 | 012 | 020 | 030 | 044 | 052 | 101 | 152 | 189 | 197 | 175 | 7 |
| | 8 | 0+ | 0+ | 0+ | 0+ | 0+ | 0+ | 0+ | 0+ | 001 | 001 | 001 | 003 | 006 | 010 | 016 | 020 | 049 | 092 | 142 | 181 | 196 | 8 |
| | 9 | 0+ | 0+ | 0+ | 0+ | 0+ | 0+ | 0+ | 0+ | 0+ | 0+ | 0+ | 001 | 001 | 002 | 004 | 006 | 019 | 044 | 084 | 132 | 175 | 9 |
| | 10 | 0+ | 0+ | 0+ | 0+ | 0+ | 0+ | 0+ | 0+ | 0+ | 0+ | 0+ | 0+ | 0+ | 0+ | 001 | 001 | 006 | 017 | 039 | 075 | 122 | 10 |
| | 11 | 0+ | 0+ | 0+ | 0+ | 0+ | 0+ | 0+ | 0+ | 0+ | 0+ | 0+ | 0+ | 0+ | 0+ | 0+ | 0+ | 001 | 005 | 014 | 034 | 067 | 11 |
| | 12 | 0+ | 0+ | 0+ | 0+ | 0+ | 0+ | 0+ | 0+ | 0+ | 0+ | 0+ | 0+ | 0+ | 0+ | 0+ | 0+ | 0+ | 001 | 004 | 011 | 028 | 12 |
| | 13 | 0+ | 0+ | 0+ | 0+ | 0+ | 0+ | 0+ | 0+ | 0+ | 0+ | 0+ | 0+ | 0+ | 0+ | 0+ | 0+ | 0+ | 0+ | 001 | 003 | 009 | 13 |
| | 14 | 0+ | 0+ | 0+ | 0+ | 0+ | 0+ | 0+ | 0+ | 0+ | 0+ | 0+ | 0+ | 0+ | 0+ | 0+ | 0+ | 0+ | 0+ | 0+ | 001 | 002 | 14 |
| | 15 | 0+ | 0+ | 0+ | 0+ | 0+ | 0+ | 0+ | 0+ | 0+ | 0+ | 0+ | 0+ | 0+ | 0+ | 0+ | 0+ | 0+ | 0+ | 0+ | 0+ | 0+ | 15 |
| | 16 | 0+ | 0+ | 0+ | 0+ | 0+ | 0+ | 0+ | 0+ | 0+ | 0+ | 0+ | 0+ | 0+ | 0+ | 0+ | 0+ | 0+ | 0+ | 0+ | 0+ | 0+ | 16 |
| 17 | 0 | 843 | 709 | 500 | 418 | 349 | 242 | 167 | 114 | 077 | 063 | 052 | 034 | 023 | 015 | 009 | 008 | 002 | 001 | 0+ | 0+ | 0+ | 0 |
| | 1 | 145 | 246 | 354 | 374 | 379 | 358 | 315 | 264 | 213 | 189 | 167 | 128 | 096 | 070 | 051 | 043 | 017 | 006 | 002 | 001 | 0+ | 1 |
| | 2 | 012 | 040 | 118 | 158 | 194 | 249 | 280 | 288 | 278 | 267 | 255 | 225 | 191 | 158 | 128 | 114 | 058 | 026 | 010 | 004 | 001 | 2 |
| | 3 | 001 | 004 | 025 | 041 | 062 | 108 | 156 | 196 | 226 | 236 | 243 | 246 | 239 | 223 | 202 | 189 | 125 | 070 | 034 | 014 | 005 | 3 |
| | 4 | 0+ | 0+ | 004 | 008 | 014 | 033 | 060 | 094 | 129 | 146 | 162 | 189 | 209 | 221 | 223 | 221 | 187 | 132 | 080 | 041 | 018 | 4 |
| | 5 | 0+ | 0+ | 0+ | 001 | 002 | 007 | 017 | 033 | 054 | 067 | 080 | 108 | 136 | 162 | 183 | 191 | 208 | 185 | 138 | 087 | 047 | 5 |
| | 6 | 0+ | 0+ | 0+ | 0+ | 0+ | 001 | 004 | 009 | 018 | 024 | 031 | 047 | 068 | 091 | 116 | 128 | 178 | 199 | 184 | 143 | 094 | 6 |
| | 7 | 0+ | 0+ | 0+ | 0+ | 0+ | 0+ | 001 | 002 | 005 | 007 | 009 | 016 | 027 | 040 | 057 | 067 | 120 | 168 | 193 | 184 | 148 | 7 |
| | 8 | 0+ | 0+ | 0+ | 0+ | 0+ | 0+ | 0+ | 0+ | 001 | 001 | 002 | 004 | 008 | 014 | 023 | 028 | 064 | 113 | 161 | 188 | 185 | 8 |
| | 9 | 0+ | 0+ | 0+ | 0+ | 0+ | 0+ | 0+ | 0+ | 0+ | 0+ | 0+ | 001 | 002 | 004 | 007 | 009 | 028 | 061 | 107 | 154 | 185 | 9 |
| | 10 | 0+ | 0+ | 0+ | 0+ | 0+ | 0+ | 0+ | 0+ | 0+ | 0+ | 0+ | 0+ | 0+ | 001 | 002 | 002 | 009 | 026 | 057 | 101 | 148 | 10 |
| | 11 | 0+ | 0+ | 0+ | 0+ | 0+ | 0+ | 0+ | 0+ | 0+ | 0+ | 0+ | 0+ | 0+ | 0+ | 0+ | 001 | 003 | 009 | 024 | 052 | 094 | 11 |
| | 12 | 0+ | 0+ | 0+ | 0+ | 0+ | 0+ | 0+ | 0+ | 0+ | 0+ | 0+ | 0+ | 0+ | 0+ | 0+ | 0+ | 001 | 002 | 008 | 021 | 047 | 12 |
| | 13 | 0+ | 0+ | 0+ | 0+ | 0+ | 0+ | 0+ | 0+ | 0+ | 0+ | 0+ | 0+ | 0+ | 0+ | 0+ | 0+ | 0+ | 001 | 002 | 007 | 018 | 13 |
| | 14 | 0+ | 0+ | 0+ | 0+ | 0+ | 0+ | 0+ | 0+ | 0+ | 0+ | 0+ | 0+ | 0+ | 0+ | 0+ | 0+ | 0+ | 0+ | 0+ | 002 | 005 | 14 |
| | 15 | 0+ | 0+ | 0+ | 0+ | 0+ | 0+ | 0+ | 0+ | 0+ | 0+ | 0+ | 0+ | 0+ | 0+ | 0+ | 0+ | 0+ | 0+ | 0+ | 0+ | 001 | 15 |
| | 16 | 0+ | 0+ | 0+ | 0+ | 0+ | 0+ | 0+ | 0+ | 0+ | 0+ | 0+ | 0+ | 0+ | 0+ | 0+ | 0+ | 0+ | 0+ | 0+ | 0+ | 0+ | 16 |
| | 17 | 0+ | 0+ | 0+ | 0+ | 0+ | 0+ | 0+ | 0+ | 0+ | 0+ | 0+ | 0+ | 0+ | 0+ | 0+ | 0+ | 0+ | 0+ | 0+ | 0+ | 0+ | 17 |
| 18 | 0 | 835 | 695 | 480 | 397 | 328 | 223 | 150 | 100 | 066 | 054 | 043 | 028 | 018 | 011 | 007 | 006 | 002 | 0+ | 0+ | 0+ | 0+ | 0 |
| | 1 | 152 | 255 | 360 | 376 | 377 | 349 | 300 | 246 | 194 | 170 | 149 | 111 | 081 | 058 | 041 | 034 | 013 | 004 | 001 | 0+ | 0+ | 1 |
| | 2 | 013 | 044 | 127 | 168 | 205 | 258 | 284 | 285 | 268 | 256 | 241 | 207 | 172 | 139 | 109 | 096 | 046 | 019 | 007 | 002 | 001 | 2 |
| | 3 | 001 | 005 | 028 | 047 | 070 | 120 | 168 | 207 | 233 | 241 | 244 | 243 | 230 | 209 | 184 | 170 | 105 | 055 | 025 | 009 | 003 | 3 |
| | 4 | 0+ | 0+ | 004 | 009 | 017 | 039 | 070 | 106 | 142 | 159 | 175 | 200 | 215 | 221 | 218 | 213 | 168 | 110 | 061 | 029 | 012 | 4 |
| | 5 | 0+ | 0+ | 001 | 001 | 003 | 009 | 022 | 040 | 065 | 079 | 093 | 123 | 151 | 175 | 193 | 199 | 202 | 166 | 115 | 067 | 033 | 5 |
| | 6 | 0+ | 0+ | 0+ | 0+ | 0+ | 002 | 005 | 012 | 023 | 030 | 038 | 058 | 082 | 107 | 132 | 144 | 187 | 194 | 166 | 118 | 071 | 6 |
| | 7 | 0+ | 0+ | 0+ | 0+ | 0+ | 0+ | 001 | 003 | 006 | 009 | 013 | 022 | 035 | 052 | 071 | 082 | 138 | 179 | 189 | 166 | 121 | 7 |
| | 8 | 0+ | 0+ | 0+ | 0+ | 0+ | 0+ | 0+ | 001 | 001 | 002 | 003 | 007 | 012 | 020 | 031 | 038 | 081 | 133 | 173 | 186 | 167 | 8 |
| | 9 | 0+ | 0+ | 0+ | 0+ | 0+ | 0+ | 0+ | 0+ | 0+ | 0+ | 001 | 002 | 003 | 006 | 011 | 014 | 039 | 079 | 128 | 169 | 185 | 9 |
| | 10 | 0+ | 0+ | 0+ | 0+ | 0+ | 0+ | 0+ | 0+ | 0+ | 0+ | 0+ | 0+ | 001 | 002 | 003 | 004 | 015 | 038 | 077 | 125 | 167 | 10 |
| | 11 | 0+ | 0+ | 0+ | 0+ | 0+ | 0+ | 0+ | 0+ | 0+ | 0+ | 0+ | 0+ | 0+ | 0+ | 001 | 001 | 005 | 015 | 037 | 074 | 121 | 11 |
| | 12 | 0+ | 0+ | 0+ | 0+ | 0+ | 0+ | 0+ | 0+ | 0+ | 0+ | 0+ | 0+ | 0+ | 0+ | 0+ | 0+ | 001 | 005 | 015 | 035 | 071 | 12 |
| | 13 | 0+ | 0+ | 0+ | 0+ | 0+ | 0+ | 0+ | 0+ | 0+ | 0+ | 0+ | 0+ | 0+ | 0+ | 0+ | 0+ | 0+ | 001 | 004 | 013 | 033 | 13 |
| | 14 | 0+ | 0+ | 0+ | 0+ | 0+ | 0+ | 0+ | 0+ | 0+ | 0+ | 0+ | 0+ | 0+ | 0+ | 0+ | 0+ | 0+ | 0+ | 001 | 004 | 012 | 14 |
| | 15 | 0+ | 0+ | 0+ | 0+ | 0+ | 0+ | 0+ | 0+ | 0+ | 0+ | 0+ | 0+ | 0+ | 0+ | 0+ | 0+ | 0+ | 0+ | 0+ | 001 | 003 | 15 |
| | 16 | 0+ | 0+ | 0+ | 0+ | 0+ | 0+ | 0+ | 0+ | 0+ | 0+ | 0+ | 0+ | 0+ | 0+ | 0+ | 0+ | 0+ | 0+ | 0+ | 0+ | 001 | 16 |
| | 17 | 0+ | 0+ | 0+ | 0+ | 0+ | 0+ | 0+ | 0+ | 0+ | 0+ | 0+ | 0+ | 0+ | 0+ | 0+ | 0+ | 0+ | 0+ | 0+ | 0+ | 0+ | 17 |
| | 18 | 0+ | 0+ | 0+ | 0+ | 0+ | 0+ | 0+ | 0+ | 0+ | 0+ | 0+ | 0+ | 0+ | 0+ | 0+ | 0+ | 0+ | 0+ | 0+ | 0+ | 0+ | 18 |

$$P(r) = {}_nC_r\, p^r q^{n-r}$$

| n | r | .01 | .02 | .04 | .05 | .06 | .08 | .10 | .12 | .14 | .15 | .16 | .18 | .20 | .22 | .24 | .25 | .30 | .35 | .40 | .45 | .50 | r |
|---|---|---|---|---|---|---|---|---|---|---|---|---|---|---|---|---|---|---|---|---|---|---|---|
| 19 | 0 | 826 | 681 | 460 | 377 | 309 | 205 | 135 | 088 | 057 | 046 | 036 | 023 | 014 | 009 | 005 | 004 | 001 | 0+ | 0+ | 0+ | 0+ | 0 |
| | 1 | 159 | 264 | 364 | 377 | 374 | 339 | 285 | 228 | 176 | 153 | 132 | 096 | 068 | 048 | 033 | 027 | 009 | 003 | 001 | 0+ | 0+ | 1 |
| | 2 | 014 | 049 | 137 | 179 | 215 | 265 | 285 | 280 | 258 | 243 | 226 | 190 | 154 | 121 | 093 | 080 | 036 | 014 | 005 | 001 | 0+ | 2 |
| | 3 | 001 | 006 | 032 | 053 | 078 | 131 | 180 | 217 | 238 | 243 | 244 | 236 | 218 | 194 | 166 | 152 | 087 | 042 | 017 | 006 | 002 | 3 |
| | 4 | 0+ | 0+ | 005 | 011 | 020 | 045 | 080 | 118 | 155 | 171 | 186 | 207 | 218 | 219 | 210 | 202 | 149 | 091 | 047 | 020 | 007 | 4 |
| | 5 | 0+ | 0+ | 001 | 002 | 004 | 012 | 027 | 048 | 076 | 091 | 106 | 137 | 164 | 185 | 199 | 202 | 192 | 147 | 093 | 050 | 022 | 5 |
| | 6 | 0+ | 0+ | 0+ | 0+ | 001 | 002 | 007 | 015 | 029 | 037 | 047 | 070 | 095 | 122 | 146 | 157 | 192 | 184 | 145 | 095 | 052 | 6 |
| | 7 | 0+ | 0+ | 0+ | 0+ | 0+ | 0+ | 001 | 004 | 009 | 012 | 017 | 029 | 044 | 064 | 086 | 097 | 153 | 184 | 180 | 144 | 096 | 7 |
| | 8 | 0+ | 0+ | 0+ | 0+ | 0+ | 0+ | 0+ | 001 | 002 | 003 | 005 | 009 | 017 | 027 | 041 | 049 | 098 | 149 | 180 | 177 | 144 | 8 |
| | 9 | 0+ | 0+ | 0+ | 0+ | 0+ | 0+ | 0+ | 0+ | 0+ | 001 | 001 | 003 | 005 | 009 | 016 | 020 | 051 | 098 | 146 | 177 | 176 | 9 |
| | 10 | 0+ | 0+ | 0+ | 0+ | 0+ | 0+ | 0+ | 0+ | 0+ | 0+ | 0+ | 001 | 001 | 003 | 005 | 007 | 022 | 053 | 098 | 145 | 176 | 10 |
| | 11 | 0+ | 0+ | 0+ | 0+ | 0+ | 0+ | 0+ | 0+ | 0+ | 0+ | 0+ | 0+ | 0+ | 001 | 001 | 002 | 008 | 023 | 053 | 097 | 144 | 11 |
| | 12 | 0+ | 0+ | 0+ | 0+ | 0+ | 0+ | 0+ | 0+ | 0+ | 0+ | 0+ | 0+ | 0+ | 0+ | 0+ | 0+ | 002 | 008 | 024 | 053 | 096 | 12 |
| | 13 | 0+ | 0+ | 0+ | 0+ | 0+ | 0+ | 0+ | 0+ | 0+ | 0+ | 0+ | 0+ | 0+ | 0+ | 0+ | 0+ | 001 | 002 | 008 | 023 | 052 | 13 |
| | 14 | 0+ | 0+ | 0+ | 0+ | 0+ | 0+ | 0+ | 0+ | 0+ | 0+ | 0+ | 0+ | 0+ | 0+ | 0+ | 0+ | 0+ | 001 | 002 | 008 | 022 | 14 |
| | 15 | 0+ | 0+ | 0+ | 0+ | 0+ | 0+ | 0+ | 0+ | 0+ | 0+ | 0+ | 0+ | 0+ | 0+ | 0+ | 0+ | 0+ | 0+ | 001 | 002 | 007 | 15 |
| | 16 | 0+ | 0+ | 0+ | 0+ | 0+ | 0+ | 0+ | 0+ | 0+ | 0+ | 0+ | 0+ | 0+ | 0+ | 0+ | 0+ | 0+ | 0+ | 0+ | 0+ | 002 | 16 |
| | 17 | 0+ | 0+ | 0+ | 0+ | 0+ | 0+ | 0+ | 0+ | 0+ | 0+ | 0+ | 0+ | 0+ | 0+ | 0+ | 0+ | 0+ | 0+ | 0+ | 0+ | 0+ | 17 |
| | 18 | 0+ | 0+ | 0+ | 0+ | 0+ | 0+ | 0+ | 0+ | 0+ | 0+ | 0+ | 0+ | 0+ | 0+ | 0+ | 0+ | 0+ | 0+ | 0+ | 0+ | 0+ | 18 |
| | 19 | 0+ | 0+ | 0+ | 0+ | 0+ | 0+ | 0+ | 0+ | 0+ | 0+ | 0+ | 0+ | 0+ | 0+ | 0+ | 0+ | 0+ | 0+ | 0+ | 0+ | 0+ | 19 |
| 20 | 0 | 818 | 668 | 442 | 358 | 290 | 189 | 122 | 078 | 049 | 039 | 031 | 019 | 012 | 007 | 004 | 003 | 001 | 0+ | 0+ | 0+ | 0+ | 0 |
| | 1 | 165 | 272 | 368 | 377 | 370 | 328 | 270 | 212 | 159 | 137 | 117 | 083 | 058 | 039 | 026 | 021 | 007 | 002 | 0+ | 0+ | 0+ | 1 |
| | 2 | 016 | 053 | 146 | 189 | 225 | 271 | 285 | 274 | 247 | 229 | 211 | 173 | 137 | 105 | 078 | 067 | 028 | 010 | 003 | 001 | 0+ | 2 |
| | 3 | 001 | 006 | 036 | 060 | 086 | 141 | 190 | 224 | 241 | 243 | 241 | 228 | 205 | 178 | 148 | 134 | 072 | 032 | 012 | 004 | 001 | 3 |
| | 4 | 0+ | 001 | 006 | 013 | 023 | 052 | 090 | 130 | 167 | 182 | 195 | 213 | 218 | 213 | 199 | 190 | 130 | 074 | 035 | 014 | 005 | 4 |
| | 5 | 0+ | 0+ | 001 | 002 | 005 | 015 | 032 | 057 | 087 | 103 | 119 | 149 | 175 | 192 | 201 | 202 | 179 | 127 | 075 | 036 | 015 | 5 |
| | 6 | 0+ | 0+ | 0+ | 0+ | 001 | 003 | 009 | 019 | 035 | 045 | 057 | 082 | 109 | 136 | 159 | 169 | 192 | 171 | 124 | 075 | 037 | 6 |
| | 7 | 0+ | 0+ | 0+ | 0+ | 0+ | 001 | 002 | 005 | 012 | 016 | 022 | 036 | 055 | 076 | 100 | 112 | 164 | 184 | 166 | 122 | 074 | 7 |
| | 8 | 0+ | 0+ | 0+ | 0+ | 0+ | 0+ | 0+ | 001 | 003 | 005 | 007 | 013 | 022 | 035 | 051 | 061 | 114 | 161 | 180 | 162 | 120 | 8 |
| | 9 | 0+ | 0+ | 0+ | 0+ | 0+ | 0+ | 0+ | 0+ | 001 | 001 | 002 | 004 | 007 | 013 | 022 | 027 | 065 | 116 | 160 | 177 | 160 | 9 |
| | 10 | 0+ | 0+ | 0+ | 0+ | 0+ | 0+ | 0+ | 0+ | 0+ | 0+ | 0+ | 001 | 002 | 004 | 008 | 010 | 031 | 069 | 117 | 159 | 176 | 10 |
| | 11 | 0+ | 0+ | 0+ | 0+ | 0+ | 0+ | 0+ | 0+ | 0+ | 0+ | 0+ | 0+ | 0+ | 001 | 002 | 003 | 012 | 034 | 071 | 119 | 160 | 11 |
| | 12 | 0+ | 0+ | 0+ | 0+ | 0+ | 0+ | 0+ | 0+ | 0+ | 0+ | 0+ | 0+ | 0+ | 0+ | 001 | 001 | 004 | 014 | 035 | 073 | 120 | 12 |
| | 13 | 0+ | 0+ | 0+ | 0+ | 0+ | 0+ | 0+ | 0+ | 0+ | 0+ | 0+ | 0+ | 0+ | 0+ | 0+ | 0+ | 001 | 004 | 015 | 037 | 074 | 13 |
| | 14 | 0+ | 0+ | 0+ | 0+ | 0+ | 0+ | 0+ | 0+ | 0+ | 0+ | 0+ | 0+ | 0+ | 0+ | 0+ | 0+ | 0+ | 001 | 005 | 015 | 037 | 14 |
| | 15 | 0+ | 0+ | 0+ | 0+ | 0+ | 0+ | 0+ | 0+ | 0+ | 0+ | 0+ | 0+ | 0+ | 0+ | 0+ | 0+ | 0+ | 0+ | 001 | 005 | 015 | 15 |
| | 16 | 0+ | 0+ | 0+ | 0+ | 0+ | 0+ | 0+ | 0+ | 0+ | 0+ | 0+ | 0+ | 0+ | 0+ | 0+ | 0+ | 0+ | 0+ | 0+ | 001 | 005 | 16 |
| | 17 | 0+ | 0+ | 0+ | 0+ | 0+ | 0+ | 0+ | 0+ | 0+ | 0+ | 0+ | 0+ | 0+ | 0+ | 0+ | 0+ | 0+ | 0+ | 0+ | 0+ | 001 | 17 |
| | 18 | 0+ | 0+ | 0+ | 0+ | 0+ | 0+ | 0+ | 0+ | 0+ | 0+ | 0+ | 0+ | 0+ | 0+ | 0+ | 0+ | 0+ | 0+ | 0+ | 0+ | 0+ | 18 |
| | 19 | 0+ | 0+ | 0+ | 0+ | 0+ | 0+ | 0+ | 0+ | 0+ | 0+ | 0+ | 0+ | 0+ | 0+ | 0+ | 0+ | 0+ | 0+ | 0+ | 0+ | 0+ | 19 |
| | 20 | 0+ | 0+ | 0+ | 0+ | 0+ | 0+ | 0+ | 0+ | 0+ | 0+ | 0+ | 0+ | 0+ | 0+ | 0+ | 0+ | 0+ | 0+ | 0+ | 0+ | 0+ | 20 |
| 21 | 0 | 810 | 654 | 424 | 341 | 273 | 174 | 109 | 068 | 042 | 033 | 026 | 015 | 010 | 005 | 003 | 002 | 001 | 0+ | 0+ | 0+ | 0+ | 0 |
| | 1 | 172 | 280 | 371 | 376 | 366 | 317 | 255 | 195 | 144 | 122 | 103 | 071 | 048 | 032 | 021 | 017 | 005 | 001 | 0+ | 0+ | 0+ | 1 |
| | 2 | 017 | 057 | 155 | 198 | 233 | 276 | 284 | 267 | 234 | 215 | 196 | 157 | 121 | 091 | 066 | 055 | 022 | 007 | 002 | 0+ | 0+ | 2 |
| | 3 | 001 | 007 | 041 | 066 | 094 | 152 | 200 | 230 | 242 | 241 | 236 | 218 | 192 | 162 | 132 | 117 | 058 | 024 | 009 | 003 | 001 | 3 |
| | 4 | 0+ | 001 | 008 | 016 | 027 | 059 | 100 | 141 | 177 | 191 | 202 | 215 | 216 | 205 | 187 | 176 | 113 | 059 | 026 | 009 | 003 | 4 |
| | 5 | 0+ | 0+ | 001 | 003 | 006 | 018 | 038 | 065 | 098 | 115 | 131 | 161 | 183 | 197 | 201 | 199 | 164 | 109 | 059 | 026 | 010 | 5 |
| | 6 | 0+ | 0+ | 0+ | 0+ | 001 | 004 | 011 | 024 | 043 | 054 | 067 | 094 | 122 | 148 | 169 | 177 | 188 | 156 | 105 | 057 | 026 | 6 |
| | 7 | 0+ | 0+ | 0+ | 0+ | 0+ | 001 | 003 | 007 | 015 | 020 | 027 | 044 | 065 | 089 | 114 | 126 | 172 | 180 | 149 | 101 | 055 | 7 |
| | 8 | 0+ | 0+ | 0+ | 0+ | 0+ | 0+ | 001 | 002 | 004 | 006 | 009 | 017 | 029 | 044 | 063 | 074 | 129 | 169 | 174 | 144 | 097 | 8 |
| | 9 | 0+ | 0+ | 0+ | 0+ | 0+ | 0+ | 0+ | 0+ | 001 | 002 | 002 | 005 | 010 | 018 | 029 | 036 | 080 | 132 | 168 | 170 | 140 | 9 |
| | 10 | 0+ | 0+ | 0+ | 0+ | 0+ | 0+ | 0+ | 0+ | 0+ | 0+ | 001 | 001 | 003 | 006 | 011 | 014 | 041 | 085 | 134 | 167 | 168 | 10 |
| | 11 | 0+ | 0+ | 0+ | 0+ | 0+ | 0+ | 0+ | 0+ | 0+ | 0+ | 0+ | 0+ | 001 | 002 | 003 | 005 | 018 | 046 | 089 | 137 | 168 | 11 |
| | 12 | 0+ | 0+ | 0+ | 0+ | 0+ | 0+ | 0+ | 0+ | 0+ | 0+ | 0+ | 0+ | 0+ | 0+ | 001 | 001 | 006 | 021 | 050 | 093 | 140 | 12 |
| | 13 | 0+ | 0+ | 0+ | 0+ | 0+ | 0+ | 0+ | 0+ | 0+ | 0+ | 0+ | 0+ | 0+ | 0+ | 0+ | 0+ | 002 | 008 | 023 | 053 | 097 | 13 |
| | 14 | 0+ | 0+ | 0+ | 0+ | 0+ | 0+ | 0+ | 0+ | 0+ | 0+ | 0+ | 0+ | 0+ | 0+ | 0+ | 0+ | 0+ | 002 | 009 | 025 | 055 | 14 |
| | 15 | 0+ | 0+ | 0+ | 0+ | 0+ | 0+ | 0+ | 0+ | 0+ | 0+ | 0+ | 0+ | 0+ | 0+ | 0+ | 0+ | 0+ | 001 | 003 | 009 | 026 | 15 |
| | 16 | 0+ | 0+ | 0+ | 0+ | 0+ | 0+ | 0+ | 0+ | 0+ | 0+ | 0+ | 0+ | 0+ | 0+ | 0+ | 0+ | 0+ | 0+ | 001 | 003 | 010 | 16 |
| | 17 | 0+ | 0+ | 0+ | 0+ | 0+ | 0+ | 0+ | 0+ | 0+ | 0+ | 0+ | 0+ | 0+ | 0+ | 0+ | 0+ | 0+ | 0+ | 0+ | 001 | 003 | 17 |
| | 18 | 0+ | 0+ | 0+ | 0+ | 0+ | 0+ | 0+ | 0+ | 0+ | 0+ | 0+ | 0+ | 0+ | 0+ | 0+ | 0+ | 0+ | 0+ | 0+ | 0+ | 001 | 18 |
| | 19 | 0+ | 0+ | 0+ | 0+ | 0+ | 0+ | 0+ | 0+ | 0+ | 0+ | 0+ | 0+ | 0+ | 0+ | 0+ | 0+ | 0+ | 0+ | 0+ | 0+ | 0+ | 19 |
| | 20 | 0+ | 0+ | 0+ | 0+ | 0+ | 0+ | 0+ | 0+ | 0+ | 0+ | 0+ | 0+ | 0+ | 0+ | 0+ | 0+ | 0+ | 0+ | 0+ | 0+ | 0+ | 20 |
| | 21 | 0+ | 0+ | 0+ | 0+ | 0+ | 0+ | 0+ | 0+ | 0+ | 0+ | 0+ | 0+ | 0+ | 0+ | 0+ | 0+ | 0+ | 0+ | 0+ | 0+ | 0+ | 21 |

$$P(r) = {}_nC_r\, p^r q^{n-r}$$

| n | r | .01 | .02 | .04 | .05 | .06 | .08 | .10 | .12 | .14 | .15 | p .16 | .18 | .20 | .22 | .24 | .25 | .30 | .35 | .40 | .45 | .50 | r |
|---|---|---|---|---|---|---|---|---|---|---|---|---|---|---|---|---|---|---|---|---|---|---|---|
| 22 | 0 | 802 | 641 | 407 | 324 | 256 | 160 | 098 | 060 | 036 | 028 | 022 | 013 | 007 | 004 | 002 | 002 | 0+ | 0+ | 0+ | 0+ | 0+ | 0 |
| | 1 | 178 | 288 | 373 | 375 | 360 | 306 | 241 | 180 | 130 | 109 | 090 | 061 | 041 | 026 | 017 | 013 | 004 | 001 | 0+ | 0+ | 0+ | 1 |
| | 2 | 019 | 062 | 163 | 207 | 241 | 279 | 281 | 258 | 222 | 201 | 181 | 141 | 107 | 078 | 055 | 046 | 017 | 005 | 001 | 0+ | 0+ | 2 |
| | 3 | 001 | 008 | 045 | 073 | 103 | 162 | 208 | 235 | 241 | 237 | 230 | 207 | 178 | 146 | 116 | 102 | 047 | 018 | 006 | 002 | 0+ | 3 |
| | 4 | 0+ | 001 | 009 | 018 | 031 | 067 | 110 | 152 | 186 | 199 | 208 | 216 | 211 | 196 | 174 | 161 | 096 | 047 | 019 | 006 | 002 | 4 |
| | 5 | 0+ | 0+ | 001 | 003 | 007 | 021 | 044 | 075 | 109 | 126 | 143 | 170 | 190 | 199 | 197 | 193 | 149 | 091 | 046 | 019 | 006 | 5 |
| | 6 | 0+ | 0+ | 0+ | 001 | 001 | 005 | 014 | 029 | 050 | 063 | 077 | 106 | 134 | 159 | 177 | 183 | 181 | 139 | 086 | 043 | 018 | 6 |
| | 7 | 0+ | 0+ | 0+ | 0+ | 0+ | 001 | 004 | 009 | 019 | 025 | 033 | 053 | 077 | 102 | 128 | 139 | 177 | 171 | 131 | 081 | 041 | 7 |
| | 8 | 0+ | 0+ | 0+ | 0+ | 0+ | 0+ | 001 | 002 | 006 | 008 | 012 | 022 | 036 | 054 | 075 | 087 | 142 | 173 | 164 | 125 | 076 | 8 |
| | 9 | 0+ | 0+ | 0+ | 0+ | 0+ | 0+ | 0+ | 0+ | 001 | 002 | 004 | 007 | 014 | 024 | 037 | 045 | 095 | 145 | 170 | 164 | 119 | 9 |
| | 10 | 0+ | 0+ | 0+ | 0+ | 0+ | 0+ | 0+ | 0+ | 0+ | 001 | 001 | 002 | 005 | 009 | 015 | 020 | 053 | 101 | 148 | 169 | 154 | 10 |
| | 11 | 0+ | 0+ | 0+ | 0+ | 0+ | 0+ | 0+ | 0+ | 0+ | 0+ | 0+ | 001 | 001 | 003 | 005 | 007 | 025 | 060 | 107 | 151 | 168 | 11 |
| | 12 | 0+ | 0+ | 0+ | 0+ | 0+ | 0+ | 0+ | 0+ | 0+ | 0+ | 0+ | 0+ | 0+ | 001 | 002 | 002 | 010 | 029 | 066 | 113 | 154 | 12 |
| | 13 | 0+ | 0+ | 0+ | 0+ | 0+ | 0+ | 0+ | 0+ | 0+ | 0+ | 0+ | 0+ | 0+ | 0+ | 0+ | 001 | 003 | 012 | 034 | 071 | 119 | 13 |
| | 14 | 0+ | 0+ | 0+ | 0+ | 0+ | 0+ | 0+ | 0+ | 0+ | 0+ | 0+ | 0+ | 0+ | 0+ | 0+ | 0+ | 001 | 004 | 014 | 037 | 076 | 14 |
| | 15 | 0+ | 0+ | 0+ | 0+ | 0+ | 0+ | 0+ | 0+ | 0+ | 0+ | 0+ | 0+ | 0+ | 0+ | 0+ | 0+ | 0+ | 001 | 001 | 016 | 041 | 15 |
| | 16 | 0+ | 0+ | 0+ | 0+ | 0+ | 0+ | 0+ | 0+ | 0+ | 0+ | 0+ | 0+ | 0+ | 0+ | 0+ | 0+ | 0+ | 0+ | 001 | 006 | 018 | 16 |
| | 17 | 0+ | 0+ | 0+ | 0+ | 0+ | 0+ | 0+ | 0+ | 0+ | 0+ | 0+ | 0+ | 0+ | 0+ | 0+ | 0+ | 0+ | 0+ | 0+ | 002 | 007 | 17 |
| | 18 | 0+ | 0+ | 0+ | 0+ | 0+ | 0+ | 0+ | 0+ | 0+ | 0+ | 0+ | 0+ | 0+ | 0+ | 0+ | 0+ | 0+ | 0+ | 0+ | 0+ | 002 | 18 |
| | 19 | 0+ | 0+ | 0+ | 0+ | 0+ | 0+ | 0+ | 0+ | 0+ | 0+ | 0+ | 0+ | 0+ | 0+ | 0+ | 0+ | 0+ | 0+ | 0+ | 0+ | 0+ | 19 |
| | 20 | 0+ | 0+ | 0+ | 0+ | 0+ | 0+ | 0+ | 0+ | 0+ | 0+ | 0+ | 0+ | 0+ | 0+ | 0+ | 0+ | 0+ | 0+ | 0+ | 0+ | 0+ | 20 |
| | 21 | 0+ | 0+ | 0+ | 0+ | 0+ | 0+ | 0+ | 0+ | 0+ | 0+ | 0+ | 0+ | 0+ | 0+ | 0+ | 0+ | 0+ | 0+ | 0+ | 0+ | 0+ | 21 |
| | 22 | 0+ | 0+ | 0+ | 0+ | 0+ | 0+ | 0+ | 0+ | 0+ | 0+ | 0+ | 0+ | 0+ | 0+ | 0+ | 0+ | 0+ | 0+ | 0+ | 0+ | 0+ | 22 |
| 23 | 0 | 794 | 628 | 391 | 307 | 241 | 147 | 089 | 053 | 031 | 024 | 018 | 010 | 006 | 003 | 002 | 001 | 0+ | 0+ | 0+ | 0+ | 0+ | 0 |
| | 1 | 184 | 295 | 375 | 372 | 354 | 294 | 226 | 166 | 117 | 097 | 079 | 053 | 034 | 021 | 013 | 010 | 003 | 001 | 0+ | 0+ | 0+ | 1 |
| | 2 | 020 | 066 | 172 | 215 | 248 | 281 | 277 | 249 | 209 | 188 | 166 | 127 | 093 | 066 | 046 | 038 | 013 | 004 | 001 | 0+ | 0+ | 2 |
| | 3 | 001 | 009 | 050 | 079 | 111 | 171 | 215 | 237 | 238 | 232 | 222 | 195 | 163 | 131 | 101 | 088 | 038 | 014 | 004 | 001 | 0+ | 3 |
| | 4 | 0+ | 001 | 010 | 021 | 035 | 074 | 120 | 162 | 194 | 204 | 211 | 214 | 204 | 185 | 160 | 146 | 082 | 037 | 014 | 004 | 001 | 4 |
| | 5 | 0+ | 0+ | 002 | 004 | 009 | 025 | 051 | 084 | 120 | 137 | 153 | 179 | 194 | 198 | 192 | 185 | 133 | 076 | 035 | 013 | 004 | 5 |
| | 6 | 0+ | 0+ | 0+ | 001 | 002 | 006 | 017 | 034 | 059 | 073 | 087 | 118 | 145 | 168 | 182 | 185 | 171 | 122 | 070 | 032 | 012 | 6 |
| | 7 | 0+ | 0+ | 0+ | 0+ | 0+ | 001 | 005 | 011 | 023 | 031 | 040 | 063 | 088 | 115 | 139 | 150 | 178 | 160 | 113 | 064 | 029 | 7 |
| | 8 | 0+ | 0+ | 0+ | 0+ | 0+ | 0+ | 001 | 003 | 008 | 011 | 015 | 028 | 044 | 065 | 088 | 100 | 153 | 172 | 151 | 105 | 058 | 8 |
| | 9 | 0+ | 0+ | 0+ | 0+ | 0+ | 0+ | 0+ | 001 | 002 | 003 | 005 | 010 | 018 | 030 | 046 | 056 | 109 | 155 | 168 | 143 | 097 | 9 |
| | 10 | 0+ | 0+ | 0+ | 0+ | 0+ | 0+ | 0+ | 0+ | 0+ | 001 | 001 | 003 | 006 | 012 | 020 | 026 | 065 | 117 | 157 | 164 | 136 | 10 |
| | 11 | 0+ | 0+ | 0+ | 0+ | 0+ | 0+ | 0+ | 0+ | 0+ | 0+ | 0+ | 001 | 002 | 004 | 008 | 010 | 033 | 074 | 123 | 159 | 161 | 11 |
| | 12 | 0+ | 0+ | 0+ | 0+ | 0+ | 0+ | 0+ | 0+ | 0+ | 0+ | 0+ | 0+ | 0+ | 001 | 002 | 003 | 014 | 040 | 082 | 130 | 161 | 12 |
| | 13 | 0+ | 0+ | 0+ | 0+ | 0+ | 0+ | 0+ | 0+ | 0+ | 0+ | 0+ | 0+ | 0+ | 0+ | 001 | 001 | 005 | 018 | 046 | 090 | 136 | 13 |
| | 14 | 0+ | 0+ | 0+ | 0+ | 0+ | 0+ | 0+ | 0+ | 0+ | 0+ | 0+ | 0+ | 0+ | 0+ | 0+ | 0+ | 002 | 007 | 022 | 053 | 097 | 14 |
| | 15 | 0+ | 0+ | 0+ | 0+ | 0+ | 0+ | 0+ | 0+ | 0+ | 0+ | 0+ | 0+ | 0+ | 0+ | 0+ | 0+ | 0+ | 002 | 009 | 026 | 058 | 15 |
| | 16 | 0+ | 0+ | 0+ | 0+ | 0+ | 0+ | 0+ | 0+ | 0+ | 0+ | 0+ | 0+ | 0+ | 0+ | 0+ | 0+ | 0+ | 001 | 003 | 011 | 029 | 16 |
| | 17 | 0+ | 0+ | 0+ | 0+ | 0+ | 0+ | 0+ | 0+ | 0+ | 0+ | 0+ | 0+ | 0+ | 0+ | 0+ | 0+ | 0+ | 0+ | 001 | 004 | 012 | 17 |
| | 18 | 0+ | 0+ | 0+ | 0+ | 0+ | 0+ | 0+ | 0+ | 0+ | 0+ | 0+ | 0+ | 0+ | 0+ | 0+ | 0+ | 0+ | 0+ | 0+ | 001 | 004 | 18 |
| | 19 | 0+ | 0+ | 0+ | 0+ | 0+ | 0+ | 0+ | 0+ | 0+ | 0+ | 0+ | 0+ | 0+ | 0+ | 0+ | 0+ | 0+ | 0+ | 0+ | 0+ | 001 | 19 |
| | 20 | 0+ | 0+ | 0+ | 0+ | 0+ | 0+ | 0+ | 0+ | 0+ | 0+ | 0+ | 0+ | 0+ | 0+ | 0+ | 0+ | 0+ | 0+ | 0+ | 0+ | 0+ | 20 |
| | 21 | 0+ | 0+ | 0+ | 0+ | 0+ | 0+ | 0+ | 0+ | 0+ | 0+ | 0+ | 0+ | 0+ | 0+ | 0+ | 0+ | 0+ | 0+ | 0+ | 0+ | 0+ | 21 |
| | 22 | 0+ | 0+ | 0+ | 0+ | 0+ | 0+ | 0+ | 0+ | 0+ | 0+ | 0+ | 0+ | 0+ | 0+ | 0+ | 0+ | 0+ | 0+ | 0+ | 0+ | 0+ | 22 |
| | 23 | 0+ | 0+ | 0+ | 0+ | 0+ | 0+ | 0+ | 0+ | 0+ | 0+ | 0+ | 0+ | 0+ | 0+ | 0+ | 0+ | 0+ | 0+ | 0+ | 0+ | 0+ | 23 |
| 24 | 0 | 786 | 616 | 375 | 292 | 227 | 135 | 080 | 047 | 027 | 020 | 015 | 009 | 005 | 003 | 001 | 001 | 0+ | 0+ | 0+ | 0+ | 0+ | 0 |
| | 1 | 190 | 302 | 375 | 369 | 347 | 282 | 213 | 152 | 105 | 086 | 070 | 045 | 028 | 017 | 010 | 008 | 002 | 0+ | 0+ | 0+ | 0+ | 1 |
| | 2 | 022 | 071 | 180 | 223 | 255 | 282 | 272 | 239 | 196 | 174 | 153 | 114 | 081 | 056 | 038 | 031 | 010 | 003 | 001 | 0+ | 0+ | 2 |
| | 3 | 002 | 011 | 055 | 086 | 119 | 180 | 221 | 239 | 234 | 225 | 213 | 183 | 149 | 117 | 088 | 075 | 031 | 010 | 003 | 001 | 0+ | 3 |
| | 4 | 0+ | 001 | 012 | 024 | 040 | 082 | 129 | 171 | 200 | 209 | 213 | 211 | 196 | 173 | 146 | 132 | 069 | 029 | 010 | 003 | 001 | 4 |
| | 5 | 0+ | 0+ | 002 | 005 | 010 | 029 | 057 | 093 | 130 | 147 | 162 | 185 | 196 | 195 | 184 | 176 | 118 | 062 | 027 | 009 | 003 | 5 |
| | 6 | 0+ | 0+ | 0+ | 001 | 002 | 008 | 020 | 040 | 067 | 082 | 098 | 129 | 155 | 174 | 184 | 185 | 160 | 106 | 056 | 024 | 008 | 6 |
| | 7 | 0+ | 0+ | 0+ | 0+ | 0+ | 002 | 006 | 014 | 028 | 037 | 048 | 073 | 100 | 126 | 149 | 159 | 176 | 147 | 096 | 050 | 021 | 7 |
| | 8 | 0+ | 0+ | 0+ | 0+ | 0+ | 0+ | 001 | 004 | 010 | 014 | 019 | 034 | 053 | 076 | 100 | 112 | 160 | 168 | 136 | 087 | 044 | 8 |
| | 9 | 0+ | 0+ | 0+ | 0+ | 0+ | 0+ | 0+ | 001 | 003 | 004 | 007 | 013 | 024 | 038 | 056 | 067 | 122 | 161 | 161 | 126 | 078 | 9 |
| | 10 | 0+ | 0+ | 0+ | 0+ | 0+ | 0+ | 0+ | 0+ | 001 | 001 | 002 | 004 | 009 | 016 | 027 | 033 | 079 | 130 | 161 | 155 | 117 | 10 |
| | 11 | 0+ | 0+ | 0+ | 0+ | 0+ | 0+ | 0+ | 0+ | 0+ | 0+ | 0+ | 001 | 003 | 006 | 011 | 014 | 043 | 089 | 137 | 161 | 149 | 11 |
| | 12 | 0+ | 0+ | 0+ | 0+ | 0+ | 0+ | 0+ | 0+ | 0+ | 0+ | 0+ | 0+ | 001 | 002 | 004 | 005 | 020 | 052 | 099 | 143 | 161 | 12 |
| | 13 | 0+ | 0+ | 0+ | 0+ | 0+ | 0+ | 0+ | 0+ | 0+ | 0+ | 0+ | 0+ | 0+ | 0+ | 001 | 002 | 008 | 026 | 061 | 108 | 149 | 13 |
| | 14 | 0+ | 0+ | 0+ | 0+ | 0+ | 0+ | 0+ | 0+ | 0+ | 0+ | 0+ | 0+ | 0+ | 0+ | 0+ | 0+ | 003 | 011 | 032 | 069 | 117 | 14 |

$P(r) = {}_nC_r\, p^r q^{n-r}$

| n | r | .01 | .02 | .04 | .05 | .06 | .08 | .10 | .12 | .14 | .15 | p .16 | .18 | .20 | .22 | .24 | .25 | .30 | .35 | .40 | .45 | .50 | r |
|---|---|---|---|---|---|---|---|---|---|---|---|---|---|---|---|---|---|---|---|---|---|---|---|
| 24 | 15 | 0+ | 0+ | 0+ | 0+ | 0+ | 0+ | 0+ | 0+ | 0+ | 0+ | 0+ | 0+ | 0+ | 0+ | 0+ | 0+ | 001 | 004 | 014 | 038 | 078 | 15 |
| | 16 | 0+ | 0+ | 0+ | 0+ | 0+ | 0+ | 0+ | 0+ | 0+ | 0+ | 0+ | 0+ | 0+ | 0+ | 0+ | 0+ | 0+ | 001 | 005 | 017 | 044 | 16 |
| | 17 | 0+ | 0+ | 0+ | 0+ | 0+ | 0+ | 0+ | 0+ | 0+ | 0+ | 0+ | 0+ | 0+ | 0+ | 0+ | 0+ | 0+ | 0+ | 002 | 007 | 021 | 17 |
| | 18 | 0+ | 0+ | 0+ | 0+ | 0+ | 0+ | 0+ | 0+ | 0+ | 0+ | 0+ | 0+ | 0+ | 0+ | 0+ | 0+ | 0+ | 0+ | 0+ | 002 | 008 | 18 |
| | 19 | 0+ | 0+ | 0+ | 0+ | 0+ | 0+ | 0+ | 0+ | 0+ | 0+ | 0+ | 0+ | 0+ | 0+ | 0+ | 0+ | 0+ | 0+ | 0+ | 001 | 003 | 19 |
| | 20 | 0+ | 0+ | 0+ | 0+ | 0+ | 0+ | 0+ | 0+ | 0+ | 0+ | 0+ | 0+ | 0+ | 0+ | 0+ | 0+ | 0+ | 0+ | 0+ | 0+ | 001 | 20 |
| | 21 | 0+ | 0+ | 0+ | 0+ | 0+ | 0+ | 0+ | 0+ | 0+ | 0+ | 0+ | 0+ | 0+ | 0+ | 0+ | 0+ | 0+ | 0+ | 0+ | 0+ | 0+ | 21 |
| | 22 | 0+ | 0+ | 0+ | 0+ | 0+ | 0+ | 0+ | 0+ | 0+ | 0+ | 0+ | 0+ | 0+ | 0+ | 0+ | 0+ | 0+ | 0+ | 0+ | 0+ | 0+ | 22 |
| | 23 | 0+ | 0+ | 0+ | 0+ | 0+ | 0+ | 0+ | 0+ | 0+ | 0+ | 0+ | 0+ | 0+ | 0+ | 0+ | 0+ | 0+ | 0+ | 0+ | 0+ | 0+ | 23 |
| | 24 | 0+ | 0+ | 0+ | 0+ | 0+ | 0+ | 0+ | 0+ | 0+ | 0+ | 0+ | 0+ | 0+ | 0+ | 0+ | 0+ | 0+ | 0+ | 0+ | 0+ | 0+ | 24 |
| 25 | 0 | 778 | 603 | 360 | 277 | 213 | 124 | 072 | 041 | 023 | 017 | 013 | 007 | 004 | 002 | 001 | 001 | 0+ | 0+ | 0+ | 0+ | 0+ | 0 |
| | 1 | 196 | 308 | 375 | 365 | 340 | 270 | 199 | 140 | 094 | 076 | 061 | 038 | 024 | 014 | 008 | 006 | 001 | 0+ | 0+ | 0+ | 0+ | 1 |
| | 2 | 024 | 075 | 188 | 231 | 260 | 282 | 266 | 228 | 183 | 161 | 139 | 101 | 071 | 048 | 031 | 025 | 007 | 002 | 0+ | 0+ | 0+ | 2 |
| | 3 | 002 | 012 | 060 | 093 | 127 | 188 | 226 | 239 | 229 | 217 | 203 | 170 | 136 | 104 | 076 | 064 | 024 | 008 | 002 | 0+ | 0+ | 3 |
| | 4 | 0+ | 001 | 014 | 027 | 045 | 090 | 138 | 179 | 205 | 211 | 213 | 206 | 187 | 161 | 132 | 118 | 057 | 022 | 007 | 002 | 0+ | 4 |
| | 5 | 0+ | 0+ | 002 | 006 | 012 | 033 | 065 | 103 | 140 | 156 | 170 | 190 | 196 | 190 | 175 | 165 | 103 | 051 | 020 | 006 | 002 | 5 |
| | 6 | 0+ | 0+ | 0+ | 001 | 003 | 010 | 024 | 047 | 076 | 092 | 108 | 139 | 163 | 179 | 184 | 183 | 147 | 091 | 044 | 017 | 005 | 6 |
| | 7 | 0+ | 0+ | 0+ | 0+ | 0+ | 002 | 007 | 017 | 034 | 044 | 056 | 083 | 111 | 137 | 158 | 165 | 171 | 133 | 080 | 038 | 014 | 7 |
| | 8 | 0+ | 0+ | 0+ | 0+ | 0+ | 0+ | 002 | 005 | 012 | 017 | 024 | 041 | 062 | 087 | 112 | 124 | 165 | 161 | 120 | 070 | 032 | 8 |
| | 9 | 0+ | 0+ | 0+ | 0+ | 0+ | 0+ | 0+ | 001 | 004 | 006 | 009 | 017 | 029 | 046 | 067 | 078 | 134 | 163 | 151 | 108 | 061 | 9 |
| | 10 | 0+ | 0+ | 0+ | 0+ | 0+ | 0+ | 0+ | 0+ | 001 | 002 | 003 | 006 | 012 | 021 | 034 | 042 | 092 | 141 | 161 | 142 | 097 | 10 |
| | 11 | 0+ | 0+ | 0+ | 0+ | 0+ | 0+ | 0+ | 0+ | 0+ | 0+ | 001 | 002 | 004 | 008 | 015 | 019 | 054 | 103 | 147 | 158 | 133 | 11 |
| | 12 | 0+ | 0+ | 0+ | 0+ | 0+ | 0+ | 0+ | 0+ | 0+ | 0+ | 0+ | 0+ | 001 | 003 | 005 | 007 | 027 | 065 | 114 | 151 | 155 | 12 |
| | 13 | 0+ | 0+ | 0+ | 0+ | 0+ | 0+ | 0+ | 0+ | 0+ | 0+ | 0+ | 0+ | 0+ | 001 | 002 | 002 | 011 | 035 | 076 | 124 | 155 | 13 |
| | 14 | 0+ | 0+ | 0+ | 0+ | 0+ | 0+ | 0+ | 0+ | 0+ | 0+ | 0+ | 0+ | 0+ | 0+ | 0+ | 001 | 004 | 016 | 043 | 087 | 133 | 14 |
| | 15 | 0+ | 0+ | 0+ | 0+ | 0+ | 0+ | 0+ | 0+ | 0+ | 0+ | 0+ | 0+ | 0+ | 0+ | 0+ | 0+ | 001 | 006 | 021 | 052 | 097 | 15 |
| | 16 | 0+ | 0+ | 0+ | 0+ | 0+ | 0+ | 0+ | 0+ | 0+ | 0+ | 0+ | 0+ | 0+ | 0+ | 0+ | 0+ | 0+ | 002 | 009 | 027 | 061 | 16 |
| | 17 | 0+ | 0+ | 0+ | 0+ | 0+ | 0+ | 0+ | 0+ | 0+ | 0+ | 0+ | 0+ | 0+ | 0+ | 0+ | 0+ | 0+ | 001 | 003 | 012 | 032 | 17 |
| | 18 | 0+ | 0+ | 0+ | 0+ | 0+ | 0+ | 0+ | 0+ | 0+ | 0+ | 0+ | 0+ | 0+ | 0+ | 0+ | 0+ | 0+ | 0+ | 001 | 004 | 014 | 18 |
| | 19 | 0+ | 0+ | 0+ | 0+ | 0+ | 0+ | 0+ | 0+ | 0+ | 0+ | 0+ | 0+ | 0+ | 0+ | 0+ | 0+ | 0+ | 0+ | 0+ | 001 | 005 | 19 |
| | 20 | 0+ | 0+ | 0+ | 0+ | 0+ | 0+ | 0+ | 0+ | 0+ | 0+ | 0+ | 0+ | 0+ | 0+ | 0+ | 0+ | 0+ | 0+ | 0+ | 0+ | 002 | 20 |
| | 21 | 0+ | 0+ | 0+ | 0+ | 0+ | 0+ | 0+ | 0+ | 0+ | 0+ | 0+ | 0+ | 0+ | 0+ | 0+ | 0+ | 0+ | 0+ | 0+ | 0+ | 0+ | 21 |
| | 22 | 0+ | 0+ | 0+ | 0+ | 0+ | 0+ | 0+ | 0+ | 0+ | 0+ | 0+ | 0+ | 0+ | 0+ | 0+ | 0+ | 0+ | 0+ | 0+ | 0+ | 0+ | 22 |
| | 23 | 0+ | 0+ | 0+ | 0+ | 0+ | 0+ | 0+ | 0+ | 0+ | 0+ | 0+ | 0+ | 0+ | 0+ | 0+ | 0+ | 0+ | 0+ | 0+ | 0+ | 0+ | 23 |
| | 24 | 0+ | 0+ | 0+ | 0+ | 0+ | 0+ | 0+ | 0+ | 0+ | 0+ | 0+ | 0+ | 0+ | 0+ | 0+ | 0+ | 0+ | 0+ | 0+ | 0+ | 0+ | 24 |
| | 25 | 0+ | 0+ | 0+ | 0+ | 0+ | 0+ | 0+ | 0+ | 0+ | 0+ | 0+ | 0+ | 0+ | 0+ | 0+ | 0+ | 0 | 0+ | 0+ | 0+ | 0+ | 25 |

# B

# Binomial Distribution – Cumulative Terms

THE TABLE presents the binomial probability for *r or more* successes in *n* trials for selected values of *p*, the probability of a success on any one trial.

Probability of $r$ or more successes in $n$ trials $= \sum_{r}^{n} {}_nC_r p^r q^{n-r}$

| n | r | .01 | .02 | .04 | .05 | .06 | .08 | .10 | .12 | .14 | .15 | p .16 | .18 | .20 | .22 | .24 | .25 | .30 | .35 | .40 | .45 | .50 | r |
|---|---|---|---|---|---|---|---|---|---|---|---|---|---|---|---|---|---|---|---|---|---|---|---|
| 2 | 0 | 1 | 1 | 1 | 1 | 1 | 1 | 1 | 1 | 1 | 1 | 1 | 1 | 1 | 1 | 1 | 1 | 1 | 1 | 1 | 1 | 1 | 0 |
| | 1 | 020 | 040 | 078 | 098 | 116 | 154 | 190 | 226 | 260 | 278 | 294 | 328 | 360 | 392 | 422 | 438 | 510 | 578 | 640 | 698 | 750 | 1 |
| | 2 | 0+ | 0+ | 002 | 002 | 004 | 006 | 010 | 014 | 020 | 022 | 026 | 032 | 040 | 048 | 058 | 062 | 090 | 122 | 160 | 202 | 250 | 2 |
| 3 | 0 | 1 | 1 | 1 | 1 | 1 | 1 | 1 | 1 | 1 | 1 | 1 | 1 | 1 | 1 | 1 | 1 | 1 | 1 | 1 | 1 | 1 | 0 |
| | 1 | 030 | 059 | 115 | 143 | 169 | 221 | 271 | 319 | 364 | 386 | 407 | 449 | 488 | 525 | 561 | 578 | 657 | 725 | 784 | 834 | 875 | 1 |
| | 2 | 0+ | 001 | 005 | 007 | 010 | 018 | 028 | 040 | 053 | 061 | 069 | 086 | 104 | 124 | 145 | 156 | 216 | 282 | 352 | 425 | 500 | 2 |
| | 3 | 0+ | 0+ | 0+ | 0+ | 0+ | 001 | 001 | 002 | 003 | 003 | 004 | 006 | 008 | 011 | 014 | 016 | 027 | 043 | 064 | 091 | 125 | 3 |
| 4 | 0 | 1 | 1 | 1 | 1 | 1 | 1 | 1 | 1 | 1 | 1 | 1 | 1 | 1 | 1 | 1 | 1 | 1 | 1 | 1 | 1 | 1 | 0 |
| | 1 | 039 | 078 | 151 | 185 | 219 | 284 | 344 | 400 | 453 | 478 | 502 | 548 | 590 | 630 | 666 | 684 | 760 | 821 | 870 | 908 | 938 | 1 |
| | 2 | 001 | 002 | 009 | 014 | 020 | 034 | 052 | 073 | 097 | 110 | 123 | 151 | 181 | 212 | 245 | 262 | 348 | 437 | 525 | 609 | 688 | 2 |
| | 3 | 0+ | 0+ | 0+ | 0+ | 001 | 002 | 004 | 006 | 010 | 012 | 014 | 020 | 027 | 036 | 045 | 051 | 084 | 126 | 179 | 241 | 312 | 3 |
| | 4 | 0+ | 0+ | 0+ | 0+ | 0+ | 0+ | 0+ | 0+ | 0+ | 001 | 001 | 001 | 002 | 002 | 003 | 004 | 008 | 015 | 026 | 041 | 062 | 4 |
| 5 | 0 | 1 | 1 | 1 | 1 | 1 | 1 | 1 | 1 | 1 | 1 | 1 | 1 | 1 | 1 | 1 | 1 | 1 | 1 | 1 | 1 | 1 | 0 |
| | 1 | 049 | 096 | 185 | 226 | 266 | 341 | 410 | 472 | 530 | 556 | 582 | 629 | 672 | 711 | 746 | 763 | 832 | 884 | 922 | 950 | 969 | 1 |
| | 2 | 001 | 004 | 015 | 023 | 032 | 054 | 081 | 112 | 147 | 165 | 183 | 222 | 263 | 304 | 346 | 367 | 472 | 572 | 663 | 744 | 812 | 2 |
| | 3 | 0+ | 0+ | 001 | 001 | 002 | 005 | 009 | 014 | 022 | 027 | 032 | 044 | 058 | 074 | 093 | 104 | 163 | 235 | 317 | 407 | 500 | 3 |
| | 4 | 0+ | 0+ | 0+ | 0+ | 0+ | 0+ | 0+ | 001 | 002 | 002 | 003 | 004 | 007 | 010 | 013 | 016 | 031 | 054 | 087 | 131 | 188 | 4 |
| | 5 | 0+ | 0+ | 0+ | 0+ | 0+ | 0+ | 0+ | 0+ | 0+ | 0+ | 0+ | 0+ | 0+ | 001 | 001 | 001 | 002 | 005 | 010 | 018 | 031 | 5 |
| 6 | 0 | 1 | 1 | 1 | 1 | 1 | 1 | 1 | 1 | 1 | 1 | 1 | 1 | 1 | 1 | 1 | 1 | 1 | 1 | 1 | 1 | 1 | 0 |
| | 1 | 059 | 114 | 217 | 265 | 310 | 394 | 469 | 536 | 595 | 623 | 649 | 696 | 738 | 775 | 807 | 822 | 882 | 925 | 953 | 972 | 984 | 1 |
| | 2 | 001 | 006 | 022 | 033 | 046 | 077 | 114 | 156 | 200 | 224 | 247 | 296 | 345 | 394 | 442 | 466 | 580 | 681 | 767 | 836 | 891 | 2 |
| | 3 | 0+ | 0+ | 001 | 002 | 004 | 009 | 016 | 026 | 039 | 047 | 056 | 076 | 099 | 125 | 154 | 169 | 256 | 353 | 456 | 558 | 656 | 3 |
| | 4 | 0+ | 0+ | 0+ | 0+ | 0+ | 001 | 001 | 003 | 005 | 006 | 007 | 012 | 017 | 024 | 033 | 038 | 070 | 117 | 179 | 255 | 344 | 4 |
| | 5 | 0+ | 0+ | 0+ | 0+ | 0+ | 0+ | 0+ | 0+ | 0+ | 0+ | 001 | 001 | 002 | 003 | 004 | 005 | 011 | 022 | 041 | 069 | 109 | 5 |
| | 6 | 0+ | 0+ | 0+ | 0+ | 0+ | 0+ | 0+ | 0+ | 0+ | 0+ | 0+ | 0+ | 0+ | 0+ | 0+ | 0+ | 001 | 002 | 004 | 008 | 016 | 6 |
| 7 | 0 | 1 | 1 | 1 | 1 | 1 | 1 | 1 | 1 | 1 | 1 | 1 | 1 | 1 | 1 | 1 | 1 | 1 | 1 | 1 | 1 | 1 | 0 |
| | 1 | 068 | 132 | 249 | 302 | 352 | 442 | 522 | 591 | 652 | 679 | 705 | 751 | 790 | 824 | 854 | 867 | 918 | 951 | 972 | 985 | 992 | 1 |
| | 2 | 002 | 008 | 029 | 044 | 062 | 103 | 150 | 201 | 256 | 283 | 311 | 368 | 423 | 478 | 530 | 555 | 671 | 766 | 841 | 898 | 938 | 2 |
| | 3 | 0+ | 0+ | 002 | 004 | 006 | 014 | 026 | 042 | 062 | 074 | 087 | 115 | 148 | 184 | 223 | 244 | 353 | 468 | 580 | 684 | 773 | 3 |
| | 4 | 0+ | 0+ | 0+ | 0+ | 0+ | 001 | 003 | 005 | 009 | 012 | 015 | 023 | 033 | 046 | 062 | 071 | 126 | 200 | 290 | 392 | 500 | 4 |
| | 5 | 0+ | 0+ | 0+ | 0+ | 0+ | 0+ | 0+ | 0+ | 001 | 001 | 002 | 003 | 005 | 007 | 011 | 013 | 029 | 056 | 096 | 153 | 227 | 5 |
| | 6 | 0+ | 0+ | 0+ | 0+ | 0+ | 0+ | 0+ | 0+ | 0+ | 0+ | 0+ | 0+ | 0+ | 001 | 001 | 001 | 004 | 009 | 019 | 036 | 062 | 6 |
| | 7 | 0+ | 0+ | 0+ | 0+ | 0+ | 0+ | 0+ | 0+ | 0+ | 0+ | 0+ | 0+ | 0+ | 0+ | 0+ | 0+ | 0+ | 001 | 002 | 004 | 008 | 7 |
| 8 | 0 | 1 | 1 | 1 | 1 | 1 | 1 | 1 | 1 | 1 | 1 | 1 | 1 | 1 | 1 | 1 | 1 | 1 | 1 | 1 | 1 | 1 | 0 |
| | 1 | 077 | 149 | 279 | 337 | 390 | 487 | 570 | 640 | 701 | 728 | 752 | 796 | 832 | 863 | 889 | 900 | 942 | 968 | 983 | 992 | 996 | 1 |
| | 2 | 003 | 010 | 038 | 057 | 079 | 130 | 187 | 248 | 311 | 343 | 374 | 437 | 497 | 554 | 608 | 633 | 745 | 831 | 894 | 937 | 965 | 2 |
| | 3 | 0+ | 0+ | 003 | 006 | 010 | 021 | 038 | 061 | 089 | 105 | 123 | 161 | 203 | 249 | 297 | 321 | 448 | 572 | 685 | 780 | 855 | 3 |
| | 4 | 0+ | 0+ | 0+ | 0+ | 001 | 002 | 005 | 010 | 017 | 021 | 027 | 040 | 056 | 076 | 100 | 114 | 194 | 294 | 406 | 523 | 637 | 4 |
| | 5 | 0+ | 0+ | 0+ | 0+ | 0+ | 0+ | 0+ | 001 | 002 | 003 | 004 | 007 | 010 | 016 | 023 | 027 | 058 | 106 | 174 | 260 | 363 | 5 |
| | 6 | 0+ | 0+ | 0+ | 0+ | 0+ | 0+ | 0+ | 0+ | 0+ | 0+ | 0+ | 001 | 001 | 002 | 003 | 004 | 011 | 025 | 050 | 088 | 145 | 6 |
| | 7 | 0+ | 0+ | 0+ | 0+ | 0+ | 0+ | 0+ | 0+ | 0+ | 0+ | 0+ | 0+ | 0+ | 0+ | 0+ | 0+ | 001 | 004 | 009 | 018 | 035 | 7 |
| | 8 | 0+ | 0+ | 0+ | 0+ | 0+ | 0+ | 0+ | 0+ | 0+ | 0+ | 0+ | 0+ | 0+ | 0+ | 0+ | 0+ | 0+ | 0+ | 001 | 002 | 004 | 8 |
| 9 | 0 | 1 | 1 | 1 | 1 | 1 | 1 | 1 | 1 | 1 | 1 | 1 | 1 | 1 | 1 | 1 | 1 | 1 | 1 | 1 | 1 | 1 | 0 |
| | 1 | 086 | 166 | 307 | 370 | 427 | 528 | 613 | 684 | 743 | 768 | 792 | 832 | 866 | 893 | 915 | 925 | 960 | 979 | 990 | 995 | 998 | 1 |
| | 2 | 003 | 013 | 048 | 071 | 098 | 158 | 225 | 295 | 366 | 401 | 435 | 501 | 564 | 622 | 675 | 700 | 804 | 879 | 929 | 961 | 980 | 2 |
| | 3 | 0+ | 001 | 004 | 008 | 014 | 030 | 053 | 083 | 120 | 141 | 163 | 210 | 262 | 316 | 371 | 399 | 537 | 663 | 768 | 850 | 910 | 3 |
| | 4 | 0+ | 0+ | 0+ | 001 | 001 | 004 | 008 | 016 | 027 | 034 | 042 | 062 | 086 | 114 | 148 | 166 | 270 | 391 | 517 | 639 | 746 | 4 |
| | 5 | 0+ | 0+ | 0+ | 0+ | 0+ | 0+ | 001 | 002 | 004 | 006 | 007 | 012 | 020 | 029 | 042 | 049 | 099 | 172 | 267 | 379 | 500 | 5 |
| | 6 | 0+ | 0+ | 0+ | 0+ | 0+ | 0+ | 0+ | 0+ | 0+ | 001 | 001 | 002 | 003 | 005 | 008 | 010 | 025 | 054 | 099 | 166 | 254 | 6 |
| | 7 | 0+ | 0+ | 0+ | 0+ | 0+ | 0+ | 0+ | 0+ | 0+ | 0+ | 0+ | 0+ | 0+ | 001 | 001 | 001 | 004 | 011 | 025 | 050 | 090 | 7 |
| | 8 | 0+ | 0+ | 0+ | 0+ | 0+ | 0+ | 0+ | 0+ | 0+ | 0+ | 0+ | 0+ | 0+ | 0+ | 0+ | 0+ | 0+ | 001 | 004 | 009 | 020 | 8 |
| | 9 | 0+ | 0+ | 0+ | 0+ | 0+ | 0+ | 0+ | 0+ | 0+ | 0+ | 0+ | 0+ | 0+ | 0+ | 0+ | 0+ | 0+ | 0+ | 0+ | 001 | 002 | 9 |
| 10 | 0 | 1 | 1 | 1 | 1 | 1 | 1 | 1 | 1 | 1 | 1 | 1 | 1 | 1 | 1 | 1 | 1 | 1 | 1 | 1 | 1 | 1 | 0 |
| | 1 | 096 | 183 | 335 | 401 | 461 | 566 | 651 | 721 | 779 | 803 | 825 | 863 | 893 | 917 | 936 | 944 | 972 | 987 | 994 | 997 | 999 | 1 |
| | 2 | 004 | 016 | 058 | 086 | 118 | 188 | 264 | 342 | 418 | 456 | 492 | 561 | 624 | 682 | 733 | 756 | 851 | 914 | 954 | 977 | 989 | 2 |
| | 3 | 0+ | 001 | 006 | 012 | 019 | 040 | 070 | 109 | 155 | 180 | 206 | 263 | 322 | 383 | 444 | 474 | 617 | 738 | 833 | 900 | 945 | 3 |
| | 4 | 0+ | 0+ | 0+ | 001 | 002 | 006 | 013 | 024 | 040 | 050 | 061 | 088 | 121 | 159 | 201 | 224 | 350 | 486 | 618 | 734 | 828 | 4 |
| | 5 | 0+ | 0+ | 0+ | 0+ | 0+ | 001 | 002 | 004 | 007 | 010 | 013 | 021 | 033 | 048 | 067 | 078 | 150 | 249 | 367 | 496 | 623 | 5 |
| | 6 | 0+ | 0+ | 0+ | 0+ | 0+ | 0+ | 0+ | 0+ | 001 | 001 | 002 | 004 | 006 | 010 | 016 | 020 | 047 | 095 | 166 | 262 | 377 | 6 |
| | 7 | 0+ | 0+ | 0+ | 0+ | 0+ | 0+ | 0+ | 0+ | 0+ | 0+ | 0+ | 0+ | 001 | 002 | 003 | 004 | 011 | 026 | 055 | 102 | 172 | 7 |
| | 8 | 0+ | 0+ | 0+ | 0+ | 0+ | 0+ | 0+ | 0+ | 0+ | 0+ | 0+ | 0+ | 0+ | 0+ | 0+ | 0+ | 002 | 005 | 012 | 027 | 055 | 8 |
| | 9 | 0+ | 0+ | 0+ | 0+ | 0+ | 0+ | 0+ | 0+ | 0+ | 0+ | 0+ | 0+ | 0+ | 0+ | 0+ | 0+ | 0+ | 001 | 002 | 005 | 011 | 9 |

Source: William A. Spurr and Charles P. Bonini, *Statistical Analysis for Business Decisions*, rev. ed. (Homewood, Ill.: Richard D. Irwin, 1973) © 1973 by Richard D. Irwin, Inc., pp. 690–95.

Probability of $r$ or more successes in $n$ trials $= \sum_{r}^{n} {}_nC_r p^r q^{n-r}$

| n | r | .01 | .02 | .04 | .05 | .06 | .08 | .10 | .12 | .14 | .15 | p .16 | .18 | .20 | .22 | .24 | .25 | .30 | .35 | .40 | .45 | .50 | r |
|---|---|---|---|---|---|---|---|---|---|---|---|---|---|---|---|---|---|---|---|---|---|---|---|
| 10 | 10 | 0+ | 0+ | 0+ | 0+ | 0+ | 0+ | 0+ | 0+ | 0+ | 0+ | 0+ | 0+ | 0+ | 0+ | 0+ | 0+ | 0+ | 0+ | 0+ | 0+ | 001 | 10 |
| 11 | 0 | 1 | 1 | 1 | 1 | 1 | 1 | 1 | 1 | 1 | 1 | 1 | 1 | 1 | 1 | 1 | 1 | 1 | 1 | 1 | 1 | 1 | 0 |
| | 1 | 105 | 199 | 362 | 431 | 494 | 600 | 686 | 755 | 810 | 833 | 853 | 887 | 914 | 935 | 951 | 958 | 980 | 991 | 996 | 999 | 1- | 1 |
| | 2 | 005 | 020 | 069 | 102 | 138 | 218 | 303 | 387 | 469 | 508 | 545 | 615 | 678 | 733 | 781 | 803 | 887 | 939 | 970 | 986 | 994 | 2 |
| | 3 | 0+ | 001 | 008 | 015 | 025 | 052 | 090 | 137 | 191 | 221 | 252 | 316 | 383 | 449 | 513 | 545 | 687 | 800 | 881 | 935 | 967 | 3 |
| | 4 | 0+ | 0+ | 001 | 002 | 003 | 009 | 019 | 034 | 056 | 069 | 085 | 120 | 161 | 208 | 260 | 287 | 430 | 574 | 704 | 809 | 887 | 4 |
| | 5 | 0+ | 0+ | 0+ | 0+ | 0+ | 001 | 003 | 006 | 012 | 016 | 021 | 033 | 050 | 072 | 099 | 115 | 210 | 332 | 467 | 603 | 726 | 5 |
| | 6 | 0+ | 0+ | 0+ | 0+ | 0+ | 0+ | 0+ | 001 | 002 | 003 | 004 | 007 | 012 | 019 | 028 | 034 | 078 | 149 | 247 | 367 | 500 | 6 |
| | 7 | 0+ | 0+ | 0+ | 0+ | 0+ | 0+ | 0+ | 0+ | 0+ | 0+ | 0+ | 001 | 002 | 004 | 006 | 008 | 022 | 050 | 099 | 174 | 274 | 7 |
| | 8 | 0+ | 0+ | 0+ | 0+ | 0+ | 0+ | 0+ | 0+ | 0+ | 0+ | 0+ | 0+ | 0+ | 0+ | 001 | 002 | 004 | 012 | 029 | 061 | 113 | 8 |
| | 9 | 0+ | 0+ | 0+ | 0+ | 0+ | 0+ | 0+ | 0+ | 0+ | 0+ | 0+ | 0+ | 0+ | 0+ | 0+ | 0+ | 001 | 002 | 006 | 015 | 033 | 9 |
| | 10 | 0+ | 0+ | 0+ | 0+ | 0+ | 0+ | 0+ | 0+ | 0+ | 0+ | 0+ | 0+ | 0+ | 0+ | 0+ | 0+ | 0+ | 0+ | 001 | 002 | 006 | 10 |
| | 11 | 0+ | 0+ | 0+ | 0+ | 0+ | 0+ | 0+ | 0+ | 0+ | 0+ | 0+ | 0+ | 0+ | 0+ | 0+ | 0+ | 0+ | 0+ | 0+ | 0+ | 0+ | 11 |
| 12 | 0 | 1 | 1 | 1 | 1 | 1 | 1 | 1 | 1 | 1 | 1 | 1 | 1 | 1 | 1 | 1 | 1 | 1 | 1 | 1 | 1 | 1 | 0 |
| | 1 | 114 | 215 | 387 | 460 | 524 | 632 | 718 | 784 | 836 | 858 | 877 | 908 | 931 | 949 | 963 | 968 | 986 | 994 | 998 | 999 | 1- | 1 |
| | 2 | 006 | 023 | 081 | 118 | 160 | 249 | 341 | 431 | 517 | 557 | 595 | 664 | 725 | 778 | 822 | 842 | 915 | 958 | 980 | 992 | 997 | 2 |
| | 3 | 0+ | 002 | 011 | 020 | 032 | 065 | 111 | 167 | 230 | 264 | 299 | 370 | 442 | 511 | 578 | 609 | 747 | 849 | 917 | 958 | 981 | 3 |
| | 4 | 0+ | 0+ | 001 | 002 | 004 | 012 | 026 | 046 | 075 | 092 | 111 | 155 | 205 | 261 | 320 | 351 | 507 | 653 | 775 | 866 | 927 | 4 |
| | 5 | 0+ | 0+ | 0+ | 0+ | 0+ | 002 | 004 | 009 | 018 | 024 | 031 | 049 | 073 | 102 | 138 | 158 | 276 | 417 | 562 | 696 | 806 | 5 |
| | 6 | 0+ | 0+ | 0+ | 0+ | 0+ | 0+ | 001 | 001 | 003 | 005 | 006 | 012 | 019 | 030 | 045 | 054 | 118 | 213 | 335 | 473 | 613 | 6 |
| | 7 | 0+ | 0+ | 0+ | 0+ | 0+ | 0+ | 0+ | 0+ | 0+ | 001 | 001 | 002 | 004 | 007 | 011 | 014 | 039 | 085 | 158 | 261 | 387 | 7 |
| | 8 | 0+ | 0+ | 0+ | 0+ | 0+ | 0+ | 0+ | 0+ | 0+ | 0+ | 0+ | 0+ | 001 | 001 | 002 | 003 | 009 | 026 | 057 | 112 | 194 | 8 |
| | 9 | 0+ | 0+ | 0+ | 0+ | 0+ | 0+ | 0+ | 0+ | 0+ | 0+ | 0+ | 0+ | 0+ | 0+ | 0+ | 0+ | 002 | 006 | 015 | 036 | 073 | 9 |
| | 10 | 0+ | 0+ | 0+ | 0+ | 0+ | 0+ | 0+ | 0+ | 0+ | 0+ | 0+ | 0+ | 0+ | 0+ | 0+ | 0+ | 0+ | 001 | 003 | 008 | 019 | 10 |
| | 11 | 0+ | 0+ | 0+ | 0+ | 0+ | 0+ | 0+ | 0+ | 0+ | 0+ | 0+ | 0+ | 0+ | 0+ | 0+ | 0+ | 0+ | 0+ | 0+ | 001 | 003 | 11 |
| | 12 | 0+ | 0+ | 0+ | 0+ | 0+ | 0+ | 0+ | 0+ | 0+ | 0+ | 0+ | 0+ | 0+ | 0+ | 0+ | 0+ | 0+ | 0+ | 0+ | 0+ | 0+ | 12 |
| 13 | 0 | 1 | 1 | 1 | 1 | 1 | 1 | 1 | 1 | 1 | 1 | 1 | 1 | 1 | 1 | 1 | 1 | 1 | 1 | 1 | 1 | 1 | 0 |
| | 1 | 122 | 231 | 412 | 487 | 553 | 662 | 746 | 810 | 859 | 879 | 896 | 924 | 945 | 960 | 972 | 976 | 990 | 996 | 999 | 1- | 1- | 1 |
| | 2 | 007 | 027 | 093 | 135 | 181 | 279 | 379 | 474 | 561 | 602 | 640 | 708 | 766 | 815 | 856 | 873 | 936 | 970 | 987 | 995 | 998 | 2 |
| | 3 | 0+ | 002 | 014 | 025 | 039 | 080 | 134 | 198 | 270 | 308 | 346 | 423 | 498 | 570 | 636 | 667 | 798 | 887 | 942 | 973 | 989 | 3 |
| | 4 | 0+ | 0+ | 001 | 003 | 006 | 016 | 034 | 061 | 097 | 118 | 141 | 194 | 253 | 316 | 382 | 416 | 579 | 722 | 831 | 907 | 954 | 4 |
| | 5 | 0+ | 0+ | 0+ | 0+ | 001 | 002 | 006 | 014 | 026 | 034 | 044 | 068 | 099 | 137 | 182 | 206 | 346 | 499 | 647 | 772 | 867 | 5 |
| | 6 | 0+ | 0+ | 0+ | 0+ | 0+ | 0+ | 001 | 002 | 005 | 008 | 010 | 018 | 030 | 046 | 068 | 080 | 165 | 284 | 426 | 573 | 709 | 6 |
| | 7 | 0+ | 0+ | 0+ | 0+ | 0+ | 0+ | 0+ | 0+ | 001 | 001 | 002 | 004 | 007 | 012 | 019 | 024 | 062 | 129 | 229 | 356 | 500 | 7 |
| | 8 | 0+ | 0+ | 0+ | 0+ | 0+ | 0+ | 0+ | 0+ | 0+ | 0+ | 0+ | 001 | 001 | 002 | 004 | 006 | 018 | 046 | 098 | 179 | 291 | 8 |
| | 9 | 0+ | 0+ | 0+ | 0+ | 0+ | 0+ | 0+ | 0+ | 0+ | 0+ | 0+ | 0+ | 0+ | 0+ | 001 | 001 | 004 | 013 | 032 | 070 | 133 | 9 |
| | 10 | 0+ | 0+ | 0+ | 0+ | 0+ | 0+ | 0+ | 0+ | 0+ | 0+ | 0+ | 0+ | 0+ | 0+ | 0+ | 0+ | 001 | 003 | 008 | 020 | 046 | 10 |
| | 11 | 0+ | 0+ | 0+ | 0+ | 0+ | 0+ | 0+ | 0+ | 0+ | 0+ | 0+ | 0+ | 0+ | 0+ | 0+ | 0+ | 0+ | 0+ | 001 | 004 | 011 | 11 |
| | 12 | 0+ | 0+ | 0+ | 0+ | 0+ | 0+ | 0+ | 0+ | 0+ | 0+ | 0+ | 0+ | 0+ | 0+ | 0+ | 0+ | 0+ | 0+ | 0+ | 001 | 002 | 12 |
| | 13 | 0+ | 0+ | 0+ | 0+ | 0+ | 0+ | 0+ | 0+ | 0+ | 0+ | 0+ | 0+ | 0+ | 0+ | 0+ | 0+ | 0+ | 0+ | 0+ | 0+ | 0+ | 13 |
| 14 | 0 | 1 | 1 | 1 | 1 | 1 | 1 | 1 | 1 | 1 | 1 | 1 | 1 | 1 | 1 | 1 | 1 | 1 | 1 | 1 | 1 | 1 | 0 |
| | 1 | 131 | 246 | 435 | 512 | 579 | 689 | 771 | 833 | 879 | 897 | 913 | 938 | 956 | 969 | 979 | 982 | 993 | 998 | 999 | 1- | 1- | 1 |
| | 2 | 008 | 031 | 106 | 153 | 204 | 310 | 415 | 514 | 603 | 643 | 681 | 747 | 802 | 847 | 884 | 899 | 953 | 979 | 992 | 997 | 999 | 2 |
| | 3 | 0+ | 002 | 017 | 030 | 048 | 096 | 158 | 232 | 311 | 352 | 393 | 474 | 552 | 624 | 689 | 719 | 839 | 916 | 960 | 983 | 994 | 3 |
| | 4 | 0+ | 0+ | 002 | 004 | 008 | 021 | 044 | 077 | 121 | 147 | 174 | 235 | 302 | 372 | 443 | 479 | 645 | 779 | 876 | 937 | 971 | 4 |
| | 5 | 0+ | 0+ | 0+ | 0+ | 001 | 004 | 009 | 020 | 036 | 047 | 059 | 091 | 130 | 176 | 230 | 258 | 416 | 577 | 721 | 833 | 910 | 5 |
| | 6 | 0+ | 0+ | 0+ | 0+ | 0+ | 0+ | 001 | 004 | 008 | 012 | 016 | 027 | 044 | 066 | 095 | 112 | 219 | 359 | 514 | 663 | 788 | 6 |
| | 7 | 0+ | 0+ | 0+ | 0+ | 0+ | 0+ | 0+ | 001 | 001 | 002 | 003 | 006 | 012 | 020 | 031 | 038 | 093 | 184 | 308 | 454 | 605 | 7 |
| | 8 | 0+ | 0+ | 0+ | 0+ | 0+ | 0+ | 0+ | 0+ | 0+ | 0+ | 001 | 001 | 002 | 005 | 008 | 010 | 031 | 075 | 150 | 259 | 395 | 8 |
| | 9 | 0+ | 0+ | 0+ | 0+ | 0+ | 0+ | 0+ | 0+ | 0+ | 0+ | 0+ | 0+ | 0+ | 001 | 002 | 002 | 008 | 024 | 058 | 119 | 212 | 9 |
| | 10 | 0+ | 0+ | 0+ | 0+ | 0+ | 0+ | 0+ | 0+ | 0+ | 0+ | 0+ | 0+ | 0+ | 0+ | 0+ | 0+ | 002 | 006 | 018 | 043 | 090 | 10 |
| | 11 | 0+ | 0+ | 0+ | 0+ | 0+ | 0+ | 0+ | 0+ | 0+ | 0+ | 0+ | 0+ | 0+ | 0+ | 0+ | 0+ | 0+ | 001 | 004 | 011 | 029 | 11 |
| | 12 | 0+ | 0+ | 0+ | 0+ | 0+ | 0+ | 0+ | 0+ | 0+ | 0+ | 0+ | 0+ | 0+ | 0+ | 0+ | 0+ | 0+ | 0+ | 001 | 002 | 006 | 12 |
| | 13 | 0+ | 0+ | 0+ | 0+ | 0+ | 0+ | 0+ | 0+ | 0+ | 0+ | 0+ | 0+ | 0+ | 0+ | 0+ | 0+ | 0+ | 0+ | 0+ | 0+ | 001 | 13 |
| | 14 | 0+ | 0+ | 0+ | 0+ | 0+ | 0+ | 0+ | 0+ | 0+ | 0+ | 0+ | 0+ | 0+ | 0+ | 0+ | 0+ | 0+ | 0+ | 0+ | 0+ | 0+ | 14 |
| 15 | 0 | 1 | 1 | 1 | 1 | 1 | 1 | 1 | 1 | 1 | 1 | 1 | 1 | 1 | 1 | 1 | 1 | 1 | 1 | 1 | 1 | 1 | 0 |
| | 1 | 140 | 261 | 458 | 537 | 605 | 714 | 794 | 853 | 896 | 913 | 927 | 949 | 965 | 976 | 984 | 987 | 995 | 998 | 1- | 1- | 1- | 1 |
| | 2 | 010 | 035 | 119 | 171 | 226 | 340 | 451 | 552 | 642 | 681 | 718 | 781 | 833 | 874 | 906 | 920 | 965 | 986 | 995 | 998 | 1- | 2 |
| | 3 | 0+ | 003 | 020 | 036 | 057 | 113 | 184 | 265 | 352 | 396 | 439 | 523 | 602 | 673 | 736 | 764 | 873 | 938 | 973 | 989 | 996 | 3 |
| | 4 | 0+ | 0+ | 002 | 005 | 010 | 027 | 056 | 096 | 148 | 177 | 209 | 278 | 352 | 427 | 502 | 539 | 703 | 827 | 909 | 958 | 982 | 4 |

Probability of $r$ or more successes in $n$ trials $= \sum_{r}^{n} {}_nC_r p^r q^{n-r}$

| n | r | .01 | .02 | .04 | .05 | .06 | .08 | .10 | .12 | .14 | .15 | .16 | .18 | .20 | .22 | .24 | .25 | .30 | .35 | .40 | .45 | .50 | r |
|---|---|---|---|---|---|---|---|---|---|---|---|---|---|---|---|---|---|---|---|---|---|---|---|
| | | | | | | | | | | | p | | | | | | | | | | | | |
| 15 | 5 | 0+ | 0+ | 0+ | 001 | 001 | 005 | 013 | 026 | 048 | 062 | 078 | 117 | 164 | 219 | 281 | 314 | 485 | 648 | 783 | 880 | 941 | 5 |
| | 6 | 0+ | 0+ | 0+ | 0+ | 0+ | 001 | 002 | 006 | 012 | 017 | 023 | 039 | 061 | 090 | 127 | 148 | 278 | 436 | 597 | 739 | 849 | 6 |
| | 7 | 0+ | 0+ | 0+ | 0+ | 0+ | 0+ | 0+ | 001 | 002 | 004 | 005 | 010 | 018 | 030 | 046 | 057 | 131 | 245 | 390 | 548 | 696 | 7 |
| | 8 | 0+ | 0+ | 0+ | 0+ | 0+ | 0+ | 0+ | 0+ | 0+ | 001 | 001 | 002 | 004 | 008 | 013 | 017 | 050 | 113 | 213 | 346 | 500 | 8 |
| | 9 | 0+ | 0+ | 0+ | 0+ | 0+ | 0+ | 0+ | 0+ | 0+ | 0+ | 0+ | 0+ | 001 | 002 | 003 | 004 | 015 | 042 | 095 | 182 | 304 | 9 |
| | 10 | 0+ | 0+ | 0+ | 0+ | 0+ | 0+ | 0+ | 0+ | 0+ | 0+ | 0+ | 0+ | 0+ | 0+ | 001 | 001 | 004 | 012 | 034 | 077 | 151 | 10 |
| | 11 | 0+ | 0+ | 0+ | 0+ | 0+ | 0+ | 0+ | 0+ | 0+ | 0+ | 0+ | 0+ | 0+ | 0+ | 0+ | 0+ | 001 | 003 | 009 | 025 | 059 | 11 |
| | 12 | 0+ | 0+ | 0+ | 0+ | 0+ | 0+ | 0+ | 0+ | 0+ | 0+ | 0+ | 0+ | 0+ | 0+ | 0+ | 0+ | 0+ | 0+ | 002 | 006 | 018 | 12 |
| | 13 | 0+ | 0+ | 0+ | 0+ | 0+ | 0+ | 0+ | 0+ | 0+ | 0+ | 0+ | 0+ | 0+ | 0+ | 0+ | 0+ | 0+ | 0+ | 0+ | 001 | 004 | 13 |
| | 14 | 0+ | 0+ | 0+ | 0+ | 0+ | 0+ | 0+ | 0+ | 0+ | 0+ | 0+ | 0+ | 0+ | 0+ | 0+ | 0+ | 0+ | 0+ | 0+ | 0+ | 0+ | 14 |
| | 15 | 0+ | 0+ | 0+ | 0+ | 0+ | 0+ | 0+ | 0+ | 0+ | 0+ | 0+ | 0+ | 0+ | 0+ | 0+ | 0+ | 0+ | 0+ | 0+ | 0+ | 0+ | 15 |
| 16 | 0 | 1 | 1 | 1 | 1 | 1 | 1 | 1 | 1 | 1 | 1 | 1 | 1 | 1 | 1 | 1 | 1 | 1 | 1 | 1 | 1 | 1 | 0 |
| | 1 | 149 | 276 | 480 | 560 | 628 | 737 | 815 | 871 | 910 | 926 | 939 | 958 | 972 | 981 | 988 | 990 | 997 | 999 | 1- | 1- | 1- | 1 |
| | 2 | 011 | 040 | 133 | 189 | 249 | 370 | 485 | 588 | 677 | 716 | 751 | 811 | 859 | 897 | 925 | 937 | 974 | 990 | 997 | 999 | 1- | 2 |
| | 3 | 001 | 004 | 024 | 043 | 067 | 131 | 211 | 300 | 393 | 439 | 484 | 570 | 648 | 717 | 777 | 803 | 901 | 955 | 982 | 993 | 998 | 3 |
| | 4 | 0+ | 0+ | 003 | 007 | 013 | 034 | 068 | 116 | 176 | 210 | 246 | 322 | 402 | 481 | 558 | 595 | 754 | 866 | 935 | 972 | 989 | 4 |
| | 5 | 0+ | 0+ | 0+ | 001 | 002 | 007 | 017 | 035 | 062 | 079 | 099 | 146 | 202 | 265 | 334 | 370 | 550 | 711 | 833 | 915 | 962 | 5 |
| | 6 | 0+ | 0+ | 0+ | 0+ | 0+ | 001 | 003 | 008 | 017 | 024 | 032 | 053 | 082 | 119 | 164 | 190 | 340 | 510 | 671 | 802 | 895 | 6 |
| | 7 | 0+ | 0+ | 0+ | 0+ | 0+ | 0+ | 001 | 002 | 004 | 006 | 008 | 015 | 027 | 043 | 066 | 080 | 175 | 312 | 473 | 634 | 773 | 7 |
| | 8 | 0+ | 0+ | 0+ | 0+ | 0+ | 0+ | 0+ | 0+ | 001 | 001 | 002 | 004 | 007 | 013 | 021 | 027 | 074 | 159 | 284 | 437 | 598 | 8 |
| | 9 | 0+ | 0+ | 0+ | 0+ | 0+ | 0+ | 0+ | 0+ | 0+ | 0+ | 0+ | 001 | 001 | 003 | 006 | 007 | 026 | 067 | 142 | 256 | 402 | 9 |
| | 10 | 0+ | 0+ | 0+ | 0+ | 0+ | 0+ | 0+ | 0+ | 0+ | 0+ | 0+ | 0+ | 0+ | 001 | 001 | 002 | 007 | 023 | 058 | 124 | 227 | 10 |
| | 11 | 0+ | 0+ | 0+ | 0+ | 0+ | 0+ | 0+ | 0+ | 0+ | 0+ | 0+ | 0+ | 0+ | 0+ | 0+ | 0+ | 002 | 006 | 019 | 049 | 105 | 11 |
| | 12 | 0+ | 0+ | 0+ | 0+ | 0+ | 0+ | 0+ | 0+ | 0+ | 0+ | 0+ | 0+ | 0+ | 0+ | 0+ | 0+ | 0+ | 001 | 005 | 015 | 038 | 12 |
| | 13 | 0+ | 0+ | 0+ | 0+ | 0+ | 0+ | 0+ | 0+ | 0+ | 0+ | 0+ | 0+ | 0+ | 0+ | 0+ | 0+ | 0+ | 0+ | 001 | 003 | 011 | 13 |
| | 14 | 0+ | 0+ | 0+ | 0+ | 0+ | 0+ | 0+ | 0+ | 0+ | 0+ | 0+ | 0+ | 0+ | 0+ | 0+ | 0+ | 0+ | 0+ | 0+ | 001 | 002 | 14 |
| | 15 | 0+ | 0+ | 0+ | 0+ | 0+ | 0+ | 0+ | 0+ | 0+ | 0+ | 0+ | 0+ | 0+ | 0+ | 0+ | 0+ | 0+ | 0+ | 0+ | 0+ | 0+ | 15 |
| | 16 | 0+ | 0+ | 0+ | 0+ | 0+ | 0+ | 0+ | 0+ | 0+ | 0+ | 0+ | 0+ | 0+ | 0+ | 0+ | 0+ | 0+ | 0+ | 0+ | 0+ | 0+ | 16 |
| 17 | 0 | 1 | 1 | 1 | 1 | 1 | 1 | 1 | 1 | 1 | 1 | 1 | 1 | 1 | 1 | 1 | 1 | 1 | 1 | 1 | 1 | 1 | 0 |
| | 1 | 157 | 291 | 500 | 582 | 651 | 758 | 833 | 886 | 923 | 937 | 948 | 966 | 977 | 985 | 991 | 992 | 998 | 999 | 1- | 1- | 1- | 1 |
| | 2 | 012 | 045 | 147 | 208 | 272 | 399 | 518 | 622 | 710 | 748 | 781 | 838 | 882 | 915 | 940 | 950 | 981 | 993 | 998 | 999 | 1- | 2 |
| | 3 | 001 | 004 | 029 | 050 | 078 | 150 | 238 | 335 | 432 | 480 | 527 | 613 | 690 | 758 | 812 | 836 | 923 | 967 | 988 | 996 | 999 | 3 |
| | 4 | 0+ | 0+ | 004 | 009 | 016 | 042 | 083 | 138 | 207 | 244 | 284 | 367 | 451 | 533 | 611 | 647 | 798 | 897 | 954 | 982 | 994 | 4 |
| | 5 | 0+ | 0+ | 0+ | 001 | 003 | 009 | 022 | 045 | 078 | 099 | 122 | 178 | 242 | 313 | 388 | 426 | 611 | 765 | 874 | 940 | 975 | 5 |
| | 6 | 0+ | 0+ | 0+ | 0+ | 0+ | 001 | 005 | 011 | 023 | 032 | 042 | 069 | 106 | 151 | 205 | 235 | 403 | 580 | 736 | 853 | 928 | 6 |
| | 7 | 0+ | 0+ | 0+ | 0+ | 0+ | 0+ | 001 | 002 | 006 | 008 | 012 | 022 | 038 | 060 | 089 | 107 | 225 | 381 | 552 | 710 | 834 | 7 |
| | 8 | 0+ | 0+ | 0+ | 0+ | 0+ | 0+ | 0+ | 0+ | 001 | 002 | 003 | 006 | 011 | 019 | 032 | 040 | 105 | 213 | 359 | 526 | 685 | 8 |
| | 9 | 0+ | 0+ | 0+ | 0+ | 0+ | 0+ | 0+ | 0+ | 0+ | 0+ | 0+ | 001 | 003 | 005 | 009 | 012 | 040 | 099 | 199 | 337 | 500 | 9 |
| | 10 | 0+ | 0+ | 0+ | 0+ | 0+ | 0+ | 0+ | 0+ | 0+ | 0+ | 0+ | 0+ | 0+ | 001 | 002 | 003 | 013 | 038 | 092 | 183 | 315 | 10 |
| | 11 | 0+ | 0+ | 0+ | 0+ | 0+ | 0+ | 0+ | 0+ | 0+ | 0+ | 0+ | 0+ | 0+ | 0+ | 0+ | 001 | 003 | 012 | 035 | 083 | 166 | 11 |
| | 12 | 0+ | 0+ | 0+ | 0+ | 0+ | 0+ | 0+ | 0+ | 0+ | 0+ | 0+ | 0+ | 0+ | 0+ | 0+ | 0+ | 001 | 003 | 011 | 030 | 072 | 12 |
| | 13 | 0+ | 0+ | 0+ | 0+ | 0+ | 0+ | 0+ | 0+ | 0+ | 0+ | 0+ | 0+ | 0+ | 0+ | 0+ | 0+ | 0+ | 001 | 003 | 009 | 025 | 13 |
| | 14 | 0+ | 0+ | 0+ | 0+ | 0+ | 0+ | 0+ | 0+ | 0+ | 0+ | 0+ | 0+ | 0+ | 0+ | 0+ | 0+ | 0+ | 0+ | 0+ | 002 | 006 | 14 |
| | 15 | 0+ | 0+ | 0+ | 0+ | 0+ | 0+ | 0+ | 0+ | 0+ | 0+ | 0+ | 0+ | 0+ | 0+ | 0+ | 0+ | 0+ | 0+ | 0+ | 0+ | 001 | 15 |
| | 16 | 0+ | 0+ | 0+ | 0+ | 0+ | 0+ | 0+ | 0+ | 0+ | 0+ | 0+ | 0+ | 0+ | 0+ | 0+ | 0+ | 0+ | 0+ | 0+ | 0+ | 0+ | 16 |
| | 17 | 0+ | 0+ | 0+ | 0+ | 0+ | 0+ | 0+ | 0+ | 0+ | 0+ | 0+ | 0+ | 0+ | 0+ | 0+ | 0+ | 0+ | 0+ | 0+ | 0+ | 0+ | 17 |
| 18 | 0 | 1 | 1 | 1 | 1 | 1 | 1 | 1 | 1 | 1 | 1 | 1 | 1 | 1 | 1 | 1 | 1 | 1 | 1 | 1 | 1 | 1 | 0 |
| | 1 | 165 | 305 | 520 | 603 | 672 | 777 | 850 | 900 | 934 | 946 | 957 | 972 | 982 | 989 | 993 | 994 | 998 | 1- | 1- | 1- | 1- | 1 |
| | 2 | 014 | 050 | 161 | 226 | 294 | 428 | 550 | 654 | 740 | 776 | 808 | 861 | 901 | 931 | 952 | 961 | 986 | 995 | 999 | 1- | 1- | 2 |
| | 3 | 001 | 005 | 033 | 058 | 090 | 170 | 266 | 369 | 471 | 520 | 567 | 654 | 729 | 792 | 843 | 865 | 940 | 976 | 992 | 997 | 999 | 3 |
| | 4 | 0+ | 0+ | 005 | 011 | 020 | 051 | 098 | 162 | 238 | 280 | 323 | 411 | 499 | 582 | 659 | 694 | 835 | 922 | 967 | 988 | 996 | 4 |
| | 5 | 0+ | 0+ | 001 | 002 | 003 | 012 | 028 | 056 | 096 | 121 | 148 | 212 | 284 | 361 | 441 | 481 | 667 | 811 | 906 | 959 | 985 | 5 |
| | 6 | 0+ | 0+ | 0+ | 0+ | 0+ | 002 | 006 | 015 | 031 | 042 | 055 | 089 | 133 | 187 | 249 | 283 | 466 | 645 | 791 | 892 | 952 | 6 |
| | 7 | 0+ | 0+ | 0+ | 0+ | 0+ | 0+ | 001 | 003 | 008 | 012 | 017 | 031 | 051 | 080 | 117 | 139 | 278 | 451 | 626 | 774 | 881 | 7 |
| | 8 | 0+ | 0+ | 0+ | 0+ | 0+ | 0+ | 0+ | 001 | 002 | 003 | 004 | 009 | 016 | 028 | 046 | 057 | 141 | 272 | 437 | 609 | 760 | 8 |
| | 9 | 0+ | 0+ | 0+ | 0+ | 0+ | 0+ | 0+ | 0+ | 0+ | 001 | 001 | 002 | 004 | 008 | 015 | 019 | 060 | 139 | 263 | 422 | 593 | 9 |
| | 10 | 0+ | 0+ | 0+ | 0+ | 0+ | 0+ | 0+ | 0+ | 0+ | 0+ | 0+ | 0+ | 001 | 002 | 004 | 005 | 021 | 060 | 135 | 253 | 407 | 10 |
| | 11 | 0+ | 0+ | 0+ | 0+ | 0+ | 0+ | 0+ | 0+ | 0+ | 0+ | 0+ | 0+ | 0+ | 0+ | 001 | 001 | 006 | 021 | 058 | 128 | 240 | 11 |
| | 12 | 0+ | 0+ | 0+ | 0+ | 0+ | 0+ | 0+ | 0+ | 0+ | 0+ | 0+ | 0+ | 0+ | 0+ | 0+ | 0+ | 001 | 006 | 020 | 054 | 119 | 12 |
| | 13 | 0+ | 0+ | 0+ | 0+ | 0+ | 0+ | 0+ | 0+ | 0+ | 0+ | 0+ | 0+ | 0+ | 0+ | 0+ | 0+ | 0+ | 001 | 006 | 018 | 048 | 13 |
| | 14 | 0+ | 0+ | 0+ | 0+ | 0+ | 0+ | 0+ | 0+ | 0+ | 0+ | 0+ | 0+ | 0+ | 0+ | 0+ | 0+ | 0+ | 0+ | 001 | 005 | 015 | 14 |
| | 15 | 0+ | 0+ | 0+ | 0+ | 0+ | 0+ | 0+ | 0+ | 0+ | 0+ | 0+ | 0+ | 0+ | 0+ | 0+ | 0+ | 0+ | 0+ | 0+ | 001 | 004 | 15 |
| | 16 | 0+ | 0+ | 0+ | 0+ | 0+ | 0+ | 0+ | 0+ | 0+ | 0+ | 0+ | 0+ | 0+ | 0+ | 0+ | 0+ | 0+ | 0+ | 0+ | 0+ | 001 | 16 |
| | 17 | 0+ | 0+ | 0+ | 0+ | 0+ | 0+ | 0+ | 0+ | 0+ | 0+ | 0+ | 0+ | 0+ | 0+ | 0+ | 0+ | 0+ | 0+ | 0+ | 0+ | 0+ | 17 |
| | 18 | 0+ | 0+ | 0+ | 0+ | 0+ | 0+ | 0+ | 0+ | 0+ | 0+ | 0+ | 0+ | 0+ | 0+ | 0+ | 0+ | 0+ | 0+ | 0+ | 0+ | 0+ | 18 |

Probability of $r$ or more successes in $n$ trials $= \sum_{r}^{n} {}_nC_r p^r q^{n-r}$

| n | r | .01 | .02 | .04 | .05 | .06 | .08 | .10 | .12 | .14 | .15 | p .16 | .18 | .20 | .22 | .24 | .25 | .30 | .35 | .40 | .45 | .50 | r |
|---|---|---|---|---|---|---|---|---|---|---|---|---|---|---|---|---|---|---|---|---|---|---|---|
| 19 | 0 | 1 | 1 | 1 | 1 | 1 | 1 | 1 | 1 | 1 | 1 | 1 | 1 | 1 | 1 | 1 | 1 | 1 | 1 | 1 | 1 | 1 | 0 |
| | 1 | 174 | 319 | 540 | 623 | 691 | 795 | 865 | 912 | 943 | 954 | 964 | 977 | 986 | 991 | 995 | 996 | 999 | 1- | 1- | 1- | 1- | 1 |
| | 2 | 015 | 055 | 175 | 245 | 317 | 456 | 580 | 683 | 767 | 802 | 832 | 881 | 917 | 943 | 962 | 969 | 990 | 997 | 999 | 1- | 1- | 2 |
| | 3 | 001 | 006 | 038 | 067 | 102 | 191 | 295 | 403 | 509 | 559 | 606 | 691 | 763 | 822 | 869 | 889 | 954 | 983 | 995 | 998 | 1- | 3 |
| | 4 | 0+ | 0+ | 006 | 013 | 024 | 060 | 115 | 187 | 271 | 316 | 362 | 455 | 545 | 628 | 703 | 737 | 867 | 941 | 977 | 992 | 998 | 4 |
| | 5 | 0+ | 0+ | 001 | 002 | 004 | 015 | 035 | 069 | 116 | 144 | 176 | 248 | 327 | 410 | 494 | 535 | 718 | 850 | 930 | 972 | 990 | 5 |
| | 6 | 0+ | 0+ | 0+ | 0+ | 001 | 003 | 009 | 020 | 040 | 054 | 070 | 111 | 163 | 225 | 295 | 332 | 526 | 703 | 837 | 922 | 968 | 6 |
| | 7 | 0+ | 0+ | 0+ | 0+ | 0+ | 0+ | 002 | 005 | 011 | 016 | 023 | 041 | 068 | 103 | 149 | 175 | 334 | 519 | 692 | 827 | 916 | 7 |
| | 8 | 0+ | 0+ | 0+ | 0+ | 0+ | 0+ | 0+ | 001 | 003 | 004 | 006 | 013 | 023 | 040 | 063 | 077 | 182 | 334 | 512 | 683 | 820 | 8 |
| | 9 | 0+ | 0+ | 0+ | 0+ | 0+ | 0+ | 0+ | 0+ | 001 | 001 | 001 | 003 | 007 | 013 | 022 | 029 | 084 | 185 | 333 | 506 | 676 | 9 |
| | 10 | 0+ | 0+ | 0+ | 0+ | 0+ | 0+ | 0+ | 0+ | 0+ | 0+ | 0+ | 001 | 002 | 003 | 007 | 009 | 033 | 087 | 186 | 329 | 500 | 10 |
| | 11 | 0+ | 0+ | 0+ | 0+ | 0+ | 0+ | 0+ | 0+ | 0+ | 0+ | 0+ | 0+ | 0+ | 001 | 002 | 002 | 011 | 035 | 088 | 184 | 324 | 11 |
| | 12 | 0+ | 0+ | 0+ | 0+ | 0+ | 0+ | 0+ | 0+ | 0+ | 0+ | 0+ | 0+ | 0+ | 0+ | 0+ | 0+ | 003 | 011 | 035 | 087 | 180 | 12 |
| | 13 | 0+ | 0+ | 0+ | 0+ | 0+ | 0+ | 0+ | 0+ | 0+ | 0+ | 0+ | 0+ | 0+ | 0+ | 0+ | 0+ | 001 | 003 | 012 | 034 | 084 | 13 |
| | 14 | 0+ | 0+ | 0+ | 0+ | 0+ | 0+ | 0+ | 0+ | 0+ | 0+ | 0+ | 0+ | 0+ | 0+ | 0+ | 0+ | 0+ | 001 | 003 | 011 | 032 | 14 |
| | 15 | 0+ | 0+ | 0+ | 0+ | 0+ | 0+ | 0+ | 0+ | 0+ | 0+ | 0+ | 0+ | 0+ | 0+ | 0+ | 0+ | 0+ | 0+ | 001 | 003 | 010 | 15 |
| | 16 | 0+ | 0+ | 0+ | 0+ | 0+ | 0+ | 0+ | 0+ | 0+ | 0+ | 0+ | 0+ | 0+ | 0+ | 0+ | 0+ | 0+ | 0+ | 0+ | 001 | 002 | 16 |
| | 17 | 0+ | 0+ | 0+ | 0+ | 0+ | 0+ | 0+ | 0+ | 0+ | 0+ | 0+ | 0+ | 0+ | 0+ | 0+ | 0+ | 0+ | 0+ | 0+ | 0+ | 0+ | 17 |
| | 18 | 0+ | 0+ | 0+ | 0+ | 0+ | 0+ | 0+ | 0+ | 0+ | 0+ | 0+ | 0+ | 0+ | 0+ | 0+ | 0+ | 0+ | 0+ | 0+ | 0+ | 0+ | 18 |
| | 19 | 0+ | 0+ | 0+ | 0+ | 0+ | 0+ | 0+ | 0+ | 0+ | 0+ | 0+ | 0+ | 0+ | 0+ | 0+ | 0+ | 0+ | 0+ | 0+ | 0+ | 0+ | 19 |
| 20 | 0 | 1 | 1 | 1 | 1 | 1 | 1 | 1 | 1 | 1 | 1 | 1 | 1 | 1 | 1 | 1 | 1 | 1 | 1 | 1 | 1 | 1 | 0 |
| | 1 | 182 | 332 | 558 | 642 | 710 | 811 | 878 | 922 | 951 | 961 | 969 | 981 | 988 | 993 | 996 | 997 | 999 | 1- | 1- | 1- | 1- | 1 |
| | 2 | 017 | 060 | 190 | 264 | 340 | 483 | 608 | 711 | 792 | 824 | 853 | 898 | 931 | 954 | 970 | 976 | 992 | 998 | 999 | 1- | 1- | 2 |
| | 3 | 001 | 007 | 044 | 075 | 115 | 212 | 323 | 437 | 545 | 595 | 642 | 725 | 794 | 849 | 891 | 909 | 965 | 988 | 996 | 999 | 1- | 3 |
| | 4 | 0+ | 001 | 007 | 016 | 029 | 071 | 133 | 213 | 304 | 352 | 401 | 497 | 589 | 671 | 743 | 775 | 893 | 956 | 984 | 995 | 999 | 4 |
| | 5 | 0+ | 0+ | 001 | 003 | 006 | 018 | 043 | 083 | 137 | 170 | 206 | 285 | 370 | 458 | 544 | 585 | 762 | 882 | 949 | 981 | 994 | 5 |
| | 6 | 0+ | 0+ | 0+ | 0+ | 001 | 004 | 011 | 026 | 051 | 067 | 087 | 136 | 196 | 266 | 343 | 383 | 584 | 755 | 874 | 945 | 979 | 6 |
| | 7 | 0+ | 0+ | 0+ | 0+ | 0+ | 001 | 002 | 007 | 015 | 022 | 030 | 054 | 087 | 130 | 184 | 214 | 392 | 583 | 750 | 870 | 942 | 7 |
| | 8 | 0+ | 0+ | 0+ | 0+ | 0+ | 0+ | 0+ | 001 | 004 | 006 | 009 | 018 | 032 | 054 | 083 | 102 | 228 | 399 | 584 | 748 | 868 | 8 |
| | 9 | 0+ | 0+ | 0+ | 0+ | 0+ | 0+ | 0+ | 0+ | 001 | 001 | 002 | 005 | 010 | 019 | 032 | 041 | 113 | 238 | 404 | 586 | 748 | 9 |
| | 10 | 0+ | 0+ | 0+ | 0+ | 0+ | 0+ | 0+ | 0+ | 0+ | 0+ | 0+ | 001 | 003 | 005 | 010 | 014 | 048 | 122 | 245 | 409 | 588 | 10 |
| | 11 | 0+ | 0+ | 0+ | 0+ | 0+ | 0+ | 0+ | 0+ | 0+ | 0+ | 0+ | 0+ | 001 | 001 | 003 | 004 | 017 | 053 | 128 | 249 | 412 | 11 |
| | 12 | 0+ | 0+ | 0+ | 0+ | 0+ | 0+ | 0+ | 0+ | 0+ | 0+ | 0+ | 0+ | 0+ | 0+ | 001 | 001 | 005 | 020 | 057 | 131 | 252 | 12 |
| | 13 | 0+ | 0+ | 0+ | 0+ | 0+ | 0+ | 0+ | 0+ | 0+ | 0+ | 0+ | 0+ | 0+ | 0+ | 0+ | 0+ | 001 | 006 | 021 | 058 | 132 | 13 |
| | 14 | 0+ | 0+ | 0+ | 0+ | 0+ | 0+ | 0+ | 0+ | 0+ | 0+ | 0+ | 0+ | 0+ | 0+ | 0+ | 0+ | 0+ | 002 | 006 | 021 | 058 | 14 |
| | 15 | 0+ | 0+ | 0+ | 0+ | 0+ | 0+ | 0+ | 0+ | 0+ | 0+ | 0+ | 0+ | 0+ | 0+ | 0+ | 0+ | 0+ | 0+ | 002 | 006 | 021 | 15 |
| | 16 | 0+ | 0+ | 0+ | 0+ | 0+ | 0+ | 0+ | 0+ | 0+ | 0+ | 0+ | 0+ | 0+ | 0+ | 0+ | 0+ | 0+ | 0+ | 0+ | 002 | 006 | 16 |
| | 17 | 0+ | 0+ | 0+ | 0+ | 0+ | 0+ | 0+ | 0+ | 0+ | 0+ | 0+ | 0+ | 0+ | 0+ | 0+ | 0+ | 0+ | 0+ | 0+ | 0+ | 001 | 17 |
| | 18 | 0+ | 0+ | 0+ | 0+ | 0+ | 0+ | 0+ | 0+ | 0+ | 0+ | 0+ | 0+ | 0+ | 0+ | 0+ | 0+ | 0+ | 0+ | 0+ | 0+ | 0+ | 18 |
| | 19 | 0+ | 0+ | 0+ | 0+ | 0+ | 0+ | 0+ | 0+ | 0+ | 0+ | 0+ | 0+ | 0+ | 0+ | 0+ | 0+ | 0+ | 0+ | 0+ | 0+ | 0+ | 19 |
| | 20 | 0+ | 0+ | 0+ | 0+ | 0+ | 0+ | 0+ | 0+ | 0+ | 0+ | 0+ | 0+ | 0+ | 0+ | 0+ | 0+ | 0+ | 0+ | 0+ | 0+ | 0+ | 20 |
| 21 | 0 | 1 | 1 | 1 | 1 | 1 | 1 | 1 | 1 | 1 | 1 | 1 | 1 | 1 | 1 | 1 | 1 | 1 | 1 | 1 | 1 | 1 | 0 |
| | 1 | 190 | 346 | 576 | 659 | 727 | 826 | 891 | 932 | 958 | 967 | 974 | 985 | 991 | 995 | 997 | 998 | 999 | 1- | 1- | 1- | 1- | 1 |
| | 2 | 019 | 065 | 204 | 283 | 362 | 509 | 635 | 736 | 814 | 845 | 872 | 913 | 943 | 962 | 976 | 981 | 994 | 999 | 1- | 1- | 1- | 2 |
| | 3 | 001 | 008 | 050 | 085 | 128 | 234 | 352 | 470 | 580 | 630 | 676 | 756 | 821 | 872 | 910 | 925 | 973 | 991 | 998 | 999 | 1- | 3 |
| | 4 | 0+ | 001 | 009 | 019 | 034 | 082 | 152 | 240 | 338 | 389 | 440 | 538 | 630 | 710 | 779 | 808 | 914 | 967 | 989 | 997 | 999 | 4 |
| | 5 | 0+ | 0+ | 001 | 003 | 007 | 023 | 052 | 098 | 161 | 197 | 237 | 323 | 414 | 505 | 592 | 633 | 802 | 908 | 963 | 987 | 996 | 5 |
| | 6 | 0+ | 0+ | 0+ | 0+ | 001 | 005 | 014 | 033 | 063 | 083 | 106 | 162 | 231 | 308 | 391 | 433 | 637 | 799 | 904 | 961 | 987 | 6 |
| | 7 | 0+ | 0+ | 0+ | 0+ | 0+ | 001 | 003 | 009 | 020 | 029 | 039 | 068 | 109 | 160 | 222 | 256 | 449 | 643 | 800 | 904 | 961 | 7 |
| | 8 | 0+ | 0+ | 0+ | 0+ | 0+ | 0+ | 001 | 002 | 005 | 008 | 012 | 024 | 043 | 070 | 108 | 130 | 277 | 464 | 650 | 803 | 905 | 8 |
| | 9 | 0+ | 0+ | 0+ | 0+ | 0+ | 0+ | 0+ | 0+ | 001 | 002 | 003 | 007 | 014 | 026 | 044 | 056 | 148 | 294 | 476 | 659 | 808 | 9 |
| | 10 | 0+ | 0+ | 0+ | 0+ | 0+ | 0+ | 0+ | 0+ | 0+ | 0+ | 001 | 002 | 004 | 008 | 016 | 021 | 068 | 162 | 309 | 488 | 669 | 10 |
| | 11 | 0+ | 0+ | 0+ | 0+ | 0+ | 0+ | 0+ | 0+ | 0+ | 0+ | 0+ | 0+ | 001 | 002 | 005 | 006 | 026 | 077 | 174 | 321 | 500 | 11 |
| | 12 | 0+ | 0+ | 0+ | 0+ | 0+ | 0+ | 0+ | 0+ | 0+ | 0+ | 0+ | 0+ | 0+ | 001 | 001 | 002 | 009 | 031 | 085 | 184 | 332 | 12 |
| | 13 | 0+ | 0+ | 0+ | 0+ | 0+ | 0+ | 0+ | 0+ | 0+ | 0+ | 0+ | 0+ | 0+ | 0+ | 0+ | 0+ | 002 | 011 | 035 | 091 | 192 | 13 |
| | 14 | 0+ | 0+ | 0+ | 0+ | 0+ | 0+ | 0+ | 0+ | 0+ | 0+ | 0+ | 0+ | 0+ | 0+ | 0+ | 0+ | 001 | 003 | 012 | 038 | 095 | 14 |
| | 15 | 0+ | 0+ | 0+ | 0+ | 0+ | 0+ | 0+ | 0+ | 0+ | 0+ | 0+ | 0+ | 0+ | 0+ | 0+ | 0+ | 0+ | 001 | 004 | 013 | 039 | 15 |
| | 16 | 0+ | 0+ | 0+ | 0+ | 0+ | 0+ | 0+ | 0+ | 0+ | 0+ | 0+ | 0+ | 0+ | 0+ | 0+ | 0+ | 0+ | 0+ | 001 | 004 | 013 | 16 |
| | 17 | 0+ | 0+ | 0+ | 0+ | 0+ | 0+ | 0+ | 0+ | 0+ | 0+ | 0+ | 0+ | 0+ | 0+ | 0+ | 0+ | 0+ | 0+ | 0+ | 001 | 004 | 17 |
| | 18 | 0+ | 0+ | 0+ | 0+ | 0+ | 0+ | 0+ | 0+ | 0+ | 0+ | 0+ | 0+ | 0+ | 0+ | 0+ | 0+ | 0+ | 0+ | 0+ | 0+ | 001 | 18 |
| | 19 | 0+ | 0+ | 0+ | 0+ | 0+ | 0+ | 0+ | 0+ | 0+ | 0+ | 0+ | 0+ | 0+ | 0+ | 0+ | 0+ | 0+ | 0+ | 0+ | 0+ | 0+ | 19 |
| | 20 | 0+ | 0+ | 0+ | 0+ | 0+ | 0+ | 0+ | 0+ | 0+ | 0+ | 0+ | 0+ | 0+ | 0+ | 0+ | 0+ | 0+ | 0+ | 0+ | 0+ | 0+ | 20 |
| | 21 | 0+ | 0+ | 0+ | 0+ | 0+ | 0+ | 0+ | 0+ | 0+ | 0+ | 0+ | 0+ | 0+ | 0+ | 0+ | 0+ | 0+ | 0+ | 0+ | 0+ | 0+ | 21 |

Probability of $r$ or more successes in $n$ trials $= \sum_{r}^{n} {}_nC_r p^r q^{n-r}$

| n | r | .01 | .02 | .04 | .05 | .06 | .08 | .10 | .12 | .14 | .15 | p .16 | .18 | .20 | .22 | .24 | .25 | .30 | .35 | .40 | .45 | .50 | r |
|---|---|---|---|---|---|---|---|---|---|---|---|---|---|---|---|---|---|---|---|---|---|---|---|
| 22 | 0 | 1 | 1 | 1 | 1 | 1 | 1 | 1 | 1 | 1 | 1 | 1 | 1 | 1 | 1 | 1 | 1 | 1 | 1 | 1 | 1 | 1 | 0 |
| | 1 | 198 | 359 | 593 | 676 | 744 | 840 | 902 | 940 | 964 | 972 | 978 | 987 | 993 | 996 | 998 | 998 | 1- | 1- | 1- | 1- | 1- | 1 |
| | 2 | 020 | 071 | 219 | 302 | 384 | 535 | 661 | 760 | 834 | 863 | 888 | 926 | 952 | 970 | 981 | 985 | 996 | 999 | 1- | 1- | 1- | 2 |
| | 3 | 001 | 009 | 056 | 095 | 142 | 256 | 380 | 502 | 612 | 662 | 707 | 785 | 846 | 892 | 926 | 939 | 979 | 994 | 998 | 1- | 1- | 3 |
| | 4 | 0+ | 001 | 011 | 022 | 040 | 094 | 172 | 267 | 372 | 425 | 477 | 578 | 668 | 746 | 810 | 838 | 932 | 975 | 992 | 998 | 1- | 4 |
| | 5 | 0+ | 0+ | 002 | 004 | 009 | 027 | 062 | 115 | 186 | 226 | 270 | 362 | 457 | 550 | 637 | 677 | 835 | 928 | 973 | 992 | 998 | 5 |
| | 6 | 0+ | 0+ | 0+ | 001 | 002 | 006 | 018 | 041 | 077 | 100 | 127 | 191 | 267 | 351 | 439 | 483 | 687 | 837 | 928 | 973 | 992 | 6 |
| | 7 | 0+ | 0+ | 0+ | 0+ | 0+ | 001 | 004 | 012 | 026 | 037 | 050 | 085 | 133 | 193 | 263 | 301 | 506 | 698 | 842 | 929 | 974 | 7 |
| | 8 | 0+ | 0+ | 0+ | 0+ | 0+ | 0+ | 001 | 003 | 008 | 011 | 017 | 032 | 056 | 090 | 135 | 162 | 329 | 526 | 710 | 848 | 933 | 8 |
| | 9 | 0+ | 0+ | 0+ | 0+ | 0+ | 0+ | 0+ | 001 | 002 | 003 | 005 | 010 | 020 | 036 | 060 | 075 | 186 | 353 | 546 | 724 | 857 | 9 |
| | 10 | 0+ | 0+ | 0+ | 0+ | 0+ | 0+ | 0+ | 0+ | 0+ | 001 | 001 | 003 | 006 | 012 | 022 | 030 | 092 | 208 | 376 | 565 | 738 | 10 |
| | 11 | 0+ | 0+ | 0+ | 0+ | 0+ | 0+ | 0+ | 0+ | 0+ | 0+ | 0+ | 001 | 002 | 004 | 007 | 010 | 039 | 107 | 228 | 396 | 584 | 11 |
| | 12 | 0+ | 0+ | 0+ | 0+ | 0+ | 0+ | 0+ | 0+ | 0+ | 0+ | 0+ | 0+ | 0+ | 001 | 002 | 003 | 014 | 047 | 121 | 246 | 416 | 12 |
| | 13 | 0+ | 0+ | 0+ | 0+ | 0+ | 0+ | 0+ | 0+ | 0+ | 0+ | 0+ | 0+ | 0+ | 0+ | 0+ | 001 | 004 | 018 | 055 | 133 | 262 | 13 |
| | 14 | 0+ | 0+ | 0+ | 0+ | 0+ | 0+ | 0+ | 0+ | 0+ | 0+ | 0+ | 0+ | 0+ | 0+ | 0+ | 0+ | 001 | 006 | 021 | 062 | 143 | 14 |
| | 15 | 0+ | 0+ | 0+ | 0+ | 0+ | 0+ | 0+ | 0+ | 0+ | 0+ | 0+ | 0+ | 0+ | 0+ | 0+ | 0+ | 0+ | 002 | 007 | 024 | 067 | 15 |
| | 16 | 0+ | 0+ | 0+ | 0+ | 0+ | 0+ | 0+ | 0+ | 0+ | 0+ | 0+ | 0+ | 0+ | 0+ | 0+ | 0+ | 0+ | 0+ | 002 | 008 | 026 | 16 |
| | 17 | 0+ | 0+ | 0+ | 0+ | 0+ | 0+ | 0+ | 0+ | 0+ | 0+ | 0+ | 0+ | 0+ | 0+ | 0+ | 0+ | 0+ | 0+ | 0+ | 002 | 008 | 17 |
| | 18 | 0+ | 0+ | 0+ | 0+ | 0+ | 0+ | 0+ | 0+ | 0+ | 0+ | 0+ | 0+ | 0+ | 0+ | 0+ | 0+ | 0+ | 0+ | 0+ | 0+ | 002 | 18 |
| | 19 | 0+ | 0+ | 0+ | 0+ | 0+ | 0+ | 0+ | 0+ | 0+ | 0+ | 0+ | 0+ | 0+ | 0+ | 0+ | 0+ | 0+ | 0+ | 0+ | 0+ | 0+ | 19 |
| | 20 | 0+ | 0+ | 0+ | 0+ | 0+ | 0+ | 0+ | 0+ | 0+ | 0+ | 0+ | 0+ | 0+ | 0+ | 0+ | 0+ | 0+ | 0+ | 0+ | 0+ | 0+ | 20 |
| | 21 | 0+ | 0+ | 0+ | 0+ | 0+ | 0+ | 0+ | 0+ | 0+ | 0+ | 0+ | 0+ | 0+ | 0+ | 0+ | 0+ | 0+ | 0+ | 0+ | 0+ | 0+ | 21 |
| | 22 | 0+ | 0+ | 0+ | 0+ | 0+ | 0+ | 0+ | 0+ | 0+ | 0+ | 0+ | 0+ | 0+ | 0+ | 0+ | 0+ | 0+ | 0+ | 0+ | 0+ | 0+ | 22 |
| 23 | 0 | 1 | 1 | 1 | 1 | 1 | 1 | 1 | 1 | 1 | 1 | 1 | 1 | 1 | 1 | 1 | 1 | 1 | 1 | 1 | 1 | 1 | 0 |
| | 1 | 206 | 372 | 609 | 693 | 759 | 853 | 911 | 947 | 969 | 976 | 982 | 990 | 994 | 997 | 998 | 999 | 1- | 1- | 1- | 1- | 1- | 1 |
| | 2 | 022 | 077 | 234 | 321 | 405 | 559 | 685 | 781 | 852 | 880 | 902 | 937 | 960 | 975 | 985 | 988 | 997 | 999 | 1- | 1- | 1- | 2 |
| | 3 | 002 | 011 | 062 | 105 | 157 | 278 | 408 | 533 | 643 | 692 | 736 | 810 | 867 | 909 | 939 | 951 | 984 | 996 | 999 | 1- | 1- | 3 |
| | 4 | 0+ | 001 | 012 | 026 | 046 | 107 | 193 | 295 | 405 | 460 | 514 | 615 | 703 | 778 | 838 | 863 | 946 | 982 | 995 | 999 | 1- | 4 |
| | 5 | 0+ | 0+ | 002 | 005 | 011 | 033 | 073 | 133 | 212 | 256 | 303 | 401 | 499 | 593 | 678 | 717 | 864 | 945 | 981 | 995 | 999 | 5 |
| | 6 | 0+ | 0+ | 0+ | 001 | 002 | 008 | 023 | 050 | 092 | 119 | 150 | 222 | 305 | 395 | 487 | 532 | 731 | 869 | 946 | 981 | 995 | 6 |
| | 7 | 0+ | 0+ | 0+ | 0+ | 0+ | 002 | 006 | 015 | 033 | 046 | 062 | 104 | 160 | 227 | 305 | 346 | 560 | 747 | 876 | 949 | 983 | 7 |
| | 8 | 0+ | 0+ | 0+ | 0+ | 0+ | 0+ | 001 | 004 | 010 | 015 | 022 | 042 | 072 | 113 | 166 | 196 | 382 | 586 | 763 | 885 | 953 | 8 |
| | 9 | 0+ | 0+ | 0+ | 0+ | 0+ | 0+ | 0+ | 001 | 003 | 004 | 007 | 014 | 027 | 048 | 078 | 096 | 229 | 444 | 612 | 780 | 895 | 9 |
| | 10 | 0+ | 0+ | 0+ | 0+ | 0+ | 0+ | 0+ | 0+ | 001 | 001 | 002 | 004 | 009 | 017 | 031 | 041 | 120 | 259 | 444 | 636 | 798 | 10 |
| | 11 | 0+ | 0+ | 0+ | 0+ | 0+ | 0+ | 0+ | 0+ | 0+ | 0+ | 0+ | 001 | 003 | 005 | 011 | 015 | 055 | 142 | 287 | 472 | 661 | 11 |
| | 12 | 0+ | 0+ | 0+ | 0+ | 0+ | 0+ | 0+ | 0+ | 0+ | 0+ | 0+ | 0+ | 001 | 001 | 003 | 005 | 021 | 068 | 164 | 313 | 500 | 12 |
| | 13 | 0+ | 0+ | 0+ | 0+ | 0+ | 0+ | 0+ | 0+ | 0+ | 0+ | 0+ | 0+ | 0+ | 0+ | 001 | 001 | 007 | 028 | 081 | 184 | 339 | 13 |
| | 14 | 0+ | 0+ | 0+ | 0+ | 0+ | 0+ | 0+ | 0+ | 0+ | 0+ | 0+ | 0+ | 0+ | 0+ | 0+ | 0+ | 002 | 010 | 035 | 094 | 202 | 14 |
| | 15 | 0+ | 0+ | 0+ | 0+ | 0+ | 0+ | 0+ | 0+ | 0+ | 0+ | 0+ | 0+ | 0+ | 0+ | 0+ | 0+ | 001 | 003 | 013 | 041 | 105 | 15 |
| | 16 | 0+ | 0+ | 0+ | 0+ | 0+ | 0+ | 0+ | 0+ | 0+ | 0+ | 0+ | 0+ | 0+ | 0+ | 0+ | 0+ | 0+ | 001 | 004 | 015 | 047 | 16 |
| | 17 | 0+ | 0+ | 0+ | 0+ | 0+ | 0+ | 0+ | 0+ | 0+ | 0+ | 0+ | 0+ | 0+ | 0+ | 0+ | 0+ | 0+ | 0+ | 001 | 005 | 017 | 17 |
| | 18 | 0+ | 0+ | 0+ | 0+ | 0+ | 0+ | 0+ | 0+ | 0+ | 0+ | 0+ | 0+ | 0+ | 0+ | 0+ | 0+ | 0+ | 0+ | 0+ | 001 | 005 | 18 |
| | 19 | 0+ | 0+ | 0+ | 0+ | 0+ | 0+ | 0+ | 0+ | 0+ | 0+ | 0+ | 0+ | 0+ | 0+ | 0+ | 0+ | 0+ | 0+ | 0+ | 0+ | 001 | 19 |
| | 20 | 0+ | 0+ | 0+ | 0+ | 0+ | 0+ | 0+ | 0+ | 0+ | 0+ | 0+ | 0+ | 0+ | 0+ | 0+ | 0+ | 0+ | 0+ | 0+ | 0+ | 0+ | 20 |
| | 21 | 0+ | 0+ | 0+ | 0+ | 0+ | 0+ | 0+ | 0+ | 0+ | 0+ | 0+ | 0+ | 0+ | 0+ | 0+ | 0+ | 0+ | 0+ | 0+ | 0+ | 0+ | 21 |
| | 22 | 0+ | 0+ | 0+ | 0+ | 0+ | 0+ | 0+ | 0+ | 0+ | 0+ | 0+ | 0+ | 0+ | 0+ | 0+ | 0+ | 0+ | 0+ | 0+ | 0+ | 0+ | 22 |
| | 23 | 0+ | 0+ | 0+ | 0+ | 0+ | 0+ | 0+ | 0+ | 0+ | 0+ | 0+ | 0+ | 0+ | 0+ | 0+ | 0+ | 0+ | 0+ | 0+ | 0+ | 0+ | 23 |
| 24 | 0 | 1 | 1 | 1 | 1 | 1 | 1 | 1 | 1 | 1 | 1 | 1 | 1 | 1 | 1 | 1 | 1 | 1 | 1 | 1 | 1 | 1 | 0 |
| | 1 | 214 | 384 | 625 | 708 | 773 | 865 | 920 | 953 | 973 | 980 | 985 | 991 | 995 | 997 | 999 | 999 | 1- | 1- | 1- | 1- | 1- | 1 |
| | 2 | 024 | 083 | 249 | 339 | 427 | 583 | 708 | 801 | 869 | 894 | 915 | 946 | 967 | 980 | 988 | 991 | 998 | 1- | 1- | 1- | 1- | 2 |
| | 3 | 002 | 012 | 069 | 116 | 172 | 301 | 436 | 563 | 673 | 720 | 763 | 833 | 885 | 924 | 950 | 960 | 988 | 997 | 999 | 1- | 1- | 3 |
| | 4 | 0+ | 001 | 014 | 030 | 053 | 121 | 214 | 324 | 439 | 495 | 550 | 650 | 736 | 807 | 862 | 885 | 958 | 987 | 996 | 999 | 1- | 4 |
| | 5 | 0+ | 0+ | 002 | 006 | 013 | 039 | 085 | 153 | 239 | 287 | 337 | 439 | 540 | 634 | 717 | 753 | 889 | 958 | 987 | 996 | 999 | 5 |
| | 6 | 0+ | 0+ | 0+ | 001 | 002 | 010 | 028 | 060 | 109 | 139 | 174 | 254 | 344 | 439 | 533 | 578 | 771 | 896 | 960 | 987 | 997 | 6 |
| | 7 | 0+ | 0+ | 0+ | 0+ | 0+ | 002 | 007 | 019 | 041 | 057 | 076 | 126 | 189 | 264 | 349 | 393 | 611 | 789 | 904 | 964 | 989 | 7 |
| | 8 | 0+ | 0+ | 0+ | 0+ | 0+ | 0- | 002 | 005 | 013 | 020 | 028 | 053 | 089 | 138 | 199 | 234 | 435 | 642 | 808 | 914 | 968 | 8 |
| | 9 | 0+ | 0+ | 0+ | 0+ | 0+ | 0+ | 0+ | 001 | 004 | 006 | 009 | 019 | 036 | 062 | 099 | 121 | 275 | 474 | 672 | 827 | 924 | 9 |
| | 10 | 0+ | 0+ | 0+ | 0+ | 0+ | 0+ | 0+ | 0+ | 001 | 002 | 002 | 006 | 013 | 024 | 042 | 055 | 153 | 313 | 511 | 701 | 846 | 10 |
| | 11 | 0+ | 0+ | 0+ | 0+ | 0+ | 0+ | 0+ | 0+ | 0+ | 0+ | 001 | 002 | 004 | 008 | 016 | 021 | 074 | 183 | 350 | 546 | 729 | 11 |
| | 12 | 0+ | 0+ | 0+ | 0+ | 0+ | 0+ | 0+ | 0+ | 0+ | 0+ | 0+ | 0+ | 001 | 002 | 005 | 007 | 031 | 094 | 213 | 385 | 581 | 12 |
| | 13 | 0+ | 0+ | 0+ | 0+ | 0+ | 0+ | 0+ | 0+ | 0+ | 0+ | 0+ | 0+ | 0+ | 001 | 001 | 002 | 012 | 042 | 114 | 242 | 419 | 13 |
| | 14 | 0+ | 0+ | 0+ | 0+ | 0+ | 0+ | 0+ | 0+ | 0+ | 0+ | 0+ | 0+ | 0+ | 0+ | 0+ | 001 | 004 | 016 | 053 | 134 | 271 | 14 |

Probability of $r$ or more successes in $n$ trials $= \sum_{r}^{n} {}_nC_r p^r q^{n-r}$

| n | r | .01 | .02 | .04 | .05 | .06 | .08 | .10 | .12 | .14 | .15 | p .16 | .18 | .20 | .22 | .24 | .25 | .30 | .35 | .40 | .45 | .50 | r |
|---|---|---|---|---|---|---|---|---|---|---|---|---|---|---|---|---|---|---|---|---|---|---|---|
| 24 | 15 | 0+ | 0+ | 0+ | 0+ | 0+ | 0+ | 0+ | 0+ | 0+ | 0+ | 0+ | 0+ | 0+ | 0+ | 0+ | 0+ | 001 | 005 | 022 | 065 | 154 | 15 |
| | 16 | 0+ | 0+ | 0+ | 0+ | 0+ | 0+ | 0+ | 0+ | 0+ | 0+ | 0+ | 0+ | 0+ | 0+ | 0+ | 0+ | 0+ | 002 | 008 | 027 | 076 | 16 |
| | 17 | 0+ | 0+ | 0+ | 0+ | 0+ | 0+ | 0+ | 0+ | 0+ | 0+ | 0+ | 0+ | 0+ | 0+ | 0+ | 0+ | 0+ | 0+ | 002 | 010 | 032 | 17 |
| | 18 | 0+ | 0+ | 0+ | 0+ | 0+ | 0+ | 0+ | 0+ | 0+ | 0+ | 0+ | 0+ | 0+ | 0+ | 0+ | 0+ | 0+ | 0+ | 001 | 003 | 011 | 18 |
| | 19 | 0+ | 0+ | 0+ | 0+ | 0+ | 0+ | 0+ | 0+ | 0+ | 0+ | 0+ | 0+ | 0+ | 0+ | 0+ | 0+ | 0+ | 0+ | 0+ | 001 | 003 | 19 |
| | 20 | 0+ | 0+ | 0+ | 0+ | 0+ | 0+ | 0+ | 0+ | 0+ | 0+ | 0+ | 0+ | 0+ | 0+ | 0+ | 0+ | 0+ | 0+ | 0+ | 0+ | 001 | 20 |
| | 21 | 0+ | 0+ | 0+ | 0+ | 0+ | 0+ | 0+ | 0+ | 0+ | 0+ | 0+ | 0+ | 0+ | 0+ | 0+ | 0+ | 0+ | 0+ | 0+ | 0+ | 0+ | 21 |
| | 22 | 0+ | 0+ | 0+ | 0+ | 0+ | 0+ | 0+ | 0+ | 0+ | 0+ | 0+ | 0+ | 0+ | 0+ | 0+ | 0+ | 0+ | 0+ | 0+ | 0+ | 0+ | 22 |
| | 23 | 0+ | 0+ | 0+ | 0+ | 0+ | 0+ | 0+ | 0+ | 0+ | 0+ | 0+ | 0+ | 0+ | 0+ | 0+ | 0+ | 0+ | 0+ | 0+ | 0+ | 0+ | 23 |
| | 24 | 0+ | 0+ | 0+ | 0+ | 0+ | 0+ | 0+ | 0+ | 0+ | 0+ | 0+ | 0+ | 0+ | 0+ | 0+ | 0+ | 0+ | 0+ | 0+ | 0+ | 0+ | 24 |
| 25 | 0 | 1 | 1 | 1 | 1 | 1 | 1 | 1 | 1 | 1 | 1 | 1 | 1 | 1 | 1 | 1 | 1 | 1 | 1 | 1 | 1 | 1 | 0 |
| | 1 | 222 | 397 | 640 | 723 | 787 | 876 | 928 | 959 | 977 | 983 | 987 | 993 | 996 | 998 | 999 | 999 | 1- | 1- | 1- | 1- | 1- | 1 |
| | 2 | 026 | 089 | 264 | 358 | 447 | 605 | 729 | 820 | 883 | 907 | 926 | 955 | 973 | 984 | 991 | 993 | 998 | 1- | 1- | 1- | 1- | 2 |
| | 3 | 002 | 013 | 076 | 127 | 187 | 323 | 463 | 591 | 700 | 746 | 787 | 853 | 902 | 936 | 959 | 968 | 991 | 998 | 1- | 1- | 1- | 3 |
| | 4 | 0+ | 001 | 017 | 034 | 060 | 135 | 236 | 352 | 471 | 529 | 584 | 683 | 766 | 832 | 883 | 904 | 967 | 990 | 998 | 1- | 1- | 4 |
| | 5 | 0+ | 0+ | 003 | 007 | 015 | 045 | 098 | 173 | 267 | 318 | 371 | 477 | 579 | 672 | 752 | 786 | 910 | 968 | 991 | 998 | 1- | 5 |
| | 6 | 0+ | 0+ | 0+ | 001 | 003 | 012 | 033 | 071 | 127 | 162 | 200 | 288 | 383 | 482 | 577 | 622 | 807 | 917 | 971 | 991 | 998 | 6 |
| | 7 | 0+ | 0+ | 0+ | 0+ | 001 | 003 | 009 | 024 | 051 | 070 | 092 | 149 | 220 | 303 | 393 | 439 | 659 | 827 | 926 | 974 | 993 | 7 |
| | 8 | 0+ | 0+ | 0+ | 0+ | 0+ | 001 | 002 | 007 | 017 | 025 | 036 | 066 | 109 | 166 | 235 | 273 | 488 | 694 | 846 | 936 | 978 | 8 |
| | 9 | 0+ | 0+ | 0+ | 0+ | 0+ | 0+ | 0+ | 002 | 005 | 008 | 012 | 025 | 047 | 079 | 123 | 149 | 323 | 533 | 726 | 866 | 946 | 9 |
| | 10 | 0+ | 0+ | 0+ | 0+ | 0+ | 0+ | 0+ | 0+ | 001 | 002 | 003 | 008 | 017 | 033 | 056 | 071 | 189 | 370 | 575 | 758 | 885 | 10 |
| | 11 | 0+ | 0+ | 0+ | 0+ | 0+ | 0+ | 0+ | 0+ | 0+ | 0+ | 001 | 002 | 006 | 012 | 022 | 030 | 098 | 229 | 414 | 616 | 788 | 11 |
| | 12 | 0+ | 0+ | 0+ | 0+ | 0+ | 0+ | 0+ | 0+ | 0+ | 0+ | 0+ | 001 | 002 | 004 | 008 | 011 | 044 | 125 | 268 | 457 | 655 | 12 |
| | 13 | 0+ | 0+ | 0+ | 0+ | 0+ | 0+ | 0+ | 0+ | 0+ | 0+ | 0+ | 0+ | 0+ | 001 | 002 | 003 | 017 | 060 | 154 | 306 | 500 | 13 |
| | 14 | 0+ | 0+ | 0+ | 0+ | 0+ | 0+ | 0+ | 0+ | 0+ | 0+ | 0+ | 0+ | 0+ | 0+ | 001 | 001 | 006 | 025 | 078 | 183 | 345 | 14 |
| | 15 | 0+ | 0+ | 0+ | 0+ | 0+ | 0+ | 0+ | 0+ | 0+ | 0+ | 0+ | 0+ | 0+ | 0+ | 0+ | 0+ | 002 | 009 | 034 | 096 | 212 | 15 |
| | 16 | 0+ | 0+ | 0+ | 0+ | 0+ | 0+ | 0+ | 0+ | 0+ | 0+ | 0+ | 0+ | 0+ | 0+ | 0+ | 0+ | 0+ | 003 | 013 | 044 | 115 | 16 |
| | 17 | 0+ | 0+ | 0+ | 0+ | 0+ | 0+ | 0+ | 0+ | 0+ | 0+ | 0+ | 0+ | 0+ | 0+ | 0+ | 0+ | 0+ | 001 | 004 | 017 | 054 | 17 |
| | 18 | 0+ | 0+ | 0+ | 0+ | 0+ | 0+ | 0+ | 0+ | 0+ | 0+ | 0+ | 0+ | 0+ | 0+ | 0+ | 0+ | 0+ | 0+ | 001 | 006 | 022 | 18 |
| | 19 | 0+ | 0+ | 0+ | 0+ | 0+ | 0+ | 0+ | 0+ | 0+ | 0+ | 0+ | 0+ | 0+ | 0+ | 0+ | 0+ | 0+ | 0+ | 0+ | 002 | 007 | 19 |
| | 20 | 0+ | 0+ | 0+ | 0+ | 0+ | 0+ | 0+ | 0+ | 0+ | 0+ | 0+ | 0+ | 0+ | 0+ | 0+ | 0+ | 0+ | 0+ | 0+ | 0+ | 002 | 20 |
| | 21 | 0+ | 0+ | 0+ | 0+ | 0+ | 0+ | 0+ | 0+ | 0+ | 0+ | 0+ | 0+ | 0+ | 0+ | 0+ | 0+ | 0+ | 0+ | 0+ | 0+ | 0+ | 21 |
| | 22 | 0+ | 0+ | 0+ | 0+ | 0+ | 0+ | 0+ | 0+ | 0+ | 0+ | 0+ | 0+ | 0+ | 0+ | 0+ | 0+ | 0+ | 0+ | 0+ | 0+ | 0+ | 22 |
| | 23 | 0+ | 0+ | 0+ | 0+ | 0+ | 0+ | 0+ | 0+ | 0+ | 0+ | 0+ | 0+ | 0+ | 0+ | 0+ | 0+ | 0+ | 0+ | 0+ | 0+ | 0+ | 23 |
| | 24 | 0+ | 0+ | 0+ | 0+ | 0+ | 0+ | 0+ | 0+ | 0+ | 0+ | 0+ | 0+ | 0+ | 0+ | 0+ | 0+ | 0+ | 0+ | 0+ | 0+ | 0+ | 24 |
| | 25 | 0+ | 0+ | 0+ | 0+ | 0+ | 0+ | 0+ | 0+ | 0+ | 0+ | 0+ | 0+ | 0+ | 0+ | 0+ | 0+ | 0+ | 0+ | 0+ | 0+ | 0+ | 25 |

# C

# Poisson Distribution – Individual Terms

THE TABLE presents individual Poisson probabilities for the number of occurrences $X$ per unit of measurement for selected values of $m$, the mean number of occurrences per unit of measurement. A blank space is left for values less than .0005.

| x | .001 | .002 | .003 | .004 | .005 | .006 | .007 | .008 | .009 | .01 | .02 | .03 | .04 | .05 | .06 | .07 | .08 | .09 | .10 | .15 | x |
|---|---|---|---|---|---|---|---|---|---|---|---|---|---|---|---|---|---|---|---|---|---|
| 0 | 999 | 998 | 997 | 996 | 995 | 994 | 993 | 992 | 991 | 990 | 980 | 970 | 961 | 951 | 942 | 932 | 923 | 914 | 905 | 861 | 0 |
| 1 | 001 | 002 | 003 | 004 | 005 | 006 | 007 | 008 | 009 | 010 | 020 | 030 | 038 | 048 | 057 | 065 | 074 | 082 | 090 | 129 | 1 |
| 2 | | | | | | | | | | | | | 001 | 001 | 002 | 002 | 003 | 004 | 005 | 010 | 2 |

| | | | | | | | | | | m | | | | | | | | | | | |
|---|---|---|---|---|---|---|---|---|---|---|---|---|---|---|---|---|---|---|---|---|---|
| x | .20 | .25 | .30 | .40 | .50 | .60 | .70 | .80 | .90 | 1.0 | 1.1 | 1.2 | 1.3 | 1.4 | 1.5 | 1.6 | 1.7 | 1.8 | 1.9 | 2.0 | x |
| 0 | 819 | 779 | 741 | 670 | 607 | 549 | 497 | 449 | 407 | 368 | 333 | 301 | 273 | 247 | 223 | 202 | 183 | 165 | 150 | 135 | 0 |
| 1 | 164 | 195 | 222 | 268 | 303 | 329 | 348 | 359 | 366 | 368 | 366 | 361 | 354 | 345 | 335 | 323 | 311 | 298 | 284 | 271 | 1 |
| 2 | 016 | 024 | 033 | 054 | 076 | 099 | 122 | 144 | 165 | 184 | 201 | 217 | 230 | 242 | 251 | 258 | 264 | 268 | 270 | 271 | 2 |
| 3 | 001 | 002 | 003 | 007 | 013 | 020 | 028 | 038 | 049 | 061 | 074 | 087 | 100 | 113 | 126 | 138 | 150 | 161 | 171 | 180 | 3 |
| 4 | | | | 001 | 002 | 003 | 005 | 008 | 011 | 015 | 020 | 026 | 032 | 039 | 047 | 055 | 063 | 072 | 081 | 090 | 4 |
| 5 | | | | | | | 001 | 001 | 002 | 003 | 004 | 006 | 008 | 011 | 014 | 018 | 022 | 026 | 031 | 036 | 5 |
| 6 | | | | | | | | | | 001 | 001 | 001 | 002 | 003 | 004 | 005 | 006 | 008 | 010 | 012 | 6 |
| 7 | | | | | | | | | | | | | | 001 | 001 | 001 | 001 | 002 | 003 | 003 | 7 |
| 8 | | | | | | | | | | | | | | | | | | | 001 | 001 | 8 |

| | | | | | | | | | | m | | | | | | | | | | | |
|---|---|---|---|---|---|---|---|---|---|---|---|---|---|---|---|---|---|---|---|---|---|
| x | 2.1 | 2.2 | 2.3 | 2.4 | 2.5 | 2.6 | 2.7 | 2.8 | 2.9 | 3.0 | 3.1 | 3.2 | 3.3 | 3.4 | 3.5 | 3.6 | 3.7 | 3.8 | 3.9 | 4.0 | x |
| 0 | 122 | 111 | 100 | 091 | 082 | 074 | 067 | 061 | 055 | 050 | 045 | 041 | 037 | 033 | 030 | 027 | 025 | 022 | 020 | 018 | 0 |
| 1 | 257 | 244 | 231 | 218 | 205 | 193 | 181 | 170 | 160 | 149 | 140 | 130 | 122 | 113 | 106 | 098 | 091 | 085 | 079 | 073 | 1 |
| 2 | 270 | 268 | 265 | 261 | 257 | 251 | 245 | 238 | 231 | 224 | 216 | 209 | 201 | 193 | 185 | 177 | 169 | 162 | 154 | 147 | 2 |
| 3 | 189 | 197 | 203 | 209 | 214 | 218 | 220 | 222 | 224 | 224 | 224 | 223 | 221 | 219 | 216 | 212 | 209 | 205 | 200 | 195 | 3 |
| 4 | 099 | 108 | 117 | 125 | 134 | 141 | 149 | 156 | 162 | 168 | 173 | 178 | 182 | 186 | 189 | 191 | 193 | 194 | 195 | 195 | 4 |
| 5 | 042 | 048 | 054 | 060 | 067 | 074 | 080 | 087 | 094 | 101 | 107 | 114 | 120 | 126 | 132 | 138 | 143 | 148 | 152 | 156 | 5 |
| 6 | 015 | 017 | 021 | 024 | 028 | 032 | 036 | 041 | 045 | 050 | 056 | 061 | 066 | 072 | 077 | 083 | 088 | 094 | 099 | 104 | 6 |
| 7 | 004 | 005 | 007 | 008 | 010 | 012 | 014 | 016 | 019 | 022 | 025 | 028 | 031 | 035 | 039 | 042 | 047 | 051 | 055 | 060 | 7 |
| 8 | 001 | 002 | 002 | 002 | 003 | 004 | 005 | 006 | 007 | 008 | 010 | 011 | 013 | 015 | 017 | 019 | 022 | 024 | 027 | 030 | 8 |
| 9 | | | | 001 | 001 | 001 | 001 | 002 | 002 | 003 | 003 | 004 | 005 | 006 | 007 | 008 | 009 | 010 | 012 | 013 | 9 |
| 10 | | | | | | | | | 001 | 001 | 001 | 001 | 002 | 002 | 002 | 003 | 003 | 004 | 005 | 005 | 10 |
| 11 | | | | | | | | | | | | | | 001 | 001 | 001 | 001 | 001 | 002 | 002 | 11 |
| 12 | | | | | | | | | | | | | | | | | | | 001 | 001 | 12 |

Source: William A. Spurr and Charles P. Bonini, *Statistical Analysis for Business Decisions*, rev. ed. (Homewood, Ill.: Richard D. Irwin, 1973) © 1973 by Richard D. Irwin, Inc., pp. 696–97.

$$f(x) = \frac{e^{-m}m^{x}}{x!}$$

| | | | | | | | | | | m | | | | | | | | | | |
|---|---|---|---|---|---|---|---|---|---|---|---|---|---|---|---|---|---|---|---|---|
| x | 4.1 | 4.2 | 4.3 | 4.4 | 4.5 | 4.6 | 4.7 | 4.8 | 4.9 | 5.0 | 5.1 | 5.2 | 5.3 | 5.4 | 5.5 | 5.6 | 5.7 | 5.8 | 5.9 | 6.0 | x |
| 0 | 017 | 015 | 014 | 012 | 011 | 010 | 009 | 008 | 007 | 007 | 006 | 006 | 005 | 005 | 004 | 004 | 003 | 003 | 003 | 002 | 0 |
| 1 | 068 | 063 | 058 | 054 | 050 | 046 | 043 | 040 | 036 | 034 | 031 | 029 | 026 | 024 | 022 | 021 | 019 | 018 | 016 | 015 | 1 |
| 2 | 139 | 132 | 125 | 119 | 112 | 106 | 100 | 095 | 089 | 084 | 079 | 075 | 070 | 066 | 062 | 058 | 054 | 051 | 048 | 045 | 2 |
| 3 | 190 | 185 | 180 | 174 | 169 | 163 | 157 | 152 | 146 | 140 | 135 | 129 | 124 | 119 | 113 | 108 | 103 | 098 | 094 | 089 | 3 |
| 4 | 195 | 194 | 193 | 192 | 190 | 188 | 185 | 182 | 179 | 175 | 172 | 168 | 164 | 160 | 156 | 152 | 147 | 143 | 138 | 134 | 4 |
| 5 | 160 | 163 | 166 | 169 | 171 | 173 | 174 | 175 | 175 | 175 | 175 | 175 | 174 | 173 | 171 | 170 | 168 | 166 | 163 | 161 | 5 |
| 6 | 109 | 114 | 119 | 124 | 128 | 132 | 136 | 140 | 143 | 146 | 149 | 151 | 154 | 156 | 157 | 158 | 159 | 160 | 160 | 161 | 6 |
| 7 | 064 | 069 | 073 | 078 | 082 | 087 | 091 | 096 | 100 | 104 | 109 | 113 | 116 | 120 | 123 | 127 | 130 | 133 | 135 | 138 | 7 |
| 8 | 033 | 036 | 039 | 043 | 046 | 050 | 054 | 058 | 061 | 065 | 069 | 073 | 077 | 081 | 085 | 089 | 092 | 096 | 100 | 103 | 8 |
| 9 | 015 | 017 | 019 | 021 | 023 | 026 | 028 | 031 | 033 | 036 | 039 | 042 | 045 | 049 | 052 | 055 | 059 | 062 | 065 | 069 | 9 |
| 10 | 006 | 007 | 008 | 009 | 010 | 012 | 013 | 015 | 016 | 018 | 020 | 022 | 024 | 026 | 029 | 031 | 033 | 036 | 039 | 041 | 10 |
| 11 | 002 | 003 | 003 | 004 | 004 | 005 | 006 | 006 | 007 | 008 | 009 | 010 | 012 | 013 | 014 | 016 | 017 | 019 | 021 | 023 | 11 |
| 12 | 001 | 001 | 001 | 001 | 002 | 002 | 002 | 003 | 003 | 003 | 004 | 005 | 005 | 006 | 007 | 007 | 008 | 009 | 010 | 011 | 12 |
| 13 | | | | | 001 | 001 | 001 | 001 | 001 | 001 | 002 | 002 | 002 | 002 | 003 | 003 | 004 | 004 | 005 | 005 | 13 |
| 14 | | | | | | | | | | | 001 | 001 | 001 | 001 | 001 | 001 | 001 | 002 | 002 | 002 | 14 |
| 15 | | | | | | | | | | | | | | | | | 001 | 001 | 001 | 001 | 15 |

| | | | | | | | | | | m | | | | | | | | | | |
|---|---|---|---|---|---|---|---|---|---|---|---|---|---|---|---|---|---|---|---|---|
| x | 6.1 | 6.2 | 6.3 | 6.4 | 6.5 | 6.6 | 6.7 | 6.8 | 6.9 | 7.0 | 7.1 | 7.2 | 7.3 | 7.4 | 7.5 | 8.0 | 8.5 | 9.0 | 9.5 | 10.0 | x |
| 0 | 002 | 002 | 002 | 002 | 002 | 001 | 001 | 001 | 001 | 001 | 001 | 001 | 001 | 001 | 001 | | | | | | 0 |
| 1 | 014 | 013 | 012 | 011 | 010 | 009 | 008 | 008 | 007 | 006 | 006 | 005 | 005 | 005 | 004 | 003 | 002 | 001 | 001 | | 1 |
| 2 | 042 | 039 | 036 | 034 | 032 | 030 | 028 | 026 | 024 | 022 | 021 | 019 | 018 | 017 | 016 | 011 | 007 | 005 | 003 | 002 | 2 |
| 3 | 085 | 081 | 077 | 073 | 069 | 065 | 062 | 058 | 055 | 052 | 049 | 046 | 044 | 041 | 039 | 029 | 021 | 015 | 011 | 008 | 3 |
| 4 | 129 | 125 | 121 | 116 | 112 | 108 | 103 | 099 | 095 | 091 | 087 | 084 | 080 | 076 | 073 | 057 | 044 | 034 | 025 | 019 | 4 |
| 5 | 158 | 155 | 152 | 149 | 145 | 142 | 138 | 135 | 131 | 128 | 124 | 120 | 117 | 113 | 109 | 092 | 075 | 061 | 048 | 038 | 5 |
| 6 | 160 | 160 | 159 | 159 | 157 | 156 | 155 | 153 | 151 | 149 | 147 | 144 | 142 | 139 | 137 | 122 | 107 | 091 | 076 | 063 | 6 |
| 7 | 140 | 142 | 144 | 145 | 146 | 147 | 148 | 149 | 149 | 149 | 149 | 149 | 148 | 147 | 146 | 140 | 129 | 117 | 104 | 090 | 7 |
| 8 | 107 | 110 | 113 | 116 | 119 | 121 | 124 | 126 | 128 | 130 | 132 | 134 | 135 | 136 | 137 | 140 | 138 | 132 | 123 | 113 | 8 |
| 9 | 072 | 076 | 079 | 082 | 086 | 089 | 092 | 095 | 098 | 101 | 104 | 107 | 110 | 112 | 114 | 124 | 130 | 132 | 130 | 125 | 9 |
| 10 | 044 | 047 | 050 | 053 | 056 | 059 | 062 | 065 | 068 | 071 | 074 | 077 | 080 | 083 | 086 | 099 | 110 | 119 | 124 | 125 | 10 |
| 11 | 024 | 026 | 029 | 031 | 033 | 035 | 038 | 040 | 043 | 045 | 048 | 050 | 053 | 056 | 059 | 072 | 085 | 097 | 107 | 114 | 11 |
| 12 | 012 | 014 | 015 | 016 | 018 | 019 | 021 | 023 | 025 | 026 | 028 | 030 | 032 | 034 | 037 | 048 | 060 | 073 | 084 | 095 | 12 |
| 13 | 006 | 007 | 007 | 008 | 009 | 010 | 011 | 012 | 013 | 014 | 015 | 017 | 018 | 020 | 021 | 030 | 040 | 050 | 062 | 073 | 13 |
| 14 | 003 | 003 | 003 | 004 | 004 | 005 | 005 | 006 | 006 | 007 | 008 | 009 | 009 | 010 | 011 | 017 | 024 | 032 | 042 | 052 | 14 |
| 15 | 001 | 001 | 001 | 002 | 002 | 002 | 002 | 003 | 003 | 003 | 004 | 004 | 005 | 005 | 006 | 009 | 014 | 019 | 027 | 035 | 15 |
| 16 | | | 001 | 001 | 001 | 001 | 001 | 001 | 001 | 001 | 002 | 002 | 002 | 002 | 003 | 005 | 007 | 011 | 016 | 022 | 16 |
| 17 | | | | | | | | | 001 | 001 | 001 | 001 | 001 | 001 | 001 | 002 | 004 | 006 | 009 | 013 | 17 |
| 18 | | | | | | | | | | | | | | | | 001 | 002 | 003 | 005 | 007 | 18 |
| 19 | | | | | | | | | | | | | | | | | 001 | 001 | 002 | 004 | 19 |
| 20 | | | | | | | | | | | | | | | | | | 001 | 001 | 002 | 20 |
| 21 | | | | | | | | | | | | | | | | | | | | 001 | 21 |

# D

# Poisson Distribution – Cumulative Terms

THE TABLE presents the Poisson probabilities of *X or more* occurrences per unit of measurement for selected values of $m$, the mean number of occurrences per unit of measurement.

The symbol 1 – indicates a value less than 1 but greater than .9995. A blank space is left for values less than .0005.

| x | .001 | .002 | .003 | .004 | .005 | .006 | .007 | .008 | .009 | .01 | .02 | .03 | .04 | .05 | .06 | .07 | .08 | .09 | .10 | .15 | x |
|---|---|---|---|---|---|---|---|---|---|---|---|---|---|---|---|---|---|---|---|---|---|
| | | | | | | | | | | | m | | | | | | | | | | |
| 0 | 1 | 1 | 1 | 1 | 1 | 1 | 1 | 1 | 1 | 1 | 1 | 1 | 1 | 1 | 1 | 1 | 1 | 1 | 1 | 1 | 0 |
| 1 | 001 | 002 | 003 | 004 | 005 | 006 | 007 | 008 | 009 | 010 | 020 | 030 | 039 | 049 | 058 | 068 | 077 | 086 | 095 | 139 | 1 |
| 2 | | | | | | | | | | | | | 001 | 001 | 002 | 002 | 003 | 004 | 005 | 010 | 2 |
| 3 | | | | | | | | | | | | | | | | | | | | 001 | 3 |

| x | .20 | .25 | .30 | .40 | .50 | .60 | .70 | .80 | .90 | 1.0 | 1.1 | 1.2 | 1.3 | 1.4 | 1.5 | 1.6 | 1.7 | 1.8 | 1.9 | 2.0 | x |
|---|---|---|---|---|---|---|---|---|---|---|---|---|---|---|---|---|---|---|---|---|---|
| | | | | | | | | | | | m | | | | | | | | | | |
| 0 | 1 | 1 | 1 | 1 | 1 | 1 | 1 | 1 | 1 | 1 | 1 | 1 | 1 | 1 | 1 | 1 | 1 | 1 | 1 | 1 | 0 |
| 1 | 181 | 221 | 259 | 330 | 393 | 451 | 503 | 551 | 593 | 632 | 667 | 699 | 727 | 753 | 777 | 798 | 817 | 835 | 850 | 865 | 1 |
| 2 | 018 | 026 | 037 | 062 | 090 | 122 | 156 | 191 | 228 | 264 | 301 | 337 | 373 | 408 | 442 | 475 | 507 | 537 | 566 | 594 | 2 |
| 3 | 001 | 002 | 004 | 008 | 014 | 023 | 034 | 047 | 063 | 080 | 100 | 121 | 143 | 167 | 191 | 217 | 243 | 269 | 296 | 323 | 3 |
| 4 | | | | 001 | 002 | 003 | 006 | 009 | 013 | 019 | 026 | 034 | 043 | 054 | 066 | 079 | 093 | 109 | 125 | 143 | 4 |
| 5 | | | | | | | 001 | 001 | 002 | 004 | 005 | 008 | 011 | 014 | 019 | 024 | 030 | 036 | 044 | 053 | 5 |
| 6 | | | | | | | | | | 001 | 001 | 002 | 002 | 003 | 004 | 006 | 008 | 010 | 013 | 017 | 6 |
| 7 | | | | | | | | | | | | | | 001 | 001 | 001 | 002 | 003 | 003 | 005 | 7 |
| 8 | | | | | | | | | | | | | | | | | | 001 | 001 | 001 | 8 |

| x | 2.1 | 2.2 | 2.3 | 2.4 | 2.5 | 2.6 | 2.7 | 2.8 | 2.9 | 3.0 | 3.1 | 3.2 | 3.3 | 3.4 | 3.5 | 3.6 | 3.7 | 3.8 | 3.9 | 4.0 | x |
|---|---|---|---|---|---|---|---|---|---|---|---|---|---|---|---|---|---|---|---|---|---|
| | | | | | | | | | | | m | | | | | | | | | | |
| 0 | 1 | 1 | 1 | 1 | 1 | 1 | 1 | 1 | 1 | 1 | 1 | 1 | 1 | 1 | 1 | 1 | 1 | 1 | 1 | 1 | 0 |
| 1 | 878 | 889 | 900 | 909 | 918 | 926 | 933 | 939 | 945 | 950 | 955 | 959 | 963 | 967 | 970 | 973 | 975 | 978 | 980 | 982 | 1 |
| 2 | 620 | 645 | 669 | 692 | 713 | 733 | 751 | 769 | 785 | 801 | 815 | 829 | 841 | 853 | 864 | 874 | 884 | 893 | 901 | 908 | 2 |
| 3 | 350 | 377 | 404 | 430 | 456 | 482 | 506 | 531 | 554 | 577 | 599 | 620 | 641 | 660 | 679 | 697 | 715 | 731 | 747 | 762 | 3 |
| 4 | 161 | 181 | 201 | 221 | 242 | 264 | 286 | 308 | 330 | 353 | 375 | 397 | 420 | 442 | 463 | 485 | 506 | 527 | 547 | 567 | 4 |
| 5 | 062 | 072 | 084 | 096 | 109 | 123 | 137 | 152 | 168 | 185 | 202 | 219 | 237 | 256 | 275 | 294 | 313 | 332 | 352 | 371 | 5 |
| 6 | 020 | 025 | 030 | 036 | 042 | 049 | 057 | 065 | 074 | 084 | 094 | 105 | 117 | 129 | 142 | 156 | 170 | 184 | 199 | 215 | 6 |
| 7 | 006 | 007 | 009 | 012 | 014 | 017 | 021 | 024 | 029 | 034 | 039 | 045 | 051 | 058 | 065 | 073 | 082 | 091 | 101 | 111 | 7 |
| 8 | 001 | 002 | 003 | 003 | 004 | 005 | 007 | 008 | 010 | 012 | 014 | 017 | 020 | 023 | 027 | 031 | 035 | 040 | 045 | 051 | 8 |
| 9 | | | 001 | 001 | 001 | 001 | 002 | 002 | 003 | 004 | 005 | 006 | 007 | 008 | 010 | 012 | 014 | 016 | 019 | 021 | 9 |
| 10 | | | | | | | 001 | 001 | 001 | 001 | 001 | 002 | 002 | 003 | 003 | 004 | 005 | 006 | 007 | 008 | 10 |
| 11 | | | | | | | | | | | | | 001 | 001 | 001 | 001 | 002 | 002 | 002 | 003 | 11 |
| 12 | | | | | | | | | | | | | | | | | | 001 | 001 | 001 | 12 |

Source: William A. Spurr and Charles P. Bonini, *Statistical Analysis for Business Decisions*, rev. ed. (Homewood, Ill.: Richard D. Irwin, 1973) © 1973 by Richard D. Irwin, Inc., pp. 698–99.

$$\sum_{x}^{\infty} \frac{e^{-m} m^x}{x!}$$

| x | 4.1 | 4.2 | 4.3 | 4.4 | 4.5 | 4.6 | 4.7 | 4.8 | 4.9 | 5.0 | m 5.1 | 5.2 | 5.3 | 5.4 | 5.5 | 5.6 | 5.7 | 5.8 | 5.9 | 6.0 | x |
|---|---|---|---|---|---|---|---|---|---|---|---|---|---|---|---|---|---|---|---|---|---|
| 0 | 1 | 1 | 1 | 1 | 1 | 1 | 1 | 1 | 1 | 1 | 1 | 1 | 1 | 1 | 1 | 1 | 1 | 1 | 1 | 1 | 0 |
| 1 | 983 | 985 | 986 | 988 | 989 | 990 | 991 | 992 | 993 | 993 | 994 | 994 | 995 | 995 | 996 | 997 | 997 | 997 | 997 | 998 | 1 |
| 2 | 915 | 922 | 928 | 934 | 939 | 944 | 948 | 952 | 956 | 960 | 963 | 966 | 969 | 971 | 973 | 976 | 978 | 979 | 981 | 983 | 2 |
| 3 | 776 | 790 | 803 | 815 | 826 | 837 | 848 | 857 | 867 | 875 | 884 | 891 | 898 | 905 | 912 | 918 | 923 | 928 | 933 | 938 | 3 |
| 4 | 586 | 605 | 623 | 641 | 658 | 674 | 690 | 706 | 721 | 735 | 749 | 762 | 775 | 787 | 798 | 809 | 820 | 830 | 840 | 849 | 4 |
| 5 | 391 | 410 | 430 | 449 | 468 | 487 | 505 | 524 | 542 | 560 | 577 | 594 | 610 | 627 | 642 | 658 | 673 | 687 | 701 | 715 | 5 |
| 6 | 231 | 247 | 263 | 280 | 297 | 314 | 332 | 349 | 366 | 384 | 402 | 419 | 437 | 454 | 471 | 488 | 505 | 522 | 538 | 554 | 6 |
| 7 | 121 | 133 | 144 | 156 | 169 | 182 | 195 | 209 | 223 | 238 | 253 | 268 | 283 | 298 | 314 | 330 | 346 | 362 | 378 | 394 | 7 |
| 8 | 057 | 064 | 071 | 079 | 087 | 095 | 104 | 113 | 123 | 133 | 144 | 155 | 167 | 178 | 191 | 203 | 216 | 229 | 242 | 256 | 8 |
| 9 | 024 | 028 | 032 | 036 | 040 | 045 | 050 | 056 | 062 | 068 | 075 | 082 | 089 | 097 | 106 | 114 | 123 | 133 | 143 | 153 | 9 |
| 10 | 010 | 011 | 013 | 015 | 017 | 020 | 022 | 025 | 028 | 032 | 036 | 040 | 044 | 049 | 054 | 059 | 065 | 071 | 077 | 084 | 10 |
| 11 | 003 | 004 | 005 | 006 | 007 | 008 | 009 | 010 | 012 | 014 | 016 | 018 | 020 | 023 | 025 | 028 | 031 | 035 | 039 | 042 | 11 |
| 12 | 001 | 001 | 002 | 002 | 002 | 003 | 003 | 004 | 005 | 005 | 006 | 007 | 008 | 010 | 011 | 012 | 014 | 016 | 018 | 020 | 12 |
| 13 | | | 001 | 001 | 001 | 001 | 001 | 001 | 002 | 002 | 002 | 003 | 003 | 004 | 004 | 005 | 006 | 007 | 008 | 009 | 13 |
| 14 | | | | | | | | | 001 | 001 | 001 | 001 | 001 | 001 | 002 | 002 | 002 | 003 | 003 | 004 | 14 |
| 15 | | | | | | | | | | | | | | | 001 | 001 | 001 | 001 | 001 | 001 | 15 |
| 16 | | | | | | | | | | | | | | | | | | | | 001 | 16 |

| x | 6.1 | 6.2 | 6.3 | 6.4 | 6.5 | 6.6 | 6.7 | 6.8 | 6.9 | 7.0 | m 7.1 | 7.2 | 7.3 | 7.4 | 7.5 | 8.0 | 8.5 | 9.0 | 9.5 | 10.0 | x |
|---|---|---|---|---|---|---|---|---|---|---|---|---|---|---|---|---|---|---|---|---|---|
| 0 | 1 | 1 | 1 | 1 | 1 | 1 | 1 | 1 | 1 | 1 | 1 | 1 | 1 | 1 | 1 | 1 | 1 | 1 | 1 | 1 | 0 |
| 1 | 998 | 998 | 998 | 998 | 998 | 999 | 999 | 999 | 999 | 999 | 999 | 999 | 999 | 999 | 999 | 1- | 1- | 1- | 1- | 1- | 1 |
| 2 | 984 | 985 | 987 | 988 | 989 | 990 | 991 | 991 | 992 | 993 | 993 | 994 | 994 | 995 | 995 | 997 | 998 | 999 | 999 | 1- | 2 |
| 3 | 942 | 946 | 950 | 954 | 957 | 960 | 963 | 966 | 968 | 970 | 973 | 975 | 976 | 978 | 980 | 986 | 991 | 994 | 996 | 997 | 3 |
| 4 | 857 | 866 | 874 | 881 | 888 | 895 | 901 | 907 | 913 | 918 | 923 | 928 | 933 | 937 | 941 | 958 | 970 | 979 | 985 | 990 | 4 |
| 5 | 728 | 741 | 753 | 765 | 776 | 787 | 798 | 808 | 818 | 827 | 836 | 844 | 853 | 860 | 868 | 900 | 926 | 945 | 960 | 971 | 5 |
| 6 | 570 | 586 | 601 | 616 | 631 | 645 | 659 | 673 | 686 | 699 | 712 | 724 | 736 | 747 | 759 | 809 | 850 | 884 | 911 | 933 | 6 |
| 7 | 410 | 426 | 442 | 458 | 473 | 489 | 505 | 520 | 535 | 550 | 565 | 580 | 594 | 608 | 622 | 687 | 744 | 793 | 835 | 870 | 7 |
| 8 | 270 | 284 | 298 | 313 | 327 | 342 | 357 | 372 | 386 | 401 | 416 | 431 | 446 | 461 | 475 | 547 | 614 | 676 | 731 | 780 | 8 |
| 9 | 163 | 174 | 185 | 197 | 208 | 220 | 233 | 245 | 258 | 271 | 284 | 297 | 311 | 324 | 338 | 407 | 477 | 544 | 608 | 667 | 9 |
| 10 | 091 | 098 | 106 | 114 | 123 | 131 | 140 | 150 | 151 | 170 | 180 | 190 | 201 | 212 | 224 | 283 | 347 | 413 | 478 | 542 | 10 |
| 11 | 047 | 051 | 056 | 061 | 067 | 073 | 079 | 085 | 092 | 099 | 106 | 113 | 121 | 129 | 138 | 184 | 237 | 294 | 355 | 417 | 11 |
| 12 | 022 | 025 | 028 | 031 | 034 | 037 | 041 | 045 | 049 | 053 | 058 | 063 | 068 | 074 | 079 | 112 | 151 | 197 | 248 | 303 | 12 |
| 13 | 010 | 011 | 013 | 014 | 016 | 018 | 020 | 022 | 024 | 027 | 030 | 033 | 036 | 039 | 043 | 064 | 091 | 124 | 164 | 208 | 13 |
| 14 | 004 | 005 | 005 | 006 | 007 | 008 | 009 | 010 | 011 | 013 | 014 | 016 | 018 | 020 | 022 | 034 | 051 | 074 | 102 | 136 | 14 |
| 15 | 002 | 002 | 002 | 003 | 003 | 003 | 004 | 004 | 005 | 006 | 006 | 007 | 008 | 009 | 010 | 017 | 027 | 041 | 060 | 083 | 15 |
| 16 | 001 | 001 | 001 | 001 | 001 | 001 | 002 | 002 | 002 | 002 | 003 | 003 | 004 | 004 | 005 | 008 | 014 | 022 | 033 | 049 | 16 |
| 17 | | | | | | 001 | 001 | 001 | 001 | 001 | 001 | 001 | 001 | 002 | 002 | 004 | 007 | 011 | 018 | 027 | 17 |
| 18 | | | | | | | | | | | | 001 | 001 | 001 | 001 | 002 | 003 | 005 | 009 | 014 | 18 |
| 19 | | | | | | | | | | | | | | | | 001 | 001 | 002 | 004 | 007 | 19 |
| 20 | | | | | | | | | | | | | | | | | 001 | 001 | 002 | 003 | 20 |
| 21 | | | | | | | | | | | | | | | | | | | 001 | 002 | 21 |
| 22 | | | | | | | | | | | | | | | | | | | | 001 | 22 |

# E

# Areas Under the Normal Curve

EACH ENTRY in this table is the proportion of the total area under a normal curve which lies under the segment between the mean and $x/\sigma$ or $z$ standard deviations from the mean. Example: $x = X - \mu = 31$ and $\sigma = 20$, so $z = x/\sigma = 1.55$. Then the required area is .4394. The area in the tail beyond the point $x = 31$ is then $.5000 - .4394 = .0606$.

| $x/\sigma$ | .00 | .01 | .02 | .03 | .04 | .05 | .06 | .07 | .08 | .09 |
|---|---|---|---|---|---|---|---|---|---|---|
| 0.0 | .0000 | .0040 | .0080 | .0120 | .0160 | .0199 | .0239 | .0279 | .0319 | .0359 |
| 0.1 | .0398 | .0438 | .0478 | .0517 | .0557 | .0596 | .0636 | .0675 | .0714 | .0753 |
| 0.2 | .0793 | .0832 | .0871 | .0910 | .0948 | .0987 | .1026 | .1064 | .1103 | .1141 |
| 0.3 | .1179 | .1217 | .1255 | .1293 | .1331 | .1368 | .1406 | .1443 | .1480 | .1517 |
| 0.4 | .1554 | .1591 | .1628 | .1664 | .1700 | .1736 | .1772 | .1808 | .1844 | .1879 |
| 0.5 | .1915 | .1950 | .1985 | .2019 | .2054 | .2088 | .2123 | .2157 | .2190 | .2224 |
| 0.6 | .2257 | .2291 | .2324 | .2357 | .2389 | .2422 | .2454 | .2486 | .2518 | .2549 |
| 0.7 | .2580 | .2612 | .2642 | .2673 | .2704 | .2734 | .2764 | .2794 | .2823 | .2852 |
| 0.8 | .2881 | .2910 | .2939 | .2967 | .2995 | .3023 | .3051 | .3078 | .3106 | .3133 |
| 0.9 | .3159 | .3186 | .3212 | .3238 | .3264 | .3289 | .3315 | .3340 | .3365 | .3389 |
| 1.0 | .3413 | .3438 | .3461 | .3485 | .3508 | .3531 | .3554 | .3577 | .3599 | .3621 |
| 1.1 | .3643 | .3665 | .3686 | .3708 | .3729 | .3749 | .3770 | .3790 | .3810 | .3830 |
| 1.2 | .3849 | .3869 | .3888 | .3907 | .3925 | .3944 | .3962 | .3980 | .3997 | .4015 |
| 1.3 | .4032 | .4049 | .4066 | .4082 | .4099 | .4115 | .4131 | .4147 | .4162 | .4177 |
| 1.4 | .4192 | .4207 | .4222 | .4236 | .4251 | .4265 | .4279 | .4292 | .4306 | .4319 |
| 1.5 | .4332 | .4345 | .4357 | .4370 | .4382 | .4394 | .4406 | .4418 | .4429 | .4441 |
| 1.6 | .4452 | .4463 | .4474 | .4484 | .4495 | .4505 | .4515 | .4525 | .4535 | .4545 |
| 1.7 | .4554 | .4564 | .4573 | .4582 | .4591 | .4599 | .4608 | .4616 | .4625 | .4633 |
| 1.8 | .4641 | .4649 | .4656 | .4664 | .4671 | .4678 | .4686 | .4693 | .4699 | .4706 |
| 1.9 | .4713 | .4719 | .4726 | .4732 | .4738 | .4744 | .4750 | .4756 | .4761 | .4767 |
| 2.0 | .4772 | .4778 | .4783 | .4788 | .4793 | .4798 | .4803 | .4808 | .4812 | .4817 |
| 2.1 | .4821 | .4826 | .4830 | .4834 | .4838 | .4842 | .4846 | .4850 | .4854 | .4857 |
| 2.2 | .4861 | .4864 | .4868 | .4871 | .4875 | .4878 | .4881 | .4884 | .4887 | .4890 |
| 2.3 | .4893 | .4896 | .4898 | .4901 | .4904 | .4906 | .4909 | .4911 | .4913 | .4916 |
| 2.4 | .4918 | .4920 | .4922 | .4925 | .4927 | .4929 | .4931 | .4932 | .4934 | .4936 |
| 2.5 | .4938 | .4940 | .4941 | .4943 | .4945 | .4946 | .4948 | .4949 | .4951 | .4952 |
| 2.6 | .4953 | .4955 | .4956 | .4957 | .4959 | .4960 | .4961 | .4962 | .4963 | .4964 |
| 2.7 | .4965 | .4966 | .4967 | .4968 | .4969 | .4970 | .4971 | .4972 | .4973 | .4974 |
| 2.8 | .4974 | .4975 | .4976 | .4977 | .4977 | .4978 | .4979 | .4979 | .4980 | .4981 |
| 2.9 | .4981 | .4982 | .4982 | .4983 | .4984 | .4984 | .4985 | .4985 | .4986 | .4986 |
| 3.0 | .49865 | .4987 | .4987 | .4988 | .4988 | .4989 | .4989 | .4989 | .4990 | .4990 |
| 3.1 | .49903 | .4991 | .4991 | .4991 | .4992 | .4992 | .4992 | .4992 | .4993 | .4993 |
| 3.2 | .4993129 | .4993 | .4994 | .4994 | .4994 | .4994 | .4994 | .4995 | .4995 | .4995 |
| 3.3 | .4995166 | .4995 | .4995 | .4996 | .4996 | .4996 | .4996 | .4996 | .4996 | .4997 |
| 3.4 | .4996631 | .4997 | .4997 | .4997 | .4997 | .4997 | .4997 | .4997 | .4998 | .4998 |
| 3.5 | .4997674 | .4998 | .4998 | .4998 | .4998 | .4998 | .4998 | .4998 | .4998 | .4998 |
| 3.6 | .4998409 | .4998 | .4999 | .4999 | .4999 | .4999 | .4999 | .4999 | .4999 | .4999 |
| 3.7 | .4998922 | .4999 | .4999 | .4999 | .4999 | .4999 | .4999 | .4999 | .4999 | .4999 |
| 3.8 | .4999277 | .4999 | .4999 | .4999 | .4999 | .4999 | .4999 | .5000 | .5000 | .5000 |
| 3.9 | .4999519 | .5000 | .5000 | .5000 | .5000 | .5000 | .5000 | .5000 | .5000 | .5000 |
| 4.0 | .4999683 | | | | | | | | | |
| 4.5 | .4999966 | | | | | | | | | |
| 5.0 | .4999997133 | | | | | | | | | |

Source: Frederick E. Croxton and Dudley J. Cowden, *Practical Business Statistics* (2d ed.; New York: Prentice-Hall, Inc., 1948), p. 511. Reprinted by permission of the publisher.

# F

# Fractiles of the Beta Distribution

THIS TABLE gives the values of $p_f$ such that $P(p \leqslant p_f) = f$. For selected values of the parameters $r$ and $n$, $p_f$ can be found for $f = 0.1$, 0.25, 0.50, 0.75, and 0.9.

| r | n | f: .1 | .25 | .5 | .75 | .9 |
|---|---|---|---|---|---|---|
| 1 | 2 | .1000 | .2500 | .5000 | .7500 | .9000 |
| | 4 | .0345 | .0914 | .2063 | .3700 | .5358 |
| | 6 | .0209 | .0559 | .1294 | .2421 | .3690 |
| | 10 | .0116 | .0315 | .0741 | .1428 | .2257 |
| 2 | 4 | .1958 | .3264 | .5000 | .6736 | .8042 |
| | 5 | .1426 | .2430 | .3857 | .5437 | .6795 |
| | 10 | .0608 | .1072 | .1796 | .2723 | .3684 |
| | 15 | .0387 | .0688 | .1170 | .1810 | .2507 |
| | 20 | .0283 | .0507 | .0868 | .1355 | .1898 |
| 4 | 8 | .2786 | .3788 | .5000 | .6212 | .7214 |
| | 10 | .2104 | .2910 | .3931 | .5020 | .5994 |
| | 15 | .1309 | .1846 | .2561 | .3377 | .4170 |
| | 20 | .0951 | .1353 | .1899 | .2541 | .3186 |
| | 25 | .0747 | .1068 | .1509 | .2036 | .2575 |
| | 30 | .0615 | .0882 | .1252 | .1698 | .2160 |
| 6 | 12 | .3177 | .4016 | .5000 | .5984 | .6823 |
| | 15 | .2432 | .3117 | .3954 | .4835 | .5631 |
| | 20 | .1751 | .2274 | .2932 | .3655 | .4340 |
| | 25 | .1369 | .1790 | .2330 | .2936 | .3525 |
| | 30 | .1125 | .1476 | .1933 | .2452 | .2965 |
| | 40 | .0829 | .1093 | .1441 | .1844 | .2249 |
| 8 | 20 | .2633 | .3239 | .3966 | .4725 | .5413 |
| | 25 | .2049 | .2544 | .3151 | .3804 | .4416 |
| | 30 | .1678 | .2096 | .2614 | .3182 | .3725 |
| | 40 | .1233 | .1550 | .1950 | .2397 | .2834 |
| | 50 | .0974 | .1229 | .1555 | .1922 | .2285 |
| | 60 | .0806 | .1019 | .1293 | .1604 | .1914 |
| 10 | 30 | .2264 | .2732 | .3296 | .3895 | .4452 |
| | 40 | .1658 | .2017 | .2458 | .2938 | .3397 |
| | 50 | .1309 | .1599 | .1960 | .2358 | .2744 |
| | 60 | .1081 | .1325 | .1630 | .1969 | .2301 |
| | 70 | .0921 | .1131 | .1394 | .1690 | .1981 |
| | 80 | .0802 | .0986 | .1219 | .1480 | .1739 |

This table was excerpted from Table 3, Beta Cumulative Functions, Robert O. Schlaifer, *Analysis of Decision Under Uncertainty*, published by McGraw-Hill Book Co., 1969. It is reproduced here by permission of the copyright holder, the President and Fellows of Harvard College.

# G

# Random Numbers

| | | | | |
|---|---|---|---|---|
| 88190 | 49712 | 11657 | 13897 | 95889 |
| 00224 | 58275 | 91339 | 22502 | 92613 |
| 16016 | 89514 | 99396 | 63680 | 67667 |
| 30432 | 15472 | 57649 | 63266 | 24700 |
| 64672 | 12120 | 28977 | 23896 | 76479 |
| | | | | |
| 13173 | 94082 | 61826 | 18555 | 64937 |
| 86716 | 85774 | 70495 | 32350 | 02985 |
| 92581 | 34108 | 33230 | 21529 | 53424 |
| 12470 | 07201 | 91050 | 13058 | 16218 |
| 01016 | 53969 | 67011 | 06651 | 16136 |
| | | | | |
| 34030 | 99236 | 97380 | 10404 | 55452 |
| 50259 | 89535 | 61764 | 97586 | 54716 |
| 73959 | 10252 | 11788 | 68224 | 23417 |
| 46874 | 27799 | 50669 | 48139 | 36732 |
| 60883 | 50241 | 86124 | 51247 | 44302 |
| | | | | |
| 45990 | 93241 | 25807 | 24260 | 71529 |
| 76668 | 92348 | 06170 | 97965 | 88302 |
| 39014 | 57411 | 60808 | 54444 | 74412 |
| 81232 | 50395 | 80940 | 44893 | 10408 |
| 76447 | 78636 | 19516 | 90120 | 46759 |
| | | | | |
| 17994 | 14924 | 88158 | 49386 | 54480 |
| 53119 | 70312 | 25240 | 06312 | 88940 |
| 58660 | 90850 | 24069 | 60942 | 00307 |
| 86861 | 24781 | 68990 | 92329 | 98932 |
| 08289 | 40902 | 37981 | 77936 | 63574 |
| | | | | |
| 78920 | 72682 | 78435 | 38101 | 77756 |
| 98041 | 21443 | 37836 | 39641 | 69457 |
| 81105 | 01176 | 04345 | 84054 | 40455 |
| 36222 | 80582 | 32192 | 47468 | 03577 |
| 71643 | 13177 | 75583 | 43321 | 31370 |
| | | | | |
| 23604 | 23554 | 21785 | 44053 | 64281 |
| 15995 | 69321 | 47458 | 91691 | 66847 |
| 11897 | 92674 | 40405 | 01748 | 72461 |
| 78284 | 46347 | 71209 | 85736 | 21032 |
| 31384 | 51924 | 85561 | 60555 | 95362 |
| | | | | |
| 43584 | 85301 | 88977 | 94770 | 27767 |
| 14338 | 54066 | 15243 | 64238 | 13025 |
| 36292 | 98525 | 24335 | 12836 | 80217 |
| 62004 | 90391 | 61105 | 22998 | 10875 |
| 57326 | 26629 | 19087 | 94050 | 54127 |
| | | | | |
| 42824 | 37301 | 42678 | 53656 | 60311 |
| 71484 | 92003 | 98086 | 07541 | 49739 |
| 51594 | 16453 | 94614 | 20483 | 78626 |
| 13986 | 99837 | 00582 | 49022 | 66692 |
| 28091 | 07362 | 97703 | 07772 | 44071 |
| | | | | |
| 41468 | 85149 | 49554 | 29490 | 35439 |
| 94559 | 37559 | 49678 | 47724 | 20094 |
| 41615 | 70360 | 64114 | 24432 | 06343 |
| 50273 | 93113 | 41794 | 57411 | 72535 |
| 41396 | 80504 | 90670 | 24472 | 47749 |

# Index